TRACTS AND OTHER PAPERS,

RELATING PRINCIPALLY TO THE

ORIGIN, SETTLEMENT, AND PROGRESS

OF THE

COLONIES IN NORTH AMERICA,

'ROM THE DISCOVERY OF THE COUNTRY TO THE YEAR 1776.

COLLECTED BY PETER FORCE.

Vol. III.

GLOUCESTER, MASS.
PETER SMITH
1963

THE MURRAY PRINTING COMPANY
FORGE VILLAGE, MASSACHUSETTS

CONTENTS

OF THE THIRD VOLUME.

~~~~~~~~~~~~~~

A
TRVE DECLARA-
TION OF THE
estate of the Colonie in
VIRGINIA,

With a confutation of such scandalous
reports as haue tended to the disgrace
of so worthy an enterprise.

Published by aduise and direction of the
Councell of VIRGINIA.

LONDON,
Printed for *William Barret,* and are to be sold
at the blacke Beare in Pauls Church-yard.
1610.

Force's Collection of Historical Tracts.

Vol. III.—No. 1.

A true declaration of the estate in VIRGINIA.

THERE is a great distance, betwixt the vulgar opinion of men, and the iudicious apprehension of wise men. Opinion is as blind *Ordipus*, who could see nothing, but would heare all things, *Hinc aucupari verba rumoris vagi*, to hawke after the winged report of a vagabond rumor. But iudgement, is as *Salomon* in his throne, able by the spirit of wisedome, to discerne betwixt *contesting* truth, and falshood: neither depending on the popular breath of fame, which is euer partiall, nor vpon the euent of good designes, which are euer casuall. These two commanders of our affections, haue diuided the vniuersall spirits of our land, whilst (in the honorable enterprise for plantation in *Virginia*) some, are carried away with the tide of vulgar opinion, and others, are encouraged, by the principles of religion, and reason. But because, it is for hawkes and not for men, to build their nests in aires, and because the honor and prosperity of this so noble an action, is eclipsed by the interposition of clamorous & tragicall narrations: the compiler of this relation endeuoureth to wash away those spots, which foule mouths (to iustifie their owne disloialty) haue cast vpon so fruitfull, so fertile, and so excellent a country. Wherein he professeth, that he will relate nothing (concerning *Virginia*) but what he hath from the secrets of the iudiciall councell of *Virginia*, from the letters of the Lord *La Ware*, from the mouth of Sir *Thomas Gates*, whose wisdomes (he conceiueth) are not so shallow, as easily to be deceiued *of others*, nor consciences so wretched, as by pretences to deceiue others.

But when a matter of such consequence, is not to be shufled ouer with supine negligence, and when no man raiseth a faire building, that laith not a firme foundation, it will not be impertinent, to dig a little deeper, that we may build a great deale higher: and from the vniuersall policie of all ciuill states (in replenishing the world with colonies of domesticall subiects) to deriue this wisedome to our populous state and country.

That

Colonies.   That which *Origen* said of Christs actions in vertues morall, holdeth proportion with Gods actions
in gouernment politicall, *Dei facta, sunt nostra præcepta*, Gods
actions, are our instructions: who (in the eleuenth of Genesis)
turned the greatest cursing, into the greatest blessing, and by
confusion of tongues, kept them from confusion of states; scattering those clouen people, into as many colonies ouer the face
of the earth, as there are diuersities of langoages in the earth.
Now if *Tertullians* rule be true, *Omne genus ab origine cen-
sendum* that euery action is most beutifull in the originall. Can
there be a better beginning then from God, whose wisedome
is not questioned, and whose footsteps in all succeeding ages
haue beene followed. Search the records of diuine truth, and
humane monuments of state, you shall find, *Salmanasar* transporting the Babilonians, and other Gentiles, to *Samaria :* and
replenishing with the captiues of Israëll, the dispeopled confines
of *Media.*

You shall find that 140. yeeres after the destruction of *Troy*,
the *Ionian* colony, was carried from *Greece*, to *Asia :* by which
that famous City of *Ephesus* was first builded, and inhabited.
You shall find the Egiptians, planted *Babilon*, *Argos*, and
Athens. The Phenicians first inhabiting *Carthage*, *Vtica*,
and *Thebes.* That *Timolcon* and the city of *Corinth*, at one
time repeopled *Sicilie*, with 10000. soules. That the Romans
deduced 53. colonies out of the City of *Rome* into the wombe of
Italy. That *Bremius* an Englishman by birth, but sonne in
law to the King of *France*, with an equall third part of the
kingdome, entred into the hart of *Italy*, gaue the prime sacke
to the City of *Rome*, and diuerted from thence to *Gallogræcia*,
whose offspring possesse that land vnto this day.

That the Admirall of *France*, among all the feares and discouragements of ciuill wars, neuer gaue ouer the proiect of
plantation in *Florida.*

Which heroicall actions, haue not beene vndertaken by so
mighty states and Princes, vpon triuiall and vulgar motiues,
when by these courses that first blessing (of *crescite* and *multi-
plicamini*, increase and multiplie) hath beene sanctified: the
meaner sorte haue beene prouided: the matter of plagues, famine and sedition, hath beene exhausted: the fennes of a state
politique were drained: the enemies of their peace were bridled:
the reuenues of their treasury were augmented: and the limites
of their dominions were enlarged.

Which diuine, humane, externall, and domesticall, examples,
doe shine before vs, as a *Pharaoes* towre, that wee should not
make shipwracke of our intentions, concerning *Virginia.*

Blacke

Blacke enuie, and pale feare, being not able to produce any arguments, why that should bee lawfull for *France*, which is (in vs) vnlawfull: that which to *Rome* was possible, (to vs) is impossible: that which to others is honourable, and profitable, (in vs) should bee traduced, as incommodious, base, and contemptible: wherefore vnder these three heads of Three Heads. lawfulnesse, possibility, and commoditie, will I Lawfull, Possible, marshall all those reasons, which may resolue the Profitable. religious, encourage the personall, confirme the noble, and satisfie the timorous aduenturer.

First, if it bee vnlawfull: it must be so, either in respect of the law of God, or in regard of the lawe of man. If in respect of Gods lawe, (considering our primarie end is to plant religion, our secondarie and subalternate ends are for the honour and profit of our nation) I demand a resolution of this plaine question: whether it bee not a determinated truth, that the Gospell should bee preached, to all the world, before the end of the world? If, it must bee preached, (as heauen and earth must passe awaie, but Gods word shall not pass awaie) then must it bee preached, one of these three waies: Either meerly Apostolically, without the helpe of man, (without so much as a staffe) or meerely imperiallie, when a Prince, hath conquered their bodies, that the Preachers may feede their soules; Or mixtly, by discouerie, and trade of marchants; where all temporall meanes are vsed for defence, and security, but none for offence, or crueltie. For the first (to preach Apostolicallie) it is simplie impossible: except wee had the gift of tongues, that euerie nation might heare the word of God in their owne language; or the guift of miracles, that it might be confirmed, with wonders from heauen; which two beeing ceased, questionlesse the identicall commission of the Apostles is expired: Or if yet the matter bee vrged, that God by fishers did conuert Emperors and therefore that wee must aduenture our liues without humane helpe; yet must it bee remembred, that there is no Apostolicall preaching, but where wee may expect either their conuersion, or our martyrdome. But we can expect neither, not their conuersion who cannot vnderstand vs, nor our martyrdome, when the people of *Florida*, did deuoure the Preachers of the word, without speaking any word. *Non quia Christiani, sed quia homines*, not because they were christian men, but because they were men, wee cannot·be said to be martyrs, when wee are not killed because wee are christians. And therefore the Iesuite *Acosta* confesseth (notwithstanding *Bellarmines* relation of Indian miracles) that they haue no tongues, they haue no signes from heauen, and they can haue no martyrdome

dome, and by consequent there is no means left of Apostolicall preaching.

For the second, to preach the Gospell to a nation conquered, and to set their soules at liberty, when we haue brought their bodies to slauerie ; It may be a matter sacred in the Preachers, but I know not how iustifiable in the rulers. Who for their meere ambition, doe set vpon it, the glosse of religion. Let the diuines of *Salamanca*, discusse that question, how the possessor of the west Indies, first destroied, and then instructed.

The third, belongs to vs, who by way of marchandizing and trade, doe buy of them the pearles of earth, and sell to them the pearles of heauen ; which action, if it be vnlawfull, it must proceede from one of these three grounds, either because we come to them, or trade with them, or tarrie and dwell and possesse part of their country amongst them.

Is it vnlawfull because wee come to them ? why is it not a dutie of christianitie, to behold the imprinted footsteps of Gods glorie, in euery region vnder heauen ? Is it not against the lawe of nations, to violate a peaceable stranger, or to denie him harbour. The Ethiopians, Egyptians, and men of *China*, are branded with a foule marke of sanguinarie and barbarous inhumanity, for blessing their Idols, with the bloud of strangers. It is not vnlawfull to trade with them, except *Salomon* shall bee condemned for sending for gold to *Ophir*, *Abraham* for making a league with *Abimilech*, and all christendome shall bee traduced, for hauing comerce with Turks and miscreants.

Finallie, it is not vnlawfull, that wee possesse part of their land and dwell with them, and defend our selues from them. Partlie because there is no other, moderate, and mixt course, to bring them to conuersion, but by dailie conuersation, where they may see the life, and learne the language each of other.

Partlie, because there is no trust to the fidelitie of humane beasts, except a man will make a league, with Lions, Beares, and Crocodiles.

Partlie because there is roome sufficient in the land (as *Sichem* sometime said) for them, and vs : the extent of an hundred miles, being scarce peopled with 2000. inhabitants.

Partlie, because they haue violated the lawe of nations, and vsed our Ambassadors as *Ammon* did the seruants of *Dauid :* If in him it were a iust cause to warre against the Ammonites, it is lawfull, in vs, to secure our selues, against the infidels.

But chieflie because *Paspehay*, one of their Kings, sold vnto vs for copper, land to inherit and inhabite. *Powhatan*, their chiefe King, receiued voluntarilie a crown and a scepter, with a full acknowledgment of dutie and submission.

Principallie

Principallie when Captaine *Newport* was with *Powhatan* at *Warow a comaco* hee desired him to come from *Iames* towne as a place vnholesome, and to take possession of an other whole kingdome which he gaue vnto him. If any man alleadge, that this was done in subtlety, not that they euer meant we should possesse them, but that they might first gaine by vs, and then destroy vs. This makes our cause, much the iuster, when God turned their subteltie, to our vtilitie: giving vnto vs a lawfull possession, (as *Pharaoe* gaue *Goshen* to *Israell;* or *Ephron* sold his caue to *Abraham*) and freeing vs, from all impious and sinister construction. If anie man alleadge, that yet wee can possesse no farther limits, than was allotted by composition, and that *fortitudo sine iustitia, est iniquitatis Materia,* fortitude without iustice, is but the firebrand of iniquitie. Let him know that *Plato* defineth it, to bee no iniustice, to take a sword out of the hand of a mad man; That *Austen* hath allowed it, for a lawfull offensiue warre, *quod vlcisitur iniurias* that reuengeth bloudie iniuries. So that if iust offences shall arise, it can bee no more iniustice to warre against infidells, than it is when vpon iust occasions wee warre against Christians. And therefore I cannot see, but that these truths, will sanne away all those chaffie imputations, which anie Romish boasters (that challenge a monopolie of all conuersions) will cast vpon it, or any scrupulous conscience can impute vnto it. Certainlie the Church of *Geneua* in the yeere 1555. determined in a Synode, whereof (*Caluine*) was president, to send *Peter Richier,* and *William Quadrigarius,* vnder a French Captaine to *Brasilia,* who although they were supplanted, by the comming of the Cardinall of *Loraine,* and the trecherie of their double hearted leader, yet would not the Church of *Geneua,* (after a Synodicall consultation) haue sent their ministers to such an aduenture, had not all scruples, (in their iudgement) béene cleared by the light of Scripture.

When therefore, it is a sweete smelling sacrifice, to propagate the name of Iesus Christ, when the Babylonish Inchantresse (if her owne Calenders, are to bee credited) hath compassed sea, and land, to make, sixe, eight, or ten millions, of Romish proselites. When there is no other, mixt, moderate, course, to transport the *Virginian* soules to heauen. When there hath beene a reall concession from their rurall Emperour, that hath licensed vs to negociate among them, and to possesse their countrie with them. When there is more vnpeopled continent of earth, than wee and they (before the dissolution of the pillars of heauen) can ouerburden with multitude. When we neuer intend to play the *Rehoboams,* and to scourge them with scorpions.

pions. It is not good, to create more sinnes, then God euer
censured: nor to brand that action with impietie, which God
hath begun for promulgating of his glorie *Nunquid ideo deforme
est, quia figura mentitur?* is the action therefore deformed,
because a false glasse doth slaunder it?

Concerning the other braunch of this discourse, wherein some
slie whisperers would seeme to cast an aspersion of iniustice
vpon the action, supposing some forraine Prince to haue a former interest.

Certainlie hee is but a rotten subiect that quarrells the actions
of his countrie, descrying a serpentine stinge vnder the faire
leaues of pietie. And though it bee not for a theoreticall Schollar, to circumscribe the dominions of Princes, yet a few proofes
from antiquitie, shall suffice to controwle ignorant or presumptuous follie.

In the yeare 1170. *Madocke* the sonne of *Owen Guyneth*
Prince of *Northwales* (leauing the land in contention betwixt
his two brethren *Howell* and *Dauid*) sailed into the West
Indies, and after a second, and a third returne, and supplie,
setled himselfe in those dominions.

In the yeere 1495. *Iohn Cabot* a Venetian, but the indenized
subiect of King *Henrie* the seauenth discouered the North parts
of *America*, to *Meta incognita*, and so it was annexed to the
Crowne of *England*.

As for the donation of *Alexander* the sixt; it is but a recipro-
call clawing, when Emperors create their seruants Bishops vniuersall, and shauelings create their Lords, Emperors generall.

If the donation of *Constantine* were not more virtuall for
Saint *Peters* partrimonie, wee should haue neede of more purga-
tories, to maintaine fuell in the Popes kitchen: for if the kingdome of Christ was not on earth, what a transubstantiated power,
doth the pretended Vicar of Christ claime, to dispose all the
kingdomes of the earth. *Petrarch* recordeth a memorable
historie, of *Sautius* brother to the King of *Spaine*, who was
elected generall against the Saracens of *Egypt*, and comming
to *Rome* for that purpose, the Bishop of *Rome*, made it to bee
proclaimed in the Consistorie that hee bestowed the kingdome
of *Egypt* vpon *Sautius*. *Sautius* vnderstanding this fauour,
(by his interpreter) commanded to proclaime the Pope, great
Caleph of *Baldacho:* perfuming the sonne of pride, with his
owne smoke.

The Pope hauing no more power, to make *Sautius* a King,
then *Sautius* had power to make the Pope a *Caleph*. Let
such retailers of Crownes remember, who it was that sometime
saide, all these will I giue thee if thou wilt fall downe, and
worship

worship me, And yet with this item that the diuell pretended to giue no more than he saw.

These points beeing thus defined, I come to the possibility. Against which three maine impediments are obiected. First the daungerous passage by sea, secondlie the barrennesse of the countrie, thirdly the vnholesomness of the climate: the storme that seperated the admirall from the fleete proouing the first, the famine amongst our men importing the second, the sicknesse of our men arguing the third. All which discouragements doe astonish our men with feare, as though our expences were vnprofitable, when our ends are impossible.

But before I shall enter into this discourse I must craue leaue to make a necessarie digression, and to iustifie his reputation whose worth is of speciall regard in this plantation.

Sir *Thomas Gates* supposeth himselfe accused publiquelie and in print of a treeble defect.

First that hee ranne so farre Southerlie and into the Tropique, that the heat caused the infection in the ships.

Secondlie that hee gaue a sealed direction, that if they were seperated by anie storme, that they should make for the *Baruada* in the West Indies, which direction himselfe following, it caused his shipwracke, but the other shippes, (vpon better iudgement) declining these instructions, ariued safelie in *Virginia*.

Thirdlie that hee caried in one bottome all the principall Commissioners who should successiuelie haue gouerned the Colonie. Against all which imputations, hee maketh this iust Apologie.

First hee confesseth that a little before they came vnto the Canaries, that hee entred into consultation with Sir *George Summers*, Captaine *Newport*, and the other of chiefe regarde in the fleete, wherein it was resolued by an vniformitie of consent, to runne southerlie into the Tropique, which they did, till they came to the height of foure and twentie, but hee denieth that this course was anie cause of infection. For in the *Faulcon*, the *Blessing*, the *Lyon*, (and in the *Admirall* wherein were one hundred and fiftie soules) there was not one sicke of the pestilence nor other disease ; In the other two ships the infection was somewhat hote, but they shipped the same from *London* ; To the second hee affirmeth, that hee first gaue them sealed instructions (not to bee opened till a time of storme) which directed them to the *Baruada*, But after when they came to the height of foure and twentie, hee countermaunded those directions by word of mouth, and assigned them, (that if they were scattered) that they should make with all speede for *Virginia*. Which himselfe (esteeming the price of time vnualuable)

able) woulde haue executed, had not the violent leake of the shippe hindred him, So that the other ships safe ariuall in *Virginia*, proceeded originallie from his aduise and authoritie.

To the third, he briefly signifieth, that no other Commissioners were in his Ship, but such, (as for especiall reasons) were precisely and peremptorily appointed, by the Councell of *Virginia*. And thus you see, that *Tacitus* wisely obserued two great enemies of great actions, *Ignorantiam veri, & Inuidiam*, the ignorance of Truth, and the emulation of Vertue.

To returne therefore vnto the maine channell of this discourse, and to dispell the clouds of feare, that threaten shipwracks, and sea-dangers: For we are not to extenuate the seas tempestuous violence, nor yet therefore to dispaire of Gods assisting providence. For true it is, that when *Sir Thomas Gates*, *Sir George Summers*, and *Captaine Newport*, were in the height of 27. and the 24. of Iuly 1609. there arose such a storme, as if *Ionas* had been flying vnto *Tarshish*: the heauens were obscured, and made an Egyptian night of three daies perpetuall horror; the women lamented; the hearts of the passengers failed; the experience of the sea Captaines was amased: the skill of the marriners was confounded: the Ship most violently leaked, and though two thousand tunne of water by pumping from Tuesday noone till Fryday noone was discharged, notwithstanding the Ship was halfe filled with water, and those which laboured to keepe others from drowning were halfe drowned themselues in labouring. But God that heard *Ionas* crying out of the belly of hell, he pittied the distresses of his seruants; For behold, in the last period of necessitie, *Sir George Summers* descryed land, which was by so much the more ioyfull, by how much their danger was despairefull. The Islands on which they fell were the *Bermudos*, a place hardly accessable, through the enuironing rocks and dangers: notwithstanding they were forced to runne their Ship on shoare, which through Gods prouidence fell betwixt two rockes, that caused her to stande firme and not immediately to be broken, God continuing his mercie vnto them, that with their long Boats they transported to land before night, all their company, men, women, and children, to the number of one hundred and fiftie, they carryed to shoare all the prouision of vnspent and vnspoyled victuals, all their furniture and tackling of the Ship, leauing nothing but bared ribs, as a pray vnto the Ocean.

These Islands of the *Bermudos*, haue euer beene accounted as an inchaunted pile of rockes, and a desert inhabitation for Diuels; but all the Fairies of the rocks were but flocks of birds, and all the Diuels that haunted the woods, were but heards of
swine

swine. Yea and when *Acosta* in his first booke of the hystories of the *Indies,* auerreth, that though in the continent there were diuerse beasts, and cattell, yet in the Islands of *Hispaniola, Jamaica, Marguarita,* and *Dominica,* there was not one hoofe, it increaseth the wonder, how our people in the *Bermudos* found such abundance of Hogs, that for nine moneths space they plentifully sufficed: and yet the number seemed not much diminished. Again, as in the great famine of *Israell,* God commanded *Elias* to flie to the brooke *Cedron,* and there fed him by Rauens; so God prouided for our disconsolate people in the midst of the Sea by foules: but with an admirable difference: vnto *Elias* the Rauens brought meat, vnto our men the foules brought (themselues) for meate: for when they whisteled, or made any strange noyse, the foules would come and sit on their shoulders, they would suffer themselues to be taken and weighed by our men, who would make choise of the fattest and fairest, and let flie the leane and lightest. An accident, I take it, that cannot be paralleld by any Hystorie, except when God sent abundance of Quayles to feed his *Israel* in the barren wildernesse. Lastly they found the berries of *Cedar,* the *Palmeto* tree, the prickle peare, sufficient fish, plentie of Tortoises, and diuers other kinds, which sufficed to sustaine nature. They found diuersity of woods, which ministred materials for the building of two Pinaces, acoording to the direction of the three prouident Gouernours.

Consider all these things together. At the instant of neede, they descryed land, halfe an hower more, had buried their memorial in the Sea. If they had fel by night, what expectation of light, from an vninhabited desart? They fell betwixt a laberinth of rockes, which they conceiue are mouldred into the Sea, by thunder and lightning. This was not *Ariadnes* threed, but the direct line of Gods prouidence. If it had not beene so neere land, their companie or prouision had perished by water: if they had not found Hogs, and foule, and fish, they had perished by famine: if there had not beene fuell, they had perished by want of fire: if there had not beene timber they could not haue transported themselues to *Virginia,* but must haue beene forgotten foreuer. *Nimium timet qui Deo non credit,* he is too impiously fearefull, that will not trust in God so powerfull.

What is there in all this tragicall Comædie that should discourage vs with impossibilitie of the enterprise? when of all the Fleete, one onely Ship, by a secret leake was indangered, and yet in the gulfe of Despair, was so graciously preserued. *Quæ videtur pæna, est medicina,* that which we accompt a punishment of euill, is but a medicine against euill.

After

After nine Moneths aboade in these Islands, on the 10th of May 1610. they imbarqued themselues in their two new built Pinaces, and after some eleuen daies saile, they arriued neere point Comfort vpon the coast of *Virginia:* where they had intelligence of so wofull miserie, as if God had onely preserued them, to communicate in an new extremitie.

From which calamitie, the other arguments of impossibilitie are framed; for if the Countrie bee barren, or the scituation contagious; as famine, and sicknesse, destroy our Nation: wee striue against the streame of reason, and make ourselues the subiects of scorne and derision. Therefore in this maine point of consequence, I will propound this plaine and simple methode; First to demonstrate that there is, and may be in *Virginia* a sufficient meanes (in all abundance) to sustaine the life of man; Next that the Climate is wholesome and temperate, agreeing with the constitutions of our men; Thirdly, that those extremities proceeded from accidentall and not inherent euils. Lastly, I will delineate the state of the Colony, as *Sir Thomas Gates* left it vnder the gouernment of the honorable *L. Laware:* whereby it shall appeare, that all difficulties are amended, and that the State of that Countrie is sufficiently mannaged.

To begin, with the staffe of bread. It is auowed vnto mee, in writing, in the words of the Author, that hath been there, as

Corne.

followeth. *They use to put their wheat into the ground, fiue cornes in one spit of earth, and two beanes with them: which wheat cornes multiplying into diuers stalks, grow up twelue, or fourteene foote high: yeelding some foure, fiue, or six eares, on euery stalke; and in euery eare, some fiue hundred, some six hundred, some seauen hundred cornes: the two beanes, runne vpon the stalkes of the wheat, as our garden pease vpon stickes, which multiplie to a wonderous increase. I cannot let slip a great secret, (saith the Author) whereof I will auouch no more, then with my hands aud eyes I haue handled and seene, and whereof to my great comfort, I haue often tasted: The wheate beeing sowen thicke, some stalkes beare eares of corne, and some (like siences in trees) beare none: but in those barren stalkes, there is as much iuice as in some sugar cane, of so delicate a tast, as no fruit in England, is comparable to it; out of which* Sir Ralph Lane *conceiued, that wee may extract sugar, in great quantity. But* Sir Thomas Gates *affirmeth that our men doe make cordiall drinke thereof, to their great comfort.*

Pease.
Fruits.
Hearbs.

Besides, the naturall Pease of the Countrie returne an increase innumerable, our garden fruits, both roots, hearbes, and flowers, doe spring vp speedily, all things committed to the earth, do multiply with an incredible vsurie.

The

The Beasts of the Countrie, as Deere, red, and fallow, do answere in multitude (people for people considered) to our proportion of Oxen, which appeareth by these experiences. First the people of the Countrie are apparelled in the skinnes of these beasts; Next, hard by the fort, two hundred in one heard haue been vsually obserued: Further, our men haue seene 4000. of these skins pyled vp in one wardroabe of *Powhaton;* Lastly, infinite store haue been presented to *Captaine Newport* vpon sundry occurrents: such a plentie of Cattell, as all the Spaniards found not in the whole kingdome of *Mexico*, when all their presents were but hennes, and ginycocks, and the bread of Maize, and Cently. Beasts.

There are *Arocouns*, and *Apossouns*, in shape like to pigges, shrowded in hollow roots of trees; There are Hares and Conies, and other beasts proper to the Countrie in plentifull manner.

Our transported Cattell, as Horses, Kine, Hogs, and Goats, do thriue most happily: which is confirmed by a double experiment; one, of *Sir Ralph Lane*, who brought Kine from the West Indian Island; the other of our Colony, who need take no other care of them, but least they should straie too farre, or be stolne from them. The Turkyes of that Countrie are great, and fat, and exceeding in plentie. The riuers from August, or September, till February, are couered with flocks of Wildfoule: as swannes, geese, ducke, mallard, teal, wigeons, hearons, bitters, curlewes, godwights, plouers, snights, dottrels, cormerants, (to vse the words of *Sir Thomas Gates*) in such abundance as are not in all the world to be equalled. Wildfoule.

The Fruits: as apples, running on the ground, in bignesse and shape of a small lemmon, in colour and tast like to a preserued Apricock: grapes and walnuts innumerable; the vines being as common as brambles, the walnut trees as the elmes in England. What should I speake of cucumbers, muske melons, pompions, potatoes, parsneps, carrets, turnups, which our gardens yeelded with little art and labour. God in this place is euer concurring with his gracious influence, if man strangle not his blessings, with carelesse negligence. It shall suffice to conclude in the words and phrase of that noble Gouernour, the *Lo. Laware*, as it is warranted to mee by the copie of his Letters sent to the Virginian Councell. Fruits.

Howsoeuer, men haue belyed both it and themselues, heretofore, yet let no rumor of the Countrie (as if in the wombe thereof lay not these elementall seedes of plenty and increase) waue any mans faire purposes, or wrest them to a declyning and falling off from the businesse.

For

For the healthinesse and temperatenesse of the Cly-
mate, agreeing to our constitutions, much neede not be
related, since in all the former written Treatises, it is expressly
obserued.

No man ought to judge of any Countrie by the fennes and
marshes (such as is the place where *James* towne standeth)
except we will condemne all England, for the Wilds and Hundreds of Kent and Essex. In our particular, wee haue an
infallible proofe of the temper of the Countrie: for of an hundred
and odd, which were seated at the *Falles*, vnder the gouernment
of *Captaine Francis West*, and of an hundred to the Sea-Ward
on the South side of the riuer, (in the Countrie of the *Nansa-
munds*) vnder the charge of *Captaine John Martin;* of all these
two hundred, there did not so much as one man miscarrie:
when in *Iames* Towne, at the same time, and in the same
moneths, 100. sickned, and halfe the number died.

The like experiment was long since in the regiment of *Sir
Raph Lane*, where, in the space of one whole yeare, not two
of one hundred perished. Adde vnto this the discourse of phi-
losophie; when in that Countrie flesh will receiue salt, and continue vnputrified (which it will not in the West Indies) when
the most delicate of all flowers, grow there as familiarly, as in
the fields of *Portingale*, where the woods are replenished with
more sweet barks, and odors, then they are in the plesantest
places of *Florida*. How is it possible that such a virgin and
temperat aire, should work such contrarie effects, but because
our fort (that lyeth as a semy-Iland) is most part inuironed with
an ebbing and flowing salt water, the owze of which sendeth
forth an vnwholsome & contagious vapour? To close vp this
part with *Sir Thomas Gates* his experiment: he professeth,
that in a fortnights space he recouered the health of most of
them by moderat labour, whose sicknesse was bred in them by
intemperate idlenes.

If any man shall accuse these reports of partiall falshood,
supposing them to be but Vtopian, and legendarie fables, because he cannot conceiue, that plentie and famine, a temperate
climate, and distempered bodies, felicities, and miseries can be
reconciled together, let him now reade with judgement, but let
him not judge before he hath read.

The ground of all those miseries, was the permissiue prouidence of God, who, in the fore-mentioned violent storme, seperated the head from the bodie, all the vitall powers of regiment
being exiled with *Sir Thomas Gates* in those infortunate (yet
fortunate) Ilands. The broken remainder of those supplies
made a greater shipwrack in the continent of *Virginia*, by the
tempest

tempest of dissention : euery man ouervaluing his own worth, would be a Commander: euery man vnderprising an others value, denied to be commanded. The emulation of *Cæsar* and *Pompey*, watered the plains of *Pharsaly* with bloud, and distracted the sinewes of the Romane *Monarchy*. The dissentions of the three besieged Captains betraied the Citie of *Hierusalem* to *Vespasian*: how much more easily might ambitious discord teare in peeces an infant Colony, where no eminent and respected magistrats had authoritie to punish presumptuous disobedience. *Tacitus* hath obserued, that when *Nero* sent his old trained souldiers to *Tarantum* and *Autium*, (but without their Captains and Centurians) that they rather made a number, then a Colony : euery souldier secretly glided into some neighbour Prouince, and forsooke their appointed places: which hatched this consequent mischiefe ; the Cities were vninhabited, and the emperour was frustrated: when therefore licence, sedition, and furie, are the fruits of a headie, daring, and vnruly multitude, it is no wonder that so many in our colony perished : it is a wonder, that all were not deuoured. *Omnis inordinatus animus sibi ipsi fit pæna*, euery inordinate soule becomes his owne punishment.

The next fountaine of woes was secure negligence, and improuidence, when euery man sharked for his present bootie, but was altogether carelesse of succeeding penurie. Now, I demand whether *Sicilia*, or *Sardinia* (sometimes the barnes of *Rome*) could hope for increase without manuring? A Colony is therefore denominated, because they should be *Coloni*, the tillers of the earth, and stewards of fertilitie : our mutinous loiterers would not sow with prouidence, and therefore they reaped the fruits of too deare-bought repentance. An incredible example of their idlenes, is the report of *Sir Thomas Gates*, who affirmeth, that after his first comming thither, he hath seen some of them eat their fish raw, rather than they would go a stones cast to fetch wood and dresse it. *Dij laboribus omnia vendunt*, God sels vs all things for our labour, when *Adam* himselfe might not liue in paridice without dressing the garden.

Vnto idlenesse, you may ioyne treasons, wrought by those vnhallowed creatures that forsooke the Colony, and exposed their desolate brethren to extreame miserie. You shall know that 28. or 30. of the companie, were appointed (in the Ship called the Swallow) to truck for Corne with the *Indians*, and hauing obtained a great quantitie by trading, the most seditious of them, conspired together, persuaded some, & enforced others, to this barbarous proiect. They stole away the Ship, they made a league amongst themselues to be professed pirates, with

dreames

dreames of mountaines of gold, and happy robberies: thus at
one instant, they wronged the hopes, and subuerted the cares of
the Colony, who depending vpon their returne, fore-slowed to
looke out for further prouision: they created the *Indians* our
implacable enemies by some violence they had offered: they
carried away the best Ship (which should haue been a refuge, in
extremites:) they weakned our forces, by substraction of their
armes, and succours.   These are that scum of men that fayling
in their piracy, that beeing pinched with famine and penurie,
after their wilde rouing vpon the Sea, when all their lawlesse
hopes failed, some remained with other pirates, they met vpon
the Sea, the others resolued to return for England, bound themselues by mutuall oath, to agree all in one report, to discredit
the land, to deplore the famyne, and to protest that this their
comming awaie, proceeded from desperate necessitie: These are
they, that roared out the tragicall historie of the man eating of
his dead wife in *Virginia;* when the master of this Ship willingly confessed before 40 witnesses, that at their comming awaie,
they left three moneths victuals, and all the cattell liuing in the
Fort: sometimes they reported that they saw this horrible action,
sometimes that *Captaine Dauies* sayd so, sometimes that one
Beadle the Lieutenant of *Captaine Dauies* did relate it, vary-
ing this report into diuersitie of false colours, which hold no
likenesse and proportion: But to cleare all doubts, *Sir Thomas
Gates* thus relateth the tragedie.

*There was one of the companie who mortally hated his wife,
and therefore secretly killed her, then cut her in pieces and hid
her in diuers parts of his house: when the woman was missing,
the man suspected, his house searched, and parts of her mangled body were discouered, to excuse himselfe he said that his
wife died, that he hid her to satisfie his hunger, and that he
fed daily vpon her. Vpon this, his house was againe searched,
where they found a good quantitie of meale, oatemeale, beanes
and pease. Hee therevpon was araigned, confessed the mur-
der, and was burned for his horrible villany.*

Now shall the scandalous reports of a viperous generation,
preponderate the testimonies of so worthie leaders? shall their
venemous tongues, blast the reputation of an auncient & worthy
Peere, who vpon the ocular certainty of future blessings, hath
protested in his Letters, that he will sacrifice himselfe for his
Countrie in this seruice, if he may be seconded; and if the
company doe giue it ouer he will yet lay all his fortunes vpon
the prosecution of the plantation? shall sworne lyes, and com-
bined oathes, so far priuiledge trechery, and piracy as to rob vs
of our hopes, & to quell our noble resolutions? God forbid: *Qui*
in

in mendacio confidit, cito diffidit, a lyers confidence, is but a blazing diffidence.

Vnto Treasons, you may ioyne couetousnesse in the Mariners, who for their priuate lucre partly imbezled the prouisions, partly preuented our trade with the *Indians,* making the matches in the night, and forestalling our market in the day : whereby the Virginians were glutted with our trifles, and inhaunced the prices of their Corne and Victuall. That Copper which before would haue prouided a bushell, would not now obtaine so much as a pottle : *Non habet euentus sordida præda bonos,* the consequent of sordid gaine is vntimely wretchednesse.

Ioyne vnto these an other euill : there is great store of Fish in the riuer, especially of Sturgeon ; but our men prouided no more of them, then for present necessitie, not barrelling vp any store against that season the Sturgeon returned to the sea. And not to dissemble their folly, they suffered fourteene nets (which was all they had) to rot and spoile, which by orderly drying and mending might haue been preserued : but being lost, all help of fishing perished. *Quanto maiora timentur dispendia, tanto promptior debet esse cautela,* fundamentall losses that cannot be repealed, ought with the greatest caution to be preuented.

The state of the Colony, by these accidents began to find a sensible declyning : which *Powhatan* (as a greedy Vulture) obseruing, and boyling with desire of reuenge, he inuited *Captaine Ratclife,* and about thirty others to trade for Corne, and under the colour of fairest friendship, he brought them within the compasse of his ambush, whereby they were cruelly murthered, and massacred. For vpon confidence of his fidelitie, they went one and one into seuerall houses, which caused their seuerall destructions, when if but any sixe had remained together, they would haue been a bulwarke for the generall preseruation. After this, *Powhatan* in the night cut off some of our boats, he draue away all the Deere into the farther part of the Countrie, hee and his people destroyed our Hogs, (to the number of about sixe hundred) he sent none of his *Indians* to trade with vs, but laied secret ambushes in the woods, that if one or two dropped out of the fort alone, they were indaungered.

Cast vp this reckoning together : want of gouernment, store of idlenesse, their expectations frustrated by the Traitors, their market spoyled by the Mariners, our nets broken, the deere chased, our boats lost, our hogs killed, our trade with the *Indians* forbidden, some of our men fled, some murthered, and most by drinking of the brackish water of *Iames* fort weakened, and indaungered, famyne and sicknesse by all these meanes increased, ed, here at home the monies came in so slowly, that the *Lo. Laware* could not be dispatched, till the Colony was worne and spent with difficulties: Aboue all, hauing neither Ruler, nor Preacher, they neither feared God nor man, which prouoked the wrath of the Lord of Hosts, and pulled downe his iudgements vpon them. *Discite iustitiam moniti.* Now, (whether it were that God in mercie to vs would weede out these ranke hemlockes; or whether in iudgement to them he would scourge their impieties; or whether in wisedome he would trie our patience, *Vt magna magnè desideremus*, that wee may beg great blessings earnestly) our hope is that our Sunne shall not set in a cloude, since this violent storme is dispersed, since all necessarie things are prouided, an absolute and powerfull gouernment is setled, as by this insuing relation shall be described.

When *Sir Thomas Gates* arriued in *Virginia*, the strange and vnexpected condition wherein he found the Colony, gaue him to vnderstand, how neuer was there more neede of all the powers of judgement, then at this present; it being now his charge, both to saue such as he found so forlorne and wretched, as to redeeme himselfe and his from falling into the like calamities. All which considered, he entred into consultation with *Sir George Summers*, and *Captaine Newport*, and the Gentlemen and councell of the former gouernment. They examined first their store, which after two cakes a day to a man, would hold out but sixteene dayes, (it being fiue moneths betwixt the stealing away of the *Swallow*, and his landing) the Corne of the *Indians* but newly sowed, not an eye of Sturgeon, as yet appeared in the riuer: And therefore at the same consultation it was concluded by a generall approbation, That they should abandon the Countrie, and in the foure Pinaces (which remained in the riuer) they should make for the New found land, where (it beeing fishing time) they might meete with many English Ships, into which they hoped to disperse the most of the Company.

This conclusion taking effect, vpon the seuenth of Iune Sir *Thomas Gates* (hauing appointed euery ship her complement and number, and deliuered likewise to each a proportionable weight of prouision) caused every man to repaire aboord; his company (and of his company himselfe) remained last on shore, to keepe the towne from being burned, which some of our owne company maliciously threatned. About noone they fell downe with the tyde to the Iland of Hogges, and the next morning to the Mulbury Iland: at what time, they discouered the long Boate of the Lord *Laware*, which his Lordship (hearing

ing of this resolution by the Captaine of the Fort, which standeth at the mouth of the riuer) suddenly dispatched with letters
to Sir *Thomas Gates*, which informed him of his Lordships
arriuall. Vpon receite of these letters, Sir *Thomas Gates* bore
vp the Helme, and that night with a fauourable winde relanded
all our men at the Fort. Before which, the tenth of Iune (being Sunday) his Lordship came with all his Fleete, went ashore
in the afternoone, heard a Sermon, read his Commission, and
entred into consultation for the good of the Colony.

In which secret counsell, I will a little leaue his Lordship,
that wee may duly obserue the reuealed counsell of God. He
that shal but turne vp his eye, and behold the spangled Cano-
pie of heauen, shall but cast down his eye, and consider the
imbroidered Carpet of the earth, and withall shall marke, how
the heauens heare the earth, the earth heare the corne and
oyle, and they relieue the necessities of man, that man wil
acknowledge Gods infinite prouidence. But hee that shall
further obserue, how God inclineth all casuall euents, to worke
the necessary helpe of his Saints, must needs adore the Lords
infinite goodnesse. Neuer had any people more iust cause to
cast themselues at the foot-stoole of God, and to reuerence his
mercy, then our distressed Colony: for if God had not sent Sir
Thomas Gates from the Bermudos within foure daies, they had
all beene famished: if God had not directed the heart of that
worthy Knight, to saue the Fort from fire at their shipping,
they had been destitute of a present harbor, and succor; if
they had abandoned the Fort any longer time, and had not so
soone returned, questionlesse the Indians would haue destroied
the Fort, which had beene the meanes of our safety among
them, and a terrour vnto them. If they had set Saile sooner,
and had lanched into the vast Ocean, who could haue promised,
that they should haue encountered the Fleet of the Lo.
La-ware? especially when they made for the New-found
land, a course contrary to our Nauies approaching. If the
Lord *La-ware* had not brought with him a yeares prouision,
what comfort could those soules haue receiued, to haue beene
relanded to a second destruction? *Brachium Domini,* this was
the arme of the Lord of Hosts, who would haue his people to
passe the redde Sea and Wildernesse, and then to possesse the
land of Canaan: It was diuinely spoken of heathen *Socrates,
Si Deus sit solicitus pro te, cur tu tibi sis solicitus?* If God
for man be carefull, why should man be ouer distrustfull?

The noble Lord gouernor, after mature deliberation, deliuered some few words to the company, laying iust blame vpon
them for their haughty vanities, and sluggish idlenesse; earn-
nestly

estly entreating them to amend those desperate follies, lest he
should be compelled to draw the sword of Iustice, and to cut off
such delinquents, which he had rather draw (euen to the shed-
ding of his vital blood) to protect them from iniuries; heartning
them with relation of that store hee had brought with him;
constituting officers of all conditions to rule ouer them, allotting
euery man his particular place to watch vigilantly and worke
painefully. This Oration and direction being receiued with a
generall applause, you might shortly behold the idle and restie
diseases of a diuided multitude, by the vnity and authority of
this gouernment, to be substantially cured. Those that knew
not the way to goodnes before, but cherished singularity and
faction, can now chalke out the path of all respectiue duetie
and seruice: euery man endeauouring to out-strip each other
in diligence: the French preparing to plant the Vines, the
English labouring in the woods and groundes; euery man
knoweth his charge, and dischargeth the same with alacrity.
Neither let any man be discouraged, by the relation of their
daily labor, (as though the sappe of their bodies should be
spent for other mens profite) the setled times of working (to
effect all themselues, or the Aduenturers neede desire) requiring no more pains then from sixe of clocke in the morning
vntill ten, and from two of the clocke in the afternoone till
foure: at both which times they are prouided of spiritual and
corporall reliefe. First, they enter into the Church, and make
their prayers vnto God; next, they returne to their houses,
and receiue their proportion of foode. Nor should it be conceiued, that this busines excludeth Gentlemen, whose breeding
neuer knew what a daies labour meant; for though they cannot
digge, vse the square, nor practise the axe and chizell; yet
may the stayde spirits of any condition finde how to employ
the force of knowledge, the exercise of counsell, the operation
and power of their best breeding and qualities. The houses
which are built are as warme and defensible against winde and
weather, as if they were tiled and slated; being couered aboue
with strong boordes, and matted round within, according to the
fashion of the Indians. Our forces are now such as are able
to tame the fury and treachery of the Sauages: our Forts
assure the Inhabitants, and frustrate all assailants. And to
leaue no discouragement in the heart of any, who personally
shall enter into this great action, I will communicate a double
comfort: first, Sir *George Summers* (that worthy Admiral)
hath vndertaken a dangerous aduenture, for the good of the
Colony.

Vpon the fifteenth of Iune (accompanied with Captaine
Samuel

Samuel Argoll) he returned in two Pinaces vnto the Bermudos; promising (if by any meanes God will open a way to that Iland of Rockes) that he would soone returne with sixe moneths prouision of flesh, and with liue Hogges to store againe Virginia. It is but eleuen daies saile, and we hope that God will send a pillar of fire to direct his iourney. The other comfort is, that the Lord gouernour hath built two new Forts (the one called Fort *Henry*, and the other Fort *Charles*, in honor of our most noble Prince and his hopefull brother) vpon a pleasant hill, and neere a little riuelet, which we call Southampton riuer. They stand in a wholsome ayre, hauing plenty of springs of sweete water; they command a great circuit of ground, containing wood, pasture and meadow; with apt places for vines, corne and gardens. In which Forts it is resolued, that all those that come out of England shall be at their first landing quartered; that the wearisomnes of the sea may bee refreshed in this pleasing part of the countrey.

The fertility of the soile, the temperature of the climate, the form of gouernment, the condition of our people, their daily inuocating of the name of God, being thus expressed; Why should the successe (by the rules of mortall iudgement) be despaired? Why should not the rich haruest of our hopes be seasonably expected? I dare say, that the resolution of *Cæsar* in Fraunce, the designes of *Alexander* in Greece, the discoueries of *Hernando Cortes* in the West, and of *Emanuel*, King of Portugale in the East, were not incouraged vpon so firme grounds of state and possibility. All which I could demonstrate out of their owne Records, were I not preuented with hast, to satisfie their longings, who with an open eare, hearken after the commodities of the countrey: whose appetites I will no longer frustrate, then their eyes can runne ouer this succinct Narration.

I called it a succinct Narration, because the commodities in former Treatises haue beene largely described, which I will here only epitomise, lest any man should change his resolution, when the same grounds remaine, which were the cause of his former aduenture.

The Councell of Virginia (finding the smalnesse of that returne, which they hoped should haue defraied the charge of a new supply) entred into a deepe consultation, and propounded amongst themselues, whether it were fit to enter into a new contribution, or in time to send for home the Lord *La-ware*, and to abandon the action. They resolued to send for sir *Thomas Gates*, who being come, they adiured him to deale plainely with them, and to make a true relation of those

things

things which were presently to be had, or hereafter to be
hoped for in Virginia.   Sir *Thomas Gates* with a solemne
and sacred oath replied, that all things before reported were
true : that the country yeeldeth abundance of wood, as Oake,
Wainscot, Walnut trees, Bay trees, Ashe, Sarsafrase, liue
Oake, greene all the yeare, Cedar and Firre ; which are the
materials, of soape ashes, and pot ashes, of oyles of walnuts,
and bayes, of pitch and tarre, of Clap boards, Pipe-stāues,
Masts and excellent boardes of forty, fifty and sixtie length,
and three foote bredth, when one Firre tree is able to make
the maine Mast of the greatest ship in England.   He
auouched, that there are incredible variety of sweet woods,
especially of the Balsamum tree, which distilleth a pretious
gum ; that there are innumerable White Mulberry trees, which
in so warme a climate may cherish and feede millions of silke
wormes, and returne vs in a very short time, as great a plenty
of silke as is vented into the whole world from al the parts of
Italy : that there are diuers sorts of Minerals, especially of Iron
oare, lying vpon the ground for ten miles circuite ; (of which
we haue made triall at home, that it maketh as good Iron as
any is in Europe:) that a kinde of hempe or flax, and silke
grasse doe grow there naturally, which will affoord stuffe for all
manner of excellent Cordage : that the riuer swarmeth with
Sturgeon ; the land aboundeth with Vines, the woodes doe
harbor exceeding store of Beauers, Foxes and Squirrils, the
waters doe nourish a great encrease of Otters ; all which are
couered with pretious furres : that there are in present discouered dyes and drugs of sundry qualities ; that the Orenges
which haue beene planted, did prosper in the winter, which is
an infallible argument, that Lymmons, sugar Canes, Almonds,
Rice, Anniseede, and all other commodities which we have from
the Staights, may be supplied to vs in our owne countrey,
and by our owne industry : that the corne yeeldeth a trebble
encrease more then ours ; and lastly, that it is one of the
goodliest countries vnder the sunne ; enterueined with fiue
maine Rivers, and promising as rich entrals as any Kingdome
of the earth, to whom the sunne is so neerer a neighbour.

VVhat these things will yeelde, the Merchant best knoweth,
who findeth by experience, that many hundreth of thousands
of pounds are yearly spent in Christendome in these commodities.   The Merchant knoweth, that Caueare and Traine
which come from Russia, can be brought hither but once in
the yeare, in regard of the Ice : and that Sturgeon which is
brought from the East countries, can come but twice a yeare ;
and that not before the end of Aprill, or the beginning of
                                                          May ;

May; which many times in regard of the heat of those moneths, is tainted in the transportation: when from Virginia they may be brought to vs in foure and twenty daies, and in al the colde seasons of the yeare. The Merchants know, that the commodity of sope and pot ashes are very scant in Prussia; that they are brought three hundred miles by land, and three hundred miles by riuers, before they come to the Sea; that they pay a custome there, and another in Denmarke, which enhanceth the prices exceedingly: But in Virginia they may haue them without carriage by land or custom (because fiue Nauigable Riuers doe lead vp fiue seuerall waies into the bowels of the whole countrey.) As therefore the like Riuers, are the cause of the riches of Holland, so will these be to vs a wondrous cause of sauing of expences. The merchant knoweth, that through the troubles in Poland & Muscouy, (whose eternall warres are like the Antipathy of the Dragon & Elephants) all their traffique for Mastes, Deales, Pitch, Tarre, Flax, Hempe, and Cordage, are euery day more and more indangered, and the woods of those countries are almost exhausted. All which are to be had in Virginia with farre lesse charge, and farre more safety. Lastly, the Merchant knoweth, that for our commodities in the Staights, as sweet wines, orenges, lemmonds, anniseeds, &c. that we stand at the deuotion of politique Princes and States, who for their proper vtility, deuise all courses to grinde our merchants, all pretences to confiscate their goods, and to draw from vs al marrow of gaine by their inquisitiue inuentions: when in Virginia, a few yeares labour by planting and husbandry, will furnish all our defects, with honour and security; especially since the Frenchmen (who are with the Lord Gouernour) do confidently promise, that within two yeares we may expect a plentifull Vintage.

VVhen therefore this noble enterprise, by the rules of Religion is expressly iustified; when the passages by Sea are all open and discouered; when the climate is so fruitfully tempered; when the naturall riches of the soile are so powerfully confirmed: will any man so much betray his owne inconsiderate ignorance, and bewray his rashnesse; that when the same Sunne shineth, he should not haue the same eies to beholde it; when the same hope remaines, he should not haue the same heart to apprehend it? At the voyage of Sir *Thomas Gates,* what swarmes of people desired to be transported? what alacrity and cheerefulnesse in the Aduenturers by free wil offerings, to build vp this new Tabernacle? Shall we now be deiected? Shall we cast downe our heads like Bull rushes?

because

because one storme at sea hath deferred our ioyes and
comforts! VVe are too effeminate in our longings, and too
impatient of delaies. Gods al-disposing prouidence, is not
compellable by mans violence : Let any wisedome giue a
solide reason, why his purpose should be changed, when those
grounds which gaue life to his first purpose, are not changed.
It is but a golden slumber, that dreameth of any humane
felicity, which is not sauced with some contingent miserie.
Dolor & voluptas, inuicem cedunt, Griefe and pleasure are
the crosse sailes of the worlds euer-turning-windmill. Let
no man therefore be ouer wise, to cast beyond the moone and
to multiplie needlesse doubts and questions. *Hannibal* by
too much wisedome, lost opportunity to haue sacked Rome.
Charles the eighth of Fraunce, by temporising, lost the Kingdome of Naples, and the gouernement of Florence : *Henry*
the seuenth by too much ouer-warines, lost the riches of the
golden Indies. Occasion is pretious, but when it is occasion.
Some of our neighbours would ioine in the action, if they
might be ioynt inheritors in the Plantation ; which is an
euident proofe, that Virginia shall no sooner be quitted by vs,
then it will be reinhabited by them. A dishonor of that
nature, that will eternally blemish our Nation ; as though we
were like the furious *Pyrrhus,* or impetuous Swissers, who in
a brunt can conquer any thing, but with wisedome can
maintaine nothing. It is time to wipe away such an imputation
of Barbarisme, especially since the consequence is so pregnant,
that without this or the like, the state cannot subsist without
some dangerous and imminent mutation. He is ouer blinde
that doth not see, what an inundation of people doth ouerflow
this little Iland : Shall we vent this deluge, by indirect and
vnchristian policies? shal we imitate the bloody and heathen-
ish counsell of the Romanes, to leaue a Carthage standing,
that may exhaust our people by forraine warre? or shall we
nourish domesticall faction, that as in the dayes of *Vitellius*
and *Vespasian,* the sonne may imbrew his hands in the blood
of the father? Or shall we follow the barbarous foot-steps of
the state of China, to imprison our people in a little circle
of the earth, and consume them by pestilence? Or shall we
like the beast of Babylon, denie to any sort the honourable
estate of mariage, and allow abhominable stewes, that our
people may not ouer increase in multitude? Or shall we take
an inhumane example from the Muscouite, in a time of famine
to put tenne thousand of the poore vnder the yce, as the Mice
and Rats of a state politique? If all these be diabolicall and
hellish proiects, what other meanes remaines to vs, but by
setling

setling so excellent a Plantation, to disimbarke some millions of people vpon a land that floweth with all manner of plenty?

To wade a little further, who euer saluted the monuments of antiquity, and doth not finde, that Carthage aspired to be Empresse of the world, by her opportunity of hauens and multitude of shipping? What hindereth the great Mahumetane Prince, from seazing vpon al the territories of Europe, but onely the want of skilfull marriners? What created the rich and free states of Holland, but their winged Nauy? It was a fit embleme that painted death standing vpon the shoares of Fraunce, Germany and Spaine, and looking ouer into England: intymating vnto vs, that so long as we are Lords of the narrow seas, death stands on the other shoares, and onely can looke vpon vs: but if our wooden wals were ruinated, death would soone make a bridge to come ouer, and deuoure our Nation. When therefore our mils of Iron, and excesse of building, haue already turned our greatest woods into pasture and champion, within these few years; neither the scattered Forrests of England, nor the diminished Groues of Ireland, will supply the defect of our Nauy. When in Virginia there is nothing wanting, but onely mens labours, to furnish both Prince, State and merchant, without charge or difficulty. Againe, whither shall wee transport our cloth, and how shall we sustaine our Artisans? Shall we send it into Turkey? Some priuate and deceitfull auarice hath discredited our merchandize. Into Spaine? it aboundeth with sheepe and wooll. Into Poland and Muscouy? the daunger doth ouerballance the gaine in times of contention. Into Fraunce and Germany? they are for the most part supplied by their owne peace. VVhen if our Colony were peopled in Virginia, *mutabit vellera merces*, we shall exchange our store of cloth for other merchandize. Let any man resolue why the Councell of Virginia, doe now most earnestly continue their aduentures? why those that were (eye witnesses) of the former supposed miseries, do voluntarily returne with ioy and comfort? why those noble and worthy personages, doe offer to make the action good vpon the hazard of their liues & fortunes? And why Sir *Thomas Gates* longeth and hasteneth to go thither again, and the Lord *La-ware* desireth so earnestly to stay there? Are not all these things as deere to them as to any other of the Aduenturers? Haue not their hopes the same wings? their feares the same fetters? their estates the same rockes? their liues and soules greater gulfes of perill and despair? And yet neither the imbracements of their wiues, nor indulgence to their babes, nor the neglect of their domesticke

ticke fortunes, nor banishment from their natiue soile, nor any
experimented dangers haue broken their noble resolution.

And therefore, he that desireth to purchase infallible hope
of priuate vtility; hee that aimeth at the honor & wealth of
his natiue country; he that esteemeth his owne repute as
deere as his owne eies; he that endeauoureth to enlarge the
dominions of his Prince, and the Kingdome of his God: let
him remember what hee hath already spent, which is all
buried; let him consider the consequences of state, which are
all vanished into smoake; let him conceiue what a scorne
we shall be made to the maligners of our state abroad, and
our il affected at home; let him meditate, the external riches
of other Kingdoms, able to buy and sell the monarch of the
west; let him heare the triumphant boasting of the Beast of
Rome, as though God would not suffer our schismaticall and
hereticall Religion, to be infused into a new conuerted Region:
O all ye worthies, follow the euer-sounding trumpet of a
blessed honour; let Religion be the first aim of your hopes,
& *cætera adijcientur*, and other things shall be cast vnto you:
your names shall be registred to posterity with a glorious
title; *These are the men, whom God raised to augment the
State of their countrey, and to propagate the Gospell of Iesus
Christ*. Neyther ought any man to liue vnder *Augustus*, as
if he liued vnder *Domitian, quibus inertia est pro sapientia;*
to whom sluggishnes & priuacy is imputed for wisedome and
pollicy. The same God that hath ioyned three Kingdomes
vnder one *Cæsar*, wil not be wanting to adde a fourth, if wee
would dissolue that frosty Icinesse which chilleth our zeale,
and maketh vs so cold in the action. But is a meere *Idæa*,
speculation and fancy, to sow sparingly, and yet expect for to
reape plentifully; when a penurious supply is like the casting
on of a little water vpon a great fire, that quencheth not the
heat, but augments it: when procrastinating delayes, and
lingring counsels, doe lose the opportunity of flying time;
whereby we rather bewray our Colony then releeue them: let
no man adore his golde as his God, nor his Mammon as his
Maker. If God haue scattered his blessings vpon you as
snow, will you retnrne no tributary acknowledgement of his
goodnesse? If you will, can you select a more excellent
subiect, then to cast downe the altars of Diuels, that you may
raise vp the Altar of Christ: to forbid the sacrifice of men,
that they may offer vp the sacrifice of contrite spirites; to
reduce Barbarisme and infidelity, to ciuill gouernment and
Christianity? *Si frigido loquor, nihil loquor;* If I speake
to a man void of piety, I speake but the words of winde and
vanity;

vanity; otherwise how doth that man groane vnder the worlds corruption, that doth not actually or vocally hasten the worldes conuersion? Doubt ye not but God hath determined, and demonstrated (by the wondrous preseruation of those principal persons which fell vpon the Bermudos) that he will raise our state, and build his Church in that excellent climate, if the action be seconded with resolution and Religion.

Nil disperandum Christo Duce, & Auspice Christo.

FINIS.

FOR

The Colony in Virginea

BRITANNIA.

Lavves Diuine, Morall and

Martiall, &c.

Alget qui non Ardet.

Res nostræ subinde non sunt, quales quis optaret,
sed quales esse possunt.

Printed at London for *Walter Burre*. 1612.

Force's Collection of Historical Tracts.

Vol. III.—No. 2.

To the Right Honorable, the Lords

of the Councell of Virginea.

NOblest of men, though tis the fashion now
    Noblest to mixe with basest, for their gaine:
Yet doth it fare farre otherwise with you,
    That scorne to turn to Chaos so againe,
And follow your supreme distinction still,
    Till of most noble, you become diuine
And imitate your maker in his will,
    To haue his truth in blackest nations shine.
VVhat had you beene, had not your Ancestors
    Begunne to you, that make their nobles good?
And where white Christians turn in maners Mores
    You wash Mores white with sacred Christā bloud
      This wonder ye, that others nothing make
      Forth thē (great LL.) for your Lords Sauiors sake.

By him, all whose duty is tributary
to your Lordships, and vnto so
excellent a cause.

William Strachey.

To the constant, mighty, and wor
thie friends, the Committies, Assistants
vnto his Maiesties Councell for the Colonie
in VIRGINEA-BRITANNIA.

W*Hen I went forth vpon this voyage, (Right worthy Gentlemen) true it is, I held it a seruice of dutie, (during the time of my vnprofitable seruice, and purpose of stay in the Colonie, for which way else might I adde vnto the least hight of so Heroicke and pious a building) to propose vnto myself to be (though an vnable) Remembrancer of all accidents, occurrences, and vndertakings thereunto,* aduentitiall : *In most of which since the time our right famous sole Gouernour then, now Lieutenant Generall Sir* Thomas Gates *Knight, after the ensealing of his Commission hasted to our fleete in the West, there staying for him, I haue both in the* Bermudas, *and since in* Virginea *beene a sufferer and an eie witnesse, and the full storie of both in due time shall consecrate vnto your viewes, as vnto whom by right it appertaineth, being vowed patrones of a worke, and enterprise so great, then which no obiect nor action (the best of bests) in these time, may carry with it the like fame, honour, or goodnesse.*

Howbet since many impediments, as yet must detaine such my obseruations in the shadow of darknesse, vntill I shall be able to deliuer them perfect vnto your iudgements why I shall prouoke and challenge) I do in the meane time present a transcript of the Toparchia *or State of those duties, by which their Colonie stands regulated and commaunded, that such may receive due checke, who malitiously and desperately heretofore haue censured of it, and by examining of which they may be right sorie so to haue defaulked from vs as if we liued there*

lawlesse,

lawlesse, without obedience to our Countrey, or obseruance of Religion to God.

Nor let it afflict the patience of such full and well instructed iudgments, vnto whom many of these constitutions and Lawes Diuine or Marshall may seeme auncient and common, since these grounds are the same constant, Asterismes, and starres, which must guide all that trauell in these perplexed wayes, and paths of publique affairs; & whosoeuer shall wander from them, shall but decline a hazardous and by-course to bring their purposes to good effect.

Nor let another kind quarrell or traduce the Printing of them to be deliuered in particular to officers and priuate Souldiers for their better instruction, especially vnto a Company for the grieuous, vnsettled and vnfurnished, since we know well how short our memories are oftentimes, and vnwilling to giue stoage to the better things, and such things as limit and bound mankind in their necessariest duties.

For which it transcends not the reach of his vnderstanding, who is conuersant, if but as for a festiuall exercise, (euery priuy Moone) in reading of a booke, that records and edicts for manners or ciuill duties, haue vsually beene fixed vpon ingrauen Tables, for the Commons daily to ouerlooke: a custome more especially cherished by those not many yeeres since in Magnuza who haue restored (as I may say) after so great a floud and rage of abused goodnesse, all Lawes, literature and Vertue againe, which had well nigh perished, had not the force of piety and sacred reason remaining in the bosomes of some few, opposed itselfe against the fury of so great a calamity, of whom it is an vndenyable truth, that the meanes and way whereby they reduced the generall defection, was by printing thereby so houlding vppe those inuolued principles, and Instructions wherein (as in a mirror, the blind and wandering iudgement might suruaye, what those knowledges were, which taught both how to gouerne, and how to obey, (the end indeed of sociable mankinds Creation) since without order and gouernement, (the onely hendges,

whereupon,

whereupon, not onely the safety, but the being of all states doe turne and depend) what society may possible subsist, or commutatiue goodnesse be practised.   And thus lawes being published, euery common eye may take suruey of their duties, and carrying away the tenour of the same, meditate, & bethinke how safe, quiet, and comely it is to be honest, iust, and ciuill.

And indeed all the sacred powers of knowledge and wisedome are strengthened by these two waies, either by a kind of diuine nature, which his happy creation hath blessed him with, the vertue whereof comprehendeth, foreseeth and vnderstandeth the truth and cleerenesse of all things : or by instruction and tradition from others, which must improue his wants, and by experience render him perfect, awaking him in all seasons a vigilant obseruer of ciuill cautions and ordinances, an excellent reason inforcing no lesse vnto the knowledge of him that will shine a starre in the firmament, where good men moue, and that is, that no man doth more ill then hee that is ignorant.

For the auoiding of which, and to take away the plea of I did not know in him that shall exorbitate or goe aside with any delinquencie which may be dangerous in example or execution, albeit true it is how hee is indeede the good and honest man that will be good, and to that needeth fewe other precepts.   It hath appeared most necessary vnto our present Ethnarches *Deputy Gouernor* Sir Thomas Dale *knight Marshall, not onely to exemplifie the old Lawes of the Colony, by* Sir Thomas Gates *published & put in execution by our Lord Generall* Laware *during his time one whole yeere of being there, but by vertue of his office, to prescribe and draw new, with their due penaltyes, according vnto which wee might liue in the Colony iustly one with another, and performe the generall seruice for which we first came thither, and with so great charges & expences, are now setled & maintained there.*

For my paines, and gathering of them, as I know they will be right welcom to such young souldiers in the Colony who are desirous to learne and performe their duties, so I assure me, that
by

by you I shall bee encouraged to go on in the discharge of greater offices by examining and fauouring my good intention in this, and in what else my poore knowledge or faithfulnesse may enable me to be a seruant in so beloued and sacred a businesse. And euen so committing to your still most obstract, graue and vnsatisfied carefulnesse, both it and myselfe, I wish returne of seuen fold into such his well inspired bosome, who hath lent his helping hand vnto this new Sion. From my lodging in the blacke Friers.

At your best pleasures, either to returne vnto the Colony, or to pray for the successe of it heere.

WILLIAM STRACHEY.

Articles, Lawes, and Orders, Diuine, Politique, and Martiall for the Colony in Virginea: *first established by Sir* Thomas Gates *Knight, Lieutenant Generall, the* 24. *of May* 1610. *exemplified and approued by the Right Honourable Sir* Thomas West *Knight, Lord Lawair, Lord Gouernour and Captaine Generall the* 12. *of Iune* 1610. *Againe exemplified and enlarged by Sir* Thomas Dale *Knight, Marshall, and Deputie Gouernour, the* 22. *of Iune.* 1611.

Hereas his Maiestie like himselfe a most zealous Prince hath in his owne Realmes a principall care of true Religion, and reuerence to God, and hath alwaies strictly commaunded his Generals and Gouernours, with all his forces wheresoeuer, to let their waies be like his ends, for the glorie of God.

And forasmuch as no good seruice can be performed, or warre well managed, where militarie discipline is not obserued, and militarie discipline cannot be kept, where the rules or chiefe parts thereof, be not certainely set downe, and generally knowne, I haue (with the aduise and counsell of Sir *Thomas Gates* Knight, Lieutenant Generall) adhered vnto the lawes diuine, and orders politique, and martiall of his Lordship (the same exemplified) an addition of such others, as I haue found either the necessitie of the present State of the Colonie to require, or the infancie, and weakenesse of the body thereof, as yet able to digest, and doe now publish them to all persons in the Colonie, that they may as well take knowledge of the Lawes themselues, as of the penaltie and punishment, which without partialitie shall be inflicted vpon the breakers of the same.

1   FIrst since we owe our highest and supreme duty, our greatest, and all our allegeance to him, from whom all power and authoritie is deriued, and flowes as from the first, and onely fountaine, and being especiall souldiers emprest in this sacred cause, we must alone expect our
successe

successe from him, who is onely the blesser of all good attempts, the King of kings, the commaunder of commaunders, and Lord of Hostes, I do strictly commaund and charge all Captaines and Officers, of what qualitie or nature soeuer, whether commanders in the field, or in towne, or townes, forts or fortresses, to haue a care that the Almightie God bee duly and daily serued, and that they call vpon their people to heare Sermons, as that also they diligently frequent Morning and Euening praier themselues by their owne exemplar and daily life, and dutie herein, encouraging others thereunto, and that such, who shall often and wilfully absent themselues, be duly punished according to the martiall law in that case prouided.

2   That no man speake impiously or maliciously, against the holy and blessed Trinitie, or any of the three persons, that is to say, against God the Father, God the Son, and God the holy Ghost, or against the knowne Articles of the Christian faith, vpon paine of death.

3   That no man blaspheme Gods holy name upon paine of death, or vse vnlawful oathes, taking the name of God in vaine, curse, or banne, vpon paine of seuere punishment for the first offence so committed, and for the second, to haue a bodkin thrust through his tongue, and if he continue the blaspheming of Gods holy name, for the third time so offending, he shall be brought to a martiall court, and there receiue censure of death for his offence.

4   No man shall vse any traiterous words against his Maiesties Person, or royall authority vpon paine of death.

5   No man shall speake any word, or do any act, which may tend to the derision, or despight of Gods holy word vpon paine of death: Nor shall any man vnworthily demeane himselfe vnto any Preacher, or Minister of the same, but generally hold them in all reuerent regard, and dutiful intreatie, otherwise he the offender shall openly be whipt three times, and ask publike forgiuenesse in the assembly of the congregation three seueral Saboth daies.

6   Euerie man and woman duly twice a day vpon the first towling of the Bell shall vpon the working daies repaire vnto the Church, to hear diuine Service vpon pain of losing his or her dayes allowance for the first omission, for the second to be whipt, and for the third to be condemned to the Gallies for six Moneths.   Likewise no man or woman shall dare to violate or breake the Sabboth by any gaming, publique, or priuate abroad, or at home, but duly sanctifie and obserue the same, both himselfe and his familie, by preparing themselues at home with private

vate prayer, that they may be the better fitted for the publique, according to the commandements of God, and the orders of our Church, as also euery man and woman shall repaire in the morning to the diuine seruice, and Sermons preached vpon the Saboth day, and in the afternoon to diuine seruice, and Catechising, vpon paine for the first fault to lose their prouision, and allowance for the whole weeke following, for the second to lose the said allowance, and also to be whipt, and for the third to suffer death.

7   All Preachers or Ministers within this our Colonie, or Colonies, shall in the Forts, where they are resident, after diuine Seruice, duly preach euery Sabbath day in the forenoone, and Catechise in the afternoone, and weekely say the diuine seruice, twice euery day, and preach euery Wednesday, likewise euery Minister where he is resident, within the same Fort, or Fortresse, Townes or Towne, shall chuse vnto him, foure of the most religious and better disposed as well to informe of the abuses and neglects of the people in their duties, and seruice to God, as also to the due reparation, and keeping of the Church handsome, and fitted with all reuerent obseruances thereunto belonging : likewise euery Minister shall keepe a faithful and true Record, or Church Booke, of all Christnings, Marriages, and deaths of such our people, as shall happen within their Fort, or Fortresses, Townes or Towne at any time, vpon the burthen of a neglectfull conscience, and vpon paine of losing their Entertainement.

8   He that vpon pretended malice, shall murther or take away the life of any man, shall bee punished with death.

9   No man shal commit the horrible, and detestable sins of Sodomie vpon pain of death ; & he or she that can be lawfully conuict of Adultery shall be punished with death. No man shall rauish or force any womā, maid or Indian, or other, vpon pain of death, and know ye that he or shee, that shall commit fornication, and euident proofe made thereof, for their first fault shall be whipt, for their second they shall be whipt, and for their third they shall be whipt three times a weeke for one month, and aske publique forgiuenesse in the Assembly of the Congregation.

10   No man shall bee found guilty of Sacriledge, which is a Trespasse as well committed in violating and abusing any sacred ministry, duty or office of the Church, irreuerently, or prophanely, as by beeing a Church robber, to filch, steale or carry away any thing out of the Church appertaining thereunto, or vnto any holy, and consecrated place, to the diuine Seruice of God,

God, which no man should doe vpon paine of death : likewise he that shall rob the store of any commodities therein, of what quality soeuer, whether prouisions of victuals, or of Arms, Trucking stuffe, Apparrell, Linnen, or Wollen, Hose or Shooes, Hats or Caps, Instruments or Tooles of Steele, Iron, &c. or shall rob from his fellow souldier, or neighbour, any thing that is his, victuals, apparell, household stuffe, toole, or what necessary else soeuer, by water or land, out of boate, house, or knapsack, shall bee punished with death.

11   Hee that shall take an oath vntruly, or beare false witnesse in any cause, or against any man whatsoeuer, shall be punished with death.

12   No manner of person whatsoeuer, shall dare to detract, slaunder, calumniate, or vtter vnseemely, and vnfitting speeches, either against his Maiesties Honourable Councell for this Colony, resident in England, or against the Committies, Assistants vnto the said Councell, or against the zealous indeauors, & intentions of the whole body of Aduenturers for this pious and Christian Plantation, or against any publique booke, or bookes, which by their mature aduise, and graue wisdomes, shall be thought fit, to be set foorth and publisht, for the aduancement of the good of this Colony, and the felicity thereof, vpon paine for the first time so offending, to bee whipt three seuerall times, and vpon his knees to acknowledge his offence and to aske forgiuenesse vpon the Saboth day in the assembly of the congregation, and for the second time so offending to be condemned to the Galley for three yeares, and for the third time so offending to be punished with death.

13   No manner of Person whatsoeuer, contrarie to the word of God (which tyes euery particular and priuate man, for conscience sake to obedience, and duty of the Magistrate, and such as shall be placed in authoritie ouer them, shall detract, slaunder, calumniate, murmur, mutenie, resist, disobey, or neglect the commaundments, either of the Lord Gouernour, and Captaine Generall, the Lieutenant Generall, the Martiall, the Councell, or any authorised Captaine, Commaunder or publike Officer, vpon paine for the first time so offending to be whipt three seuerall times, and vpon his knees to acknowledge his offence, with asking forgiuenesse vpon the Saboth day in the assembly of the congregation, and for the second time so offending to be condemned to the Gally for three yeares : and for the third time so offending to be punished with death.

14   No man shall giue any disgracefull words, or commit any act to the disgrace of any person in this Colonie, or any part thereof,

thereof, vpon paine of being tied head and feete together, vpon the guard euerie night for the space of one moneth, besides to bee publikely disgraced himselfe, and be made vncapable euer after to possesse any place, or execute any office in this imployment.

15 No man of what condition soeuer shall barter, trucke, or trade with the Indians, except he be thereunto appointed by lawful authority, vpon paine of death.

16 No man shall rifle or dispoile, by force or violence, take away any thing from any Indian comming to trade, or otherwise, vpon paine of death.

17 No Cape Marchant, or Prouant Master, or Munition Master, or Truck Master, or keeper of any store, shall at any time imbezell, sell, or giue away any thing vnder his Charge to any Fauorite, of his, more then vnto any other, whome necessity shall require in that case to haue extraordinary allowance of Prouisions, nor shall they give a false accompt vnto the Lord Gouernour, and Captaine Generall, vnto the Lieuetenant Generall, vnto the Marshall, or any deputed Gouernor, at any time hauing the commaund of the Colony, with intent to defraud the said Colony, vpon paine of death.

18 No man shall imbezel or take away the goods of any man that dyeth, or is imployed from the town or Fort where he dwelleth in any other occasioned remote seruice, for the time, upon pain of whipping three seuerall times, and restitution of the said goods againe, and in danger of incurring the penalty of the tenth Article, if so it may come vnder the construction of theft. And if any man die and make a will, his goods shall bee accordingly disposed; if hee die intestate, his goods shall bee put into the store, and being valued by two sufficient praisers, his next of kinne (according to the common Lawes of England, shall from the Company, Committies, or aduenturers, receiue due satisfaction in monyes, according as they were praised, by which meanes the Colonie shall be the better furnished ; and the goods more carefully preserued, for the right heire, and the right heire receiue content for the same in *England*.

19 There shall no Capttain, Master, Marriner, saylor, or any else of what quality or conditiñ soeuer, belonging to any Ship or Ships, at this time remaining, or which shall hereafter arriue within this our Riuer, bargaine, buy, truck, or trade with any one member in this Colony, man, woman, or child, for any toole or instrument of iron, steel or what else, whether appertaining to Smith Carpenter, Ioyner, Shipwright, or any manuall occupation, or handicraft man whatsoeuer, resident within our Colonie, nor shall they buy or bargaine, for any apparell,

rell, linnen, or wollen, housholdstuffe, bedde, bedding, sheete towels, napkins, brasse, pewter, or such like, eyther for ready money, or prouisions, nor shall they exchange their prouisions, of what quality soeuer, whether Butter, Cheese, Bisket, meal, Oatmele, Aquauite, oyle, Bacon, any kind· of Spice, or such like, for any such aforesaid instruments, or tooles, Apparell, or householdstuffe, at any time, or so long as they shall here remain, from the date of these presents vpon paine of losse of their wages in *England*, confiscation and forfeiture of such their monies and prouisions, and vpon peril beside of such corporall punishment as shall be inflicted upon them by verdict and censure of a martiall Court : Nor shall any officer, souldier, or Trades man, or any else of what sort soeuer, members of this Colony, dare to sell any such Toole, or instruments, necessary and vsefull, for the businesse of the Colonie, or trucke, sell, exchange, or giue away his apparell, or household stuffe of what sort soeuer, vnto any such Sea-man, either for mony, or any such foresaid prouisions, vpon paine of 3 times seuerall whipping, for the one offender, and the other vpon perill of incurring censure, whether of disgrace, or addition of such punishment, as shall bee thought fit by a Court martiall.

20　Whereas sometimes heeretofore the couetous and wide affections of some greedy and ill disposed Seamen, Saylers, and Marriners, laying hold vpon the aduantage of the present necessity, under which the Colony sometimes suffered, haue sold vnto our people, prouisions of Meale, Oatmeale, Bisket, Butter, Cheese &c, at vnreasonable rates, and prises vnconscionable : for auoiding the like to bee now put in practise, there shall no Captain, Master, Marriner, or Saylor, or what Officer else belonging to any ship, or shippes, now within our riuer, or heereafter which shall arriue, shall dare to bargaine, exchange, barter, truck, trade, or sell, vpon paine of death, vnto any one Landman member of this present Colony, any prouisions of what kind soeuer, aboue the determined valuations, and prises, set downe and proclaimed, and sent therefore vnto each of your seuerall ships, to bee fixed uppon your Maine mast, to the intent that want of due notice, and ignorance in this case, be no excuse, or plea, for any one offender herein.

21　Sithence we are not to bee a little carefull, and our young Cattell, & Breeders may be cherished, that by the preseruation, and increase of them, the Colony heere may receiue in due time assured and great benefite, and the aduenturers at home may be eased of so great a burthen, by sending vnto vs yeerely supplies of this kinde, which now heere for a while,

carefully

carefully attended, may turne their supplies vnto vs into prouisions of other qualities, when of these wee shall be able to subsist our selues, and which wee may in short time, be powerful enough to doe, if we wil according to our owne knowledge of what is good for our selues, forbeare to work into our own wants, againe, by ouer hasty destroying, and deuouring the stocks, apu authors of so profitable succeeding a Commodity, as increase of Cattel, Kine, Hogges, Goates, Poultrie &c. must of necessity bee granted, in euery common mans iudgement, to render vnto us: Now know yee therefore, these promises carefully considered, that it is our will and pleasure, that euery one, of what quality or condition soeuer hee bee, in this present Colony, to take due notice of this our Edict, whereby wee do strictly charge and command, that no man shall dare to kill, or destroy any Bull, Cow, Calfe, Mare, Horse, Colt, Goate, Swine, Cocke, Henne, Chicken, Dogge, Turkie, or any tame Cattel, or Poultry, of what condition soeuer ; whether his owne, or appertaining to another man, without leaue from the Generall, upon paine of death in the Principall, and in the accessary, burning in the Hand, and losse of his eares, and unto the concealer of the same foure and twenty houres whipping, with addition of further punishment, as shall be thought fitte by the censure, and verdict of a Martiall Court.

22   There shall no man or woman, Launderer or Launderesse, dare to wash any vncleane Linnen, driue bucks, or throw out the water or suds of fowle cloathes, in the open streete, within the Pallizadoes, or within forty foote of the same, nor rench, and make cleane, any kettle, pot, or pan, or such like vessell within twenty foote of the olde well, or new Pumpe : nor shall any one aforesaid, within lesse then a quarter of one mile from the Pallizadoes, dare to doe the necessities of nature, since by these vnmanly, slothfull, and loathsome immodesties, the whole Fort may bee choaked, and poisoned with ill aires, and so corrupt (as in all reason cannot but much infect the same) and this shall they take notice of, and auoide, vpon paine of whipping and further punishment, as shall be thought meete, by the censure of a martiall Court.

23   No man shall imbezell, lose, or willingly breake, or fraudulently make away, either Spade, Shouell, Hatchet, Axe, Mattocke, or other toole or instrument vppon paine of whipping.

24   Any man that hath any edge toole, either of his owne, or which hath heeretofore beene belonging to the store, see that he bring it instantly to the storehouse, where he shall receiue it againe by a particular note, both of the toole, and of his name

taken

taken, that such a toole vnto him appertaineth, at whose hands, vpon any necessary occasion, the said toole may be required, and this shall he do, vpon paine of seuere punishment.

25   Euery man shall haue an especiall and due care, to keepe his house sweete and cleane, as also so much of the streete, as lieth before his door, and especially he shall so prouide, and set his bedstead whereon he lieth, that it may stand three foote at least from the ground, as he will answere the contrarie at a martiall Court.

26   Euery tradsman in their seuerall occupation, trade and function, shall duly and daily attend his worke vpon his said trade or occupation, vpon perill for his first fault, and negligence therein, to haue his entertainment checkt for one moneth, for his second fault three moneth, for his third one yeare, and if he continue still vnfaithfull and negligent therein, to be condemned to the Gally for three yeare.

27   All ouerseers of workemen, shall be carefull in seeing that performed, which is giuen them in charge, vpon paine of such punishment as shall be inflicted vpon him by a martiall Court.

28   No souldier or tradesman, but shall be readie, both in the morning, & in the afternoone, vpon the beating of the Drum, to goe out vnto his worke, nor shall hee return home, or from his worke, before the Drum beate againe, and the officer appointed for that businesse, bring him of, vpon perill for the first fault to lie vpon the Guard head and heeles together all night, for the second time so faulting to be whipt, and for the third time so offending to be condemned to the Gallies for a yeare.

29   No man or woman, (vpon paine of death) shall runne away from the Colonie, to Powhathan, or any sauage Weroance else whatsoeuer.

30   He that shall conspire any thing against the person of the Lord Gouernour, and Captaine Generall, against the Lieutenant Generall, or against the Marshall, or against any publike seruice commaunded by them, for the dignitie, and advancement of the good of the Colony, shall be punished with death: and he that shall haue knowledge of any such pretended act of disloyalty or treason, and shall not reveale the same vnto his Captaine, or vnto the Gouernour of that fort or towne wherein he is, within the space of one houre, shall for the concealing of the same after that time, be not onely held an accessary, but alike culpable as the principall traitor or conspirer, and for the same likewise he shall suffer death.

31   What man or woman soeuer, shall rob any garden, publike

like or priuate, being set to weed the same, or wilfully pluck vp
therin any roote, herbe, or flower, to spoile and wast or steale the
same, or robbe any vineyard, or gather vp the grapes, or steale
any eares of the corne growing, whether in the ground belonging to the same fort or towne where he dwelleth, or in any other,
shall be punished with death.

32 Whosoeuer Seaman, or Landman of what qualitie, or in
what place of commaund soeuer, shall be imployed vpon any
discouery, trade, or fishing voiage into any of the riuers within
the precincts of our Colonie, shall for the safety of those men
who are committed to his commaund, stand vpon good and
carefull guard, for the preuention of any treachery in the Indian,
and if they touch vpon any shore, they shal be no lesse circumspect, and warie, with good and carefull guard day and night,
putting forth good Centinell, and obseruing the orders and discipline of watch and ward, and when they haue finished the
discouery, trade, or fishing, they shall make hast with all speed,
with such Barke or Barkes, Pinisse, Gallie, Ship. &c. as they
shall haue the commaund of, for the same purpose, to *Iames
towne* againe, not presuming to goe beyond their commission,
or to carry any such Barke or Barkes, Gally, Pinnice, Ship. &c.
for England or any other countrey in the actuall possession of
any Christian Prince, vpon perill to be held an enemie to this
plantation, and traitor thereunto, and accordingly to lie liable
vnto such censure of punishment (if they arriue in England) as
shall be thought fit by the Right Honourable Lords, his Maiesties Councell for this Colonie, and if it shall so happen, that he
or they shall be preuented, and brought backe hither againe into
the Colonie, their trecherous flight to be punished with death.

33 There is not one man nor woman in this Colonie now
present, or hereafter to arriue, but shall giue vp an account of
his and their faith, and religion, and repaire vnto the Minister,
that by his conference with them, hee may vnderstand, and gather, whether heretofore they have beene sufficiently instructed,
and catechised in the principles and grounds of Religion, whose
weaknesse and ignorance herein, the Minister finding, and advising them in all loue and charitie, to repaire often vnto him,
to receiue therein a greater measure of knowledge, if they shal
refuse so to repaire vnto him, and he the Minister giue notice
thereof vnto the Gouernour, or that chiefe officer of that towne
or fort, wherein he or she, the parties so offending shall remaine,
the Gouernour shall cause the offender for his first time of refu-
sall to be whipt, for the second time to be whipt twice, and to
acknowledge his fault vpon the Saboth day, in the assembly of
the

the congregation, and for the third time to be whipt euery day vntil he hath made the same acknowledgement, and asked forgiuenesse for the same, and shall repaire vnto the Minister, to be further instructed as aforesaid : and vpon the Saboth when the Minister shall catechise, and of him demaund any question concerning his faith and knowledge, he shall not refuse to make answere vpon the same perill.

34 What man or woman soeuer, Laundrer or Laundresse appointed to wash the foule linnen of any one labourer or souldier, or any one else as it is their duties so to doe, performing little, or no other seruice for their allowance out of the store, and daily prouisions, and supply of other necessaries, vnto the Colonie, and shall from the said labourer or souldier, or any one else, of what qualitie whatsoeuer, either take any thing for washing, or withhold or steale from him any such linnen committed to her charge to wash, or change the same willingly and wittingly, with purpose to giue him worse, old and torne linnen for his good, and proofe shall be made thereof, she shall be whipped for the same, and lie in prison till she make restitution of such linnen, withheld or changed.

35 No Captaine, Master, or Mariner, of what condition soeuer, shall depart or carry out of our riuer, any Ship, Barke, Barge, Gally, Pinnace &c. Roaders belonging to the Colonie, either now therein, or hither arriuing, without leaue and commission from the Generall or chiefe Commaunder of the Colonie vpon paine of death.

36 No man or woman whatsoeuer, members of this Colonie, shall sell or giue vnto any Captaine, Marriner, Master, or Sailer, &c. any commoditie of this countrey, of what quality soeuer, to be transported out of the Colonie, for his or their owne priuate vses, vpon paine of death.

37 If any souldier indebted, shall refuse to pay his debts vnto his creditor, his creditor shall informe his Captaine, if the Captaine cannot agree the same, the creditor shall informe the Marshals ciuill & principall officer, who shall preferre for the creditor a bill of complaint at the Marshals Court, where the creditor shal haue Iustice.

All such Bakers as are appointed to bake bread, or what else, either for the store to be giuen out in generall, or for any one in particular, shall not steale nor imbezell, loose, or defraud any man of his due and proper weight and measure, nor vse any dishonest and deceiptfull tricke to make the bread weigh heauier, or make it courser vpon purpose to keepe backe any part or measure of the flower or meale committed vnto him, nor

aske,

aske, take, or detaine any one loafe more or lesse for his hire or paines for so baking, since whilest he who deliuered vnto him such meale or flower, being to attend the businesse of the Colonie, such baker or bakers are imposed vpon no other seruice or duties, but onely so to bake for such as do worke, and this shall hee take notice of, vpon paine for the first time offending herein of losing his eares, and for the second time to be condemned a yeare to the Gallies, and for the third time offending, to be condemned to the Gallies for three yeares.

All such cookes as are appointed to seeth, bake or dresse any manner of way, flesh, fish, or what else, of what kind soeuer, either for the generall company, or for any priuate man, shall not make lesse, or cut away any part or parcel of such flesh, fish, &c. Nor detaine or demaund any part or parcell, as allowance or hire for his so dressing the same, since as aforesaid of the baker, hee or they such Cooke or Cookes, exempted from other publike works abroad, are to attend such seething and dressing of such publike flesh, fish, or other prouisions of what kinde soeuer, as their seruice and duties expected from them by the Colony, and this shall they take notice of, vpon paine for the first time offending herein, of losing his eares, and for the second time to be condemned a yeare to the Gallies : and for the third time offending to be condemned to the Gallies for three yeares.

All fishermen, dressers of Sturgeon or such like appointed to fish, or to cure the said Sturgeon for the vse of the Colonie, shall giue a iust and true account of all such fish as they shall take by day or night, of what kinde soeuer, the same to bring vnto the Gouernour : As also of all such kegges of Sturgeon or Cauiare as they shall prepare and cure upon perill for the first time offending heerein, of loosing his eares, and for the second time to be condemned a yeare to the Gallies, and for the third time offending, to be condemned to the Gallies for three yeares.

Euery Minister or Preacher shall euery Sabboth day before Catechising, read all these lawes and ordinances, publikely in the assembly of the congregation vpon paine of his entertainment checkt for that weeke.

The

The Summarie of the Marshall Lawes.

Yee are now further to vnderstand, that all these prohibited, and forefended trespasses & misdemenors, with the inioyned obseruance of all these thus repeated, Ciuill and Politique Lawes, prouided, and declared against what Crimes soeuer, whether against the diuine Maiesty of God, or our soueraigne, and Liege Lord, King *Iames*, the detestable crime of Sodomie, Incest, Blasphemie, Treason against the person of the principall Generals, and Commaunders of this Colonie, and their designs, against detracting, murmuring, calumniating, or slaundering of the Right Honourable the Councell resident in England, and the Committies there, the general Councell, and chiefe Commaunders heere, as also against intemperate raylings, and base vnmanly speeches, vttered in the disgrace one of another by the worser sort, by the most impudent, ignorant, and prophane, such as haue neither touch of humanitie, nor of conscience amongst our selues, against Adultery, Fornication, Rape, Murther, Theft, false witnessing in any cause, and other the rest of the Ciuill, and Politique Lawes and Orders, necessarily appertaining, & properly belonging to the Gouernment of the State and Condition of the present Colony, as it now subsisteth: I say ye are to know, that all these thus ioyned, with their due punishments, and perils heere declared, and published, are no lesse subiect to the Martiall law, then vnto the Ciuill Magistrate, and where the Alarum, Tumult, and practise of arms, are not exercised, and where these now following Lawes, appertaining only to Martiall discipline, are diligently to be obserued, and shall be seuerely executed.

1 No man shall willingly absent himselfe, when hee is summoned to take the oath of Supremacy, vpon paine of death.

2 Euery Souldier comming into this Colonie, shall willingly take his oath to serue the King and the Colonie, and to bee faithfull, and obedient to such Officers, and Commaunders, as shall be appointed ouer him, during the time of his aboad therein,

according

according to the Tenor of the oath in that case prouided, vpon paine of being committed to the Gallies.

3 If any Souldier, or what maner of man else soeuer, of what quality or condition soeuer he be, shal tacitely compact, with any Sea-man, Captain, Master, or Marriner, to conuay him-selfe a Board any shippe, with intent to depart from, and aban-don the Colony, without a lawful Passe from the Generall, or chiefe commander of the Colonie, at that time, and shall happen to bee preuented, and taken therwith, before the shippe shall depart out of our Bay, that Captaine, Maister or mariner, that shall so receiue him, shall lose his wages, and be condemned to the Gallies for three yeeres, and he the sworne seruant of the Colony, Souldier, or what else, shall bee put to death with the Armes which he carrieth.

4 When any select, and appointed Forces, for the execu-tion and performance of any intended seruice, shall bee drawne into the field, and shall dislodge from one place vnto another, that Souldier that shall quit, or forsake his Colors, shall be pun-ished with death.

5 That Souldier that shall march vpon any seruice, shall keepe his Ranke, and marching, the Drum beating, and the En-signe displayed, shall not dare to absent himselfe, or stray and straggle from his ranke, without leaue granted from the cheefe Officer, vpon paine of death.

6 All Captaines shall command all Gentlemen, and Common Souldiers in their Companies, to obey their Sergeants, and Cor-porals, in their offices, without resisting, or iniuring the said Officers, vpon paine, if the iniurie be by words, he the offender shal aske his Officer pardon in the place of Arms, in the mead of the troopes. If by Act, he the offender shall passe the pikes.

7 That Souldier that in quarrel with an other shall call vpon any of his companions, or Countrimen to assist, and abette him, shall bee put to death with such Armes as he carrieth.

8 Hee that shall begin a mutiny, shall bee put to death with such Armes as he carrieth.

9 Where a quarrell shall happen betweene two or more, no man shall betake him vnto any other Arms then his sword, ex-cept he be a Captaine or Officer, vpon paine of being put to death with such Armes as he shall so take.

10 If a Captaine or Officer of a Companie shall come where two or more are fighting with their drawne swords, so soone as hee shall cry Hold, and charge them to forbeare, those that haue their swords in their hands so drawne, shall not dare to strike or thrust once after upon paine of passing the Pikes.

11 That

11 That Souldier that hauing a quarrell with an other, shall gather other of his acquaintance, and Associates, to make parties, to bandie, braue second, and assist him therin, he and those braues, seconds, and assistants shall passe the Pikes.

12 He that shall way-lay any man by aduantage taken, thereby cowardly to wound, or murther him shall passe the Pikes.

13 If any discontentment shall happen betweene Officers, or Souldiers, so as the one shall giue words of offence, vnto the other, to mooue quarrell, the Officer or Souldier shall giue notice thereof, to his Corporall, or superior officer, and the Corporall, or superior officer, shall commit the offender, and if it happen between Commanders, the officer offended shall giue notice to the Generall, or Marshal, that he may be committed, who for the first offence shall suffer three daies imprisonment, and make the officer wronged, satisfaction before his squadron to repaire him, and satisfie him, without base submission, which may vnworthy him to carry Armes. And the officer, or Souldier so offended, hauing satisfaction offered, shall with all willingnes receiue it, for which both producing it to his Officer, and accepting of satisfaction, hee shall bee reputed an officer, or souldier well gouerned in himselfe, and so much the fitter to be aduanced in Commaund ouer others, and if any shall vpbraid him, for not hauing sought a sauage headlong reuenge against his fellow, the officer or souldier so vpbraiding, shall bee punished and make satisfaction as the first offender, and if any shal so offend the second time he shall suffer ten nights lying head and heeles together, with Irons vpon the guard, and haue his entertainement checkt for one month, and make satisfaction to the officer or souldier, as before remembred, and for the third offence, hee shall bee committed to the Gallies three yeeres. And if vpon the first offence giuen by any officer or souldier, vnto any other, in words as aforesaid, and the other returne iniurious words againe, they shall both be taken as like offenders, and suffer like punishment, sauing that he who gaue the first offence, shall offer first repaire vnto the offended, which he the offended shall accept, and then shal hee proceed to returne the like satisfaction vnto the other, and if any shall bee obstinate in this point of repaire, and satisfaction, hee shall suffer sharpe and seuere punishment, vntil hee shall consent vnto it, the words or manner of satisfaction, to be giuen vnto the Party, or parties offended, shall be appointed by the chiefe officer of the Company, vnder whom the officer, or souldier shall happen to bee, with the knowledge of the prouost Marshall, prouided, that if the Officer

or

or souldier shall desire it, hee may appeale vnto the chiefe officer of the Garrison, or vnto the Marshall, if hee shall be present
to Iudge of the equity of the satisfaction. And if any Lanceprizado, Corporall, or other officer, shall happen to bee present,
or shall take knowledge of any such offence offered of one partie, or Quarrell sought and accepted of more parties, he shall
presently cause the partie, or parties so offending to bee committed to prison, that due execution may follow, as is formerly
prouided. And if any Lanceprizado, Corporall, or superior officer shall neglect his or their duty, or duties heerein appointed,
by not bringing the offender, and their offences, to the knowledge of the superior office, that satisfaction as aforesaid, vpon
the fault committed, may orderly follow, the officer so offending,
shal for his first omission, negligence, and contempt, suffer ten
daies Imprisonment, for the second twenty, and for the third
losse of his place, and to bee put to the duty of a Centinell:
And if any officer or Souldier shall be present when two or
more shall draw weapons, with intent to fight, or shall fight,
they shall presently doe their best to part them, and if he be an
officer he shall commit them, or put them vnder safe guard to
bee committed, and if hee bee a priuate souldier, hee shal giue
notice to the prouost, marshall, or vnto the first officer that he
shal meet with, of the parties offending, who shall presently take
order, that they may be apprehended, and committed to the
Prouost Martialcy, and if any officer or souldier, shall happen to
see any officer or souldier so fighting, and shall not doe his best
to part them, without fauouring one part or other, hee shall bee
punished at the discretion of the officer in chiefe, and the punishment shall extend to the taking away of life, if the cause shal
so require, and if any officer, or souldier shall know of any purpose in any to fight, and shall not stay them, or discouer them
to such officers, as are competent to stay them, but that they
goe to fight, and doe accordingly fight, that officer, or souldier
shall bee taken, and shall bee punished cleerely and in the
same sort, as the offence deserueth punishment betweene them
fighting.

14 That officer, or Souldier that shall challenge another to
fight, and hee that shall carry any Challenge, knowing it to be a
Challenge, and he that accepteth any such Challenge with a purpose and returne of answere, to meete the saide Challenger to
fight with him, in this case they shall all three be held alike
culpable, and lie subiect to the Censure of a Martiall Court.

15 That officer who shal command the guard and let such
Challengers and Challenged, passe the ports, vpon his knowledge
to

to fight, shall be casseird, and if the officer be vnder the degree of a Captaine, hee shall bee put to doe the duty of a Centinell.

16 No officer shall strike any souldier, for any thing, not concerning the order, and duty of seruice, and the publique worke of the Colony, and if any officer shall so doe, hee shall bee punished as a priuate man in that case, and bee held vnworthy to command, so peruerting the power of his place and authority.

17 No man shall be Captaine of the watch at any time, vnder the degree of an Ensigne.

18 He that shall take the name of God in vain or shall play at Cards or dice, vpon the Court of guard, for the first time so offending, he shall bee committed to prison, there to lie in Irons for three daies, for the second time so offending, hee shall be whipt, and for the third time so offending hee shall bee condemned to the Gallies for one yeere.

19 Hee that shall absent himselfe from the Court of Guard, vppon his watch aboue one houre without leaue of his Corporall or superior officer, shall for his first time so offending, at the relieuing of the watch bee committed to prison, and there to lye in Irons for 3. dayes, for the second time he shall be committed to prison and there lye in irons for one weeke, and haue his entertainement checkt for one weeke, and for the third time, hee shall be committed to the Gallies for sixe moneths.

20 He that shall swagger, and giue iniurious words vpon the court of guard, for the first offence, hee shall aske forgiuenesse vpon his knees, of the officers, and rest of the Guard, before the Captain of the watch at that time : for his second time so offending, he shall bee committed to the Gallies for one veere.

21 He that draweth his sword vpon the Court of Guard, shall suffer death by the Armes which he weareth.

22 Hee that should draw his sword in a towne of Garrison, or in a Campe shall lose his right hand.

23 That souldier that shall goe out of the Fort, Towne or Campe, other then by the ordinary guards, issues, waies, or ports, shall suffer death by the Armes which he carrieth.

24 He that shall abuse and iniurie the Serieant Maior, the prouost Marshall, either by word, or deede, if hee bee a Captaine, hee shall be casseird, if a Souldier he shall passe the pikes.

25 When the Officer or Souldier shall haue committed any Crime, or haue made breach of the publique Lawes, his Captaine shall commit him vnto the serieant Maior, who hauing taken his examination, shall send him to the Prouost Marshall, committed

committed vnto prison, that he may bee brought to be censured by a court Marshall.

26 No Souldier shall withstand or hinder the Prouost Marshall, or his men in the execution of his office, vpon paine of death.

27 All Captaines, Lieutenants, Serieants, and Corporals, shall be diligent at conuenient times, to traine and exercise their Companies, & shall haue a care of their Armes, as they tender their entertainment, and vpon paine of casseiring, and other corporall punishment, as shall be inflicted by vertue of a Marshall court.

28 No man shall goe twelue score from the quarter, his colours, towne or fort, without leaue of his Captaine, vpon paine for the first time of whipping, for the second offence to be committed to the Gallies for one yeare, and for the third offence to suffer death.

29 No man shall sell, giue, imbezell, or play away his Armes, or any part thereof, vpon paine of death.

30 No common Souldier shall sell, or make away any of his apparell, which is deliuered vnto him by the Colonie, or out of the store, vpon paine of whipping.

31 No man shall depart from his guard without leaue of his officer, vpon paine of punishment: and who so shall be set Centinell, shall not depart from it, vntill he be relieued, nor sleepe thereof vpon paine of death.

32 No man shall offer any violence, or contemptuously resist or disobey his Commaunder, or doe any act, or speake any words which may tend to the breeding of any disorder or mutinie in the towne or field, or disobey any principall Officers directions vpon paine of death.

33 He that shall not appeare vpon the guard, or not repaire vnto his colours, when the Drum upon any occasion shall beate either vpon an Alarum, or to attend the businesse which shall be then commaunded, shall for his first offence lie in Irons vpon the court of guard all one night, and for his second be whipt, and for the third be condemned to the Gallies for one yeare.

34 That Souldier who fighting with an enemie, shall lose his Armes, or runne away cowardly, or yeeld himselfe but vpon ap parant and great constraints or without hauing performed, first the part of a good souldier, and an honest man, shall suffer death with the armes which he carrieth.

35 That Souldier that shall let go any caution deliuered vpon a treatie, or any prisoner of warre by his negligence, shall be punished with death.

36 No

36 No Souldier shall let goe any prisoner of war, which he hath taken without consent of his Captaine, who shall aduertise the chiefe Commaunder, upon paine of being committed to the Gallies for one yeare.

37 That Souldier which vpon an assault, or taking of any towne, that shall not follow his colours, and the victory, but shall fall to pillage for his priuate profit, after the place taken, shall suffer death with the armes which he weareth.

38 No Souldier may speake or haue any priuate conference with any of the saluages, without leaue of his Captaine, nor his Captaine without leaue of his chiefe Officer, vpon paine of death.

39 When the Marshall or Gouernour of a towne, shall demaund a Souldier that hath made breach of these lawes, that Captaine or any other that shall conceale him, or assist him to flie away, shall bee punished with the punishment which the fact of the said fugitiue deserued.

40 That Captaine that shall *ipso facto*, find any Souldier breaking these fore declared lawes and ordinances, of whatsoeuer company he shall be, he shall commit him to the Prouost Marshall to be punished according as the offence committed commeth vnder the construction of the Martiall law in that case prouided.

41 No Souldier shall vnprofitably waste his pouder, shot, or match, by shooting it idly away, or at birds, beasts, or fowle, but shall giue an account vnto his Corporall of the same, who shall certifie his Captain vpon peril for his first fault so cōmitted, to be cōmitted to prison, there to lie in Irons head & heeles togither eight & forty hours, for the second to be condemned sixe moneths to the Gallies, and for the third offence to be condemned two yeares to the Gallies.

42 All Captaines, Officers, and common Souldiers, or others of what condition soeuer, members of the Colonie, shall doe their endeauours to detect, apprehend, and bring to punishment all offenders, and shall assist the officer of that place for that purpose, as they will answere the contrary at our Marshall court.

43 All other faults, disorders, and offences that are not mentioned in these Lawes, Articles, and Orders shall be & are supplied in the instructions which I haue set downe, and now shall be deliuered vnto euery Captain, and other Officer, so farre forth as the infancie, and as yet weake condition of this our present Colony will suffer, and which shall be punished according to the generall custome, and therefore I commaund all men to looke

to

to their charges, and him that hath no charge to looke to his owne carriage, and to keepe himselfe within the bounds of dutie, for the discipline shall be strictly kept, and the offenders against the lawes thereof seuerely punished.

44 Whosoeuer shall giue offence to the Indians in that nature, which truly examined, shall found to haue beene cause of breach of their league, and friendship, which with so great trauaile, desire, and circumspection, we haue or shall at any time obtaine from them without commission so to doe, from him that hath authoritie for the same, shall be punished with death.

45 Whosouer shall wilfully, or negligently set fire on any Indian dwelling house, or *Quioquisock* house or temple, or vpon any storehouse, or garner of graine, or prouision of what quality soeuer, or disualedge, ransacke, or ill intreat the people of the countrey, where any warre, or where through any march shall be made except it be proclaimed, or without commandement of the chiefe officers shall be punished with death.

46 Whosoeuer shall not do his endeauour and best to regaine & recouer his colours, if by hap it fall into the Indians hands shall lie subject to the censure of a Marshall court.

47 Whosoeuer shall faine himself sick, vpō the point of fight, or when any worke is to be done or slip away from the seruice of either, shall be punished by death.

48 VVhosoeuer shall raise any question, brabble or braule in the watch, or Amboscado, or in Scout, or Sētinel in any other effect, or make any noise or rumor where silence, secrecie, and couert is to be required, shall be punished with death.

49 Whosoeuer shall not retreat when the drum or trumpet soundeth the same, whether it be vpon any sallies, made out of any town or fortres, or in skirmish, or in any incounter, shall be punished with death.

50 It now resteth, that all Captaines and supreme officers, whether gouernor in towne, fort or fortes, or Captaine of companies shall be aduised to do their indeuors ioyntly, and to agree in one accord, that the true and neuer failing Iustice, may be executed with all integrity of all these foredeclared lawes, according to the dignitie, power, and censure of the Martiall court, that by the exemplar liues, and honourable practises of all that is good & vertuous, all things may be gouerned in good order, as no doubt, our Right Honorable Lord Generall doth assure himselfe, that all good and vpright men that haue the feare of God, and his seruice, and their owne honour in regard, will demean themselues no lesse, then according to the dignity of their place, and charge of their command, the vnited powers of his
Lordships

Lordships knowledge, being so full of approued noblenesse, and
the well knowne, and long time exercised grounds of Piety, as
without question he cannot but desire rather a little number of
good men, obedient & tractable, submitting to good order &
discipline, then a great armie, composed of vitious prophane,
quarrellous, disobedient, and ignoble persons, wherefore in his
Lordships behalfe, I must intreat all Gouernors, Captains, Officers, and Soldiers, and neuerthelesse do inioyne, ordaine and
command them to carry themselues in their seuerall duties and
charges, according to the intention of his Lordship, declared by
these present Ordinances.

51 Euery Captaine shall cause to be read all these lawes
which concerne martiall discipline, euery weeke vpon his guard
day, vnto his company vpon paine of censure of a Martiall court.

---

*Instructions of the Marshall for better inhabling of
the Colonell or Gouernour, to the executing of his or their
charges in this present Colony the 22. of Iune. 1611.*

ALbeit the zeale which I beare vnto this businesse that we
haue all now in hand touching the subsistance of this plantation, might iustly take vp all my spirits, and would require a
large and passionate explanation of mine owne thoughts and
promptnesse to gaine & possesse the hearts of all vnderstanding,
noble and religious spirits thereunto, yet I must craue pardon
(considering at this time many present impediments) if I wrap
vp any impatient desires & good affection hereunto, to all such
vnto whom these necessarie effects of my dutie and office shall
appertaine, and must be declared in few words and aduises, appertinent yet (if not essentiall, as heat to bloud, to the aduancement hereof) my desire then by these is chiefly to let all the
worthier & better sort to vnderstand, how well it shall become
their Honors, birthes, breedings, reputations & faithes, to do their
bests, and emulously to actuate in this worke, the vtmost of their
cleerest powers of body and mind, where the trauaile of both is
so deerely valued, and highly interpreted by al good and wise
men, who knowing the grounds of all goodnes, cannot but know
this, how this hazardous voyage (as yet but in her earely daies,
reflecting onely the comfort of faire hopes) is vndertaken by you,
more to honour God, your country, & to profit your knowledges,
then for any other ends of profit, which speakes for you (in despight of enuie and calumnie) that you haue mindes much in
loue

loue with vertue, & are right noble and worthy instruments, to
be imployed in so sacred and heroicke a cause, if it were well
knowne heere, the care that is had of this plantation in England,
and the trauel that is taken therein, and the fire that doth not
only burne in the generall body of our deare countrymen, to the
encouragemet & ioy one of another amongst themselues, but
flames out (euen to the view of strange nations, as well our
neighbours, as far remote) for the furtherance & aduancement of
this honorable enterprise, there is no man here would thinke
that this my induction, had either fashion or purpose of a complement. If the wisest man that euer spake or writ (except
him that was both God & man) summed vp all the reckonings
of worldly felicities in these two words *Lætari & benefacere*,
imploying a cheereful mirth with well doing (from which it cannot be seuered) who hath more cause to be cheerefull, and inlie
glad then you that haue the comfort of so great weldoing, to
which no other may be compared? for what weldoing can be
greater then to be stocks & authors of a people that shall serue
and glorifie God, which is the end of all our Creation, & to redeeme thē from ignorance and infidelity, to the true knowledge
and worship of God, whereby you are made partakers of this
promise, that they which lead others into Righteousnesse, shal
shine like the starres in the firmament, wherein be right well
assured, that your happinesse is enuied by many a right knowing, and excellent vertuous man in *England*, who cannot hap-
ply by reason of other their imployments and callings, bee
partakers of that Comfort heere, as they are by their Endeauors
there at home. I shall not need to aduise any Colonel, or Gouernor here for the present how to carry himself, for each mans
owne experiēce here hath made him out go al vse of my admo-
nitiō, which my affection wold willingly else afford if there were
cause. Only to discharge my seruice to god whose souldier I
doe now professe my selfe imprest, in this so glorious and great
a cause of his, my duty to my Soueraigne Liege Lord and King,
& to his Highnesse my Royall Prince and Master, to my Country and the expectation of many Honorable select, painful, and
Religious aduenturers, Patrones of this businesse, I haue conceiued no whit impertinent to deliuer and publish to euery imminent officer in this Colony heere present, and for the direction
and guiding of such who may heereafter arriue heere such and
so many few in structions as may the better inable them to execute their charges, no whit doubting, but euery Colonell, Gouernour Captaine, and other Officer may sufficiētly vnderstand his
and their duties, as they are Souldiers, but happily not yet as
they

they are, or may be Coloni, members of a Colony, which compriseth and inuolueth here, as well all the industrious knowledges & practises of the husbandman & of his spade, as of the Souldier, and of his Sword, since as Monie is the paiment & wages of the one, so of the other are the fruits of the earth the tillage and manuring of the Land, and in very truth of more necessity & vse shall we heere be of the latter then of the other, whether of you be comprehended the souldier himselfe or his Salarie, since more easie it is to make a Husbandman a Souldier, then a Souldier a husbandman. And indeed the necessity of our subsisting, and the very daunger which our enemies of this Country can any way put vs vnto (our Companies and people well commaunded) requiring the choise rather of the one then the other. These being then the ends and intents of this work, and so vnderstood, by euery supreme and chiefe commander, I refer him to these following instructions.

All Gouernors of Town or Towns, Fort or Forts, shall be ready (when·so be it they shall be summoned thereunto) to take their Oaths of Allegeance vnto his Maiestie & of faithfulnes vnto such his maiesties Lieftenant, or to his Deputy or Deputies (authorised by Commission to command ouer and within the precincts of this whole Colony, or Colonies, by the Tenor of which Oathes they shall solemnly attest to perform all Integrity, vprightnesse, Iustice and sincere administration of the discipline and Lawes in all causes and cases, for the good of the Colony or Colonies, prouided and declared, and shal indeuor the best they may, with all carefulnesse to aduance the dignity, and subsistance of the same, as well by giuing often in charge, and taking no lesse in to their owne care, both the particular preseruation of all such helpes of what condition soeuer (especially of cattell, and all kinde of such breeders, which mayest soones redound vnto the vtility, and profit of the same, as by rendring the prouisions of the store, and the well husbanding of the same, be they of what seuerall qualitie soeuer. Nor is he meanely to be watchfull, and iealous ouer his own waies and carriage in all particulars, making profession, and practise of all vertue and goodnes for examples vnto others to imitate, it being true that examples at all times preuaile farre aboue precepts, men beeing readier to bee led by their eies, then their eare, for seeing a liuely pattern of industry, order and comlinesse, wee are all of vs rather swayed vnto the same by a visible obiect, then by hearing much more in wel instructed Arguments.

Euery such Gouernor therefore shall make it his first duty to resort dayly and vsually to the diuine Seruice, next to put in execution

ecution the Lawes duly against offenders, and withall cherish
and reward the well deseruing, and lastly with all worthines &
circumspection, abeare himselfe vnto and towards his Garrison,
intreating all men as well strangers as others, with al Grace, humanity, and sweetnes of a noble nature, & manlinesse, vnto all
which I hartily aduise, and withall inioyne euery such Gouernor
of Town or Towns, to be most indulgent, and carefull to performe, as hee will answer the contrary (beside with the losse of
his own Honor, with such other penalties, as the neglect of so
behoofefull and necessary businesse in him, may draw vpon the
Colony.

Further he ought to be most vigilant, circumspect, and prouident for the conservatiõ, defending, & keeping the Town or
Fort, for & vnto his Maiesty, wherin he is placed cheefe commander, & therfore ought the more duely to strengthen his
Iudgement, and remember his reputation, that he fall into neither of those extreames, which the needy and prodigall are most
what culpable of, the one wasting the stocks, commodities and
prouisions of the store, by which he must subsist, and the other
by being rauenous and corrupt in himselfe become likewise enforced to tolerate the same in his inferior captaines, and so leaue
the poore Souldier and Labourer, miserably pilled, oppressed
and starued.

Further he ought to prouide that the companies be trained,
and that they may bee made ready for the publique seruice, and
for that the condition of this country doth require rather shot
then other Armes, either for offence or defence, and time being
pretious with vs in respect of our dayly labours and works abroad
belonging to our subsisting, in so much, as a small portion therof may bee affoorded and allowed vnto such exercising and
training, therefore it is appointed by the Marshall, that the Captains that shall haue the Guard, during their time of Guard (their
people as then being exempted from their dayly labour and
work abroad) and their Officers shall teach euery Souldier to
handle his peece, first to present it comely, and souldier like,
and then to giue fire, by false firing, and so to fall his Piece to
the right side with the nose vp, & when their souldiers are hardy
and expert in this, they shall set vp a conuenient mark fast by
the court of Guard, at which euery Souldier shall twice discharge his peece, at the releeuing of the watch, morning and
euening, and he that shall shoot neerest the Gouernor shall do
wel to allow some addition of victuals, or pay, or some prize of
incouragement, that euery one may therby emulously contend
to do best : Concerning the training, and cleanely exercising of
their

their Armes, & their postures, the captains shall haue order and directions for the same vnder the Marshals hand which they shall put in Execution during the time of their Guard.

41 It is also required that the Gouernor neuer lie out of his Towne or Fort whereby hee may the better keepe good espiall vpon all officers, that they perform their seuerall duties each one in his place especially in good observatiō of the watch & Guard, for the more confidēt securing the charge cōmitted to him :

Hee shall not suffer in his Garrison any Souldier to enter into Guard, or to bee drawne out into the field without being armed according to the Marshals order, which is, that euery shot shall either be furnished with a quilted coate of Canuas, a headpeece, and a sword, or else with a light Armor, and Bases quilted, with which hee shall be furnished : and euery Targiteer with his Bases to the small of his legge, and his headpeece, sword and pistoll, or Scuppet prouided for that end. And likewisee euery Officer armed as before, with a firelocke, or Snaphaūse, headpeece, and a Target, onely the Serieant in Garrison shall vse his Halbert, and in field his Snaphaunse and Target.

The Gouernour shall haue a Principall care, that he vse his Garrison to the dayly wearing of these Armors, least in the field, the souldier do finde them the more vncouth strange and troublesome.

Lastly the Gouernor shall haue a singular care to put in execution all such Orders and Instructions as shall bee deliuered vnto him from the Generall, or his deputie or deputies, concerning the imployments of his Garrison vpon such manuall works and duties, as shall be thought necessary and conuenient for the better subsisting both of the Laborer, and Garrison committed vnto him : In which is not to bee forgotten the chary conseruation of powder, and munition, which will the better inhable him for the defence of his Charge.

The Gouernor shall be better instructed by taking notice of the Lawes published, that these following abuses are prouided for, impious and malicious speaking against the holy and blessed Trinity, Blasphemy, and taking Gods holy name in vain, traiterous words against his maiesties person, or Royall Authority, vnreuerent Demeanor towards the Ministers and preachers of the same, the detestable crime of Sodomie, incest, theft, murther, false witnessing, treason against the Person of the Generall, and principall Commaunders of this Colony, and their designes, against Detracting, Murmuring or slaundering of the Right Honourable, the Councell resident in England, and the Committies there, the Generall Councel and Subalternate Commanders, heere,

heere, as also against intemperate raylings & ᵇase vnmanly speeches vttered in the disgrace one of another, all which the Marshall Law, as well as the Ciuil Magistrate is to punish, but these which concerne in particular the military Discipline, to inable your iudgement for your sentence to be required, that it may with greater cleerenes, and vnderstanding, called to censure offences in the Marshal court be deliuered, I haue abstracted, as followeth

1 Conference with the enemy, without leaue or warrant, frō the Lord Generall, Lieutenant Generall, Marshal, or chief & principal cōmand for the presēt.

2 The designes, enterprises, and estate of the Colony, reuealed to what enemy soeuer, by priuy messengers, or missiues, or otherwise in what sort soeuer.

3 The not present aduertising, & giuing notice vnto a cheefe Commaunder, of such things as any man knoweth intended· any way, or by any body, for the domage, mischiefe, or ill of the Colony, or the concealement in any one of any matter of importance, and moment for the good of the Colony.

4 Running vnto the enemy, or intending, and plotting to runne albeit preuented.

5 Of any one taken prisoner by the enemy, hauing meanes to escape, & not returning to the Colony againe, vnlesse hee haue giuen faith.

6 Of attempting commotion, giuing occasion of sedition, or Muteny in the Colony, or seducing any labourer or souldier from their duty, diuine, ciuill, or martiall, or from their appointed works and labours.

7 Of disclosing or giuing the word vnto the enemy, or vnto any other, where it ought not to be giuē.

8 Of receiuing, or protecting any Indian, stranger, or suspected spie, or supposed enemy, into house, or any couert, without making it knowne to the General, or chiefe officer, and without leaue from him so to do.

9 Suspitious and priuily entring into the Campe Town, or Fort, or going out by any other waies and issues, then those which are accustomed, as ouer the Ramparts, Pallizadoes, Trenches, &c.

10 Of doing any act, or contriuing any practise, which may preiudice the seruice of his Maiesty commanded for the good of the Colony, by the Generall, or chiefe Officer.

11 Of breaking the Truce, or peace at any time cōcluded with the Indian, without leaue & warrant expresly giuen, by him who hath power so to doe.

12 Of

12 Of pillaging, or violently forcing from any Indian to friend, without leaue.

13 Of ransacking, ransoming, or violently outraging, and dispoiling the Country people, or making war vpon them, be it in body or goods, vnles they be declared enemies, & warrant giuen to make prise of.

14 Of laying violent hands on his Captaine or other superiour officer, and generally vppon any one whatsoeuer, to whom duty & obedience is due, especially if it be in the executing of his Office.

15 Of him who shall see his superior, or chiefe officer in danger, and shall not doe his indeauour to rescue and relieue him with all his force, and power.

16 Of him who shall violently or hardly intreate, or kill his souldier, without good, & lawfull occasion, or that he haue deserued so to be intreated, not to satisfie his owne pleasure and appetite, to punish in colour, and reuenge, thereby thinking to make himselfe more redoubted, a braue man, & to be feared, remembring well, the life of a souldier, or a laborer, belongs to none to take away, but to the Lord Generall, Lieftenant General, Marshal, or their deputy or deputies.

17 Of killing any one, except it be in his own defēce.

18 Of striking or fighting with an other man, hauing a quarrell vnto him, and not holding his or their hands when an officer or third party comes between and cries, Holah.

19 Of making debate, raising question, or laying his hand on his sword, and drawing it in the Court of Guard, in Ambush, or other place, where he ought to be modest, peaceable, silēt, & to keep himself in couert.

20 Of assaying or indeuouring by brauery, & chiefly by trechery, to outrage or iniury any one without a cause, in deed or in words, priuately behind his backe like a slie coward, or openly to his face, like an arrogāt ruffian, since words are the parents of blowes, & from quarrels infinite disorders, and mischiefes gather head whether in Campe, Towne, or Fort.

21 Of reuenging a new wrong, or old iniury, by any course, contrary to the peace of the camp or Colony.

22 Of running where any quarrell is a foote, and companies gathered together, furnished with other Armes then his sword.

23 Of taking away any mony in brauery, wonne from another, or gotten by play otherwise without the will and consent of him, from whom he wonne it, or cheating or cosenage in play.

24 Of not repairing to the place of Armes, or Colors at the publique beating of the Drum.

25 Of

25 Of wilfully firing any place, without order from the superior officer.

26 Of sacriledge or taking any goods out of Churches, or Temples, be they sacred or prophane, without license from the chiefe commander.

27 Of a souldier enrowling himself in two companies at one time.

28 Of going out of one company into another, without leaue of his Captaine.

29 Of absenting himselfe from the Campe, towne, or fort, without permission of a superiour officer.

30 Of him that shall receiue his pay, and shall go away without speaking a word, it is a case capital, and worthy of death.

31 Of suborning souldiers the one from the other, which is an euill example, and which doth draw many inconueniences with it.

32 Of quarrels, debates, and reuenge.

33 Of failing to go, or refusing to follow, where his ensigne shall march, or else where that he shall be commaunded by those who haue authoritie so to commaund without enquiring the cause.

34 Of abandoning his ensigne without leaue or going from the place assigned him, be it in fight, in the court of guard, Centinels, or other part, not brought of by those who placed him there, or others hauing the same authority.

35 Of a Souldier not doing his endeuour to recouer his ensigne, if the enemie haue taken it.

36 Of being wanting at his watch, vpon his time appointed, or of going of the Guard without leaue, albeit vnder a colour of espie.

37 Of being found sleeping in Centinell, or of him who placed vpon some Guard or watch by his negligence hath giuen meanes to the enemie, to do some spoile in the campe, towne, or fort, and to surprise them at vnawares.

38 Of running away from the battell, conflict, or assault, &c. and of him that marcheth too slowly, or maketh delaies in any other sort.

39 Of a Souldier faining himselfe sicke, when any seruice is to be performed.

40 Of yeelding vnto the enemy, a place which he hath in gard, without doing first his duty to the vttermost, & be not cōstraind vnto it, according to the quality of the same, & the state whereunto he shall be drawn.

41 Of

41 Of being appointed to defend a breach, trench, or pas sage, cōmitted vnto his charge, & do forsake it altogether, with out being forced thereunto by the enemy.

42 Of entring into any place taken by force, & pillaging the same, not following his colors, or forsaking the same, without a publike proclamatiō, made by the chiefe commander, that it shal be lawful so to pillage.

43 Of a soldier being found vnfurnished of his arms, and of such furniture, as he is appointed to weare and ought to haue, by losing them in play, or in cowardly runing away, or otherwise by his default or negligēce.

44 Of a souldiers going from his quarter, town, or fort, without he haue leaue from a superior officer.

45 Of a souldier aduancing himselfe, to go before the troopes, be it to come first to his lodging, or for any other occasion, or wandring heere and there, and stragling when he should march.

46 Of not retiring so soone as the drum or trumpet shall sound retreat, whether it be comming out of any towne, or skirmish, or any other fight.

47 Of speaking loud, or making a noise in the battel or any other place, where silence is to be vsed, except those who haue power to command.

Instructions of the Marshall for the better inhabling of the Captaine of the watch, to the executing of his charge in this present Colony. the 22. of Iune. 1611.

S Ithence, as in euery liuing creature, there be many and sundry members, & those distinct in place, and office, and all yet vnder the regiment of the soule, and heart, so in euery army, commonwealth, or Colonie (all bodies a like compounded) it cannot be otherwise for the establishment of the same in perfect order and vertue, but that there should be many differing parts, which directed by the chiefe, should helpe to gouerne and administer Iustice vnder him. And if it be thus in this ciuill Audit, & courts of a well setled State, much more sure as it required, to be in their beginnings, and no lesse shall we read, how that first & great commander ouer the Colony of the children of Israel, conducting them from Ægypt to make their plantation in the land of Promise, appointed Captains ouer Tribes and hundreds for the wars, and Elders to sit upon the bench (whilest vnto himselfe all great causes were brought, whether martial, or ciuil to direct and determine it otherwise being impossible,

possible, so many and infinite occasions both being to be thought vpon, and requiring iudiciall audience, should euer come by one mā (of how indefatigable a spirit soeuer) to be decided or determined. Out of this example cōmended vnto vs by the holy writ, it may wel be, that many Officers are still continued in all vnited societies, religious and wel gouerned : hauing then thus religion, beside prescription and reason, (which mine owne breeding hath taught me how to make the best vse of, to be my guids in this new settlement, and in this strange and heathenous (contending with all the strength and powers of my mind and body, I confesse to make it like our natiue country, I am not a little careful to adhere & take vnto mine owne endeuours, as many furtherances, as may helpe to work out with me the ends of this great imployment, which hath now possessed and furnished all states of Christendom with discourse and expectatiō what may be the issue thereof, & to what perfection so great, & frequent leuies of monies, & annuall transportations for these foure yeares of men, and prouisions, may bring this English plantation vnto . And as I haue constituted subalterne officers according both to the ancient & moderne order of the wars, and well approued the gouernment & magistracy, resembling and maintaining the lawes of England, so I haue taken paines to present so many & such instructions to such speciall officers (whom our necessity teacheth to establish amongst vs) as may most neerest concerne them for the present, (leauing out yet I confesse many appertinent ones, which the time & our earely daies here of settlement may not yet admit of. Let me aduise therfore euery officer now established, to hold it a seruice of duty faithfully to execute such orders and instructions, as I haue made it my mindes labour to expresse and draw out for him : and amongst the rest (our no little safety consisting in our watch & guard as wel by day as night, we being set down in a stranger land, sauage, and trecherous, and therfore many sodaine and barbarous accidents to be feared, I haue as followeth extracted the duty of the captaine of the. wrath an office not meanly appertaining and necessary vnto this Colony, and whose ignorance, and supine negligence may much indanger the safetie thereof.

That Captaine who is Captaine of the watch, must haue a speciall care of the safeguard and preseruation of the Towne or Fort committed to his charge, and of the liues and goods of the soldiers, and Inhabitants, that through his defect, negligence, or Ignorance in his charge, he giues not opportunity to the enemie to execute any of his deseignes, for the indamaging of the place or the Inhabitants: Now for the more faithfull executing of his charge,

charge, he shall doe well to take notice, that being the chiefe commander of the watch, he is to answere for all Disorders, Misrules, Riots, Tumults and what vnquietnesse soeuer, shall happen in the Towne or Fort, and that if any of these shall fall out to be, he is to commit the parties so offending, to the Prouost Marshall, making the Gouernour there-with acquainted, that the offender may receiue such punishment, as his fault shall deserue, of what quality soeuer he be.

At the setting of the watch, he is to repayre to the place of Arms, with his Gorget about his neck, if his company haue not the Guard, there to be present with the Sargeant Maior, at the drawing of the Billets for the Guards, that he may the better know the strength of his watch, and how the companies are disposed vpon their Guards.

He is to remaine from the setting of the watch vpon the main court of Guard, or Guard appointed for him & his Rounders, that if any occasion present it selfe wherin his endeauour is to be vsed, hee may be the readier found to receiue the cheife Officers direction, or to reforme any abuses that shall come to his knowledge, by the misdemeanors of any to bee found in the campe, towne or fort.

The Ports being shut, and the word deliuered out from the Gouernor, he is to see that al his Gentlemen, appointed for his assistants, doe come vpon their guard, where he is so to order it that by drawing of Billets according to their lots, they may execute their rounds, whither first, second, third, &c. and after the Corporalls haue set out their centinells, hee is to passe from his court of guard, with three or foure of his assistants, and so to make the round about the campe, towne, or fort, from guard to guard, receiuing from euery Corporall the word of guet, that their be no error, or abuse, by variety of word : after which he is to goe into the conrt of guard, to see that such officers, rounders, and soldiers, apoynted for that guard, bee there present vpon their guard, then hee shall search the peices whither they be charged with Bullet, and that the soldiers bee furnished with poulder and match for the better defence of the guard, committed to his charge, so commanding and inioyning euery officer, and soldier to execute his duty, for ther better security of the campe, towne, or fort : hee shall depart to the next guard there to doe the like, and so from guard to guard, vntil he hath visited all the guards and centinells of his watch, giuing in charge to the officers of each guard to send forth their rounders, according to their order and directions.

Further hee shall command all disordred people vntimely (sitting

ting vp late in vsuall assemblies, whither in priuat meetings, publike tap-houses or such like places) vnto their rests, for which he shall cause all fire and candles to bee put out and raked vp in the towne, and such night-walkers, or vnruly persons whome hee shall meete in the streets, he shall either send to their lodgings, or to the Prouost Marshall, according as their misdemeanour shall require.

Hee being returned to his owne court of guard shall see his rounders set forth euery one according to his order of Billet, from houre to houre, and he shall informe him-selfe from these rounders which walke their rounds, two bowers before day breake, whither the Captaines and their guards, and their companies bee in armes according to their duties : if they bee not hee shall walke a round towards the morning vnto those Guards, and cause them to be put in armes, and shall informe the gouernour of those Officers neglects, that they may receiue punishment : after this at the discharge of the watch, hee is with his guard to attend the Serjeant Major for the safe opening of the Ports.

At the opening of the Ports, hee shall cause the people to stay that are to goe out of the Towne, a pretty distance from his guard, that they may giue no incombrance to his guard, vntill such time, as he hath sent out certaine Serjeants to discouer forth right, and vpon each side, as farre as the limmits of that fort are prescribed : At the returne of the Serjeant, hee shall cause those of the Towne to goe out leisurely and without thronging or confusion, and those without to come in, in like manner, warning the Gards to stand in armes one houre after.

From thence hee shall returne to the maine Guard or place of armes to assist the Serieant Maior for the disposing of such men as are appoynted vnto their seuerall busines and workes of the Colony for the whole day following : and likewise to see that those Captaines, who haue the Guard, do put in execution the cōmandements of the Marshall for the trayning and disciplining of their men for the better inabling them to the seruice of the Colony.

After which he shall do well to present himselfe before the Gouernour, or chiefe Officer, to vnderstand his further commaunds.

It shall bee his duty the time beeing come, when the general morning worke is to be left off, to cause the Drum to beate, and with his Guard of Rounders to assist the Captaines or Capt. to bring the laborers into the Church to heare diuine seruice, which beeing ended hee is to returne to the maine Court of Guard, there to be present for the ordering of all matters whatsoeuer to

happen,

happen, during his time of being Captaine of the watch, and when it shall so fall out that the Indians do at any time come in way of trade or visitation vnto the Camp, towne or fort, he shal leaue order with the Guards that they suffer not them to enter before such time as they haue made him acquainted first of their beeing there, who shall informe the Gouernor to know his pleasure, which beeing vnderstood hee shal so accomplish, at al times, appointing Guards vppon such Indians, that they do not steale any of our Tooles, Axes, Howes, Swords, Peeces or what thing else ; and that none of our people talke publikely or priuately with them, or that they truck or trade with them, or doe any other vnorderly Act, without leaue granted for the same from the Gouernour, or chiefe Officer, the omission of which duty, will be required at his bands.

Hee must likewise take notice of all such breaches of the publique Lawes and Articles, as shall bee committed in the time of his Guard, and accordingly command such persons to the Prouost Marshall, as shall bee found trespassers and breakers of the said Lawes and Articles.

At the time or houres appoynted for the afternoone worke of the Colony, euery labourer to his worke, and euery crafts man to his occupation, Smiths, Ioyners, Carpenters, Brick makers &. He shall cause the drumme to beate againe, to draw and call forth the people vnto their labour, when againe the worke on all hands towards night being to bee left off, hee is to cause the drumme likewise then to beate, and as before assist the Capt: with the whole company to bring them to euening prayer.

If it shall so bee that hee bee Capt. of the watch vpon Sonday, it shall be his duety to see that the Saboath be no waies prophaned, by any disorders, gaming, drunkennes, intemperate meeting, or such like, in publike or priuate, in the streetes or within the houses.

It shall be his duty halfe an houre before the diuine seruice, morning & euening, to shut the Ports and place Centinels, and the Bell hauing tolled the last time, he shal search all the houses of the towne, to command euery one, of what quality soeuer (the sick and hurt excepted) to repaire to Church, after which he shall accompany all the guards with their armes, (himselfe being last) into the Church, and lay the keyes before the Gouernor.

If at any time any alarme be taken, he is to strengthen himselfe from the maine court of gard, taking a competent proportion of that guard, for the securing of his person, and so to repaire to the place where the alarme was giuen, to enforme
himselfe

himselfe by what means the alarum came, causing his rounders to command all guards to be in armes for the readier execution and resistance of any perill, and conseruation of their charge, and if he find the alarum to be truly giuen, and that the enemy approch the Fort, towne, or campe, he is to send to aduertise the Gouernor or chiefe officers to know his directions for the assembling of guards, and ordering and drawing a force for the better preuention of the enemies designes.

Lastly, when the guard is set, and another Captaine hath the watch, hee shall present himselfe before the Gouernor or chiefe Commander, to giue account vnto him of all such accidents, trespasses and neglects, as haue been committed during the time of his watch.

Thus to conclude, though his office amongst many others be a chief and principall office, and there be many weighty and frequent duties required in this great duty of the Captaine of the watch, yet these are the most essentiall and necessariest which I can yet aduise, the neerest to concerne vs.

Instructions of the Marshall, for the better inabling of a Captaine, to the executing of his charge in this present Colonie. Iune the 22. 1611.

THat Captaine that will honestly and religiously discharge himselfe, and the duty entrusted to him, shall doe well to conceiue of himselfe, as the maister of a family, who is at all times so to gouerne himselfe, as knowing assuredly that all the crimes and trespasses of his people vnder him shall bee exacted at his hands, not onely by his superior officer and Iudge here, but by the great Iudge of Iudges, who leaues not vnpunished the sinnes of the people, vpon the Magistrates, in whose hands the power and sword of Iustice and authority is committed, to restraine them from all delinquences, misdeeds and trespasses. And moreouer since the Captaine is to know, that not onely the command of their ciuill duties is at his directions, for which he is to answer, but likewise al their actions and practises which shall breake forth in them, contrary to the diuine prescriptions of Piety and Religion : their periuries, blasphemies, prophanenesse, ryots, and what disorders soeuer, and generally all their breaches of both the sacred Tables, diuine, and morrall, to G O D and man, and in this place most especially, where the worke assumed, hath no other ends but such as may punctually aduance the glory, and propagation of the heauenly goodnesse,

for

for which so many religious lawes and ordinances are established, and declared, all tending to the subsisting of a Colony, the first seed-plot and settlement of such a new temporary kingdom and state, as may reduce, and bring poore misbeleeuing miscreants, to the knowledge of the eternall kingdom of God (therefore by him first shut vp in misbeliefe, that in his due time, when it should so please him, hee might againe on them shew mercy) It is carefully therefore by each Captaine to be considered, how pretious the life of a poore souldier is, but how much more pretious his soule, and that he make conscience how he expose the first to apparant ruine and mischiefe, or suffer the other to run on into headlong destruction: for the first let his wisedom, knowledge, and circumspection be euer awake, and ready how to imploy, and when and with what assurances, regards and cautions, either left to his owne power, or prescribed him by vertue of these from the Marshall, and for the other, let him first be mindfull to giue witnesses in his owne life, how carefull hee is to please God, who must blesse all that he vndertakes, and walke himselfe in a noble example of Iustice and truth; which doth not onely enforce a reputation and respect from other men, but an imitation and following of the like by other men: And vnto this may the diuerse and frequent changes and strictnesse of the place where we are, and the hardnesse of the many with whom he shal haue to do, with other chances & difficulties be motiues sufficient to perswade him, in which yet let him remember this, that it is in vaine in such place as heere, to pretend onely to bee vertuous and religious, except a man bee vertuous and religious indeed, and that vertue extend it selfe to example. But since I assure my selfe that of this aduice no Capt. voluntarily imploying himselfe in such a busines as this is, and onely for the businesse sake, hath any need, I commend him to the following instructions.

Euery Captaine shall (if conueniently hee may) present himselfe before his Colonel or Gouernor, once a day, to vnderstand his commands, the which hee must bee carefull, neither to exceed at any time, nor bee defectiue in their full accomplishment, albeit he shall haue a shew and presentment at any time of a better aduantage, since concerning his imployment hee may bee ignorant of the chiefe commaunders ends.

Hee shall doe well to haue a speciall eye and regard ouer his company, that they as well breake not the publique Lawes, and Orders prescribed them, but also performe all dueties and seruices vnto which they shall bee for the present commaunded, the which that hee may with the better aptnesse and conueniency

ency draw them vnto, it shal be his duty to haue knowledg, and take notice of euery one of his vnder Officers, offices and duties; that he may the readier reforme faults committed, eyther by negligence, or ignorance, and at the time of watch he shall send his Serieant to the Serieant maior for the word, and if he haue the watch himselfe, hee shall after the word giuen out, call vpon his court of guard, all his company (vnlesse his Centinels) and assembled together, humbly present themselues on their knees, and by faithful and zealous prayer vnto almighty God commend themselues and their indeauours to his mercifull protection.

After prayer, either the Captaine himselfe, or some one of his vnder officers, shall accompany the Centinell to the place of Guet, after which he shall search all the pieces vpon the court of guard, that they be charged with bullet against the Captaine of the watch or Serieant Maior shall come to visit them, and also that they be furnished with Poulder and Match, for the discharge of their duties, during the time of their watch and ward : and it is his duty, after that the Serjeant Major or Captaine of the watch haue made their round some time after midnight to walke his round, to see that his Centinels do hold good watch in their guet, & that all things be quiet and peaceable, and no disorders in the towne, and that if alarum be giuen, he giue order to his Centinels to take it with al secrecy, without any tumult or noise made, for the exact performance whereof, he must haue especiall care that he weaken not his guard, by giuing leaue vnto any of them to be absent from the guard, but vpon iust and lawfull cause, & reason to be alledged : likewise he is to appoint certaine gentlemen for rounders in his company, the which are to make their said rounds from houre to houre, according to the directions of the Captaine of the watch.

Further, about two houres before day, the Captaine shall put on his armes, and cause all his company to arme themselues, and so to stand in armes vntil one houre after the discharge of the watch in the morning, which time expired, he shall returne with his company vnto the court of guard, and there, with publike praier, giue vnto almighty God humble thankes and praises, for his mercifull and safe protection that night, and commend himselfe and his, to his no lesse mercifull protection and safegard for the day following.

And because that, during the watch, that time is appointed for the exercising of his men, and fashioning them to their armes, he shall set vp a conuenient marke by his court of guard, where

hee

hee shall teach his men the exercise of their armes, both for the comely and needful vse thereof, as the offensiue practise against their enemies, at which marke his men shall discharge their pieces twice, both morning and euening, at the discharge of the watch, hauing procured from the Gouernor some prize of incouragement due vnto him that shall shoot neerest, then he shall file and ranke, & exercise his men in such military actions, actions, according vnto such forme and exercise, as he shall receiue from the Marshall, not forgetting by the way, that all the Courts of guard, and all the members of the watch and ward, are under the command of the Capt. of the watch.

Further, the Captaine is to make it his especial duty to haue religious and manly care ouer the poore sick soldiers or labourers vnder his command, for which cause he shall visite such as are sick, and prouide so that they bee attended, their lodgings kept sweet, and their beds standing the same heigth from the ground which is prouided for in the publique Iniunctions, as likewise hee shall call for such things for them out of the store, or from the Phisitions or Surgeons chest, as the necessitie of their sicknesse shall require.

Further he is to know, because we are not onely to exercise the duty of a Souldier, but of the husbandman, and that in time of the vacancie of our watch and ward wee are not to liue idely, therefore the Captaine sending his Serieant to the Serieant Maior for the word, shall likewise giue in charge vnto his Serjeant to make demand of the Serieant Major, what seruice, worke, and businesse he hath in charge, from the Gouernor, to command him and his men to goe vppon him the next morning, after notice whereof, he shall so prouide, that he and his men be ready at the relieuing of the morning watch, the Drum summoning him there-vnto to effect the same, for which he shall bring his men vnto the place of Armes, by the maine Court of guard, where the Serjeant Major, or the Captaine of the watch, shall conduct them to the place of the subsisting businesse, prouiding them such labouring and needfull Instruments or tooles, as the worke for the present shall require, in which worke the Captaine himselfe shall do exceeding worthily to take paines and labour, that his Souldiers seeing his industry and carefulnesse, may with more cheerfulnesse loue him, and bee incouraged to the performance of the like in that businesse wherevpon they are imploied, contrariwise himselfe taking his ease, and inioyning them to toile and worke, may breed both a weariness of the businesse in the imployed, and giue a way vnto much hatred, and contempt vnto himselfe.

Now

Now concerning the tooles and instruments, and the furnishing his soldiers therewith, the Captaine shall send his Serieant
to the store to make demand thereof, and leauing a note vnder
his hand for the receipt of the same, thereby charging him-selfe
to the redeliuerie of them againe at the finishing of the worke.
The companies thus furnished, and being assembled in the place
of armes, the Serieant Maior or Captaine of the watch, vpon
their knees shall make their publike and faithfull prayers vnto
almighty God for his blessing and protection to attend them in
this their businesse the whole day after succeeding, which done,
the Serieant Maior or Captaine of the watch shal extract out of
the companies howsoeuer deuided, and deliuer vnto euery Maister of the worke appointed, his propper and seuerall Ging, to
take their wayes therevnto, where the said Maisters and ouerseers of such workes shal be present with them to labour, and
hold to labour such his Ginge vntill 9. or ten of the clock, according vnto the coldnesse or heat of the day, at which time he
shall not suffer any of his company to be negligent, and idle, or
depart from his worke, vntill the Serieant maior, or Capt. of the
watch causing the drum to beat shall fetch them in vnto the
Church to heare diuine seruice, which beeing effected, euery man
shall repaire to his lodging, to prouide himselfe of his dinner, and
to ease and rest himselfe vntill two or three of the clocke in the
after-noone, acording to the heat and coldnesse of the day, at
which time the drumme beating, the Capt: shall againe draw
forth his company vnto the place of Armes as aforesaid, to bee
disposed of as before vppon their worke vntil fiue or six of the
clocke, at which time the drumme beating as before, at the command of the Sarjeant maior or Capt. of the watch, they shalbe
by one of them brought in againe vnto the Church to Euening
prayer, which beeing ended they shall dismisse the company;
those that are to set the watch, with charge to prepare their
Armes, the others vnto their rests and lodgings.

All these duties the Captaine must not be ignorant nor negligent to put in execution, as being duties which will be exactly
required at his hands by the Marshall, as also so to behaue himselfe that he may be as well beloued as obeyed of his souldiers,
that thereby they may as well know, how to obey, as he to command, and that he endeuour by all meanes to conserue his men,
as annoy his enemy, & painefully to execute with al diligence
such matters as he is inioyned by his superiors, and to haue no
apprehension of feare, but of shame and infamie.

Instructions

Instructions of the Marshall for the better enabling of a Lief-tenant to the executing of his charge in this present Colonie
Iune *the* 22. 1611.

WHen the Captaine is present he is to be assisting to his Captaine, in prouiding that all directions that are commanded by the Superior Officer, as well his Captain as other, be put in execution, that the company be well and orderly gouerned, and such duties duly and dayly performed as are inioyned by the Gouernor or chiefe officer : and likewise that the duties of the inferiour officers or Soldiers be no lesse diligently and sedulously discharged, for he being, as is said, a helpe, and aide vnto his Captaine, is therefore accountant to and with his Captain for such omissions, disorders and neglects, as the company shall be found faulty in.

He ought faithfully to informe his Capt: of all abuses, disorders, neglects, and contempts that shall happen in the company, of what nature or condition soeuer they bee.

If his Captain shal at any time demand his opinion in any matter of consequence, he shall faithfully and sincerely deliuer it, but not presume to aduise his Capt. vndemanded, vnles it be vpon extraordinary occasiō of present and imminent perill.

It shalbe his duty in all quarrels, braules, debates, and discontentments of his soldiers to accord and agree them without partiallity, and with the least troubling of his Cap. with the same, & if he cannot with his curtesies, and gentle interposition worke them into peaceable agreement, hee shall then acquaint his Captaine, and afterwards faithfully put in execution his Captaines directions.

He ought to traine & exercise the company that they may be expert in the vse of their armes when they shall be commanded to publike seruice.

He ought likewise to see that the inferiour officers be duly obei'd the one by the other without singularity or contradictiō, & the soldiers obey thē all in generall, each one according to his place.

By his care euery Squadron shal haue his armes seruiceable and cleane, and at the setting of the watch that they be prouided of pouder, match, and bullet, for the defence of the guard, and if the company be vnfurnished to aduertise his Captaine, or send his Serieant to the munition Maister, that order may bee presently taken for the supplie thereof.

Hee shall doe well, if conueniently he may, morning and euening (or at least once a day) to present him-selfe before his
Captaine,

Captaine, to know his commands, and to informe his Captaine, of the state of his Companie.

It shalbe his duty to haue care that the company bee ready (as is exprest in the Captaines duty) to go forth and attend the daily businesse, and publike labour appertayning to the Colonie, which shalbe commaunded by the chiefe officer, In which hee shall haue a hand in executing, and an eye in ouer-seeing, that euery one take his due paines, and not loyter, and idlely mis-pend the time appoynted vnto the dispatch of such businesse.

Hee is to haue a hearty and religious care that the souldiers doe not make breach of the lawes, and duties, diuine, ciuill, or martiall, inioyned them to obserue vpon so necessary reasons and strict penalties, but that he informe, correct and punish to the vtmost of his authority limited, the trespassers of the same, or the omission of any duty whatsoeuer, with the approbation of his Captaine.

Hee is not to make it his least care to ouer-see and take charge of the lodging and bedding of all in generall in his com-pany, that according vnto the publike edict the preseruation of their healths be prouided for, and that one point of slothfullnesse in the common soldier preuented, and met with, of lying vpon or to neere the ground, which neglect in the officer hath bin the losse of many a man.

For his order of command and march in the field, and quar-tering he shal be appoynted the manner thereof by the Marshall, when occasion of seruice shall so require, like-wise the order of trayning and exercising his Captaines company he shall haue vnder the marshalls hand.

Hee is amongst other his duties most carefully, like a cha-ritable and wel instructed Christian, mercifull and compassion-ate, make often and daily suruey of such of his company as shalbe visited with sicknesse, or wounded by any casualty of warre, gunpoulder, or other-wise, in which hee shall take such order that the lodgings of such as shalbe so sicke or hurt, be sweet and cleanely kept, them-selues attended and drest, and to the vttermost of his power to procure either from the store, or Phisition and Surgeons chest, such comforts, healps, and reme-dies, as may be administred and applied vnto them, and to haue care that they be not defrauded of those meanes and remedies which are for them deliuered out of the said store or chests.

And for that this officer is in the abscence of his Captaine to be called vnto the Marshall Court as his deputie, for the better inhabling of his iudgement, when his opinion is to be required in the censure of offences and crimes of what quality soeuer,

which

which shalbe brought thither to be sentenced, I refer him to the abstract of the lawes in breefe anexed vnto the duty of his Capt.

Instructions of the Marshall for the better enabling of an En- signe to the executing of his charge in this present Colo- nie, Iune *the* 22. 1611.

IT is requisite for euery soldier to stand vpon his credit and reputation, proposing vnto himselfe that there can be no lesse equall, or to be compared with dishonour, & sure in matters of armes and their execution, what dishonour can bee greater then the losse of the ensigne, for which it ought to be committed to the charge of a right valiant, and well gouerned soldier, who may not leaue nor loose it, but where the losse of his life shall quit him of that duty.

So farre as toucheth his command, or gouernment in the com- pany, he is to know that he hath no command where his Cap- taine or Lieftenant are present, but in their absence I referre him to the duty of the Capt: which he is to execute as reli- giously, painfully, and circumspectly as the Captaine: he bee- ing answerable vnto his Captaine for all defects, neglects, dis- orders, and contempts of duties, in his company whatsouer.

In the gouernment of his company he is to be asistant vnto his superiour officers, in teaching and inabling all his inferiours, euery one his perticular duty, with faire perswasion and all gen- tlenes, and sweetnes of command, and if any thing shall happen, either disorders or neglects of duties, it shall be fit for him to aduertise his superior officers that redresse may be had, for he hath no power of himselfe in their presence to punish, correct, or do any act of executions vpon his companions.

When the time of exercise and training shalbe of the com- panie, he shall be there ready and assistant vnto his superiour officer (if so be it his colours be not drawne forth) for the bet- ter furtherance of him in the so training, and disciplining of the men.

Hee shall see all commands of his superior Officers put in execution, and not stand ignorantly in defence (as some haue) and it is the property of the ignorant so to do, that he is tyed to no other duties, but to the carrying of his coulours. For no in- feriour officers duty, whether Sargeant or corporalls, but he is to performe and execute (if they shall be by any disaster, defeate, or visitation of sicknesse disabled personally to discharge it themselues)

themselues) being so commanded by his Superior officers, during the time of guard, yea the duty of the Centinell he is to vndergoe, and from which neither the Captaine nor Lieftenant are exempted vpon vrgent occasion.

In the hapning of any dispute, quarrell, or debate amongst the soldiers, the same being brought to his knowledge, he shall do his best to end and compound, whose authority & perswasions, if they shal not be powerfull enough to reconcile & set at one, he shal then informe his Lieftenant, or Captaine : that order with the most speed & conuenience, may be taken therein.

He shall hold it his duty to visit the sick or hurt in his company, and to his power of them take the same care, and make the same charitable prouision for, as is inioynd both the Captaine and Lieftenant.

It is his duty to command the Corporalls to bring their squadrons to his lodging, who shal conduct them to his Lieftenant, and they both conduct them to their Captaine, at the beating of the Drum, whither for any manuall labour and worke, for the Colony, or whither to bee lead vnto the Church at any time to heare diuine seruice.

He is to visit the armes of the Company, and at the setting of the watch to take care, and so at all time, that they be not vnseruiceable, and if any want bee then of match, poulder, or bullet, or what else defect, hee is to aduertise his Superior Officers, that they may then and at all other times bee supplied and amended.

To bee breefe hee is an assistant to the Lieftenant in the same nature that the Lieftenant is to the Captaine, and may not by any meanes intrude into the command of the one or other, they being present.

In the absence of the Captaine, and Lieftenant (when hee is then to bee Captaine of the watch) I referre him to the duty of the sayd Captayne of the watch.

For his Order of march, and flying of his collours, and his carriage in the field, and vpon seruice, he shalbee ordred and instructed by word of mouth from the Marshall, when occasion shalbe offered.

Thus mutch is needfull for him to know touching his command, and his carriage to his officers and company, so far forth as hee and they are soldiers, and as the necessity of this present state and condition which we are in doth require. But concerning the publike and dayly manuall businesse which appertaine to our setling there as Planters of a Colonie, he is to make it his duty, to be a diligent not onely ouer-seer, but labourer,

himselfe

hiinselfe accompanying therein, and seconding the example
of his Captaine, and industrious Lieutenant, that the necessary
and daily taskes of such workes and husbandry (without which
we cannot here keepe footing, nor possibly subsist) may be in
due time accomplisht and brought to passe.

Instructions of the Marshall for the better enabling
of a Serjeant to the executing of his charge in this present Colonie, Iune the 22. 1611.

That Captaine who shall dispose of a Halbert,
by vertue whereof a Serjeant is knowne, ought
to make choise of a man well approoued, that
hath passed the inferior grades of a resolute
spirit, quick apprehension, and actiue body, for
it is a place of great paines and promptitude,
and that Serjeant who will be able to execute his duty in sin-
ceritie and vprightnesse, must not be slack to punish where it is
deserued, nor ouer rash to abuse his authority, vnbefitting an
officer of such moment.

This officer hath in the absence of his superior officers the
command of the company, to see them doe their duties, and
obserue lawes and orders in all things, and punishment of them
by his Halbert, or otherwise in his discretion, for defect or negligence in any part of order.

This officer is to attend vpon the Serjeant Major for the word
vpon the shutting in of the Ports, at the Gouernors lodging or
place of armes, according as the Serjeant Major shall appoint,
then he is to giue the word to his Captaine, Lieftenant, and
Ensigne, and vnto his corporall or corporalls hauing the guard.

Hee must see the Soldiers of his company furnished and prouided with munition, as shotte, poulder, and match, at the setting of the watch.

Hee is to call, or cause to bee called the Corporalls roule, to
see who are absent or negligent in the discharge of their duties.

Hee is to see each souldiers armes cleanly kept, and seruiceable, and if default be, he is to reprooue the corporall for his
negligence in the ouer-sight of that dutie, and to punish the
souldier. .

Hee must see the souldiers practise their armes, and therefore it is requisite that he know the vse of all sorts of armes
himselfe.

If the watch be set by squadrons, he shall leade that squadron,
that

that is to watch to the *Parado*, and there draw Billets for his guard, and from thence lead them to the guard.

He shall see the setting out of the Centinels, and after shall haue care that silence and good order be kept vpon the guard, and that no man depart from the guard without the leaue of him, or his corporall, and that no man be absent aboue one halfe houre, hauing a special regard that hee weaken not his guard, by giuing leaue vnto aboue two at a time to be absent, least he disable himselfe in the performance of that duty of trust and charge which is committed vnto him of the guard.

Hee shall see that his corporall or corporals, do put his or their squadrons into armes, two houres before the relieuing of the watch, who shall so abide in armes, at least one whole houre after.

If the watch be set by whole companies, it is his duty to place euery souldier in his order, and to see them march in ranke and file, and himselfe being eldest Serjeant to march vpon the right point in the vaunt-guard: if he be the yongest he is to march vpon the left point in the rere-ward, each taking care of halfe of the company, vnlesse when more companies march together, they be appointed any other place by a superior officer.

When the Serjeant is appointed to lead out any shot, he shall goe vpon the side of the vtmost ranke, and see that they take their leuell, & giue fier, and do all things with comlinesse and leisure, & so likewise in the retrait.

A Serjeant of each company, presently after the discharge of the watch shall bee in the place of armes, or market place, to attend the Captaine of the watch to the opening of the Ports, that they may be imploied by him, for the discouery without the forts, of any ambushes or attempts of the enemy, with such guard as hee shall appoint them, the Captaine of the watch hauing caused all those of the towne, about, to go forth, to forbeare and stay vntill the said Serjeants returne, which Serjeants are to command those that are comming in, to stay vntill those in the towne are comming forth, & and then they shal discouer right forth before the Port, and to both sides of the Port, so farre vntill the discouerers of the other forts meete where they end; the discouerers being returned, those of the towne shall be suffered to passe out leisurely, & after those being without shal come in as leisurely, without throng or crowd, that they be the better discerned by the guard what they are. The Ports beeing open, the Serjeants shall returne to their guards, where they shall instruct their souldiers in the practise of their armes, and shall shew them the ready vse of them, and do their indeauours

by

by their best meanes, to incourage the towardly, and instruct the ignorant.

If vpon his guard, in the absence of his superior officer, any soldier of his guard shall offend, hee shall eyther punish him by his Halbert, or if the qualitie of the offence so deserue, he shall disarme him, and keepe him prisoner vpon the guard, vntill the watch bee relieued, and then hee shall bring him to his superior officers, that he may receiue condigne punishment according to the condition of his offence.

The Serjeant ought to know euery souldier, and to take notice of their particular lodgings, and to make it a point of his duty to see that they keepe their lodgings cleane, and that their beds doe stand a yard aboue the ground, to haue an eye into their diet, their thriftinesse and conuersation, to aduise them to the best, whereof he is to make report vnto the Captaine or chiefe officer, that they may receiue estimation for good, and punishment for euill behauiour.

He is to informe himselfe of the sick, or hurt, in the company, and to visit them once a day, and to inquire whether they bee not defrauded by the Phisitions and Surgeons, of such necessary helpes as are deliuered vnto them, for their preseruations and recoueries, and to informe his Captaine of the negligence and abuse of such, who should in that case deale vniustly with them that their dishonesty may receiue due punishment.

He is likewise to addresse himselfe vnto the Serjeant Major, and Store-maister, for the supplying of his company with munition, and victuals, vpon any occasion : and concerning the munition, he is to haue a principall care, that the souldier doe not spend it away in vaine, but onely at such times as they are appointed for exercising and training.

He is likewise to take notice of all defects and abuses in his company, and to enforme his superiour officers, that they may be redressed, and Iustice take place.

He shall with great diligence attend the commands of his Captaine, and of the Serjeant Major, and at all times put them in present execution, rebuking such as do amisse, shewing them their faults, and teaching them by a good example in himselfe, to tread in the way of all ciuilitie and goodnesse. If any debate shall happen betweene souldier and souldier, hee hauing knowledge thereof, shall doe his indeauor to agree, and reconcile them, that it come not to his superior officers, and if through obstinacie hee cannot agree them, hee shall commit them, or informe his superior officers, who may take order therein.

He is to prouide that none of the company be absent when
the

the Drum shall call them forth to worke, in which workes he is to be a president himselfe, both by labouring in the same, and calling vpon others to doe the like.

He is to goe to the Store, to take out such Tooles, as are required for the workes in hand, and there to vnder-write vnto the booke of the store-Maister, or vnto a note to be filed, thereby charging himselfe to be accountable for the said tooles, when the worke shall be performed, ouer which he is to haue a regard, that they be not neglectfully layed vp, spoyled nor broken without examining by what meanes they came so broken, that the wilfull breaker thereof may receiue punishment, and the said toole or tooles so broken, withall the pieces, he shall bring vnto the store, to shew the same for his better discharge.

Instructions of the Marshall for the better enabling of a Corporall vnto the discharge of his duty in this present Colonie, Iune *the* 22. 1611.

He Corporall is in grade and dignity aboue the priuate soldier, and therefore care ought to bee had in the choosing of this officer, for that it is an office of good account, and by neglect of this duty, many inconueniences may come upon a camp, towne, or fort, therefore it is fit that hee surmount and excell his inferiors in valour, diligence and iudgment, and likewise in the practise and vse of all sorts of armes, whereby he may the better bee enabled to instruct and teach this squadron committed to his charge.

The Corporall ought (hauing the third part of the company giuen him in command) to sort and assist them in their quartering or lodging, to haue a care that they be cleane and sweet, and that their beds in the same bee laide three foote from the ground, hee is to carry a hand ouer their dyet, thriftinesse, and conuersation, and to aduise and instruct them at all times to demeane themselues as good Christians ought to do, and to make report thereof vnto his Captaine or chiefe officer, that from them they may receiue credit and estimation for good behauiour, and punishment and disgrace for their misdemenours.

Hee is to haue a speciall care of their Armes to see them duly furnished and kept in order, and when the Drum beateth to bee in a readinesse at the Colonies, and if any bee absent, hee shall make it knowne to his Serjeant or superior officer.

When he marcheth, hee is to lead a file, hee ought to bee

daily

daily conuersant with his little company committed vnto his charge, and the company beeing in the field, to lodge with them, and prouide to his power for their wants, and to instruct and teach them how to vse and handle the weapon they carry: Likewise, to remember well how each one is armed and appointed when hee receiueth him into charge, then to see no part of his furniture or armes bee broken or spoiled, but to haue care that they bee preserued cleane and seruice-able.

Hee ought to haue a vigilant eye vpon the good behauiour of his company, not suffering them to vse any unlawfull and prohibited games, nor that they giue them selues to excesse of drinking, surfitting and ryot, but that they bee conformable to all the Martiall lawes: that they likewise make spare of their pay or victuals, the better to furnish themselues in comely and decent manner, with apparell and other necessaries fitte and requisite for them, wherein the Corporall ought to vse his vtmost endeauour.

In presence of his Captaine, or superior officer, he is to take vppon him no more then the condition of his office doth require, but diligently to attend and execute what they shall command, that his example may serue for a President to the rest of his squadron.

At the setting of the watch hee is to see that they be furnished with poulder, Bullet and match, and that their armes be seruiceable and soldier-like.

If the company watch by squadrons, he and his squadron shall be brought by the Serjeant vnto the place of watch, and from him receiue the word and directions, in what maner, and where he shall place his Centinels, whether by day or night, which hee is to see performed.

When the Corporall with his squadron shall bee brought to the place where he and they shall watch, he and they must prouide eft-soones for wood for fyring vpon the guard, that beside for their owne comfort, they may haue fire ready alwayes vpon the guarde to light their match vpon any proffered occasion.

Hee is to cause silence to bee kept vppon the court of guard, and to guarde, and to gouerne the watch, so that the labour bee equally diuided of his squadron, either in watch, worke, or seruice, and to take care in all respects, that they performe the duties of good and honest soldiers.

His Centinels being placed, hee is to let none passe without the word, vnlesse it bee the Captaine of the watch, or Serjeant Major, vnto whom (after hee shall haue perfect knowledge of them,) hee is to deliuer the word at their first round, but before
the

the deliuery of the word, hee shall take the Captaine of the watch and Serjeant Major alone within his guard, the corporall beeing accompanied with halfe a dozen of shot with Match in Cock, to haue an eye ouer the rest of the rounders that accompany the Captaine of the watch or Sarjeant Major, and not to suffer the rounders to come within the centinell, & if at any time of the night after their first round, the Serjeant Maior or Captaine of the watch shall goe their round, as it is their duties, then they are to giue the word to the Corporal, vnlesse they mistrust and doubt the memory of any Corporall: the Corporall is not to goe out single to take the word of any round but to take two, or three, or more of his guard with him, and if it shalbe a round of more then two, then hee shall draw out all his men in his guard in their armes, the Corporall shall at no time (to receiue the word) passe beyond the Centinell, but make him that hath the word to come forward within the Centinell, and shall cause the rest to stand without the Centinell, and those that are out by the Corporall for his guard shall keepe their eies and armes in a readinesse ouer him that is to giue or take the word of the Corporall, vntill such time as the Corporall be satisfied of him.

He must make good his guard vntill he bee releiued the which hee shall the better doe if hee keepe his men together vpon the guard; he must visite the Centinels sometimes vnawares to them, and must be ready to go to them at the first call.

Hee shall put his men in armes two houres before the discharge of the watch, so to remayne one houre after.

Hee shall warne his Centinells to make noe alarum but vpon iust cause, and then with as much silence as may be, and in like silence hee must aduertise the Captaine of the watch, and the next guards vnto him, and so without notice or signe of confusiō from one guard vnto another.

If vpon his guard any of his soldiers shal misdemeane himselfe, or offend in any of the publique lawes, diuine, ciuill, or martiall, he shall bring him to his superior officer, then vpon the guard, that he may receiue punishment.

His duty is to prouide that none of his Squadron, be absent, when the drumme shall call to any labour, or worke, or at what time soeuer they shall be commanded thereunto for the seruice of the Collonie, in the performance of which said workes he is to be an example of the rest of his Squadron by his owne labouring therein, and by encouraging and calling vpon others at any time negligent, idle and slothfull, that thereby giuing encoraging to his superior officers he may be held by them worthy of a higher place.

Hee

Hee must likewise receiue such instruments and tooles, as spades, shouels, axes, &c. imployed in the worke, from his Sarjeant to dispose, and to deliuer the same vnto the labourers with all the care he may, to his vtmost, that none of them be broken, lost, or wilfully spoiled, without drawing the parties so breaking, loosing and wilfully spoyling the same into punishment; and after the worke done he shall gather the said tooles in againe and re-deliuer them vp vnto his Sargeant, all, and the same, who is to be accountable vnto the maister of the store vnto whose booke he hath underwritten for the receipt of them.

And by reason he is well knowing of euery man in his Squadron, and thereby cannot but misse the pretence of any man from any duty whatsoeuer, sooner then haply the superiour officers may, his care shall bee to attend his squadron to the vsuall workes and day-labours, and vnto frequent prayers, and the deuine seruice at all times, and vppon all the dayes in the weeke, giuing due notice vnto his superiour officer, of the neglect of eyther duties in their kinde, that reformation may follow.

He shall not suffer any gaming, heare any prophane lewd speeches, swearing, brawling, &c. or see any disorder whatsoever vppon his court of guard, or else-where, without present information giuen thereof vnto his superiour officer, that the offenders may be duly punished.

Hee shall take notice of all bands and proclamations published by the Generall, procuring a copie of the same from the Prouost Marshall, the same duly to bee read vnto his squadron, that they may be made the perfecter in the knowledge of them, and thereby learne the better to forbeare the trespassing in forbidden things, remembring the penaltie of the same, and execute things commanded, considering the reward thereof, whether in Campe, Towne or Forte, Field or garrison.

Hee shall read, or cause to bee read, the Souldiers dutye, euery time of his guarde in some conuenient time and place, during the same, thereby to remember them the better of their generall duties.

Instructions of the Marshall for the better enabling of a priuat soldier, to the executing of his duty in this present Colonie. Iune 22. 1611.

IT is requisite that he who will enter into this function of a soldier, that he dedicate himselfe wholly for the planting and establishing of true religion, the honour of his Prince, the safety of his country, and to learne the art which he professeth, which is in this place to hold warre, and the seruice requisite to the subsisting of a
colonie

colonie : There be many men of meane descent, who haue this way attained to great dignity, credit, and honor.

Hauing thus dedicated himselfe with a constant resolution, he ought to be diligent, carefull, vigilant and obedient, and principaly to haue the feare of God, and his honor in greatest esteeme.

In making choyse of his familiar acquaintance, let him haue care that they be of religious and honest conditions, not factious nor mutenous murmurers, nor euill languaged and worse disposed persons : his choyse beeing made he is to carry hirn selfe discreete, temperate, quiet and friendly, withholding himselfe from being to lauish of speech, for such as take liberty vnto themselues to talke licentiously, to slander, raile, and backbite others, do vsually make bankrout of their friends, of estimation, and of their own peace and quiet of conscience.

He must be carefull to serue God priuately and publiquely ; for all professions are therevnto tied, that carry hope with them to prosper, and none more highly then the souldier, for hee is euer in the mouth of death, and certainly hee that is thus religiously armed, fighteth more confidently and with greater courage, and is thereby protected through manifold dangers, and otherwise vnpreuentable euents.

He must bee no blasphemer nor swearer, for such an one is contemptible to God and the world, and shall be assured to be found out and punished by the diuine Iustice : whereof we haue instant examples.

He must refraine from dicing, carding, and Idle gaming : for common gamsters, although they may haue many good parts in them, yet commonly they are not esteemed according to their better qualities, but censured according to their worst, procuring enemies, questions, brawles, and a thousand following inconueniences.

He must not set his minde ouer-greedily vpon his belly, and continuall feeding, but rest himselfe contented with such prouisions as may be conueniently prouided, his owne labour purchase, or his meanes reach vnto : aboue all.things he must eschew that detestable vice of drunkennesse ; for then a man is not apt nor good for any thing, and by that beastly disorder, many great armies haue miscarried, and much disquiet and tumults raised in campe, and ciuill townes, wherevpon doth fall the sword of Iustice vpon their necks, which in that case they haue compelled to be drawne.

Chastitie is a vertue much commended in a souldier, when vncleannesse doth defile both body and soule, and makes a man

stinke

stinke in the nostrils of God & man, and laieth him open to the malice & sword of his enemy, for commonly it makes a man effeminate, cowardly, lasie, and full of diseases, & surely such who haue vnlawful women stil trudging about with thē, or in whom custome hath taken away the sence of offending in that kind, commonly come to dishonorable ends.

He is tyed in his entring or inrowling into any company, to take his oath of faithfulnesse, and sincere seruice to his Prince, Generall and Captaine: to be conformable to the lawes prouided for the aduancement of the intended businesse, and for the cherishing of the good therein, and punishment of the euill.

He must be true-hearted to his Capt. and obey him and the rest of the officers of the Campe, Towne, or Fort, with great respect, for by the very oath which he taketh hee doth binde himselfe and promise to serue his Prince, and obey his officers: for the true order of warre is fitly resembled to true religion ordeined of God, which bindeth the souldier to obserue iustice, loyaltie, faith, constancie, patience, silence, and aboue all, obedience, through the which is easily obteined the perfection in armes, and is as a meanes to atchieue great enterprises, though neuer so difficult: certainly, who wanteth the vertue of obedience and patience, though neuer so valiant otherwise, yet is he vnworthy of the same name.

A souldier must patiently suffer the aduersities and trauailes which do fall out in the courses and chances of warre: he must not be ouer-greedy, nor hasty of his pay, albeit he may stand in some want thereof, but must with a chearfull alacrity shew his constancy, auoyding by al possible meanes, rebellions and mutenies, which most vpon such pettish occasiones are runne into: by no meanes must hee bee a pertaker with such mutiners, for the end of such is sharpe and shamefull death.

If in Skirmishes Incounters, or surprise of towne the enimies be vanquished, let him set all his care and diligence in execution of the victorie with his Armes, & not in rifling and spoiling for trash, for so he shal be accounted an vnruly freebooter, beside innumerable are the disorders and mischefes which do happen by rauenous Pillagers, many times to the dishonor of the action, and to the losse of their liues, therfore he shall pursue the victorie vntil the enimy be wholy ended & and the place fully caried and possessed, the Guards placed, and liberty granted from the chiefe Commander to sack & spoile, wherein by any meanes let him auoid murther and crueltie, and violation of women, for those are odious to God and man, rather in such cases let him shew himselfe pittiful and mercifull vnto the vanquished

quished, rather defending the sillie women and Children then procuring their hurt and damage, for in so doing it will be right acceptable to God and his Commanders.

Such Armes as he is apointed to serue with, whither Musket, Caliuer or Target, let him be very dilligent to vse all his industrie to excell in the vse of them, for therby he may conserue his owne life and his fellows, for the which purpose he shall call vpon his Serjeant and his Corporall to instruct him therein, vntill hee come vnto perfection.

He must learne the seuerall sounds of the Drumme, whereby hee may obey that which he is commanded; for the Drum often-times is the voice of the Commander, hee shall carefully note and marke the signes made by the Captaine and officers, without talking or pratling vnto his next companions: for that is vnbefitting a Souldier, and makes him vncapable to heare what is giuen in command.

In skirmishes and incounters he shal be resolute and valiant, for that souldier which is timorous and fearfull can neuer bring his heart to any hearty enterprise, nor dareth to attempt any hotte, bold, or audacious charge or seruice, by reason of his cowardly spirit and feare.

Hee must bee carefull to bee alwayes vigilant and ready, beeing placed for a Centinell, or in the Court of guard, where he shall not put of his armes, vntill hee haue leaue from the Captaine : for therein consisteth the security of the Campe, Towne, or Fort.

Hee shall doe well to keepe his fidelity vnspotted to his Prince and Generall, although his sufferings may bee intolerable and infinite, and shall not flye vnto the enemy: for to bee branded with infamie of a traytor is a fowle and odious offence, and rigorously punished among all nations, and neuer yet traitor came to good end; of which we haue examples infinite.

Hee must not bee shifting from company to company, but serue in the company where hee first began, and if at any time hee shall depart for his preferment, let him demand the good liking of his Captaine, who if hee shall denie it him in such a case, it shall bee imputed no offence in him to appeale vnto the Generall or chiefe officer.

At the sound of the Drumme, for the setting of the watch with his arms being fix and seruiceable he shall repaire to his colours, and it shall be commendable in him by the way to call vpon his Corporall, so that all the Squadron meeting together at the Corporals lodging may attend the Corporall vnto the colours, and if he be vnprouided of munition he shall acquaint his Corporall therewith, who shall see him furnished.

When

When the company or squadron march to the guard he shall hold that order in which he was placed by his Serjeant, marching in a comely and gracefull manner, and being armed at the place of guard he shall pose his armes according vnto the Corporalls direction, and behaue himselfe in all his actions as befitting a religious Soldier in that holy place of guard, without doing any act of prophanenesse, disorder, or ought els, tending to the pollution of the same either in word or deed.

When his Corporall shall appoint him forth for Centinell, he shall shoulder his peice, both ends of his match being alight, and his peice charged, and prined, and bullets in his mouth, there to stand with a carefull and waking eye, vntill such time as his Corporall shall relieue him, and to let no man passe nor come vp to him, but to force him stand, and then to call his Corporall.

He must harken diligently and looke well about him from his place of Centinell for the approch of any about the Camp, Towne, or Fort, or the dich thereof, or if he heare any noyse, to call his Corporall to aduertise him of the same.

He must haue a speciall care that he sleepe not vpon his Centinell, nor set his armes out of his hands: for therein he maketh himselfe subiect for any passenger by to take away his life, beside the generall inconuenience that may come vpon the Camp, Towne or Fort.

His Corporall hauing releiued him and brought him to the guard, he shall do well to read the Lawes and ordinances for the gouernment of the Camp, Towne, or Fort, constituted and prescribed by the Marshall, the better to enable his memory for the exact obseruance of those lawes whereby he shall not only auoyd the trespassing against the same, but also get the reputation of a well ordered and gouerned soldier.

Such gentlemen or others, as are appointed by their Captaine for rounders, and approoued by the Serjeant Major or Captaine of the watch, amongst them those rounders that are appointed to attend the Captaine of the watch on his guard are to receiue their directions from him, as Likewise those of the companies vpon the guards for their order of rounding, according to the time of the night in what hower they shal make their Rounds.

The Rounders from the guard, from the Captaine of the watch, are to visit the Centinells, and Courts of guards, making their rounds vpon the rampart, harkning and listening and looking ouer into the ditches, if they can heare or see, or discouer any troopes, or men neere the town, taking care besides that there be good watch kept both by the Centinells, and vpon the

court

court of guard, and if any noyse or tumult be neere the rampart, they may step downe and informe themselues of it, and bring the trespassers to the next guard, committing them there vntill after the round made they haue acquainted the Capt. of the watch of such disorders.

The rounds frō the Ports are to round the streets to take in charge that no disorders, breaking vp, or fiering of houses of yͤ store, or roberies, *magazin*, riots or tumult in Taphouses, or in the streetes, or in priuat houses at houres vntimely be committed, and the offenders to bring to the next guard, and to informe the Captaine of the watch; All rounders are to be subiect and obedient vnto the Captaine of the watch and his commands during his time of watch.

Two houres before day he must be ready in arms with his peice charged & prouided, & a match alight at both ends and bullets in mouth, there to attend the command of the Corporall vntill further directions be giuen, and at the time appoynted for the exercise of his armes, he shall be tractable and obedient to his officers executing such commands as they shall impose vpon him, that he may be the better trained and inhabled to offend his enemy, and to defend himselfe.

He shal be carefull to obserue al words of command, postures and actions, according to the order of training published by the marshall.

The exercise being ended and the prise won and lost he shall pose his armes at the court of Guard, and ther giue diligent attendance that he be at no time absent from his Guard, aboue one houre, without leaue from his Officer, and that not without leaue of his Officer.

The watch being relieued and he free from the guard he is to dispose of the rest of the time for his owne perticular vse vntill next morning at the discharge of the watch: when at the call of the drumme, he shall attend at his corporalls lodging ther to receiue such instrument, or toole as the busines of that day shall require, from whence he shall march to the place of armes or maine court of guard; there to be disposed of by the captaine of the watch for that day seruice of the Colonies, in which he shall doe his best indeauour like a painfull and industrious seruant of the Colonies to discharge his duty for the furtherance of his worke, and incouragment of such who shall be the more stirred vp by his example of goodnes, to the imitation of the like: and thus doing, he shall giue cause vnto the Generall, vnto his Captaine, and chiefe officers, to take notice of his
                                                                painfulnesse,

painfulnesse, who may according to his desert in time giue him aduancement for the same.

He shall continue at his worke vntill the drumme beate, and that his Captaine, his officers or ouerseers of the worke, giue order vnto a cessation for the time, and for the same purpose attendeth to lead him in, whom he shall orderly and comely follow into the Camp, Towne or Fort, by his said Captaine, officer or ouerseer him meeting, to be conducted vnto the church to heare diuine seruice, after which he may repayre to his house or lodging to prepare for his dinner, and to repose him vntill the drumme shall call him forth againe in the afternoone, when so (as before) he shall acompany his chiefe officer vnto the field, or where els the work lieth, and there to follow his easie taske untill againe the drumme beat to returne home : at which time according as in the forenoone, he shall follow his chiefe officer vnto the church to heare diuine seruice and after dispose of himselfe aṣ he shall best please, and as his owne businesse shall require ; with this caution carefully to preserue the toole or Instrument with which he wrought to serue his turne againe the next day as he will answere the contrary vpon the perill pre-scribed.

Concerning his order of march and carriage in the field when occasion shall present it selfe, he will easily acquire and learne the same by experience, prouided that he be carefull to march, ranke, and file, and not straggle, or be disobedient vnto procla-mations of the General for therin consisteth the principall part of his duty, vntill when I leaue him with this caueat, that he di-ligently marke, consider and remember the orders, which the higher officers do obserue, in ordering their files and rankes, and surueying their squadrons of footmen, and to the placing of the great Artillery in the march and setled campe, and the plot of the quartering, according to the disposition of the ground where the campe shall then be, with the manner of entrenching, placing of Ordinances & Guards for the defence of the same, that in the knowledge and execution of these duties, the Generall hauing vnderstanding of his promptitude and diligence may conferre vpon him, and call him vnto place of preferment and com-maund.

That there be no neglect found in him, in his marching to the Guard or Field, and that in the same he doe not forget or leaue behinde him any peece or parcell of his Armes appointed him by the Marshall for his owne defence, or offence of the enemie.

A

A *Praier* duly said *Morning* and *Eue-*
ning vpon the Court of Guard, either by
the Captaine of the watch himselfe, or by
some one of his principall officers.

Erciful Father, and Lord of heauen and earth, we come before thy presence to worship thee in calling upon thy name, and giuing thankes unto thee, and though our duties and our verie necessities call us heereunto : Yet we confesse our hearts to be so dull and untoward, that unlesse thou be mercifull to vs to teach vs how to pray, we shall not please thee, nor profit our selues in these duties.

Wee therefore most humbly beseech thee to raise vp our hearts with thy good spirit, and so to dispose vs to praier, that with true feruencie of heart, feeling of our wants, humblenesse of minde, and faith in thy gracious promises, we may present our suites acceptably vnto thee by our Lord and Sauiour Jesus Christ.

And thou our Father of al mercies, that hast called vs vnto thee, heare vs and pitie thy poore seruants, we haue indeed sinned wonderously against thee through our blindnesse of mind, prophanesse of spirit, hardnesse of heart, selfe loue, worldlinesse, carnall lusts, hypocrisie, pride, vanitie, vnthankfulnesse, infidelitie, and other our natiue corruptions, which being bred in vs, and with vs, haue defiled vs euen from the wombe, and vnto this day, and haue broken out as plague sores into innumerable transgressions of all thy holy lawes, (the good waies whereof we haue wilfully declined,) & haue many times displeased thee, and our own consciences in chusing those things which thou hast most iustly & seuerely forbidden vs. And besides all this wee haue outstood the gracious time and meanes of our conuersion, or at least not stooped and humbled our selues before thee, as wee ought, although we haue wanted none of those helpes, which thou vouchsafest vnto thy wandering children to fetch them home withall, for we haue had together with thy glorious workes, thy word calling vpon vs without, and thy spirit within, and haue been solicited by promises, by threatnings, by blessings, by chastisings, & by examples, on all hands : And yet our corrupted spirits cannot become wise before thee, to humble themselves, and to take heede as we ought, and wish to do.

Wherefore O Lord God, we do acknowledge thy patience to haue beene infinite and incomparable, in that thou hast been able

to

to hold thy hands frō reuenging thy self vpō vs thus long, &
yet pleasest to hold open the dore of grace, that we might come
in vnto thee and be saued.

And now O blessed Lord God, we are desirous to come vnto
thee, how wretched soeuer in our selues, yea our very wretchednesse sends vs vnto thee : vnto thee with who the fatherlesse,
and he that hath no helper findeth mercy, we come to thee in thy
Sons name not daring to come in our owne : In his name that
came for vs, we come to thee, in his mediation whom thou hast
sent : In him O Father, in whom thou hast professed thy selfe
to be well pleased, we come vnto thee, and doe most humbly
beseech thee to pittie vs, & to saue vs for thy mercies sake in
him.

O Lord our God our sins haue not outbidden that bloud of
thy holy Son which speaks for our pardon, nor can they be so
infinite, as thou art in thy mercies, & our hearts (O God thou
seest them,) our hearts are desirous to haue peace with thee, and
war with our lusts, and wish that they could melt before thee,
and be dissolued into godly mourning for all that filth that hath
gone through them, and defiled them. And our desires are now
to serue and please thee, and our purposes to endeuour it more
faithfully, we pray thee therefore for the Lord Jesus sake seale
vp in our consciences thy gracious pardon of all our sinnes past,
and giue vs to feele the consolation of this grace shed abroad in
our hearts for our eternall comfort and saluation : and that we
may know this perswasion to be of thy spirit, and not of carnall
presumption, (blessed God) let those graces of thy spirit, which
doe accompanie saluation, be powred out more plentifully vpon
vs, encrease in vs all godly knowledge, faith, patience, temper-
ance, meekenesse, wisedome, godlinesse, loue to thy Saints and
seruice, zeale of thy glory, iudgement to discerne the difference
of good & ill, and things present which are temporary, and
things to come which are eternall.

Make vs yet at the last wise-hearted to lay vp our treasure
in heauen, and to set our affections more vpon things that are
aboue, where Christ sits at thy right hand : And let all the
vaine and transitory inticements of this poore life, appeare vnto
vs as they are, that our hearts may no more be intangled and
bewitched with the loue of them.

O Lord, O God, our God, thou hast dearely bought vs for
thine owne selfe, guie vs so honest hearts as may be glad to
yeeld the possession of thine owne. And be thou so gracious, as yet to take them vp, though we haue desperately held
thee out of them in times past, and dwell in vs, and raigne in
vs

vs by thy spirit, that we may be sure to raigne with thee in thy glorious kingdome, according to thy promise through him that hath purchased that inheritance for all that trust in him.

And seeing thou doest so promise these graces to vs, as that thou requirest our industrie and diligence in the vse of such meanes as serue thereto (good Lord) let vs not so crosse our praiers for grace, as not to seeke that by diligence, which we make shew to seeke by prayer, least our owne waies condemne vs of hypocrisie. Stirre vs vp therefore (O Lord) to the frequent vse of prayer, to reading, hearing, and meditating of thy holy word, teach vs to profit by the conversation of thy people, and to be profitable in our owne, make vs wise to apprehend all oportunities of doing or receiuing spirituall good, strengthen vs with grace to obserue our hearts and waies, to containe them in good order, or to reduce them quickly, let vs neuer thinke any company so good as thine, nor any time so well spent, as that which is in thy seruice, and beautifying of thine Image in our selues or others.

Particularly we pray thee open our eies to see our naturall infirmities, and to discouer the aduantages which Satan gets thereby. And giue vs care to striue most, where we are most assaulted and endamaged.

And thou O God, that hast promised to blesse thine owne ordinances, blesse all things vnto vs, that we may grow in grace & in knowledge, and so may shine as light in this darke world, giuing good example to all men, and may in our time lie downe in peace of a good conscience, embaulmed with a good report, and may leaue thy blessings entailed vnto ours after vs for an inheritance.

These O Father, are our speciall suits, wherein wee beseech thee to set forth the wonderful riches of thy grace towards vs, as for this life, and the things thereof, we craue them of thee so farre as may be for our good, and thy glory, beseeching thee to prouide for vs as vnto this day in mercy. And when thou wilt humble or exalt vs, gouerne vs so long, and so farre in all conditions and changes, as we may cleaue fast vnto thee our God vnchangeably, esteeming thee our portion & sufficiēt inheritance for euermore. Now what graces we craue for our selues, which are here before thy presence, we humbly begge for all those that belong vnto . vs, and that by dutie or promise wee owe our praiers vnto, beseeching thee to be as gracious vnto them, as vnto our own souls, and specially to such of them, as in respect of any present affliction or temptation may be in speciall neede of some more speedie helpe or comfort from thy mighty hand.

Yea

Yea our Lord God we humbly desire to blesse with our praiers the whole Church more specially our nation, and therein the kings Maiestie our Soueraigne, his Queene and royall seede, with all that be in authoritie vnder him, beseeching thee to follow .him and them with those blessings of thy protectiõ and direction, which may preserue them safe from the malice of the world, and of Satan, and may yeeld them in their great places faithfull to thee for the good of thy people, and their owne eternall happinesse and honour.

We beseech thee to furnish the Churches with faithfull and fruitfull ministers, and to blesse their liues and labours for those mercifull vses, to which thou hast ordained them, sanctifie thy people O God, and let them not deceiue themselues with a formalitie of religion in steed of the power thereof, giue them grace to profit both by those fauours, and by those chastice-ments which thou hast sent successiuely or mixedly amongst them. And Lord represse that rage of sinne, and prophanesse in all Christian states which breeds so much Apostacy and de-fection, threatning the taking away of this light from them: Confound thou O God all the counsel and practises of Satan and his ministers, which are or shall be taken vp against thee, and the kingdome of thy deare sonne. And call in the Jewes together with the fulnesse of the gentiles, that thy name may be glorious in al the world, the dayes of iniquity may come to an end, and we with all thine elect people may come to see thy face in glorie, and be filled with the light thereof for euermore.

And now O Lord of mercie, O Father of the spirits of all flesh, looke in mercie vpon the Gentiles, who yet know thee not, O gracious God be mercifull to vs, and bless vs, and not vs alone, but let thy waies be knowne vpon earth, & thy sauing health amongst all nations : we praise thee, and we blesse thee : But let the people praise thee O God, yea let all the people praise thee, and let these ends of the world remember them-selues and turne to thee the God of their saluation. And see-ing thou hast honoured vs to choose vs out to beare thy name vnto the Gentiles : we therefore beseech thee to bless vs, and this our plantation, which we and our nation haue begun in thy feare, & and for thy glory. We know O Lord, we haue the diuel and all the gates of hel against vs, but if thou O Lord be on our side, we care not who be against vs. O therfore vouch-safe to be our God, & let vs be a part and portion of thy peo-ple, cõfirme thy couenãt of grace & mercy with vs, which thou hast made to thy Church in Christ Jesus. And seeing Lord the highest end of our plantation here, is to set vp the standard,

&

& display the banner of Jesus Christ, euē here where satans throne is Lord, let our labor be blessed in laboring the conversiō of the heathē. And because thou vsest not to work such mighty works by vnholy means, Lord sanctifie our spirits, & giue vs holy harts, that so we may be thy instrumēts in this most glorious work : lord inspire our souls with thy grace, kindle in vs zeale of thy glory : fill our harts with thy feare, & our tongues with thy praise, furnish vs all from the highest to the lowest with all gifts & graces needful not onely for our saluation, but for the discharge of our duties in our seuerall places, adorne vs with the garments of Justice, mercy, loue, pitie, faithfulnesse, humility, & all vertues, & teach vs to abhor al vice, that our lights may so shine before these heathen, that they may see our good works, & so be brought to glorifie thee our heauenly Father. And seeing Lord we professe our selues thy seruants, & are about thy worke, Lord blesse vs, arme vs against difficulties, strength vs against all base thoughts & temptations, that may make vs looke backe againe. And seeing by thy motion & work in our harts, we haue left our warme nests at home, & put our liues into our hands principally to honour thy name, & aduance the kingdome of thy son, Lord giue vs leaue to commit our liues into thy hands : let thy Angels be about vs, & let vs be as Angels of God sent to this people, And so blesse vs Lord, & so prosper all our proceedings, that the heathen may neuer say vnto vs, where is now your God : Their Idols are not so good as siluer & gold, but lead ·& copper, & the works of their own hands. But thou *Iehouah* art our God, & we are yᵉ works of thy hands : O then let *Dagon* fall before thy Arke, let Satan be confounded at thy presence, & let the heathen see it & be ashamed, that they may seeke thy face, for their God is not as our God, thēselues being Judges. Arise therfore O Lord, & let thine enemies be scattered, & let them that hate thee flie before thee : As the smoke vanisheth, so let Satan & his delusions come to nought & as wax melteth before the fire, so let wickednes, superstitiō, ignorance & idolatry perish at yᵉ presēce of thee our God. And wheras we haue by vndertaking this plantatiō vndergone the reproofs of the base world, insomuch as many of our owne brethren laugh vs to scorne, O Lord we pray thee fortifie vs against this temptation : let *Sanballat*; & *Tobias*, Papists & players, & such other *Amonits* & *Horonits* the scum & dregs of the earth, let the mocke such as helpe to build vp the wals of Jerusalem, and they that be filthy, let thē be filthy still, & let such swine still wallow in their mire, but let not yᵉ rod of the wicked fal vpon the lot of the righteous, let not them put forth their hands to

such

such vanity, but let them that feare thee, reioyce & be glad in thee, & let them know, that it is thou O Lord, that raignest in England, & vnto the ends of the world.   And seeing this work must needs expose vs to many miseries, & dangers of soule & bodie, by land & sea, O Lord we earnestly beseech thee to re- ceiue vs into thy fauour & protection, defend vs from the delu- sion of the diuel, the malice of the heathē, the inuasions of our enemies, & mutinies & dissentions of our own people, knit our hearts altogether in faith & feare of thee, & loue one to another, giue vs patience, wisedome & constancy to goe on through all difficulties & temptations, til this blessed work be accomplished, for the honour of thy name, & glory of the Gospel of Jesus Christ: That when the heathē do know thee to be their God, and Jesus Christ to be their saluation, they may say, blessed be the King & Prince of England, & blessed be the English nation, and blessed for euer be the most high God, possessor of heauen & earth, that sent them amongst vs :   And heere O Lord we do vpon the knees of our harts offer thee the sacrifice of praise & thanksgiuing, for that thou hast moued our harts to undertake the performance of this blessed work, with the hazard of our person, and the hearts of so many hundreds of our nation to assist it with meanes & prouision, and with their holy praiers, Lord looke mercifully vpon them all, and for that portion of their substance which they willingly offer for thy honour & seruice in this action, recompence it to them and theirs, and reward it seuen fold into their bosomes with better blessings : Lord blesse England our sweet natiue countrey, saue it from Popery, this land from heathenisme, & both from Atheisme. And Lord heare their praiers for vs, and vs for them, and Christ Jesus our glorious Mediator for vs all.   Amen.

A PLAINE

DESCRIPTION

OF THE BARMVDAS,

NOW CALLED SOMMER

ILANDS.

With the manner of their discouerie
Anno 1609. by the shipwrack and admirable deliuerance
of Sir *Thomas Gates*, and Sir *George Sommers*, wherein
are truly set forth the commodities and profits of
that Rich, Pleasant, and Healthfull

COVNTRIE.

WITH

An Addition, or more ample relation of
diuers other remarkeable matters concerning those
Ilands since then experienced, lately sent
from thence by one of the Colonie now
there resident.

ECCLESIASTES 3: 11.

God hath made euery thing beautifull in his time.

LONDON,
Printed by *W. Stansby*, for *W. Welby.*
1613.

Force's Collection of Historical Tracts.

VOL. III.—No. 3.

TO THE TRVLY HO-
NORABLE AND RIGHT WOR-
THY KNIGHT SIR Thomas Smith,

TREASVRER for the Colonies and Companies of VIRGINIA: *and Gouernour of* Mus-
couia, East-India, North-west Passage,
and SOMMER Ilands
Companies.

HONORABLE SIR, the wisest of Men, or
rather the wisedome of God tells vs, *Eccles.* 3. I.
that *there is a time for all things* :
and that the great God, who at his owne will
beganne Time it selfe, doth at his owne time
beginne all things else : the foolishnesse of
men may aske and muse why was this so soone, and that so
late ? but the wisedome of God knowes what is fit for euery
time : And surely amongst the sensible signes, and euident demonstrations of Gods all-gouerning prouidence, this is not the
least, that he brings not forth his mightie works altogether, but
makes euery thing beautifull in his time.   And as in *Eccl.* 3. 11.
his creation he made not al at once, but produced them
in their seuerall daies : so in his gubernation, he reueileth not the
knowledge of all things in one Age, but discouers them in the
seuerall ages of the World.   And if man aske why God doth thus,
holy *David* giues the answere ; *The Lord hath so done Psal.* 111.4.
his marvailous works, that they should be had in re-
membrance ; for were they all in one age (such is our corruption)
they would bee lesse obserued and sooner forgotten, but being
declared in their seuerall times, euery Age finds matter to mag-
nifie God ; And therefore He *whose glorious name Psal.* 72.19.
is to be praised for euer, reueils some meruailous thing
in euery generation, that so his name may be praised from
Generation to Generation.

Mans works are for the most part (as Christ saith of the
Wine that is serued in at feasts) best at first, and afterwards
worse : but with God it is cōtrarie ; for as in the *Creation*,
though euery daies worke was good, yet each daies was *Gen.* 1.
better then the former, and the last best of all : So in
his dispensation and gouernement of the world, all knowledge
was

was not reueiled, nor all good things made knowne at the first, *Psal.* 19.2. but *day vnto day vttereth, and night to night* (and why not also, age vnto age) *teacheth knowledge.* And hence is it that as great secrets in nature, and as admirable perfections in art, and as rare inuentions, and profitable experiments (euery way) are daily discouered in these latter ages, as were in the former. There be not yet two hundred yeares It began past since the admirable art of Printing was found out, about the an inuention so excellent and so vsefull, so much tend- yeare 1450. ing to the honour of God, the manifestation of the truth, propagation of the Gospell, restoration of learning, diffusion of knowledge, and consequently the discouerie and destruction of Poperie, that the Pope and Popish Politicians wish it had neuer beene, and haue bestowed many a secret curse vpon him that first reueiled it ; and no meruaile, for it hastens and helps forward his confusion more then all the Mechanicke mysteries in the World. Nor is yet foure hundred yeares agoe, since the superadmirable vse of the Loadstone was found out. The attraction of yron vnto it was seene by *Aristotle*, and the Ancients, and it amazed them : But the correspondencie it hath with the Pole-starre, and consequently the excellent vse of it for Nauigation (being one of the greatest wonders of the world) was not knowne to them : nay (which is more strange) not the Apostles themselues ; for had it beene, *Acts* 27. surely Saint *Paul* and his companie had not beene almost halfe a yeare in his voyage betwixt Iudæa and Italie, and that through so many difficulties, and at last shipwrack ; *Vers.* 20. Nor would it haue beene said, that *when neither Sunne nor Starre appeared for many dayes, all hope of being saued was taken away.* For when neither Sunne nor Starre appeares ; yet by the helpe of this poore dead Creature, the Pilot can tell where he is, and knowes his course, more certainely now in the wide and vnmeasurable Ocean, then they could in the narrow Mediterran Sea ; and more easily now will an ordinarie Sea-man goe to the West Indies, then S. *Paul* with all the knowledge God had then reueiled, from Ierusalem to Rome : for howsoeuer the Lord was miraculously powerfull in the Apostles, and glorious and wonderfull in the Primitiue Church, in giuing knowledge of tongues, and other learning, and power of miracles, yet he did bound and limit it at his owne pleasure, and reserued this and other of his wonderfull works to be made knowne in the later times, that so all men in all ages *Psa.*102.26. may know, that *though all things perish, yet God endures ;* and though all creatures *waxe old as a garment, yet He is the same* still and for euer.

It

It is yet but a hundreth yeares agoe, that (after the world had scarce dreamed of any other habitable place of the earth, more then Asia, Africke, and Europe) God discouered to vulgar knowledge another, and as it were the new world of America, which if it had beene foretold in the elder ages, millions of men would neuer haue beleeued it. And that we in this present and peruerse age may also knowe, that *Times and Sea-* *sons are in Gods hand*, He hath vouchsafed amongst   *Acts.* 1. the many excellent inuentions and wonderfull discoueries of these times, to make knowne to vs of the poore *Virginian* plantation, and by vs to the world, the hidden and long concealed truth, touching the state of the *Barmuda* Ilands. Who did not thinke till within these foure yeares, but that those Ilands had beene rather a habitation of Diuells, then fit for men to dwell in? who did not hate the name when hee was on Land, and shunne the place when he was on the Seas? But behold the misprision and misconceits of the world! For true and large experience hath now told vs, it is one of the sweetest Paradises that be vpon the earth. Let them hearken to this and make vse of it, that mislike all new inuentions, and suspect all new discoueries, and hold it for a rule, That whatsoeuer is new is nought. If any had said seuen yeares agoe, the *Barmuda* Ilands are not only accessible and habitable, but also fertile, fruitfull, plentifull, and a safe, secure, temperate, rich, sweet, and healthfull habitation for Man, and especially for English bodies; oh how loudly would he haue beene laught at, and hist out of most mens companies! And yet no more then He would haue beene, who foure hundred yeares agoe should haue told the world, that by the vse and helpe of a stone a man should more safely saile vpon the Ocean, round about the earth, then formerly in the narrow Seas: Or then He who two hundred yeares agoe should haue said, there was an Art by which all writing of bookes should be saued, and that two men should Print more in a day, then two hundred can write: Or then He who 100. yeares agoe did tell vs, there was another world. as it were vnder our feete, wherein men liued like vs, and a richer part of the world then ours. And yet all these are now proued true before our eyes, and all the world can witnesse it: and who is he that feeles not the benefit of these three blessings? Now therefore let the iealous and suspitious world ceare his due reproofe, and let God haue his due glorie and praise who brings to light things that lie hidde in darkenesse. and reuecles his meruailous works in his due time. And let the Planters and Patrons of the *Virginia* Colonies take heart and comfort themselues;

themselues ; for that God, who by discouering these Ilands to
them hath deliuered the world from that old inueterate errour,
and giuen them the rightfull possession (vnder God and his
Maiestie) of so rich so wholesome, and healthfull Ilands, which
may be as nurseries to *Virginia*, hath hereby let the world see
that he will vphold that Christian plantation, if men should be so
base and beastly to forsake it. But (worthy Sir) if other men
were like you, I needed not to make that (If) if all as able as
you were as willing, and forward as you, wee should soone see
a flourishing Christian Church, and Common-wealth in *Virginia* ; But let this be your comfort, there is one that is more
able, is also more willing then you, euen the God of heauen and
earth : it is his worke you manage, and his cause you haue in hand ;
he may worke with comfort that works with God and for God ;
he that works with God is sure to preuaile ; he that works for
God is sure to be rewarded. You know good Sir (and you better
then many) that *He is well kept whom God keepes*, and know
also that hee shall bee roially rewarded whom God rewards.
And know further for your comfort, that though the burden lye
vpon you and a few more, yet are there many honorable &
worthy men of all sorts, who will neuer shrinke from you : Goe
on therefore with courage and constancie, and be assured that
though by your Honorable Embassages, and imploiments, and
by your charitable & vertuous courses, you haue gained a worthy reputation in the world, yet nothing that you euer did or
suffred more honours you in the eyes of all that are godly-
wise, then your faithfull and vnwearied prosecution, your continuall and comfortable assistance of these foraine Plantations.
A worke so honorable to God, our Religion, our King, and our
Countrie ; so comfortable to the Soules of the poore Saluages,
and so profitable to the Aduenturers (that of *Virginia* for our
Posterities, but this of the *Barmudas* for the present) as the
like (for all these put together) hath not been attempted in the
Christian world these many Ages. And because it is the glorie
of God to declare his works : I cannot but commend your wisdomes in publishing those strange and welcome newes from the
Barmudas : the stile is base and broken, I confesse, but it better beseemes the bare and naked truth. Now then let the
Christian world reioyce to see, that God is worshipped in the
Deuills Ilands, and that English men liue safelie and sweetly
there where neuer any liued before them. It is almost foure
yeares agoe since our valorous Commanders Sir *Thomas Gates*,
and Sir *George Sommers*, with a hundred and fiftie Persons
more, were in a terrible tempest cast away vpon these Ilands,

and

and so found it, when they sought it not: and though they suffered shipwrack vpon the Rocks that compasse these Ilands (as all other did that euer pitcht vpon them) yet were they preserued euery man; which neuer befell any but themselues, such was the fauour of God vnto them; And there they liued in health and safetie almost a yeare, when all the world held them dead, and had liued there till this day, and for ought we know, for euer, had they not made themselues two little ships of Cedar, in which they went to *Virginia*, yet leauing two men in the Ilands, whom Sir *George Sommers* comming back againe from *Virginia* the same yeare, and our Colonie sent thither the last yeare, found in health and good liking: Our Colonie, consisting of some threescore men, hath now beene there almost a yeare, from whom we receiue this plaine and simple, but comfortable Narration, and to whom we now send a supply, not of victualls, or such prouisions, for they neede none such, but of men and vvomen, for habitation and plantation, which by the blessing of God now goes away this present moneth, there to plant a Christian Church, to endure to the worlds end, where neuer man dwelt before, since the worlds beginning: Oh happie men who there find God & his Angels, where the world thought had beene nothing, but the Deuill and *his Swine into which he enter-ed.* The God that led them to it, saued them vpon it, fed ^Math. 8. them in it and sends vs so comfortable newes from it, still ^31. 32. blesse it and defend it, and all his children in it, and all that now or hereafter goe to it, and all that loue it, and assist the plantation of Gods Church in it: Peace bee vpon them and Mercie, and vpon the Israel of God, *Amen.* And to you my Bretheren that be there and haue the honour to lay the first foundation of Gods Church there, and to you much honored Knight, and the rest, who by your care and charge doe beare the burthen, and maintaine the life of such glorious actions which lie neglected in this base and vnworthy world; for this your holy and heroicall resolutions, and your loue therein appearing to the *Lord Iesus Christ* and his holy Gospell, to our King and Countrie, I professe and denote my selfe in all offices and duties of a Christian

Your Seruant in Christ Iesus.

W. C.

To the Reader.

GOod Reader, this is the first Booke published to the world touching Sommer Ilands : but who shall liue to see the last? A more full and exact description of the Countrie, and Narration of the nature, site, and commodities, together with a true Historie of the great deliuerance of Sir Thomas Gates and his Companie vpon them, which was the first discouerie of them ; thou maiest surely expect, if God will, to come into thy hands. This short Narration, in the meane time, shall rather prepare thee for it, then preuent thee of it.

A DISCOVERY

OF THE BARMV_
DAS, NOW CALLED
THE SOMMER
Ilands.

Being in ship called the sea-venture, with *Sir Thomas Gates* our Gouernour, *Sir George Sommers*, & Captain *Newport*, three most worthy honoured Gentlemen, (whose valour and fortitude the world must needes take notice of, and that in most Honourable designes) bound for Virginia, in the height of thirty degrees of northerly Latitude, or thereabouts : we were taken with a most sharpe and cruell storme vpon the fiue and twentieth day of July, *Anno* 1609. which did not onely separate vs from the residue of our fleet, (which were eight in number) but with the violent working of the Seas our ship became so shaken, torne, and leaked, that shee receiued so much water as couered two tire of hogsheads aboue the ballast ; that our men stood vp to the middles, with buckets, baricos, and kettles, to baile out the water, and continually pumped for three dayes and three nights together, without any intermission ; and yet the water seemed rather to encrease, then to diminish : in so much that all our men, being vtterly spent, tyred, and disabled for longer labour, were euen resolued, without any hope of their liues, to shut vp the hatches, and to haue committed themselues to the mercie of the sea, (which is said to be mercilesse) or rather to the mercie of their mightie God and Redeemer, (whose mercies exceed al his works) seeing no helpe, nor hope, in the apprehension of mans reason, that any mothers childe could escape that ineuitable dãger, which euery man had proposed and digested to himselfe of

of present sinking. So that some of thē hauing some good and
comfortable waters in the ship, fetcht them, and drunke one to
the other, taking their last leaue one of the other, vntill their
more ioyfull and happy meeting in a more blessed world ; when
it pleased God out of his most gracious and mercifull prouidence
so to direct and guide our ship, (being left to the mercy of the
sea) for her most aduantage ; that *Sir George Sommers* sitting
vpon the poope of the ship, (where he sate three dayes and
three nights together, without meales meat, and little or no
sleepe) couning the ship to keep her as vpright as he could (for
otherwise shee must needes instantly haue foundred) most wish-
edly and happily descried land ; wherevpon he most comforta-
bly encouraged the company to follow their pumping, and by
no meanes to cease bayling out of the water, with their buckets,
baricos, and kettles ; whereby they were so ouer-wearied, and
their spirits so spent with long fasting, and continuance of their
labour, that for the most part they were fallen asleepe in corners, and wheresoeuer they chanced first to sit or lie : but hearing
newes of land, wherewith they grew to be somewhat reuiued,
being caried with will and desire beyond their strength, euery
man busled vp, and gathered his strength and feeble spirits
together, to performe as much as their weake force would per-
mitte them : through which weake meanes, it pleased God to
worke so strongely as the water was staid for that little time,
(which as wee all much feared, was the last period of our
breathing) and the ship kept from present sinking, when it
pleased God to send her within halfe an English mile of that
land that *Sir George Sommers* had not long before descried :
Which were the Ilands of the Barmudas. And there neither
did our shippe sincke, but more fortunately in so great a misfortune fell in betweene two rockes, where shee was fast lodged
and locked, for further budging : whereby wee gained not only
sufficient time, with the present help of our Boate, and Skiffe,
safelye to set and conuey our men ashore, (which were one
hundred and fifty in number) but afterwards had time and leasure
to saue some good part of our goods and prouision, which the
water had not spoyled, with all the tackling of the ship, and
much of the yron about her, which were necessaries not a little
auaileable for the building and furnishing of a new shippe and
pinnace, which we made there, for the transporting and carrying
of vs to Virginia. But our deliuery was not more strange in
falling so opportunely and happily vpon the land, as our feeding & preseruation was beyond our hopes, & all mens expectations, most admirable. For the Ilands of the Barmudas, as
euery

euery man knoweth that hath heard or read of them, were
neuer inhabited by any Christian or Heathen people, but euer
esteemed, and reputed, a most prodigious and inchanted place,
affoording nothing but gusts, stormes, and foule weather ; which
made euery Nauigator and Mariner to auoide them, as Scylla
and Charibdis ; or as they would shun the Diuell himselfe ;
and no man was euer heard to make for the place, but as
against their willes, they have by stormes and dangerousnesse of
the rockes, lying seuen leagues into the Sea, suffered shipwracke ; yet did we finde there the ayre so temperat, and the
Country so abundantly fruitfull of all fit necessaries for the
sustentation and preseruation of mans life, that most in a manner of all our prouisions of bread, beere, and victuall, being
quite spoyled, in lying long drowned in salt water ; notwithstanding, wee were there for the space of nine moneths (few
dayes ouer) not onely well refreshed, comforted, and with good
satietie contented, but out of the abundance thereof, prouided vs
some reasonable quantitie and proportion of prouision, to carry
vs for Virginia, and to maintaine our selues, and that companie
wee found there, to the great releefe of them, as it fell out in
their so great extremities, and in respect of the shortnes of
time, vntill it pleased God, that by my Lord *de la Wars* comming thither, their store was better supplied. And greater ; &
better prouision wee might haue made, if we had had better meanes
for the storing and transportation thereof. Wherefore my opinion sincerely of this Iland is, that whereas it hath beene, and is
still accounted, the most dangerous, infortunate, and most forlorne place of the world, it is in truth the richest, healthfullest,
and pleasing land, (the quantitie and bignesse thereof considered) and meerely naturall, as euer man set foote vpon : the
particular profits and benefits whereof, shall be more especially
inserted, and hereunto annexed, which euerie man to his owne
priuate knowledge, that was there, can auouch and iustifie for a
truth. Vpon the eight and twentieth day of July 1609. (after
the extremity of the storme was something qualified) we fell
vpon the shore at the Barmudas ; where after our Generall
Sir Thomas Gates, Sir George Sommers, and Captaine *Newport,* had by their prouident carefulnesse Landed all their men,
and so much of the goods and prouisions out of the ship, as was
not vtterly spoyled, euerie man disposed and applyed himselfe
to search for, and to seeke out such releefe and sustentation, as
the Countrie afforded : and *Sir George Sommers,* a man inured
to extremities, (and knowing what thereunto belonged) was in
this seruice neither idle nor backward, but presently by his
carefull

carefull industry went, and found out sufficient of many kind of fishes, and so plentifull thereof, that in half an houre he tooke so many fishes with hookes, as did suffice the whole company one day. And fish is there so abundant, that if a man steppe into the water, they will come round about him; so that men were faine to get out for feare of byting. These fishes are very fat and sweete, and of that proportion and bignesse, that three of them will conueniently lade two men: those we called rock-fish. Besides there are such abundance of Mullets, that with a seane might be taken at one draught one thousand at the least, and infinite store of pilchards, with diuers kinds of great fishes, the names of them vnknowne to me: of tray fishes very great ones, and so great store, as that there hath beene taken in one night with making lights, euen sufficient to feed the whole company a day. The Countrie affordeth great abundance of Hogges, as that there hath beene taken by *Sir George Sommers,* who was the first that hunted for them, to the number of two and thirtie at one time, which he brought to the company in a boate, built by his owne hāds. There is Fowle in great number vpon the Ilands, where they breed, that there hath beene taken in two or three houres, a thousand at the least; the bird being of the bignes of a good Pidgeon, and layeth egges as big as Hen egges vpon the sand, where they come and lay them dayly, although men sit downe amongst them; that there hath beene taken vp in one morning by *Sir Thomas Gates* men, one thousand of egges: and *Sir George Sommers* men, comming a little distance of time after them, haue stayed there whilst they came and layed their eggs amongst them, that they brought away as many more with them; with many young birds very fat and sweet. Another Sea fowle there is that lyeth in little holes in the ground, like vnto a cony-hole, and are in great numbers, exceeding good meate, very fat and sweet (those we had in the winter) and their eggs are white, and of that bignesse, that they are not to be knowne from Hen egges. The other birds egges are speckled, and of a different colour: there are also great store and plenty of Herons, and those so familiar and tame, that wee beate them downe from the trees with stones and staues; but such were young Herons: besides many white Herons, without so much as a blacke or gray feather on them; with other small birds so tame and gentle, that a man walking in the woods with a sticke, and whistling to them, they wil come and gaze on you, so neare that you may strike and kill many of them with your sticke; and with singing and hollowing you may doe the like. There are also great store of
Tortoses,

Tortoses, (which some call Turtles) and those so great, that I haue seene a bushell of egges in one of their bellies, which are sweeter then any Henne egge : and the Tortose it selfe is all very good meate, and yeeldeth great store of oyle, which is as sweete as any butter ; and one of them will suffice fifty men a meale, at the least : and of these hath beene taken great store, with two boates, at the least forty in one day. The Country yeeldeth diuers fruits, as prickled peares, great aboundance, which continue greene vpon the trees all the yeare ; also great plenty of Mulberries, white and red : and on the same are great store of Silke-wormes, which yeeld cods of silke, both white and yellow, being some course, and some fine. And there is a tree called a Palmito tree, which hath a very sweet berry, vpon which the hogs doe most feede ; but our men finding the sweetnesse of them, did willingly share with the hogs for them, they being very pleasant and wholesome, which made them carelesse almost of any bread with their meate ; which occasioned vs to carry in a manner all that store of flower and meale wee did or could saue, for Virginia. The head of the Palmito tree is verie good meate, either raw or sodden, it yeeldeth a head which weigheth about twentie pound, and is farre better meate, then any cabbidge. There are an infite number of Cedar trees, (the fairest I thinke in the world) and those bring forth a verie sweete berrie, and wholesome to eate. The Countrey (for as much as I could finde my self, or heare by others) affords no venimous creature, or so much as a Rat or Mouse, or any other thing vnwholesome. There is greate store of Pearle, and some of them very faire, round, and Orientall ; and you shall finde at least one hundred seede of Pearle in one Oyster ; there hath beene likewise found some good quantitie of Amber Greece, and that of the best sort. There are also great plentie of Whales, which I conceaue are very easie to bee killed, for they come so vsually, and ordinarilie to the shore, that wee heard them oftentimes in the night a bed ; and haue seene many of them neare the shoare, in the day time. There was borne vpon the Barmudas, at the time of our being there, two children, the one a man child, there baptised by the name of Barmudas : and a woman childe, baptised by the name of Barmuda : as also there was a marriage between two Englsh people vpon that Iland. This Iland, I meane the maine Iland, with all the broken Ilands adiacent, are made in the forme of a halfe Moone, but a little more rounder, and diuided into many broken Ilands, and there are many good harbours in it, but we could find but one especiall place to goe in, or rather

to

to goe out from it, which was not altogether free from some Danger, where there is three Fathoms water at the entrance thereof, but within, sixe, seauen, or eight Fathoms at the least, where you may safely lie Land-locked, from the daunger of all Winds and Weathers, and moore to the Trees. The comming into it is so narrow & straight betweene the Rockes, as that it will with small store of Munition bee fortified, and easily defended, against the forces of the Potentest King of Europe, such aduantage the place affoords. There are also plentie of Hawkes, and verie good Tobacco, as I thinke, which through forgetfulnesse, I had almost omitted. Now hauing finished and rigged our ship, and Pinnesse, the one called the Deliuerance, the Pinnace which wee built there, the Patience, wee prepared and made our selues readie, to ship for Virginia, hauing powdred some store of Hogges flesh for prouision thither, and the company thereof, for some reasonable time : but were compelled to make salt for the same purpose, for all our salt was spent and spoiled, before wee recouered the shore. We carried with vs also a good portion of Tortoise-oyle, which either for frying or baking did vs very great pleasure, it being very sweete, nourishing, and wholesome : the greatest defects we found there, was tarre and pitch for our ship and pinnace, in stead whereof wee were forced to make lime there of a hard kinde of stone, and vse it : which for the present occasion and necessitie, with some wax wee found cast vp by the Sea, from some shipwracke, serued the turne to pay the seames of the pinnace *Sir George Sommers* built, for which hee had neither pitch nor tarre : so that God in the supplying of all our wants, beyond all measure, shewed himselfe still mercifull vnto vs, that we might accomplish our intended voyage to Virginia, for which I confidently hope, hee doth yet reserue a blessing in store, and to the which I presume every honest and religious hart will readily giue their Amen. When all thinges were made ready, and commodiously fitted, the winde comming faire, wee set saile and put off from the Barmudas, the tenth day of May, in the yeare 1 6 1 0. and arriued at *Iames* towne in Virginia, the foure and twentieth day of the same Moneth : where we found some threescore persons liuing. And being then some three weeks or there abouts passed, and not hearing of any supply, it was thought fitting by a generall cōsent, to vse the best means for the preseruation of all those people that were liuing, being al in number two hundred persons. And so vpon the eight of June one thousand six hundred and ten, wee imbarked at James Towne, not hauing aboue fourteene dayes victuall, and so were determined to direct our course for

New-found-land,

New-found-land, there to refresh vs, and supply our selves with victuall, to bring vs home; but it pleased God to dispose otherwise of vs, and to giue vs better meanes. For being all of vs shipped in foure pinnaces, and departed from the towne, almost downe halfe the Riuer, we met my Lord *de la Warre* comming vp with three ships, wel furnished with victuall, which reuiued all the company, and gaue them great content. And after some few dayes, my Lord vnderstanding of the great plentie of Hogges and Fish was at the Barmudas, and the necessitie of them in Virginia, was desirous to send thither, to supply himselfe with those things, for the better comforting of his men, and the plantation of the Countrey. Whereupon *Sir George Sommers* being a man best acquainted with the place, and being willing to do seruice vnto his Prince and Countrey, without any respect of his own priuate gaine, and being of threescore yeares of age at the least, out of his worthy and valiant minde, offered himselfe to vndertake to performe with Gods helpe that dangerous voyage for the Barmudas, for the better releefe and comfort of the people in Virginia, and for the better plantation of it, which offer my Lord *de la Warre* very willingly and thankfully accepted: and so vpon the nineteenth of June, *Sir George Sommers* imbarked himselfe at James towne in a small Barge of thirtie tonne, or thereabout, that he built at the Barmudas: wherein hee laboured from morning vntill night, as duelie as any workeman doth labour for wages, and built her all with Cedar, with little or no yron worke at all: hauing in her but one boult, which was in the kilson:

notwithstanding thankes be to God, shee brought vs
in safety to Virginia, and so I trust he will
protect him, and send him wel back
againe, to his harts desire, and
the great comfort of all
the company there.

AN ADDITION
SENT HOME BY
THE LAST SHIPS
from our Colonie in the
Barmudas

Eing bound for the Sommer Ilands, in the shippe called the Plough, wee imbarked the 28. of Aprill 1612. So passing downe to Grauesend, wee anchored at Tilbery-hope vntill the fifth of May. The winde comming faire, wee put foorth and came to the Downes the sixth of May, where we stayed till the ninth. And then setting forward, wee had a faire and comfortable passage, and by Gods blessing found so direct a course, that on the eleuenth of July in the morning betwixt nine and ten of the clocke wee discried our hoped and desired Ilands, and in the afternoone of the same day about three a clocke we arriued in a very safe harbour neare S. *Georges* Iland, there we landed all our men and women, and had beene at an anchor aboue an houre before wee could heare of our three men which had been left there. As soone as wee had landed all our company, we went all to prayer, and gaue thankes vnto the Lord for our safe arriuall ; and whilest we were at prayer, wee saw our three men come rowing downe to vs, the sight of whom did much reioyce vs : so they welcomming vs, and we the like to them againe, we sung a Psalme and praised the Lord for our safe meeting, and went to supper.

The next day being the Sabbath day, which wee dedicated to God in the best manner we could, wee abode still in the foresaid Iland with all the rest of our company till munday morning, being the thirteenth of July : then we went vp with our ship and company higher into the harbour, to the place where these three men had planted themselues. And wheras many English men would haue thought that wee should haue found these three men either dead, or more like sauage then ciuill, I assure you al my friends and acquaintance (and so

generally

generally to all my country men in England) we found them
ciuill, honest and religious, and making conscience of their
waies: you shall not heare an oath proceed out of their mouths;
vaine and idle talke they vsed not: and it seemed apparantly
vnto our eyes that they haue not beene idly giuen. For howsoeuer to be but three of them left in such a desolate place not
inhabited, nor assured of any to come to them: would haue
made most men fainted in any thing they should haue took in
hād: yet was it not so with these mē: nay they shewed vnto
vs a good example, who are now come to them. For they
haue planted corne, great store of Wheate, Beanes Tobacco and
Mellons, with many other good things for the vse of man: besides they haue wrought vpon timber, in squaring and sawing of Cedar trees, for they intended to build a small Pinnace
to carry them into Virginia, being almost out of hope and comfort of our comming; because Captaine *Dauies* his time was to
haue beene with them long before we came. And thus they
spent their time in labor, imploying themselues in one good
action or other.

Now to certifie you the truth of the state of the Country, I
am loath to write that which I haue seene, by reason you would
condemne my writing (as I feare) and thinke it to be but false
reports come from vs to draw more company hither, for I per-
ceiue the world is giuē too much to such surmises. But why
should I feare to write that which I know to be true, when as
all the shippes company will or may approue it, but cannot re-
proue it: As first the Captaine, the Master and his Mate, and
all the rest of the Saylers: first I will begin with the Fish
and Fowle which the Countrey doth yeeld.

We were no sooner come within a league of the land, but a
company of Fish, as it were, met vs, and neuer left vs til we
were come to an ankor within the harbour; and as soone as
we had passed ouer our busines, and all things safe and in order,
with a hooke and line wee tooke more then all our whole company was able to eate, so that there was enough to feed many
more. The next day after the Sabbath wee went with our net
and boat, and if we would have loaded two boats we might; and
so may you doe day by day, Fishes doe so abound, and they
be of these sorts, Mullets, Breames, Hogge-fish, Rock-fish and
Lobstars, with more sorts of other Fish which I cannot name.

Turkles there bee of a mightie bignesse; one Turkle will serue
or suffice three or foure score at a meale, especially if it be a
shee Turkle, for she will have as many egges as will suffice fiftie or threescore at a meale; this I can assure you, they are very
good

good and wholesome meate, none of it bad, no not so much as the very guts and maw of it, for they are exceeding fat, and make as good tripes as your beastes bellies in England. And for Fowle wee went the third day of our arriuall vnto the Bird-Ilands (as we call them) and vsing neither sticke nor stone-bow, nor gunne, wee tooke them up with our hands so many as we would that euery one of the company were to haue some three, some foure a peece; three for a childe, boy or girle, for a man foure; then reckon what those that serued some fourescore people did amount vnto. But this is for certaine, if we would haue brought away twice so many more wee might, but our order is not to take Fish or Fowle but for one or two meales, because that by reason of the flies, and heate of the countrey, they will not keepe, especially these two monthes, June and July, and some part of August.

Some sixe dayes after our comming, we sent out for Hogges, so the company which went out brought home some : for the meate of them, I hould your mutton of England not of so sweet and pleasant a taste.

Fowles there are of diuers sorts, but amongst all there is a bird like vnto yours, which you call in England a Crow, which though they talke in the Barmuda language, yet their tongues shall walke as fast as any English womans : wee cannot goe vp into the woods, but they will follow after vs with such an out-cry, that it would fret a man to heare them ; they are very good meate, fat, and as white flesh as a Chicken, we many times make some of them leaue their talking with stones or cudgels, for they will sit and face you hard at your hand.

And whereas it is reported that this Land of the Barmudas, with the Ilands about it (which are many, at the least an hundred) are inchanted and kept with euill and wicked spirits ; it is a most idle and false report. God grant that we haue brought no wicked spirits with vs, or that there comes none after vs, for we found none there so ill as our selues, nor the three men neuer saw any euill or hurtfull thing in the Land all the time since their comming, and wee haue found the like since our landing : no nor any noysome thing or hurtfull, more then a poore flie which tarries not aboue two or three moneths.

For the inclination of the weather, considering in what cli-mate it lies, wee haue had for the space of some fortie dayes no raine, but very coole and fresh gales of winde, yet in the day-time very hotte ; but wee agree with it very wel, and not a man that hath lien sicke or diseased, but all likes well, and followes & imployes themselues to one businesse or other.

For

For the fruits which the Land yeelds, they bee the Mulberie, great store, and Peares which haue in them a red liquor, as the Pomgranat hath, or somewhat redder, but very wholesome : if you eat an hundred at one time, you shall neuer surfet of them ; if you eat som proportion of them they will bind, but if you exceed in eating of them, then are they of the contrary operation : yet neuer any that hurt themselues by them, eat they neuer so many.   It is certaine that one man eat aboue a peck of them in some ten houres and was neuer the worse.   We haue a kinde of Berrie vpon the Cedar tree, verie pleasant to eat ; and for the Palmito tree, the top of it is a great deale sweeter and wholesomer then any Cabedge.

In some of our Ilands there growes Pepper, but not so good as our Indian Pepper : diuers sorts of other good things there is, which the seuerall times of the yeare bring forth one after another; but the top of the Palmito tree is in season and good all the yeare.

For the ground; I hold it the richest ground to beare forth fruit, (whatsoeuer one shall lay into it) that is in the world, and very easie and light for digging; so that if a man wil labour, he may turne vp a great quantitie in a day, for it is a fat sandy ground, & of colour a browne red.

After the time of our landing many of the company digged certaine plats of ground, and sowed diuers sortes of seedes to make triall of the ground, and for certaine they were seen aboue the ground sprung vp the fourth day after their sowing : and amongst all the rest of the seeds, the Cowcumber and the Mellon were forward : we haue set and sowed fourescore and one sorts of seeds, it was ten'dayes before the shippes comming away, and for the most part they are all come vp.

Of necessitie I must needs mention the Palme-tree once againe, I haue found it so good; take a hatchet and cut him, or an augar and bore him, and it yeelds a very pleasant liquour, much like vnto your sweete wines ; it beares likewise a berry in bignes of a prune, and in taste much like.

Also we haue Oliues grow with vs, but no great store: many other good excellent things we haue grow with vs, which this short time will not permit me to write of so largely as I might ; but this is of truth, that Hogges, Turkles, Fish and Fowle doe abound as dust of the earth: for Amber-greece and Pearle wee haue not had leasure in so few dayes since our arriuall to goe looke out for the one, or to fish for the other, but the three men which were left there, haue found of them both.   Also they haue made a great deale of Tobacco, and if some would come that

haue

haue skill in making it, it would bee very commodious both to the Merchant, and to the maker of it. And for the Silke-worme, if any were brought ouer, and some of skill to vse them, there would be very much good done with them, for the verie Spider in these our Ilands doth weaue perfect fine Silke, both yellow and white.

The Timber of the Countrey consisteth of three sorts, the one is the Cedar, verie fine Timber to worke vpon, of colour redde, and verie sweete : the other sorts wee haue no name for, for there is none in the company hath seene the like in other Countries, before we came, some did thinke it to be *Lignum vitæ*, but it is not so, it is verie fine wood, of colour yellow, and it beares a leafe like vnto a Walnut, and the rine or barke is much like a Walnut tree, and the barke, if one taste of it, will bite ones tongue, as if it were Ginney Pepper, that wood also is very sweet; the other is much like vnto the second, but onely it is white ; the Palme-tree is no timber, but it growes vp of a great height, and no tree growes like vnto it ; for other trees as they grow vp in length, so they grow in bignesse, but the Palme-tree the higher it growes, so the smaller it growes : there is another kinde of wood, which some also thinke is *Lignum vitæ*, and some of it is come ouer for example.

Other kinde of trees there be, but no timber trees they are ; but amongst all the rest there growes a kinde of tree called Mangrowes, they grow very strangely, & would make a man wonder to see the manner of their growing, whereof you shall heare at more leasure.

Also amongst al the sorts of Fish, there is one very strange Fish, and bewtifull to behold, wee call it an Angell-fish (as well it may be) for as you see the picture of an Angell made, so is this, and it shewes of many colours both in the water swimming, and out of the water, and as a daintie a fish of meat as a Salmon, or rather better.

The plentifull time of our fruits is in your Winter, from October till it be May, or about the latter end of May is the plentifullest time of our fruits, but some we haue al the yeare of one fruit or other.

The Climate I hold to be verie good, and agreeable with our constitutions of England, and for the victuall very wholesome and good : for the three men which were left there are very fat and faire, not tanned or burned in the Sun so much as we which came last, & they say theselues they neuer were sicke all the time of their being there, and one of them hath beene there three yeares and vpwards, (one *Christopher Carter* by
name,

name, a Buckingham-shire man, borne in Wickham or there-abouts.)

And for such extraordinarie weather, for thunder and lightning, as it is reported of these Ilands, I can see no such matter, but more temperate and better weather then you haue in England : we haue gone a hunting, and lien out night by night for Hogges : and if wee had beene wette by weather or by wading, wee may lay vs downe so wette to sleepe with a Palme-tree leafe or two vnder vs, and one aboue vs, and we sleepe soundly without any taking cold or being disturbed with any thing else : your aires in England are far more subiect to diseases then these Ilands are.

Whales there are great store at that time of the yeare, when they come in, which time of their comming is in Februarie, and tarrie till June. Likewise there commeth in two other Fishes with them, but such, as the Whale had rather bee without their company ; one is called a Sword-fish, the other a Threasher : the Sword-fish swimmes vnder the Whale, and pricketh him vpward ; the Threasher keepeth aboue him, and with a mightie great thing like vnto a flaile, hee so bangeth the Whale, that hee will roare as though it thundered, and doth giue him such blowes, with his weapon, that you would thinke it to be a cracke of great shot.

Hastie occasion of businesse doth make mee write somewhat hastilie, and leaue out many things which were fitte to bee spoken of, wherefore against my will I am forced to leaue my worke, which I haue begunne, before I come into the middest of it, but I hope it will suffice you that are my friends to passe it ouer in the best manner you can, for there is much broken English of it, & badly penned : regard I pray you the matter, not the manner, the truth of the storie, and not the stile.

But this I say to them that haue aduentured in Virginia, especially to such as thinke they shall lose by that worthy action : let them do the like to vs, and I make no doubt but wee shall in short time giue them satisfaction.

For our Inchanted Ilands which is kept, as some say, with spirits, will wrong no friend nor foe, but yeeld all men their expectations :

If we can praise God for so great a blessing and labour to make benefit of it to his glory, the honour of our Religion, the strength of our Country, and good of our selues. And if you in England will do what is fit for you, as we will, by Gods helpe, what is fit for vs, we hope shortly to see the day that men shal say, Blessed bee God that suffered Sir Thomas Gates, and Sir George Sommers to be cast away vpon these Ilands.

A

A Copie of the Articles which Master

R. MORE, *Gouernour Deputie of the* Sommer Ilands, *pro-pounded to the Companie that were there with him to bee subscribed vnto, which both hee and they subscribed the second of August, in his house,* Anno 1612. *which about the same time he sent into England to the worshipfull Companie of the Adventurers.*

WE who haue here vnder subscribed our names, being by the great goodnesse of God safely arriued at the *Sommer Ilands,* with purpose here to inhabit, doe hereby promise and binde our selues to the performance of the seuerall Articles hereafter following, and that in the presence of the most glorious God, who hath in mercie brought vs hither.

First, We doe faithfully promise, and by these presents solemnely binde our selues euer-more to worship that aforesaid only true and euer-liuing God, who hath made the Heauens, and the Earth, the Sea, and all that therein is, and that accord-ing to those rules that are prescribed in his most holy Word, and euer to continue in that faith into the which we were bap-tised in the Church of England, and to stand in defence of the same against all Atheists, Papists, Anabaptists, Brownists, and all other Heretiques and Sectaries whatsoeuer, dissenting from the said Word and Faith.

Secondly, because the keeping of the Sabboth-day holy is that wherein a principall of Gods worship doth consist, and is as it were the Key of all the other parts thereof, wee doe there-fore in the presence aforesaid promise, That we will set a-part all our owne labours and imploiments on that day, vnlesse it be those that be of meere necessitie, much more vaine and vnfruit-full practises, and apply our selues to the hearing of Gods word, Prayer, and all other exercises of Religion in his word required, to the vttermost of our power.

Thirdly, Seeing the true worship of God and a holy Life cannot bee seuered, wee doe therefore promise in the presence aforesaid, That to the vttermost of our power we will liue to-gether in doing that which is iust, both towards God and Man, and in particular we will forbeare to take the most holy name of God in vaine, in ordinarie swearing by it, or any other thing, or by scoffing, or vaine abusing of his most holy Word, or to vse cursing or filthy speeches, or any other thing forbidden in

Gods

Gods most holy Word, as also to liue together without stealing one from another, or quarrelling one with another, or slandering one of another : And to auoide all things that stand not with the good estate of a Christian Church and well gouerned Com- monwealth, as also to embrace the contrarie, as Iustice, and Peace, Loue, and all other things that stand with the good and comfort of Societie.

Fourthly, Whereas we are here together farre remote from our natiue soile of England, and yet are indeed the naturall Subiects of our most royall and gratious King I A M E S of Eng- land, Scotland, France, and Ireland, King, Defender of the Faith, &c. We doe therefore in the presence aforesaid solemne- ly promise euer more to continue the loyall Subiects of our said Soueraigne King, his Heires and Successors, and neuer to re- uolt from him, or them, vnto any other whatsoeuer, but euer- more to acknowledge his Supreme Gouernment.

Fiftly, Whereas wee were sent hither by diuers Aduenturers of the Citie of London, and other parts of the Realme of England, we doe here in the presence aforesaid promise to vse all diligence for the good of the Plantation, and not to purloine or imbesell any of the prohibited Cōmodities out of the gene- rall estate, but to vse all faithfulnesse as it becommeth Chris- tians to doe, as also to bee obedient to all such Gouernour or Gouernours, or their Deputie or Deputies, as are, or shall bee by them sent to gouerne vs ; As also to yeeld all reuerence to- wards the Ministerie or Ministers of the Gospell, sent, or to be sent.

Sixtly and lastly, Wee doe here in presence aforesaid promise, the Lord assisting vs, that if at any time hereafter any forraine power shall attempt to put vs out of this our lawfull possession, not cowardly to yeeld vp the same, but manfully to fight as true English men, for the defence of the Common-wealth we liue in, and Gospell wee professe, and that whiles we haue breath we will not yeeld to any, that shall inuade vs vpon any condi- tions whatsoeuer.

FINIS.

NEVVES
Of S^r. Walter Rauleigh.
WITH
The true Description of GVIANA:
As also a Relation of the excellent Gouernment, and much hope of the prosperity of the Voyage.
Sent from a Gentleman of his Fleet,
to a most especial Friend of his in London.

From the Riuer of Caliana, on the Coast of Guiana, Nouemb. 17. 1617.

LONDON,
Printed for *H. G.* and are to be sold by *I. Wright*, at the signe of the Bible without New-gate. 1618.

Force's Collection of Historical Tracts.

VOL. III.—No. 4.

NEWES OF

Sr. Walter Rauleigh.

IN these queasie and most dangerous times, wherein Truth is manacled by Opinion and Imagination, euery man making his owne thoughts a Comment vpon other mens labours, and by scrues or wrests winding euery designe to that which best suites with their fancies : I could not chuse but borrow so much time from the necessitie of mine occasions, as to acquaint you with some particular passages in our voyage : Which though in the value it may be much short both of what your selfe and others expect, because at this time our designe is but an Embrion, conceiued, and farre from that happy perfection to which I doubt not (the diuine will assisting vs) but wee shall, to the comfort of our noble and good friends, and the honour of our Nation, with all prosperitie of fortune bring to passe : Yet in as much as I know the malice of many enuious and euill disposed people, who build the ground-worke of their owne honors vpon other mens ^{Against Backbiters.} disgraces, and with the venome of their aspersions seeke (as much as in their malice lies) to poyson the worthy labours of the most noble attempters. To which our Voyage (being most hopefull to our friends, and most dreadfull to our contraries) is infinitely subiect, and that such rancour doth await and follow vs, as the great *Leuiathan* of the Sea pursueth the *Bonittos*, I doubt not but my present Relation shall giue you (whose vertue I seeke onely to satisfie) that assurance of good hope in our attemptings, as shall arme you against whatsoeuer slander or imputation shall be able (in misty thicke fogs of disdaine) to throw before you.

And albeit to the iudgement of euery vertuous good man, there needeth no other Apologie for the hope of our successe, then the wisdome, experience, and vndefatigable labors, in the like designes, of our Generall, who now setting all Christendome; nay, almost the whold world at gaze vpon him, if hee should

not

not to such beholders giue a renowned satisfaction; it were against
all rules of worth and policie to imagine. Yet aboue all, this mee
thinkes should satisfie euery reasonable soule, and make Enuy
feede onely vpon his owne Serpent, when not alone the entyre
wisdome of our Land, but the suffrage and allowance of our Soueraigne (who is the very soule of that wisdome) doth both giue
way to our action, whose goodnes what man would be so ingratefull to abuse, or what folly could be so strong in any sencible
soule, as to seeke to goe inuisible before God.

But Sir, these arguments are needlesse against a slander of such
weaknesse, nor will I trouble your eares with a confutation of
them, who stand already confounded in all good mens opinions :
suffice it, that hitherto our successe is answerable to our hopes,
and our hope as strong as any that hath passed from our Kingdome since the first discouery, and no doubt but the end will
bring forth as worthy, if not a much better issue: In as much as
wee haue had both the cleare lights of all other mens experience,
and the approued knowledge of a great part of our designe in
our Generals noble and personall tryall.

Besides, wee know that the tops of hye Scales, Mountaines,
or Pyramides are not to be attained vnto by leaping or iumping
at, but by slow degrees, and by secure and safe steps, euen *lento
pede*, as the Parrat climbes with both beake and feete : For if
wee looke into the courses of all the most excellent men of our
Nation which haue made it as famous for sea-actions as any Nation in the world, we shall finde, how euen by little and little, as
Hanibal with Vinegar wasted the *Alpes*, and made a passage
(where neuer any before was discerned) for not himselfe alone,
but a whole Army to passe ouer : So our famous and excellent
Attempters haue by degrees, man after man, adding step vnto
step, made such a way ouer the whole world, that except the
very heart of all, (which as in the Anatomy of mans body, it is
not to be found out, or toucht, till a man haue past through first
both all the exteriour and interiour members, and so likewise of
the braine : Nature as it were defending all her most excellent
workes from euery ordinary assault and inuasion) so there is at
this day not left any Climate unsearcht or vndiscouered, but
onely this, which as for its site and place, being the middle of
the world, and also for the excellency of it, may well be stiled
The heart of the world, as the most principall and renowned
part of it. At which if it be our fortunes to arriue, the worke will
be worthy the Doer, and a fayre Iewell for his Crowne, who is
the Royall Author and Comforter of so great an Attempt, by so
many Kings and Princes attempted, and yet vnachiued.

And that wee may walke vp this Scale, with as much ease and
                                                                                      safety,

safety, as all mortall hope can allow vs, let vs turne backe our eyes and looke into the actions of most of the most famous & noble Gentlemen which haue gone before vs, and made those most fayre and large paths, through which we daily walke : wee shall see that M. *William Haukins,* the Father of Sir *Iohn* M. *William* made his first Discouries but to the Southerne Ilands, *Haukins a man of infinite vertue and great action Haukins his* trauell.

called the *Grand Canaria,* and found there great Trade, and great Commoditie : which for the benefit might well haue taken vp the rest of any mans minde (whose end had beene wealth and no other) but the Gentleman hauing a more worthy ayme, (though then in the winter and last quarter of his age) from thence discouered some part of the small Ilands which belonged to the West Indies, learnt intelligence of the maine : and out of his iudgement saw what was fittest both for Traffique and other more materiall Discoueries. This (not able to furnish himselfe) hee imparted to his most worthy Sonne Sir *Iohn* *Haukins,* and making him rich with his knowledge, Sr. *Iohn Hau-kins* Trauell. so armd him for the Enterprise, that in the yeare 1562. hee made a Voyage thither, with three small Ships, and but 100. men, and made Discouery of the Iland of *Hispaniola, De Plata, Monte Christi,* and the Ilands of *Caicos,* where by way of traffique hee made such merchandise that hee not onely laded all his owne ships, but diuers other Hulkes which he there hyred, and so returned home with more wealth and honour then ever any had done before his time.

Yet since he had gone not a steppe higher then his father had done before him, and made the scale no larger nor easier for others that should pursue him : out of the excellency of his disposition and loue to his Country, in the yeare 1 5 6 4. hee betooke himselfe to the Sea againe, and with a Fleet of foure Ships and 170. men, went againe to the West *Indies,* Sr. *Iohns* second Voyage. and in his way did discouer the Iland *Sambula,* and other partes of *Affricke :* thence to the Iland called *Sancta Dominica,* so to *Margarita,* thence to *Tortuga,* after to *Barbarotta,* then to the Ilands of *Curasao, Ranchario, Rio de la Hacha,* and others, thence to Cape St. *Anthony,* and so to the sandy Ilands : and lastly by *Florida,* where he showed that excellency of good nature and rare humanity to certaine distressed Frenchmen, that the remembrance will liue whilst there liues any record of goodnes, or any thankfulnesse in France : and thus hee returned home the second time, laden with as much wealth and honor, as euer any had done before him, and to this braue heroicall scale of Discouery, had now added diuers noble and

spacious

spacious Stayres, which albeit might haue very well deterd him
from any more trouble and vexation, both considering the goods
and goodnes he had gotten, and the honourable places, with the
fauour of his dearest Soueraigne.

Yet all this not valued with the debt hee owed his Country,
he went againe the third time to Sea with a Fleet
of sixe faire Ships, and traded in all such places as
he had traded in before: and moreouer discouered
Carthagena, and diuers other Ilands about it, after went to St.
Iohn Vllua, and other parts bordering vpon *Mexico,* where hee
made him selfe Master of twelue Ships, in value, worth two
hundred thousand pounds, and seazed the Iland: But out of his
noble nature (considering the amity at that time betwixt Spaine
and England) restored all againe; which, had his ends tended as
much to lucre as his enemies did to perfidie and trechery, he
might not onely haue brought home that, but sixe millions of
treasure more, all which was at his commandement: thence he
searched the whole Bay of *Mexico,* and thence went to *Ponte
Vedra,* and so returned home.

In this Discouery hee got great perfection of knowledge touching the wonderfull wealth and riches of those Southerne parts,
and though hee had done more than any English man before his
time, yet he saw there was a super excellence remayning as it
were hidden, and possible to bee found out; at which, with all
his endeauours, he aymed most earnestly, onely he found that a
greater strength & a greater industry: then either he was yet
maister of, or had occasion to vse, must be imployed in the same,
and therefore the fourth time hee returned vnto the
Sea with 27 tall Ships, and 2500. men: But it
pleased God the designe should bee preserued
either for some other man, or some other time, so that Sir *Iohn
Haukins,* falling sicke, dyed at St. *Iohn de Puertorico,* and by
that meanes the great end of the iourney failed, yet did hee leaue
behind him such braue examples for imitation, and so fayre a
scale for others to ascend by; that many became his Schollers,
and howsoeuer their renownes wanne to themselues particular
names of particular eminence, yet they arriued not beyond him,
or got a skill that was to him vnacquainted.

Onely that most famous and worthy Knight Sir
Francis Drake, who had (as it is reported) taken
from him the most and greatest part of his breeding,
being (as some men say) for a long time his ordinary houshold
Seruant, and one that had attended him in the successe of some
of his voyages, seeing and aquainting himselfe with the happy

Sir Iohns third
Voyage.

Sir Iohns fourth
Voyage.

*Sir Francis
Drakes* trauell.

rules

rules of such a happy maister, betooke himselfe to the Sea in the yeare of our Lord 1572. and discouered most of the hithermost parts of the small Ilands of *America,* and returned home with more knowledge then substance, and yet with more substance then might defray the charge of three times such a voyage, by the strength of which successe he made himselfe fit for the Sea the second time, in the yeare 1577. in which Voyage hee made himselfe more familiar with all the richest parts of the West *Indies,* and with some parts Sir *Francis* second Voyage. of the maine body of the same : and so returned home with a competent substance, yet farre inferior to the largenes of his mind, because these two first attempts still opened to his iudgement matters of much greater hope and renowned consequence, so that the third time againe he put to Sea, in the year of our Lord 1585. with a full resolution to doe some- Sir *Francis* 3. Voyage. thing answerable to the greatnes of his heart, and the honor of the Nation he challenged, and in this voyage he went about the circumference of the whole World, and returned home with his Ship laden with gold and treasure, of that infinite and inestimable value, that neuer any man before him attained to any small degree in his comparison, and yet in this vnspeakeable Iourney for infinite wealth and infinite labour (not any mortall man hauing formerly done the like) the experience hee gained did so farre precede his riches, that hee made it of no value, and knew that there yet remained that vndiscouered (at least out of Christian commandement) which would make all hee knew pittifully poore, & of no reconing: and therfore to achiue this *Magisteri* or true Philosophers stone, being indeed the mother of all mines and perfect treasure, he againe betooke himselfe to the Sea in the yeare of our Lord 1595. with a very goodly Nauy, and many most noble and worthy personages, admirably well experienced both in Land and Sea seruices : But it was not the pleasure of the euerliuing God, that by him the worke should bee finished and therefore in this voyage he sickened, and in the West *Indies* died, so that the end of the Iourney being by a twofold way defeyted, as by his death, and the taking of a certaine surgeon which belonged to a Ship, called the *Salomon,* as also by the taking of another Ship called the *Francis,* and by them the whole Voyage discouered to the enemy, the rest of the Fleet was inforced to returne home altogether vnsatisfied.

Now whilst these Gentlemen were thus searching the South and South-west parts of the world, and had almost brought their hopes within a step or two of the high- Sir *Hugh Wil-loughbies* tra-
est

uolls to the North. est scale, an honorable emulation raised vp diuers other Gentlemen of like vertue and fitnes for action, to search into the North and North-west Seas, for the finding out of the easiest and most safe wayes into the East *Indies*, a place esteemed for riches equall with the former: but in merchandise by much far beyond it, and in this Discouery Sir *Hugh Willoughby* was exceeding well deseruing, who made diuers faire steps to the Scale, and though he perished and died in the action, yet hee left such excellent hopes behind him that many became pursuers of his proiect, amongst whom none is more remarkable and exquisite then that famous worthy Gentleman, Sir *Martin* *Forbisher* Knight, who by many experiences and intelligences of the state, condition, Climate, and height, of *China:* knew that if a way might by any industry bee found out from the North-west to lead vnto the same, that then it must needs be most short, most easie, & most safe, and that doubtlesse the wealth which would arise by rich Merchandise from thence, would exceed the whole trade of the world beside, nay that the mines, which was hopefull there to bee found, might goe neere to counteruayle the great hopes which were built on the South-west, if not exceed it. And therevpon hauing all those experiences, which Sir *Hugh Willoughby* had left behind, together with his owne knowledge, he betook himselfe to the Sea in the yeare 1576 with two good Ships, and hauing past the faire Iland, and *Swinborne* in Scotland, he came to *Fowlay* in Friesland, thence to *Labrador*, so to the Ilands *Gabriels* and *Bourchers*, where he saw and conferred with many people of that Iland, being a Sauage people, much like vnto the *Tartars*, with broad faces, flat noses, and long black hayres below their shoulders, their attire onely Seale skinnes, nor is there betweene the men and women any difference, more then a few blew streakes downe their cheekes and about their eyes, these hee saw on the water, not on the land, in certaine small Boates which were made of Seale skinnes, being sharpe at each end and broad in the bottome, with small wooden keeles made of broad splinters, and in shape or proportion not much unlike vnto the Spanish Shallops. With these people, whom he inticed to come to him by all faire and gentle meanes, and by giuing them certaine thrid poynts and other toyes, in which they infinitely delighted, hee had **very** much conference, both touching the nature of those Seas, and other occurrents meet for his Discouery, by whome he vnderstood that the yeare time being then spent, and the Ice in those places infinitely increasing, it was at that time imposssble

Sir Martin Forbisher to China.

possible to attempt further, without most assured losse, which
accordingly hee found by his owne experience, and therefore returned homeward by *Trumpets* Iland, and other places which
both for victuall and fresh water he found of great consequence
for the furthering of this Discouery hereafter.

Now having thus erected these few steps to this much wisht
for Scale, and finding great hope likely to ensue vpon the attempt,
hee betooke himselfe againe to the Sea, in the yeare Sir *Martins* se-
of our Lord 1577. and taking a better aduantage of cond Voyage
the yeare time, passed all the former places, which to Cataya.
before he had discouered and from thence held his course euen
vnto the maine of *Cataia*, though with many dangers and inter-
ruptions, for not any man that seeketh wayes vnknowne, but must
of necessity many times erre, neither can the iudgement be satisfied by the first superficiall sight of the eye, but by a more serious time to contemplate and meditate vpon the same, discourse
euer crowning all actions with perfection. And hence it came
that making a longer stay vpon this Coast, then before hee imagined any necessity would haue drawne him, the year time so
passed on, that hee could by no possible meanes proceed further
in the discouery, but was forced to approue what particular profits he could find in that place to recompence his trauell, finding
by the Climat & all other good likelihoods that of force there
must bee something of great valuation, wherevpon after some curious search of many well experienst men in mynerall busines,
(which at that time attended vpon him) he found at
length certaine strange mynes which yeelded a kind Gold Mynes in
of black shining Ore, both massy and wealthy, which Cataya.
they called the blacke stone, and by such small triall as that
place (with the accommodation of their Shipping) could afford
them, they found it a very rich gold Ore, so that not being able
to stay there to refine any great quantity thereof, as well for the
necessity of the yeare time, as the want of other most necessary
prouisions, hee presently laded all his Ships with that Oare, being
one tall Ship and two smaller Barks, and then taking a man, a
woman, and a child of that Country into his Ship also, hee returned with them home into England, to the much contentment
of the Queenes Maiesty his Soueraigne, and all other aduenturers which had then shared in his fortunes; and still hee found
an increase of his hopes and made his way larger and
larger, so that the third time hee put forth to the *Sr. Martins*,
Sea in the yeare of our Lord 1588. But it pleased third Voyage.
God that he could not perfect his intent, onely returned home
with much wealth and a great deale of knowledge, which hath
since

since beene pursued by diuers worthy Aduenturers, and though
not perfited in that exquisite height and perfection which the
greatnes of their minds and wishes aymed at, yet still it gaue that
lustre and strong hope of successe in the action, that a very no-
Mr. *Thomas* ble and worthy Gentleman, Mr. *Thomas Cauendish*
Cauendish led as well by their former attempts and experiences,
Trauell.   as also by his owne knowledge, drawne from certaine
approued assurances and intelligences, touching the wonderfull
and almost vnexpressible wealth of *China*, with great iudgement
and aduice of many most excellent Seamen, ingaged himselfe
into this worthy discouery, and finding many hard difficulties in
the North-west passage, by good aduice resolued to try the contrary, which is the South-west, knowing that of necessity those
lines must in the end meet in one period: And therefore with
all good accommodations he betooke himselfe to the Sea in the
yeare of our Lord 1586. and passing the *Grand Canaries*, came
to *Cape Verde*, and thence to the Tropicke Line, discouering
all the hithermost parts of the East Indies ; and from thence attained the very maine and body of *China*, where he fraught his
Ships with that wealth (as Cloth of Gold, Tyssue, Veluets, Sat-
tens, Damaskes, and a world of other commodities of `no lesse
value) that it is thought, excepting *Drake*, not any Englishman
euer returned with the like wealth, insomuch that it set a world
of noble hearts on fire, to enter into the like action.

But hee hauing compassed an end of his profit, (but not of his
experience) refused to returne back againe by one and the same
way, but keeping his course forward, went round about the whole
Circumference of the earth ; and in the end came into England
without any abatement of the great substance hee had formerly
attained, to the infinite ioy of all his friends, the great honour of
the Kingdom, and the much admiration of all forraine Nations.

But did this Experience giue him a full satisfaction, or shew
that end to his designes, that hee might with his honour or reputation say with *Hercules, Ne plus vltra?* No surely, but after
a cleane contrary manner, opened vnto him such a fayre way to
greater glory and renowne, that he accounted this neyther worthy of his boast, nor fit in any small degree to contayne the least
part of his actions : being in comparison of those things which
hee heard there related, (and indeed not farre remoued from that
Continent) but poore, base and beggarly.

M. *Cauendish* his   The glory of which famous action so inticed
second Voyage. him, that the second time he went to the Sea, in the
          yeare of our Lord 1591. so accommodated with all
necessary prouisions, both of men, munition, and victuals, that
                                                              not

not any Gentleman euer went forth (in his owne particular) better or more brauely prouided. But it pleased God (who is the strength and guide of these actions) not to marke him out for this great work: for in this Voyage hee sickned and dyed, whose greatest directions liuing inclosed in his owne brest, the Voyage queld, and his ships returned home againe for England, but the infinite profit which hath sprung from his example may be beheld in our East Indian Trade, the like whereof I thinke no Nation in the world can boast, being of all other the wealthiest, the fruitfullest, and the most certaine, affording vs not onely a nurcery of Merchants and Sea-men, but such an inuincible strength of Shipping, and other warlike acoustrements, that any Nation vnder the Sunne may tremble to offend vs.

To these Discoueries I could adde the Discouery Sr. *Richard* of *Virginia,* by the euer memorable and valiant *Grinuile* his Knight Sir *Richard Grinuile,* and the Plantation Virginia. there: which doubtlesse promiseth and already restoreth much benefit to our Kingdome, hauing continued there almost from the yeare 1585. till this hower; and how euen in that Discouery hee both heard and vnderstood of the incomparable and not to be equald wealth which yet lay hidden in the South parts of *America.*

But I feare I haue troubled your eares already too much with my tedious digression, which is not altogether vaine and impertinent, since by it you may see how euen from the infancy of our English trauell, euery man hath had a noble ambition, and most probable assurances of good hope to attaine a height of honour and wealth, which yet rests vnattained: At which questionless our Generall bends his ayme, being diuers Sir *Walter Rauleigh.* wayes wooed and induced thereunto, more then any Englishman whatsoeuer, both in respect of his former experience (at this day not to be paralleld) his wisdome, learning, and conference, with the experience of places hee hath formerly held, that it is impossible any thing of note should be hidden from him: Therefore to reconcile those things already written, with the Relation I intend to pursue, you shall vnderstand that whatsoeuer hath beene done formerly by any of those already rehearsed, or by any other, whether English, Spanish, Dutch, French, or any other Nation of Christendome, all their knowledges and experiences haue liberally beene brought to his remembrance; Loue, Dutie, his place of Authoritie, or the chance of Warre, tendering the same vnto him as a rent due to his noble minde and actions. And aboue all an English Knight, Sir *Ro-* Sir *Robert* *bert Dudley* was an especiall man that long since both *Dudley.*

from

from his experience at sea, (hauing consumed infinite wealth and much time in these Discoueries) as also by meanes of certaine Letters which he had intercepted from the Spaniards and taken in his trauells, gaue our Generall a strong assurance, that yet there remained out of the hands of all the Kings and Princes in Christendome, in the South parts of *America*, the very Magazine of all rich Mettalls, and such an Empire as whosoeuer shall haue the fortune to conquer it, shall so darken all the actions either of *Cortez* or *Pescaro*, that nothing but pouerty will appeare in their deeds, neyther *Mexico* nor *Peru* bee worthy to be compared with it, and what Prince soeuer shall possesse it, shall bee Lord of more gold, of a more beautifull Empire, and of more Citties and people then either the King of Spaine or the great Turke. At this questionlesse our hopes promise that his noble ends doe bend, for being full as great, and hauing beene much greater then any man whatsoeuer of our nation that hath followed the like course, to what should his great hart look? or what should hee dedicate to so gracious and mercifull a King as hee enioyeth, but the very toppe and Garland of all Heroyicall actions? But in as much as yet nothing is done worthy relation, because we are not yet ariued at the hithermost end of our designes, all our successe remayning in hope, and least my too much loue might make me too saucy in prophesie, I will leaue all to his holy will which gouernes all; onely I will acquaint you with some particulars touch-iug the generall gouernment of our Fleete, which although other men doubtlesse in their Voyages haue in some measure obseru'd, yet in all the great Volumes which haue beene written touching Voyages, there is no president of so godly, seuere and Martiall gouernment, which not onely in it selfe is laudable and worthy imitation, but also fit to bee written and ingrauen in euery mans Soule, that couets to doe honor to his King and Country in these or the like attempts: The true Coppy of which Lawes, Articles, and especiall Commandements, are these which heere after fol-low; and at this present we obserue.

Orders

Orders to bee obserued by the
Commanders of the Fleet, and land

Companies, vnder the charge and conduct
of Sr. *Walter Rauleigh* Knight,
bound for the South parts of Ame-
rica or elsewhere. Giuen at *Pli-*
mouth in *Deuon.* the third
of *May.* 1617.

Irst, because no action nor Enterprise can prosper (be it by Sea or Land) without the fauour and as- sistance of Almighty God, the Lord and strength of Hoasts and Armies, you shall not fayle to cause Diuine Seruice to be read in your Shippe morning and euening, in the morning before Dinner, and at night before Supper, or at least (if there be interruption by foule weather) once the day, praysing God euery night with singing of a Psalme at the setting of the Watch.

Secondly, you shall take especiall care that God be not blas- phemed in your Ship, but that after admonition giuen, if the of- fenders doe not refraine themselues, you shall cause them of the better sort to be fined out of their aduentures, by which course, if no amendment bee found, you shall acquaint me withall : For if it be threatned in the Scriptures, that *The Curse shall not de- part from the house of the Swearer,* much lesse from the Ship of the Swearer.

Thirdly, no man shall refuse to obey his Officer in all that he is commaunded, for the benefit of the Iourney : no man (being in health) refuse to wayte his turne as he shall be directed : the Saylors by the Maister and Boatswaine : the Landmen by their Captaine, Liefetenant and others.

You shall make in euery Ship two Captaines of the watch, who shall make choyce of two Soldiers euery night to search be- tweene the Decks, that no fire nor candle light be carried about the Ship, after the watch set, nor that any Candles be burning in any Caben without a Lanthorne, and that neither but while they are to make themselues vnready, for there is no danger so

ineuitable

ineuitable as the Ships firing, which may also as well happen by taking of Tobacco betweene the Decks, & therefore forbidden to all men but aloft the vpper Decke.

You shall cause the Land-men to learne the names and places of the ropes, that they may assist the Sailors in their labours vpon the Decks, though they cannot goe vp to the tops and yards.

You shall traine and instruct your Sailers, (so many as shall bee found fit) as you doe your Land-men, and register their names in the Lists of your Companies, making no difference of professions; but that all bee esteemed Saylors and all Soldiers, for your troupes will bee very weake when you come to Land, without the assistance of your Sea-faring-men.

You shall not giue chase, or send aboard any Shippe, but by order from the Generall: And if you come neere any Shippe in your course, if shee bee belonging to any Prince or State in league or amitie with his Maiestie, you shall not take any thing from them by force, vppon paine of punishment as a Pirate, although in manifest extremity or want you may, (agreeing for the price) relieue your selues with things necessary, (giuing bond for the same) prouided that it bee not to the disfurnishing of any such Ship, whereby the Owner or Merchants be endangered for the Ship or goods.

You shall euery night fall a sterne the Generalls Shippe, and follow his light, receiuing instructions in the Morning what course to holde, and if you shall at any time bee seperated by foule Weather, you shall receiue certaine Billettes sealed vp, the first to bee opened on this side the North Cape, (if there bee cause) the second to be opened at the South Cape: the third, after you shall passe 23. degrees, and the fourth from the height of Cape *de Vert*.

If you discouer any sayle at Sea, either to wind-ward or to lee-ward of the Admirall, or if any two or three of our Fleet, shall discouer any such saile which the Admirall cannot discerne: If shee bee a great Shippe and but one, you shall strike your maine top-saile, and hoyst it againe so often as you shall iudge it to bee 100. Tunnes of burthen, as if you iudge her to bee 200. Tunnes to strike & hoyst twise, if 300. thrice and so answerable to her greatnes.

If you discerne a small Ship, you shall doe the like with your fore top-saile, but if you discouer many great Ships, you shall not onely strike your maine top-Saile often, but put out your Ensigne in the maine top, and if such Ships or Fleet goe large before the winde, you shall also (after your signes giuen) goe large,

and

and stand as any of the Fleet doth, I meane no longer then that you may iudge the Admirall and the rest haue seene your signes and your so standing. And if you went large at the time of the Discouery, you shall hale oft your sheats for a little time, and then goe large againe, that the rest may know that you goe large, to shew vs that the Ships or Fleet discouered keep that course, so you shall doe if the Ships or Fleet discouered haue their tacks aboard, namely if you had also your tacks aboard at the time of the discouery, you shall beare vp for a little time and after hale your sheat oft againe to show vs what course the Ship or Fleet holds.

If you discouer any Ship or Fleet by night, if the Ship or Fleete bee to windeward of you, and you to windeward of the Admirall, you shall presently beare vp to giue vs knowledge : but if you thinke you might speake with her, then you shall keepe your loose and shoot off a piece of Ordnance to giue vs knowledge thereby.

For a Generall rule, let no man presume to shoote off any piece of Ordinance but in discouering a Ship or Fleet by night, or by being in danger of the enemy, or in danger of fire, or in danger of sinking, it may bee vnto vs all a most certaine intelligence of some matter of importance, and you shall make vs know the difference by this, for if you giue chase, and being neere a Ship, you shoot to make her strike, wee shall see and know you shoot to that end, (if it be by day) if by night, we shall then know that you haue seene a Ship or Fleet more then our owne, and if you suspect wee doe not heare the first piece, then you may shoote a second but not otherwise, and you must take almost a quarter of an hower betweene your two pieces : If you bee in danger by a leake (I meane in present danger) you shall shoote two pieces presently one after another. And if in danger of fire three pieces presently one after another.

In foule weather euery man shall fit his Sailes to keepe company with the rest of the Fleet, and not run so farre a head by day, but that hee may fall a sterne the Admirall before night : in case we should be set vpon by Sea, the Captaine shall appoint sufficient company to assits the Gunners, after which (if the fight require it) the Cabens betweene the Decks shall be taken downe, all beds and sacks imployed for Bulwarks; the Musketiers of euery Ship shall bee diuided vnder Captaines, or other Officers, some for the fore-Castell, others for the wast, the rest for the poope, where they shall abide (if they bee not otherwise directed) the Gunners shall not shoot any great Ordnance at other distance then poynt blanke. An Officer or two shall bee

appointed

appointed to take care that no loose pouder bee carried betweene
the Decks, or neere any linstocke, or match in hand : you shall
saw diuers Hogs-heads in two parts, and filled with water, set
them aloft the Deckes : you shall deuide your Carpenters some
in the hold, (if any shot come betweene wind and water) and the
rest betweene the Decks, with plates of lead, plugs, with all things
necessary laid by them : you shall also lay by your tubs of water,
certaine wet blankets to cast vpon and choke any fire, the Maister
and Boat-swaine shall appoynt a certaine number of Sailers to
euery saile, and to euery such company a Maisters mate, Boat-
swaines Mate, or quarter Maister, so as when euery man knowes
his charge and place, things may be done without noyse or confusion, and no man to speake but the Officers : As for example,
if the Maister or his Mate bid heaue out the maine Top-saile, the
Maisters mate, Boat-swains mate, or quarter Maister which hath
charge of that saile, shall with his company performe it without
calling out to others, and so for the fore-saile, fore top-saile,
sprit-saile, and the rest : the Boat-swaine himselfe taking no particular charge of any Saile, but ouerlooking all, and seeing euery
one doe his duty.

No man shall bord a Ship of the enemy without order, because
the losse of a Ship to vs is of more importance, then of ten to
the enemy, as also by one mans bording all our Fleet may be ingaged, it being a great dishonour to loose the least of our Fleet,
Euery Ship being vnder the lee of the enemy shall labour to recouer the wind, if the Admirall indeauour it, and find an enemy
to leeward of vs, the whole Fleet shall follow the Admirall, Vice-
Admirall, or other leading Ships within Musquet shot of the
enemy, giuing so much liberty to the leading Ships after her
broad side discouered, she may stay and trim her sailes, then is
the second Ship to giue her side, and the third and fourth, which
done they shall all take as the first Ship, and giuing the enemy
the other side shall keepe him vnder a perpetuall volley : Thus
must you doe to the windermost Ship of the enemy, which you
shall batter in pieces, or force her to beare vp and intangle the
rest falling foule one of another to their great confusion.

If the Admirall giue chase and bee head-most man, the next
Ship shall take vp his Boat if other order bee not giuen : or if
any other Ship bee appointed to giue chase, the next Ship, if the
chasing Ship haue a boat at her sterne, shall take her vp : if any
make a Ship to strike, hee shall not enter her till the Admirall
come vp.

The Musketiers deuided into certaine quarters of the Ship
shall not deliuer their shot but at such distances as their Commander

mander shall direct them: you shall take a speciall care for the keeping of the Ship cleane betweene the Decks, to haue your Ordnance in order and not cloyd with trunkes, and chests. Let those that haue prouision of victualls, deliuer it to the Steward, and euery man put his apparrell in canuase Clokebags, except some few Chests which doe not pester the Ship: Euery one that vseth any weapon of fire, bee it Musket or other Piece, shall keepe it cleane, and if hee bee not able to amend it being out of order, hee shall presently acquaint his Officer therewith who shall command the Armorer to amend it.

No man shall keepe any feasting or drinking betweene meales, nor drinke any healths on the Ships prouision: Euery Captaine by his Purser, Steward, or other Officer shall take a weekely account how the Victualls wast: The Steward shall not deliuer any Candles to any priuate man, or to any priuate vse.

Whosoeuer shall steale from his fellowes, either apparrell or any thing else, shall be punished as a thiefe, or if any one steale any victualls, either by breaking into the hold, or otherwise, hee shall receiue the punishment of a thiefe and the murtherer of his fellowes.

There is no man shall strike any Officer, be hee Captaine, Lieftenant, Ensigne, Sergeant, Corporall of the Field, a quarter Maister, nor the Maister of any Ship, Maisters mate, Boat-swaine, or quarter Maister, I say no man shall offer any violence to any of these, but the Supreame Officer to the inferior, in time of Seruice vpon paine of death: No priuate man shall strike one another vpon paine of receiuing such punishment as a Marshall' Court shall thinke him worthy of.

No man shall play at Cards or Dice, either for his Apparill or Armes vpon paine of being disarmed, & made a Swabber; and whosoeuer shall shew himselfe a coward vpon any landing or otherwise, hee shall bee disarmed, and made a Labourer and carrier of victualls for the rest.

No man shall land any men in any forraigne parts, without order from the Generall, the Sergeant Mayor or other chiefe Officer, vpon paine of death; and wheresoeuer wee shall haue cause to land, no Man shall force any Woman, bee shee Christian or Heathen vpon paine of death: And you shall take especiall care when God shall suffer vs to land in the *Indies*, not to eat any fruits vnknowne, such fruits as you doe not find eaten by birds on the tree or beasts vnder the tree you shall auoyd.

You shall not sleepe on the ground nor eat any new flesh till it bee salted, two or three houres, which otherwise, will breed a most dangerous fluxe, so will the eating of ouer fat hoggs or Turkies:

Turkies : you shall also haue a great care, that you swim not in any Riuers but where you see the Indians swim, because most of the Riuers are full of *Allegators :* you shall not take any thing from any Indian by force, for from thenceforth we shall neuer be releeued ; but you must vse them with all courtesie. And for trading or exchanging with them it must be done by one or two of euery Ship for all the rest, and the price to be directed by the Cape Merchant, for otherwise all our commodities will bee of small price, and greatly to our hinderance.

For other orders on the Land we will establish them (when God shall send vs thither) by generall consent, in the meane time I will value euery mans honor according to their degree and valor, and taking care for the seruice of God and prosperity of our enterprise.

When the Admirall shall hang out a Flag or Ensigne on the Missen shrouds, you shall know it to be a Flag of Counsaile to come aboard.

A

A Reference of the Voyage to *the Directions*.

BY these orders and Commandements, you may see to what Coast wee are bound, and namely to the South parts of *America*, and no doubt to the onely best part therof: For as all the Springs and Riuers in the world haue but one head, namely, the Sea: so it is thought all the wealthy Mynes in the world haue but one Soueraigne, which is an Empire placed in these parts, and that is the great Empire of *Guiana*, ruled by the great Emperour *Of Guyana, and the wealth.*
Inga: of the great wealth and riches whereof *Francisco Lopez* and others thus report; That all the vessels of the Emperours house, Tables, and Kitchen were of Siluer and Gold, and the very meanest of all of Siluer and Copper, for the strength and hardnesse of the mettall: That in his Wardrobe were hollow Statues of gold, which seemed gyants, and Figures in proportion and bignes of all the Beasts, Birds, Trees, and Hearbs, that the earth bringeth forth in pure Gold also, and of all the Fishes that the Sea and waters of that Empyre breedeth. Also there was Ropes, Budgets, Chests, and Troughs of Gold and Siluer; great heaps of Billets of Gold, which seemed wood marked out to burne; nay, that there was nothing in all that Empire (the most flourishing of the whole world) whereof there was not a counterfeit in pure Gold.

Besides, there was seene in a certaine Iland neare the Emperours Court, a Garden of pleasure, in which was all kinde of Garden-hearbs, flowers and trees, of Gold and Siluer. As also in other places diuers great infinits of Gold and siluer vnwrought, as in one place to the value of fifty two thousand Markes of pure Siluer, and one Million and three hundred twenty and sixe thousand and fiue hundred *Pesoes* in Gold.

Now it is to be vnderstood that all this wealth *A very strange* belonged but to one Emperour: for the custome *custome.* of the Country is, that whosoeuer dyeth hath all his Treasure buryed with him, so that euen from the first Ruler to the Emperour now liuing, it is thought no lesse Treasure will be found in euery Monument; which how vnspeakable it is, I leaue to iudgement.

And

Martines his
testimony, and
first Christian
that saw *Guy-*
ana.

And this doth also witnesse *Martines*, a Spanyard, who liued seauen Moneths in the great Citie
Manoa (which hee called *El Dorado*, the place of
gold) with the great Emperour *Inga*, and saw with
his eyes what *Lopez* had written.   And further, he did affirme
of himselfe, that when hee first entred into that Citie, (which
for buildings, state and popularitie, and all other outward excellencies, hee thought the goodliest in the whole world) it was
neare noone, and then they vncouered his face (for in his whole
trauell hee was led by the Indians blindfold before) and hee tra-
uelled all that day till darke night, and the next day from Sunne-
rise till Sunne-set, directly forward within the Citie, before hee
came to the Emperours Court which expresseth a masse of
buildings farre beyond our apprehensions.

A curious Ob-
iection answer-
ed.

But here it will be obiected by the curious, that
without all question if this were possible to be so,
that the Conquest thereof had beene attempted
many yeares agoe, and that the Spanyard who hath
got *Peru* and *Mexico*, would not haue slept in a Designe of this
great consequence: Or if he had, that then these knowledges
would haue inflamed all the great Spirits of Christendome to haue
ioyned their forces together in so worthy a Conquest. And surely the Obiection is true, nor hath eyther the Spanyard or other
Princes beene sloathfull in this attempt, though it hath pleased
God their labours haue not hitherto taken effect.   For first, the

Oreliano the 1.
attempter for
Guyana.

Marquesse of *Pescaro* imployed *Oreliano* about the
Discouery of this Empire in the yeare 1542. and
hee was the first that found out the Riuer of *Ama-*
zons, but failed in his first purpose.

Ordace the 2.
attempter.

After him *Ordace*, who was Knight of the order
of St. *Iago*, did attempt the same designe, vnder
whom *Martines* (before mentioned) was maister of
the Munition, this *Ordace* was slaine by a mutiny vpon the Coast
of *Guiana*, with all such as likewise fauoured him; by reason
whereof the attempt fayled, and few or none of the Company returned, beeing sixe hundred foote, and thirty horse.

Pedro de Osua,
the third attem-
ptor.

After the death of *Ordace*, *Pedro de Osua* a
Knight vndertooke the attempt, and hauing spent
much time and search in the Riuer *Amazons*, and
wearied his soldiers, was also by a mutiny stird vp by one *Agiri*,
a man of meane quality, put to the sword, and with him all such
as loued him.

Agiri the fourth
attemptor.

Then *Agiri* being chiefe, tooke on him the attempt; but not being able by that Riuer to finde
any passage to *Guiana*, he returned back, and
                                    committing

committing diuers rebellious outrages, was in the end ouerthrowne in *Naeuo reigno*, and finding no way to escape, first slew his Children to saue them from defamation, and after himselfe.

After him succeded in this enterprise *Ieronimo Ortal de Saragosa*, but failing of his entrance was cast on a contrary Coast, and so proceeded no further.

Ieronimo Ortal de Saragosa, the fift attemptor.

Then followed *Don Pedro de Siluas*, but hee also entring by the Riuer *Amazons*, was by those warlike Woemen defeated, and but seauen of his Company escaped, whereof but two onely returned.

Don Pedro de Siluas, the sixt attemptor.

Then came *Pedro Hernandez de Serpa*, and vndertooke the action, but marching by Land to the Riuer *Orenoque*, was met by an Army of the *Indians* and ouerthrowne, so that of his whole power returned but eighteene persons.

Pedro Hernandez, the seuenth attemptor.

This ouerthrow, heard of the *Adalantado, Don Gonzales Cemenes de Casada* vndertooke the action, and sought his passage by the Riuer which is called *Papamene*, but he also, fayling in the true entrance, returned with the losse of much labour and cost : This *Gonzales* gaue his Daughter in marriage to a very braue and stoute Spaniard (but a little perfidious) called *Bereo*, binding him by his oath and honour to pursue the Action to his last substance, or the losse of his life, which *Bereo* vndertooke ; and all be it hee had the experience of all those which had gone before, and of diuers others, and was well perswaded of their errours and mistakings, yet he fayled as much as any other, nor euer could come to any true light thereof till hee got conference with an antient King of that Country called *Carapana*. This *Bereo* was after taken Prisoner by Sir *VValter Rauleigh*, our noble Generall at Trinidado, from whom he exacted much of that hath beene formerly written in the yeare of our Lord 1595. at which time *Sir VValther* attempted the discouery of Guiana, and proceeded further therein (being but himselfe and one hundred followers of all sorts) then euer any man had done before ; he entred by one of the maine branches of *Orenoque*, being nine in number which fall out of the North side, and seauen out of the South, and passed the Country of the *Tiuitiuas*, which are people that in the Sommer dwell in houses on the ground, but in the VVinter, vpon the tops of trees.

Gonzales Cemenes, the eight attemptor.

Anthonio Bereo the ninth attemptor.

Bereo taken Prisoner.

Sir Walter Rauleigh first Discouerer of Guiana.

Of the *Tiuitiuas.*

Thence

Thence he came into the goodly Riuer of *Ama-*
na, on whose borders he saw grow aboundance of
fruit Trees, good and pleasant to eat, which was a
very great reliefe to his Company when their victualls were
spent, and such strange plants and flowers as was most wonderfull.

Of the Riuer
Armana.

Then hee went to a Towne of the *Arcoacas,*
where hee found reliefe of victualls, and other necessaries, and a most delicate and sweet Country,
and in lesse then fifteene dayes after hee came to descry the
mountaines of *Guiana:* thence he went to the Towne of *Topa-*
rimaca an Indian Casiquy, which Towne is called *Arcoacas,*
and there feasted, was refreshed, and got a Pilot to bring him to
Guiana ; so that thence hee passed by the Iland
Assapano,. and the Iland *Icoana :* thence to the
Ile *Ocaycoita,* whence hee sent two *Gutanians* to
tell the Lord of that Country of his comming, so he passed by
the plaines of the *Samay,* which reach to *Cumana* and *Caracas;*
thence hee went vp to *Aromaia,* which was the Country of *Mo-*
requito, that was formerly slaine by *Bereo,* where in the Port
thereof hee anchored, and the King of *Aromaia*
came a foote, vnto him, being fourteene English
miles, and brought him all sorts of prouisions, with
this King (beeing a man of an hundred and tenne
yeares old) Sir *Walter* discoursed in priuate, and
vnderstood that Country to bee a part of *Guiana,* and with all
he learnd from him the waies & passages to *Manoa,* the strength
& gouernment of the great Empire, and lastly, the nature &
disposition of the people, and what Nations and Countries were
aduerse vnto them. After this discourse Sir *Walter* gaue him
leaue to depart, the old man promising him vpon his returne, all
things necessary that hee should want : Thence Sir
Walter went to view the famous Riuer *Caroli,*
and so to the Iland *Caiama :* thence to *Canuria,*
where he had conference with the *Cassique* therof, and from
him learned also more of the state of *Guiana,* and of the
great wealth and of certaine Siluer Mynes, which
were then vpon the borders of that Riuer, where
hee then anchored, and that also hee was then very
neere vnto *Macureguarai* the first ciuill Towne of *Guiana :* But
now the time of the yeare being past, and the Riuers beginning
to rise and breake forth, hee could assend no further vpward by
water, yet hee sent diuers especiall Gentlemen of good iudgement ouer the land, who discouered a great part of that Country,

Of the Arroa-
cas.

The Iland As-
sapano, and
others.

Sir Walters con-
ferrence with
the King of
Aromaia.

The great riuer
Caroli.

Discouery of
Siluer Mynes.

try, & himselfe in person diuers places of especiall account also, amongst which hee beheld the wonderfull strange fall of waters which fell from the Riuer *Caroli,* being about ten or twelue ouer-falls, euery one higher then another aboue the height of an ordi-nary Church steeple, but touching the excellency The excellency of the Country, the beauty, riches, sweet ayre, and of those border-plenty of all things necessary for pleasure as deere, ing Countries. foule, fish, and other commodities no Nation in the world could exceed it, and in this place hee found diuers very precious stones, and other Minerall things of great value, heere also he saw the great Lake of *Cassipa,* from which in the Summer time is gathered great aboundance of The great Lake grains of pure gold, and tooke also a full suruay of *Cassipa.* of many other Nations adioying to both sides of that Riuer, but by this time the Riuers grew to an extraordinary height aboue their bankes, so as hee was compeld to proceed no further in the attempt at that time, but returned back vnto his Shippes by the Easterly Coast, discouering all such Nations as on that side they had not beheld, and in this returne he had conferrence with di-uers Kings and Cassiques of those Nations, whom with his ver-tue, wisedome, clemency, and noble carriage, he so wan vnto him, that they offered him all the aide and assistance (to any attempt he should take in hand) that either their liues or estates were able to accomplish; withall, giuing him an accompt for the defects of other mens attempts vppon that Country, and shewing him the safe and readiest way how he might heereafter make himselfe Maister of the same, with diuers other cautions of great consequence, and heere also he got some store of gold, of gold Oare, and other Iewels: hence hee came into the Country of the Cassique *Putyma* who shewed him a wonderfull great Myne Of gold mines. of Gold in manner of a Rock or hard golden stones, which without especiall strong engines which they wanted, was not to bee pierst: Hence hee came into another branch of the Riuer of *Orenoque,* called *Winicapora,* where hee beheld a mountaine of Christall, which to Of a Mountaine there eyes appeared like a white Church Tower of of Christall. a most exceeding height: where also he saw and heard the greatest fall of water that any part of the world can produce. And in this place hee was assured there was many rich Diamonds and other precious stones of inestimable value, which were to be be-held a great way off. But the yeare time being spent, the ouer flow of waters comming, and the way much impassible, at that time he would not come neare vnto it: here hee receiued a great number of Spleene-stones, and other wealth, besides much pro-uision of food and other necessaries. Here also he got further

intelligence,

intelligence, and further assurances of ayd, if he should attempt any thing. Hence he came backe to *Assapano*, and thence with much danger to *Trinidado*, where hee found his ships, the sight and ioy whereof hardly any can expresse that hath not tryed the same hazard ; and so thence returned home for England.

Neyther hath this Attempt beene approued onely by the Spanyard and English (as is before rehearsed) but hath also beene taken in hand by diuers braue spirits of France, as *Mounseir Villieres* and diuers others, which were here very tedious to repeate : but they all likewise fayled therein. For making their way by the Riuer *Amazons*, they were euer crost in their purpose, and could finde no certaine entrance into that wealthy Empire : yet notwithstanding, in that Riuer, and in the branches thereof they found great trade of Gold, which came from the borders of *Guyana*, and so euer returned home very wealthy, together with other rich merchandise of great estimation.

Attempts by the French, for Guiana.

Thus you may see this *El Dorado*, or golden seate, hath beene sought by many worthy Spanyards, one Noble Englishman, and diuers Frenchmen, yet none so successefull as the English, which makes me Prophetiquely suppose, that the glory of the action is reserued for vs only, and the Kingdome such a Paragon and rich stone as shall adorne no crowne but the crowne of King *Iames*.

Hope of good hap.

The rest I leaue to their iudgement which shall reade what hath beene formerly written of it, or else these few protestations which doe follow.

First, Sir *Walter Rauleigh* himselfe protesteth from his owne sight and knowledge, that vpon this maine Riuer in which he sailed, whose branches doe runne and diuide into diuers Nations and Countries, aboue two thousand miles to the East and West, and eight hundred miles South and North, a man may see as many seuerall Kingdomes and Prouinces as may satisfie any industrious iudgement whatsoeuer ; and of them, the most, eyther rich in Gold or in other Merchandise : that in this place the Souldier may fight for Gold, and pay himselfe in stead of pence with plates of gold a foot broad : that the Commanders which shoot at honor and abundance, may finde there more beautifull Cities, more Temples adorned with Golden Images, more Sepulchers filled with Treasure, then eyther was found in *Mexico* or *Peru :* and that the shining glory of this Conquest would eclypse all the beames of the Spanish Nation.

Sir Walters protestation touching the welth of Guyana.

Also hee saith, there is no Country which yeeldeth more pleasure to the Inhabitants, for the delights of Hunting, Hawking, Fishing,

Fishing, Fowling, and the rest, then these Lands which hee saw did. They haue also so many Plaines, cleare Riuers, abundance of Pheasants, Partridges, Quailes, Rayles, Cranes, Herons, and all other Fowle : Deere of all sorts, Porkes, Hares, Lyons, Tygers, Leopards, and diuers other sorts of Beasts eyther for chase or foode, that no Nation of the world can exceede them.

And to conclude, hee saith, that both for health, good Ayre, pleasure and riches, it is not to be equald by any Region eyther in the East or West : and that there is in it great store of Brasill-wood, and diuers Berryes which dye a most perfect Crimson and Carnation ; and for painting, not all France, Italy, nor the East-Indies yeeld any such, for the more the skinne is washed, the fairer the colour appeareth.

Also there is great store of Cotton, of Silke, of Balsamum, and of those kindes most excellent, and neuer knowne in *Europe.* There are all sorts of Gummes, of Indian Pepper, besides what the Country may afford inwardly, which hee had not leasure to search, is yet vnknowne. Also the Soyle is so excellent and so full of Riuers, that it will beare Sugar, Ginger, and all commodities that the West Indies hath.

Now for the easinesse of the Nauigation, hee saith it may be sayled in sixe weekes thither, and in sixe weekes backe againe : and by the way ney-ther be shoare, enemies coast, rockes, nor sands ; all which other Voyages are subiect vnto. *Easines for Nauigation.*

Also hee saith, the best time to sayle from England thither, is in Iuly, because the Summer in *Guyana* is in October, Nouember, December, Ianuary, February, and March, and so shipping may returne from thence in Aprill, and arriue at home in England, in Iune ; and by that means neuer be subiect to winter weather, eyther comming, going, or staying, which no doubt is an excellent comfort to all men that shall vndertake the Action.

And thus much touching his worthy and noble Relation, who being an eye-witnesse, would not for his honour and vertues sake abuse his Soueraigne with vntruths.

Now let vs see what the Spanyards say of this rich Kingdome. First, *Alonso*, a chiefe Gouernour in the *Grand Canaria*, saith ; that there was a Land newly discouered, called *Nueuo Dorado*, in which *The testimony of the Spaniards for the wealth of Guiana.* was abundance of Gold, and wonderfull riches aboue imagination : that the course to fall with it, was fifty leagues to the winde-ward to the *Marguarita.*

Againe hee saith in another affirmation, that in *Nueuo Dorado* lately found out there was gold in that abundance, as the like hath neuer formerly been heard of, nor was any part of the world

world to be compared with it; and the like affirmeth *Domingo de Vera* who was Campe Maister and Generall for *Anthony Bereo* in this Discouery, and no lesse saith *Rodrigo de Caranoa*

The conclusion. Register for the Sea, and many others: So that to conclude your trouble and the tediousnes of my weary discourse, this Empire is that rich *Magazany* which yet hath her Maidenhead neuer sackt, turn'd, nor wrought, the face of the earth hath not beene turnd nor the vertue and salt of the soyle spent by manurance, The graues haue not been opened for Gold, the Mines not broken with the sledge or pickaxe, nor their Images puld downe out of their Temples. It hath neuer beene entred by any army of strength, and neuer conquered or possessed by any Christian Prince: Besides by the report of all former Discouerers, especially our Generall, it is so defensible and easie to bee kept from the assaults of any inuaders, that if two Forts bee builded in one of the Prouinces which he beheld and tooke especiall note of; the flood setteth in so neere the banke where the channell also lyeth that no Ship can passe vp, but within a pikes length, of the artillery, first of the one, and afterwards of the other, which two Forts he supposeth will bee sufficient guard, both to the Empire of *Inga*, and to one hundred other seuerall Kingdomes, all lying within the great Riuer of *Orenoque*, euen to the Citty of *Quito* in *Peru*.

Of this Empire if it shall please God to make the King our Maister Soueraigne, what honor and reward it will bring him and his Subiects may easily bee coniectured by what is before written; and since it is or may bee vndertaken by his owne vassaile, and one who is bound in extraordinary bonde more then euery common Subiect, to spend the vttermost of his life in the same, no doubt but hee will effect it with that wisedome, diligence, and care which shall bee sutable to the greatnes of the action, and the trust reposed, being thus far forth further encouraged by *Anthonio Bereo* the Spaniard, who in great earnestnes, and

A strange Prophesie. vpon his Soules health protested, that hee had seene amongst diuers most antient Prophesies in

Peru (at such time as that Empire was reduced to the Spanish obedience) one that affirmed, that from *Inglatierra* (which is to say, England) those *Ingas* should bee againe in time to come restored and deliuered from the seruitude of the former Conquerors, and this hee auowed to haue seene in diuers of their most principall and chiefest Temples, preserued with great reuerence and care, and till this day beleeued of all the Indians: Now an entrance in former yeares our Generall did make, as you haue read, with that successe that not any before or since hath euer equalled & displanted the first garrisons, if then now he succeed

ceed and haue fortune answerable to his rare wisedome, industry and direction, whether it bee in this or any other to himselfe onely concealed, there is no doubt but (God assisting) hee will with such honor and high thoughts, passe and go thorow the same, that his nation shall haue praise, his friendes comfort, and himselfe the true aduancement of his merits.

But to giue you a little tast of what hath succeeded in our present Iourney, you shall vnderstand that we departed from *Plimouth* to *Corke* in Ireland, where after some refreshment wee set saile out of the riuer of *Corke,* and thence sailed more than three Moneths before we came to the Coast of *Guiana,* which albeit generally it bee euer run in seauen or eight weekes, yet were the windes so strangely crosse vnto vs, (a thing seldome seene in that passage) that in lesse time we could not effect our purpose: So that vpon the seauenth day of Nouember last past, 1 6 1 7. wee discouered the Coast of *Guiana,* during which time of our being at Sea, we had a great visitation of Sicknesse, so that many were sick, and some are dead, amongst which, the most eminent persons that dyed were these. Captaine *Iohn Pygot* our Lieftenant Generall, worthy Captaine *Hastings,* my Lord of *Huntingtons* brother, a Gentleman of so much foreward hope, and goodnes, that that he was couered with many teares, and much mourning; also there died Maister *Talbot* Scholler, which hath been long imployed by our Generall; M. *Newball,* the maister Chirurgeon of our Generalls Ship, and others, with which I will not trouble your eares.

Vpon the discouering of the Coast, we came into the faire Riuer of *Caliana,* being (as it appeareth to me) a branch of *Oerenoque,* where my Lord, our Generall cast Anchor, and doth purpose to refresh his sick men, and to take in fresh water and other necessary prouisions, of which that Coast aboundeth, and so to proceed in his enterprise which God in his mercy prosper, for our hopes euery day grow stronger and stronger. This part of *Guiana* in which we now are, is to me a very Paradise, and so excellent in all perfections and beauties, that Nature seemes only here to haue her Temple; we haue euen now (being the Month of Nouember) a much more delicate Sommer, then is in England at Mid-sommer, the Sun and Ayre so wholesome & pleasant without offence or scorching, the trees & ground so brauely flourishing, and euery thing in Generall so absolute and full of fruitfull promise, that more cannot be by man desired: for mine own part I dare assure you, that in my life time I neuer saw or tasted more strange, more delicate, & more pleasant fruits, then heere we may continually gather in most infinite aboundance, being besides so wondrous wholsome and vnoffensiue, that I haue not heard

any

any complaine either of surfet, or other accidentall sicknes, as wormes, fluxes & such like, which commonly follow the much eating of sweet and pleasant fruit.   To enter into a Description of the beautifull prospect of this Country which wee now see, although it be but the out-borders and skirts of the Empire, so neare a neighbour to the maine Ocean, that in reason it should promise the least fertilitie ; yet I say againe, to describe the good-linesse thereof, the brauery of the Hils, and comlinesse of the vallies, both shadowed and adorned with goodly tall green trees ; the pleasantnesse and coolnesse of the Riuers which runne and mixe themselues in the most conuenientest places, plentifully stored with fish of seuerall natures ; the variety of rare coloured Birds which flie vp and down in euery place about vs, no colour almost vnder the Sun but being reuealed in their fea-thers : were to draw a Landskip of that excellent perfection, which no Art could better, hardly imitate. For truely hitherto to mine eye this Country hath appeared a very earthly Paradise, and therefore doubtlesse is full of strong promises, that our at-temptings cannot returne without much honour and reward, a rent hopefully due to euery such noble action.   But since it yet resteth in hope, I will leaue it to the will and direction of the great G O D of Heauen : To whose protection I refer you, with this assurance, that as our successe shall happen, and the action either decrease or diminish, so you shall by writing more amply vnderstand thereof.

From the Riuer of *Caliana* on the Coast of *Guiana*, this seauen-teenth of *Nouember*, 1617.   *R. M.*

FINIS.

A
DECLARATION
OF THE STATE OF
the COLONIE and Affaires
in *VIRGINIA:*

WITH

The Names of the Aduenturors,
and Summes aduentured in

that Action.

By his Maiesties Counseil for
VIRGINIA. 22. Iunij. 1620.

LONDON:
Printed by *T. S.* 1620.

Force's Collection of Historical Tracts.

Vol. III.—No. 5.

By his Maiesties Counseil

for VIRGINIA.

Fter the many disasters, wherewith it pleased Almighty God to suffer the great Enemy of all good Actions, and his Instruments, to encounter and interrupt, to oppresse and keepe weake, this noble Action for the planting of *Virginia*, with Christian Religion, and English people : It hauing pleased him now, contrarily, of his especiall great grace, so to blesse and prosper our late carefull endeuours, as well for the repairing of all former breaches, as for supplying of the present defects, wherewith the Colony was kept downe, that it hath as it were on a sodaine growne to double that height, strength, plenty, and prosperity, which it had in former times attained : We haue thought it now the peculiar duety of our place, accordingly as it hath beene also ordered by a generall Court, to Summon, as it were by a kinde of louing inuitement, the whole Body of the Noble and other worthy Aduenturors, as well to the conseruing and perfecting of this happy worke, as to the reaping of the fruit of their great expenses and trauailes.

And first to remoue that vnworthy aspersion, wherewith ill disposed mindes, guiding their Actions by corrupt ends, haue, both by Letters from thence, and by rumours here at home, sought vniustly to staine and blemish that Countrey, as being barren and vnprofitable ;—Wee haue thought it necessary, for the full satisfaction of all, to make it publikely knowne, that, by diligent examination, wee haue assuredly found, those Letters and Rumours to haue been false and malicious ; procured by practise, and suborned to euill purposes : And contrarily disadvowed by the testimony, vpon Oath, of the chiefe Inhabitants of all the Colony ; by whom we are ascertained, that the Countrey is rich, spacious, and well watered ; temperate as for the Climate ;

mate ; very healthfull after men are a little accustomed to it ;
abounding with all Gods naturall blessings : The Land replenished with the goodliest Woods in the world, and those full of
Deere, and other Beasts of sustenance : The Seas and Riuers
(whereof many are exceeding faire and nauigable,) full of excellent Fish, and of all sorts desireable ; both Water and Land
yeelding Fowle in very great store and variety : In Summe, a
Countrey, too good for ill people ; and wee hope reserued by
the prouidence of God, for such as shall apply themselues faithfully to his seruice, and be a strength and honour to our King
and Nation. But touching those Commodities for which that
Countrey is proper, and which haue beene lately set vp for the
Aduenturors benefit : we referre you to a true note of them,
lately deliuered in a great and generall Court, and hereunto annexed for your better information. By which and other approued informations brought vnto vs, Wee rest in great assurance, that this Countrey, as it is seated neere the midst of the
world, betweene the extreamities of heate and cold ; So it also
participateth of the benefits of bothe, and is capable (being assisted with skill and industry) of the richest commodities of most
parts of the Earth. The rich Furres, Cauiary, and Cordage,
which we draw from *Russia* with so great difficulty, are to be
had in *Virginia*, and the parts adioyning, with ease and plenty.
The Masts, Planckes, and Boords, the Pitch and Tarre, the
Pot-ashes and Sope-ashes, the Hempe and Flax, (being the
materials of Linnen,) which now we fetch from *Norway*, *Denmarke*, *Poland*, and *Germany*, are there to be had in abundance
and great perfection. The *Iron*, which hath so wasted our *English* Woods, that it selfe in short time must decay together with
them, is to be had in *Virginia* (where wasting of Woods is a
benefit) for all good conditions answerable to the best in the
world. The Wines, Fruite, and Salt of *France* and *Spaine*;
The Silkes of *Persia* and *Italie*, will be found also in *Virginia*,
and in no kinde of worth inferior. Wee omit here a multitude
of other naturall Commodities, dispersed vp and downe the diuers parts of the world : of Woods, Rootes, and Berries, for
excellent Dyes : Of Plants and other Drugges, for Physicall seruice : Of sweet Woods, Oyles, and Gummes, for pleasure and
other vse : Of Cotton-wooll, and Sugar-Canes : all which may
there also be had in abundance, with an infinity of other more :
And will conclude with these three, Corne, Cattle, and Fish,
which are the substance of the foode of man. The Graines of
our Countrey doe prosper there very well : Of Wheate they
haue great plenty : But their *Maze*, being the naturall Graine
of

of that Countrey, doth farre exceede in pleasantnesse, strength, and fertility. The Cattle which we haue transported thither, (being now growne neere to fiue hundred,) become much bigger of Body, then the breed from which they came: The Horses also more beautifull, and fuller of courage. And such is the extraordinary fertility of that *Soyle*, that the *Does* of their *Deere* yeelde two Fawnes at a birth, and sometimes three. The Fishings at *Cape Codd*, being within those Limits, will in plenty of Fish be equall to those of *Newfound Land*, and in goodnesse and greatnesse much superiour. To conclude, it is a Countrey, which nothing but ignorance can thinke ill of, and which no man but of a corrupt minde and ill purpose can defame.

Now touching the present estate of our Colony in that Country, Wee haue thought it not vnfit thus much briefly to declare. There haue beene sent thither this last yeare, and are now presently in going, twelue hundred persons and vpward, as particularly appeareth in the note aboue specified: and there are neere one thousand more remaining of those that were gone before. The men lately sent, haue beene most of them choise men, borne and bred vp to labour and industry. Out of *Deuonshire*, about an hundred men, brought vp to Husbandry. Out of *Warwickshire* and *Staffordshire*, aboue one hundred and ten; and out of *Sussex* about forty; all framed to *Iron*-workes: the rest dispersedly out of diuers Shires of the Realme. There haue been also sundry persons of good quality, much commended for sufficiency, industry and honesty, prouided and sent to take charge and gouernment of those people. The care likewise that hath beene taken by directions, Instructions, Charters, and Commissions to reduce the people and affaires in *Virginia* into a regular course, hath beene such and so great, that the Colony beginneth now to haue the face and fashion of an orderly State, and such as is likely to grow and prosper. The people are all diuided into seuerall Burroughs; each man hauing the shares of Land due to him set out, to hold and enioy to him and his Heires. The publique Lands for the Company here, for the Gouernor there, for the College, and for each particular Burrough, for the Ministers also, and for diuers other necessary Officers, are likewise laid out by order, and bounded. The particular Plantations for diuers priuate Societies, are setled in their Seates, being alotted to their content, and each in conuenient distance. The rigour of Martiall Law, wherewith before they were gouerned, is reduced within the limits prescribed by his Maiesty: and the laudable forme of Iustice and gouernment

vsed

vsed in this Realme, established, and followed as neere as may be. The Gouernour is so restrained to a Counseil ioyned with him, that hee can doe wrong to no man, who may not haue speedy remedy. Each Burrough, and each particular Plantation, partly hath, partly is bound to haue in short time, a sufficient Minister: for whom maintenance is ordained, to each of two hundred pounds a yeere value. Which orderly proceeding there, by direction from hence, hath caused the Colony now at length to settle themselues in a firme resolution to perpetuate the Plantation. They fall to building of Houses, each for his owne priuate; and the Generalitie to the rearing of publique Guest houses, for intertaining of new men vpon their first arriuall. They fall to set vp their Ploughes; to the planting of *Vineyards;* to the pursuing of the Staple Commodities furnished and commended from hence. In summe they are now so full of alacritie and cheerefulnesse, that in a late generall Assembly, they haue in the name of the Colony presented their greatest possiule thankes to the Company, for the care that hath beene taken for the setling of the Plantation. Neither is it to be omitted, the care which hath beene had here lately at home, for the reducing of all the proceedings and affaires of the Company, to an orderly course of good gouernment and Iustice. Wherein to begin with the fountaine thereof, his Maiesties authority and pleasure, there hath beene a Collection made of all the branches of the same, dispersed in his *Letters Patents,* now three times renewed: as also out of other Instructions proceeding from his Maiestie. Out of bothe which, together with such other Orders as (authorised by his Maiestie) the Company themselues haue thought necessary to make, hath beene compiled a Booke of standing Lawes and orders, approued by the generall Consent of all the Company: whereby both the company here, and the Colony in *Virginia,* haue their businesse carried regularly, industriously, and iustly, euery man knowing both his right and duety, to their generall great content, and the great aduancement of the Action. And whereas the Colony likewise haue beene often Sutors in effect, to reduce into a compendious and orderly forme in writing, the Lawes of *England* proper for the vse of that Plantation, with addition of such other, as the nature of the place, the nouitie of the Colony, and other important circumstances should necessarily require: a course is likewise taken for the effecting of this worke; yet so as to submit it first to his Maiesties view and approbation; it being not fit that his Maiesties Subjects should be gouerned by any other Lawes, then such as receiue the influence of their life from him.

And

And now to come to that which concerneth the Aduenturors in particular, by whose charges, care and labour (next vnto his Maiesties especiall grace,) this famous Plantation hath not one-ly beene vndertaken, but through so many difficulties vpheld and continued: wee should be very greatly iniurious to them, if we should not acquaint them with this seasonable time, for the reap-ing of that benefit and reward which is due vnto them. Wee therefore let them knowe, that in this last yeare now ended, there haue beene granted by the Company vnder their legall Seale, eleuen seuerall Patents for particular Plantations; and more are in hand to be passed this next Quarter-Court. It is not vnprobable, that vpon each of these Patents, diuers hun-dreds of persons will soone Plant in *Virginia:* there hauing beene already transported vpon the first, aboue three hundred men. These and other like Planters, hauing priority of time, will haue priority also in choise of the Seat of their Plantations. Seeing therefore the onely matter of retribution to the Aduen-turors, is by a faire proportion of Land to them & their heires; namely of one hundred acres for euery share of twelue pounds and ten shillings, vpon a first diuision; and as much more vpon a second, the first being peopled; with fiftie acres for euery per-son, (to be doubled in like manner) which at their owne charges they shall transport to inhabit in *Virginia* before the 24. day of *Iune* 1625. if hee continue there three yeares, either at one or seuerall times, or dye after he is shipped for that voyage: It standeth them vpon, who are not willing to be the last in the benefit to be partaked, not to be the least in setting forth to the choise and peopling of their Land. Wherein what fauour or assistance may by vs be giuen them, they shall be well assured of it, in equall proportion with our selues, as their charges and long expectance haue well deserued. And to the end that not onely the Aduenturors now liuing, but the Heires also of the de-ceased, may take certaine notice of the seuerall proportions of Land, which ratably to their Aduentures in mony are due and belonging to them: And likewise that Posteritie may truely know, by whose charges this Plantation (next vnder his Maie-stie) hath beene happily founded, maintained, and continued: Wee haue here, according to an Order of Court, set downe in an Alphabeticall Table the names of all the Aduenturors, with all their seuerall sums aduentured. Wherein if by error, or other mis-accident, there haue wrong beene done to any man; if within one twelue moneth after the date hereof, he giue no-tice and make proofe thereof to the Companies Auditors; hee shall be set right, and the Table reformed: there being not any
thing

thing more deere vnto vs, then to doe Right vnto them with all Iustifiable curtesie, who haue beene beginners and continuers of this glorious worke, tending so much to the propagating of the true seruice of Almighty God, to the adding of greatnesse and honour to our King, and to the benefit of our whole Nation in disburdening their multitude.   22. *Iunij*
1620.

A
NOTE OF THE
Shipping, Men, and Prouisions
sent to *VIRGINIA*, by the
Treasvrer and Company
in the yeere, 1 6 1 9.

Ships.

THe *Bona Noua* of 200. Tun sent } 120 per-
in August 1 6 1 9. with——— } sons.

The *Duty*, of 70. Tunne, sent in } 51. per-
Ianuary 1619. with ——— } sons.

The *Ionathan*, of 350. Tun, sent in } 200.per-
February, 1619. with ——— } sons.

The *Triall*, of 200. Tun, sent in February, } 40. persons,
1619. with ——————————— } & 60. Kine.

The *Faulcon*, of 150. Tun, sent in Feb- } 36. persons, and 52.
ruary, 1 6 1 9. with ——————— } Kine, and 4. Mares.

The *London Merchant*, of 300. Tun, sent in } 200. persons.
March, 1619. with —————————— }

The *Swan of Barnstable*, of 100. Tun, in } 71. persons.
March, 1 6 1 9. with ————————— }

The *Bonauenture*, of 240. Tun, sent in } 153. persons.
Aprill, 1 6 2 0. with—————— }

Besides these, set out by the *Treasurer* and Company, there
haue been set out by particular aduenturers for priuate *Plantations.*

The *Garland*, of 25. Tunne, sent in Iune, 1619, } 45. persons.
for Mr. *Iohn Ferrars* Plantation, with ——— }

Who are yet detained in the *Summer Islands.*

A Ship of *Bristoll*, of 80. Tunne, sent in Sep- } 45. persons.
temb. 1 6 1 9. for Mr. *Barkleys* Plantation, with }

There are also two Ships in prouiding to be shortly } 300. per-
gone, for about 300 persons more, to be sent by } sons.
priuate Aduenturers to *Virginia.* }

Summe

Summe of the persons ————————————1261.

Whereof in the eight Ships set out by the *Treasurer* and Company ——————————— } 871.

People.

Of these persons there are sent for publicke and other pious vses, these ensuing :

Tenants for the Gouernours Land, (besides fiftie sent the former spring.)——————————— } 80.
Tenants for the Companies Land. ———————— 130.
Tenants for the Colleges Land. ————————— 100.
Tenants for the Ministers glebe-Lands.———————— 50.
Young maids to make Wiues for so many of the former Tenants. ——————————— } 90.
Boyes to make Apprentices for those Tenants. ——— 100.
Seruants for the publicke. ——————————— 50.
Men sent, by their labours to beare vp the charge of bringing vp Thirty of the *Infidels* children in true Religion and ciuility. ——————————— } 50.

Summe of Persons for publicke vse, &c.————————650.

The 611. remaining, are sent for priuate *Plantations.*

Commodities.

The Commodities which these people are directed principally to apply, (next to their owne necessary maintenance) are these ensuing :

IRON: for which are sent 150. Persons, to set vp three *Iron* workes ; proofe hauing beene made of the extraordinary goodnesse of that *Iron.*
CORDAGE : for which (besides Hempe) direction is giuen for the planting of *Silke-grasse*, (naturally growing in those parts) in great abundance : which is approued to make the best Cordage and Linnen in the world. Of this, euery householder is bound to set 100 Plants : and the Gouernour himselfe hath set fiue thousand.
POT-ASHES and SOPE-ASHES, PITCH and TARRE:
for

for the making whereof the *Polackers* are returned to their
workes.

T I M B E R of all sorts, with Masts, Planks and Boords for prouision of Shipping, &c, there being not so good Timber for
all vses in any one knowne Countrey whatsoeuer. And for
the ease and encrease of diuers of these workes, prouision is
sent of men and materials, for the setting vp of sundry Sawing Milles.

S I L K E : for which that Countrey is exceeding proper, hauing innumerable store of Mulbery Trees of the best, and some
silke-wormes naturally found vpon them, producing excellent
Silke : some whereof is to be seene. For the setting vp of
which Commoditie, his Maiesty hath beene graciously pleased now the second time (the former hauing miscarried) to
bestow vpon the Company plenty of Silke-wormes seed of
his owne store, being the best.

V I N E S : whereof the Countrey yeeldeth naturally great store,
and of sundry sorts : which by culture will be brought to excellent perfection. For the effecting whereof, diuers skilfull
Vignerons are sent, with store also from hence of *Vine* plants
of the best sort.

S A L T : which workes hauing been lately suffered to decay, are
now ordered to be set vp in so great plenty, as not onely to
serue the Colony for the present ; but as is hoped in short
time also the great Fishings on those Coast.

For the following, working, and perfecting of these *Commodities*, all prouisions necessary for the present are sent in good
abundance. As likewise the People that goe, are plentifully
furnished with apparell, bedding, victuall for sixe moneths :
Implements both for House and labour, Armour, weapons,
tooles, and sundry other necessaries. And a supply of Armour,
Powder, and many necessary prouisions is made for those
of the Colonie which were there before ; yet without any preiudice to the former *Magazin*.

Gifts.

*There haue beene giuen to the Colonie this yeere by deuout
Persons, these gifts ensuing.*

Two Persons vnknowne, haue giuen faire Plate, and other rich
Ornaments for two Communion Tables ; whereof one for the
College

College, and the other for the Church of Mistrisse *Mary Robinsons* founding : who in the former yeere by her Will, gaue 200. pounds towards the founding of a Church in *Virginia*.

Another vnknowne person, (together with a godly letter) hath lately sent to the *Treasurer* 550. pounds in gold, for the bringing vp of children of the *Infidels :* first in the Knowledge of God and true Religion ; and next, in fit Trades whereby honestly to liue.

Master *Nicolas Ferrar* deceased, hath by his Will giuen 300. pounds to the College in *Virginia*, to be paid, when there shall be ten of the *Infidels* children placed in it. And in the meane time foure and twenty pounds by yeere, to be distributed vnto three discreet and Godly men in the Colony, which shall honestly bring vp three of the *Infidels* children in Christian Religion, and some good course to liue by.

An vnnamed person sent to the *Treasurer* the summe of ten pounds, for aduancing of the *Plantation*.

Patents.

There haue beene Patents granted this yeere for particular Plantations, as here ensueth :

To the Society of *Southampton* hundred.
To Master *Heath,* Recorder of *London.*
To Master *Wincopp.*
To Master *Tracie.*
To Doctor *Bohun.*
To Master *Pierce.*
To Master *Delbridge.*
To Master *Pointz.*
To Master *Barkley.*
To Captaine *Bargraue.*
To Captaine *Ward.*

Who haue vndertaken to transport to *Virginia* great multitudes of people, with store of Cattell.

It is to be knowne, that touching the College for the *Infidels* Children, it hath beene thought more expedient to beginne first with the planting and peopling of the Lands : (which hath beene done this yeere :) and afterwards to proceede to the erecting of the Fabricke, which is to be performed out of the reuenues of the Lands.

FINIS.

A
DECLARATION
of the Supplies intended to be
sent to *VIRGINIA*, in this
yeare 1 6 2 0.

By his Maiesties Counseil for
Virginia. 18.*Iulij* 1 6 2 0.

Hereas the Right Honourable, *Henry* Earle of Southampton, with the aduise and consent of the *Counseil* and *Company* for *Virginia*, hath resolued and concluded to imploy all good meanes in this present yeare, 1 6 2 0. not onely for the aduancing of the *Plantation* in strength and multitude of good people, but also for the enriching thereof with store of cattell of diuers sorts, and by setting vp or encreasing such Staple *Commodities*, as, being proper for that Countrey, may be also of most necessary vse for this Realme, and redound in fine to the greatest benefit of both *Aduenturors* and *Planters*, and lastly for the establishing there of such good *Gouernment* (originally deriued from the King's most excellent Maiestie, the first and chiefe Founder of this glorious worke) as whereby the people there, diuided in soyle onely, but still participating in the religious and happy gouernment of this their natiue Countrey, may continue alwayes as one and the same people with vs, according to the most Princely direction of his Maiestie : We haue thought it very necessarie for the seconding and forwarding of those so noble Designes, not onely to publish them to the *Aduenturors* in generall, thereby to inuite them to concurre with vs in the same, but also to set downe such particularities requisite, as whereby the preparations of all sorts needful, may vpon this timely warning, both better and more seasonably be made and compassed.

First

First therefore we haue thought fit, to make it publikely knowne, that, besides the great store of particular *Plantations*, now in prouiding, and like very shortly in large proportion to augment, the Company haue resolued in a late generall Court, by the blessing of God, to set out this yeere at the publike charge, and to send to *Virginia*, eight hundred choise persons, of the qualities ensuing : First, foure hundred, to be Tenants of the general land of the *Company*, to make vp the number of those Tenants ful 500. whereof 200. to be placed at *Elizabeth* Citie, with the *Companies* Deputie : 100 at *Henrico*, 100. at *Charles* Citie : And at *Iames* Citie there are a hundred and more already, Secondly, one hundred, to be Tenants to such Officers, &c. as the Court already hath, or shall shortly appoint : *viz.* 10. for the Deputy of the College, 40. for the *Companies* Deputy : 20. for the *Secretary :* 10. more (besides 50. already sent) for the Ministers : and 20. for the Phisitian : their care for the ease and prosperity of the *Colonie*, being such and so great, as to cause them to endowe those Offices and places, (as they haue formerly done others,) with faire possessions, furnished with Tenants and other fit prouisions : that the people may haue the benefit by them, and yet be freed from the burden. Thirdly one hundred yong Maides, to make wiues for these Tenants, as the former 90. which haue been lately sent. Fourthly, one hundred Boyes, to be apprentizes likewise to the publike Tenants. Fiftly, one hundred seruants to be disposed amongst the old *Planters*, which they greatly desire, and haue offered to defray their charges with very great thankes. And although, by reason of the preparations already made, the difficulty may be well conceiued to be in great part ouercome, and the profit much more neere, and more easie to come by, yet the *Companie* wholly affecting the peoples prosperity, haue determined to deale both as fauourably in the Contracts, and as bountifully in all sorts of furniture and prouisions, with the Tenants which shall now goe, as they haue done with those, which haue been formerly sent. Which conditions it hath beene thought fit here to reinsert and publish.

EVery man transported into Virginia, *with intent there to inhabit, as Tenants to the Common land of the* Company, *or to the publike land, shall be freely landed there at the charge of the* Company : *And shal be furnished with prouisions of victuall for one whole yeare, next after his arriuall, as also of Cattle : And with apparell, weapons, tooles and implements, both of house and labour, for his ne-*
cessary

cessary vse.   *He shall enioy the ratable moytie of all the*
profits that shall be raised of the land on which he shall be
Planted, as well Corne and Cattle, as other commodities
whatsoeuer : the other halfe being due to the Owners *of the*
Land.

   He shall be tyed by Couenant, to continue vpon that Land
for the Terme of seauen yeares : which being expired, it shal
be in his choyse, whither to continue there, or to remoue to
any other place, at his owne will and pleasure.

Of these persons, one hundred and twenty (such as are to be
Tenants) are to be shipped here for *Virginia,* by the midst of
August now at hand : and the rest in *Ianuary* and *February*
ensuing.

The next preparations are of Cattle of diuers sorts : whereof
there are intended, in the next Spring, to be sent these ensuing : One hundred Kine, for this addition of 500. Tenants : One
hundred Kine more, to remaine in a perpetuall stock vpon the
Companies Land, to be lent to new *Planters,* as hath bin formerly ordered.   Foure hundred Goats, twenty Mares, fourescore
Asses, to be procured from France : The care of prouiding
which, is commended to diuers select persons by parts, and the
whole to the ouersight of the generall *Committies.*

The last prouisions appointed to be made, are for the setting
vp, or increasing of diuers principall Commodities.   For *Silke,*
there is prouision to be made, of great store of *Silke-worme-*
seede, about *Michaelmas* next : as also of men skilfull in the ordering as well of the Wormes, as of their *Silke,* which are to
be sent away in a *Pinnace,* in *October* betimes.   For *Hempe*
and *Flaxe, Pot-ashes* and *Sope-ashes, Pitch* and *Tarre,* there
is a Treaty already on foote, for procuring of men skilfull in
those Trades from the Easterne parts : besides the *Polakers* yet
remaining in *Virginia.* For *Wines,* it is also ordered, that men
skilfull be procured, in the planting and dressing of Vines, out of
France and from the *Rhene :* and from thence also, and other
parts, to procure Plants of the best kindes.   For *Oyle,* besides
great quantitie to be made out of the Walnuts, growing naturally in *Virginia* in great abundance, *Oliue-Plants* are to be prouided from *Marseilles* and *Ligorno.* For *Fish,* which on those
Coasts are taken in great plenty, and in worth much better then
in *New-found-Land,* there is care and a course taken, to preserue the *Companies* Liberties, and to set vp the Fishings in
better sort then heretofore.   For *Salt,* order is giuen for the
making of it in abundance, and after the manner of those hotter
Climates

Climates, which may prooue a great helpe to increase the *Plantation*. For *Iron*, there is sufficient done alreadie.

And for *Sawing-Milles*, besides those already gone this Spring, there are lately come from *Hamborough*, diuers Workemen very skilfull, to be sent in the next ship. And that nothing may be wanting for the *Companies* Tenants, there is a *Pinnace* already, and other Boates shall be prouided, to remaine there at the *Deputies* commaund, to traffique and trade for the *Company* and their Tenants vnder his charge.

These large supplies of men, Cattle, and Commodities, as they tend to the accomplishing of this great worke of the Plantation ; so can they not be themselues effected, without large prouision of money, being the sinewes and mouing Instruments in these great Actions.

To which end, wee desire the noble and worthy Aduenturors, to be assisting to vs, by such meanes as they shall please : especially that the remaine of all promised Aduentures, may in Michaelmas Terme next be paid in without faile, which we trust will now be done cheerefully on all parts, the inuitements of this yeere being well considered : that as the presenting of their first payments, hath been the beginning, so the performance of the later, may be the perfecting and finishing of this worke, so glorious before God and man.

And here by the way, for the clearing of some scruples and errors, through mistaking of our writings lately published, we are to aduertise, that the *Alphabet* of Aduenturers and summes aduentured, neither then conueniently could, nor was intended to extend any further, then to such summes as haue been paid in to the Treasurors of the Company, and to Sir *Baptist Hicks*, by speciall order of Court. And whereas diuers other bils of Aduenture, haue bin heretofore deliuered, partly vpon personall aduenture, and no money paid in, partly vpon gift from the Company, in regard of deserts, partly for summes paid to other men, whose *Accounts* hang yet vncleared (and not to the *Treasurors*) and partly for goods which neuer came within the *Treasurors Accounts*, but of other inferiour Officers, into whose hands they were deliuered (for which notwithstanding bils of Aduenture haue been deliuered, mentioning as if it were money paid to the *Treasuror* : If the Aduenturors shall be pleased within the time prefixed, to put in their iust claimes, by these or any other wayes whatsoeuer, there shall be right done to them, and a new Alphabeticall booke shall be published, embracing exactly all kinde of Aduenturors, with their seuerall summes either really aduentured, or otherwise accepted, allowed or bestowed, be it vpon what cause, or in what kinde soeuer.

Now

Now if the Aduenturors be thus requested, with much greater reason are all *Accountants* to the Company to be prayed and required, to prepare and make perfect their seuerall *Accounts,* and to pay in those monyes, which shall remaine due to the Company : that so all parts concurring with their duties and endeuours, the worke may proceede with generall ioy.

Lastly, as heretofore, so we now also declare, that the persons to be admitted to goe, as the Companies-Tenants, and with the foresaid conditions, shall be no other then good men, that is to say, of good Trades, of skill in husbandry, or industrious labourers ; and such of those as shall be commended for their honest conuersation : which persons repairing to the Citie of *London* in the beginning of *August,* and in the middle of *Ianuary,* next, according to the seuerall numbers at those times to be sent, shall from thence-forward be entertained, at the *Companies* charges, till such time as they be shipped for *Virginia :* there being especiall care likewise taken, for the prouiding of good Commanders and Directors of their workes.

Giuen in a Generall Court held for *Virginia* the eighteenth of *Iuly,* 1 6 2 0.

The seuerall Trades-men to be entertained.

Husbandmen.	Potters.
Gardners.	Fowlers.
Brewers.	Fishermen.
Bakers.	Fish-hookemakers.
Sawyers.	Net-makers.
Carpenters.	Shooe-makers.
Ioyners.	Rope-makers.
Ship-wrights.	Tile-makers.
Boat-wrights.	Edgetoole-makers.
Plough-wrights.	Bricke-makers.
Mil-wrights.	Bricke-layers.
Masons.	Dressers of Hempe and Flaxe.
Turners.	Lime-burners.
Smiths of all sorts.	Lether-dressers.
Coopers of all sorts.	Men skilfull in Vines.
Weauers.	Men for Iron-workes.
Tanners.	Men skilfull in Mines.

THE

The Names of the Aduenturers,

with their seuerall sums aduentured,
paid to Sir *Thomas Smith*, Knight,
late Treasurer of the Company
for Virginia.

A

	li.	s.
Sir William Aliffe - - -	50.	
Sir Roger Aston - - -	10.	
Sir Anthony Ashley - - -	37.	10
Sir Iohn Akland - - -	12.	10
Sir Anthony Aucher - - -	12.	10
Sir Robert Askwith - - -	37.	10
Doctor Francis Anthony - - -	100.	
Charles Anthony - - - -	137.	10
Edward Allen - - - -	100.	
Edmund Allen Esquire - - -	25.	
Iohn Allen - - - -	12.	10
Thomas Allen - - - -	12.	10
William Atkinson, Esquire - -	37.	10
Richard Ashcroft - - -	25.	
Nicholas Andrews - - -	62.	10
Iohn Andrews the elder - -	25.	
Iohn Andrews the younger - -	25.	
Iames Ascough - - -	37.	10
Giles Allington - - -	25.	
Morris Abbott - - -	50.	
Ambrose Asten - - -	12.	10
Iames Askew - - -	25.	
Anthony Abdey - - -	37.	10
Iohn Arundell, Esquire - -	25.	

B

	li.	s.
Edward, Earle of Bedford - -	120.	
Iames, Lord Bishop of Bathe & Wells -	75.	
Sir Francis Barrington - - -	37.	10
Sir Morice Barkley - - -	80.	
Sir Iohn Benet - - - -	25.	

Sir

				li.	s.
Sir Thomas Beamont	-	-	-	-	25.	
Sir Amias Bamfield	-	-	-	-	12.	10
Sir Iohn Bourcher	-	-	-	-	37.	10
Sir Edmund Bowyer	-	-	-	-	12.	10
Sir Thomas Bludder	-	-	-	-	25.	
Sir George Bolles	-	-	-	-	37.	10
Sir Iohn Bingley	-	-	-	-	125.	
Sir Thomas Button	-	-	-	-	25.	
Company of Barber-surgeons	-	-	-	25.	
Company of Bakers	-	-	-	-	40.	
Richard Banister -	-	-	-	-	50.	
Iohn Bancks	-	-	-	-	112.	10
Miles Bancks	-	-	-	-	50.	
Thomas Barber	-	-	-	-	62.	10
William Bonham -	-	-	-	-	120.	
Iames Bryerley	-	-	-	-	87.	10
William Barners -	-	-	-	-	37.	10
Anthony Barners, Esquire	-	-	-	100.	
William Brewster	-	-	-	-	20.	
Richard Brooke	-	-	-	-	50.	
Hugh Brooker, Esquire	-	-	-	50.	
Ambrose Brewsey	-	-	-	-	12.	10
Iohn Brooke	-	-	-	-	12.	10
Matthew Bromridge	-	-	-	-	50.	
Christofer Brooke, Esquire	-	-	-	50.	
Martin Bond	-	-	-	-	12.	10
Gabriel Beadle	-	-	-	-	12.	10
Iohn Beadle	-	-	-	-	12.	10
Dauid Borne	-	-	-	-	25.	
Edward Barnes	-	-	-	-	50.	
Iohn Badger	-	-	-	-	12.	10
Edmund Branduell	-	-	-	-	25.	
Robert Bowyer, Esquire	-	-	-	25.	
Robert Bateman -	-	-	-	-	25.	
Thomas Britton	-	-	-	-	25.	
Nicholas Benson -	-	-	-	-	75.	
Edward Bishop	-	-	-	-	75.	
Peter Burgoney -	-	-	-	-	25.	
Thomas Burgoney	-	-	-	-	12.	10
Robert Burgoney	-	-	-	-	12.	10
Christofer Baron	-	-	-	-	62.	10
Peter Benson	-	-	-	-	25.	
Iohn Baker	-	-	-	-	25.	
Iohn Bustoridge -	-	-	-	-	25.	

Francis

	li.	s.
Francis Burley - - - - -	25.	
William Browne - - - - -	12.	10
Robert Barker - - - - -	25.	
Samuel Burnham - - - -	12.	10
Edward Barkley - - - - -	12.	10
William Bennet - - - -	25.	
Captain Edward Brewster - -	30.	
Thomas Brocket - - - -	25.	
Iohn Bullock - - - -	25.	
George Bache - - - -	12.	10
Thomas Bayly - - - -	12.	10
William Barkley - - - -	12.	10
George Butler - - - -	25.	
Timothy Bathurst - - -	25.	
George Burton - - - -	12.	10
Thomas Brett - - - -	35.	
Captaine Iohn Brough - - -	25.	
Thomas Baker - - - -	100.	
Iohn Blunt - - - -	12.	10
Thomas Bayly - - - -	25.	
Richard and Edward Blunt - -	12.	10
Mineon Burrell - - - -	12.	10
Richard Blackmore - - -	25.	
William Beck - - - -	25.	
Beniamin Brand - - - -	12.	10
Iohn Busbridge - - - -	37.	10
William Burrell - - - -	37.	10
William Barret - - - -	25.	
Francis Baldwin - - - -	12.	10
Edward Barber - - - -	12.	10
Humfrey Basse - - - -	25.	
Robert Bell - - - -	37.	10
Matthew Bromrick - - -	16.	
Iohn Beaumont - - - -	12.	10
George Barkeley - - - -	12.	10
Peter Bartle - - - -	37.	10
Thomas Bretton - - - -	12.	10
Iohn Blount - - - -	25.	
Arthur Bromfeld Esquire - -	25.	
William Berbloke - - -	12.	10
Charles Beck - - - -	25.	

C

George, Lord Archbishop of Canterbury - - 75.

William

	li.	s.
William Lord Cranborne, now Earle of Salisbury -	25.	
William, Lord Compton, now Earle of North-hampton	100.	
William, Lord Cauendish, now Earle of Deuonshire	137.	10
Richard, Earle of Clanricard - - -	20.	
Sir William Cauendish, now Lord Cauendish -	25.	
Gray, Lord Chandos - - - -	50.	
Sir Henry Cary - - - - -	20.	
Sir George Caluert - - - -	25.	
Sir Lionell Cranfield - - - -	12.	10
Sir Edward Cecill - - - -	25.	
Sir Robert Cotten - - - -	25.	
Sir Oliuer Cromwell - - - -	65.	
Sir Anthony Cope - - - -	40.	
Sir Walter Cope - - - - -	165.	
Sir Edward Carr - - - - -	12.	10
Sir Thomas Conisbie - - - -	50.	
Sir George Cary - - - -	45.	
Sir Edward Conwey - - - -	100.	
Sir Walter Chute - - - -	25.	
Sir Edward Culpeper - - - -	12.	10
Sir Henry Cary, Captaine - - -	25.	
Sir Walter Couert - - - -	12.	10
Sir William Crauen - - - -	75.	
Sir George Coppin - - - -	115.	
Sir George Chute - - - -	12.	10
Sir Thomas Couentry - - - -	12.	10
Lady Cary - - - - -	12.	10
Company of Clothworkers - - -	100.	
City of Chichester - - - -	25.	
Robert Chamberlaine - - - -	100.	
Richard Chamberlaine - - - -	150.	
Francis Couill - - - - -	112.	10
William Coyse, Esquire - - -	100.	
Abraham Chamberlaine - - - -	112.	10
Thomas Carpenter - - - -	49.	3
Anthony Crew - - - - -	25.	
Richard Cox - - - - -	25.	
William Crosley - - - - -	75.	
Iames Chatfield - - - - -	12.	10
Richard Caswell - - - -	125.	
Iohn Cornelis - - - - -	62.	10
Randall Carter - - - - -	100.	
Executors of Randall Carter - - -	25.	
Richard Champion - - - -	37.	10

Rawley

				li.	s.
Rawley Crashaw -	-	-	-	25.	
Henry Collins -	-	-	-	12.	10
Henry Cromwell -	-	-	-	25.	
Iohn Cooper -	-	-	-	25.	
Richard Cooper -	-	-	-	25.	
Thomas Colthurst	-	-	-	25.	
Iohn Casson -	-	-	-	50.	
Allen Cotten -	-	-	-	62.	10
Edward Cage -	-	-	-	87.	10
Abraham Carthwright	-	-	-	75.	
Robert Coppin -	-	-	-	12.	10
Thomas Conock -	-	-	-	25.	
Iohn Clapham -	-	-	-	25.	
Thomas Church -	-	-	-	62.	10
William Carpenter	-	-	-	37.	10
Laurence Campe	-	-	-	100.	
Iames Cambell -	-	-	-	25.	
Christofer Cletheroe	-	-	-	50.	
Matthew Cooper -	-	-	-	25.	
George Chamber	-	-	-	12.	10
Captaine Iohn Cooke -	-	-	-	25.	
Captaine Thomas Conwey, Esquire	-	-	37.	10
Edward Culpeper, Esquire	-	-	-	25.	
Master William Crashaw -	-	-	37.	10
Abraham Colmer -	-	-	-	12.	10
Iohn Culpeper -	-	-	-	37.	10
Edmund Colbey -	-	-	-	12.	10
Richard Cooper -	-	-	-	12.	10
Robert Creswell -	-	-	-	12.	10
William Crowe -	-	-	-	12.	10
Abraham Carpenter	-	-	-	12.	10
Iohn Crowe -	-	-	-	37.	10
Thomas Cordel -	-	-	-	50.	
Richard Connock, Esquire	-	-	-	20.	
William Compton	-	-	-	25.	
William Chester -	-	-	-	12.	10
Thomas Couel -	-	-	-	25.	
Richard Carmarden, Esquire	-	-	-	25.	
William and Paul Canning	-	-	37.	10
Henry Cromwell, Esquire	-	-	37.	10
Simon Codrington	-	-	-	12.	10
Clement Chichley	-	-	-	25.	
Iames Cullemore	-	-	-	25.	
William Cantrel -	-	-	-	12.	10

D Richard

D

	li.	s.
Richard Eale of Dorset - - - -	120.	
Edward Lord Denny - - - -	13.	6. 8
Sir Iohn Digbie, now Lord Digbie - -	25.	
Sir Iohn Doderidge - - - -	25.	
Sir Drew Drewry the elder - - -	75.	
Sir Thomas Dennis - - : -	30.	
Sir Robert Drewry - - - -	10.	
Sir Iohn Dauers - - - -	25.	
Sir Dudley Diggs - - - -	37.	10
Sir Marmaduke Dorrel - - -	50.	
Sir Thomas Dale - - - -	25.	
Dompany of Drapers - - -	150.	
Company of Dyers - - - -	75.	
Towne of Douer - - - -	25.	
Master Richard Deane, Alderman - -	37.	10
Henry Dawkes - - - -	25.	
Edward Dichfeild - - -	68.	15
William Dunne - - - -	25.	
Iohn Dauis - - - -	25.	
Matthew Dequester - - -	87.	10
Philip Durdent - - - -	25.	
Abraham Dawes - - - -	62.	10
Iohn Dyke - - - -	50.	
Thomas Draper - - - -	87.	10
Lancelot Dauis - - - -	25.	
Rowley Dawsey - - - -	25.	
William Dobson Esquire - - -	37.	10
Anthony Dyot Esquire - - -	25.	
Auery Dranfield - - - -	25.	
Roger Dye - - - -	37.	10
Iohn Downes - - - -	37.	10
Iohn Drake - - - -	12.	10
Iohn Delbridge - - - -	37.	10
Beniamin Decroe - - -	37.	10
Thomas Dyke - - - -	25.	
Ieffrey Duppa - - - -	50.	
Daniel Darnelly - - - -	45.	
Sara Draper - - - -	12.	10
Clement and Henry Dawkney - -	20.	

E

Thomas, Earle of Exeter - - -	140.	

Sir

				li.	s.
Sir Thomas Euerfield	-	-	-	- 12.	10
Sir Francis Egiock	-	-	-	- 37.	10
Iohn Eldred, Esquire	-	-	-	- 137.	10
William Euans	-	-	-	- 87.	10
Richard Euans	-	-	-	- 50.	
Hugh Euans	-	-	-	- 50.	
Raph Ewens, Esquire	-	-	-	- 37.	10
Iohn Elkin	-	-	-	- 75.	
Iohn Elkin	-	-	-	- 25.	
Robert Euelin	-	-	-	- 17.	
Nicholas Exton	-	-	-	- 74.	10
Iohn Exton	-	-	-	- 12.	10
George Etheridge	-	-	-	- 62.	10

F

Sir Moyle Finch	-	-	-	- 50.	
Sir Henry Fanshaw	-	-	-	- 70.	
Sir Thomas Freake	-	-	-	- 25.	
Sir Peter Fretchuile	-	-	-	- 37.	10
Sir William Fleetwood	-	-	-	- 37.	10
Sir Henry Fane	-	-	-	- 12.	10
Company of Fishmongers	-	-	-	- 150.	
Iohn Fletcher	-	-	-	- 62.	10
Iohn Farmer	-	-	-	- 100.	
Martin Freeman, Esquire	-	-	-	- 75.	
Raph Freeman	-	-	-	- 62.	10
William, and Raph Freeman	-	-	-	- 25.	
Michael Fetiplace	-	-	-	- 12.	10
William Fetiplace	-	-	-	- 10.	
Thomas Forrest	-	-	-	- 50.	
Edward Fleetwood, Esquire	-	-	-	- 62.	10
William Felgate	-	-	-	- 62.	10
William Field	-	-	-	- 25.	
Nicholas Ferrar	-	-	-	- 50.	
Giles Francis	-	-	-	- 50.	
Edward Fawcet	-	-	-	- 75.	
Richard Farrington	-	-	-	- 25.	
Iohn Francklin	-	-	-	- 25.	
Richard Frith	-	-	-	- 25.	
Iohn Ferne	-	-	-	- 25.	
George Farmer	-	-	-	- 25.	
Thomas Francis	-	-	-	- 12.	10
Iohn Fenner	-	-	-	- 50.	

Nicholas

	li.	s.
Nicholas Fuller, Esquire -	20.	
Thomas Foxall -	37.	10
William Fleet -	37.	10
Peter Franck, Esquire -	12.	10
Richard Fishborne -	25.	
William Faldoe -	12.	10
Iohn Fletcher, and Company -	75.	
William Ferrers -	37.	10

G

Lady Elizabeth Gray -	25.	
Sir Iohn Gray -	12.	10
Sir William Godolfine -	37.	10
Sir Thomas Gates -	100.	
Sir William Gee -	25.	
Sir Richard Grobham -	50.	
Sir William Garaway -	83. 6. 8	
Sir Francis Goodwin -	37.	10
Sir George Goring -	25.	
Company of Grocers -	487.	10
Company of Goldsmiths -	200.	
Company of Girdlers -	50.	
Iohn Geeringe -	112.	10
Iohn Gardiner -	75.	
Richard Gardiner -	12.	10
Iohn Gilbert -	62.	10
Thomas Graue -	25.	
Iohn Gray -	25.	
Nicholas Greice -	25.	
Richard Goddard -	25.	
Thomas Gipps -	12.	10
Peter Gates -	12.	10
Thomas Gibbs Esquire -	12.	10
Laurence Grene -	37.	10
William Greenwell -	100.	
Robert Garset -	12.	10
Robert Gore -	37.	10
Thomas Gouge -	12.	10
Francis Glanuile Esquire -	37.	10

H

| Henrie, Earle of Huntingdon - | 120. | |

Lord

		li.	s.
Lord Theophilus Haward, L. Walden -	-	137.	10
Sir Iohn Harington, L. Harington	-	187.	10
Sir Iohn Hollis, now Lord Hautein	-	50.	
Sir Thomas Holecroft - - -	-	10.	
Sir William Harris - - -	-	75.	
Sir Thomas Harefleet - - -	-	12.	10
Sir George Haiward ﹙ - -	-	12.	10
Sir Warwick Heale - - -	-	37.	10
Sir Baptist Hicks - - -	-	100.	
Sir Iohn Hanham - - -	-	12.	10
Sir Thomas Horwell - - -	-	37.	10
Sir Thomas Hewit - - -	-	75.	
Sir William Herrick - - -	-	25.	
Sir Eustace Hart - - -	-	25.	
Sir Arthur Harris - - -	-	37.	10
Sir Edward Heron - - -	-	25.	
Sir Ferdinando Heiborne - - -	-	37.	10
Sir Laurence Hide - - -	-	37.	10
Master Hugh Hamersley, Alderman	-	25.	
Master Richard Herone, Alderman	-	37.	10
Richard Humble Esquire -	-	100.	
Master Richard Hackleuit -	-	21.	
Edward Harrison - - -	-	112.	10
George Holeman - - -	-	100.	
Robert Hill - - -	-	87.	10
Griffin Hinton - - -	-	12.	10
Iohn Hawkins - - -	-	25.	
William Hancock - - -	-	62.	10
Iohn Harper - - -	-	62.	10
George Hawger - - -	-	25.	
Iohn Holt - - -	-	12.	10
Iohn Huntley - - -	-	25.	
Ieremy Heidon - - -	-	75.	
Raph Hamor - - -	-	133. 6. 8	
Raph Hamor, Iunior - -	-	25.	
Iohn Hodgeson - - -	-	25.	
Iohn Hanford - - -	-	37.	10
Thomas Harris - - -	-	25.	
Richard Howell - - -	-	12.	10
Thomas Henshaw - - -	-	75.	
Leonard Harwood - - -	-	37.	10
Tristram Hill - - -	-	25.	
Francis Haselridge - - -	-	12.	10
Tobias Hinson - - -	-	45.	

Peter

	li.	s.
Peter Heightley - - - - -	25.	
George Hawkenson - - - -	12.	10
Thomas Hackshaw - - - -	12.	10
Charles Hawkens - - - -	62.	10
Iohn Hodgis - - . - -	50.	
William Holland - - - -	12.	10
Robert Hartley - - - - -	12.	10
Gregory Herst - - - - -	12.	10
Thomas Hodgis - - - - -	37.	10
William Hodgis - - - - -	25.	
Roger Harris - - - - -	68.	15
Iohn Harris - - - - -	37.	10
Master Iohn Haiward - - -	100.	
Iames Haiward - - ᴸ - -	12.	10
Nicholas Hide, Esquire - - -	37.	10
Iohn Hare, Esquire - - -	37.	10
William Hackwell, Esquire - -	12.	10
Gressam Hoogan - - - -	37.	10
Humfrey Hanford - - - -	50.	
William Haselden - - - -	12.	10
Nicholas Hooker - - - -	25.	
Doctor Anthony Hunton - - -	25.	
Iohn Hodsale - - - -	12.	10
George Hooker - - - - -	25.	
Anthony Hinton - - - -	12.	10
Iohn Hogsell - - - - -	25.	
Thomas Hampton - - - -	25.	
William Hicks - - - - -	30.	
William Holiland - - - -	37.	10
Ralph Harison - - - - -	25.	
Harman Harison - - - -	25.	

I

	li.	s.
Sir Thomas Iermyn - - - -	12.	10
Sir Robert Iohnson - - - -	56.	
Sir Arthur Ingram - - - -	25.	
Sir Francis Iones - - - -	37.	10
Company of Ironmongers - - -	33. 6.	8
Company of Inholders - - -	25.	
Company of Imbroyderers - - -	25.	
Bailiffes of Ipswich - - - -	100.	
Henry Iackson - - - - -	25.	
Richard Ironside - - - -	75.	

Master

	li.	s.
Master Robert Iohnson, Alderman - -	185.	
Thomas Iones - - - -	12.	10
William Iobson - - - -	25.	
Thomas Iohnson - - - -	62.	10
Thomas Iadwine - - - -	75.	
Iohn Iosua - - - -	12.	10
George Isam - - - -	37.	10
Philip Iacobson - - - -	62.	10
Peter Iacobson - - - -	25.	
Thomas Iuxson senior - - -	25.	
Iames Iewell - - - -	25.	
Gabriel Iacques - - - -	25.	
Walter Iobson - - - -	25.	
Edward Iames - - - -	37.	10
Zachary Iones Esquire - - -	10.	
Anthony Irbye Esquire - - -	12.	10
William I-anson - - - -	37.	10
Humfrey Iobson - - - -	12.	10

K

Sir Valentine Knightley - - -	37.	10
Sir Robert Killegrew - - -	110.	
Sir Charles Kelke - - -	25.	
Sir Iohn Kaile - - - -	25.	
Richard Kirrill - - - -	37.	10
Iohn Kirrill - - - -	75.	
Raph King - - - -	62.	10
Henry Kent - - - -	25.	
Towne of Kingslynne - - -	75.	
Iohn Kettleby, Esquire - - -	25.	
Walter Kirkham, Esquire - - -	16.	

L

Henry, Earl of Lincolne - - -	50.	
Robert, L. Lisle, now Earle of Leicester -	90.	
Thomas, Lord Laware - - -	500.	
Sir Francis Leigh - - -	33. 6. 8	
Sir Iohn Lewson - - -	12.	10
Sir William Lower - - -	37.	10
Sir Samuel Leonard - - -	37.	10
Sir Samson Leonard - - -	12.	10
Company of Lethersellers - -	50.	
Thomas Laughton - - -	62.	10

William

	li.	s.
William Lewson - - - - -	37.	10
Peter Latham - - - - -	12.	10
Peter Van Lore - - - - -	112.	10
Henry Leigh - - - - -	12.	10
Thomas Leuer - - - - -	62.	10
Christofer Landman - - -	50.	
Morris Lewellin - - - - -	37.	10
Edward Lewis - - - -	37.	10
Edward Lewkin - - - -	87.	10
Peter Lodge - - - -	12.	10
Thomas Layer - - - -	12.	10
Thomas Lawson - - -	12.	10
Francis Lodge - - - -	25.	
Iohn Langley - - - -	25.	
Dauid Loide - - - -	12.	10
Iohn Leuitt - - - -	25.	
Thomas Fox and Luke Lodge - -	25.	
Captaine Richard Linley - - -	25.	
Arnold Lulls - - -	50.	
William Laurence - - -	12.	10
Iohn Landman - - - -	25.	
Nicholas Lichfield - - -	6.	5
Nicholas Leate - - - -	25.	
Gedeon de Laune - - -	37.	10

M

Philip Earle of Montgomerie - - -	40.	
Doctor George Mountain, now Lord Bishop of Lincolne - - - -	12.	10
William Lord Mounteagle now Lord Morley -	50.	
Sir Thomas Mansell - - -	50.	
Sir Thomas Mildmay - - -	12.	10
Sir William Maynard - - -	12.	10
Sir Humfrey May - - -	31.	10
Sir Peter Manhood - - -	50.	
Sir Iohn Merrick - - -	75.	
Sir George More - - -	75.	
Sir Robert Mansell - - -	97.	10
Sir Arthur Mannering - - -	25.	
Sir Dauid Murrey - - -	37.	10
Sir Edward Michelborn - - -	12.	10
Sir Thomas Middleton - - -	62.	10
Sir Robert Miller - - -	37.	10

Sir

				li.	s.
Sir Caualiero Maicott	-	-	-	- 125.	
Doctor Iames Meddus	-	-	-	- 15.	
Richard Martin, Esquire	-	-	-	- 75.	
Company of Mercers	-	-	-	- 200.	
Company of Merchant Taylors	-	-	-	- 200.	
Otho Mawdite	-	-	-	62.	10
Captaine Iohn Martin	-	-	-	- 70.	
Arthur Mouse	-	-	-	- 37.	10
Adrian More	-	-	-	- 100.	
Thomas Mountford	-	-	-	20.	
Thomas Morris	-	-	-	- 87.	10
Ralph Moorton	-	-	-	- 30.	
Francis Mapes	-	-	-	12.	10
Richard Maplesden	-	-	-	- 50.	
Iames Monger	-	-	-	- 25.	
Peter Monsell	-	-	-	- 75.	
Robert Middleton	-	-	-	- 37.	10
Thomas Maile	-	-	-	- 25.	
Iohn Martin	-	-	-	- 25.	
Iosias Maude	-	-	-	- 12.	10
Richard Morton	-	-	-	- 12.	10
George Mason	-	-	-	- 12.	10
Thomas Maddock	-	-	-	- 25.	
Richard Moore	-	-	-	- 25.	
Nicholas Moone	-	-	-	- 12.	10
Alfonsus van Medkerk	-	-	-	- 25.	
Captaine Henry Meoles	-	-	-	- 25.	
Philip Mutes	-	-	-	- 12.	10
Thomas Mayall	-	-	-	- 12.	10
Humfrey Marret	-	-	-	- 12.	10
Iarius Mundz	-	-	-	- 12.	10
Robert Mildmay	-	-	-	- 37.	10
William Millet	-	-	-	- 37.	10
Richard Morer	-	-	-	- 25.	
Iohn Miller	-	-	-	- 37.	10
Thomas Martin	-	-	-	- 37.	10
Iohn Middleton	-	-	-	- 6.	5
Francis Middleton	-	-	-	12.	10

N

Dudlie, Lord North	-	-	-	- 13. 6. 8	
Francis, Lord Norris	-	-	-	- 50.	
Siɪ Henry Neuill, of Barkshire	-	-	37.	10	

Thomas

				li.	s.	
Thomas Nicols -	-	-	-	- 62.	10	
Christopher Nicols	-	-	-	- 62.	10	
William Nicols -	-	-	-	- 50.		
George Newce -	-	-	-	- 12.	10	
Ioseph Newberow	-	-	-	- 20.		
Christopher Newgate	-	-	-	- 25.		
Thomas Norincott	-	-	-	- 37.	10	
Ionathan Nuttall	-	-	-	- 12.	10	
Thomas Norton -	-	-	-	- 13.	6.	8

O

William Oxenbridge, Esquire	-	-	- 112.		
Robert Offley -	-	-	- 100.		
Francis Oliuer - . -	-	-	- 25.		

P

VVilliam, Earle of Pembroke	-	-	- 400.		
VVilliam, Lord Paget -	-	-	- 60.		
Iohn, Lord Petre -	-	-	- 95.		
George Percy, Esquire -	-	-	- 20.		
Sir Christofer Parkins -	-	-	- 50.		
Sir Amias Preston -	-	-	- 100.		
Sir Nicolas Parker -	-	-	- 12.	10	
Sir VVilliam Poole -	-	-	- 37.	10	
Sir Steuen Powell -	-	-	- 100.		
Sir Henry Peyton -	-	-	- 25.		
Sir Iames Perrot -	-	-	- 12.	10	
Sir Iohn Pettus -	-	-	- 25.		
Sir Robert Payne -	-	-	- 25.		
VVilliam Payne -	-	-	- 100.		
Iohn Payne -	-	-	- 12.	10	
Edward Parkins -	-	-	- 37.	10	
Edward Parkins widow -	-	-	- 12.	10	
Aden Perkins -	-	-	- 25.		
Thomas Perkin -	-	-	- 12.	10	
Richard Partridge -	-	-	- 25.		
VVilliam Palmer -	-	-	- 62.	10	
Miles Palmer -	-	-	- 12.	10	
Robert Parkhurst -	-	-	- 75.		
Richard Perciuall, Esquire -	-	-	- 62.	10	
Richard Poyntell -	-	-	- 62.	10	
George Pretty -	-	-	- 12.	10	

George

					li.	s.
George Pit	-	-	-	-	- 112.	10
Allen Percy	-	-	-	-	- 12.	10
Abraham Peirce	-	-	-	-	- 12.	10
Edmund Peirce	-	-	-	-	- 25.	
Phenice Pet	-	-	-	-	- 37.	10
Thomas Philips	-	-	-	-	- 12.	10
Henry Philpot	-	-	-	-	- 25.	
Master George Procter	-	-	-	-	- 25.	
Robert Penington	-	-	-	-	- 25.	
Peter Peate	-	-	-	-	- 12.	10
Iohn Prat	-	-	-	-	- 12.	10
William Powell	-	-	-	-	- 25.	
Edmund Peashall	-	-	-	-	- 25.	
Captaine William Proude	-	-	-	-	- 25.	
Henry Price	-	-	-	-	- 12.	10
Nicholas Pewriffe	-	-	-	-	- 12.	10
Thomas Pelham	-	-	-	-	- 6.	5
Richard Piggot	-	-	-	-	- 25.	
Iohn Pawlet, Esquire	-	-	-	-	- 12.	10
Robert Pory	-	-	-	-	- 25.	
Richard Paulson	-	-	-	-	- 37.	10

Q

William Quick	-	-	-	-	- 62.	10

R

Sir Robert Rich, now Earle of Warwick	-	-	- 75.	
Sir Thomas Rowe	-	-	-	- 60.	
Sir Henry Rainsford	-	-	-	- 37.	10
Sir William Romney	-	-	-	- 170.	
Sir Iohn Ratcliffe	-	-	-	- 50.	
Sir Steuen Ridleson	-	-	-	- 56.	
Sir William Russell	-	-	-	- 50.	
Master Edward Rotheram, Alderman	-	- 25.	
Robert Rich	-	-	-	- 12.	10
Tedder Roberts	-	-	-	- 37.	10
Henry Robinson	-	-	-	- 87.	10
Iohn Russell	-	-	-	- 12.	10
Richard Rogers	-	-	-	- 75.	
Arthur Robinson	-	-	-	- 25.	
Robert Robinson	-	-	-	- 25.	
Millicent Ramsden	-	-	-	- 37.	10

Iohn

	h.	s.
Iohn Robinson - - - - -	75.	
George Robins - - - - -	62.	10
Nicholas Rainton - - - - -	25.	
Henry Rolffe - - - - -	12.	10
Iohn Reignolds - - - - -	12.	10
Elias Roberts - - - - -	25.	
Henry Reignolds, Esquire - - -	87.	10
William Roscarrock, Esquire - - -	37.	10
Humfrey Raymell - - - -	12.	10
Richard Robins - - - - -	12.	10

S

	h.	s.	d.
Henry, Earle of Southampton - - -	350.		
Thomas, Earle of Suffolke - - -	200.		
Robert, Earle of Salisbury - - -	333.	6.	8
Mary, Countesse of Shrewsburie - - -	50.		
Edmund, Lord Sheffeld - - -	140.		
Robert, Lord Spencer - - -	33.	6.	8
Iohn, Lord Stanhope - - -	50.		
Sir Iohn Saint-Iohn - - -	37.	10	
Sir Thomas Smith - - -	145.		
Sir Iohn Samms - - - -	50.		
Sir Iohn Smith - - - -	26.	13.	4
Sir Edwin Sandys - - -	212.	10	
Sir Samuel Sandys - - -	87.	10	
Sir Steuen Some - - - -	25.		
Sir Raph Shelton - - -	12.	10	
Sir Thomas Stewkley - - -	37.	10	
Sir VVilliam Saint-Iohn - - -	50.		
Sir VVilliam Smith - - -	45.		
Sir Richard Smith - - -	37.	10	
Sir Martin Stuteuill - - -	12.	10	
Sir Nicolas Salter - - -	125.		
Doctor Matthew Sutcliffe, Deane of Exeter	20.		
Thomas Sandys, Esquire - - -	25.		
Henry Sandys, Esquire - - -	25.		
George Sandys, Esquire - - -	12.	10	
Company of Skinners - - -	100.		
Company of Salters - - -	50.		
Company of Stationers - - -	125.		
Iohn Stokley - - - -	50.		
Captaine Iohn Smith - - -	9.		
Richard Staper - - - -	75.		

Robert

					li.	s.
Robert Shingleton	-	-	-	-	75.	
Thomas Shipton	-	-	-	-	62.	
Cleophas Smith	-	-	-	-	87.	10
Richard Strongtharm	-	-	-	-	100.	
Hildebrand Spruson	-	-	-	-	59. 9. 9	
Matthew Scriuener	-	-	-	-	100.	
Othowell Smith	-	-	-	-	42. 6. 8	
George Scot	-	-	-	-	125.	
Hewet Stapers	-	-	-	-	40.	
Iames Swift	-	-	-	-	25.	
Richard Stratford	-	-	-	-	75.	
Edmund Smith	-	-	-	-	12.	10
Robert Smith	-	-	-	-	37.	10
Matthias Springham	-	-	-	-	25.	
Richard Smith	-	-	-	-	25.	
Edward Smith	-	-	-	-	12.	10
Ionathan Smith	-	-	-	-	12.	10
Humfrey Smith	-	-	-	-	37.	10
Iohn Smith	-	-	-	-	37.	10
George Swinhow	-	-	-	-	62.	10
Ioseph Some	-	-	-	-	25.	
William Sheckley	-	-	-	-	25.	
Iohn Southick	-	-	-	-	12.	10
Henry Shelley	-	-	-	-	25.	
Walter Shelley	-	-	-	-	12.	10
Richard Snarsborow	-	-	-	-	12.	10
George Stone	-	-	-	-	12.	10
Hugh Shepley	-	-	-	-	12.	10
William Strachey	-	-	-	-	25.	
Vrion Spencer	-	-	-	-	12.	10
Iohn Scarpe	-	-	-	-	12.	10
Thomas Scott	-	-	-	-	50.	
VVilliam Sharpe	-	-	-	-	25.	
Steuen Sparrow	-	-	-	-	75.	
Thomas Stokes	-	-	-	-	12.	10
Richard Shepard	-	-	-	-	25.	
Henry Spranger	-	-	-	-	12.	10
VVilliam Stonnard	-	-	-	-	25.	
Steuen Sad	-	-	-	-	12.	10
Iohn Stockley	-	-	-	-	50.	
Thomas Steuens	-	-	-	-	37.	10
Matthew Shepard	-	-	-	-	50.	
Thomas Sherwell	-	-	-	-	12.	10
VVilliam Seabright, Esquire	-	-	-	12.	10

Nicholas

					li.	s.
Nicholas Sherwell	-	-	-	-	12.	10
Augustine Steward	-	-	-	-	25.	10
Thomas Stile	-	-	-	-	62.	10
Abraham Speckhard	-	-	-	-	12.	10
Edmund Scott	-	-	-	-	25.	
Francis Smalman	-	-	-	-	12.	10
Gregory Sprint, Esquire	-	•	-	-	37.	10
Thomas Stacey	-	-	-	-	25.	
VVilliam Sandbatch	-	-	-	-	10.	

T

					li.	s.
Sir VVilliam Twisden	-	-	-	-	37.	10
Sir VVilliam Throckmorton	-	-	-	-	50.	
Sir Nicholas Tufton	-	-	-	-	80.	
Sir Iohn Treuer	-	-	-	-	70.	
Sir Thomas Tracy	-	-	-	-	37.	10
George Thorpe, Esquire	-	-	-	-	25.	
Doctor William Turner	-	-	-	-	12.	10
The Trinity house	-	-	-	-	150.	
Richard Turner	-	-	-	-	37.	10
Iohn Tauerner	-	-	-	-	37.	10
Daniel Tucker	-	-	-	-	31.	5
Charles Towler	-	-	-	-	12.	10
William Tayler	-	-	-	-	12.	10
Leonard Townson	-	-	-	-	25.	
Richard Tomlins	-	-	-	-	25.	
Francis Tate, Esquire	-	-	-	-	25.	
Andrew Troughton	-	-	-	-	25.	
George Tucker	-	-	-	-	12.	10
Henry Timberlake	-	-	-	-	37.	10
William Tucker	-	-	-	-	25.	
Lewis Tite	-	-	-	-	25.	
Robert Thornton	-	-	-	-	25.	

V

					li.	s.
Sir Horatio Vere	-	-	-	-	121.	
Henry Vincent	-	-	-	-	37.	10
Richard Venne	-	-	-	-	12.	10
Christopher Vertue	-	-	-	-	12.	10
Iohn Vassell	-	-	-	-	25.	
Arthur Venne	-	-	-	-	12.	10

Henry

W

	li.	s.	
Henry Bishop of Worcester - - -	13.	6.	8
Francis West, Esquire - - -	25.		
Sir Raph Winwood - - -	75.		
Sir Iohn Wentworth - - -	12.	10	
Sir William Waad - - -	144.	10	
Sir Robert Wroth - - -	50.		
Sir Perciuall Willoby - - -	50.		
Sir Charles Wilmott - - -	27.	10	
Sir Iohn Watts - - -	162.	10	
Sir Hugh Worrell - - -	25.		
Sir Edward Waterhouse - - -	25.		
Sir Thomas Wilsford - - -	50.		
Sir Richard Williamson - - -	25.		
Sir Iohn Wolstenholm - - -	137.	10	
Sir Thomas Watson - - -	62.	10	
Sir Thomas Wilson - - -	37.	10	
Sir Iohn Weld - - -	37.	10	
Mistris Kath. West, now Lady Conway -	25.		
Iohn Wroth, Esquire - -	87.	10	
Captaine Maria Winckfield, Esquire -	88.		
Thomas Webb - - -	12.	10	
Rice Webb - - -	62.	10	
Edward Webb - - -	100.		
Sands Webb - - -	12.	10	
Felix Wilson - - -	25.		
Thomas White - - -	62.	10	
Richard Wiffen - - -	12.	10	
William Williamson - - -	50.		
Humfrey Westwood - - -	62.	10	
Hugh Willeston - - -	12.	10	
Thomas Wheatley - - -	87.	10	
William Wattey - - -	25.		
William Webster - - -	37.	10	
Iames White - - -	25.		
Edmund Winne - - -	62.	10	
Iohn West - - -	50.		
Iohn Wright - - -	25.		
Edward Wooller - - -	50.		
Iohn Wooller - - -	25.		
Thomas Walker - - -	25.		
Iohn Westrow - - -	37.	10	
Edward Welch - - -	25.		

Nathaniel

	li.	s.
Nathaniel Waad - - - - -	25.	
Richard Wydowes - - - -	25.	
Dauid Waterhouse, Esquire - - -	37.	10
Captaine Owen Winne - - - -	50.	
Randall Wetwood - - - -	25.	
George Wilmer, Esquire - - -	25.	
Edward Wilkes - - - - -	25.	
Leonard White - - - - -	25.	
Andrew Willmer - - - - -	25.	
Clement Willmer - - - - -	25.	
George Walker - - - - -	25.	
William Welby - - - - -	87.	10
Francis Whistler - - - -	25.	
Thomas Welles - - - - -	25.	
Captaine Thomas Winne - - -	25.	
Iohn Whittingham - - - -	12.	10
Thomas Wheeler - - - -	12.	10
William Willet - - - - -	12.	10
Deuereux Woogam - - - -	50.	
Iohn Walker - - - - -	37.	10
Thomas Wood - - - - -	25.	
Iohn VVillet - - - - -	37.	10
Nicholas Wheeler - - - -	12.	10
Thomas Wale - - - - -	75.	
William Wilston - - - - -	12.	10
Iohn Waller - - - - -	5.	
VVilliam VVard - - - -	37.	10
VVilliam VVilleston - - - -	25.	
Iohn VVater - - - - -	12.	10
Thomas Warr, Esquire - - -	25.	
Dauid VViffen - - - - -	12.	10
Garret VVeston - - - - -	12.	10

Y

Sir George Yeardley, now Gouernour of Virginia -	25.	
VVilliam Yong - - - - -	12.	10
Simon Yeomons - - - - -	12.	10

Z

| Edward, Lord Zouch - - - - | 60. | |

Names of the Aduenturers,

with the Sums paid by order to Sir *Baptist Hicks*, Knight.

A

	li.	s.
Sir Anthony Ashley - - - -	25.	

B

Sir Iohn Benet - - - - -	12.	10
Sir Edmund Bowyer - - - -	25.	
Sir Henry Beddingfield - - -	37.	10
Edward Barnes - - - - -	12.	10
Humfrey Basse - - - - -	12.	10

C

Sir Henry Cary - - - - -	75.	
Sir Lyonell Cranfield - - - -	25.	
Sir Walter Cope - - - - -	50.	
Sir Edward Carr - - - - -	25.	
Sir George Coppin - - - -	20.	
Sir Iohn Cuts - - - - -	75.	
Edward Carn, Esquire - - - -	37.	10
Thomas Cannon, Esquire - - - -	12.	10

D

Sir Thomas Dennis - - - -	75.	
Sir Thomas Denton - - - -	37.	10

E

Sir Robert Edolph - - - -	37.	10

F

Richard Fishborne - - - -	12.	10

Sir

G

				li.	s.
Sir Thomas Grantham	-	-	-	37.	10
Sir William Garaway	-	-	-	16.	13.4
Thomas Gouge	-	-	-	25.	

H

Sir Iohn Hollis, now L. Houghton	-	-	25.	
Sir Perciuall Hart	-	-	-	37.	10
Sir Warwick Heale	-	-	-	25.	
Sir Baptist Hicks	-	-	-	50.	
Sir Iohn Hanham	-	-	-	25.	
Sir William Herick	-	-	-	12.	10
Sir George Huntley	-	-	-	25.	
Nicholas Hooker	-	-	-	12.	10

I

Sir Arthur Ingram	-	-	-	50.

L

Sir Iohn Lewson	-	-	-	25.	
Sir Richard Louelace	-	-	-	25.	
Sir Samuel Leonard	-	-	-	25.	
Sir William Litton	-	-	-	37.	10

M

Philip, Earle of Mountgomery	-	-	120.	
Sir William Maynard	-	-	-	25.
Sir George More	-	-	-	75.
Sir Caueliero Maycott	-	-	-	50.

P

Robert Parkhurst	-	-	-	25.

S

Sir Iohn Stradling	-	-	-	12.	10
Sir William Smith, of Hill Hall	-	-	-	25.	

Sir

Sir William Smith, of London	-	-	- 25.
Sir Nicholas Salter	-	-	- 12. 10
Augustine Steward, Esquire	-	-	- 12. 10
Abraham Speckard	-	-	- 12. 10

T

			li.	s.
Sir William Throkmorton -	-	-	- 25.	
Richard Tomlins	-	-	- 12.	10

V

Sir Walter Vaughan	-	-	- 37. 10

W

Sir Thomas Walsingham -	-	-	- 37. 10
Sir Charles Wilmot	-	-	- 25.
Sir Thomas Watson	-	-	- 50.

The Names of the Aduenturers, with

the Sums paid to Sir *Edwin Sandys*, Knight,

Treasurer of the Company for Virginia,
from the 28. *of Aprill,* 1619.
to the 27. *of Iune,* 1620.

	li.	s.
William, Lord Cauendish - - -	50.	
Iohn Zouch, Esquire - - -	25.	
Thomas Bond, Esquire - - -	37.	10
Dauid Benet, Esquire - - - -	37.	10
Iohn Cage, Esquire - - - -	12.	10
Iohn Ferrar - - - - -	12.	10
Elias Roberts - - - - -	12.	10
Matthew Cauell - - - - -	12.	10

ORDERS

AND

CONSTITVTIONS,

Partly collected out of his Maiesties
Letters Patents, and partly ordained vpon
mature deliberation, by the TREASVROR,
COVNSEIL and COMPANIE of
VIRGINIA, for the better gouerning of the Actions and affaires
of the said COMPANIE here
in *England* residing. *An-*
no 1619. and 1620.

Courts.

I.

THERE are foure great generall Courts, commonly called Quarter Courts, appointed to be
held by the *Treasuror, Counseil* and *Compa-*
nie of *Virginia*, vpon the foure last Wednes-
dayes saue one of euery Tearme : which onely
haue and shall haue power to choose Counseil-
ours and Officers, as well for the *Companie* here, as also for the
Colonie and *Planters* in *Virginia* : to make Lawes and ordinances : to distribute and dispose of the Lands in *Virginia* :
and to settle matter of Trade for the behoofe of the *Companie*
and *Colonie.*

II.

EVery Munday before a Quarter-Court, shall be held a
Court to prepare all kinde of businesse reserued to the
power of the Quarter Court to determine.

EVery

I I I.

EVery Wednesday fortnight, reckoning from the great Courts shall also be held an ordinary Court for this Company, for dispatch of ordinary and extraordinary businesse. And it is not to be counted a perfect Court, vnlesse there be five of the *Counseil* there (the *Treasuror* or *Deputie* being one) and fifteene of the Generality.

I V.

IT shall be in the power of the *Treasuror*, or the *Deputie* in his absence, vpon extraordinary cause to call an extraordinary Court.

V.

IT shall not be in the power of any other then a Quarter Court, to make any contract whereby to binde the Company for any continuance of yeares. In which case it shall be proposed also in the *Preparatiue* Court next preceding.

V I.

PVblique businesse shall haue the precedence in the Courts before priuate, vnlesse there be extraordinary important cause to the contrary.

V I I.

IF any thing ordered in an ordinary or lesser Court, be afterward reuersed in one of the great and generall Courts: It shall be from thence forward as though it had neuer beene so ordered.

V I I I.

ALL Courts shall begin at two of the clocke in the afternoone, and dissolue at the rising of the *Treasuror*, or of the *Deputie* in his absence.

I X.

NOthing shall be put to the question after sixe of the Clocke in the after-noone.

X.

IN regard of the great businesse for *Virginia* yearely encreasing, It shall be in the power of the *Treasuror*, (if hee

see

see it so necessary) to assemble the Quarter Courts both in the fore-noones and after-noones of the dayes appointed for them.

X I.

THe *Companie* shall be summoned to the Quarter Courts, and Courts extraordinary, by the Officer: But of the ordinary Courts themselues shall take notice. And the Secretary shall keepe a booke of the proceedings of the Courts: who with the Booke-keeper, Husband, and Bedle, shall at all Courts giue diligent attendance.

X I I.

IT shall be lawfull at a generall Court, and with consent thereof, to dispence with all meetings in long Vacations, or in such part of them as may be spared; vnlesse some extraordinary matter befall, in which case may be called extraordinary Courts.

X I I I.

THe *Treasuror* and *Company*, being a Body and Commonaltie perpetuall, shall haue one faire and common Seale, to be kept by the Treasuror; and not to be affixed to any Grants or Instruments whatsoeuer, otherwhere then in publique Courts, or by warrant from thence.

X I V.

THe *Treasuror* and the *Counseil*, or the *Court*, haue power to admit any into this Society.

Elections.

X V.

AT the great and generall Court, commonly called the Quarter Court, in Easter Terme, all Offices of this Company (excepting the *Counseil*) shall be voide: And the Court shall proceede to an election of new Officers, in manner following.

X V I.

THE *Treasuror* in the beginning of the Court, at the giuing vp of his Office, shall declare by word or writing the present estate of the *Colonie* and Planters in *Virginia*. And
deliuer

deliuer into the Court a Booke of his accounts for the yeere past, examined and approued vnder the Auditors hands : Declaring withall the present estate of the Cash.

X V I I.

AFter the choise of a *Treasuror*, a *Deputie* shall be chosen; then the *Auditors*, and *Comitties*; and lastly the *Secretarie, Booke-keeper, Husband,* and *Bedle*.

X V I I I.

AT the choise of each Officer, the persons nominated for the election, shall withdraw themselues till the party chosen be publiquely so pronounced. And generally no man shall be present in the Court, whilst himselfe or his matter passeth the iudgement of the Court.

X I X.

IN regard of the weighty and manifold businesse of this *Companie*, which is also like daily to encrease : No man shall be chosen Treasuror of the Company of *Virginia*, who at the time of his election is Gouernor of any other Company; but vpon condition that before the next Quarter Court hee effectually resigne that other Gouernement : except it seeme good for the behalfe of both Companies, that the same man be also Gouernour of the *Somer Ilands* Company.

X X.

IT is for weighty reasons thought very expedient, that no man continue in the place of *Treasuror* or *Deputie,* aboue three yeares at once.

X X I.

FOr the auoiding of diuers inconueniences, It is thought fit, that all elections of principall Officers in or for *Virginia,* as also of the *Treasuror* and *Deputie* here, be performed by a Ballating box, as in some other Companies.

X X I I.

EVery Officer as he is chosen, shall openly in Court take his oath : or if he be absent, at the next Court he commeth to.

X X I I I.

THe *Treasuror, Deputie, Auditors,* and *Comitties,* hauing no certaine allowance for their cares and labours : the reward

ward of these former Officers according to their deserts, is referred to the pleasure of the Court wherein new Officers are chosen.

Treasuror.

X X I V.

THe *Treasurors* duetie is to keepe the ordinary Courts of *Virginia :* and vpon cause extraordinary, to call Courts extraordinarily. And in all Courts, and other meetings, hee is to haue a casting voyce.

X X V.

HE is to moderate the Courts in qualitie of a *President :* and to cause grauity, decency, and good order to be obserued : And for breach thereof, after a graue admonition, first giuen, and not preuailing; to proceede to reformation by the iudgement of the Court.

X X V I.

HE is to propound and put all things to the question which the Court requires, vnder paine of being immediately put from his Office, if he refuse. In which case the *Deputie* shall doe it, vnder the like paine. And if he refuse, then any of the *Counseil* there present.

X X V I I.

WHereas the *Treasuror* is to put to the question all things which the Court requires : It is explained to be intended of such things as are not contrary to his Maiesties *Letters Patents* or Instructions, nor to the standing Lawes and Orders of the Companie.

X X V I I I.

HE is to haue care that the extraordinary *Comitties* appointed by the Courts to seuerall businesse, doe prosecute the same ; and giue seasonable account of their doings to the Court.

X X I X.

HE is also to haue an especiall care, that no *Grant* or *Patent* doe passe from the *Companie,* but upon examination
thereof

thereof by a select *Comittie*, who are exactly to obserue the Orders made concerning them. And to this end, with diuers others, he is to haue a vigilant eye on the Companies and Counseils Seales, that they be not wronged by abusing of them.

X X X.

THe *Treasuror*, vpon receipt of publique Letters from or concerning *Virginia*, shall assemble at least foure of the *Counseil* to impart them to them ; and by their assents shall cause them to be read in Court, vnlesse there be some cause of secresie : In which case he shall communicate them with the *Counseil* onely. In like sort the publique Letters and Instructions to be sent to the *Gouernour*, *Counseil*, or People in *Virginia*, or otherwise concerning them, hee shall cause to be publiquely read and approued by the *Court*, or *Counseil*, as the case shall require. And neither he, nor any other, shall of his owne head or authoritie, write or send any directions, swaruing from such as the Court or *Counseil* shall giue, vpon paine to be dis-franchized.

X X X I.

THe *Treasuror* shall assemble the *Counseil* vpon all weightie occasions requiring serious deliberation : And shall haue care with them, that the Lords of his Maiesties priuie *Counseil* be acquainted with all matters of extraordinary and greatest importance concerning the *State*.

X X X I I.

HE is to doe his best that fit Counsailors be chosen : And being chosen, is to haue care that they take their oathes.

X X X I I I.

THe *Treasuror* is to haue care also, that the generall *Comitties* keepe their Courts with the *Deputie*, vpon all occasions of businesse.

X X X I V.

HE is to doe his best that fit men be chosen also to that place : And that they which are chosen, be sworne.

X X X V.

THe *Treasuror* at his pleasure shall sit in any Assembly of *Comitties*, ordinary, or extraordinary ; vnlesse it concerne himselfe.

The

XXXVI.

THe *Treasuror* shall stand charged with the publique *Treasure* of the Company. And is to haue care that it be duely got in: And not issued out, but by lawfull warrant, and to the *Companies* vse.

XXXVII.

A Lawfull warrant for charges of the present yeare, is that which is signed by the *Deputie* and foure of the *Committies*: And for former charges or Debts; that which is signed by three of the *Auditors*, whereof one to be of the *Quorum*. And vnderneth, or vpon the backes of euery Warrant, an Acquittance shall be taken for the receipt vnder the parties hand.

XXXVIII.

THe *Treasuror* is also to yeelde vp a true and perfect account of the generall Cash at the end of his yeare: And to bring it in a fortnight before to the *Auditors*, to be examined. And at all times, being requested by the *Auditors*, to shew in what case the Cash doth stand.

XXXIX.

IF any complaint or suspition growe concerning the Account, there shall be a reuiew made by twelue chosen by the Court. And the account being accepted and approued by the Court; the *Treasuror* shall haue his *Quietus est* vnder the *Companies Seale*, at the Quarter Court in *Trinitie Term* then next ensuing.

X L.

THe standing wages of the Cashier shall be suspended: and his reward such as that Quarter Court in *Easter Term* shall appoint.

Deputie.

X L I.

FOR matter of the Courts, in the *Treasurors* absence, the *Deputie* shall performe his Office: and in his presence, be assisting to him.

Hee

XLII.

HEe shall ouersee the Secretary for entring the Orders of Courts. And shall giue instructions for the writing of Letters, as he shall be directed : and haue care that accordingly they be written.

XLIII.

THe *Deputie* shall also keepe the Courts of *Comitties*, vpon all occasions requisite. And in them shall haue a casting voyce.

XLIV.

HE shall suffer no Warrants to be made and signed for issuing out of money, but in the open Court of *Comitties*, after due examination of the cause : vnto all which Warrants his owne hand shall be first set; and after it, other foure hands or more of the *Comitties*. And the *Deputie* and *Comitties* shall not intermedle with disbursments for any other charges, then such as arise within the compasse of their owne yeare.

XLV.

VVHere a Warrant is directed to the *Treasuror*, to pay any grosse Summe to the *Deputie*; to be issued out by him and the *Committies* for the vse of the *Companie* : In that case it shall not be requisite that the *Deputies* hand be to the warrant; so it be to the receipt.

XLVI.

GEnerally he shall ouersee all inferiour Officers, that they performe their dueties.

Counseil.

XLVII.

THe names of his Maiesties *Counseil* for *Virginia*, shall be publiquely read in euery Quarter-Court in *Michelmas Term :* They requested by the *Treasuror* to attend the seruice, and warned to take their Oathes.

XLVIII.

IF there be defect in the number, or attendance of the *Counseil*; then addition shall be made : And that but onely of

men

men of especiall worth and qualitie, and such as are likely to giue attendance to that seruice. They are to continue *Counseilors* during life: vnlesse they be displaced by a great and generall Court.

XLIX.

IN regard of the present great number of the *Counseil*, and to preserue vnto them that reputation which is fit for their place and employment: None hereafter vnder the degree of a *Lord* or principall Magistrate, shall be chosen to be of his Maiesties Counseil for *Virginia;* but such as by diligent attendance at the Courts and seruice of Virginia for one yeare at least before, haue approued their sufficiency and worth to the *Companie.*

L.

SEuen of the *Counseil*, being assembled by order, without practize or purpose to exclude the rest, shall be counted the *Counseil.*

LI.

THe *Counseil* are to assemble vpon all important occasions, being requested by the *Treasuror*, or the *Deputie* in his absence; and in defect of bothe, being desired by the Court: And without fauour or displeasure, priuate or sinister respect, to giue their faithfull aduise in all matters tending to the aduancement or benefit of the *Plantation:* and especially touching the making of *Lawes* and Constitutions, for the better gouerning as well of the *Companie* here, as also of the *Colonie* planted in *Virginia.* Wherein the policie and forme of *England* is to be followed as neere as may be.

LII.

THe *Counseil* shall haue an especiall regard, by pious constitutions, and by other good politique Lawes and Orders, to hold the people there, in the true religion and seruice of God: and in assured allegeance to his Maiestie and the Crowne of *England :* In due respect also to his Maiesties *Counseil* here, and to this *Company* of *Virginia :* And in Iustice, Peace, vniformitie, and amitie amongst themselues.

LIII.

THey shall also according to the first institution and profession of this *Companie*, aduise and deuise to the utmost of their powers, the best meanes for the reclaiming of the *Barbarous Natiues;*

Natiues; and bringing them to the true worship of God, ciuilitie of life, and vertue.

LIV.

ALL Instructions to the *Gouernour* and *Counseil,* and all
other principall Officers in *Virginia,* shall proceede from the
Counseil, and vnder their hands and Seale : which Seale shall
be in the custodie of the *Treasuror.*

LV.

IF any principall Officer of the *Companie* here ; or Magistrate,
great Officer, or Counseilor in *Virginia;* shall by the fame of
his misdeserts, or particular accusation, merit to be called in
question of being remoued from his place, or otherwise reformed
or censured : He shall be first conuented and examined by the
Counseil, before his cause be produced in publique Court. And
in case of his absence, the like course shall be held for his businesse.

Auditors.

LVI.

THe *Auditors* shall be seauen : whereof two at the least of the
Counseil, and three of them of the *Quorum.*

LVII.

THe *Auditors* shall haue care of the generall accounts : to
examine the receipts and disbursments according to the Orders of the *Companie :* and in all cases of difficultie, or of breach
of those Orders, they shall acqnaint the *Treasuror* and the generall Court therewith : and from thence receiue resolution and
direction.

LVIII.

THey shall also cause to be reduced into a seuerall Booke,
the whole receipts and disbursements of that yeare : and the
same vnder foure of their hands at the least (whereof two to be
of the *Quorum*) shall be presented by the *Treasuror* at the
Quarter Court in *Easter Term,* at the giuing vp of his and their
Office.

LIX.

THey shall signe no warrants for the issuing of money, but
onely for olde charges or debts ; that is to say, due before
that

that yeare of their Office : And that not otherwise, then after due examination of the matter had in their appointed meetings : vnto which warrant shall be first set the hand of one at the least of the *Quorum*, and then two other or more of the rest of the Auditors.

L X.

THe *Auditors* shall also employ their best industry and care, for the recouery of the olde debts due to the *Company :* And their receipts shall transmit to the generall Cash.

L X I.

ANd touching the olde accounts now depending in Audite, that is to say from the beginning of the *Plantation* till the 30. day of Nouember, 1 6 1 6. the *Auditors* shall proceede in the examining and reducing them to order, and to the finall auditing of them, with what expedition they well can. And shall from time to time acquaint the *Treasuror* and Court, with such impediments and difficulties as shall be incident.

L X I I.

IN digesting of the olde accounts, the *Auditors* shall take especiall care, to cause the *Secretary* or *Booke-keeper*, in a seuerall Booke, to set downe particularly and exactly the names of all the Aduenturors, with their seuerall sums aduentured : as also what is paid, or yet remaining vnpaid : as well that right may be done to the Aduenturors, as also the debts preserued which are due to the Company. And this booke of the Aduenturors, shall be extended till the Quarter Court in *Easter Term*, 1619.

L X I I I.

THe *Auditors* shall keepe their meetings, once at the least euery weeke in the *Term time ;* or oftner, if need require : and once euery moneth at least in the vacation times : to ouersee the accounts, and dispatch such other businesse as shall be committed to them.

L X I V.

THey shall also haue the authoritie of the Court, to call before them such persons, as are indebted or accomptable to the Company.

In

L X V.

IN regard of the greatnesse of the businesse for the present: the *Auditors* are allowed an Officer to attend vpon them: who shall be salariated at the pleasure of the Court.

Comitties.

L X V I.

THe *Comitties* being to be sixteene; and to be yearely chosen; there shall be a yearelie alteration made of one fourth part at the least, to the end many be trained vp in the businesse.

L X V I I.

THe *Comitties* office is, together with the *Deputie,* to perform the orders of Courts, for setting out Ships, and buying prouisions for *Virginia.* Wherein especiall care is to be had, that neither the *Husband,* nor any one man alone, be entrusted with the making of those prouisions; but two at the least, to be appointed thereunto by the *Deputie* and *Comitties* in their Court: who shall also bring in their bils and accounts, to be examined and approued by the *Comitties.* The like care shall they haue at the returne of Ships from *Virginia,* for the goods belonging to the Companie, to be safely kept, and sould to the best aduantage, either in Court, or otherwise by the Courts direction. The accounts of all which, shall be transmitted to the *Auditors:* and the money remaining, returned to the Cash. The *Deputie* and *Comitties* shall also haue care of the *Inuoices* to be made for the prouisions sent to *Virginia:* and of the Certificats of the receipt to be thence returned: As likewise of the *Inuoices* of the goods sent from *Virginia.* All which shall be registred fairely in a booke.

L X V I I I.

THe *Comitties* shall diligently keepe their Courts, whensoeuer occasion of businesse shall require. They shall be summoned by order of the *Treasuror,* or *Deputie.* And it shall not be counted a Court of *Comitties,* vnlesse the *Treasuror* or *Deputie* with sixe *Comitties* be present. The *Secretary* of the *Company* shall keepe a booke also of their proceedings.

Secretary.

Secretary.

LXIX.

THe *Secretary* shall attend the *Treasuror,* and *Deputie,* in such seruice of the *Companie* as wherein they shall haue cause to vse him. And besides the generall Courts, he shall of duety attend the Courts of *Comitties;* and keepe seuerall bookes of their proceedings. The *Counseil, Auditors,* and *Comitties* extraordinary, he shall then also attend, when and so often as he shall be thereunto required.

LXX.

HE shall be bound by oath to keepe secret all matters of secrecy : And not to discouer the proceedings of the *Counseil,* and *Comitties* extraordinary, till such time as themselues shall publish the same.

LXXI.

THe *Secretary,* vpon reference of any businesse from the Court to a select *Comittie;* shall giue a note to the Messenger, containing the businesse, time, & place.

LXXII.

HIs office is also to be a Remembrancer to the generall Courts, and to the Courts of *Comitties;* for the prosequuting and performing of matters formerly ordered : As also touching motions formerly made, and referred to speciall *Comitties,* or other farther consideration.

LXXIII.

IF at any time a generall Court shall order any money to be issued out of the Cash ; the *Secretarie* vnder his hand shall deliuer a Copie thereof to the *Auditors,* if it be of old Debts ; and if otherwise, then to the *Deputie* and *Comitties :* who respectiuely shall vnder that Order make their warrant for the payment of that money : vnlesse they find the Court, by wrong information, to haue been abused and deceiued in that Order ; whereof at the next Court they shall giue aduertisement.

LXXIV.

THe *Secretaries* Office is to keepe the Bookes of the *Companie,* and fairely and orderly to enter in them the particulars
here-vnder

here-vnder expressed; and in such manner as he shall be directed by the *Treasuror, Deputie*, or *Auditors*. First, a Booke containing the Copies of the *Kings Letters Patents* to the *Companie:* Also of all Letters, Orders, Directions, and other writings, from his Maiestie, the Lords of the *Counseil*, and other great Officers, concerning the *Companie*, or the affaires of *Virginia;* together with the answeres made vnto them.

L X X V.

A Second Booke shall be kept of all the Lawes and standing Orders established hence-forward in the Quarter-Courts, and beginning with this day; as well such as concerne the Gouernement of the *Companie* and businesse here; as also the Gouernment of the *Colonie* and affaires in *Virginia*.

L X X V I.

IN a third Booke shall be registred all the Patents, Chartres, and Indentures of validitie, heretofore granted, or that hereafter shal be granted, by the *Treasuror* and *Companie:* all instructions from the *Counseil:* all publique Letters written to *Virginia*, or from thence receiued.

L X X V I I.

A Fourth Booke shall be of the Acts of the generall Courts; beginning with a new Booke at the last Quarter-Court.

L X X V I I I.

A Fift Booke shall be of the Acts of the *Comitties*, beginning from the same Court. In which Booke shall be registred all Inuoyces of the prouisions sent to *Virginia* from the *Companie;* and the Certificats of the receipts to be thence returned: As likewise the Inuoyces of the Goods sent from *Virginia*; with the Husbands certificat of the receipt or defect.

L X X I X.

IN a sixt booke, at the one end, shall be registred the names of all the Aduenturors here by money; or otherwise by seruice, for which shares of Land in *Virginia* haue beene giuen by the *Companie* in their Quarter-Courts; together with the number of Shares to each person belonging. Where shall also be entred in a place by it selfe, the lawfull Transports of Shares from one to another. Here shall also be entred, the names of his
Maiesties

Maiesties *Counseil* for *Virginia*. At the other end of the same Booke, shall be registred the names of all the *Planters* in *Virginia*, as well for the publique, as vpon priuate *Plantations :* which is to be done distinctly for each *Plantation* by it selfe. And this is to be done vpon the Certificates hereafter returned from the *Gouernour* and *Counseil* in *Virginia :* And from the Heads and Bodies of particular *Plantations*, according to the tenor and effect of the Grants made vnto them, and other Lawes and Orders made by the *Companie*. All which shall be first published and allowed in a generall Court : and not registred in this Booke, but by direction from thence.

L X X X.

THe *Secretarie* shall also keepe safe in the *Companies* Chest of euidences, the originals of all the Letters Patents, and other writings afore mentioned : all the Bookes also aforesaid : All the *Treasurors* Bookes of their yearely accounts : The *Husbands* Bookes of accounts of euery voyage to *Virginia :* and all other accounts perfected and approued by the *Auditors*. In the same Chest shall be kept all Charter Parties, as well cancelled as vncancelled : All Bonds made to the *Companie*, or for their vse : And all Bonds of the *Companies* discharged and cancelled : And all other writings and muniments whatsoeuer belonging to the *Companie*. And the *Secretarie* shall deliuer out none of the *Companies* writings, but by direction from the *Treasuror, Counseil,* or Court : taking a note of the parties hand for the true restoring of them. And in conuenient time he shall make Calenders of all the foresaid writings.

L X X X I.

THe *Secretaries* Salarie shall be twenty pounds *per annum :* and of his paines extraordinary, the Court shall take con-consideration.

Booke Keeper.

L X X X I I.

THe *Booke keeper,* so long as he shall seeme necessarie, shall be wholy directed and ordered by the *Treasuror*, and *Auditors :* And shall receiue his *Salarie* from the Quarter-Courts, as the *Auditors* shall report of his paines and deserts.

The

LXXXIII.

THe *Booke keeper*, vpon conference with the *Secretarie* and the *Husband*, and they two in his defect, shall in euery Quarter Court present openly to the *Treasuror*, a true note of the Debts, both owing by the *Companie*, and ought vnto them: together with the ground from whence they haue risen : that the Court may take order for discharge of thé one, and recouery of the other.

Husband.

LXXXIV.

THe *Husband* is to be ordered by the *Treasuror, Deputie,* and *Comitties;* and to keepe his accounts in exact and iustifiable manner : and to bring them from time to time to the *Deputie* and *Comitties,* to be first examined there, and approued vnder their hands; and then to be presented to the *Auditors.*

LXXXV.

HE shall at the end of euery voyage set out by the *Companie,* make a seuerall Booke of the charges of that voyage ; to be presented by him to the *Auditors ;* and by them to the Court.

LXXXVI.

THe *Husband* shall also (being required by the Court) be assisting to other *Aduenturors* vpon particular *Plantations,* in making their prouisions, and setting out their Ships. His wages shall be fortie pounds *per annum.*

Bedel.

LXXXVII.

THe *Bedel* or Messenger is to be at command of the *Treasuror, Deputie,* and Courts. He is to warne all Quarter-Courts, and Courts extraordinary : all meetings of the *Counsail,* Generall *Comities,* and Select *Comitties.* His wages, forty pound *per annum.*

Generalitie.

Generalitie.

LXXXVIII.

THe particular Members of the *Companie*, shall be subiect to the generall Courts, in matters concerning the *Companie* or *Plantation*. If any man finde himselfe agrieued by a lesser or ordinary Court, he may appeale to a great and Quarter-Court, where the matter shall be heard and finally ordered. If any man refuse to obay both the one Court and other, he shall be dis-franchized.

LXXXIX.

EVery man speaking in Court, shall addresse his speech to the *Treasuror*, or *Deputie* in his absence, as representing the Court: And all priuate speeches, or directed to particular persons, shall be forborne.

XC.

NO man in one Court shall speake aboue thrise to one matter: saue the *Treasuror* and the *Deputie*, being to moderate the businesse.

XCI.

NO man with his speech shall interrupt the speech of another, before he haue finished: Except the *Treasuror*, or in his absence the *Deputie*, (with approbation of the Court) fee cause to put any to silence, for impertinency, or other vnseemely speaking.

XCII.

IF any man be found by sinister course, to practise his owne aduantage, to the damnifying of the publique, or be found with the *Companies* Mony or Goods in his hands, and refuse to deliuer the fame being lawfully thereunto required: If being summoned to the Court, he refuse to appeare, or appearing, performe not the Order of the Court; he shall be both disfran-chized, and farther proceeded against, as an vnworthy Member, and wrong-doer to the *Companie*.

XCIII.

IF any man out of euill minde, practize to raise faction or dis-sention in the *Companie*; he shall for the first time, be ad-monished by the Court or *Counseil*, and at the second, disfran-chized.

Whosoeuer

XCIV.

VVHosoeuer shall attempt by priuate solicitation to packe the Court to any vniust or vnlawfull end; shall vpon complaint, be conuented before the *Counseil*, and being conuicted, shall be disfranchized.

XCV.

IF any man be found, through corrupt reward, to make a Motion in the Court, tending to the publique hurt, or to the priuate wrong of another; he shall be forthwith disfranchized.

XCVI.

NO man shall presume to intercept Letters, written by, or to, the *Counseil*, or *Companie;* or to spread false rumors, vpon sinister intent, to the wrong of the *Counseil, Companie,* or *Colonie:* The offender shall be disfranchized.

XCVII.

NO man shall traduce any Member of this *Companie* in any other Court, for any thing done or spoken in this Court. The offender for the first time, shall be admonished; for the second, suspended from the Court for one yeere; and the third time, disfranchized.

XCVIII.

TO auoyd the drawing of the *Companie* into Debt henceforward: It is ordered, that no particular man make or propound any new proiect of charge to the *Companie*, but he withall offer good meanes how to defray that charge, and to vphold his proiect, in such sort as the *Companie* neuer be drawne againe into any farther debt. And the breakers of this Order, shall be excluded from the generall Courts, and from hauing voyce, or bearing Office, for one yeare after.

XCIX.

IF any man moue for any charge to the *Companie*, by way of gift in what sort soeuer: It shall be first referred to a select *Comittie:* and if the charge fall out to be vnder thirtie pound, it may be ordered by the next Court; if aboue, it shall be reserued till the Quarter Court ensuing.

C.

IT shall not be lawfull for any *Aduenturor*, to sell or transport his shares to another, otherwise then in open Court: And

not

not before it doe appeare vnder three of the *Auditors* hands, that the partie transporting his shares stand cleere, and is not indebted to the *Companie;* or the partie to whom they are passed, doe pay the said Debt.

Officers in Virginia.

C I.

ALL principall Officers in *Virginia*, namely the *Gouernour, Lieutenant Gouernour, Admirall, Marshal*, chiefe *Iustice*, and *Treasuror*, shall be chosen here by Ballating in a Quarter-Court.

C II.

THe *Counseil* established in *Virginia*, and all other Officers there reserued to the choise of the *Companie* here, shall be chosen in a Quarter-Court by onely erection of hands; vnlesse the Court desire to haue it passe by Ballating.

C III.

THe Commissions to all Officers there, shall be onely for three yeares in certaine, and afterwards during the *Companies* pleasure. Onely the *Gouernour* shall vpon no occasion hold that place aboue six yeares.

C IV.

THe *Companie* here shall not be charged with the maintenance of the Officers there: But they shall be maintained there, out of the publique Lands.

Lawes.

C V.

NO Lawes or standing Orders shall be made by the *Companie*, but in this manner. First, after the proposing of them in Court, they shall be referred to the examination of a select *Comittie*. The *Comitties* shall present their Labours to the view of the *Counseil*. The *Counseil* approuing them, they shall be

brought·

brought to the Court of preparation on the Munday before the Quarter-Court, and there openly read. And lastly they shall passe the iudgement of the Quarter-Court.

C V I.

THe Lawes and Orders thus made, shall be fairely registred by the *Secretary* in a parchment Booke: which he shall bring in every Court, and lay on the table, that all men may peruse them that are so disposed.

C V I I.

IN the Quarter-Court in *Hillarie Term*, all Lawes and standing Orders concerning the *Companie* here, shall be publiquely read in the beginning of the Court.

C V I I I.

THe abrogating of a Law or Order, shall proceede by the same degrees, by which the making.

C I X.

ALL Orders heretofore made, repugnant or swaruing from these, shall be henceforth voyd.

Grants of Land.

C X.

ALL *Grants* of Lands and Liberties in *Virginia*, shall be passed by Indenture: the Counterpane wherof shall be sealed by the *Grantees*, and kept in the *Companies* Chest of Euidences. And the *Secretary* shall haue the engrossing of all such Indentures.

C X I.

NO *Patents* or Indentures of *Grants* of Lands in *Virginia*, shall be sealed, but being read and approoued in a Quarter-Court: the same hauing been also first examined and allowed vnder the hands of a select *Comittie* for that purpose.

C X I I.

NO libertie shall be granted, tending to the exempting of any man from the authoritie of the Gouernor of *Virginia*, or of the Supreame *Counseils* or Courts there established; in any case

of

of Treason, Rebellion, or Sedition : or vpon any dutie to be performed for the necessary defence of the Countrey ; or the perseruation of the publique peace, and suppressing Tumults within the Land ; or for trials in matters of Iustice by way of appeale ; or otherwise by lawfull Orders to be from hence deliuered : or in cases consented vnto, as well by a generall Assembly of the *Colonie* there, as by the *Companie* here in a Quarter-Court. And all Grants, former or future, swaruing from this Order, shall be so farre forth deemed vnlawfull and surreptitious : as being repugnant to the Limitations in his Maiesties *Letters Patents.*

CXIII.

IN all *Grants* of Lands, a fift of the Roiall Mines of Gould and Siluer shall be reserued to the *Companie :* as an other fift is alreadie referued to the Crowne.

CXIV.

IN all *Patents* or Indentures of *Grants* of Lands, the *Grantees* shall couenant to employ their people in great part in Staple Commodities, as Corne, Wine, Silke, Silke grasse, Hempe, Flax, Pitch and Tar, Pot-ashes and Sope-ashes, Iron, Clap-boord, and other Materialls : and not wholly or chiefly about *Tabacco,* and *Sassaphras.*

CXV.

ALL *Grants* of Land in *Virginia* to the old Aduenturors their Heires and Assignes, that is, to such as haue heretofore brought in their money to the *Treasurie* for their seuerall shares, (being of twelve pound ten shillings the share) shall be of one hundred Acres the share vpon the first diuision ; and of as many more vpon a second diuision, when the Land of their first diuision shall be sufficiently peopled. And for euery person which they shall transport thither before *Midsomer* day one thousand sixe hundred twentie fiue, if he continue there three yeares, or dye in the meane time after he is shipped, it shall be to the Transporters, of fiftie acres the person vpon the first diuision, and fiftie more vpon a second diuision in like manner, without paying any Rent to the *Companie* for the one or the other. And in all such Grants, the names of the Aduenturors, and the seuerall number of each of their shares, shall be expressed. *Prouided* alwayes, that if the said Aduenturors or any of them, doe not truely and effectually within one yeare next after the sealing of the said Grant, pay and discharge all such summes of money, wherein by subscription (or otherwise vpon notice

thereof

thereof giuen from the *Auditors*,) they stand indebted to the *Companie* : Or if the said Aduenturors, or any of them, hauing not lawfull right, either by purchase from the *Companie*, or by assignement from some other former Aduenturor, within one yeare after the said Grant; or by speciall gift of the *Companie* (vpon merit preceding) in a full Quarter Court; to so many shares as he or they pretend; doe not within one yeare after the said Grant, satisfie and pay to the said *Treasuror* and *Companie* for euery share so wanting, after the rate of twelue pounds ten shillings the share : that then the said Grant, for so much as concerneth the whole part, and all the Shares of the said person so behinde, and not satisfying as aforesaid, shall be vtterly voide.

C X V I.

ALL *Grants* of Land in *Virginia* to new Aduenturors, that is to say, to such as hereafter shall be free of the *Companie*, paying the *Companie* for their Shares before *Midsomer*, 1625. shall for their owne persons and shares be of like condition with the former to all intents and purposes. But for such other as shall at their charges be transported into *Virginia*, before the said *Midsomer*, 1625. in manner afore said; shall be reserued a yearely Rent of twelue pence for euery fiftie acres acrewing to them by vertue of such transportation; to be answered to the said *Treasuror* and *Companie*, and their Successors for euer, after the first seuen yeares of euery such *Grant*.

C X V I I.

ALL *Grants* to all other persons not comprised in the two Orders last before set downe, that is to say, to such Planters as before *Midsomer* day, 1625. shall goe into *Virginia* with intent there to inhabit : if they continue there three yeares, or dye after they are shipped, there shall be grant made of fiftie acres for euery person vpon a first diuision, and as many more vpon a second diuision (the first being peopled) which Grant shall be made respectiuely to such persons and their Heires, at whose charges the said persons going to inhabit in *Virginia* shall be transported; with reseruation of twelue pence yearely Rent, as aforesaid.

C X V I I I.

IN all the foresaid *Grants*, shall be inserted a Condition or *prouiso*, that the *Grantees* shall from time to time, make a true Certificat to the said *Treasuror*, *Counseil*, and *Companie*, from the chiefe Officer or Officers of the places respectiuely, of the number, names, ages, sex, trades, and conditions of euery such

such person so transported, or shipped, before the said *Midsomer* day, 1625. to be entred by the *Secretarie* into a Register Booke for that purpose to be made.

CXIX.

FOr the preuenting of fraud, and dammage to the *Companie* in their Rents; by drawing new Aduenturors or Planters, vpon purchase of a few old Aduentures, into th'immunitie of the old Aduenturors of not paying any Rent for the shares of fiftie acres the person transported by them before the foresaid day : it is ordered, that in all Indentures of *Grant* of Lands to old Aduenturors, being for fewer then fiftie shares of the old aduenture, the immunitie of not paying Rent for the shares obtained by transporting of persons as aforesaid, shall not be generall ; but restrained to the proportion of foure persons to euery share of the old aduenture, transported before *Midsomer* day, 1625.

CXX.

ALL *Grants* of Land shall be made with equall fauours, and *Grants* of like Liberties and Immunities as neere as may be, (except the differences of Rent aboue set downe :) to the end that all complaint of partialitie or vnindifferency may be preuented.

Trade.

CXXI.

IT shall be free for all his Maiesties Subiects, after the determination of the present Ioynt Stocke for the *Magazine*, to trade into *Virginia* with the *Colonie ;* paying the duties set down in his Maiesties *Letters Patents.*

CXX·II.

IF any ioynt Stocke for a *Magazine*, being requested by the Court, refuse or forbeare to send Corne, Cattle, or Munition, for the necessary reliefe and supply of the *Colonie* in *Virginia :* it shall be lawfull from that day forward for any person freely to trade to and with the *Colonie* in *Virginia*, carrying thither onely Cattle, Corne, and Munition, without paying any duties to the *Companie* for seuen yeares next coming ; any former restraint to the contrarie notwithstanding.

If

CXXIII.

IF either in the present ioynt Stocke for the *Magazine*, or any other hereafter to be erected, the generall *Companie* out of their common Cash beare part as an Aduenturor : they shall ratably partake like profit, and vndergoe like losse, with other Aduenturors. And any Order made to the contrary shall be voide.

CXXIV.

DVring the time that the common Cash beareth part as an Aduenturor in any Ioynt Stocke for the *Magazine* ; the meetings of the Aduenturors shall be in the same place, and on the same dayes, that the Generall Courts are kept : and either before the beginning, or after the ending of the Court : vnlesse the Court vpon extraordinary cause appoint some other time.

College.

CXXV.

THE Quarter Court in euery *Trinitie Term*, shall appoint a choise *Comittie* of fiue or seuen, to continue for that yeare, to take into their care and charge the matter of the *College* to be erected in *Virginia* for the conuersion of *Infidels :* which *Comittie* shall take a course for the recouering of the mony that hath beene collected for that worke. And shall likewise consult how the same may be best imployed, for the beginning, pursuing, and perfecting of the same worke. And shall from time to time acquaint the generall Courts with their doings, from thence to receiue approbation and direction.

CXXVI.

THE *Treasuror* shall keepe a seuerall Cash and account of this money, to be presented to the *Auditors*, and from them to the Court. And he shall not issue any money out of this Cash, otherwise then by warrant vnder the great part of these *Comitties* hands.

CXXVII.

THE *Auditors* shall forthwith pervse the account of this Cash ; and if any money haue beene issued out thereof by order of Court, otherwise then for the proper end to which it was
intended ;

intended; it shall be restord out of the common cash of the *Companie.*

Accounts.

CXXVIII.

NO *Auditors* extraordinary shall presume to intermedle with the auditing of any Account, wherein the body of the *Companie* is interrested, but being appointed in the face, and with the approbation of the Court.

CXXIX.

ALL *Accountants* whatsoeuer, and Auditors extraordinary, if the Court so require, shall haue an Oath ministred vnto them in the face of the Court; the one for true accounting, the other for true auditing.

CXXX.

NO *Account* shall be held cleered, nor *Accountants* discharged; till the *Account,* being approued vnder the *Auditors* hands, be presented to the Court: And there lye openly in Court, two Court dayes, to be viewed by any that are so disposed.

CXXXI.

IF exception be taken to any *Account* whatsoeuer, the Court shall proceede to a review, as in like case of the *Treasuror.* If no exception be taken in the two Court dayes; or vpon the reuiew returned, and the *Account* approued: the *Treasuror* then, or *Deputie* in his absence shall signe the *Account* in open Court: wherby the *Accountants* shall be clearely discharged.

CXXXII.

IF any Officer, or other *Accountants,* be slowe in bringing in their Accounts to the *Auditors,* ordinary, or extraordinary; Or within one moneth after their *Account* is perfected, doe not pay to the Cash the due summe remaining, vnlesse the Court see cause to giue longer time: the *Auditors* or *Treasuror* shall impart the same to the Court, that order be thence giuen for redresse thereof.

THese Orders hauing beene first framed and digested by a select *Comittie;* and then presented to the *Counseil,* and by them approued; were afterwards publiquely read in the

Preparatory

Preparatory Court, held on Munday the 7. of Iune, 1619. And lastly were againe read distinctly and deliberately in a great and generall Quarter Court held on Wednesday, the 9. of Iune, 1619. where with a full & general consent, by erection of hands, they were ratified and ordained to be the perpetuall standing Orders of the *Companie* of *Virginia*.

Some few additions, and small alterations, haue
since been made, in the Quarter Courts
in *Easter Term* and *Trinitie Terme*,
1620.

FINIS

Force's Collection of Historical Tracts.

VOL. III.—No. 6.

A TRUE
RELATION
OF
VIRGINIA
AND
Mary-Land;

With the Commodities therein, which in
part the Author saw; the rest he had from knowing and Credible persons in the Moneths of
February, March, April and *May:*

By *Nathaniel Shrigley*, Anno. 1669.

Published by Allowance.

LONDON,
Printed by *Tho. Milbourn* for *Thomas Hudson* Book-binder,
Living the next door to the Signe of the *Blew-Boar* in
Redcross Street.

Force's Collection of Historical Tracts.

Vol. III.—No. 7.

A TRUE
RELATION
OF
VIRGINIA and *MARY-LAND*,

With the Commodities therein, &c.

IMprimis, the *Capes* are in the Latitude of 37 Longitude of 302. from whence a Large *Bay* called *Chesebeack Bay* flowes about seven Leagues broad *N*. by *E*. betwixt three and four degrees in length; then it branches it self into many small Rivers: the depth of the *Bay* is seaven, ten, twelve, or fourteen Fatham; it hath several small Islands in it. Out of which *Bay* on the *East* side, these are the principal Rivers, *Anamesax, Ockahanock, Nantecocke,* little *Choptanke,* great *Choptanke,* St. *Michaels, Wy River, Chester, Sacifrax River.*

On the *West* side these are the principle Rivers, *Elizabeth, Nansemum, James, Back, Yorke, Rapahanock, Petomock, Patuxon, Soueth, Severn, Gunpowder* River, *Patapsco;* from which River the *Bay* draws straiter, and devides it self into many lesser Rivers.

Out of which *Bay* and Rivers, there are branched many Navigable Rivers and Creeks, the which no Ten men in the Land are able to nominate.

The shore on the *East* from the *Bay* to the Ocean, is but about twenty miles broad.

The Rivers on the *West* of the *Bay* are Navigable, some 40. some 50. some 100. some 200. some 300. miles; which Bay, Rivers and Creeks are plentiful of Fowle from *September* till *March,* of all sorts, as Swans, Geese, Brants, Ducks, Widgeon, Teale, with many other sorts too tedious to relate, some of which tarry with them all *Summer:* And Fish multitudes, as

Porposses,

Porposses, Grampases, Herring-Hoggs, Drums, Sheepsheads, Bass, Mullets, Pearch, Sturgeon, Eales, Salmon, Trouts, Thornbacks, Garrs, Cats, Oysters, Crabs, Turtles, with many more too tedious to relate.

The Cattle naturally of the Country, are Bucks, Does, Staggs, Hindes, Hares, Ratoons, Possums, Beavers, Otters, Lyous, Bears, Wolves, Panthers, Leopards, Foxes, Wilde Cats, with many more.

Fowle naturally to the Land are Eagles, Hawks, Vultures, Cranes, Crows, Turkies, Partridges, Pidgions, Larks, Red-birds, the Baltenore.bird, being black and yellow, blew Birds, mocking Birds, Woodpickers, and many sorts more.

English Cattle; plenty of Cows, Bulls, Oxen, Sheep, Goats, Swine, Horses, and all manner of English Poultrey.

The Country is naturally full of *Vines, Fruit Trees,* and *Timber,* As,

F. *Mulberries.*		T. *Ash.*	
F. *Plumbs.*		*Holly*	
F. *Pesimmons.*		T. *Elder.*	
F. *Cherries.*		*Locust.*	
M. *Beach.*		T. *Hasle.*	
T. *Chesnut.*		*White.*	
T. *Poplar.*	Oaks.	*Red.*	
T. *Pine.*	A. T.	*Black.*	
Sasifrax.		*Chesnut.*	
T. *Ceder.*		*Spanish.*	
T. *Cypress.*		*Gum Trees*	
Syccamore.		*being cut,*	
T. *Wallnut.*		*runns Bal-*	
Pekickery.		*some,* with	
Sasiperella.		many others.	

These Trees marked *F.* are fruite, *M.* are Mass or feeding for Swine, T. timber or plank, A. Acorns, N. Nutts, with Grape-Vines climbing up the trees very fruitfull; and Hops
also

also in the Woods; multitudes of Rasberies, Strawberies, Barberies, Cranberies, with infinite of all sorts of Hearbs; the best Garden in *England* affords not better.

In Orchards all sorts of Apple-Trees, Pear-Trees, Quince, Peach, Apricocks, Cherries, Figg-Trees, and Vines; Gardens as good as *England* affords for flowers, hearbs and roots of all sorts; with Colworts, Musmillions, Cuccumbers, Watermillions, May-cocks, Hornes, Peshaues, Rose-Trees, sweet-Bryers, and many things more.

There is a Root common in the Woods called *Tuckaho*, the Natives eat it for bread; our swine eat it; with Acorns and Nuts of all sorts, they are Fat; and is the sweetest Bacon that ever man tasted.

The planters feed not their Swine nor Cattle, but kill them fat out of the Woods.

There is Fullers-Earth, Marle, Salt-peter, Iron, Stone, Lead, Tin and Silver Oar.

There is plenty of English graine, as Wheat, Barley, Beanes, Peas and Oats.

The ground is very fruitful, and produceth plentiful Crops with great speed, what ever is planted or Sown; as for example, one careful laborious man will plant, tend, and get in 50. barrels of Indian Wheat, without the help of Man, Horse or Oxe; each barrel is five English bushels. And if the stone or seed of any fruit be sown, it will bear the third year without grafting; each Planter makes great Crops of Tobacco; the *Western* limits of the Land are unknown In *Mary-Land*; their Religion is free to all that profess to believe in Jesus Christ.

F I N I S.

THE

Simple Cobler

OF

A G G A W A M in America.

WILLING

To help Mend his Native Country, lamentably tattered, both in the upper-Leather
and sole, with all the honest stitches he
can take.

And as willing never to be paid for his work
by Old English wonted pay.

It is his Trade to patch all the year long, gratis.

Therefore

I Pray Gentlemen keep your Purses.

By *Theodore de la Guard.*

The Fifth Edition, with some Amendments.

---

*In rebus arduis ac tenai spe, fortissima
quæque consilia tutissima sunt.* Cic.

In English,

When boots and shoes are torn up to the lefts,
Coblers must thrust their awles up to the hefts.

This is no time to fear *Appelles gramm :
Ne Sutor quidem ultra crepidam.*

LONDON: Printed by *J. D. & R. I.* for *Stephen Bowtell,* at
the Sign of the Bible, in Pope's Head Alley, 1 6 4 7. Re-
printed at *BOSTON* in *N. England,* for *Daniel Henchman,*
at his Shop in King Street, 1 7 1 3.

Force's Collection of Historical Tracts.

Vol. III.—No. 8.

TO THE
READER,

Gentlemen,

I Pray make a little room for a Cobler, his work was done in time, but a Ship setting Sail one day too soon makes it appear some Weeks too late; Seeing he is so reasonable as to demand no other pay for his labour and leather, but leave to pay us well for our faults, let it be well accepted, as Counsel in our occasions to come, and as Testimony to what is past,

By a Friend.

SUTOR ULTRA CREPIDEM.

EITHER I am in Apoplexy, or that man is in a Lethargy, who doth not now sensibly feel God shaking the Heavens over his head, and the Earth under his feet: The Heavens so, as the Sun begins to turn into darkness, the Moon into blood, the Stars to fall down to the ground; So that little Light of Comfort or Counsel is left to the Sons of Men: The Earth so, as the foundations are failing, the righteous scarce know where to find rest, the inhabitants stagger like drunken men: it is in a manner dissolved both in Religions and Relations: And no marvel; for, they have defiled it by transgressing the Laws, changing the Ordinances, and breaking the Everlasting Covenant. The Truths of God are the Pillars of the World, whereon States aud Churches may stand quiet if they will; if they will not, He can easily shake them off into delusions, and distractions enough.

Satan is now in his passions, he feels his passion approaching; he loves to fish in royled waters. Though that Dragon cannot sting the vitals of the Elect mortally, yet that Beelzebub can fly-blow their Intellectuals miserably: The finer Religion grows, the finer he spins his Cobwebs, he will hold pace with Christ so long as his wits will serve him. He sees himself beaten out of gross Idolatries, Heresies, Ceremonies, where the Light breaks forth with power; he will therefore bestir him to prevaricate Evangelical Truths, and Ordinances, that if they will needs be walking, yet they shall *laborare varicibus*, and not keep their path, he will put them out of time and place; Assassinating for his Engineers, men of Paracelsian parts; well complexioned for honesty; for such are fittest to Mountebank his Chimistry into sick Churches and weak Judgments.

Nor shall he need to stretch his strength overmuch in this work: Too many men having not laid their foundations sure, nor ballasted their Spirits deep with humility and fear, are prest enough of themselves to evaporate their own apprehensions. Those that are acquainted with Story know, it hath ever been so in new Editions of Churches: Such as are least able, are most busy to pudder in the rubbish, and to raise dust in the eyes of more steady Repayrers. Civil Commotions make room for uncivil practises: Religious mutations, for irreligious opinions:

nions: Change of Air, discovers currupt bodies; Reformation
of Religion, unsound minds.   He that hath any well-faced
phansy in his Crown, and doth not vent it now, fears the pride
of his own heart will dub him dunce for ever.   Such a one will
trouble the whole *Israel* of God with his most untimely births,
though he makes the bones of his vanity stick up, to the view
and grief of all that are godly wise.   The devil desires no better sport than to see light heads handle their heels, and fetch
their carreers in a time, when the Roof of Liberty stands open.

The next perplexed Question, with pious and ponderous
men, will be: What should be done for the healing of these
comfortless exulcerations.   I am the unablest adviser of a thousand, the unworthiest of ten thousand; yet I hope I may presume to assert what follows without just offence.

First, such as have given or taken any unfriendly reports of
us *New-English*, should doe well to recollect themselves.   We
have been reputed a Colluvies of wild Opinionists, swarmed into
a remote wilderness to find elbow-room for our Phanatic Doc-
trines and practises; I trust our diligence past, and constant se-
dulity against such persons and courses, will plead better things
for us.   I dare take upon me, to be the Herauld of *New-England* so far, as to proclaim to the World, in the name of our
Colony, that all Familists, Antinomians, Anabaptists, and other
Enthusiasts shall have free Liberty to keep away from us, and
such as will come to be gone as fast as they can, the sooner the
better.

Secondly, I dare aver, that God doth no where in his word
tolerate Christian States, to give Tolerations to such adversa-
ries of his Truth, if they have power in their hands to suppress them.

Here is lately brought us an Extract of a *Magna Charta,*
so called, compiled between the Sub-planters of a *West-Indian*
Island; whereof the first Article of constipulation, firmly pro-
vides free stable-room and litter for all kind of Consciences, be
they never so dirty or jadish; making it actionable, yea, trea-
sonable, to disturb any man in his Religion, or to discommend
it, whatever it be.   We are very sorry to see such professed
Prophaneness in *English* Professors, as industriously to lay their
Religious foundations on the ruine of true Religion; which
strictly binds every Conscience *to contend earnestly for the
Truth: to preserve unity of Spirit, Faith and Ordinances, to
be all like minded, of one accord; every man to take his Brother into his Christian care, to stand fast with one spirit, with
one mind, striving together for the faith of the Gospel;* and
by no means to permit Heresies or Erronious Opinions: But
God

God abhorring such loathsome beverages, hath in his righteous judgment blasted that enterprize, which might otherwise have prospered well, for ought I know; I presume their case is generally known ere this.

If the Devil might have his free option, I believe he would ask nothing else, but liberty to enfranchize all false Religions, and to embondage the true; nor should he need: It is much to be feared that lax Tolerations upon State-pretences and planting necessities, will be the next subtle Stratagem he will spread to distate the Truth of God, and supplant the Peace of the Churches. Tolerations in things tolerable, exquisitely drawn out by the lines of the Scripture, and pensil of the Spirit, are the sacred favours of Truth, the due latitudes of Love, the fair Compartiments of Christian fraternity: but irregular dispensations, dealt forth by the facilities of men, are the frontiers of error, the redoubts of Schisme, the perillous irritaments of carnal and spiritual enmity.

My heart hath naturally detested four things: The standing of the Apocrypha in the Bible; Forainers dwelling in my Country, to crowd out Native Subjects into the corners of the Earth; Alchymized Coines; Tolerations of divers Religions, or of one Religion in segregant shapes: He that willingly assents to the last, if he examines his heart by day-light, his Conscience will tell him, he is either an Atheist, or an Heretick, or an Hypocrite, or at best a captive to some Lust: Poly-piety is the greatest impiety in the World. True Religion is *Ignis probationis*, which doth *congregare homogenea & segregare heterogenea*.

Not to tolerate things meerly indifferent to weak Consciences, argues a Conscience too strong: pressed uniformity in these, causes much disunity: To tolerate more than indifferents, is not to deal indifferently with God: He that doth it, takes his Scepter out of his hand, and bids him stand by. Who hath to do to institute Religion but God. The power of all Religion and Ordinances, lies in their Purity: their Purity in their Simplicity: then are mixtures pernicious. I lived in a City, where a Papist Preached in one Church, a Lutheran in another, a Calvinist in a third; a Lutheran one part of the day, a Calvinist the other, in the same Pulpit: the Religion of that Place was but motly and meagre, their affections Leopard-like.

If the whole Creature should conspire to do the Creator a mischief, or offer him an insolency, it would be in nothing more, than in erecting untruths against his Truth, or by sophisticating his Truths with humane medleyes: the removing of some one iota in Scripture, may draw out all the life, and traverse all the

Truth

Truth of the whole Bible: but to authorise an untruth, by a Toleration of State, is to build a sconce against the walls of Heaven, to batter God out of his Chair: To tell a practical lye, is a great Sin, but yet transient; but to set up a Theorical untruth, is to warrant every lye that lyes from its root to the top of every branch it hath, which are not a few.

I would willingly hope that no Member of the Parliament hath skilfully ingratiated himself into the hearts of the House, that he might watch a time to Midwife out some ungracious Toleration for his own turn, and for the sake of that, some other, I would also hope that a word of general caution should not be particularly misapplied. I am the freer to suggest it, because I know not one man of that mind, my aim is general, and I desire may be so accepted. Yet good Gentlemen, look well about you, and remember how *Tiberius* play'd the Fox with the Senate of *Rome*, and how *Fabius Maximus* cropt his ears for his cunning.

That State is wise, that will improve all pains and patience rather to compose, than tolerate differences in Religion. There is no divine Truth, but hath much Cœlestial fire in it from the Spirit of Truth: nor no irreligious untruth, without its proportion of Antifire from the spirit of Error to contradict it: the zeal of the one, the virulency of the other, must necessarily kindle Combustions. Fiery diseases seated in the Spirit, imbroil the whole frame of the body: others more external and cool, are less dangerous. They which divide in Religion, divide in God; they who divide in him, divide beyond *Genus Generalissimum*, where there is no reconciliation, without atonement; that is, without uniting in him, who is One, and in his Truth, which is also one.

Wise are those men who will be perswaded rather to live within the pale of Truth, where they may be quiet, than in the purlieves, where they are sure to be hunted ever and anon, do Authority what it can. Every singular Opinion, hath a singular opinion of it self, and he that holds it a singular opinion of himself, and a simple opinion of all contra-sentients: he that confutes them, must confute all three at once, or else he does nothing; which will not be done without more stir than the Peace of the State or Church can indure.

And prudent are those Christians, that will rather give what may be given, than hazard all by yielding nothing. To sell all Peace of Country, to buy some Peace of Conscience unseasonably, is more avarice than thrift, imprudence than patience: they deal not equally, that set any Truth of God at such a rate; but they deal wisely that will stay till the Market is fallen.

My Prognosticks deceive me not a little, if once within three
seven

seven years, Peace prove not such a Penny-worth at most Marts in Christendom, that he that would not lay down his Money, his Lust, his Opinion, his Will, I had almost said the best flower of his Crown for it, while he might have had it; will tell his own heart, he plaid the very ill husband.

Concerning Tolerations, I may further assert.

That Persecution of true Religion, and Toleration of false, are the *Jannes* and *Jambres* to the Kingdom of Christ, whereof the last is far the worst. *Augustines* Tongue had not owed his Mouth one Penny-rent though he had never spake word more in it, but this, *Nullum malum pejus libertate errandi.*

Frederick Duke of *Saxon,* spake not one foot beyond the mark when he said. He had rather the Earth should swallow him up quick, than he should give a toleration to any Opinion against any Truth of God.

He that is willing to tolerate any Religion, or discrepant way of Religion, besides his own, unless it be in matters meerly indifferent, either doubts of his own, or is not sincere in it.

He that is willing to tolerate any unsound Opinion, that his own may also be tolerated, though never so sound, will for a need hang God's Bible at the Devils girdle.

Every toleration of false Religions, or Opinions hath as many Errors and Sins in it, as all the false Religions and Opinions it tolerates, and one sound one more.

That State that will give Liberty of Conscience in matters of Religion, must give Liberty of Conscience and Conversation in their Moral Laws, or else the Fiddle will be out of Tune, and some of the strings crack.

He that will rather make an irreligious quarel with other Religions than try the Truth of his own by valuable Arguments, and peaceable Sufferings; either his Religion, or himself is irreligious.

Experience will teach Churches and Christians, that it is far better to live in a State united, though a little Corrupt, than in a State, whereof some Part is incorrupt, and all the rest divided.

I am not altogether ignorant of the eight Rules given by Orthodox Divines about giving Tolerations, yet with their favour I dare affirm,

That there is no Rule given by God for any State to give an affirmative Toleration to any false Religion, or Opinion whatsoever; they must connive in some Cases, but may not concede in any.

That the State of *England* (so far as my Intelligence serves) might in time have prevented with ease, and may yet without any great difficulty deny both Toleration, and irregular connivences *salva Republica.*

That

That if the State of *England* shall either willingly Tolerate, or weakly connive at such Courses, the Church of that Kingdom will sooner become the Devils dancing-School, than Gods Temple : The Civil State a Bear-garden, than an Exchange : The whole Realm a Pais base than an *England*. And what pity it is, that that Country which hath been the Staple of Truth to all Christendom, should now become the Aviary of Errors to the whole World, let every fearing heart judge.

I take Liberty of Conscience to be nothing but a freedom from Sin, and Error. *Conscientia in tantum libera, inquantum ab errore liberata.* And Liberty of Error nothing but a Prison for Conscience. Then small will be the kindness of a State to build such Prisons for their Subjects.

The Scripture saith, there is nothing makes free but Truth, and Truth saith, there is no Truth but one : If the States of the World would make it their sum-operous Care to preserve this One Truth in its purity and Authority, it would ease you of all other Political cares. I am sure Satan makes it his grand, if not only task, to adulterate Truth ; Falshood is his sole Scepter, whereby he first ruffled, and ever since ruined the World.

If Truth be but One, methinks all the Opinionists in *England* should not be all in that One Truth, some of them I doubt are out. He that can extract an unity out of such a disparity, or contract such a disparity into an unity ; had need be a better Artist, than ever was *Drebell*.

If two Centers (as we may suppose) be in one Circle, and lines drawn from both to all the points of the Compass, they will certainly cross one another, and probably cut through the Centers themselves.

There is talk of an universal Toleration, I would talk as loud as I could against it, did I know what more apt and reasonable Sacrifice *England* could offer to God for his late performing all his heavenly Truths than an universal Toleration of all hellish Errors, or how they shall make an universal Reformation, but by making Christs Academy the Devils University, where any man may commence Heretick *per saltum;* where he that is *filius Diabolicus,* or *simpliciter pessimus,* may have his grace to go to Hell *cum Publico Privilegio;* and carry as many after him, as he can.

Religio docenda est, non coercenda is a pretty piece of *album Latinum* for some kind of throats that are willingly sore, but *Hæresis dedocenda est non permittenda,* will be found a far better *Diamoron* for the Gargarisms this Age wants, if timely and throughly applyed.

If

If there be room in *England* for

Familists		*Manes*
Libertines		*Lemures*
Erastians		*Dryades*
Antitrinitarians		*Homodryades*
Anabaptists		*Potamides*
Antiscripturists		*Naiades*
Arminians		*Hinnides*
Manifestarians		*Pierides*
Millinarians	the room	*Nereides*
Antinomians	for	*Pales*
Socinians		*Anonides*
Arrians		*Parcades*
Perfectists		*Castalides*
*Brownists**		*Monidès*
Mortalians		*Charites*
Religious *Seekers*	Good Spi-	*Heliconides*
Men but *Enthusiasts*,	rits, but ve-	*Pegasides.*
pernicious &c.	ry Devils.	&c.
Hereticks		

In a word room for Hell above ground.

It is said, Though a man have light enough himself to see the Truth, yet if he hath not enough to enlighten others, he is bound to tolerate them, I will engage my self, that all the Devils in *Britanie* shall sell themselves to their shirts, to purchase a Lease of this Position for three of their Lives, under the Seal of the Parliament.

It is said, That Men ought to have Liberty of their Conscience, and that it is Persecution to debar them of it : I can rather stand amazed than reply to this : it is an astonishment to think that the braines of men should be parboyl'd in such impious ignorance ; Let all the wits under the Heavens lay their heads together and find an Assertion worse than this (one excepted) I will Petition to be chosen the universal Ideot of the World.

It is said, That Civil Magistrates ought not to meddle with Ecclesiastical matters.

I would answer to this so well as I could, did I not know that some Papers lately brought out of *New-England*, are going to

---

* *By Brownists, I mean not Independents, but dew-clawd Seperatists : far be it from me to wrong godly Independents. I truly acknowledge that I judge my self neither able nor worthy to honour some of them as they deserve.*

the Press, wherein the Opinions of the Elders there in a late Synod, concerning this point are manifested, which I suppose will give clearer satisfaction than I can.

The true English of all this their false Latin, is nothing but a general Toleration of all Opinions; which motion if it be like to take, it were very requisite, that the City would repair *Pauls* with all the speed they can, for an English *Pantheon*, and bestow it upon the Sectaries, freely to assemble in, then there may be some hope that *London* will be quiet in time.

But why dwell I so intolerable long about Tolerations, I hope my fears are but Panick, against which I have a double cordial. First, that the Parliament will not though they could: Secondly, that they cannot though they would grant such Tolerations. God who hath so honoured them with eminent Wisdom in all other things, will not suffer them to cast both his, and their Honour in the dust of perpetual Infamy, do what they can; nor shall those who have spent so great a part of their substance in redeeming their Civil Liberties from Usurpation, lose all that remains in enthralling their spiritual Liberty by Toleration.

It is said Opinionists are many, and strong, that *de sunt Vires*, that it is *turbata respublica*, I am very sorry for it, but more sorry, if despondency of mind shall cause the least tergiversation in Gods Worthies, who have receiv'd such pledges of his presence in their late Counsels, and Conflicts. It is not thousands of Opinionists that can pinion his Everlasting armes, I can hardly believe there is a greater unbeliever than my Self, yet I can verily believe that the God of Truth will in a short time scatter them all like smoke before the wind. I confess, I am troubled to see Men so over-troubled about them; I am rather glad to hear the Devil is breaking up house in *England*, and removing some whither else, give him leave to sell all his rags, and odd-ends by the out-cry; and let his petty Chapmen make their Market while they may, upon my poor Credit it will not last long. He that hath done so much for *England* will go on to perfect his own Praise, and his Peoples Peace: Let good men stand still, and behold his further Salvation. He that sitteth in the Heavens laughs at them, the most High hath them in Derision, and their folly shall certainly be manifested to all men.

Yet I dare not but add, and in the Name of God will add, that if any Publick members of Church or State, have been either open fautors, or private abetters of any blasphemous, contagious Opinions; It will be their wisdom to proportion their repentance to their Sin, before God makes them Publick Monuments of Ignominy, and Apostasy.

Thirdly,

Thirdly, That all Christian States, ought to disavow and decry all such Errors, by some peremptory Statutory Act, and that in time, that Subjects knowing fully the mind of the State, might not delude themselves with vain hopes of unsufferable Liberties. It is less to say, *Statuatur veritas, ruat Regnum*, than *Fiat justitia, ruat Cœlum :* but there is no such danger in either of them. Fear nothing Gentlemen, *Rubiconem transistis, jacta est alea*, ye have turned the Devil out of doors ; fling all his old parrel after him out at the windows, lest he makes another errand for it again. *Quæ relinquunter in morbis post indicationem, recidivas facere consuevere.* Christ would have his Church without spot or wrinckle ; They that help make it so, shall lose neither honour nor labour : If ye be wise, suffer no more thorns in his sides or your own. When God kindles such fires as these, he doth not usually quench them, till the very scum on the Pot sides be boyled clean away, *Ezek.* 24. 10, 11. Ye were better to do it your selves, than leave it to him : the Arm of the Lord is mighty, his hand very heavy ; who can dwell with his devouring fire, and long lasting burnings ?

Fourthly, to make speedy provisions against Obstinates and Disseminaries : were under favour, two things will be found requisite. First, variety of Penalties, I mean certain, not indefinite : I am a Crabbat against Arbitrary Government. Experience hath taught us here, that political, domestical, and personal respects, will not admit one and the same remedy for all, without sad inconveniences. Secondly, just severity : Persecution hath ever spread Truth, Prosecution scattered Error : Ten of the most Christian Emperors, found that way best ; Schollars know whom I mean : Five of the ancient Fathers perswaded to it, of whom *Augustine* was one, who for a time argued hard for indulgency : but upon conference with other Prudent Bishops, altered his judgment, as appears in three of his Epistles, to *Marcellinus, Donatus*, and *Boniface.* I would be understood, not only an Allower, but an humble Petitioner, that ignorant and tender conscienced Anabaptists may have due time and means of conviction.

Fifthly, That every Prophet, to whom God hath given the Tongue of the Learned, should teach, and every Angel who hath a Pen and Inkhorn by his side write against these grieving extravagancies : writing of many Books, I grant is irksome, reading endless. A reasonable man would think Divines had declaimed sufficiently upon these Themes. I have ever thought the Rule given, *Titus* 3. 10. which cuts the work short and sharp to be more properly prevalent, than wearisome waiting upon unweariable Spirits. It is a most toylsome task to run the
wild-goose

wild-goose chase after a well-breath'd Opinionist: they delight in vitilitigation: it is an itch that loves a life to be scrub'd: they desire not satisfaction, but satisdiction, whereof themselves must be judges: yet in new eruptions of Error with new objections, silence is sinful.

As for my self, I am none of the disputers of this world: all I can do, is to guess when men speak true or false Divinity: If I can but find the Parental root, or formal reason of a Truth, I am quiet; if I cannot, I shore up my slender judgement as long as I can, with two or three the handsomest Props I can get: I shall therefore leave Arguments to acuter heads, and only speak a word of Love, with all Christian respect to our dear Brethren in *England,* which are against Baptizing of Infants: I intreat them to consider these few things seriously and meekly. First, what a high pitch of boldness it is for man to cut a principal Ordinance out of the Kingdom of God; If it be but to make a dislocation, which so far disgoods the Ordinance, I fear it altogether unhallows it, to transplace or transtime a stated Institution of Christ, without his direction, I think, is to destroy it. Secondly, what a Cruelty it is to devest Children of that only external Priviledge which their heavenly Father hath bequeathed them, to interest them visibly in Himself, His Son, His Spirit, His Covenant of Grace, and the tender bosome of their careful Mother the Church. Thirdly, what an Inhumanity it is, to deprive Parents of that comfort they may take from the Baptism of their Infants dying in their Childhood. Fourthly, How unseasonable and unkindly it is, to interturbe the State and Church with these Amalekitish on-sets, when they are in their extream pangs of travail with their lives. Fifthly, to take a through view of those who have preambled this by path. Being sometimes in the Crowds of foraign Wederdopers, that is, Anabaptists, and prying into their inward frames with the best eyes I had; I could not but observe these disguised guises in the generality of them. First, a flat formality of Spirit without salt or savour in the spiritualties of Christ, as if their Religion began and ended in their Opinion. Secondly, a shallow flighting of such as discent from them, appearing too often in their faces, speeches and carriages. Thirdly, a feeble, yet peremptory obstinacy; seldome are any of them reclaimed. Fourthly, a shameful sliding into other such tarpauling tenets, to keep themselves dry from the showers of Justice, as a rational mind would never entertain, if it were not Error-blasted from Heaven and Hell. I should as shrewdly suspect that Opinion, that will cordially corrive with two or three sottish errors, as that faith that can professedly live with two or three sordid sins. I dare
not

not fear our godly Brethren in *England* to be yet coming to this pass; how soon they may, themselves know not, the times are slippery : They will undoubtedly find God as jealous of his Ordinances, as themselves are zealous of their Opinions.

Sixthly, that Authority ought to see their Subjects Children Baptized, though their Parents judgments be against it, if there be no other Evangelical bar in the way.

Seventhly, that prudent men, especially Young, should do well not to ingage themselves in conference with Errorists, without a good calling and great caution : their breath is contagious, their leprey spreading : receive not him that is weak, saith the Apostle to doubtful disputations ; much less may they run themselves into dangerous Sophistications. He usually hears best in their Meetings, that stops his ears closest; he opens his Mouth to best purpose, that keeps it shut, and he doth best of all, that declines their company as wisely as he may.

Brethren, have an extraordinary care also of the late Theosophers, that teach men to climb to Heaven upon a ladder of lying figments. Rather than the Devil will lose his game, he will out-shoot Christ in his own bow; he will out-law the Law, quite out of the Word and World: over-Gospel the Gospel, and quidanye Christ, with Sugar and Rats-bane. He was Professor not long since at *Schlestat* in *Alsatia*, where he learned, that no Poyson is so deadly as the Poyson of Grace.

The wisest way, when all is said, is with all humility and fear, to take Christ as himself hath revealed himself in his Gospel, and not as the Devil presents him to prestigiated fansies. I have ever hated the way of the Rosie-Crucians, who reject things as Gods Wisdom hath tempered them, and will have nothing but their Spirits. If I were to give Physick to Spryts, I would do so too : but when I want Physick for my body, I would not have my Soul tartared : nor my Animal Spirits purged any way, but by my Natural, and those by my bodily humours, and those by such Ordinaries, as have the nearest vicinage to them, and not by the Metaphysical Limbeckings. I cannot think that *materia prima* or *secunda*, should be good for me, that am at least, *Materia minessima sexcentesima quadragesima-quinta.*

Here I hold my self bound to set up a Beacon, to give warning of a new-sprung Sect of Phrantasticks, which would perswade themselves and others, that they have discovered the Norst-west passage to Heaven. These wits of the game, cry up and down in Corners such bold ignotions of a new Gospel, new Christ, new Faith, and new gay-nothings, as trouble unsetled heads, querulous hearts, and not a little grieve the Spirit of
God.

God. I desire all good men may be saved from their Lunatick Creed, by Infidelity; and rather believe these torrid overtures will prove in time nothing but horrid raptures down to the lowest hell, from which he that would be delivered, let him avoid these blasphemers, a late fry of croaking Frogs, not to be indured in a Religious State, no, if it were possible, not an hour.

As some are playing young Spaniel, questing at every bird that rises; so others, held very good men, are at a dead stand, not knowing what to do or say; and are therefore called Seekers, looking for new Nuntio's from Christ, to assoil these benighted questions, and to give new Orders for new Churches. I crave leave with all respect to tell them, that if they look into *Act.* 20. 20, 25. *Gal.* 1. 8, 9. 1 *Tim.* 6. 13, 16. and find them not there; they may happily seek as the young Prophets did for *Elijah's* corps, where it never was, nor ever will be found.

I cannot imagine why the Holy Ghost should give *Timothy* the solemnest charge, was ever given Mortal man, to observe the Rules he had given, till the coming of Christ, if new things must be expected.

Wo to them, who ever they be, that so trouble the ways of God that they who have found the way to Heaven cannot find the way to Church: And wo be to them, that so gaze at the glorious light, they say, will break forth in the thousand years to come, that they make little of the gracious Truth that hath been revealed these sixteen hundred years past. And wo be to them that so under-value the first Master Builders, I mean the Apostles of Christ, that unless he sends wiser than they, He must be accounted less faithful in his house than *Moses* was.

I have cause enough to be as Charitable to others as any man living; yet I cannot but fear, that those men never Moored their Anchors well in the firm soil of Heaven; that are weather-waft up and down with every eddy-wind of every new doctrine. The good Spirit of God doth not usually tie up the Helm, and suffer Passengers to Heaven to ride a drift, hither and thither, as every wave and current carries them : that is a fitter course for such as the Apostle calls wandring Stars and Meteors, without any certain motion, hurried about with tempests, bred of the Exhalations of their own Pride and Self-wittedness: whose damnation sleepeth not, and to whom the mist of darkness is reserved for ever, that they may suffer irreparable shipwrack upon the Sands and Rocks of their own Errors, being of old ordained to condemnation.

Eightly, let all considerate men beware of ungrounded Opinions in Religion : Since I knew what to fear, my heart hath
dreaded

dreaded three things: a blazing Star appearing in the Air: a State Comet, I mean a favourite rising in a Kingdom; a new Opinion spreading in Religion: these are Exorbitances: which is a formidable word; a *vacuum* and an exorbitancy, are mundicidious evils. Concerning Novelties of Opinions; I shall express my thoughts in these brief passages. First, that Truth is the best boone God ever gave the World: there is nothing in the World, World, any further than Truth makes it so, it is better than any creat' *Ens* or *Bonum,* which are but Truths twins. Secondly, the least Truth of Gods Kingdom, doth in its place, uphold the whole Kingdom of his Truths; Take away the least *vericulum* out of the World, and it unworlds all, potentially, and may unravel the whole texture actually, if it be not conserved by an Arm of Superiordinary Power. Thirdly, the least Evangelical Truth is more worth than all the Civil Truths in the World, that are meerly so. Fourthly, that Truth is the Parent of all liberty whether Political or Personal; so much untruth, so much thraldom, *Joh.* 8. 32.

Hence it is, that God is so jealous of his Truths, that he hath taken order in his due justice: First, that no practical Sin is so Sinful as some error in judgment; no man so accursed with indelible infamy and dedolent impenitency, as Authors of Heresie. Secondly, that the least Error, if grown sturdy and pressed, shall set open the Spittle-door of all the squint-ey'd, wry-necked, and brasen-faced Errors that are or ever were of that litter; if they be not enough to serve its turn, it will beget more, though it hath not one crust of reason to maintain them. Thirdly, that that State which will permit Errors in Religion, shall admit Errors in Policy unavoidably. Fourthly, that that Policy which will suffer irreligious Errors, shall suffer the loss of so much Liberty in one kind or other, I will not exempt *Venice, Rhaguse,* the *Cantons,* the *Netherlands,* or any.

An easie head may soon demonstrate, that the Pre-mentioned Planters, by Tolerating all Religions, had immazed themselves in the most intolerable confusions and inextricable thraldoms the World ever heard of. I am perswaded the Devil himself was never willing with their proceedings, for fear it would break his wind and wits to attend such a Province. I speak it seriously, according to my meaning. How all Religions should enjoy their liberty, Justice its due regularity, Civil cohabitation moral honesty, in one and the same Jurisdiction, is beyond the Artique of my comprehension. If the whole conclave of Hell can so compromise, exadverse, and diametrical contradictions, as to compolitize such a multimonstrous maufrey of heteroclytes and quicquidlibets quietly; I trust I may say with all humble reverence,

they

they can do more than the Senate of Heaven. My *modus la-quendi* pardoned : I intirely wish much welfare and more wisdom to that Plantation.

It is greatly to be lamented, to observe the wanton fearlessness of this Age, especially of Younger Professors, to greet new Opinions and Opinionists : as if former truths were grown Superannuate, and Sapless, if not altogether antiquate. *Non senescet veritas.* No man ever saw a gray hair on the head or beard of any Truth, wrinckle, or morphew on its face : The bed of Truth is green all the year long. He that cannot solace himself with any saving truth, as affectionately as at the first acquaintance with it, hath not only a fastidious, but an adulterous Heart.

If all be true we hear, Never was any People under the Sun, so sick of new Opinions as *English-men*, nor of new fashions as *English-women :* If God help not the one, and the Devil leave not helping the other, a blind man may easily foresee what will become of both. I have spoken what I intend for the present to men ; I shall speak a word to the Women anon : in the mean time I intreat them to prepare Patience.

Ninthly, that godly humble Christians ought not to wonder impatiently at the wonderful works of God in these times : it is full Season for him to work Soveraign work, to vindicate his Soveraignty, that men may fear before him. States are unstated, Rulers grown Over-rulers, Subjects worse than men, Churches-decayed. Tofts, Professors, empty casks filled with unholy humours ; I speak not of all, but too many ; I condemn not the generation of the just, God hath his remnant, whom he will carefully preserve. If it be time for men to take up Defensive Arms against such as are called Gods, upon the point of *Salus populi*, it is high time for him that is God indeed, to draw his Sword against Worms and no Men, upon the point of *Majestas imperij :* The piercing of his Sword shall discover the thoughts of many hearts.

Lastly, I dare aver, that it ill becomes Christians any thing well-shod with the preparation of the Gospel, to meditate flight from their dear Country upon these disturbances. Stand your grounds ye *Eleazars* and *Shammahs*, stir not a foot so long as you have half a foot of ground to stand upon : after one or two such Worthies, a great Victory may be regained, and flying *Israel* may return to a rich spoil. *English-men*, be advised to love *England*, with your hearts and to preserve it by your Prayers. I am bold to say that since the pure Primitive Time, the Gospel never thrived so well in any soil on Earth, as in the *British*, nor is the like goodness of Nature, or Cornucopian plenty else-where

else-where to be found : if ye lose that Country and find a better before you come to Heaven, my Cosmography fails me. I
am far from discouraging any, whom necessity of Conscience or
Condition thrusts out by head and shoulders : if God calls any
into a Wilderness, He will be no Wilderness to them, *Jer.* 2. 31.
witness his large beneficence to us here beyond expectation.

Ye say, why come not we over to help the Lord against the
Mighty, in these Sacred Battailes?

I answer, many here are diligently observing the counsel of
the same Prophet, 22. 10. *Weep not for him that is dead, neither bemoan him ; but weep for him that is gone away and shall
return no more to see his Native Country.* Divers make it an
Article of our *American* Creed, which a celebrate Divine of
England hath observed upon *Heb.* 11. 9. That no man ought
to forsake his own Country, but upon extraordinary cause, and
when that cause ceaseth, he is bound in Conscience to return
if he can : We are looking to him who hath our hopes and seasons in his only wise hand.

In the mean time we desire to bow our knees before the
Throne of Grace day and night, that the Lord would be pleased
in his tender mercy to still the sad unquietness and per-peracute
contentions, or that most comfortable and renowned Island, that
at length He may have Praise in his Churches, and his Churches
Peace in Him, through Jesus Christ.

SHould I not keep Promise in speaking a little to Womens
fashions, they would take it unkindly : I was loath to pester
better matter with such stuff; I rather thought it meet to let
them stand by themselves, like the *Quæ Genus* in the Gram-
mar, being Deficients, or Redundants, not to be brought under
any Rule : I shall therefore make bold for this once, to borrow
a little of their loose tongued Liberty, and mispend a word or
two upon their long-wasted, but short-skirted Patience : a little
use of my stirrup will do no harm.

Ridentem dicere verum, quid prohibet?

Gray Gravity it self can well beteam,
That Language be adapted to the Theme.
He that to Parrots speaks, must parrotise :
He that instructs a fool, may act th' unwise.

It is known more than enough, that I am neither Nigard, nor
Cinick, to the due bravery of the true Gentry : if any man mis-
likes a bullymong drossock more than I, let him take her for his
labour :

labour : I honour the Woman that can honour her self with her attire : a good Text always deserves a fair Margent; I am not much offended if I see a trimme far trimmer than she that wears it : in a word, whatever Christianity or Civility will allow, I can afford with *London* measure : but when I hear a nugiperous Gentledame inquire what dress the Queen is in this week : what the nudiustertian fashion of the Court; with egge to be in it in all haste, what ever it be ; I look at her as the very gizzard of a trifle, the product of a quarter of a cypher, the epitome of of Nothing, fitter to be kickt, if she were of a kickable substance, than either honour'd or humour'd.

To speak moderately, I truly confess it is beyond the ken of my understanding to conceive, how those Women should have any true Grace, or valuable vertue, that have so little wit, as to disfigure themselves with such exotick garbes, as not only dismantles their native lovely lustre, but transclouts them into gantbar-geese, ill-shapen-shotten shell-fish, Egyptian Hyeroglyphicks, or at the best into French flurts of the pastery, which a proper English Woman should scorne with her heels : it is no marvel they wear drailes on the hinder part of their heads, having nothing as it seems in the fore-part, but a few Squirrils brains to help them frisk from one ill-favour'd fashion to another.

These whimm' Crown'd shees, these fashion-fansying wits,
Are emty thin brain'd shells, and fidling Kits.

The very troublers and impoverishers of mankind, I can hardly forbear to commend to the World a saying of a Lady living sometime with the Queen of *Bohemia*, I know not where she found it, but it is pitty it should be lost.

The world is full of care, much like unto a bubble,
Women and care, and care and Women, and Women and care
(and trouble.

The Verses are even enough for such odd pegma's, I can make my self sick at any time, with comparing the dazling splender wherewith our Gentlewomen were imbellished in some former habits, with the gut-foundred goosdom, wherewith they are now surcingled and debauched. We have about five or six of them in our Colony : if I see any of them accidentally, I cannot cleanse my phansie of them for a Month after. I have been a solitary Widdower almost twelve years, purposed lately to make a step over to my Native Country for a yoke-fellow : but when I consider how Women there have tripe-wifed themselves with their cladments, I have no heart to the Voyage, least their
　　　　　　　　　　　　　　　　　　　　　　　　　nauseous

nauseous shapes and the Sea, should work too sorely upon my stomach. I speak sadly ; methinks it should break the hearts of English-men, to see so many goodly English-women imprisoned in French Cages, peering out of their hood holes for some men of mercy to help them with a little wit, and no body relieves them.

It is a more common than convenient saying, that nine Taylors make a man : it were well if nineteen could make a Woman to her mind : if Taylors were men indeed, well furnished but with meer Moral Principles, they would disdain to be led about like Apes, by such mymick Marmosets. It is a most unworthy thing, for men that have bones in them, to spend their lives in making fidle-cases for futulous Womens phansies ; which are the very pettitoes of Infirmity, the giblets of perquisquilian toyes. I am so charitable to think, that most of that mystery would work the cheerfuller while they live, if they might be well discharged of the tyring slavery of mis-tyring Women : it is no little labour to be continually putting up English-women, into Out-landish caskes ; who if they be not shifted a new, once in a few Months, grow too sowre for their Husbands. What this Trade will answer for themselves when God shall take measure of Taylors Consciences is beyond my skill to imagine. There was a time when,

> *The joyning of the Red-Rose with the White,*
> *Did set our State into a Damask plight.*

But now our Roses are turned to *Flore de lices*, our Carnations to Tulips, our Gilliflowers to Dayzes, our City-Dames, to an indenominable Quæmalry of overturcas'd things. He that makes Coates for the Moon, had need take measure every noon : and he that makes for Women, as often, to keep them from Lunacy.

I have often heard divers Ladies vent loud feminine complaints of the wearisome varieties and chargeable changes of fashions : I marvel themselves prefer not a Bill of redress. I would *Essex* * Ladies would lead the *Chore*, for the honour of their County and Persons ; or rather the thrice honourable Ladies of the Court, whom it best beseems : who may well presume of a *Le Roy le veult* from our sober King, a *Les Seigneurs ont assentus* from our prudent Peers, and the like *Assentus*, from our considerate, I dare not say Wife-worn Commons :

---

* *All the Counties and Shires of England have had Wars in them since the Conquest, but Essex, which is only free, and should be thankful.*

who

who I believe had much rather pass one such Bill, than pay so many Taylors Bills as they are forced to doe.

Most dear and unparallel'd Ladies, be pleased to attempt it : as you have the precellency of the Women of the World for beauty and feature ; so assume the honour to give, and not take Law from any, in matter of attire : if ye can transact so fair a motion among your selves unanimously, I dare say, they that most renite, will least repent. What greater honour can your Honours desire, than to build a Promontory president to all foraign Ladies, to deserve so eminently at the hands of all the English Gentry present and to come : and to confute the opinion of all the wise men in the World ; who never thought it possible for Women to do so good a work.

If any man think I have spoken rather merrily than seriously he is much mistaken, I have written what I write with all the indignation I can, and no more than I ought. I confess I veer'd my tongue to this kind of Language *de industriæ* though unwillingly, supposing those I speak to are uncapable of grave and rational arguments.

I desire all Ladies and Gentlewomen to understand that all this while I intend not such as through necessary modesty to avoid morose singularity, follow fashions slowly, a flight shot or two off, shewing by their moderation, that they rather draw countermont with their hearts, than put on by their examples.

I point my Pen only against the light-heel'd beagles that lead the chase so fast, that they run all civility out of breath, against these Ape-headed Pullets, which invent Antique fool-fangles, meerly for fashion and novelty sake.

In a word, if I begin once to declaim against fashions, let Men and Women look well about them, there is somewhat in the business ; I confess to the World, I never had Grace enough to be strict in that kind ; and of late years, I have found syrrope of Pride very wholsome in a due *Dos*, which makes me keep such store of that drugg by me, that if any body comes to me for a question-full or two about fashions, they never complain of me for giving them hard measure, or under-weight.

But I address my self to those who can both hear and mend all if they please : I seriously fear, if the Pious Parliament do not find time to state fashions, as ancient Parliaments have done in part, God will hardly find a time to state Religion or Peace : They are the surquedryes of pride, the wantonness of idleness, provoking sins, the certain prodromies of assured judgment, *Zeph.* 1. 7, 8.

It is beyond all account, how many Gentlemens and Citizens Estates are deplumed by their feather-headed Wives, what useful

ful supplies the pannage of *England* would afford other Countries, what rich returns to it self, if it were not slic'd out into Male and Female fripperies : and what a multitude of mis-imploy'd hands, might be better improv'd in some more manly Manufactures for the Publick Weal : it is not easily credible, what may be said of the Preterpluralities of Taylors in *London:* I have heard an honest man say, that not long since there were numbered between *Temple-bar* and *Charing-Cross*, eight thousand of that Trade : let it be conjectured by that proportion how many there are in and about *London*, and in all *England*, they will appear to be very numerous. If the Parliament would please to mend Women, which their Husbands dare not do, there need not so many men to make and mend as there are. I hope the present doleful estate of the Realm, will perswade more strongly to some considerate course herein, than I now can.

Knew I how to bring it in, I would speak a word to long Hair, whereof I will say no more but this : if God proves not such a Barbor to it as he threatens, unless it be amended, *Isai*. 7. 20. before the Peace of the State and Church be well setled, then let my Prophesie be scorned, as a sound mind scornes the riot of that sin, and more it needs not. If those who are tearmed Rattle-heads and Impuritans, would take up a Resolution to begin in moderation of hair, to the just reproach of those that are called Puritans and Round-heads ; I would honour their manliness, as much as the others godliness, so long as I knew what man or honour meant : if neither can find a Barbors shop, let them turn in, to *Psal*. 68. 21. *Jer*. 7. 29. 1 *Cor*. 11. 14. If it be thought no wisdom in men to distinguish themselves in the field by the Scissers, let it be thought no Injustice in God, not to distinguish them by the Sword. I had rather God should know me by my sobriety, than mine enemy not know me by my vanity. He is ill kept, that is kept by his own sin. A short promise, is a far safer guard than a long lock : it is an ill distinction which God is loth to look at, and his Angels cannot know his Saints by. Though it be not the mark of the Beast, yet it may be the mark of a beast prepared to slaughter. I am sure men use not to wear such Manes ; I am also sure Souldiers use to wear other Marklets or Notadoes in time of battel.

HAving done with the upper part of my work, I would now with all humble willingness set on the best piece of Soul-leather I have, did I not fear I should break my All, which though it may be a right old English blade, yet it is but little and weak. I should esteem it the best piece of workmanship my Cobling hand ever wrought, if it would please Him whose work
it

it is, to direct me to speak such a word over the Sea, as the good
old Woman of *Abel* did over the wall, in the like exigent : but
alas, I am but simple.   What if I be ?

> *When States dishelv'd are, and Laws untwist,*
> *Wise men keep their tongues, fools speak what they list.*

I would not be so unwise as to grieve the wise, if I were wise
enough to foresee it : I would speak nothing to the Cause or
Continuance of these wearisome Wars hitherto ; the one is
enough debated, the other more than enough peracted.   Nor
would I declaim of the uncomliness, unbrotherliness, unseason-
ableness and unreasonableness of these direful digladiations : every stroak struck sounds too loud upon this harsh string.   I would
much rather speak perswasives to a comely brotherly seasonable
and reasonable Cessation of Arms on both sides, by a drawn battail : Wherein if I shall adventure a few over-bold words, I intreat my ignorance, impartiality, and Loyalty may plead pardon
for me.

Four means there are, and no more, within the compass of
my consideration, conducing to what is desired.   Either to get
the Standard fixed in Heaven by the Lord of Hosts taken down,
I mean by Reformation : Or to set up white colours instead
of red, on one side or other, I mean by Composition : Or by
furling up all the Ensignes on both sides, I mean by mutual and
general Cessation : Or by still displaying all the Colours and
Cornets of every battallion, I mean by prosecution : without Reformation there will hardly be any Composition ; without Composition little hope of Cessation ; without Cessation there must
and will be Prosecution ; which God forbid.

Reformation.

WHen the Roman Standard was defixed with such difficulty at the battail between *Hannibal* and *Flaminius* at
Trasimene, it proved an ill Omen.   *When God gives quietness,*
who can make trouble ; when he hideth his face, who can be-
hold him?   Whether it be against a Nation or a man only.
That the Hypocrite reign not, lest the People be insnared, Job
34. 29, 30.   How can the Sword of the Lord put it self up into
its scabbard and be quiet.   When himself hath given it a charge
to the contrary ? *Jer.* 47. 6, 7.   It was a Cardinal Truth which
Cardinal *Poole* spake to *H.* 8. *Penes Reges est inferre bellum,*
penes autem Deum terminare.   If Kings will make their beginnings, God will make his ends : much more when himself begins :
When I begin, I will also make an end, 1 *Sam.* 3. 12.   Far
better

better were it, for men to make an end with him in time, than put him to make such an end with them as he there intends.

Political Reformation he seems to call for now *indigitanter*. When he beholds Christian Kingdoms and States unsound in their foundations, illineal in their superstructures, unjust in their administrations; he kicks them in pieces with the foot of his Indignation : But when Religious Statesmen frame and build by the level and plummet of his wisdom, then People may say as his Servants of old, *Look upon* Zion *the City of our Solemnities; Your eyes shall see it a quiet Habitation, a Tabernacle that shall not be taken down; not one of the stakes thereof shall be removed, neither shall any of the cords thereof be broken,* Isai. 33. 20. Neither by civil Commotions nor foraign Invasions. When the cords of a State are exquisitely tight, and the stakes firmly pitched, such a Tent though but a Tent shall not easily flutter or fall : But *if the Tacklings be so loose, that the main Mast cannot stand steady, nor the Sail be well spread ; then may the lame take and devide a great prey,* ver. 23. If Religion, Laws, Liberties, and foraign Federacies be slight ; the strength of strong men shall be weakness, and the weakness of the weak victorious.

Pura politeja ne unum admittit solœcismulum, neque valet, præscriptio in politicis aut moralibus. It may maintain a bright conjecture, against a rusty Truth : a legible possession, against an obliterate Claim : an inconvenience, against a convenience ; where no clear remedy may be had : but never any thing that is formally sinful, or materially mischievous. When rotten States are soundly mended from head to foot, proportions duly admeasured, Justice justly dispenced ; then shall Rulers and Subjects have peace with God and themselves : but till then, the gayest Kingdoms shall be but ruffling scuffling, removing and commoving hovels. For *England,* however the upper Stories are shroadly shattered ; yet the foundations and frame being good or mendable by the Architectors now at work, there is good hope, when Peace is setled, People will dwell more wind-tight and water-tight than formerly, I earnestly wish our Mr. Builders to remember, that punctuality in Divinity and Politie, is but regularity ; that what is amiss in the mould, will misfashion the prosult : and that if this market be slipt, things may grow as dear as ever they were. Most expert Gentlemen, be intreated at length to set our Head right on our Shoulders, that we may once look upwards and go forwards like proper English-men.

God will also have Ecclesiastical Reformation now, or nothing : And here he stands not upon Kings, Parliaments or Assemblies, but upon his own Terms. I fear He will have all dross.

and

and base metals throughly melted away by these combustions, before He quenches them; all his Ordinances and vessels cast into his own fashion, in his own mould, to his own *amussim*, before he restores Peace. If this first work be throughly and throughoutly dispatched as I hope it is, the great *Remora* is removed. If the Parliament and Assembly be pleased to be as curious and industrious as I have seen a great Popish Bishop in execrating a Protestant Par. Church one day, and consecrating it the next ; they may adjourn a while with leave enough.

Some ten or twelve years before these Wars there came to my view these two Predictions.

1. *When God shall purge this Land with soap & nitre,*
   Wo be to the Crown, wo be to the Mitre.

The Accent of the blow shall fall there.
He that pities not the Crown, pities not his own Soul. He that pities not those that wore the Mitre, more than they pittied themselves, or the Churches over which they insulted, or the State then corrupted and now Corruined by their pride & negligence, is to blame.

2. *There is a set of Bishops coming next behind,*
   Will ride the Devil off his legs, and break his wind.

Poor men ! they might have kept his back till this time for ought I know, had they not put him beyond his pace : but Schollers must gallop, though they tumble for it. Yet I commend them for this, they gave him such straynes as made him blow short ever since. I doubt the Assembly troubles him ; and I doubt he troubles them. Well, the Bishops are gone: If they have carried away with them all that was in the Pockets of their Holliday hose, fare them well ; let them come again when I give them a new *Conge d'slier*, or send a pursuivant for them ; which if I do, I shall never trust my self more, though they have often done it for me, who never deserved that honour. Some of them I confess were very honest men, and would have been honester if they dared for their fellows.

The sad work now is to institute better things in their Room, and to induct better men in their room ; rather where and how to find those things, they having cunningly laid them so far out of the way ; I doubt some good men cannot see them, when they look full upon them : it is like, the Bishops carryed away their eyes with them, but I fear they left their Spectacles behind them. I use no Spectacles, yet my eyes are not fine enough,

nor

nor my hand steady enough to cut by such fine threads as are now spun. I am I know not what; I cannot tell what to make of my self, nor I think no body else : My Trade is to find more faults than others will mend ; and I am very diligent at it; yet it scarce finds me a living, though the Country finds me more work than I can turn my hand to.

For Church work, I am neither Presbyterian, nor plebsbyterian, but an Interpendent: My task is to sit and study how shapeable the Independent way will be to the body of *England,* then my head akes on one side ; and how suitable the Presbyterian way, as we hear it propounded, will be to the mind of Christ, then my head akes on the other side : but when I consider how the Parliament will commoderate a way out of both, then my head leaves aking. I am not, without some contrivals in my patching braines ; but I had rather suppose them to powder, than expose them to preregular, much less to preter-regular Judgments : I shall therefore rejoyce that the work is faln into so good hands, heads, & hearts, who will weigh Rules by Troy-weight, and not by the old Haber-dupois : and rather than meddle where I have so little skill, I will sit by and tell my fears to them that have the patience to hear them, and leave the red-hot question to them that dare handle it.

I fear many holy men have not so deeply humbled themselves for their former mis-worshippings of God as he will have them before he reveals his secrets to them : as they accounted things indifferent, so they account indifferent repentance will serve turn. *Son of man, if my People be ashamed of all that they have done, then shew them the form of the House, and the fashion thereof,* else not, *Ezek.* 43. 11. A sin in Gods worship, that seems small in the common beam of the world, may be very great in the scoals of his Sanctuary. Where God is very jealous, his Servants should be very cautelous.

I fear the furnace wherein our new forms are casting, is overheat, and cast smoke in the eyes of our founders, that they cannot well see what they do, or ought to do ; *Omne perit judicium cum res transit in affectum.* Truth and Peace are the *Castor* and *Pollux* of the Gospel : they that seek the one without the other, are like to find neither : Anger will hinder domestick Prayers, much more Ecclesiastick Counsels. What is produced by tumult, is either defficient or redundant. When the judgments of good men concur with an harmonious Diapason, the result is melodious and commodious. Warring and jarring men are no builders of houses for God, though otherwise very good. Instruments may be well made and well strung, but if they be not well fretted, the Musick is marred. The great Turk hearing

Musitians

Musitians so long a tuning he thought it stood not with his state to wait for what would follow. When Christ whips Market-makers out of his Temple, he raises dust: but when he enters in with Truth and Holiness, he calls for deep silence, *Hab.* 2. 20. There must not a tool be heard when the Tabernacle is reared : Nor is that amiable or serviceable to men that passeth through so many ill animadversions of Auditors and Spectators. If the Assembly can hardly agree what to determine, People will not easily agree what to accept.

I fear, these differences and delayes have occasioned men to make more new discoveries than otherwise they would. If Pub-lick Assemblies of Divines cannot agree upon a right way, pri-vate Conventicles of illiterate men, will soon find a wrong. Bi-vious demurs breed devious resolutions. Passengers to Heaven are in haste, and will walk one way or other. He that doubts of his way, thinks he loses his day : and when men are gone a while, they will be loth to turn back. If God hide his path, Satan is at hand to turn Convoy : if any have a mind to ride post, he will help them with a fresh spavin'd Opinion at every Stage.

> *Where clocks will stand, and Dials have no light,*
> *There men must go by guess, be't wrong or right.*

I fear, if the Assembly of all Divines, do not consent, and con-center the sooner, God will breath a spirit of wisdom and meek-ness, into the Parliament of no Divines, to whom the Imperative and Coactive power supremely belongs, to consult such a contem-perate way, as shall best please him, and profit his Churches, so that it shall be written upon the door of the Assembly ; *The Lord was not there.*

I fear the importunity of some impatient, and subtlety of some malevolent minds, will put both Parliament and Assembly upon some preproperations, that will not be safe in Ecclesiastical Constitutions. To procrastinate in matters clear, as I said even now, may be dangerous ; so, not to deliberate in dubious cases, will be as perilous. We here, though I think under favour, we have some as able Steersmen as *England* affords, have been driven to tack about again to some other points of Christs Com-pass, and to make better observations before we hoyse up sailes. It will be found great wisdom in disputable cases, not to walk on by twilight, but very cauteously ; rather by probationers for a time, than peremptory positives. Reelings & wheelings in Church acts, are both difficult and disadvantageous. It is rather Christian modesty than shame, in the dawning of Reformation,

to

to be very perpensive.   Christs mind is, that Evangelical Policies, should be framed by Angelical measures; not by a line of
flax, but by a golded Reed, *Rev.* 21. 15.

I fear, he that sayes the Presbyterian and Independent way,
if rightly carryed do not meet in one, he doth not handle his
Compasses so considerately as he should.

I fear if Authority doth not establish a suitable and peaceable
Government of Churches the sooner, the bells in all the steeples
will ring awke so long, that they will hardly be brought into
tune any more.

My last, but not least fear, is, That God will hardly replant
his Gospel in any part of Christendome, in so fair an Edition as
is expected, till the whole field hath been so ploughed and har-
rowed, that the soile be throughly cleansed and fitted for new
seed : Or whether he will not transplant it into some other Regions, I know not : This fear I have feared these Twenty years,
but upon what grounds I had rather bury than broach.

I dare not but add to what preceded about Church-reforma-
tion, a most humble Petition, that the Authority of the Ministry
be kept in its due altitude : if it be dropp'd in the dust, it will
soon be stifled : Encroachments on both sides, have bred detri-
ments enough to the whole.   The Separatists are content their
teaching Elders should sit highest on the Bench, so they may
sit in the Chair over-against them ; and that their Ruling Elders
shall ride on the saddle, so they may hold the bridle.   That they
may likewise have seasonable and honourable maintenance, and
that certainly stated : which generally we find and practise here
as the best way.   When Elders live upon Peoples good wills,
People care little for their ill wills, be they never so just.   Voluntary Contributions or non tributions of Members, put Ministers upon many temptations in administrations of their Offices,
two hours care does more dis-spirit an ingenuous man than two
dayes study : nor can an Elder be given to hospitality, when he
knows not what will be given him to defray it : it is pity men of
gifts should live upon mens gifts.   I have seen most of the Reformed Churches in Europe, and seen more misery in these two
respects, than it is meet others should hear : the complaints of
painful *Pareus, David Pareus,* to my self, with tears, concerning the Germane Churches are not to be related.

There is yet a Personal Reformation, as requisite as the Political.   When States are so reformed, that they conform such as
are profligate into good civility : civil men, into religious morality : When Churches are so constituted, that Faith is ordained
Pastor, Truth Teacher, Holiness and Righteousness ruling Elders : Wisdom and Charity Deacons : Knowledge, love, hope,
zeal,

zeal, heavenly-mindedness, meekness, patience, watchfulness, humility, diligence, sobriety, modesty, chastity, constancy, prudence, contentation, innocency, sincerity, &c. admitted Members, and all their opposites excluded : then there will be Peace of Country and Conscience.

Did the Servants of Christ know what it is to live in Reformed Churches with unreformed Spirits, under strict order with loose hearts, how formes of Religion breed but formes of Godliness, how men by Church-discipline, learn their Church-postures, and there rest; they would pray as hard for Purity of heart, as Purity of Ordinances: If we mock God in these, He will mock us; either with defeat of our hopes, or which is worse : when we have what we so much desire, we shall be so much the worse for it. It was a well salted speech, uttered by an English Christian of a Reformed Church in the Netherlands We have the good Orders here, but you have the good Christians in *England*. He that prizes not Old *England* Graces, as much as New *England* Ordinances, had need go to some other market before he comes hither.   In a word, he that is not Pastor, Teacher, Ruler, Deacon and Brother to himself, and looks not at Christ above all, it matters not a farthing whether he be Presbyteran or Independent : he may be a zealot in bearing witness to which he likes best, and yet an Iscariot to both, in the witness of his own Conscience.

I have upon strict observation, seen so much power of Godliness, and spiritual mindedness in English Christians, living meerly upon Sermons and private duties, hardly come by, when the Gospel was little more than symptometical to the State ; such Epidemical and lethall formality in other disciplinated Churches, that I profess in the hearing of God, my heart hath mourned, and mine eyes wept in secret, to consider what will become of Multitudes of my dear Countrymen when they shall enjoy what they now covet : Not that good Ordinances breed ill Consciences, but ill Consciences grow stark nought under good Ordinances ; insomuch that might I wish an hypocrite the most perilous place but Hell, I should wish him a Membership in a strict Reformed Church : and might I wish a sincere Servant of God, the greatest grief earth can afford, I should wish him to live with a pure heart, in a Church impurely Reformed ; yet through the improvement of Gods Spirit, that grief may sanctifie him for Gods service and presence, as much as the means he would have, but cannot.

I speak this the rather to prevent, what in me lyes the imprudent romaging that is like to be in *England*, from Villages to Towns, from Towns to Cities, for Churches sake, to the undo-

ing

ing of Societies, Friendships, Kindreds, Families, Heritages, Callings, yea, the wise Providence of God in disposing mens habitations, now in the very Infancy of Reformation: by forgetting that a little leaven may season a large lump: and it is much better to do good than receive. It were a most uncharitable and unserviceable part, for good men to desert their own Congregations, where many may glorifie God in the day of his Visitation, for their presence and assistance. If a Christian would pick out a way to thrive in Grace, let him study to administer Grace to them that want; or to make sure a blessing upon his Family, let him labour to multiply the Family of Christ, and believe, that he which soweth liberally, shall reap abundantly; and he that spareth more than is need, from them that have more need, shall surely come to poverty: yea, let me say, that he who forsakes the means of Grace for Christ and his Churches sake, shall meet with a better bargain, namely, Grace it self. It is a time now, when full flocks should rather scatter to lean Churches than gather from other places to make themselves fat; when able Christians should rather turn Jesuites and Seminaries, than run into Covents and Frieries: had this been the course in the Primitive time, the Gospel had been pinfolded up in a few Cities, and not spread as it is.

What more ungodly sacriledge or man-stealing can there be, than to purloin from Godly Ministers the first born of their fervent Prayers and faithful Preachings, the leven of their flocks, the incouragement of their Souls, the Crown of their labours, their Epistle to Heaven? I am glad to hear our *New-England* Elders generally detest it *dispuenter*, and look at it as a killing *Cordolium:* If men will needs gather Churches out of the World (as they say) let them first plough the World, sow it, and reap it with their own hands, and the Lord give them a liberal Harvest. He is a very hard man that will reap where he hath not sowed, and gathered where he hath not strowed, *Mat.* 25. 24.

'He that saith, it is or was our case, doth not rightly understand himself or us, and he that takes his warrant out of *Joh.* 4. 37, 38. is little acquainted with Expositors. Wisemen are amazed to hear that conscientious Ministers dare spoil many Congregations to make one for themselves.

In matter of Reformation, this would be remembred, that in premonitory judgments, God will take good words, and sincere intents; but in peremptory, nothing but real performances.

Composition.

IF Reformation were come thus near, I should hope Composition were not far off: When hearts meet in God, they will

soon

soon meet in Gods ways and upon Gods termes. But to avoid prolixity, which steals upon me; For Composition, I shall compose half a dozen distichs concerning these kind of Wars; wishing I could sing asleep these odious stirs, at least on some part, with a dull Ode. He is no Cobler that cannot sing, nor no good Cobler that can sing well:

Si natura negat, facit indignatio versum } They are
Qualemcunque potest————Juvenal. } these.

1.

THey seldome lose the field, but often win,
        They end their Wars, before their Wars begin.

2.

Their Cause is oft the worst, that first begin,
And they may lose the field, the field that win. *

3.

In Civil Wars 'twixt Subjects and their King,
There is no conquest got, by conquering.

4.

War ill begun, the onely way to mend,
Is t'end the War before the War do end.

5.

They that will end ill Wars, must have the skill,
To make an end by Rule, and not by Will.

6.

In ending Wars 'tween Subjects and their Kings,
Great things are sav'd, by losing little things.

We hear that *Majestas Imperij* hath challenged *Salus Populi* into the field; the one fighting for Prerogatives, the other defending Liberties: Were I a Constable big enough, I would set one of them by the heels to keep both their hands quiet; I mean only in a pair of stocks, made of sound reason, handsomly fitted for the leggs of their Understanding.

If *Salus Populi* began, surely it was not that *Salus Populi* I left in *England*: that *Salus Populi* was as mannerly a *Salus Populi* as need be: if I be not much deceived, that *Salus Populi* suffer'd its nose to be held to the Grindstone, till it was al-

---

Victrix causa Diis placuit, sed Victa Catoni. Lucan.

most

most ground to the grisles and yet grew never the sharper for ought I could discern; What was, before the world was made, I leave to better Antiquaries than my self; but I think, since the World began, it was never storied that *Salus Populi* began with *Majestas Imperij*, unless *Majestas Imperij* first unharbour'd it, and hunted it to a stand, and then it must either turn head and live, or turn tail and die: but more have been storyed on the other hand than *Majestas Imperij* is willing to hear: I doubt not but *Majestas Imperij* knows, that Common-wealths cost as much the making as Crowns; and if they be well made, would yet outsell an ill fashioned Crown, in any Market overt, if they could be well vouched.

But *Preces & Lachrymæ*, are the Peoples weapons: so are Swords and Pistoles, when God and Parliaments bid them Arm. Prayers and Tears are good weapons for them that have nothing but knees and eyes; but most men are made with teeth and nailes; only they must neither scratch for Liberties, nor bite Prerogatives, till they have wept and prayed as God would have them. If Subjects must fight for their Kings against other Kingdoms, when their Kings will; I know no reason, but they may fight against their Kings for their own Kingdoms, when Parliaments say they may & must: but Parliaments must not say they must, till God sayes they may.

I can never believe that *Majestas Imperij*, was ever so simple as to think, that if it extends it self beyond its due Artique at one end, but *Salus Populi* must Antartique it as far at the other end, or else the World will be Excentrick, and then it will whirle, and if it once fall a whirling, ten to one, it will whirle them off first, that sit in highest Chaires on cushions fill'd with Peacocks feathers; and they are like to stand their ground fastest, that own not one foot of ground to stand upon. When Kings rise higher than they should, they exhale Subjects higher than they would: if the *Primum Mobile* should ascend one foot higher than it is, it would hurry all the nether wheels, and the whole World on fire in Twenty-four hours. No Prince exceeds in Soveraignty, but his Subjects will exceed as far in some vicious Liberty, to abate their grief; or some pernicious mutiny, to abate their Prince.

> *The crazy world will crack, in all the middle joynts,*
> *If all the ends it hath, have not their parapoynts.*

Nor can I believe that Crowns trouble Kings heads, so much as Kings heads trouble Crowns: nor that they are flowers of Crowns that trouble Crowns, but rather some Nettles or Thistles mistaken for flowers.
To

To speak plainer English, I have wondred these thirty years what Kings aile : I have seen in my time, the best part of twenty Christian Kings and Princes ; Yet as Christian as they were, some or other were still scuffling for Prerogatives.   It must be granted at all hands, that *Prærogativæ Regis* are necessary Supporters of State : and stately things to stately Kings : but if withal, they be *Derogativæ Regno*, they are but little things to wise Kings.   Equity is as due to People, as Eminency to Princes : Liberty to Subjects, as Loyalty to Kings : If they cannot walk together lovingly hand in hand, *pari passu*, they must cut girdles and part as good friends as they may : Nor must it be taken offensively, that when Kings are hailing up their topgallants, Subjects lay hold on their slablines ; the head and body must move alike : it is nothing meet for me to say with *Horace*,

Ut tu fortunam, sic nos te Car'le feremus.

But I hope I may safely say,

The body bears the head, the head the Crown,
If both bear not alike, then one will down.

Distracting Nature, calls for distracting Remedies ; perturbing Policies for disturbing cures : if one Extream should not constitute its Anti-Extream, all things would soon be in *extremo :* if ambitious winds get into Rulers Crowns, rebellious vapours will into Subjects Caps, be they stopt never so close : Yet the tongues of Times tell us of ten Preter royal Usurpations, to one contra-civil Rebellion.

Civil Liberties and Proprieties admeasured, to every man to his true *suum*, are the *prima pura principia, propria quarto modo*, the *sine quibus* of humane States, without which, men are but women. Peoples prostrations of these things when they may lawfully help it, are prophane prostitutions ; ignorant Ideotismes, under-natural noddaries ; and just it is that such as undersell them, should not re-inherit them in haste, though they seek it carefully with teares. And such usurpations by Rulers, are the unnaturalizings of nature, disfranchisements of Freedom, the Neroman nullifyings of Kingdoms : yea, I believe the Devil himself would turn Round-head, rather than suffer these Columns of Commonwealths to be slighted : as he is a creature, he fears decreation ; as an Angel, dehominations ; as a Prince, dis-common-wealthings ; as finite, these pen-infinite insolencies, which are the most finite Infinites of misery to men on this side the Worlds dissolution ; therefore it is, that with Gods leave, he
hath

hath sounded an alarm to all the *susque deques* pell-mels, one and alls, now harrasing sundry parts of Christendom. It is enough for God to be Infinite, too much for man to be Indefinite. He that will flye too high a quarry for Absoluteness, shall stoop as much too low before he remounts his proper pitch : If *Jacob* will over top his Brother out of Gods time and way, we will so hamstring him, that he shall make legs whether he will or no, at his brothers approach : and such as over-run all humane measure, shall seldom return to humane mercy : There are sins besides the sin against the Holy Ghost, which shall not be expiated by sacrifice for temporal revenge. I mean when they are boyled up to a full consistence of contumacy and impenitency. Let absolute Demands or Commands be put into one scale, and indefinite refusals into the other : All the Goldsmiths in *Cheapside*, cannot tell which weighs heaviest. Intolerable griefs to Subjects, breed the *Iliaca passio* in a body Politick, which inforces that upwards which should not. I speak these things to excuse what I may, my Countrymen in the hearts of all that look upon their proceedings.

There is a quadrobulary saying, which passes current in the Western World, That the Emperour is King of Kings, the *Spaniard*, King of Men, the *French* King of Asses, the King of *England*, King of Devils. By his leave that first brayed the speech, they are pretty wise Devils and pretty honest; the worse they do, is to keep their Kings from devillizing, and themselves from Assing : Were I a King (a simple supposal) I would not part with one good English Devil, for some two of the Emperours Kings, nor three of the *Spaniards* Men, nor four *French* Asses; If I did, I should think my self an Ass for my labour. I know nothing that *Englishmen* want, but true Grace, and honest Pride; let them be well furnisht with these two, I fear they would make more Asses, than *Spain* can make men, or the Emperour Kings. You will say I am now beyond my latchet; but you would not say so, if you knew how high my latchet will stretch; when I hear a lye with a latchet, that reaches up to his throat that first forged it.

He is a good King that undoes not his Subjects by any one of his unlimited Prerogatives : and they are a good People, that undoe not their Prince, by any one of their unbounded Liberties, be they the very least. I am sure either may, and I am sure neither would be trusted, how good soever. Stories tell us in effect, tho' not in termes, that over-risen Kings, have been the next evils to the World, unto fallen Angels : and that over-franchised people, are devils with smooth snaffles in their mouths. A King that Lives by Law, lives by love; and he that lives

above

above Law, shall live under hatred do what he can. Slavery and knavery go as seldom asunder, as Tyranny and Cruelty.

I have a long while thought it very possible, in a time of Peace, and in some Kings Reign, for disert Statesmen, to cut an exquisite thred between Kings Prerogatives, and Subjects Liberties of all sorts, so as *Cæsar* might have his due, and People their share, without such sharp disputes. Good Casuists would case it, and case it, part it, and part it; now it, and then it, punctually. *Aquinas, Suarez,* or *Valentia,* would have done it long ere this, had not they been Popish, I might have said Knavish; for if they be so any where, it is in their Tractates of Priviledges. Our Common Law doth well, but it must do better before things do as they should. There are some *Maxims* in Law, that would be taught to speak a little more mannerly, or else well *Anti-Maxim'd :* we say, the King can do a Subject no wrong; why may we not say the Parliament can do the King no wrong? We say, *Nullum tempus occurrit Regi* in taking wrong; why may we not say, *Nullum tempus succurrit Regi* in doing wrong? which I doubt will prove as good a Canon if well examined.

Authority must have power to make and keep people honest; People, honestly to obey Authority; both, a joynt-Council to keep both safe. Moral Laws, Royal Prerogatives, Popular Liberties, are not of Mans making or giving, but Gods: Man is but to measure them out by Gods Rule: which if mans wisdom cannot reach, Mans experience must mend: And these Essentials, must not be Ephorized or Tribuned by one or a few mens discretion, but lineally sanctioned by Supreme Councils. In *pro-renascent* occurrences, which cannot be foreseen; Diets, Parliaments, Senates, or accountable Commissions, must have power to consult & execute against intersilient dangers and flagitious crimes prohibited by the light of Nature: Yet it were good if States would let People know so much before hand, by some safe woven *Manifesto*, that gross Delinquents may tell no tales of Anchors and Buoyes, nor palliate their presumptions with pretence of ignorance. I know no difference in these Essentials, between Monarchies, Aristocracies, or Democracies; the rule will be found, par-rational say Schoolmen and Pretorians what they will. And in all, the best standard to measure Prerogatives, is the Plough staffe, to measure Liberties, the Scepter: if the tearms were a little altered into Loyal Prerogatives and Royal Liberties, then we should be sure to have Royal Kings and Loyal Subjects.

> *Subjects their King, the King his Subjects greets,*
> *Whilome the Scepter and the Plough-staffe meets.*

But

But Progenitors have had them for four and twenty predecessions : that would be spoken in the Norman tongue or Cimbrian, not in the English or Scottish : When a Conquerour turns Christian, Christianity turns Conquerour : if they had had them time out of mind of man, before *Adam* was made, it is not a pin to the point in *foro recta rationis :* Justice and Equity were before time, and will be after it : Time hath neither Politicks nor Ethicks, good nor evil in it ; it is an empty thing, as empty as a *New-English* purse, and emptier it cannot be : a man may break his neck in time, and in a less time than he can heal it.

But here is the deadly pang, it must now be taken by force and dint of Sword : I confess it is a deadly pang to a Spirit made all of flesh, but not to a mortified heart : it is good to let God have his will as he please, when we have not reason to let him have it as we should ; remembring, that hitherto he hath taken order that ill Prerogatives gotten by the Sword, should in time be fetcht home by the Dagger, if nothing else will do it : Yet I trust there is both day and means to intervent this bargain. But if they should, if God will make both King and Kingdom the better by it, what should either lose ? I am sure there is no great cause for either to make great brags.

Pax quo carior, eo charior.

A Peace well made, is likeliest then to hold,
When 'tis both dearly bought and dearly sold.

I confess, he that parts with such pearls to be paid in old iron, had need to be pityed more by his faithful friends, than he is like to be by his false flatterers. My heart is surcharged, I can no longer forbear.

MY Dearest Lord, and my more than *dearest King* ; I most humbly beseech you upon mine aged knees, that you would please to arm your mind with patience of proof, and to intrench your self as deep as you can, in your wonted Royal meekness ; for I am resolved to display my unfurled Soul in your face, and to storm you with volyes of Love and Loyalty. You owe the meanest true Subject you have, a close account of these open Wars : they are no *Arcana imperij.* Then give me leave to inquire of your Majesty, what you make in fields of blood, when you should be amidst your Parliament of Peace : What you do sculking in the suburbs of Hell, when your Royal Palaces stand desolate, through your absence ? What moves you to take up Armes against your faithful Subjects, when your

Armes should be embracing your mournful Queen? What in-
censes your heart to make so many Widows and Orphans, and
among the rest your own? Doth it become you, the King of
the stateliest Island the World hath, to forsake your Throne,
and take up the Manufacture of cutting your Subjects throats,
for no other sin, but for Deifying you so over-much, that you
cannot be quiet in your Spirit, till they have pluckt you down
as over-low? Do your three Kingdoms so trouble you, that they
must all three be set on fire at once, that when you have done,
you may probably run away by their light into utter darkness?
Do your three Crowns sit too heavy on your head, that you will
break the backs of the three bodies that set them on, and helpt
you to bear them so honourably? Have your three Lamb-like
flocks so molested you, that you must deliver them up to the
ravening teeth of evening Wolves? Are you so angry with those
that never gave you just cause to be angry, but by their too
much fear to anger you at all, when you gave them cause
enough? Are you so weary of Peace, that you will never be
weary of War? Are you so willing to War at home, who were
so unwilling to War abroad, where and when you should? Are
you so weary of being a good King, that you will leave your
self never a good Subject? Have you Peace of Conscience, in
inforcing many of your Subjects to fight for you against their
Conscience? Are you provided with Answers at the great Tri-
bunal, for the destruction of so many thousands, whereof every
man was as good a man as your Self, *qua* man?

Is it not a most unworthy part for you to be running away
from your Subjects in a day of battel, upon whose Pikes you may
come safe with your naked breast and welcome? Is it honourable for you to be flying on horses, from those that would esteem it their greatest honour, to bear you on their humble
Shoulders to your Chair of Estate, and set you down upon a
Cushion stuffed with their hearts? Is it your prudence to be
inraged with your best friends, for adventuring their lives to rescue you from your worst enemies? Were I a King, pardon the
supposal, I would hang that Subject by the head, that would
not take me by the heels and dragg me to my Court, when he
sees me shifting for life in the ruined Country, if nothing else
would do it; And I would honour their very heels, that would
take me by the very head, and teach me, by all just means, to
King it better, when they saw me un-Kinging my self, and
Kingdom: Do you not know Sir, that, as when your people are
sick of the Kings-evil, God hath given you a gift to heal them?
so when your self is sick of it, God hath given the Parliament
a gift to heal you: Hath your Subjects love been so great to
you.

you, that you will spend it all, and leave your Children little or none? Are you so exasperated against wise *Scotland*, that you will make *England* your fool or foot-stool? Is your Fathers Son grown more Orthodox, than his most Orthodox Father, when he told his Son, that a King was for a Kingdom, and not a Kingdom for a King? Parallel to that of the Apostle; the Husband is but by the Wife, but the Wife of the Husband.

Is *Majestas Imperij* grown so kickish, that it cannot stand quiet with *Salus Populi*, unless it be fettered? Are you well advised, in trampling your Subjects so under your feet, that they can find no place to be safe in, but over your head: Are you so inexorably offended with your Parliament, for suffering you to return as you did, when you came into their house as you did, that you will be avenged on all whom they represent? Will you follow your very worst Council so far as to provoke your very best, to take better counsel than ever they did? If your Majesty be not Popish, as you profess, and I am very willing to believe, why do you put the Parliament to resume the Sacrament of the Altar in saying, the King and Parliament, the King and Parliament? breaking your simple Subjects braines to understand such mystical Parlee-ment? I question much, whether they were not better, speak plainer English, than such Latin as the Angels can hardly construe, and God happily loves not to perse; I can as well admit an ubiquitary King as another, if a King be abroad in any good affair; but if a King be at home, and will circumscribe himself at *Oxford*, and proscribe or discribe his Parliament at *Westminster*, if that *Parliament* will prescribe what they ought, without such paradoxing, I should think God would subscribe a *Le Dieu le veult* readily enough.

Is your *Advisera* such a *Suavamen* to you, that hath been such a *Gravamen* to Religion and Peace? Shall the chief bearing womb of your Kingdom, be ever so constituted, that it cannot be delivered of its own deliverance, in what pangs soever it be, without the will of one man-midwife, and such a man as will come and not come, but as he list: nor bring a Parliament to bed of a well-begotten Liberty without an entire Subsidy? Do not your Majesty being a Schollar, know that it was a truth long before it was spoken, that *Mundus est unus aut nullus*, that there is *Principum purum unum*, which unites the World and all that is in it; where that is broken, things fall asunder, that whatsoever is durable or triable, is fryable.

Is the *Militia* of your Kingdom, such an orient flower of your Crown, which all good Herbalists judge but a meer nettle, while it is in any one mans hand living? May not you as well challenge the absolute disposal of all the wealth of the Kingdom

as

as of all the strength of your Kingdom? Can you put any difference? unless it be this, that mens hearts and bones are
within their skins, more proper and intrincical, their lands and
cattle more external: dare you now *contredit* the *Militia*, with
those to whom you may betrust your heart, better than your
own breast? Will they ever harm you with the *Militia*, that
have no manner of *Malitia* against you, but for mis-imploying
the *Militia* against them by the *Malitia* of your ill Counsellours? What good will the *Militia* do you when you have
wasted the Realm of all the best *Milites* it hath? May not your
Majesty see through a pair of Spectacles, glazed with inch-board,
that while you have your *Advisera* in one hand, and the *Militia* in the other, you have the necks of your Subjects under your
feet, but not your heart in your own hand? do you not know
that *malum est, posse malum*?

Hath Episcopacy been such a religious Jewel in your State ;
that you will sell all or most of your Coronets, Caps of honour,
and blue Garterts, for six and twenty cloth Caps? and your Ba-
rons Clokes, for so many Rockets, whereof usually twenty have
had scarce good manners enough to keep the other six sweet?
Is no Bishop no King, such an oraculous Truth, that you will
pawn your Crown and life upon it? if you will, God may make
it true indeed on your part: Had you rather part with all, than
lose a few superfluous tumours, to pare off your monstrousness?
Will you be so covetous as to get more than you ought, by loosing more than you need? Have you not driven good Subjects
enough abroad, but you will also slaughter them that stay at
home? Will you take such an ill course, that no Prayers can
fasten that good upon you we desire? Is there not some worse
root than all these growing in your Spirit, bringing forth all this
bitter fruit? Against which you should take up Arms, rather
than against your harmless Subjects? Do you not foresee, into
what importable head-tearings & heart-searchings you will be
ingulfed, when the Parliament shall give you a mate, though
but a Stale?

Methinks it should break your heart, to see such a one as I,
presume so much upon your clemency and too much upon your
Majesty, which your self have so eclipsed by the interposal your
Self between your Self and your Self, that it hath not ray's
enough left to dazle down the height of my affections to the
awe of my judgment?

Tres-Royal Sir, I once again beseech you, with tears drop-
ping from my hoary head, to cover your Self as close as you
may, with the best shield of goodness you have: I have somewhat more to say, which may happily trouble not your Self, but
                                                              your

your followers, more than what is already said. There lived in
your Realm and Reign two whom I may well tearm Prophets,
both now in a better Kingdom ; whereof one foretold two things
concerning your Majesty, of these very proceedings, long before
they began ; which being done and past shall be buried in silence : the other made this prediction about the same time.

> *King* Charles *will joyn himself to bitter Grief,*
> *Then joyn to God, and prove a Godly Chief.*

His words were in prose these, King *Charles* will come into
fetters, meaning strong afflictions, and then prove as good a
King, as such a good King of *Israel*, whom he then named, but
I need not : he was as inwardly acquainted with the mind of
God, as fervent and frequent a Beadsman for your welfare, and
had as religious Opticks of State, as any man I know : four
other Predictions he made, full as improbably as this, whereof
three are punctually performed. A good Christian being sometime in conflicts of Conscience, hurried with long tentations,
used this speech to my self, I am now resolved to be quiet, for
I plainly see, God will save me whether I will or no : If your
Majesty would be pleased to think so in your heart, and say so
with your mouth, all the good Subjects you have, would say,
Amen, till the heavens rang, and I hope you have few so bad,
but would say, *So be it*.

Much lamented Sir, if you will please to retire your Self to
your Closet, whither you may most safely come, and make your
Peace with God, for the vast heritage of Sin your Intombed
Father left upon your score, the dreadful Imprecation he poured
upon the heads of his tender Posterity in *Summersets* and *Over-
buryes* Case, published in Starchamber by his Royal command ;
your own sinful Mariage, the Sophistication of Religion and Policy in your time, the Luxury of your Court and Country, your
connivence with the Irish butcheries, your forgetful breaches
upon the Parliament, your compliance with Popish Doegs, with
what else your Conscience shall suggest : and give us, your
guilty Subjects example to do the like, who have held pace
and proportion with you in our evil wayes : we will help you
by Gods assistance, to pour out rivers of tears, to wash away
the streams of blood, which have been shed for these heavy accounts ; we will also help you, God helping us, to believe, that
there is hope in *Israel* for these things ; and Balme enough in
his *Gilead* to heal all the broken bones of your three Kingdoms, and to redouble your honour and our Peace ; His Arm is
infinite ; to an infinite power all things are equally faisible, to an
infinite

infinite Mercy all sins equally pardonable. The Lord work these things in us and for us, for his compassions sake in Jesus Christ.

Sir, you may now please to discover your Self where you think meet; I trust I have not indangered you: I presume your Ear-guard will keep far enough from you, what ever I have said: be it so, I have discharged my duty, let them look to theirs. If my tongue should reach your ears, which I little hope for; let it be once said; the great King of great *Britain*, took advise of a simple Cobler, yet such a Cobler, as will not exchange either his blood or his pride, with any Shoe-maker or Tanner in your Realm, nor with any of your late Bishops which have flattered you thus in pieces: I would not speak thus in the ears of the World, through the mouth of the Press for all the Plunder your Plunderers have pillaged; where it not somewhat to abate your Royal indignation toward a Loyal Subject; a Subject whose heart hath been long carbonado'd, *des veniam verbo*, in flames of affection towards you. Your Majesty knows or may know, time was, when I did, or would have done you a better piece of Service, than all your Troops and Regiments are now doing. Should I hear any Gentleman that follows you, of my years, say he loves you better than I, if it were lawful, I would swear by my Sword, he said more than his Sword would make good.

Gracious Sir, Vouchsafe to pardon me my no other sins, but my long Idolatry towards you, and my loving you too hard in this speech, and I will pardon you your Treason against me, even me, by committing Treason against your Self my Lord and King; * and your Murther, in Murthering me, even me, by Murthering my dear fellow Subjects, bone of my bone, and flesh of of my flesh, and of yours also. If you will not pardon me, I will pardon my self, dwell in my own Clothes as long as I can, and happily make as good a shift for my proportion, as he that hath a lighter pair of heels: And when you have done what you please, I am resolved to be,

> *As Loyal a Subject to your Majesty when I have never a head on my Shoulders, as you a Royal King to me, when you have your three Crowns on your head,*

Theod : de la Guard.

Sir,

I Cannot give you over thus; I most earnestly implore you, that you would not defer to consider your self throughly, you

---

* *I speak in Termes of Divinity not of Law and am deeply grieved that I am forced to suck necessary over-boldness.*

are

are now returned to the brink of your Honour and our Peace, stand not too long there, your State is full of distractions, your people of expectations, the importune Affairs of your Kingdom perplexedly suspended, your good Subjects are now rising into a resolution to pray you on to your Throne, or into your Tomb, into Grace with your Parliament and People, or into Glory with the Saints in Heaven; but how you will get into the one, without passing first through th'other, is the riddle they cannot untye. If they shall ply the Throne of Grace hard, God will certainly hear, and in a short time mould you to his mind, and convince you, that it had and will be far easier to sit down meekly upon the *Rectum,* than to wander resolutely in obliquities, which with Kings, seldom fail to dissembogue into bottomless Seas of sorrows.

Dearest Sir, be intreated to do what you do sincerely; the King of Heaven and Earth can search and discover the hiddenest corner of your heart, your Parliament understands you far better than you may conceive, they have many ears and eyes, and good ones, I believe they are Religiously determined to recement you to your Body so exquisitely, that the Errors of State and Church, routed by these late stirs, may not re-alle hereafter, nor Themselves be made a curse to the issue of their own bodies, nor a Scoff, to all Politique Bodies in Europe. The Lord give your Majesty and all your Royal Branches *the spirit of wisdom and understanding, the Spirit of knowledge and his fear,* for His mercy and Christ His sake.

I would my skill would serve me also, as well as my heart, to translate Prince *Rupert,* for his Queen-mothers sake, *Eliz,* a second. Mismean me not. I have had him in my arms when he was younger, I wish I had him there now: if I mistake not, he promised then to be a good Prince, but I doubt he hath forgot it: if I thought he would not be angry with me, I would pray hard to his Maker, to make him a right Roundhead, a wise hearted Palatine, a thankful man to the English; to forgive all his sins, and at length to save his soul, notwithstanding all his Goddamme mee's: yet I may do him wrong; I am not certain he useth that oath; I wish no man else would; I dare say the Devils dare not. I thank God I have lived in a Colony of many thousand English these twelve years, am held a very sociable man; yet I may considerately say, I never heard but one Oath sworn, nor never saw one man drunk, nor ever heard of three women Adulteressess, in all this time, that I can call to mind: If these sins be amongst us privily, the Lord heal us. I would not be understood to boast of our Innocency; there is no cause I should, our hearts may be bad enough, and our lives much better. But to follow my business. Prosecutions

Prosecutions of Wars between a King and his Parliament, are the direful dilacerations of the world, the cruel Catastrophes of States, dreadful to speak of: they are *nefanda & n'agenda:* I know no grounds can be given of them but two: Either upon Reason founded upon some surmisal of Treason, which my reason cannot reach: I could never conceive why a rational King should commit Treason against a reasonable Parliament; or how a faithful Parliament against their lawful King: the most I can imagine, is a misprision of Treason, upon a misprision of Reason. He that knows not the spirit of his King, is an Atheist. Our King is not *Charles le simple* sometime of France: he understands not our King that understands him not to be understanding. The Parliament is supposed Omniscient, because under God they are Omnipotent: if a Parliament have not as much knowledge and all other Vertues, as all the Kingdom beside, they are no good Abridgment of the Common-wealth. I believe Remonstrances have demonstrated enough concerning this point of Reason, to give such satisfaction to such as satisfaction will satisfie.

Or upon Will.

The Will of a King is very numinous; it hath a kind of vast universality in it, it is many times greater than the will of his whole Kingdom, stiffened with ill Counsel and ill Presidents: if it be not a foot and a half lesser than the Will of his Council, and three foot lesser than the Will of his Parliament, it is too big. I think it were well for a King if he had no will at all, but were all Reason. What if he committed his Moral will to Divines, that were no Bishops? his Political, to his Parliament, and a Council chosen by Parliament? that if ever it miscarry, they may blame themselves most, and him least. I scarce know any King that hath such advantage as ours; his three Kingdoms lye so distinct and entire, that if he please, he might keep them like three Gardens without a weed, if he would let God keep his will, without wilfulness and rashness.

I have observed men to have two kind of Wills, a Free-hold will, such as men hold in *Capite* of themselves; or a Copy-hold will, held at the will of other Lords or Ladies. I have read almost all the Common Law of *England*, and some Statutes; yet I never read that the Parliament held their will in such a *Capite*: their Tenure is *Knight-service*, and good *Knight-service* too, or else they are to blame. And I am sure, a King cannot hold by Copy, at the will of other Lords; the Law calls that *base tenure*, inconsistent with Royalty; much more base is it, to hold at the will of Ladies: Apron-string *tenure* is very weak, tyed but of a
slipping-knot,

slipping-knot, which a Child may undoe, much more a King. It stands not with our Queens honour to wear an Apron, much less her Husband, in the strings; that were to insnare both him and her self in many unsafeties. I never heard our King was Effeminate: to be a little Uxorious personally, is vertuous vice in Oeconomics; but Royally, a vitious vertue in Politicks. To speak English, Books and Tongues tell us, I wish they tell us true, that the Error of these Wars on our Kings part, proceeds only from ill Counsellours.

Ill Counsellours, are very ill Gamesters; if they see their own stake a losing, they will play away King, Queen, Bishops, Knights, Rooks, Pawns, and all, before they will turn up the board; they that play for lusts, will play away themselves, and not leave themselves so much as a heart to repent; and then there is no Market left but Hell; if the case be thus, it is to no end to look for any end, till one side make an end of the other.

> *They that at stake their Crowns and Honours set,*
> *Play lasting games, if Lust or Guilt do bet.*

Cessation.

IF God would vouchsafe to give his Majesties Religion and Reason, power to fling his Wills head over the Wall, in matter of Composition, and his Subjects strength to throw their lusts after it, Arms would be soon laid down, and Peace soon taken up. They that are not at Peace with God, are not at Peace with themselves, whatever they think; and they that are not at Peace with themselves, cannot be at Peace with others, if occasion provokes, be their nature never so good.

So far as I can conjecture, the chief impediment to a general & mutual Cessation of Armes, is, a despair of mutual and general forgiveness. If ever *England* had need of a general Jubile in Heaven and Earth, it is now. Our King and Parliament have been at great strife, who should obtain most Justice: if they would now strive, who should shew most Mercy, it would hear well throughout the World. Here also my speech must be twofold and blind-fold. It is now nine Months and more since the last credible News was acted: it is possible by this, the Parliament may be at the Kings Mercy? Did I say a Kings Mercy? what can I say more? no man on earth, can shew more mercy than a King, nor shall need more, when he comes to give an Account of his Kingdom: nor did ever any Parliament merit more mercy than this, for they never sinned, that I know, I mean against the Common and Statute Law of *England:* it is pity they who have given so many general pardons, should want one now.

If

If our King hath lost his way, and thereby learned to look to his path better hereafter, and taught many Successors to King it right for many Ages; Methinks it should impetrate a Royal Redintegration, upon a Royal acknowledgment and ingagement. But how should an erring King trust a provoked Parliament? Surely he may trust God safe enough; who will never trust that State more with a good King, that will do ill to a King that is turned so good. Methinks those passages of Scripture, *Isai*. 43. 24, 25. *Chap*. 57. 17, 18. The strange illation, *Hos*. 2. 13, 14. should melt a heart of steel into floods of mercy.

For others, were my head, one of the heads which first gave the King Counsel to take up these Armes, or to persist in them, when at any time he would have disbanded, I would give that head to the Kingdom, whether they would or no; if they would not cut it off, I would cut it off my self, and tender it at the Parliament door, upon condition that all other heads might stand, which stand upon penitent hearts, and will do better on than off; then I would carry it to *London-Bridge*, and charge my tongue to teach all tongues, to pronounce Parliament right hereafter.

When a Kingdom is broken just in the neck joynt, in my poor policy, ropes and hatchets are not the kindliest instruments to set it: Next to the spilling of the blood of Christ for sin, the sparing of the blood of sinners, where it may be as well spared as spilt, is the best way of expiation. It is no rare thing for Subjects to follow a leading King; if he will take his truncheon in his hand, it is to be expected many will put their Swords in their Belts. Sins that rise out of mistake of judgment, are not so sinful as those of malice ordinarily: and when multitudes sin, multitudes of mercy are the best Anodines.

—gratia gratis data, gratissima.

Grace will dissolve, but rigour hardens guilt:
Break not with Steely blows, what oyle should melt.
In Breaches integrant, 'tween Principals of States,
Due Justice may suppress, but Love redintegrates.

Whosoever be pardoned, I pray let not *Britanicus* scape, I mean a pardon. I take him to be a very serviceable Gentleman; Out of my intire respect to him, I shall presume to give him half a dozen stitches of advice:

I intreat him to consider that our King is not onely a man, but a King in affliction; Kings afflictions are beyond Subjects apprehensions; a Crown may happily ake as much as a whole Common-wealth.   I

I desire him also to conceal himself as deeply as he can, if he cannot get a special pardon, to wear a Latitat, about his neck, or let him lie close under the Philosophers stone, and I'le warrant him for ever being found.

If he be discovered, I counsel him to get his head set on faster than our *New-England* Taylors use to set on Buttons ; Kings, and Kings Childrens memories are as keen as their Subjects wits.

If he fears any such thing, that he would come over to us, to help recruit our bewildred brains : we will promise to maintain him so long as he lives, if he will promise to live no longer then we maintain him.

If he should be discovered and his head chance to be cut off against his will, I earnestly beseech him to bequeath his wits to me and mine in Fee-simple, for we want them, and cannot live by our hands in this Country.

Lastly, I intreat him to keep his Purse, I give him my Counsel *gratis*, confessing him to be more than my match, and that I am very loath to fall into his hands.

Prosecution.

IF Reformation, Composition, Cessation, can find no admittance, there must and will be Prosecution : to which I would also speak briefly and indifferently still to both sides ; and first to that, which I had rather call Royalists than Malignants ; who if I mistake not, fight against the Truth.

Foolish Cowardly man (I pray patience, for I speak nothing but the pulse of my own heart) dreads and hates, nothing in Heaven or Earth, so much as Truth : it is not God, nor Law, nor Sin, nor Death, nor Hell, that he fears, but only because he fears there is Truth in them : Could he detruth them all, he would defie them all : Let Perdition it self come upon him with deadly threats, fiery swords, displayed vengeance, he cares not ; Let Salvation come cap in hand, with naked Reason, harmless Religion, lawny imbracements, he will rather flye or dye, than entertain it : come Truth in what shape it will, he will reject it : and when he can beat it off with most steely prowess, he thinks himself the bravest man when in truth it is nothing but exsanguine feeble exility of Spirit. Thy heart, saith the Prophet *Ezek.* 16. 30, is weak, like the heart of an imperious Whorish woman : a man would think, the heart of an imperious Whore, were the very pummel of *Scanderbergs* ; sword ; alas, she is hen-hearted, she dares not look Truth in the face ; if she dared, she would neither be Whorish, nor imperious, nor weak. He shews more true fortitude, that prayes quarter of the least

Truth

Truth, at a miles distance, than he that breaks through and
hewes down the most Theban Phalanx that ever field bore. *Paul*
expressed more true valour, in saying, I can do nothing against
the Truth, than *Goliah*, in defying the whole hoste of *Israel.*

Couragious Gentlemen, Ye that will stab him that gives you
the lye ; take heed ye spend not your bloods, limbs and souls,
in fighting for some untruth : and ye that will fling out the
gantlet to him that calls you Coward, dishonour not your selves
with such Cowardise, as to fight against Truth, meerly for fear
of it.   A thousand pities it is such gallant Spirits should spend
their lives, honours, heritages, and sweet relations in any Wars,
where, for ought many of them know, some false mistake commands in Chief.

Honoured Country men, be intreated to love Truth : if it loves
not you again, and repaires not all your losses, then install some
Untruth in its room for your General.   If you will needs War,
be perswaded to contend lawfully, wisely and stedfastly against
all errors in Divinity and Policy : they are the cursed Counter-
mures, dropt Portcullises, scouring Angi-ports, sulphurious Gra-
nado's, laden murtherers, peevish Galthropes, and rascall despa-
radoes, which the Prince of lyes imployes with all his skill and
malice, to maintain the walls and gates of his kingdom, when
Truth would enter in with Grace and Peace to save forlorn sinners, and distressed common-wealthes ; witness the present deplorable estate of sundry States in Europe.

Give me leave to speak one word more : it is but this ; Ye
will find it a far easier field, to wage War against all the Armies
that ever were or will be on Earth, and all the Angels of Heaven, than to take up Armes against any truth of God : It hath
more Counsel and Strength than all the World besides ; and will
certainly either gain or ruine, convert or subvert every man that
opposes it.   I hope ingenuous men will rather take advice, than
offence at what I have said : I had rather please ten, than grieve
one intelligent man.

If this side be resolute, I turn me to the other.

Go on brave Englishmen, in the Name of God, go on pros-
perously, because of Truth and Righteousness : Ye that have
the cause of Religion, the life of your Kingdom and of all the
good that is in it in your hands : Go on undauntedly : As you
are Called and Chosen, so be faithful : Ye fight the battels of
the Lord, be neither desidious nor perfidious : You serve the
King of Kings, who stiles you his heavenly Regiments, Consider well, what impregnable fighting it is in heaven, where the
Lord of Hosts is your General, his Angels your Colonels, the
                                                          Stars

Stars your Fellow-souldiers, his Saints your Oratours, his Promises your Victuallers, his Truth your Trenches ; where Drums are Harps, Trumpets joyful sounds ; your Ensigns Christs Banners ; where your weapons and armour are spiritual, therefore irresistable, therefore impierceable ; where Sun and Wind cannot disadvantage you, you are above them ; where hell it self cannot hurt you, where your Swords are furbushed and sharpened by him that made their Metal, where your wounds are bound up with the oyl of a good Cause, where your blood runs into the Veines of Christ, where sudden death is present Martyrdom and Life ; your Funerals Resurrections your honour Glory ; where your Widows and Babes are received into perpetual Pensions ; your Names listed among *Davids* Worthies ; where your greatest losses are greatest gains ; and where you leave the troubles of War, to lye down in beds of eternal rest.

What good will it do you, dear Countrymen, to live without Lives, to enjoy *England* without the God of *England*, your Kingdom without a Parliament, your Parliament without Power, your Liberties without Stability, your Laws without Justice, your honours without Vertue, your Beings without well-Being, your Wives without honesty, your Children without Morality, your Servants without Civility, your Lands without Propriety, your Goods without Immunity, the Gospel without Salvation, your Churches without Ministry, your Ministers without Piety, and all you have or can have, with more tears and bitterness of heart, than all you have and shall have will sweeten or wipe away ?

Go on therefore Renowned Gentlemen, fall on resolvedly, till your hands cleave to your Swords, your Swords to your enemies hearts, your hearts to Victory, your Victories to triumph, your triumphs to the everlasting Praise of him that hath given you Spirits to offer your selves willingly, and to jeopard your lives in high Perils, for his Name and Service sake.

And We your Brethren, though we necessarily abide beyond *Jordan*, and remain on the American Sea-coasts, will send up Armies of Prayers to the Throne of Grace, that the God of Power and Goodness, would incourage your hearts, cover your heads, strengthen your arms, pardon your sins, save your Souls, and bless your Families, in the day of Battel. We will also pray, that the same Lord of Hosts, would discover the Counsels, defeat the Enterprizes, deride the hopes, disdain the insolencies, and wound the hairy scalpes of your obstinate Enemies, and yet pardon all that are unwillingly misled. We will likewise help you believe that God will be seen on the Mount, that it is all one with him to save by many or few, and that he doth but humble

ble

ble and try you for the present, that he may do you good at the latter end. All which he brings to pass who is able to do exceeding abundantly, above all we can ask or think, for his Truth and Mercy sake in Jesus Christ.   *Amen, Amen.*

A Word of IRELAND:

Not of the Nation universally, nor of any man in it, that hath so much as one hair° of Christianity or Humanity growing on his Head or Beard, but onely of the truculent Cut-throats, and such as shall take up Armes in their Defence.

THese *Irish* anciently called *Antropophagi*, man-eaters: Have a Tradition among them, That when the Devil shewed our Saviour all the Kingdoms of the Earth and their glory, that he would not shew him *Ireland*, but reserved it for himself: it is probably true, for he hath kept it ever since for his own peculiar; the old Fox foresaw it would eclipse the glory of all the rest: he thought it wisdom to keep the Land for a Boggards for his unclean spirits imployed in this Hemisphere, and the people, to do his Son and Heir, I mean the Pope, that Service for which *Lewis* the eleventh kept his Barbor *Oliver*, which makes them so blood-thirsty. They are the very Offall of men, Dregs of Mankind, Reproach of Christendom, the Bots that crawl on the Beasts taile, I wonder *Rome* it self is not ashamed of them.

I beg upon my, hands and knees, that the Expedition against them may be undertaken while the hearts and hands of our Souldiery are hot, to whom I will be bold to say briefly: Happy is he that shall reward them as they have served us, and Cursed be he that shall do that work of the Lord negligently, Cursed be he that holdeth back his Sword from blood: yea, Cursed be he that maketh not his Sword stark drunk with *Irish* blood, that doth not recompence them double for their hellish treachery to the *English*, that maketh them not heaps upon heaps, and their Country a dwelling place for Dragons, an Astonishment to Nations: Let not that eye look for pity, nor that hand to be spared, that pities or spares them, and let him be accursed, that curseth not them bitterly.

A

A Word of Love to the Common People of ENGLAND.

IT is, your, now or never, to muster up puissant Armies of Prayers to the Mercy Seat; your Body Representative, is now to take in hand, as intricate a piece of work, as ever fell into the hands of any Parliament in the World, to tye an indissoluble knot upon that webb which hath been woven with so much cost and bloud, wherein if they happen to make one false maske, it may re-imbarque themselves and you all into deadly relapse of scorn and calamity. It is the work of God, not of man, pray speedily therefore, and speedingly, give him no rest till your rest be thoroughly re-established, Your God is a God whose Name is All-sufficient, abundant in Goodness and Truth, on whom the sons of *Jacob* never did, nor shall call in vain, you have a Throne of Grace whereto you may go boldly; a Christ to give you a leading by the hand and liberty of speech, an Intercessor in Heaven to offer up your Prayers wrapp'd in his own; a large Charter *aske and have*, a Spirit to help all your infirmities in that duty, a sure Covenant that you shall be heard, and such late incouragement as may strengthen your feeble hands for ever. If you who *may command God concerning the work of his hand*, shall fail to demand the workmanship of his hand in this work, your Children will proclaim you un-thrifts with bitter teares to the Worlds end.

If you see no cause to pray, read,

Jer. 18. 1.----10.

Be also intreated to have a continual and conscientious care not to impeach the Parliament in the hearts one of another by whispering complaints, easilier told than tryed or trued. Great bodies move but slowly, especially when they move on three leggs and are over-loden with weighty occasions. They have now sat full six years without intermission to continue your being, many of their heads are grown gray with your cares,.they are the High Council of the Kingdom, the great Gilead of your Balm, the Physitians of all your sickness; if any of them do amiss, blame your selves, you chose them, be wiser hereafter; you cannot do the State, your selves, your Posterity a more ungrateful office than to impair them with disparagements and discouragements who are so studious to repair your almost irreparable ruines.

Be likewise beseeched, not to slight good Ministers, whom you were wont to reverence much, they are Gods Embassadours, your Ephods, your Stars, your Horse-men & Chariots, your

Watchmen,

Watchmen, and under Christ your Salvation, I know no deadlier Symptom of a dying People than to undervalue godly Ministers, whosoever despiseth them shall certainly be despised of God and man at one time or other.

A most humble heel-piece,

TO THE

Most Honourable Head-piece

THE

Pàrliament of *England*.

I Might excuse my self in Part, with a speech *Lycurgus* used in the like exigent of State, *senectute fio audacior, publica necessitate loquacior,* but it much better becomes me with all lowliness and uprightness, wherein I have failed to pray pardon on both my knees, which I most humbly and willingly do ; only, before I rise, I crave leave to present this six-fold Petition.

That you would be pleased,

To preserve the Sacred reputation of Parliaments, or, we shall have no Common-wealth.

To uphold the due estimation of good Ministers, else, we shall have no Church.

To heal the sad dislocation of our Head, throughly, perfectly, or, we shall have no King.

To oppugne the bold violation of divine Truths, else we shall have no God.

To proceed with what zeal you began, or what you began can come to little end.

To expedite work with what speed you safely may, else ignorant people will fear they shall have no end at all.

He that is great in Counsel, and Wonderful in Working, guide and help you in all things, that doing all things in Him, by Him, and for Him, you may do all things like Him.

So be it.

A

A respective word to the Ministers
of E N G L A N D.

FAR be it from me, while I dehort others to slight you my
self, or to despise any man but my self, whom I can never
despise enough: I rather humbly intreat you to forgive my boldness, who have most just cause to judge myself less and less
faithful than the least of you all, yet I dare not but be so faithful to you and my self, as to say,

They are the Ministers of *England,* that have lost the Land;
for Christs sake, put on His bowels, His wisdom, His zeal, and
recover it.

I pray let me drive in half a dozen plain honest
Country Hobnailes, such as the Martyrs were wont
to wear; to make my work hold the surer; and I
have done.

1. *There, lives cannot be good,*
   There, Faith cannot be sure,
Where Truth cannot be quiet,
   Nor Ordinances pure.

2. *No King can King it right,*
   Nor rightly sway his Rod;
Who truely loves not Christ,
   And truely fears not God.

3. *He cannot rule a Land,*
   As Lands should ruled been,
That lets himself be rul'd
   By a ruling Roman Queen.

4. *No earthly man can be*
   True Subject to this State;
Who makes the Pope his Christ,
   An Heretique his Mate.

5. *There Peace will go to War,*
   And Silence make a noise:
Where upper things will not
   With nether equipoyse.

6. *The*

6. *The upper World shall* **Rule,**
   While Stars will run their race :
The nether World obey,
   While People keep their place.

The Clench.

I *F any of these come out*
   So long's the World do last
Then credit not a word
   Of what is said and past.

ERRATA
AT NON CORRIGENDA.

N O W I come to rub over my work, I find five or **six things** like faults, which would be mended or commended, I know not well which, nor greatly care.

1. For *Levity*, read *Lepidity*, ——— and that a very little, and that very necessary, if not unavoidable.

> *Misce stultitiam Consilijs brevem*
> ---*Dulce est desipere in loco.* Horat.

To speak to light heads with heavy words, were to break their Necks: to cloathe Summer matter, with Winter Rugg, would make the Reader sweat. It is Musick to me, to hear **every** Dity speak its spirit in its apt tune : every breast, to sing **its** proper part, and every Creature, to express it self in its natural Note : should I hear a Mouse roar like a Bear, a Cat lowgh like an Ox, or a Horse whistle like a Red-breast, it would **scare** ——— me.

> *The World's a well strung fidle, mans tongue the quill,*
> *That fills the World with fumble for want of skill,*
> *When things and words in tune and tone do meet,*
> *The universal Song goes smooth and sweet.*

2. For *audacity*, read *veracity*, or *Verum Gallice non liben-*
ter audis. Mart. Flattery never doth well, but when it is whispered through a pair of lisping teeth ; Truth best, when it is

spoken

spoken out, through a pair of open lips, Ye make such a noise there, with Drums and Trumpets, that if I should not speak loud, ye could not hear me. Ye talk one to another, with whole Culvering and Cannon; give us leave to talk Squibs and Pistoletto's charged with nothing but Powder of Love and shot of Reason: if you will cut such deep gashes in one anothers flesh, we must sow them up with deep stitches, else ye may bleed to death: ye were better let us, your tender Country-men do it, than forraign Surgeions, who will handle you more cruelly, and take no other pay, but your Lives & Lands.

——————— *Aspice vultus,*
Ecce meos, utinamque oculos in pectore posses
Inserere : & patrias intus deprendere Curas.

(Ovid. Phœb.

He that to tall men speaks, must lift up's head ;
    And when h'hath done, must set it where he did :
He that to proud men talks, must put on pride ;
    And when h'hath done, 'tis good to lay't aside.

3. For, *Yes, but you speak at three thousand Miles distance,* which *every Coward dare doe,* read, *if my heart deceives me not, I would speak thus, in the Presence Chamber or House of Commons;* hoping *Homer* will speak a good word for me.

Θαρσαλεȣ γαρ ανηρ εν πασιν αμεινων
'Εργοισι————————

Omnibus in rebus potior vir fortis & audàx
Sit licet hospes, & e longinquis venerit oris.

When Kings are lost, and Subjects cast away,
    A faithful heart should speak what tongue can say :
It skils not where this faithful heart doth dwell,
    His faithful dealing should be taken well.

4. For, *affected termes,* read, *I hope not* ———————— If I affect termes, it is my feebleness; friends that know me, think I do not: I confess, I see I have here and there taken a few finish stitches, which may haply please a few Velvet ears ; but I cannot now well pull them out, unless I should seam-rend all. It seems it is in fashion with you to sugar your papers with Carnation phrases, and spangle your speeches with new quodled words. Ermins in Minifer is every mans Coat. Yet we hear
some

some are raking in old·musty Charnel books, for old mouldy mo-
nesyllables; I wish they were all banisht to *Monmouthshire,* to
return when they had more wit.

*Multa renascentur qua jam cecidere, cadentque
Quæ nunc sunt in honore vocabula, si volet usus.*
(Hor.

I honour them with my heart, that can express more than
ordinary matter in ordinary words: it is a pleasing eloquence;
them more that study wisely and soberly to inhance their native
language; them most of all, that esteem the late significant speech,
the third great blessing of the Land; it being so enriched, that
a man may speak many Tongues in his Mothers mouth and an
uplandish Rustick, more in one word than himself and all the
Parish understands. Affected termes are unaffecting things to
solid hearers; yet I hold him prudent, that in these fastidious
times, will help disedged appetites with convenient condiments,
and bangled ears, with pretty quick plucks. I speak the rather
because, not long since, I met with a book, the best to me I ever
saw, but the Bible, yet under favour, it was somewhat underclad,
especially by him who can both excogitate and express what he
undertakes, as well as any man I know.

*The World is grown so fine in words and wit,
That pens must now Sir* Edward Nich'las *it.
He that much matter speaks, speaks ne'r a whit.
If's tongue doth not career't above his wit.*

5. For, *You verse it simply, what need have we of your thin
Poetry;* read, I confess I wonder at it my self, that I should turn
Poet: I can impute it to nothing, but to the flatuousness of our
diet: they are but sudden raptures soon up, soon down.

--*Deductum dicere Carmen,* is highly commended by *Macro-
bius.*

Virgil himself said,
  Agrestem tenui meditabor arundine musam.

*Poetry's a gift wherein but few excell,
  He doth very ill, that doth not passing well.*

*But he doth passing well, that doth his best,
  And he doth best, that passeth all the rest.*

6. For

6. For, *tediousness*, read, *I am sorry for it*———We have a strong weakness in N. E. that when we are speaking, we know not how to conclude : we make many ends, before we make an end : the fault is in the Climate ; we cannot help it though we can, which is the Arch infirmity in all morality : We are so near the West pole, that our Longitudes are as long, as any wise man would wish, and somewhat longer : I scarce know any Adage more gratefull : than *Grata brevitas.*

> *Verba confer maxime ad compendium.*   Plaut.

> *Coblers will mend, but some will never mend,*
>   *But end, and end, and end, and never end.*
> *A well-girt hour gives every man content,*
>   *Six ribs of beef, are worth six weeks of Lent.*

For, *all my other faults, which may be more and greater than I see* ; read, *I am heartily sorry for them,* before I know them, least I should forget it after ; and humbly crave pardon at adventure, having nothing that I can think of, to plead but this,

> *Quisquis inops peccat, minor est reus.*   Petron.

> *Poor Coblers well may fault it now and then,*
>   *They'r ever mending faults for other men.*
> *And if I work for nought, why is it said,*
>   *This bungling Cobler would be soundly paid?*

> SO *farewell* England *old*
>   *If evil times ensue,*
> *Let good men come to us,*
>   *Wee'l welcome them to New.*

> *And farewell Honor'd Friends,*
>   *If happy dayes ensue,*
> *You'l have some Guests from hence.*
>   *Pray Welcome us to you.*

> *And farewell simple World,*
>   *If thou'lt thy Cranium mend,*
> *There is my Last and All.*
> *And a Shoem-Akers*

E N D .

Postscript.

Postscript.

THis honest Cobler has done what he might :
    That Statesmen in their Shoes might walk upright.
But rotten Shoes of Spannish running-leather :
No Coblers skill, can stitch them strong together.
It were best to cast such rotten stuff away :
And look for that, that never will decay.

If all were shod with Gospel's lasting Peace ;
Hatred abroad, and Wars at home would cease.

                          Jerome Bellamie.

F I N I S.

AN
ABSTRACT
OF THE
LAWES
OF
NEW ENGLAND

As they are novv established.

LONDON,

Printed for *F. Coules*, and *W. Ley* at Paules Chain,

1641.

Force's Collection of Historical Tracts.

Vol. III.—No. 9.

AN ABSTRACT
Of the Lavves of Nevv
ENGLAND.

CHAP. I.

Of Magistrates.

1 First, All Magistrates are to be chosen.
 First, By the free Burgesses. Deut. **1. 13.**
 Secondly, Out of the free Burgesses. 17.15.
 Thirdly, Out of the ablest men and Ex.18.21.
most approved amongst them.
 Fourthly, Out of the ranck of No- Eccl.10.17.
ble men or Gentlemen among them, the best that God Ier.30.21.
shall send into the Countrey, if they be qualified with
gifts fit for Government, either eminent above others,
or not inferior to others.

2 The Governor hath power with the Assistants
to governe the whole Countrey, according to the Laws
established hereafter mentioned; He hath power of
himselfe, and in his absence the Deputy Governor, to
moderate all publike actions of the Common-wealth, as
 First, To send out warrants for the calling of the Iosh.24.1.
generall Court.
 Secondly, To order and ransacke all actions in the
Court' where he sitteth : as, to gather Suffrages and
Voyces, and to pronounce Sentences according to the
greater part of them.

3 The power of the Governor with the rest of the
Counsellors, is
 First, To consult and provide for the maintenance Num.11.4.
of the State and People. to 16.
 Secondly, To direct in all matters wherein Appeale Ex.18.22.
is made to them from inferiour Courts. Deu. 17.8.9.
 Thirdly, To preserve Religion. Ex.32.25.27

4 To

2 Cor. 19.11.
32 23. 45 6.
Ex. 17.9.
Prov.24.5.

4 To oversee the Forts and Munition of the Countrey, and to take order for the protection of the Countrey from forraine invasion, or intestine sedition, as need shall require, with consent of the people to enterprise wars.

1 Kings 12.6

And because these great affaires of the State cannot be attended, nor administred, if they be after changed ; therefore the Counsellors are to be chosen for life, unlesse they give just cause of removall, which if they do, then they to be removed by the Generall Court.

Ex. 18. 22.

Deu.1.16.17.

4 The power of the Governor, sitting with the Counsellors and Assistants, is to heare and determine all causes whether Civill or Criminall, which are brought before him through the whole Commonwealth: Yet reserving liberty of Appeale from him to the generall Court.

Deu. 16.18.

5 Every Town is to have Iudges within themselves, whose power shall be once in the month, or in three months at the furthest to heare and determine both Civill Causes and Pleas of lesse value, and crimes also, which are not capitall: Yet reserving liberty of Appeale to the Court of Governor and Assistants.

Deu. 16.18.
Ier. 36. 10.
& 12.

6 For the better expedition and execution of Iustice, and of all affaires incident unto every Court. Every Court shall have certaine Officers, as a Secretary to inroll all the Acts of the Court: And besides Ministers of Iustice, to attach, and fetch, and set persons before the Magistrates: and also to execute the Sentence of the Court upon offenders: And for the

1 Sam. 20.
24.25.

same end, it shall be lawfull for the Governor or any one or two of the Counsellors, or Assistants, or Iudges, to give warrant to an Officer, to fetch any delinquent before them, and to examine the cause, and if

Acts 5.26:27

he be found culpable of that crime, to take order by surety or safe custody for his apparance at the Court.

And further for the same end, and to prevent the offendours lying long in prison, it shall be lawfull for the Governor, with one of the Counsell, or any two of the Assistants or Iudges, to see execution done upon any offenders for any crime that is not capitall, according to the Lawes established : Yet still reserving a liberty of Appeale from them to the Court, and from an Inferiour Court to an Higher Court.

CHAP.

Chap. II.

Of the free Burgesses and free Inhabitants.

1 First, All the free Burgesses excepting such as were admitted men before the establishment of Churches in the Countrey, shall bee received and admitted out of the members of some or others of the Churches in the Countrey, such Churches as are gathered or herafter shall be gathered with the consent of other Churches already established in the Countrey, and such members as are admitted by their own Church unto the Lords-Table.

2 These free Burgesses shall have power to choose in their owne Townes fit and able men out of themselves, to be the ordinary Iudges of inferiour Causes, in their own Town, and against the approach of the Generall Court to choose two or three, as their Deputies and Committees, to joyne with the Governour and Assistants of the whole Countrey, to make up and constitute the Generall Court.

3 This Generall Court shall have power,

First, By the Warrant of the Governor or deputy Governor, to assemble once every quarter or halfe a yeare or oftner, as the affaires of the Countrey shall require, and to sit together till their affaires bee dispatched.

2 To call the Governour and all the rest of the publike Magistrates and Officers into place, and to call them also to accoumpt for the breach of any Laws established, or other misdemeanour, and to censure them as the quality of the fact may require.

Thirdly, To make and repeale Laws.

Fourthly, To dispose all Laws in the Countrey, and to assigne them to severall Towns or persons, as shall be thought requisite.

Fifthly, To impose a leavy of moneys, for the publike service of the Common-wealth, as shall be thought requisite for the provision and protection of the whole.

Sixthly, To heare and determine all causes, wherein appeale shall be made unto them, or which they shall see cause to assume, into their own cognisance or judicature.

Seventhly, To assist the Governors and Counsellors in the maintenance of the purity and unity of Religion, and accordingly to set forward and uphold all such good causes as shall be thought fit, for that end, by the advice with consent of the Churches, and to represse the contrary.

Eighthly,

Eighthly, In this generall Court nothing shall be concluded but with Common consent of the greater part of the Governors, or Assistants, together with the greater part of the Deputies of the Towns, unlesse it be in election of Officers, where the liberty of the people is to be preferred, or in judging matters of offence against the Law, wherein both parties are to stand to the direction of the Law.

Ninthtly, All the housholders of every Town, shalbe accompted as the free Inhabitants of the Countrey, and accordingly shall enjoy freedome of Commerce and Inheritance of such lands, as the generall Court or the severall Townes wherein they dwell shall allot unto them, after they have taken an Oath, or given other security to be true and faithfull to the State, and subject to the good and wholesome Laws established in the Countrey by the generall Court.

Chap. III.

Of the protection and provision of the Countrey.

1 First, A Law to be made (if it be not made already) for the trayning of all men in the Countrey fit to beare armes unto the exercise of military Discipline; and withall another Lawe to be made for the maintenance of military Officers and Forts.

2 Because fishing is the chiefe staple commodity of the Countrey, therefore all due encouragement to be given, unto such hands as shall set forwards the trade of fishing; and for that end a Law to be made. That whosoever shall apply themselves to set forward the trade of fishing, as Fisher-men, Marriners and Shipwrights, shall be allowed, man for man, or some or other of the Labourers of the Countrey, to plant and to reape for them, in the season of the yeare, at the publike charge of the Common-wealth, for the space of these seven yeares next ensuing; and such Labourers to be appointed and paid by the Treasurer of the Common-wealth.

3 Because no Common-wealth can maintaine either their authority at home, or their honour and power abroad, without a sufficient Treasury : a Law therefore to be made for the electing and furnishing of the Treasury of the Common-wealth, which is to be supplyed and furnished.

1 By the yearely payment.

First

First, Of one penny, or halfe penny an Acre of Land to be occupied throughout the Countrey.

Land in common by a Towne to be paid for out of the Stocke or Treasury of the same Town.

Secondly, Of a penny for every beast, Horse or Cow.

Thirdly, Of some proportionable rate upon Marchants.

This rate to be greater or lesse as shall be thought fit.

2 By the payment of a barrel of Gun-powder, or such goods, or other munitions out of every ship, that bringeth forraine Commodities.

3 By fines and mulcts upon trespassers beasts.

4 A Treasurer to be chosen by the free Burgesses out of the Assistants, who shall receive and keep the Treasury and make disbursements out of it, according to the direction of the generall Court, or of the Governor or Counsellors, whereof they are to give an accompt at the generall Court.

It shall pertaine also to the Office of the Treasurer, to survey and oversee all the munitions of the Countrey, as Cannons, Culvering, Muskets, Powder, Match, Bullets, and to give accompt thereof to the Governor and Counsell.

5 A Treasury also or Magazin, or Storehouse to be erected, and furnished in every Town, as *Deut.* 14. 28. distinct from the Treasury of the Church, that provision of Corne and other necessaries, may be laid up at the best hand, for the reliefe of such poore, as are not members of the Church ; and that out of it such Officers may be mainteined, as Captaines and such like, who do any publike service for the Town: But chiefly this Treasury will be requisite for the preserving of the livelyhood of each Town within it selfe.

That in case the Inheritance of the Lands belong to any Towne, come to be alienated from the Townesmen, which may unavoydably fall out: Yet a supply may be had and made to the livelyhood of the Town by a reasonable Rent charge, upon such alienations laid by the common consent of the Land-owners and Townesmen, and to be paid unto the Treasury of the Town.

This Treasury to be supplyed.

1 First, By the yearely payment of some small rate upon Acres of Land.

2 By fines or amerciaments put upon trespassours beasts.

A Town Treasurer to be appointed for the oversight and ordering of this chosen out of the free Burgesses of the same Town, who is to dispose of things under his charge, according to the directions of the Iudges of the Towne, and to give accompt at the Townes Court to the Iudges and free Burgesses of the Town or to some elected by them. CHAP.

Chap. IV.

Of the right of Inheritance.

1 First, Forasmuch as the right of disposals of the Inheritanceof all Lands in the Countrey, lyeth in the Generall Court, whatsoever Lands are given and assigned by the Generall Court, to any Town or person shall belong and remaine as right of Inheritance to such Townes and their successors, and to such persons and to their heires and Assignes as their propriety for ever.

Whatsoever Lands belong to any Town, shall be given and assigned by the Town or by such Officers therein, as they shall appoint unto any person, the same shall belong and remaine, unto such person and his heires and assignes as his proper right for ever.

3 And in dividing of Lands to the severall persons in each Town, as regard is to be had partly to the number of the persons in family : To the more assigning the greater allotment, to the fewer lesse, and partly by the number of beasts, by the which a man is fit to occupy the Land assigned to him, and subdue it : Eminent respect (in this case may be given to men of eminent quality and descent) in assigning unto them more large and honorable accommodations, in regard of their great disbursements to publike charges.

Num. 26. 53 54.
Num.35.3.

4 Forasmuch as all Civill affaires are to be administred and ordered, so as may best conduce to the upholding and setting forward of the worship of God in Church fellowship. It is therefore ordered, that wheresoever the Lands of any mans Inheritance shall fall, yet no man shall set his dwelling house above the distance of halfe a mile or a mile at the furthest, from the meeting of the Congregation, where the Church doth usually assemble for the worship of God.

Num.17.7. to 11.

5 Inheritances are to descend naturally to the next of kinne, according to the Law of Nature, delivered by God.

Deu.21.17.

6 If a man have more Sonnes than one, then a double portion to be assigned, and bequeathed to the eldest Son, according to the Law of Nature, unlesse his own demerit do deprive him of the dignity of his Birth right.

1 Chr.5.1.

7 The will of a Testatour, is to be approved, or
disallowed

disallowed by the Court of Governours, and Assistants, or by the Court of Iudges in each Towne ; yet not to be disallowed by the Court of Governours, unlesse it appeare either to be counterfeit or unequall, either against the Law of God, or against the publike weale, or against the due right of the Legatours.

8 As God in old time, in the Common-wealth of *Israell*, forbad the alienation of Lands from one Tribe to another, so to prevent the like inconvenience in the alienation of Lands, from one Towne to another it were requisite to be ordered.

1 First, that no free Burgesse, or free Inhabitant of any Town shall sell the Land allotted to him in the Towne, (unlesse the free Burgesse of the Towne give consent unto such sale, or refuse to give due price answerable to what other offer without fraud) but to some one or other of the free Burgesses, or free inhabitants of the same Towne.

2 That if such Lands be sould to any others, the sale shall be made with reservation of such a rent charge to be paid to the Town Stock, or Treasury of the Towne, as either the former occupiers of the Land were wont to pay towards all the publike charges thereof; whether in Church or Town, or at least after the rate of three shillings the acre or some such like proportion, more or lesse, as shall be thought fit.

3 That if any free Burgesses, or free Inhabitants of any Towne, or the heire of any of their Lands, shal remove their dwelling from one Towne to another, none of them shall carry away the whole benefit of the Lands which they possessed, from the Townes whence they remove : But if they shall keepe the right of Inheritance, in their own hands, & not sell it as before, then, they shall reserve a like proportion of Rent charge out of their Land, to be paid to the publike Treasury of the Towne, as hath beene wont to be paid out of it to the publike charges of the Town and Church, or at least after the rate of three or five shillings an Acre, as before.

4 That if the Inheritance of a free Burgesse, or free Inhabitants of any Town fal to his daughters, as it wil do for defect of heires males, that then if such daughters doe not marry to some of the Inhabitants of the same Towne where their Inheritance lyeth, nor sell their

their Inheritance to some of the same Towne as before, that then they reserve a like proportion of rent
charge out of their Lands to be paid to the publike
Treasury of the Towne, as hath beene wont to be paid
out of them, to the publike charge of the Towne and
Church; or at least after the rate of three or five
shillings an Acre, provided alwayes that nothing be
payed to the maintenance of the Church out of the
Treasury of the Church or Towne, but by the free
consent and direction of the free Burgesses of the
Towne.

Chap. V.

Of Commerce.

1 First it shall be lawfull for the Governour with one
or more of the Counsell, to appoint a reasonable
rate of prizes upon all such commodities as are out of
the Ships, to be bought and sould in the Countrey.

2 In trucking or trading with the *Indians* no man
shall give them for any commodity of theirs, Silver or
Gold, or any weapons of war, either Guns or Gun-
powder, nor Sword, nor any other munition, which
might come to be used against our selves.

3 To the intent that all oppression in buying and
selling may be avoyded, it shall be lawfull for the
Iudges in every Towne, with the consent of the free
Burgesses to appoint certaine select men, to set reasonable rates upon all comodities, and proportionably
to limmit the wages of workemen and labourers, and
the rates agreed upon by them, and ratified by the
Iudges, to bind all the Inhabitants of the Towne. The
like course to be taken by the Governour, and Assistants, for the rating of prizes throughout the Countrey,
and all to be confirmed if need be by the generall
Court.

4 Iust weights and ballances to be kept betweene
buyers and sellers, and for default thereof the profit so
wickedly and corrruptly gotten, with as much more
added thereto, is to be forfeited to the publike Treasury of the Common-wealth.

Lev.19.35.
36.
Pro. 11. 1.
and 16. 11.
and 20. 10.

5 If

5 If any borrow ought of his neighbour upon a Deu. 24. 10. pledge, the lender shall not make choyce of what 11, 12, 13. pledge he will have, nor take such pledge as is of dayly Exod. 22. necessary use unto the debtor, or if he do take it, he 26. 27. shall restore it againe the same day.

6 No increase to be taken of a poore brother or Ex. 22. 25. neighbour, for any thing lent unto him. Lev. 25. 36.
37.

7 If borrowed goods be lost or hurt in the owners absence, the borrower is to make them good, but in the owners presence wherein he seeth his goods no otherwise used than with his consent, the borrower shall not make them good: If they were hired, the Ex. 22. 14, hire is to be paid and no more. 15.

CHAP. VI.

Of Trespasses.

1 IF a man's Swine or any other beast, or a fire kin- Ex. 22. 5, 6, dled, breake out into another mans field or corne, he shal make full restitution both of the dammage made by them, and of the losse of time, which others have had in carrying such Swine or beasts unto the owners, or to the fould.

But if a man put his beasts or Swine into anothers field, restitution is to be made of the best of his owne, though it were much better than that which were destroyed or hurt.

2 If a man kills another mans beast, or digge and Lev. 24. 18. open a pit, and leave it uncovered, and a beast fall Ex. 21. 34. into it; he that killed the beast, or the owner of the pit shall make restitution.

3 If any man's beast kill the beast of another, the Exo. 21. 35. owner of the beast shall make restitution.

4 If a man's Oxe or other beast, gore or bite and Ex. 21. 28, kill a man or a woman, whether Child or of riper age, 23, 30, 31. the beast shall be killed, and no benefit of the dead beast reserved to the owner, but if the Oxe or beast were wont to push or bite in times past, and the owner hath beene told it, and hath not kept him in; then both the Oxe or beast shall be forfeited and killed, and the owner also put to death, or fined to pay what the Iudges and the persons dampnified shall lay on him.

5 If

5 If a man deliver goods to his neighbour to keepe, and they be said to be lost or stolne from him, the keeper of the goods shall be put to his oath touching his own innocency, which if he take, & no evidence appeare to the contrary, he shall be quit, but if he be found false or unfaithfull, he shall pay double unto his neighbour.

Ex. 22. 11. 12.

But if a man take hire for the goods committed to him, and they be stolne, the keeper shall make restitution : But if the beast so kept for hire dye or be hurt, or be driven away, no man seeing it, then oath shall be taken of the keeper, that it was without his default, and it shall be accepted : but if the beast be torne in pieces, and a peece be brought for witnesse, it excuseth the keeper.

Chap. VII.

Of Crimes.

ANd first, of such as deserve capitall punishment, or cutting off from a mans people, whether by death or banishment.

Blasphemy.
Lev. 24. 11 to 16.

1 First, Blasphemy which is a cursing of God by Atheisme or the like, to be punished with death.

Idolatry.
Deu: 13. 10 15, 16.

2 Idolatry to be punished with death.

Witchcraft.
Ex. 22: 18. 20. 27.
Lev. 19, 31.

3 Witchcraft which is fellowship by covenant with a familiar Spirit to be punished with death.

4 Consulters with Witches not to be tollerated, but either to be cut off by death, or by banishment.

Consulters with witches.
Heresie.
Zac. 13. 3.

5 Heresie which is the maintenance of some wicked errors, overthowing the foundation of Christian Religion, which obstinacy if it be joyned with endeavour, to seduce others thereunto to be punished with death : because such an Hereticke no less than an Idolater seeketh to thrust the soules of men from the Lord their God.

False worship.
Ex. 32. 27, 28.

6 To worship God in a molten or graven Image, to be punished with death.

Scandalous livers.
1 Cor. 5. 5.

7 Such members of the Church, as doe wilfully reject to walke after due admonition, and conviction, the Churches establishment, and their christian admonition and censures, shall be cut off by banishment.

8 Whosoever

8 Whosoever shall revile the Religion and Worship of God, and the Government of the Church as it is now established, to be cut off by banishment. *Revilers of Religion.*

9 Wilfull perjury, whether before the judgement seat or in private conference, to be punished with death. *Wilful perjury.*

10 Rash perjury whether in publike or in private, to be punished with banishmēt, just it is that such a mans name should be cut off from his people, who prophans so grossly the name of God before his people. *Rash perjury.*

11 Profaning of the Lords day, in a carelesse and scornefull neglect or contempt thereof to be punished with death. *Sabbath Breakers.* Num 15. 35.

12 To put in practice the betraying of the Countrey, or any principall fort therein to the hand of any forraigne State, *Spanish, French, Dutch,* or the like: contrary to the allegeance we ow, and professe to our Dread Soveraign Lord King *Charles,* His Heires and Successors; whilst he is pleased to protect us as his loyal subjects, to be punished with death. *Treason.*

13 Vnreverend and dishonorable carriage to Magistrates, to be punished with banishment for a time, till they acknowledge their fault, and professe reformation. *Vnreverend to Magistrates.* Num. 12. 1. 14, 15.

14 Reviling of the Magistrates in highest rancke amongst us, to wit of the Governours and Counsell to be punished with death. *Reviling the Magistrate.*

15 Rebellion, Sedition, or Insurrection, by taking up armes against the present Government established in the Country to be punished with death. *Rebellion &c.* 1 King 22. 8, 9. & 44.

16 Rebellious children whether they continue in riot or drunkennesse after due correction from their parents, or whether they curse or smite their Parents, to be put to death. *Rebellious Children.* Deu. 21. 18. 19. 20. Ex. 21. 15. Lev. 20. 9.

17 Murther which is a wilfull man-slaughter, not in a mans necessary and just defence, nor casually committed, but out of hatred or cruelty, to be punished with death. *Murther.* Ex. 21. 12, 13. Num. 35. 16, 17, 18. to 33.

18 Adultery which is the defiling of the marriage bed, to be punished with death. Defiling of a woman espoused, is a kind of Adultery, and punishable by death, of both parties; but if a woman be forced, then by the death of the man only. *Gen. 9. 6. Adultery.* Lev. 20. 10. Deu. 22. 22, 23. Deu. 24. 25. 26.

19 Incest,

Incest.
Lev. 20. 11.
12 19. 20.

19 Incest, which is the defiling of any neer of kin, within the degrees prohibited in *Leviticus*, to be punished with death.

Sodomy.

20 Vnnaturall filthinesse to be punished with death, whether Sodomy, which is carnall fellowship of man with man, or woman with woman.

Buggery.

Or Buggery which is carnall fellowship of man or woman, with beasts or fowles.

Pollution &c.
Lev. 20. 18.
19.

21 Pollution of a woman known to be in her flowers to be punished with death.

Whordome.
Ex. 21. 16.
Deu. 24. 7.

22 Whordome of a maiden in her fathers house, kept secret till after her marriage with another, to be punished with death.

Man-stealing.
False witnesse.

23 Man-stealing to be punished with death.
24 False witnesse bearing to be punished with death.

Chap. VIII.

Of other Crimes lesse hainous such as are to be punished with some Corporall punishment or Fine.

1 **F**Irst rash and prophane swearing and cursing to be punished.

1 First, with losse of honour, or office, if he be Magistrate, or Officer : meet it is, their name should be dishonoured who dishonour Gods name.

2 With losse of freedome.

3 With disability to give Testimony.

4 With corporall punishment either by stripes, or by branding him with a hot iron, or boring through the tongue, who hath bored and pierced Gods name.

2 Drunkennesse, as transforming Gods Image into a beast, is to be punished with the punishment of *Pro. 26. 3.* beasts : A whip for the horse, and a rod for the fooles backe.

3 Forcing or a maid or a rape is not to bee punished with death by Gods Law, but

1 First, with Fine or penalty to the father of the maid.

Deut. 22. 8.
9.

2 With marriage of the maide defiled, if shee and her father consent.

3 With

3 With corporall punishment of stripes for his wrong, as a reall slander: And it is worse to make a whore, than to say one is a whore.

4 Fornication to be punished.   Ex. 22. 16.

1 First, with marriage of the maide, or giving her a sufficient Dowrie.

2 Secondly, with stripes though fewer, from the equity of the former Cause.

5 Mayming or wounding of a freeman, whether free Burgesse, or free Inhabitant, to be punished with a Fine; to pay

First, for his cure.   Ex. 21. 18, 19.

Secondly, for his losse.

And with losse of member for member, or some valuable recompence.   Lev. 24. 19, 20.

But if it be but the mayming or wounding of a servant, the servant is to go forth free from such a service.   Ex. 21. 26, 27.

6 If a man steale a beast, if it be found in his hand, he shall make restitution two for one; if it be kild & sould, restitution is to be made, of five Oxen for one: If the Theefe be not able to make restitution, then he to be sould by the Magistrate for a slave, till by his labour he may make due restitution.   Ex. 22. 4, & 1, 22, 3.

7 If a Theefe bee found breaking a house by night, if he be slaine, his smiter is guiltlesse, but in the day time, the Theefe is to make full restitution, as before, or if he be not able, then to be sould as before.   Ex. 22, 2,3.

8 Slanders are to be punished,

First, with a publike acknowledgment as the slander was publike.

Secondly, by mulcts or Fine of Money, when the slander bringeth damage.

Thirdly, by stripes if the slander be grosse, or odious, against such persons whom a man ought to honour and cherish: whether they be his Superiours, or in some degrees of equality with himselfe and his wife.

CHAP. IX.

Of the triall of Causes, whether Civil or Criminall, and the execution of Sentence.

1 IN the tryall of all Causes, no judgement shall passe, but either upon confession of the party, or upon the Testimony of two witnesses.   Deu. 19.10. 17. 6.

2 Triall

2 Triall by judges shall not be denied, where either the delinquent requireth it in causes Criminall, or the Plaintife or Defendant in Civill causes, partly to prevent suspition of partiality, of any Magistrates in the Court.

3 The Iurours are not to be chosen by any Magistrates, or Officers, but by the free Burgesses of each Town, as can give best light, to the Causes depending in Court, and who are least obnoxious to suspition of partiality : And the Iurours then chosen, to be nominated to the Court, and to attend the service of the Court.

4 The sentence of judgement given upon Criminall causes, and persons shall be executed in the presence of the Magistrates, or some of them at least.

5 No free-man whether free-Burgesse, or free-Inhabitant to be imprisoned, but either upon conviction or at least probable suspition, or some crime formerly mentioned, and the cause of his imprisonment, be declared and tried at the next Court following, at the furthest.

6 Stripes are not to be inflicted, but when the crimes of the offendour are accompanied with childish or brutish folly, or with lewd filthinesse, or with stubborne insolency, or with bruitish cruelty, or with idle vagrancy : But when stripes are due, not above 40 are to be inflicted.

Chap. X.

Of causes Criminall between our People and Forraine Nations.

Mat. 7. 12. 1 IN case any of our people should do wrong to any of another Nation, upon complaint made to the Governour or some other of the Counsell or Assistants, the fact is dilligently to be inquired into, and being found to be true, restitution is to be made of the goods of offendors, as the case shall require, according to the quality of the crime.

2 In case the people of another Nation have done Deuter. 20. any important wrong, to any of ours, right is first to be 10. 11. demanded of the Governor of that people, and Iustice
upon

upon the malefactors, which if it bee granted and per- formed, then no breach of peace to follow. 2 Sam. 20. 18, 19.

3 If right and Iustice be denied, and it will not stand with the honour of God and safety of our Nation, that the wrong be passed over, then war is to be undertaken and denounced.

4 Some Minister is to be sent forth to go along with the Army for their instruction and incouragement. Deut. 20. 2, 3, 4.

5 Men betrothed and not married, or newly married, or such as have newly built or planted, and not received the fruits of their Labours, and such as are fainthearted men, are not to be pressed or forc'd against their wils to go forth to wars. Dent. 20. 5, 6, 7, 8. & 24. 5.

6 Captaines are to be chosen by the Officers.

7 All wickednesse is to bee removed out of the Campe by severe discipline. Deut. 23. 9, 14.

8 And in war from men of a corrupt or false Religion, is not to be accepted, much lesse sought for. 2 Chro. 25. 7. 8.

9 Women, especially such as have not lyen by man, little children and cattell, are to be spared and reserved for spoyle. Deu. 20. 1.

10 Fruit Trees, whilst they may bee of use for meat to our owne Souldiers, are not to be cut down or destroyed, and consequently no Corne. Deut. 20. 19. 20.

11 The spoyles got by warre are to be divided into two pars, between the Souldiers and the Commonwealth that sent them forth. Num. 31. 21.

12 A Tribute from both is to be levyed to the Lord, and given to the Treasury of the Church, a fift part out, of the Common-wealth's part, and a 500 part out of the Souldiers part. Num. 31. 18. & 47.

13 If all the Souldiers return again in peace, not one lacking, it is acceptable to the Lord, if they offer over and above the former Tribute, a voluntary oblation unto the Treasury of the Church for a memoriall of the Redemption of their lives, by the especiall providence and Salvation of the Lord of Hoasts.

The Lord is our Iudge,
The Lord is our Law-giver,
The Lord is our King, He will save us. Isay. 33. 22.

FINIS.

The Table of the
Chapters.

Of

The Table of the Chapters.

F I N I S.

A

VOYAGE

TO

VIRGINIA.

BY

Colonel *NORWOOD*.

Force's Collection of Historical Tracts.

Vol. III.—No. 10.

A
VOYAGE
TO
VIRGINIA.

THE month of *August, Anno* 1649. *Time of* *setting out.* being the time I engag'd to meet my two comrades, Major *Francis Morrison*, and Major *Richard Fox*, at *London*, in order to a full accomplishment of our purpose to seek our fortunes in *Virginia*, (pursuant to our agreement the year before in *Holland*) all parties very punctually appear'd at the time and place assign'd, and were all still in the same mind, fully bent to put in practice what we had so solemnly agreed upon, our inclinations that way being nothing abated, but were rather quicken'd, by the new changes that we saw in the state of things, and that very much for the worse : For if our spirits were somewhat depress'd in contemplation of a barbarous restraint upon the person of our king in the *Isle of Wight ;* to what horrors and despairs must our minds be reduc'd at the bloody and bitter stroke of his assassination, at his palace of *Whitehall ?*

This unparallel'd butchery made the rebels cast away the scabbards of their swords with both their hands, in full resolution never to let them meet again, either by submission or capitulation ; so that the sad prospect of affairs in this juncture, gave such a damp to all the royal party who had resolved to persevere in the principle which engaged them in the war, that a very considerable number of nobility, clergy, and gentry, so circumstanc'd, did fly from their native country, as from a place infected with the plague, and did betake themselves to travel any where to shun so hot a contagion, there being no point on the compass that would not suit with some of our tempers and circumstances, for transportation into foreign lands.

Of the number who chose to steer their course for *America,*
such

such of them as inclin'd to try their fortunes at *Surinam*, *Barbados*, *Antigua*, and the *Leeward Islands*, were to be men of the first rate, who wanted not money or credit to balance the expence necessary to the carrying on the sugar works: And this consideration alone was enough to determine our choice for *Virginia*, had we wanted other arguments to engage us in the voyage. The honour I had of being nearly related to Sir *William Barkeley* the governor, was no small incitation to encourage me with a little stock to this adventure: Major *Morrison* had the king's commission to be captain of the fort; and Mr. *Fox* was to share in our good or bad success: But my best cargaroon was his majesty's gracious letter in my favour, which took effect beyond my expectation, because it recommended me (above whatever I had or could deserve) to the governor's particular care.

To proceed then, without any further *exordium*, to the subject of this narrative: It fell out to be about the first day of *September*, *Anno* 1649, that we grew acquainted on the *Royal-Exchange* with Capt. *John Locker*, whose bills upon the posts made us know he was master of a good ship, (untruly so call'd) *The Virginia Merchant*, burden three hundred tons, of force thirty guns, or more: We were not long in treaty with the captain, but agreed with him for ourselves and servants at six pounds a head, to be transported into *James River*; our goods to be paid for at the current price.

About the fifteenth day, we were ordered to meet the ship at *Gravesend*, where the captain was to clear with his merchants, and we to make our several payments; which when we had performed, we staid not for the ship, but took post for the *Downs*, where, with some impatience, we expected her coming there. About the sixteenth *ditto*, we could see the whole fleet under sail, with a south-west wind; which having brought them to that road, kept them there at anchor, until our money was almost spent at *Deal*.

September 23. the wind veered to the east, and we were summoned by signs and guns to repair on board. We had a fresh large gale three days, which cleared us of the channel, and put us out of soundings. With this propitious beginning we pursued our course for about twenty days, desiring to make the western islands; at which time the cooper began to complain, that our water-cask was almost empty, alledging, that there was not enough in hold, for our great family (about three hundred and thirty souls) to serve a month.

Scarcity of water. Our early want of water gave the master an alarm, and an occasion to consult with his officers for a remedy

to

to so important an evil as that might be, if not timely helped. We were now, by all accounts, very near the western islands : *Fyall* was that we were likely first to see, and our captain resolved to touch there to supply this defect, as the most commodious port for our purpose; and this was good news to the passengers, who are always glad at sight of land.

The day-break of *October* 14th, shewed us the peek of that island, the highest and most conspicuous land of any I have heard the seamen mention for land-marks, except that of the *Teneriff*. We stood directly for the harbour, which is also a good road, land-lock'd by the peek, which stands easterly about a mile distant from the town.

Assoon as we had saluted the castle, and returned thanks for being civilly answered, captain *John Tatam*, our countryman, did the same from aboard his goodly ship the *John*. He was newly returned from *Brasil*, in the kingdom of *Portugal's* service, and now bound for *Lisbon*, with a rich freight, and some lady of great note, who with her family took passage with him.

The *English* merchants from the town came soon on board our ship, and gave us a very civil welcome. Of them, one Mr. *Andrews* invited me, with my two comrades, to refresh ourselves with fruit and meat such as the island produced. Our captain dined with us at his house, and so did captain *Tatam*, who in like courteous manner engaged us all to dine on board his ship the next day. We visited the peach-trees for our desert, of which I took at least a double share, and did not fail to visit and revisit them in the dead of night, to satisfy a ravenous appetite nature has too prodigally given me for that species.

The next morning we surveyed the island, and thought the castle well fortified, especially on the sea-barr'd parts. The governor very civilly declared, he had lately received command from his majesty the king of *Portugal*, to treat all ships that belonged and were faithful to the king of *Great Britain*, with more than common courtesy, as he, for his part, did in all we could desire.

A little before the time of dinner captain *Tatam* had sent his boats to bring us on board his ship; and it was well for us he did so, our ship's long-boat having been staved in pieces the night before, by the seamens neglect, who had all tasted so liberally of new wine, by the commodiousness of the vintage, that they lay up and down dead drunk in all quarters, in a sad pickle.

The loss of our long-boat, as it was likely to make our watering tedious, and chargeable to the owners, so did it expose us to the hazard of many inconveniencies and perils in the whole course of our voyage, wherein frequent occasions occur that render

der

der that boat necessary to preserve the whole fabrick and lives of the ship and company; but to this breach no other reparation was applicable, but by recourse to that great stock of patience we were to be furnished withal for our support in the mighty straights we must encounter before we come to safe port.

Our captain disabled hereby to take the best course for our dispatch, made choice of the next best way to effect it, by the island boats; and having ordered his officers to use all diligence, and greater care than before, he led the van into *Tatam's* boat, which brought us safe on board the *John*.

At our arrival we were welcomed with a whole tyre of guns, and with a very kind aspect in the captain. He gave us excellent wines to drink before dinner, and at our meat as good of other sorts for concoction. There was a handsome plenty of fish and fowl, several ways cooked, to relish the *Portuguese*'s and the *English* palates; and, which made our entertainment more complete, he had prevailed with that great lady, with her pretty son of about twelve years old (tho' contrary to the custom even of the meaner sort at land) to sit at the table with us. She was taller than the ordinary stature of that nation, finely shap'd, had a very clear skin; her eyes and hair vying for the blackness and beauty of the jet; her modesty served, without any other art, to put a tincture of red upon her face; for when she saw herself environed with a company of strange faces, that had or might have had beards upon them, her blushes raised in her face a delicate complexion of red and white.

The captain was our interpreter to tell her how much we esteemed our selves honoured with her presence, which (for her better justification) she was in a manner forced to grant us, the ship affording her no other place fit for her retreat whilst we were there. Her young son sat by her, on whom all our eyes were fix'd; and our minds united with one opinion, that the air and lineaments of his face, full of sweetness, made him so like our king when he was of that age, that, every one whispering his thoughts to his neighbour, we all broke out at length in an open admiration of so great resemblance.

The healths of the two kings were passing about with thundering peals of cannon; the youth was permitted by his mother to kiss the cup, and drink a small portion to that of our king; and she was in so pleasant an humour at this honour done to her son, that, to close our feast, she ordered the table to be covered anew, and a handsome banquet placed upon it, which we must partake of before we parted. To conclude this rare treat, she repeated the health of our king in a sort of choice rich wine that they make in *Brasil*, and drank the proportion she would take, with-

out

out the allay of water, which till then she drank with little or no wine.

The approaching night made us take leave sooner than our inclinations would have led us ashore, the merchants having told us, there was no safe walking the streets in the night, for fear the *Pycaroes* (a sort of land-pyrates) should snatch away our hats and looser garments, as they use to treat strangers.

When we had paid our thanks to the captain, we desired his best language to make our compliments to the lady and her son, which she returned with her wishes for our happy voyage.

Whilst we were caress'd in this manner on shipboard, the seamen on shore continued in their debauchery, with very little advance of our dispatch; the getting water was so tedious in itself for lack of our boat, and so full of delays by drunken contests of ours with the islanders, and with themselves, that, after some days stay upon the island, when our captain resolved to sail away, he found the ship in worse condition for liquors, than when we came on shore; for if we got a new supply of water, the proportion was hardly enough to balance the expence of beer that was spent in the time we got it.

Some days before we parted, we saw the *John* under sail, bound for *Lisbon;* where the captain no sooner arrived and discharged his ship, but he listed himself as a man of war in a squadron of ships then there, under command of the prince *Rupert:* which I mention for his honour, because I have heard the prince acknowledge in his favour, that he did his duty very well when there was like to be an occasion of trying his valour.

It was about the 22d of *October* that we took leave October 22. of our landlord and *Fyal.* We had store of black pigs for fresh meat, and I carry'd peaches without number. We parted with an easterly wind a topsail gate, which soon brought us into a trade-wind that favoured us at fifty or sixty leagues in twenty-four hours, till we came to the height of *Bermudas.* In that latitude it is the general observation of seamen, that the seas are rough, and the weather stormy. It was my fortune to have a curiosity to look out, when the officer on the watch shewed me a more than ordinary agitation of the sea in one particular place above the rest; which was the effect of what they call a spout, a raging in the bowels of the sea, (like a violent birth) striving to break out, and at last springs up like a mine at land, with weight and force enough to have hoised our ship out of her proper element, into the air (had the helm been for it) and to have made her do the supersalt; but God's providence secured us from that danger.

The sight of the island was welcome to all: the mariners
learned

learned thereby our true distance from cape *Hatteras;* and the passengers were relieved with hopes to be soon at shore from a hungry pester'd ship and company.

Nov. 8.   The gale continued fair till *November* 8: then we observed the water changed; and having the lead, we had thirty-five fathom of water, which was joyful news; our want of all things necessary for human life, made it so.

Towards break of day, weary of my lodging, I visited mate *Putts* on the watch, and would have treated him with brandy, but he refused that offer, unless I could also give him tobacco, which I had not. He said, it was near break of day, and he would look out to see what change there was in the water. No sooner were his feet upon the deck, but with stamps and noise he calls up the seamen, crying out, *All hands aloft! Breaches, breaches on both sides! All hands aloft!*

The seamen were soon on deck with this dismal alarm, and saw the cause thereof; but instead of applying their hands for their preservation (through a general despondency) they fell on their knees, commending their souls as at the last gasp. The captain came out at the noise to rectify what was amiss; but seeing how the case stood, his courage failed. Mate *Putts* (a stout seaman) took heart again, and cryed out, Is there no good fellow that will stand to the helm, and loose a sail? But of all the ship's crew there were but two foremast men that would be perswaded to obey commands, namely, *Thomas Reasin* and *John Smith*, men of innate courage, who, for their good resolution on that and divers other occasions in the various traverses of this voyage, deserve to have their names kept in lasting remembrance.

One of them got up and loosed the fore top-sail, to put the ship (if possible) in steerage way, and under command; the other stood to the helm, and he shifted it in a nick of time; for the ship was at the point of dashing on the starboard breach: and altho', in the rest of the voyage, she was wont to be blamed for the ill quality of not feeling the helm, she did, in this important instance, redeem her credit, and fell round off for our rescue from that danger. But the sense of this escape lasted but a moment; for no sooner was she fallen from that breach, but another on the larboard-bow was ready to receive her. The ship's crew, by this time (reproached by the courage of *Reasin* and *Smith*) were all at work; and the helm shifting opportunely, she fell off again as before. The light of the day (which now broke forth) did discover our condition to be altogether as perillous as possible; for we now saw our selves surrounded with breaches; scarce any water like a channel appeared for a way to shun them.

In

In this sad condition the ship struck ground, and raised such a war of water and sand together, which fell on the main-chains, that now all hopes of safety were laid aside ; but the ship being still afloat, and the seamen all of them now under command, nothing was omitted for our preservation that was in their power.

Tom Reasin, seeing the ship go a-head in the likeliest water for a channel, and ordering the helm accordingly, heaved the lead ; and after a little further advance into that new channel, wholly against his hopes, he had a good deal of water more than the ship drew, which soon mended upon us, the next cast of the lead affording eighteen or twenty foot. We stood to this channel, and the light of the morning enabling the quarter-masters to con the ship, we were by this miraculous mercy of God, soon clear of the breaches at cape *Hatteras*, and got out to sea.

No sooner was the ship freed of this danger, and gotten a little into the offing, but the seamen (like so many spirits) surveyed each other, as if they doubted the reality of the thing, and shook hands like strangers, or men risen from the other world, and did scarce believe they were, what they seemed to be, men of flesh and blood. As they recovered force, they made what sail they could to stand to sea-ward.

The gale came fresh at north-west, and this fresh gale   *A storm.* did soon grow up to a violent storm, which increased to so great a rigour, separating us from the land at the rate of eight leagues a watch, merely with our fore-courses, insomuch that the master thought it necessary to stop that career ; and, in order thereunto, he did advise with his officers to bring the ship about, to furl all sails, and to try with the mizzen.

The mountainous towring north-west seas that this storm made, were so unruly, that the seamen knew not how to work the ship about. We were already at a great distance from land, and something must be done to hinder our running off at that excessive rate. The first thing they did, was to lower the mainyard, to give some ease to that mast, by laying it on the ship's waste. Our great difficulty was, how to deal so with the foresails, that the ship might work about with safety, or at least with as little hazard as possible. All hands were too little to hale the sheet close, in order to bring the ship about. Many great seas were shipp'd as she came to work thro' the trough of the sea : amongst the rest one chanc'd to break upon the poop (where we were quartered) and that with so sad a weight, that we guess'd a tun of water (at the least) did enter the tarpaulin, and set us all on float who were in the round-house. The noise it made by discharging itself in that manner, was like the report of a great gun, and did put us all into a horrible fright, which we

could

could not soon shake off. This shock being past, the ship about, and our fore-sail handled, we now lay trying with our mizzen.

Great   I cannot forget the prodigious number of porpoises *numbers of* that did that evening appear about the ship, to the *porpoises.* astonishment of the oldest seamen in her. They seemed to cover the surface of the sea as far as our eyes could discern; insomuch that a musket bullet, shot at random, could hardly fail to do execution on some of them. This the seamen would look upon as of bad portent, predicting ill weather; but in our case, who were in present possession of a storm, they appeared too late to gain the credit of foretelling what should come upon us in that kind.

The seas thus enraged, and all in foam, the gale still increasing upon us, the officers on the watch made frequent visits to the round-house, to prepare the captain for some evil encounter which this mighty tempest must bring forth: and their fears proved reasonable; for, about the hours of ten or eleven, our new disasters did begin with a crash from aloft. All hands were summon'd up with loud cries, that the fore-topmast was come by the board, not alone, but in conjunction with the fore-mast head broken short off, just under the cap.

This was a sore business, and put all to their wits end to recover to any competent condition; what could be done was done to prevent further mischiefs; but the whole trim and rigging of a ship depending much upon stays and tackle fixed to that mast, we had reason to expect greater ruins to follow, than what had already befallen us. Mate *Putt* was then on the watch, and did not want his apprehension of what did soon ensue, which in all likelihood was to end in our utter perdition; for about the hours of twelve or one at night, we heard and felt a mighty sea break on our fore-ship, which made such an inundation on the deck where the mate was walking, that he retired back with all diligence up to his knees in water, with short ejaculations of prayers in his mouth, supposing the ship was foundering, and at the last gasp. This looked like a stroke of death in every seaman's opinion: the ship stood stock still, with her head under water, seeming to bore her way into the sea. My two comrades and myself lay on our platform, sharing liberally in the general consternation. We took a short leave of each other, men, women, and children. All assaulted with the fresh terror of death, made a most dolorous outcry throughout the ship, whilst mate *Putts* perceiving the deck almost freed of water, called out aloud for hands to pump. This we thought a lightning before death, but gave me occasion (as having the best sea legs) to look and learn the subject of this astonishing alarm, which proved to arise from

no

no less cause than the loss of our forecastle, with six guns, and
our anchors (all but one that was fastened to a cable) together
with our two cooks, whereof one was recovered by a strange providence.

This great gap, made by want of our forecastle, did open a
passage into the hold for other seas that should break there before a remedy was found out to carry them off, and this made
our danger almost insuperable; but it fell out propitiously, that
there were divers land-carpenter passengers, who were very
helpful in this distress; and, in a little time, a slight platform of
deal was tack'd to the timbers, to carry off any ordinary sea in
the present straight we were in; every moment of this growing
tempest cutting out new work to employ all hands to labour.

The bowsprit, too top-heavy in itself, having lost all stays
and rigging that should keep it steady, sway'd to and fro with
such bangs on the bows, that at no less rate than the cutting it
close off, could the ship subsist.

All things were in miserable disorder, and it was evident our
danger increas'd upon us: the stays of all the masts were gone,
the shrouds that remained were loose and useless, and it was
easy to foretel, our main-topmast would soon come by the board.
Tom Reasin (who was always ready to expose himself) with an
ax in his hand, ran up with speed to prevent that evil, hoping
thereby to ease the main-mast, and preserve it; but the danger
of his person in the enterprize, was so manifest, that he was
called down amain; and no sooner was his foot upon the deck,
but what was feared came to pass with a witness, both main and
topmast all came down together, and, in one shock, fell all
to the windward clear into the sea, without hurt to any man's
person.

Our main-mast thus fallen to the broadside, was like to incom-
mode us more in the sea, than in her proper station; for the
shrouds and rigging not losing the hold they had of the ship,
every surge did so check the mast (whose but-end lay charg'd
to fall perpendicular on the ship's side) that it became a ram to
batter and force the plank, and was doing the last execution upon
us, if not prevented in time by edge-tools, which freed the ship
from that unexpected assault and battery.

Abandon'd in this manner to the fury of the raging sea,
tossed up and down without any rigging to keep the ship steady,
our seamen frequently fell overboard, without any one regarding
the loss of another, every man expecting the same fate, tho' in
a different manner. The ceilings of this hulk (for it was no
better) were for the same cause so uneasy, that, in many tumbles,
the deck would touch the sea, and there stand still as if she would

never

never make another.   Our mizzen mast only remained, by which
we hoped to bring the ship about in proper season, which now
lay stemming to the east.

In this posture did we pass the tenth and eleventh days of *November ;* the twelfth in the morning we saw an *English* merchant, who shewed his ensign, but would not speak with us, tho'
the storm was abated, and the season more fit for communication.
We imagined the reason was, because he would not be compelled
to be civil to us : he thought our condition desperate, and we
had more guns than he could resist, which might enable us to take
what he would not sell or give.   He shot a gun to leeward, stood
his course, and turn'd his poop upon us.

Before we attempted to bring the ship about, it was necessary to refresh the seamen, who were almost worn out with toil
and want of rest, having had no leisure of eating set meals for
many days.   The passengers overcharged with excessive fears,
had no appetite to eat; and (which was worst of all) both seamen and passengers were in a deplorable state as to the remaining victuals, all like to fall under extreme want ; for the storm,
by taking away the forecastle, having thrown much water into
the hold, our stock of bread (the staff of life) was greatly dam-
nified ; and there remained no way to dress our meat, now that
the cook-room was gone ; the incessant tumbling of the ship (as
has been observ'd) made all such cookery wholly impracticable.
The only expedient to make fire betwixt decks, was, by sawing
a cask in the middle, and filling it with ballast, which made a
hearth to parch pease, and broil salt beef ; nor could this be
done but with great attendance, which was many times frustrated by being thrown topsy-turvy in spite of all circumspection,
to the great defeat of empty stomachs.

Nov. 17.   The seas were much appeas'd the seventeenth day,
         and divers *English* ships saw, and were seen by us, but
would not speak with us ; only one, who kept the pump always
going, for having tasted too liberally of the storm, he was so kind
as to accost us.   He lay by till our wherry (the only surviving
boat that was left us) made him a visit.   The master shewed
our men his leaks, and proposed, that ours would spare him
hands to pump in lieu of any thing he could spare for our relief.
He promised however to keep us company, and give us a tow
to help to weather the cape, if occasion offered ; but that was
only a copy of his countenance ; for in the night we lost each
other, and we never heard more of him, tho' he was bound to our
port.

Nov. 13.   The weather now invited us to get the ship about with
         our mizzen ; and having done so, the next consideration
                                                            was,

was, how to make sail. The fore mast, all this while (as much as was of it) stood its ground: and as it was without dispute, that a yard must in the first place be fixed to it, so was it a matter of no small difficulty how to advance to the top of that greasy slippery stump, since he that would attempt it, could take no hold himself, nor receive any help for his rise, by other hands. This was a case that put all the ship's crew to a nonplus, but *Tom Reasin* (a constant friend at need, that would not be baffled by any difficulty) shewed by his countenance, he had a mind to try his skill to bring us out of this unhappy crisis. To encourage him the more, all passengers did promise and subscribe to reward his service, in *Virginia*, by tobacco, when God should enable us so to do. The proportions being set down, many were the more generous, because they never thought to see the place of payment, but expected to anticipate that by the payment of a greater debt to nature, which was like to be exacted every hour by an arrest of the merciless sea, which made small shew of taking bail for our appearance in *Virginia*.

The manner of *Tom Reasin's* ascent to this important work, was thus. Among the scatter'd parcels of the ship's stores he had the luck to find about half a dozen iron spikes fit for his purpose. His first onset was to drive one of them into the mast, almost to the head, as high as he could reach; which being done, he took a rope of about ten foot long, and having threaded the same in a block or pulley, so as to divide it in the middle, he made both ends meet in a knot upon the spike, on both sides of the mast; so that the block falling on the contrary side, became a stirrup to mount upon for driving another spike in the same manner: and thus from step to step, observing the best advantage of striking with his hammer in the smoothest sea, he got aloft, drove cleats for shrouds, to rest upon, and was soon in a posture of receiving help from his comrades, who got a yard and sails (with other accommodation) such as could be had, and thus we were enabled, in few hours time, to make some sail for our port.

The main-yard, that in the storm had been lowered to the wast to lie out of harm's way, was now preferred to the place of a main mast, and was accordingly fitted and accoutred, and grafted into the stump of what was left in the storm, some eight or ten foot from the deck. It was a hard matter to find out rigging answerable to that new-fashioned mast and yard; top-gallant sails and yards were most agreeable to this equipage, and was the best part of our remaining stores. The seas grew every moment smoother, and the weather more comfortable; so that for a while we began to shake off the visage of utter despair, as hoping ere

long

long to see our selves in some capacity to fetch the cape. We
discovered another ship bound to *Virginia*, who as frankly promised to stand by us, the wind at N. N. W. We did what could
be done by a ship so mangled, to get the weather-gage of the
cape *Henry*, conceiving our selves to the southward of cape
Hatteras : but by taking an observation on a sun-shine day, we
found our selves carryed by a current we knew not of, to the
windward, much beyond all our dead reckonings and allowances
for sailing, insomuch that when we thought we had been to the
southward of the cape, we found our selves considerably shot to
the north of *Achomat*, and that in the opinion of mate *Putts*,
who was as our north star.

We passed this night with greater alacrity than we had done
any other since we had left *Fyall ;* for mate *Putts*, our trusty
pilot, did confidently affirm, that, if the gale stood, there would
be no question of our dining the next day within the capes. This
was seasonable news, our water being long since spent, our meat
spoiled (or useless) no kind of victuals remaining to sustain life,
but a bisket cake a day for a man ; at which allowance there was
not a quantity to hold out many days. In the dark time of the
night, in tacking about, we lost our new comrade, and with much
impatience we expected the approaching day ; the wind N. W.

The morning appeared foggy, as the wind veered to *Nov.* 15:
the east, and that did cover and conceal the land from
our clearer sight ; howbeit we concluded by mate *Putts's* computation, we were well to the northward of the capes. Many times
he would mount the mizzen top for discovery, as the weather
seemed to clear up, and would espy and point at certain hum-
works of trees that used to be his several land-marks in most of
the twenty-two voyages he had made to that plantation. Under
this confidence he made more sail, the day-light confirming him
in what he thought was right.

All the forenoon we lost the sight of land and marks by trees,
by reason of the dark fogs and mists that were not yet dispelled ;
but assoon as the sun, with a north-west gale, had cleared all the
coast (which was about the hours of two or three o'clock) mate
Putts perceived his error from the deck, and was convinced, that
the hum-works of trees he had seen and relied on for sure land-
marks, had counter points to the south cape, which had misguid-
ed him ; and that it was the opening of the bay which made the
land at distance out of sight.

This fatal disappointment (which was now past human help)
might have met an easy remedy, had our sails and rigging been
in any tolerable condition to keep the windward gage (for we
had both the capes in our sight) but under our circumstances it
was

was vain to endeavour such a thing; all our equipage, from stem
to stern, being no better than that of a western barge, and we
could not lie within eleven or twelve points of the wind.

Defeated thus of lively hopes we had the night before entertain'd to sleep in warm beds with our friends in *Virginia*, it was
a heavy spectacle to see our selves running at a round rate from
it, notwithstanding all that could be done to the contrary.   Nothing was now to be heard but sighs and groans thro' all that
wretched family, which must be soon reduced to so short allowance, as would just keep life and soul together.   Half a bisket
cake a day to each (of which five whole ones made a pound)
was all we had to trust to.   Of liquors there remained none to
quench thirst: *Malaga* sack was given plentifully to every one,
which served rather to inflame and increase thirst, than to extinguish it.

The gale blew fresh (as it uses to do) towards night, and
made a western sea that carry'd us off at a great rate.   Mate
Putts, extremely abash'd to see his confidence so miserably deluded, grew sad and contemplative, even to the moving compassion in those whom his unhappy mistake had reduc'd to this
misery.   We cherish'd him the best we could, and would not
have him so profoundly sad, for what was rather his misfortune
than his fault.

The wind continued many days and nights to send us out into
the ocean, insomuch that until we thought our selves at least an
hundred leagues from the capes, the north-west gale gave us no
truce to consider what was best to do. All little helps were used
by top-gallant sails, and masts placed where they could be fixed,
to keep the windward gage ; but, for lack of borolins and other
tackle to keep them stiff to draw, every great head-sea would
check them in the wind, and rend and tear them in pieces ; so
that it was an ordinary exercise with us to lie tumbling in the sea
a watch or two together, driving to leeward, whilst the broken
sails were in hand to be repaired.

It would be too great a trial of the reader's patience to be entertain'd with every circumstance of our sufferings in the remaining part of this voyage, which continued in great extremity for
at least forty days from the time we left the land, our miseries
increasing every hour: I shall therefore omit the greatest number of our ill encounters, which were frequently repeated on us,
and remember only what has in my thoughts been most remarkable, and have made the deepest impression in my memory.

To give us a little breathing, about the nineteenth *Nov.* 19.
day the wind shifted to the east, but so little to our avail
(the gale so gentle, and the seas made against us like a strong
current)

current) that, with the sail we were able to make, we could hardly reckon the ship shortened the way, but that she rather lost ground. In less than two watches the gale faced about; and if we saved our own by the change, it was all we could pretend unto.

Our mortal enemy, the north-west gale, began afresh to send us out to sea, and to raise our terrors to a higher pitch. One of our pumps grew so unfix'd, that it could not be repair'd; the other was kept in perpetual motion; no man was excus'd to take his turn that had strength to perform it. Amongst the manifold perils that threatened every hour to be our last, we were in mortal apprehension, that the guns which were all aloft, would shew us a slippery trick, and some of them break loose, the tackle that held them being grown very rotten: and it was another providence they held so long, considering how immoderately the ship rolled, especially when the sails were mending that should keep them steady, which was very near a third part of our time, whilst we plyed to the windward with a contrary gale.

To prevent this danger which must befal when any one gun should get loose, mate *Putts* found an expedient by a more than ordinary smooth water; and by placing timber on the hatchway, to supply the place of shrouds, he got them safe in hold; which tended much to our good, not only in removing the present danger, but by making the ship (as seamen say) more wholesome, by haveing so great weight removed from her upper works into her centre, where ballast was much wanted.

But the intolerable want of all provisions, both of meat and drink, jostled the sense of this happiness soon out of our minds. And to aggravate our misery yet the more, it was now our interest to pray, that the contrary gale might stand; for whilst the westerly wind held, we had rain water to drink, whereas at east the wind blew dry.

In this miserable posture of ship and provision, we reckoned our selves driven to the east, in less than a week's time, at least two hundred leagues, which we despaired ever to recover without a miracle of divine mercy. The storm continued so fresh against us, that it confounded the most knowing of our ship's company in advising what course to take. Some reckoned the ship had made her way most southerly, and therefore counselled we should put our selves in quest of the *Bermudas* islands, as to the nearest land we could hope to make: but that motion had great opposition in regard of the winter season, which would daily produce insuperable difficulties, and give greater puzzle in the discovery of it, than our circumstances would admit. Others would say, The furthest way about, in our case, would prove the nearest

way

way home; and judged it best to take advantage of the westerly winds, and impetuous seas made to our hands, to attempt returning back to the western islands, as a thing more likely to succeed (tho' at a great distance) than thus to strive against the stream without any hopeful prospect of gaining the capes. But that motion met with a more general aversion, because the run was so long, that, tho' the gale had been in our own power to continue it, we could not have subsisted. Backwards we could not go, nor forwards in the course we desired: it followed then of consequence, that we must take the middle way; and it was resolved, that, without further persisting in endeavouring to gain our port by a close hale, we should raise our tackle, and sail tardy for the first *American* land we could fetch, tho' we ran to the leeward as far as the coast of *New England*.

Whilst this determination was agreed and put in practice, the famine grew sharp upon us. Women *A famine.* and children made dismal cries and grievous complaints. The infinite number of rats that all the voyage had been our plague, we now were glad to make our prey to feed on; and as they were insnared and taken, a well grown rat was sold for sixteen shillings as a market rate. Nay, before the voyage did end (as I was credibly inform'd) a woman great with child offered twenty shillings for a rat, which the proprietor refusing, the woman died.

Many sorrowful days and nights we spun out in this manner, till the blessed feast of *Christmas* came upon us, which we began with a very melancholy solemnity; and yet, to make some distinction of times, the scrapings of the meal-tubs were all amassed together to compose a pudding. *Malaga* sack, sea water, with fruit and spice, all well fryed in oyl, were the ingredients of this regale, which raised some envy in the spectators; but allowing some privilege to the captain's mess, we met no obstruction, but did peaceably enjoy our *Christmas* pudding.

My greatest impatience was of thirst, and my dreams were all of cellars, and taps running down my throat, which made my waking much the worse by that tantalizing fancy. Some relief I found very real by the captain's favour in allowing me a share of some butts of small claret he had concealed in a private cellar for a dead lift. It wanted a mixture of water for qualifying it to quench thirst; however, it was a present remedy, and a great refreshment to me.

I cannot forget another instance of the captain's kindness to me, of a like obligation. He singled me out one day to go with him into the hold to seek fresh water in the bottoms of the empty casks. With much ado we got a quantity to satisfy our longing,
tho'

tho' for the thickness thereof it was not palatable. We were now each of us astride on a butt of *Malaga*, which gave the captain occasion to taste of their contents. We tasted and tasted it again ; and tho' the total we drank was not considerable, yet it had an effect on our heads that made us suspend (tho' we could not forget) our wants of water. The operation this little debauch had upon the captain, was very different from what it wrought on me, who felt myself refresh'd as with a cordial ; but the poor captain fell to contemplate (as it better became him) our sad condition ; and being troubled in mind for having brought so many wretched souls into misery, by a false confidence he gave them of his having a good ship, which he now thought would prove their ruin ; and being conscious, that their loss would lie all at his door, it was no easy matter to appease his troubled thoughts. He made me a particular compliment for having engaged me and my friends in the same bottom, and upon that burst into tears. I comforted him the best I could, and told him, We must all submit to the hand of God, and rely on his goodness, hoping, that the same providence which had hitherto so miraculously preserved us, would still be continued in our favour till we were in safety. We retired obscurely to our friends, who had been wondering at our absence.

The westerly wind continued to shorten our way to the shore, tho' very distant from our port ; but this did not at all incline us to change our resolution of sailing large for the first land ; it did rather animate and support us in our present disasters of hunger and thirst, toil and fatigue. The hopes of touching land was food and raiment to us.

In this wearisome expectation we pass'd our time for eight or nine days and nights, and then we saw the water change colour, and had soundings. We approach'd the shore the night of Jan. 3. *January* 3d. with little sail ; and, as the morning of the —— 4. fourth day gave us light, we saw the land ; but in what latitude we could not tell, for that the officers, whose duty it was to keep the reckoning of the ship, had for many days past totally omitted that part ; nor had we seen the sun a great while, to take observations, which (tho' a lame excuse) was all they had to say for that omission. But in truth it was evident, that the desperate estate of the ship, and hourly jeopardy of life did make them careless of keeping either log or journal ; the thoughts of another account they feared to be at hand, did make them neglect that of the ship as inconsiderable.

About the hours of three or four in the afternoon of the twelfth eve, we were shot in fair to the shore. The evening was clear and calm, the water smooth ; the land we saw nearest was

some

some six or seven *English* miles distant from us, our soundings twenty-five fathoms in good ground for anchor-hold.

These invitations were all attractive to encourage the generality (especially the passengers) to execute what we had resolved on for the shore: but one old officer who was husband for the ship's stores whilst there were any, would not consent on any terms to trust the only anchor that was left us for preservation, out of his sight at sea. His arguments to back his opinion were plausible; as, *first,* The hazard of losing that only anchor by any sudden storm, bringing with it a necessity to cut or slip, on which every life depended. 2*dly.* The shortness of the cable, very unfit for anchorage in the ocean: And 3*dly.* The weakness of the ship's crew, many dead and fallen over board, and the passengers weakened by hunger, dying every day on the decks, or at the pump, which with great difficulty was kept going, but must not rest.

Against the old man's reasonings was urged the very small remains of bisket, at our short allowance, which would hardly hold a week; the assurance of our loss by famine if we should be forced to sea again by a north-west storm, and the great possibility of finding a harbour to save our ship, with our lives and goods, in some creek on the coast. These last reasons prevailed upon the majority against all negatives: and when the anchor was let loose, mate *Putts* was ordered to make the first discovery of what we might expect from the nearest land. He took with him twelve sickly passengers, who fancied the shore would cure them; and he carry'd major *Morrison* on shore with him in pursuit of such adventures as are next in course to be related; for according to the intelligence that could be got from land, we were to take our measures at sea, either to proceed on in our voyage in that sad condition that has been in some proportion set forth, or to land our selves, and unload the ship, and try our fortunes amongst the *Indians.*

In four or five hours time we could discover the boat returning with mate *Putts* alone for a setter, which we look'd upon as a signal of happy success. When he came on board his mouth was full of good tidings, as namely, That he discovered a creek that would harbour our ship, and that there was a depth of water on the bar, sufficient for her draught when she was light. That there was excellent fresh water, (a taste whereof major *Morrison* had sent me in a bottle.) That the shore swarm'd with fowl, and that major *Morrison* stayed behind in expectation of the whole ship's company to follow.

I opened mine ears wide to the motion, and promoted the design of our landing there with all the rhetorick and interest I had.

The

The captain was no less forward for it, hoping thereby to save the lives of the passengers that remained: and that he might not wholly rely on mate *Putts*'s judgment in a matter wherein he was most concern'd, he embark'd with me in the wherry, with a kinsman of his, and some others; and the seamen were glad of my help to put the boat to shore, my hands having been very well season'd at the pump, by taking my turn for many weeks at the rate of three hours in twenty four. My passionate desires to be on shore at the fountain head to drink without stint, did not a little quicken me, insomuch that the six or seven miles I rowed on this occasion, were no more than the breadth of the *Thames* at *London*, at another time, would have been toilsome to me.

In our passage to the shore, the darkness of the evening made us glad to see the fires of our friends at land, which were not only our beacons to direct us to their company, but were also a comfortable relief to our chill bodies when we came near them, the weather being very cold (as it ever is) the wind north-west on that coast.

Land.   Assoon as I had set my foot on land, and had rendred thanks to almighty God for opening this door of deliverance to us, after so many rescues even from the jaws of death at sea, major *Morrison* was pleased to oblige me beyond all requital, in conducting me to the running stream of water, where, without any limitation of short allowance, I might drink my fill. I was glad of so great liberty, and made use of it accordingly, by prostrating myself on my belly, and setting my mouth against the stream, that it might run into my thirsty stomach without stop. The rest of the company were at liberty to use their own methods to quench their thirst; but this I thought the greatest pleasure I ever enjoyed on earth.

After this sweet refreshment, the captain, myself, and his kinsman crossed the creek in our wherry, invited thither by the cackling of wild-fowl. The captain had a gun charged, and the moon shining bright in his favour, he killed one duck of the flock that flew over us, which was roasted on a stick out of hand by the seamen, whilst we walk'd on the shore of the creek for further discovery.

In passing a small gullet we trod on an oyster bank that did happily furnish us with a good addition to our duck. When the cooks had done their parts, we were not long about ours, but fell on without using the ceremony of calling the rest of our company, which would have been no entertainment to so many, the proverb telling us, *The fewer the better chear.* The bones, head, legs, and inwards were agreed to be the cook's fees; so

we

we gave God thanks, and return'd to our friends, without making boast of our good fortunes.

Fortify'd with this repast, we inform'd our selves of the depth of water at the bar of the creek, in which the captain seem'd satisfy'd, and made shews in all his deportment, of his resolution to discharge the ship there in order to our safety. Towards break of day he ask'd me in my ear, If I would go back with him on board the ship? I told him, No, because it would be labour lost, in case he would persist in his resolution to do what he pretended, which he ratify'd again by protestations, and so went off with his kinsman, who had a large coarse cloth gown I borrow'd of him to shelter me from the sharpest cold I ever felt. That which had sometimes been a paradox to me, was by this experience made demonstrable, (*viz.*) That the land on the continent is much colder than that of islands, tho' in the same latitude; and the reason is evident to any who shall consider the many accidents on the continent that cool the air by winds that come from the land; as in those parts of *America*, the mighty towring mountains to the north-west, covered all the year with snow, which does refrigerate the air even in the heat of summer; whereas winds coming from the sea are generally warm: and this hath proved a fatal truth to the inhabitants of *Virginia*, who, in the south-east winds, have gone to bed in sultry heat and sweat, without any covering, and have awaked in the night stiff and benumb'd with cold, without the use of their limbs, occasion'd by a shifting of the wind in the night from sea to land.

No sooner had the captain cleared himself of the shore but the day-break made me see my error in not closing with his motion in my ear. The first object we saw at sea was the ship under sail, standing for the capes with what canvass could be made to serve the turn. It was a very heavy prospect to us who remained (we knew not where) on shore, to see our selves thus abandon'd by the ship, and more, to be forsaken by the boat, so contrary to our mutual agreement. Many hours of hard labour and toil were spent before the boat could fetch the ship: and the seamen (whose act it was to set sail without the captain's order, as we were told after) car'd not for the boat whilst the wind was large to carry them to the capes. But mate *Putts*, who was more sober and better natur'd, discovering the boat from the mizzen-top, lay by till she came with the captain on board.

In this amazement and confusion of mind that no words can express, did our miserable distress'd party condole with each other our being so cruly abandon'd and left to the last despairs of human help, or indeed of ever seeing more the face of man. We entred into a sad consultation

Left on an island.

what

what course to take ; and having, in the first place, by united
prayers, implored the protection of Almighty God, and recommended our miserable estate to the same providence which, in so
many instances of mercy, had been propitious to us at sea ; the
whole party desired me to be as it were the father of this distressed family, to advise and conduct them in all things I thought
might most tend to our preservation.   This way of government
we agreed must necessarily reside in one, to avoid disputes, and
variety of contradictory humours, which would render our deliverance the more impracticable ; and it was thought most reasonable to be placed in me, for the health and strength it had
pleased God to preserve unto me above my fellows, more than
for any other qualification.

At the time I quitted the ship my servant *Thomas Harman*,
a *Dutchman*, did, at parting, advertise me (for I left him on
board to look to my goods) that, in the bundle I ordered to be
carry'd with me on shore, I should find about thirty bisket cakes
which he, by unparallel'd frugality, had saved out of his own belly
in the great dearth and scarcity we lived in.   The thoughts of
these biskets entring upon me at the time I was press'd to accept
this charge, I thought myself obliged, in christian equity, to let
every one partake of what I had ; and so dividing the bread into
nineteen parts (which was our number) perhaps I added the
fraction to my own share.

Jan. 5.   It was, to be best of my remembrance, upon the fifth
day of *January* that we entred into this method of life,
or rather into an orderly way unto our graves, since nothing but
the image of death was represented to us : but that we might
use our outmost endeavours to extract all the good we could out
of those evil symptoms that did every way seem to confound us,
I made a muster of the most able bodies for arms and labour ;
and, in the first place, I put a fowling-piece into every man's
hand that could tell how to use it.   Amongst the rest, a young
gentleman, Mr. *Francis Cary* by name, was very helpful to me
in the fatigue and active part of this undertaking. He was strong
and healthy, and was very ready for any employment I could put
upon him. He came recommended to me by Sir *Edward Thur-
lan*, his genius leading him rather to a planter's life abroad, than
to any course his friends could propose to him in *England* ; and
this rough entrance was like to let him know the worst at first.

All our woodmen and fowlers had powder and shot given
them, and some geese were killed for supper. Evening came on
apace, and our resolution being taken to stay one night more in
these quarters, I sent my cousin *Cary* to head the creek, and
make what discovery he could as he passed along the shore,
                                                    whether

whether of *Indians* or any other living creatures that were likely to relieve our wants, or end our days. To prepare like men for the latter, we resolved to die fighting, if that should be the case; or if, on the contrary, the *Indians* should accost us in a mein of amity, then to meet them with all imaginable courtesy, and please them with such trivial presents as they love to deal in, and so engage them into a friendship with us.

My cousin *Cary* was not absent much above an hour, when we saw him return in a contrary point to that he sallied out upon. His face was clouded with ill news he had to tell us, namely, that we were now residing on an island without any inhabitant, and that he had seen its whole extent, surrounded (as he believed) with water deeper than his head; that he had not seen any native, or any thing in human shape, in all his round, nor any other creature besides the fowls of the air, which he would, but could not, bring unto us.

This dismal success of so unexpected a nature, did startle us more than any single misfortune that had befallen us, and was like to plunge us into utter despair. We beheld each other as miserable wretches sentenc'd to a lingering death, no man knowing what to propose for prolonging life any longer than he was able to fast. My cousin *Cary* was gone from us without notice, and we had reason, (for what followed) to believe he was under the conduct of an angel; for we soon saw him return with a chearful look, his hands carrying something we could not distinguish by any name at a distance; but by nearer approach we were able to descry they were a parcel of oysters, which, in crossing the island, as he stept over a small current of water, he trode upon to his hurt; but laying hands on what he felt with his feet, and pulling it with all his force, he found himself possessed of this booty of oysters, which grew in clusters, and were contiguous to a large bank of the same species, that was our staple subsistance whilst we remained there.

Whilst this very cold season continued, great flights of fowl frequented the island, geese, ducks, curlieus, and some of every sort we killed and roasted on sticks, eating all but the feathers. It was the only perquisite belonging to my place of preference to the rest, that the right of carving was annexed to it, wherein, if I was partial to my own interest, it was in cutting the wing as large and full of meat as possible; whereas the rest was measured out as it were with scale and compass.

But as the wind veered to the south-ward, we had greater warmth and fewer fowl, for they would then be gone to colder climates. In their absence we were confined to the oyster bank, and a sort of weed some four inches long, as thick as houseleek,

and

and the only green (except pines) that the island afforded. It was very insipid on the palate; but being boiled with a little pepper (of which one had brought a pound on shore) and helped with five or six oysters, it became a regale for every one in turn.

In quartering our family we did observe the decency of distinguishing sexes: we made a small hut for the poor weak women to be by themselves; our cabbin for men was of the same fashion, but much more spacious, as our numbers were. One morning, in walking on the shore by the sea side, with a long gun in my hand loaden with small shot, I fired at a great flight of small birds called *Oxeyes*, and made great slaughter among them, which gave refreshment to all our company.

But this harvest had a short end ; and as the weather by its warmth, chased the fowl to the north, our hunger grew sharper upon us. And in fine, all the strength that remained unto us was employed in a heartless struggling to spin out life a little longer ; for we still deemed our selves doom'd to die by famine, from whose sharpest and most immediate darts tho' we seemed to be rescued for a small time, by meeting these contingent helps on shore, yet still we apprehended (and that on too great probability) they only served to reprieve us for a little longer day of execution, with all the dreadful circumstances of a lingering death.

For the south-west winds that had carry'd away the fowl, brought store of rain ; which meeting with a spring-tide, our chief magazine, the oyster bank, was overflown ; and as they became more accessible, our bodies also decayed so sensibly, that we could hardly pull them out of their muddy beds they grew on. And from this time forward we rarely saw the fowl ; they now grew shy and kept aloof when they saw as contriving against their lives.

Add to this, our guns most of them unfix'd and out of order, and our powder much decayed, insomuch that nothing did now remain to prolong life, but what is counted rather sauce to whet, than substance to satisfy the appetite; I mean the oysters, which were not easily gotten by our crazy bodies after the quantity was spent that lay most commodious to be reach'd, and which had fed us for the first six days we had been on the island. And thus we wish'd every day to be the last of our lives (if God had so pleased) so hopeless and desperate was our condition, all expectation of human succour being vanished and gone.

They feed on their dead companions. Of the three weak women before-mentioned, one had the envied happiness to die about this time; and it was my advice to the survivors, who were following her apace, to endeavour their own preservation by converting her dead carcase into food, as they did to good effect.

effect. The same counsel was embrac'd by those of our sex : the living fed upon the dead ; four of our company having the happiness to end their miserable lives on *Sunday* night the ————— day of *January*. Their chief distemper, 'tis true, was hunger; but it pleased God to hasten their *exit* by an immoderate access of cold, caused by a most terrible storm of hail and snow at north-west, on the *Sunday* aforesaid, which did not only dispatch those four to their long homes, but did sorely threaten all that remained alive, to perish by the same fate.

Great was the toil that lay on my hands (as the strongest to labour) to get fuel together sufficient for our preservation. In the first place I divested myself of my great gown, which I spread at large, and extended against the wind in nature of a screen, having first shifted our quarters to the most calm commodious place that could be found to keep us, as much as possible, from the inclemency of that prodigious storm.

Under the shelter of this traverse I took as many of my comrades as could be comprehended in so small a space ; whereas those who could not partake of that accommodation, and were enabled to make provision for themselves, were forced to suffer for it. And it was remarkable, that notwithstanding all the provision that could possibly be made against the sharpness of this cold, either by a well-burning fire consisting of two or three loads of wood, or shelter of this great gown to the windward, we could not be warm. That side of our wearing cloaths was singed and burnt which lay towards the flames, whilst the other side that was from the fire, became frozen and congeal'd. Those who lay to the leeward of the flame, could not stay long to enjoy the warmth so necessary to life, but were forced to quit and be gone to avoid suffocation by the smoke and flame.

When the day appeared, and the sun got up to dissipate the clouds, with downcast looks and dejected, the survivors of us entred into a final deliberation of what remained to be done on our parts (besides our prayers to Almighty God) to spin out a little longer time of life, and wait a further providence from heaven for our better relief. There were still some hands that retained vigour, tho' not in proportion to those difficulties we were to encounter, which humanly did seem insuperable. The unhappy circumstance of our being coop'd up in an island, was that which took from us all probable hopes of escaping this terrible death that did threaten us every hour. Major *Morrison*, on whose counsel I had reason to rely most, was extremely decayed in his strength, his legs not being able to support him. It was a wonderful mercy that mine remained in competent strength, for our common good, which I resolved, by God's help, to employ for that end to the last gasp.   In

In this last resolution we had to make, I could not think on any thing worthy my proposal, but by an attempt to cross the creek, and swim to the main (which was not above an hundred yards over) and being there to coast along the woods to the southwest (which was the bearing of *Virginia*) until I should meet *Indians,* who would either relieve or destroy us. I fancied the former would be our lot when they should see our conditions, and that no hurt was intended to them ; or if they should prove inhuman, and of a bloody nature, and would not give us quarter, why even in that case it would be worth this labour of mine to procure a sudden period to all our miseries.

I open'd my thoughts to this purpose to the company, who were sadly surprized at the motion ; but being fully convinc'd in their judgment, that this was the only course that could be depended on (humanly speaking) for our relief, they all agreed it must be done.

To fortify me for this expedition, it was necessary that some provision should be made for a daily support to me in this my peregrination. Our choice was small ; our only friend the oyster bank was all we had to rely on ; which being well stew'd in their own liquor, and put up into bottles, I made no doubt, by God's blessing, but that two of them well filled, would suffice to prolong my life in moderate strength, until I had obtain'd my end. To accomplish this design, my cousin *Cary* laboured hard for oysters, hoping to make one in the adventure.

About the ninth day of our being in the island, I fell to my oyster-cookery, and made a good progress that very day ;
Jan. 14.
when in the heat of my labour my cousin *Cary* brought me word, That he had just in that instant seen *Indians* walking on the main. I suspended my cookery out of hand, and hastened with all possible speed to be an eye-witness of that happy intelligence ; but with all the haste I could make I could see no such thing, but judg'd it a chimera that proceeded from some operation in my cousin's fancy, who was more than ordinary of a sanguine nature, which made him see (as it were by inchantment) things that were not, having many times been deluded (as I judg'd) by the same deception.

Defeated in this manner of my hopes to see *Indians* without the pains of seeking them, I returned to my work, and continued at it till one bottle was full, and myself tired : wherefore, that I might be a little recreated, I took a gun in my hand ; and hearing the noise of geese on our shore, I approach'd them privately, and had the good hap to be the death of one. This goose, now in my possession without witnesses, I resolved to eat alone (deducting the head, bones, guts, &c. which were the cook's fees)
hoping

hoping thereby to be much the better enabled to swim the creek, and perform the work I had upon my hand. I hung my goose upon the twist of a tree in a shrubby part of the wood, whilst I went to call aside our cook with his broach, and a coal of fire to begin the roast. But when we came to the place of execution, my goose was gone all but the head, the body stollen by wolves, which the *Indians* told us after, do abound greatly in that island.

The loss of this goose, which my empty stomach look'd for with no small hopes of satisfaction, did vex me heartily. I wish'd I could have taken the thief of my goose to have serv'd him in the same kind, and to have taken my revenge in the law of retaliation. But that which troubled me more, was an apprehension that came into my mind, that this loss had been the effect of divine justice on me, for designing to deal unequally with the rest of my fellow-sufferers; which I thought, at first blush, look'd like a breach of trust: but then again when I consider'd the equity of the thing, that I did it merely to enable myself to attain their preservation, and which otherwise I could not have done, I found I could absolve myself from any guilt of that kind. Whatever I suffer'd in this disappointment, the cook lost not all his fees; the head and neck remained for him on the tree.

Being thus over-reach'd by the wolf, it was time to return to my cookery, in order to my sally out of the island; for I had little confidence in the notice frequently brought me of more and more *Indians* seen on the other side, since my own eyes could never bear witness of their being there.

The next morning, being the ninth or tenth of our being there, I fell to work afresh, hoping to be ready to begin my journey that day; and being very busy, intelligence was brought, that a canoe was seen to lie on the broken ground to the south of our island, which was not discovered till now, since our being there: but this I thought might be a mistake cast in the same mould of many others that had deceived those discoverers, who fancy'd all things real according to their own wishes. But when it was told me, That *Indians* had been at the poor *Relieved by Indians.* womens cabbin in the night, and had given them shell-fish to eat, that was a demonstration of reality beyond all suspicion. I went immediately to be inform'd from themselves, and they both avowed it for truth, shewing the shells (the like whereof I ne'er had seen) and this I took for proof of what they said.

The further account these women gave of the *Indians*, was, that they pointed to the south-east with their hands, which they know not how to interpret, but did imagine by their several gestures, they would be with them again to morrow. Their pointing to the south-east was like to be the time they would come,

meaning

meaning nine o'clock to be their hour, where the sun will be at that time. Had the women understood their language, they could not have learned the time of the day by any other computation than pointing at the sun. It is all the clock they have for the day, as the coming and going of the *Cabuncks* (the geese) is their almanack or prognostick for the winter and summer seasons.

This news gave us all new life, almost working miracles amongst us, by making those who desponded, and totally yielded themselves up to the weight of despair, and lay down with an intent never more to rise again, to take up their beds and walk. This friendly charitable visit of the *Indians* did also put a stop to my preparations to seek them, who had so humanely prevented me, by their seeking ways to preserve and save our lives.

Instead of those preparations for my march which had cost me so much pains, I passed my time now in contriving the fittest posture our present condition would allow us to put on when these angels of light should appear again with the glad tidings of our relief; and the result was, that every able man should have his gun lying by his side, laden with shot, and as fit for use as possible, but not to be handled unless the *Indians* came to us like enemies (which was very unlikely, the premises considered) and then to sell our lives at as dear a rate as we could; but if they came in an amicable posture, then would we meet them unarm'd, chearfully, which the *Indians* like, and hate to see a melancholy face.

In these joyful hopes of unexpected deliverance by these *Indians*, did we pass the interval of their absence. Every eye look'd sharply out when the sun was at south-east, to peep thro' the avenues of the wood to discover the approaches of our new friends. When the sun came to the south we thought our selves forgotten by them, and began to doubt the worst, as losing gamesters, at play for their last estate, suspect some stabcast to defeat the hopes of the fairest game. We feared some miscarriage, either from their inconstancy by change of their mind, or that some unlook'd-for misfortune that our evil fates reserved for us, had interposed for our ruin.

Scouts were sent out to the right and left hands, without discovery of any body all the forenoon: and then, considering our case admitted no delay, I began to resume my former resolution of swiming to them that would not come to us. But how wholesome soever this counsel might seem in itself, it was most difficult to be put in practice, in regard of the cold time.

The northerly wind that in these climates does blow very cold in the heat of summer, does much more distemper the air in the
winter

winter season (as our poor comrades felt that *Sunday* night to their cost) and did send so cold a gale upon the surface of the water in the creek I was to pass, that, in the general opinion of all the concern'd, it was not a thing to be attempted; and that if I did, I must surely perish in the act. I was easily perswaded to forbear an action so dangerous, and the rather, because I verily believed the *Indians* would bring us off, if our patience would hold out.

About the hours of two or three o'clock it pleased God to change the face of our condition for the best; for whilst I was busy at the fire in preparations to wait on them, the *Indians*, who had placed themselves behind a very great tree, discovered their faces with most chearful smiles, without any kind of arms, or appearance of evil design; the whole number of them (perhaps twenty or thirty in all) consisting of men, women and children; all that could speak accosting us with joyful countenances, shaking hands with every one they met. The words *Ny Top*, often repeated by them, made us believe they bore a friendly signification, as they were soon interpreted to signify my friend.

After many salutations and *Ny Tops* interchang'd, the night approaching, we fell to parley with each other; but perform'd it in signs more confounded and unintelligible than any other conversation I ever met withal; as hard to be interpreted as if they had express'd their thoughts in the *Hebrew* or *Chaldean* tongues.

They did me the honour to make all applications to me, as being of largest dimensions, and equip'd in a camlet coat glittering with galoon lace of gold and silver, it being generally true, that where knowledge informs not, the habit qualifies.

The ears of *Indian* corn they gave us for present sustenance, needed no other interpreter to let them know how much more acceptable it was to us than the sight of dead and living corpses, which raised great compassion in them, especially in the women, who are observed to be of a soft tender nature.

One of them made me a present of the leg of a swan, which I eat as privately as it was given me, and thought it so much the more excellent, by how much it was larger than the greatest limb of any fowl I ever saw.

The *Indians* stayed with us about two hours, and parted not without a new appointment to see us again the next day: and the hour we were to expect them by their pointing to the sun, was to be at two o'clock in the afternoon. I made the chief of them presents of ribbon and other slight trade, which they lov'd, designing, by mutual endearment, to let them see, it would gratify their interest as well as their charity, to treat us well. *Ha-na*
Haw

Haw was their parting word, which is farewel, pointing again at the place where the sun would be at our next meeting. We took leave in their own words *Ha-na Haw.*

The going away of the *Indians*, and leaving us behind, was a separation hard to be born by our hungry company, who nevertheless had received a competent quantity of corn and bread to keep us till they returned to do better things for our relief; we did not fail to give glory to God for our approaching deliverance, and the joy we conceiv'd in our minds in the sense of so great a mercy, kept us awake all the night, and was a cordial to the sick and weak to recover their health and strength.

The delay of the *Indians* coming next day, beyond their set time, we thought an age of tedious years: At two o'clock we had no news of them, but by attending their own time with a little patience, we might see a considerable number of them, men, women, and children, all about our huts, with reeruits of bread and corn to stop every mouth. Many of them desir'd beads and little truck they use to deal in, as exchange for what they gave us; and we as freely gave them what we had brought on shore; but to such of us as gave them nothing, the *Indians* failed not however to give them bread for nothing.

One old man of their company, who seem'd, by the preference they gave him, to be the most considerable of the party, apply'd himself to me by gestures and signs, to learn something, (if possible) of our country, and occasion of the sad posture he saw us in, to the end that he might inform his master, the king of *Kickotamk*, (on whose territories we stood) and dispose him to succour us, as we had need.

I made return to him in many vain words, and in as many insignificant signs as himself had made to me, and neither of us one jot the wiser. The several nonplus's we both were at in striving to be better understood, afforded so little of edification to either party, that our time was almost spent in vain. It came at last into my head, that I had long since read Mr. *Smith's* travels thro' those parts of *America*, and that the word *Werowance* (a word frequently pronounced by the old man) was in *English* the king. That word, spoken by me, with strong emphasis, together with the motions of my body, speaking my desire of going to him, was very pleasing to the old man, who thereupon embrac'd me with more than common kindness, and by all demonstrations of satisfaction, did shew that he understood my meaning. This one word was all the *Indian* I could speak, which (like a little armour well plac'd) contributed to the saving of our lives.

In order to what was next to be done, he took me by the
hand

hand and led me to the sea side, where I embark'd with himself and one more *Indian* in a canoe, that had brought him there, which the third man rowed over to that broken ground, where, not long before, we made discovery of a canoe newly laid there, and (as they told us) was lodg'd there on purpose to be ready for our transport, at such time as they thought fit to fetch us off; and the reason of their taking me with them was to help launch this weighty embarkation, which was very heavy for its proportion, as being made of the body of an oak or pine, some twenty-two foot in length, hollowed like a pig-trough, which is the true description of a canoe. The manner of its being put into motion is very particular; the labourers with long booms place their feet on the starboard and larboard sides of the boat, and with this fickle footing do they heave it forward.

I cannot omit a passage of one major *Stephens*, who had been an officer in the late civil war, under Sir *William Waller*, and was now one of our fellow-sufferers. He could not be persuaded by any means to give his vote for prosecuting the way we were in for our relief, but differ'd as much in judgment with us, in this our design of going to the king of this country, as he had done in *England*, by engaging against his natural sovereign; he cry'd out these rogues would draw us into their power, and take away our lives, advising, rather than to put our trust in this king, we should put ourselves into one of these canoes, and taking advantage of the calm time, we should try to get the north cape.

His fears and objections were so unreasonable, that they were not worth an answer, and his project of going thus by sea was so ridiculous, that it did exceed all chimera's of knight-errantry, and his apprehending the king would ensnare us, we all esteemed vain, as nothing could be more childish: We had been in the king's power (though we knew it not) ever since we set foot on that ground, so that had his mind been that way bent, he need use no other stratagem to end our lives, than to have forborn the sending us relief; every one dissented to the main project, and I did unfeignedly profess, for my own part, that I would much rather expose my life to the honour of a king (tho' never so mean) than to the billows of the sea, in such a bottom; which would be to tempt God to destroy us, and punish our presumption by his justice, at the same time that he was saving us by a miracle of his mercy.

I should not have remembred this passage of major *Stephens*, had he only shew'd his antipathy in this single instance, but because he repeated the rancor of his mind, in two other very small occasions, which will follow, 'tis just that the malignity of so ill an humour should suffer some reprimand.

                                                                The

The canoes being fitted to take us in and waft us to the main, I made a fair muster of the remnant we had to carry off, and found we wanted six of the number we brought on shore (*viz.*) four men and two women: five of those six we knew were dead, but missing one of our living women, we made the *Indians* understand the same, who as readily made us know that she was in their thoughts, and should be cared for assoon as we were settled in our quarters.

In passing the creek that was to lead us to an honest fisherman's house, we entred a branch of it to the southward, that was the road-way to it. The tide was going out, and the water very shoal, which gave occasion to any one that had a knife, to treat himself with oysters all the way. At the head of that branch we were able in a short time to discover that heaven of happiness where our most courteous host did, with a chearful countenance, receive and entertain us. Several fires were kindled out of hand, our arms and powder were laid up in safety, and divers earthen pipkins were put to boil with such varieties as the season would afford. Every body had something or other to defend and save them from the cold; and my obligation to him, by a peculiar care that he had of me, exceeded all the rest. I had one intire side of the fire, with a large platform to repose on, to myself; furrs and deer skins to cover my body, and support my head, with a priority of respect and friendly usage, which, to my great trouble, I was not able to deserve at his hands, by any requital then in my power to return.

Our kind entertainment in the house of this poor fisherman, had so many circumstances of hearty compassion and tenderness in every part of it, that as it ought to be a perpetual motive to engage all of us who enjoyed the benefit of it, to a daily acknowledgement of the Almighty's goodness for conducting us in this manner by his immediate hand, out of our afflictions, so may it ever be look'd upon as a just reproach to christians, who, on all our sea-coasts, are so far from affording succour to those who, by shipwreck and misfortunes of the sea, do fall into their power, that they treat with all inhuman savage barbarity, those unhappy souls whom God hath thus afflicted, seizing on their goods as their proper perquisites, which the waves of the sea (by divine providence) would cast upon the shore for the true proprietors; and many times dispatching them out of the world to silence complaints, and to prevent all after-reckonings. And the better to intitle themselves to what they get in this way of rapine, they wickedly call such devilish acquests by the sacred name of God's good, prophaning and blaspheming at the same time that holy name, as they violate all the laws of hospitality :
and

and human society: whereas, on the contrary, our charitable host, influenced only by natural law, without the least shew of coveting any thing we had, or prospect of requital in the future, did not only treat in this manner our persons, but did also, with as much honesty, secure for us our small stores of guns, powder, &c. as if he had read and understood the duty of the gospel, or had given his only child as a hostage to secure his dealing justly with us; so that I can never sufficiently applaud the humanity of this *Indian*, nor express the high contentment that I enjoyed in this poor man's cottage, which was made of nothing but mat and reeds, and bark of trees fix'd to poles. It had a loveliness and symmetry in the air of it, so pleasing to the eye, and refreshing to the mind, that neither the splendor of the *Escurial*, nor the glorious appearance of *Versailles* were able to stand in competition with it. We had a boiled swan for supper, which gave plentiful repasts to all our upper mess.

Our bodies thus refresh'd with meat and sleep, comforted with fires, and secured from all the changes and inclemencies of that sharp piercing cold season, we thought the morning (tho' clad in sunshine) did come too fast upon us. Breakfast was liberally provided and set before us, our arms faithfully delivered up to my order for carriage; and thus in readiness to set forward, we put our selves in a posture to proceed to the place where the king resided. The woman left behind at the island, had been well look'd to, and was now brought off to the care of her comrade that came with us; neither of them in a condition to take a journey, but they were carefully attended and nourished in this poor man's house, till such time as boats came to fetch them to *Virginia*, where they did soon arrive in perfect health, and lived (one or both of them) to be well married, and to bear children, and to subsist in as plentiful a condition as they could wish.

In beginning our journey thro' the woods, we had not advanced half a mile till we heard a great noise of mens voices, directed to meet and stop our further passage. These were several *Indians* sent by the king to order us back to our quarters. Major *Stephens* (not cured of his jealous humour by the experience of what he felt the night before) took this alarm in a very bad sense, and as much different from the rest of the company as in his former fit. He was again deluded with a strong fancy, that these violent motions in the *Indians* who approach'd us, were the effect of some sudden change in their counsels to our detriment, and that nothing less than our perdition could be the consequence thereof, which he feared would immediately be put in practice by the clamorous men that made such haste to meet us, and (as he would apprehend) to kill and destroy us.

This

This passion of major *Stephens*, cast in the same mould with that other he discovered in the island, had not (as we all thought and told him) whereon to raise the least foundation of terror to affright a child; for besides the earnest we had received of their good intentions the night before, these men who came so fast upon us, were all unarm'd; nor was it likely, that king would now possibly imbrew his hands in our blood, and provoke he knew not how powerful a nation to destroy him, after such kind caresses, and voluntary expressions of a temper very contrary to such cruelty. In fine, we saw no cause in all the carriage of the *Indians* on which I could ground any fear, and therefore I long'd with all impatience to see this king, and to enjoy the plenty of his table, as we quickly did.

When these *Indians* came up to us, this doubt was soon clear-ed. The good-natur'd king being inform'd of our bodily weak-ness, and inability to walk thro' the woods to his house, on foot (which might be about four miles distant from our setting out) had a real tenderness for us, and sent canoes to carry us to the place nearest his house, by the favour of another branch of the same creek; and to the end we might take no vain steps (as we were going to do) and exhaust our strength to no purpose, these *Indians* made this noise to stop us.

We entred the canoes that were mann'd, and lay ready to receive us. We had a pleasant passage in the shallow water, eat oysters all the way: for altho' the breakfast we had newly made, might well excuse a longer abstinence than we were like to be put to, our arrear to our stomachs was so great, that all we swallowed was soon concocted, and our appetite still fresh and craving more.

Having pass'd this new course for some three *English* miles in another branch of the creek, our landing place was contriv'd
Queen of to be near the house of the queen then in waiting.
the country She was a very plain lady to see to, not young, nor
describ'd. yet ill-favour'd. Her complexion was of a sad white: but the measures of beauty in those parts where they are ex-posed to the scorching sun from their infancy, are not taken from red and white, but from colours that will better lie upon their tawny skins, as hereafter will be seen.

The beauty of this queen's mind (which is more permanent than that of colour) was conspicuous in her charity and gene-rosity to us poor starved weather-beaten creatures, who were the object of it. A mat was spread without the house, upon the ground, furnish'd with *Pone*, *Homini*, oysters, and other things. The queen made us sit down and eat, with gestures that shewed more of courtesy than majesty, but did speak as hearty welcome

as

as could in silence be expected : and these were the graces that, in our opinion, transcended all other beauties in the world, and did abundantly supply all defects of outward appearance in the person and garb of the queen. The southerly wind made the season tolerable; but that lasted but little, the north-west gale coming violently on us again.

When this collation of the queen was at an end, we took leave of her majesty with all the shews of gratitude that silence knew how to utter. We were now within half an hour's walk of the king's mansion, which we soon discovered *The king's* by the smoak, and saw it was made of the same stuff *palace.* with the other houses from which we had newly parted, namely, of mat and reed. Locust posts sunk in the ground at corners and partitions, was the strength of the whole fabrick. The roof was tied fast to the body with a sort of strong rushes that grow there, which supply'd the place of nails and pins, mortises and tenants.

The breadth of this palace was about eighteen or twenty foot, the length about twenty yards. The only furniture was several platforms for lodging, each about two yards long and more, plac'd on both sides of the house, distant from each other about five foot ; the space in the middle was the chimney, which had a hole in the roof over it, to receive as much of the smoak as would naturally repair to it ; the rest we shared amongst us, which was the greatest part ; and the sitters divided to each side, as our soldiers do in their *corps de guarde.*

Fourteen great fires, thus situated, were burning all at once. The king's apartment had a distinction from the rest ; it was twice as long, and the bank he sat on was adorn'd with deer skins finely dress'd, and the best furrs of otter and beaver that the country did produce.

The fire assign'd to us was suitable to our number, to which we were conducted, without intermixture of any *Indian* but such as came to do us offices of friendship. There we were permitted to take our rest until the king pleased to enter into communication with us. Previous to which he sent his daughter, a well-favour'd young girl of about ten or *King's* twelve years old, with a great wooden bowl full of *daughter.* homini (which is the corn of that country, beat and boiled to mash). She did in a most obliging manner give me the first taste of it, which I would have handed to my next neighbour after I had eaten, but the young princess interposed her hand, and taking the bowl out of mine, delivered it to the same party I aimed to give it, and so to all the rest in order. Instead of a spoon there was a well-shap'd muscle-shell that accompanied the bowl.

The linen of that country grows ready made on the branches
of

of oak trees (or pine) the *English* call it *moss*. It is like the threads of unwhited cotton-yarn ravelled, and hangs in parcels on the lower boughs, divine providence having so ordered it for the conveniency and sustenance of the deer, which is all the food they can get in times of snow. It is very soft, sweet and cleanly, and fit for the purpose of wiping clean the hands, and doing the duty of napkins.

About three hours after this meal was ended, the king sent to have me come to him. He called me *Ny a Mutt*, which is to say, My brother, and compelled me to sit down on the same bank with himself, which I had reason to look upon as a mighty favour. After I had sat there about half an hour, and taken notice of many earnest discourses and repartees betwixt the king and his *crotemen* (so the *Indians* call the king's council) I could plainly discover, that the debate they held was concerning our adventure and coming there. To make it more clear, the king address'd himself to me with many gestures of his body, his arms display'd in various postures, to explain what he had in his mind to utter for my better understanding. By all which motions I was not edify'd in the least, nor could imagine what return to make by voice or sign, to satisfy the king's demands in any thing that related to the present straights of our condition. In fine, I admir'd their patient sufferance of my dulness to comprehend what they meant, and shew'd myself to be troubled at it; which being perceiv'd by the king, he turn'd all into mirth and jollity, and never left till he made me laugh with him, tho' I knew not why.

Audience of the king.

I took that occasion to present the king with a sword and long shoulder-belt, which he received very kindly; and to witness his gracious acceptance, he threw off his *Mach coat* (or upper covering of skin) stood upright on his bank, and, with my aid, did accoutre his naked body with his new harness, which had no other apparel to adorn it, besides a few skins about his loyns to cover his nakedness. In this dress he seem'd to be much delighted; but to me he appear'd a figure of such extraordinary shape, with sword and belt to set it off, that he needed now no other art to stir me up to laughter and mirth, than the sight of his own proper person.

Having made this short acquaintance with the king, I took leave, and returned to my comrades. In passing the spaces betwixt fire and fire, one space amongst the rest was blinded with a traverse of mat; and by the noise I heard from thence, like the beating of hemp, I took it to be some kind of elaboratory. To satisfy a curiosity I had to be more particularly inform'd, I edg'd close to the mat; and, by standing on tiptoe for a full dis-

covery,

covery, I saw a sight that gave me no small trouble. The same specifical queen (whose courtesy for our kind usage the other day, can never be enough applauded) was now employed in the hard servile labour of beating corn for the king's dinner, which raised the noise that made me thus inquisitive. I wish'd myself in her place for her ease: but the queens of that country do esteem it a privilege to serve their husbands in all kind of cookery, which they would be as loth to lose, as any christian queen would be to take it from them.

Several *Indians* of the first rank followed me to our quarters, and used their best endeavours to sift something from us that might give them light into knowing what we were. They sought many ways to make their thoughts intelligible to us, but still we parted without knowing what to fix upon, or how to steer our course in advance of our way to *Virginia*.

In this doubtful condition we thought it reasonable to fall upon a speedy resolution what was next to be done on our parts, in order to the accomplishment of our voyage by land, which we hop'd (by the divine aid) we might be able to effect after a little more refreshment by the plenty of victuals allowed us by the king, who was no less indulgent and careful to feed and caress us, than if we had been his children.

Towards morning we were treated with a new regale brought to us by the same fair hand again. It was a sort of spoon-meat, in colour and taste not unlike to almond-milk temper'd and mix'd with boiled rice. The ground still was *Indian* corn boiled to a pap, which they call *Homini*, but the ingredient which performed the milky part, was nothing but dry pokickery nuts, beaten shells and all to powder, and they are like our walnuts, but thicker shell'd, and the kernel sweeter; but being beaten in a mortar, and put into a tray, hollow'd in the middle to make place for fair water, no sooner is the water poured into the powder, but it rises again white and creamish; and after a little ferment it does partake so much of the delicate taste of the kernel of that nut, that it becomes a rarity to a miracle.

Major *Morrison*, who had been almost at death's door, found himself abundantly refreshed and comforted with this delicacy; he wished the bowl had been a fathom deep, and would say, when his stomach called on him for fresh supplies, that if this princess royal would give him his fill of that food, he should soon recover his strength.

Our bodies growing vigorous with this plenty, we took new courage, and resolv'd (as many as were able) to attempt the finding out of *Virginia*. We guess'd the distance could not be great, and that it bore from us S. by W. to S. W. Our igno-

rance

rance of the latitude we were'in, was some discouragement to us; but we were confident, from what the seamen discoursed, we were to the southward of the *Menados,* then a *Dutch* plantation, now *New York :* Fair weather and full stomachs made us willing to be gone. To that end we laid out for a quantity of pone; and for our surer conduct we resolved to procure an *Indian* to be our pilot through the wilderness, for we were to expect many remora's in our way, by swamps and creeks, with which all those sea-coasts do abound.

The king remarking our more than ordinary care to procure more bread than amounted to our usual expence, gathered thence our design to leave him, and shift for ourselves. To prevent the rashness and folly of such attempt, he made use of all his silent rhetorick to put us out of conceit of such design, and made us understand the peril and difficulty of it by many obstacles we must meet with. He shew'd us the danger we should expose ourselves unto, by rain and cold, swamps and darkness, unless we were conducted by other skill than we could pretend to: He pointed to his fires and shocks of corn, of which he had enough, and made it legible to us in his countenance, that we were welcome to it. All the signs the king made upon this occasion, we were content to understand in the best sense; and taking for granted our sojourning there was renewed to another day, we retired to our quarters.

About midnight following, the king sent to invite me to his fire. He placed me near him as before, and in the first place shewing me quarters of a lean doe, new brought in. He gave me a knife to cut what part of it I pleased, and then pointing to the fire, I inferr'd, I was left to my own discretion for the dressing of it. I could not readily tell how to shew my skill in the cookery of it, with no better ingredients then appear'd in sight; and so did no more but cut a collop and cast it on the coals. His majesty laugh'd at my ignorance, and to instruct me better, he broach'd the collop on a long scewer, thrust the sharp end into the ground (for there was no hearth but what nature made) and turning sometimes one side, sometimes the other, to the fire, it became fit in short time to be served up, had there been a dining-room of state such as that excellent king deserved.

I made tender of it first to the king, and then to his nobles, but all refused, and left all to me, who gave God and the king thanks for that great meal. The rest of the doe was cut in pieces, stewed in a pipkin, and then put into my hands to dispose of amongst my company.

Assoon as I had dispatch'd this midnight venison feast, and sent the rest to my comrades, the king was greatly desirous to

make

make me comprehend, by our common dialect of signs and motions, the ingenious stratagem by which they use to take their deer in the winter season, especially when the surface of the earth is cover'd with snow. He shewed me in the first place a small leather thong, in which (said he) any kind of deer should be invited to hamper himself and lie fast ty'd on his back, until the engineer (or some body else for him) should take quiet possession of him. I could not conceive the particular structure of this machine, so as to direct the making of it elsewhere; but thus much in the general I did understand; they would fasten a pine green branch at the end of a pole (such as hops grow upon) which should lie athwart an oak, like the pole of a turner's lath, and the green hanging dingle-dangle at the pole end, fastened by a string; it should be set at a heighth for a deer to reach, but not without mounting and resting on his hinder legs, that so in pulling the branch, as at a trigger, the machine discharging, his heels are struck up to fly in the air, and there he remains on his back so straitly hamper'd, that the least child may approach to touch and take him.

Before I parted, the king attack'd me again, with reiterated attempts to be understood, and I thought by these three or four days conversation, I had the air of his expression much more clear and intelligible than at first. His chief drift for the first essay seemed to be a desire to know which way we were bound, whether north or south; to which I pointed to the south. This gave him much satisfaction, and there-upon steps in the little grotman before described, who by the motion of his hand seemed to crave my regard to what he was going about. He took up a stick, with which he made divers circles by the fire-side, and then holding up his finger to procure my attention, he gave to every hole a name; and it was not hard to conceive that the several holes were to supply the place of a sea-chart, showing the situation of all the most noted *Indian* territories that lay to the southward of *Kickotank.*

That circle that was most southerly, he called *Achomack,* which, tho' he pronounc'd with a different accent from us, I laid hold on that word with all demonstrations of satisfaction I could express, giving them to understand, that was the place to which I had a desire to be conducted.

The poor king was in a strange transport of joy to see me receive satisfaction, and did forthwith cause a lusty young man to be called to him, to whom, by the earnestness of his motions, he seemed to give ample instructions to do something for our service, but what it was we were not yet able to resolve. In two or three days time, seeing no effect of what he had so seriously

said,

said, we began again to despond, and did therefore resume our former thoughts of putting ourselves in posture to be gone ; but the king seeing us thus ready at every turn to leave him, shewed in his looks a more than ordinary resentment; still describing (as he could) the care he had taken for us, and impossibility of accomplishing our ends by ourselves, and that we should surely faint in the way and die without help, if we would not be ruled by him.

He shewed me again his stores of corn, and made such reiterated signs, by the chearfulness of his countenance, that we should not want, whilst he had such a plenty, as made us lay aside all thoughts of stirring till he said the word. But as oft as he look'd or pointed to the coast of *Achomack*, he would shake his head, with abundance of grimaces, in dislike of our design to go that way till he saw it good we should do so. I was abundantly convinced of our folly in the resolution we were ready to take of going away without better information of the distance from *Achomack*, and way that led to it; and having so frank a welcome where we were, we resolved to stay till the king should approve of our departure, which he was not able to determine till the messenger came back, that he had sent to *Achomack*, who, it now seemed more plainly, was dispatch'd upon my owning that place to be our home, tho' we knew it not from any cause we could rely upon, before we saw the effect.

While we liv'd in this suspense, the king had a great mind to see our fire-arms, and to be acquainted with the use and nature of them. That which best did please his eye I presented to him, and shew'd him how to load and discharge it. He was very shy at first essay, fearing it might hurt him, but I made him stand upon his lodging place, and putting him in a posture to give fire, he presented the mouth of his gun to the chimney hole, and so let fly. The combustible nature of the king's palace not well consider'd, the fabrick was endangered by the king's own hand, for the flashing of the powder having taken hold of the roof at the smoke-hole, all was in a flame; but a nimble lad or two ran up to quench it, and did soon extinguish it without considerable damage to the building, which was of mat and boughs of oak as aforesaid.

The king's eldest son, of about eighteen years of age, was hugely enamour'd with our guns, and look'd so wistfully on me, when he saw what wonders they would do, that I could not forbear presenting him with a birding-piece. Some of our company, who knew that by the laws of *Virginia*, it was criminal to furnish the *Indians* with fire-arms, gave me caution in this case, but I resolved, for once, to borrow a point of that law ; for
tho'

tho' it might be of excellent use in the general, yet as our condition was, I esteemed it a much greater crime to deny those *Indians* any thing that was in our power, than the penalty of that law could amount to.

Father and son abundantly gratify'd in this manner, the king thought himself largely requited for the cost we put him to in our entertainment. I taught his son to shoot at fowls, to charge his gun and clean it, insomuch that in a few minutes, he went among the flocks of geese, and firing at random he did execution on one of them to his great joy, and returned to his father with the game in his hand, with such celerity, as if he had borrowed wings of the wind.

About three o'clock this afternoon, the king was Jan. 24. pleased in great condescension to honour me with a visit, a favour which I may (without vanity) assume to myself, and my better habit, from the many particular applications that he made to me, exclusive of the rest of the company. He thought I was too melancholy, (for the *Indians*, as has been observ'd, are great enemies to that temper) and shew'd me by his own chearful looks, what humour he would have put me on; he would not have me in the least apprehensive of wanting any thing his country afforded, as his mien and gesture witnessed; and for the higher proof of his reality, he found me out a divertisement, that was very extraordinary. He came at this time attended by his young daughter, who had done us the good offices before mention'd, and having first by kind words and pleasant gestures given us renewed assurance of hearty welcome, he singled me out, and pointed with his hand to a way he would have me take, but whither, or to what end, I was at liberty to guess; upon that he produced his little daughter for my conductrix to the place to which I should go, and shewed his desire that I should follow her where-ever she should lead me.

Major *Stephens*, not yet enough convinc'd of the *Indians* fidelity, would have discouraged me from leaving the company in that manner, unreasonably fancying that this was a contrivance in the king to take away my life in a private way; but this I thought did so much out-strip all his other senseless jealousies, that after I had acknowledg'd the obligation I had to his care of my person, his needless caution had no other effect on me than to turn it into ridicule. These inordinate fears of this major in three foregoing instances, might (I confess) have been very well omitted, as not worthy the mention, and so they should have been, had his humour and constitution in prosperous times been any way suitable to this wary temper; but because his habits on shore were scandalously vicious his mouth always

belching

belching oaths, and his tongue proving him the vainest hector I
had seen, I thought it was pity to lose such a strong confirmation of that known truth, (*viz.*) That true innate courage does
seldom reside in the heart of a quarrelling and talking hector.

The weather (as I have said) was excessive cold, with frost,
and the winds blowing very fresh upon my face, it almost stopt
my breath.   The late condition I had been in, under a roof, with
great fires, and much smoke, did conduce to make me the more
sensible of the cold air : but in less than half an hour that pain
was over ; we were now in sight of the house whereto we were
bound, and the lady of the place was ready to receive us, (who
proved to be the mother of my conductrix) and to shew me my
apartment in the middle of her house, which had the same accommodation to sit and rest upon, as before has been described
in other instances.

The lusty rousing fire, prepared to warm me, would have
been noble entertainment of itself, but attended (as it was quickly) with good food for the belly, made it to be that compleat
good chear, I only aimed at ; a wild turkey boiled, with oysters,
was preparing for my supper, which, when it was ready, was
served up in the same pot that boiled it. It was a very savoury
mess, stew'd with muscles, and I believe would have passed for
a delicacy at any great table in *England,* by palates more competent to make a judgment than mine, which was now more gratify'd with the quantity than the quality of what was before me.

This queen was also of the same mould of her majesty whom
we first met at our landing place, somewhat antient (in proportion to the king's age) but so gentle and compassionate, as did
very bountifully requite all defects of nature ; she passed some
hours at my fire, and was very desirous to know the occasion that
brought us there (as her motion and the emphasis of her words did
shew) but I had small hopes to satisfy her curiosity therein, after
so many vain attempts to inform the king in that matter. In fine,
I grew sleepy, and about nine o'clock every one retired to their
quarters, separated from each other by traverses of mat, which
(besides their proper vertue) kept the ladies from any immodest
attempts, as secure as if they had been bars of iron.

Assoon as the day peeped in, I went out and felt the same
cold as yesterday, with the same wind, N. W. I was not forward
to quit a warm quarter, and a frank entertainment, but my young
governess, who had her father's orders for direction, knew better
than myself what I was to do : she put herself in a posture to
lead the way back from whence we came, after a very good repast of stew'd muscles, together with a very hearty welcome
plainly appearing in the queen's looks.

My

My nimble pilot led me away with great swiftness, and it was necessary so to do; the weather still continuing in that violent sharpness, nothing but a violent motion could make our limbs useful. No sooner had I set my foot in the king's house to visit my comrades, but a wonderful surprize appeared to me in the change of every countenance, and as every face did plainly speak a general satisfaction, so did they with one voice explain the cause thereof, in telling me the messengers of our delivery were arriv'd, and now with the king.

I hastened to see those angels, and addressing my- *Messengers* self to one of them in *English* habit, ask'd him the *from* Vir- occasion of his coming there? He told me his busi- *ginia.* ness was to trade for furs, and no more; but assoon as I had told him my name, and the accidents of our being there, he acknowledg'd he came under the guidance of the *Kickotank Indian* (which I imagin'd, but was not sure the king had sent) in quest of me and those that were left on shore, sent by the governor's order of *Virginia* to enquire after us, but knew not where to find us till that *Indian* came to his house; he gave me a large account of the ship's arrival, and the many dangers and difficulties she encountred before she could come into *James* river, where she ran ashore, resolving there to lay her bones. His name was *Jenkin Price*, he had brought an *Indian* of his neighbourhood with him that was very well acquainted in those parts, for our conduct back to *Achomack*, which *Indian* was called *Jack*.

The king was very glad of this happy success to us, and was impatient to learn something more of our history than hitherto he had been able to extract from signs and grimaces. *Jenkin Price*, with his broken *Indian*, could make a shift to instruct *Jack* to say any thing he pleased, and *Jack* was the more capable to understand his meaning by some sprinklings of *English*, that he had learnt at our plantations. Betwixt them both they were able to satisfy the king in what he pleased to know. *Jack* told them of himself what a mighty nation we were in that country, and gave them caution not to imbezzle any goods we had brought with us, for fear of an after-reckoning. I wondered, upon this serious discourse he had with the king, to see guns and stockings, and whatever trifles we had given, offer'd to be return'd, and being told the reason of it by *Jenkin Price*, I was very much ashamed of *Jack*'s too great zeal in our service, which tho' it did proceed from a principle of honesty, and good morality in him, we were to consider that our dearest lives, and all we could enjoy in this world, was (next to divine providence) owing to the virtue and charity of this king, and therefore not

only

only what they had in possession, but whatever else he should desire that was in my power, would be too mean an acknowledgment for so high obligations. I took care to let them know that I had no hand in the menace by which *Jack* brought them to refund what they had got of us; the right understanding whereof increased our good intelligence, and became a new endearment of affection betwixt us.

By better acquaintance with these our deliverers, we learn'd that we were about fifty *English* miles from *Virginia:* That part of it where *Jenkin* did govern, was call'd *Littleton's Plantation*, and was the first *English* ground we did expect to see. He gave me great encouragement to endure the length of the way, by assuring me I should not find either stone or shrub to hurt my feet thorow my thin-soaled boots, for the whole colony had neither stone nor underwood; and having thus satisfy'd my curiosity in the knowledge of what *Jenkin Price* could communicate, we deferred no longer to resolve how and when to begin our journey to *Achomack*.

The *Indian* he brought with him (who afterwards lived and died my servant) was very expert, and a most incomparable guide in the woods we were to pass, being a native of those parts, so that he was as our sheet-anchor in this our peregrination. The king was loth to let us go till the weather was better temper'd for our bodies; but when he saw we were fully resolved, and had pitch'd upon the next morning to begin our journey, he found himself much defeated in a purpose he had taken to call together all the flower of his kingdom to entertain us with a dance, to the end that nothing might be omitted on his part for our divertisement, as well as our nourishment, which his small territory could produce. Most of our company would gladly have deferred our march a day longer, to see this masquerade, but I was wholly bent for *Achomack*, to which place I was to dance almost on my bare feet, the thoughts of which took off the edge I might otherwise have had to novelties of that kind.

When the good old king saw we were fully determined to be gone the next day, he desired as a pledge of my affection to him, that I would give him my camblet coat, which he vowed to wear whilst he lived for my sake; I shook hands to shew my willingness to please him in that or in any other thing he would command, and was the more willing to do myself the honour of compliance in this particular, because he was the first king I could call to mind that had ever shew'd any inclinations to wear my old cloaths.

To the young princess, that had so signally obliged me, I presented a piece of two-penny scarlet ribbon, and a *French* tweezer,

that

that I had in my pocket, which made her skip for joy, and to shew how little she fancy'd our way of carrying them concealed, she retired apart for some time, and taking out every individual piece of which it was furnish'd, she tied a snip of ribbon to each, and so came back with scissars, knives and bodkins hanging at her ears, neck and hair. The case itself was not excus'd, but bore a part in this new dress: and to the end we might not part without leaving deep impressions of her beauty in our minds, she had prepared on her forefingers, a lick of paint on each, the colours (to my best remembrance) green and yellow, which at one motion she discharg'd on her face, beginning upon her temples, and continuing it in an oval line downwards as far as it would hold out. I could have wish'd this young princess would have contented herself with what nature had none for her, without this addition of paint (which, I thought, made her more fulsome than handsome); but I had reason to imagine the royal family were only to use this ornament exclusive of all others, for that I saw none other of her sex so set off; and this conceit made it turn again, and appear lovely, as all things should do that are honour'd with the royal stamp.

I was not furnish'd with any thing upon the place, fit to make a return to the two queens for the great charity they used to feed and warm me; but when I came into a place where I could be supply'd, I was not wanting that way, according to my power.

Early next morning we put our selves in posture to be gone, (*viz.*) major *Stephens*, myself, and three or four more, whose names are worn out of my mind. Major *Morrison* was so far recovered as to be heart-whole, but he wanted strength to go thro' so great a labour as this was like to prove. We left him with some others to be brought in boats that the governor had order'd for their accommodation; and with them the two weak women, who were much recover'd by the good care and nourishment they receiv'd in the poor fisherman's house.

Breakfast being done, and our pilot *Jack* ready to set out, we took a solemn leave of the good king. He inclosed me in his arms with kind embraces, not without expressions of sorrow to part, beyond the common rate of new acquaintance. I made *Jack* pump up his best compliments, which at present *Their departure.* was all I was capable to return to the king's kindness; and so, after many *Hana haes*, we parted.

We were not gone far till the fatigue and tediousness of the journey discovered itself in the many creeks we were forc'd to head, and swamps to pass (like *Irish* bogs) which made the way at least double to what it would have amounted to in a strait line: and it was our wonder to see our guide *Jack* lead on the

way

way with the same confidence of going right, as if he had had a *London* road to keep him from straying. Howbeit he would many times stand still and look about for land-marks; and when on one hand and the other his marks bore right for his direction, he would shew himself greatly satisfied. As to the purpose, an old deform'd tree that lay north-west, opposite to a small hammock of pines to the southeast, would evidence his going right in all weathers. It is true, they know not the compass by the loadstone, but, which is equivalent, they never are ignorant of the north-west point, which gives them the rest ; and *North-west point distinguished by moss on the trees.* that they know by the weather-beaten moss that grows on that side of every oak, different from the rest of the tree, which is their compass. Towards evening we saw smoak (an infallible sign of an *Indian* town) which *Jack* knew to arise from *Gingo Teague*. We went boldly into the king's house (by advice of his brother of *Kickotank*) who was also a very humane prince. What the place and season produc'd was set before us with all convenient speed, which was enough to satisfy hunger, and to fit us for repose.

I was extremely tir'd with this tedious journey; and it was the more irksome to me, because I perform'd it in boots (my shoes being worn out) which at that time were commonly worn to walk in ; so that I was much more sleepy than I had been hungry. The alliance I had newly made at *Kickotank* did already stand me in some stead, for that it qualified me to a lodging apart, and gave me a first taste of all we had to eat, tho' the variety was not so great as I had seen in other courts.

And yet (as we see in all worldly honours) this grandeur of mine was not without its allay ; for as it gave me accommodation of eating and sleeping in preference to my comrades, so did it raise the hopes of the royal progeny of gifts and presents, beyond what I was either able or willing to afford them : for when I would have taken my rest, I was troubled beyond measure with their visits, and saw by their carriage what they would be at ; wherefore, to free myself of further disturbance, and to put myself out of the pain of denials, I resolv'd to comply with the necessities of nature, which press'd me hard to sleep ; and to that end I took the freedom by *Jack*, to desire they would all withdraw until I found myself refresh'd.

I pass'd the night till almost day-break in one intire sleep ; and when I did awake (not suddenly able to collect who, or where I was) I found myself strangely confounded, to see a damsel plac'd close to my side, of no meaner extract than the king's eldest daughter, who had completely finish'd the rape of
all

all the gold and silver buttons that adorn'd the king of *Kicko-tank's* coat, yet on my back. When I was broad awake, and saw this was no enchantment (like those trances knights-errant use to be in) but that I was really despoiled of what was not in my power to dispense withal, I called for *Jack*, and made him declare my resentment and much dislike of this princess's too great liberty upon so small acquaintance, which made me have a mean opinion of her. *Jack* shew'd more anger than myself to see such usage by any of his country, and much more was he scandaliz'd, that one of the blood royal should purloin.

But the king, upon notice of the fact and party concerned in it, immediately caused the buttons to be found out and returned, with no slight reprimand to his daughter, and then all was well, and so much the better by the gift of such small presents as I was able to make to the king and princess. Breakfast was given ns, and we hasten'd to proceed in our journey to *Achomack*.

The uneasiness of boots to travel in, made me by much the more weary of the former day's journey, and caus'd me to enter' very unwillingly upon this second day's work. We reckon'd our selves about twenty-five miles distant from *Jenkin's* house. It pleased God to send us dry weather, and not excessive cold. We had made provision of *Pone* to bait on by the way, and we found good water to refresh us; but all this did not hinder my being tir'd and spent almost to the last degree. *Jack* very kindly offer'd his service to carry me on his shoulders (for I was brought to a moderate weight by the strict diet I had been in) but that would have been more uneasy to me, in contemplation of his more than double pains, and so I resolved to try my utmost strength, without placing so great a weight on his shoulders.

The hopes of seeing *English* ground in *America*, and that in so short a time as they made us expect, did animate my spirits to the utmost point. *Jack* fearing the worst, was of opinion, that we should call at his aunt's town, the queen of *Pomumkin*, not far out of the way : but *Jenkin Price* opposed that motion, and did assure me our journey's end was at hand. His words and my own inclination carried the question, and I resolved, by God's help, that night to sleep at *Jenkin's* house.

But the distance proving yet greater than had been described, and my boots trashing me almost beyond all sufferance, I became desperate, and ready to sink and lie down. *Jenkin* lull'd me on still with words that spurr'd me to the quick ; and would demonstrate the little distance betwixt us and his plantation, by the sight of hogs and cattle, of which species the *Indians* were not masters. I was fully convinc'd of what he said, but would however have consented to a motion of lying without

doors

doors on the ground, within two or three flights shot of the place, to save the labour of so small a remainder.

The close of the evening, and a little more patience (thro' the infinite goodness of the Almighty) did put a happy period to our cross adventure. A large bed of sweet straw was spread ready in *Jenkin's* house for our reception, upon which I did hasten to extend and stretch my wearied limbs. And being thus brought into safe harbour by the many miracles of divine mercy, from all the storms and satigues, perils and necessities to which we had been exposed by sea and land for almost the space of four months, I cannot conclude this voyage in more proper terms, than the words that are the burthen of that psalm of providence, *O that men would therefore praise the Lord for his goodness, and for his wondrous works unto the children of men!*

Our landlord *Jenkin Price,* and conductor *Jack* took great care to provide meat for us; and there being a dairy and hens, we could not want. As for our stomachs, they were open at all hours to eat whate'er was set before us, assoon as our wearied bodies were refresh'd with sleep. It was on *Saturday* the —— day of *January,* that we ended this our wearisome pilgrimage, and entred into our king's dominions at *Achomat,* called by the *English, Northampton* county, which is the only county on that side of the bay belonging to the colony of *Virginia,* and is the best of the whole for all sorts of necessaries for human life.

Having been thus refresh'd in *Jenkin's* house this night with all our hearts could wish, on the next morning, being *Sunday,* we would have been glad to have found a church for the performance of our duty to God, and to have rendred our hearty thanks to him in the publick assembly, for his unspeakable mercies vouchsafed to us; but we were not yet arrived to the heart of the country where there were churches, and ministry perform'd as our laws direct, but were glad to continue our own chaplains, as formerly. As we advanced into the plantations that lay thicker together, we had our choice of hosts for our entertainment, without money or its value; in which we did not begin any novelty, for there are no inns in the colony; nor do they take other payment for what they furnish to coasters, but by requital of such courtesies in the same way, as occasions offer.

When I came to the house of one *Stephen Charlton,* he did not only outdo all that I had visited before him, in variety of dishes at his table, which was very well order'd in the kitchen, but would also oblige me to put on a good farmer-like suit of his own wearing cloaths, for exchange of my dirty habit; and this gave me opportunity to deliver my camlet coat to *Jack,* for the

use

use of my brother of *Kickotank*, with other things to make it worth his acceptance.

Having been thus frankly entertain'd at Mr. *Charlton*'s, our company were in condition to take care for themselves. We took leave of each other, and my next stage was to esquire *Yardly*, a gentleman of good name, whose father had sometimes been governor of *Virginia*. There I was received and treated as if I had in truth and reality been that man of honour my brother of *Kickotank* had created me. It fell out very luckily for my better welcome, that he had not long before brought over a wife from *Rotterdam*, that I had known almost from a child. Her father (*Custis* by name) kept a victualling house in that town, liv'd in good repute, and was the general host of our nation there. The esquire knowing I had the honour to be the governor's kinsman, and his wife knowing my conversation in *Holland*, I was receiv'd and caress'd more like a domestick and near relation, than a man in misery, and a stranger. I stay'd there for a passage over the bay, about ten days, welcomed and feasted not only by the esquire and his wife, but by many neighbours that were not too remote.

About the midst of *February*, I had an opportunity to cross the bay in a sloop, and with much ado landed $_{Feb. 13.}$ in *York* river, at esquire *Ludlow*'s plantation, a most pleasant situation. I was civilly receiv'd by him, who presently order'd an accommodation for me in a most obliging manner. But it fell out at that time, that captain *Wormly* (of his majesty's council) had guests in his house (not a furlong distant from Mr. *Ludlow*'s) feasting and carousing, that were lately come from *England*, and most of them my intimate acquaintance. I took a sudden leave of Mr. *Ludlow*, thank'd him for his kind intentions to me, and using the common freedom of the country, I thrust myself amongst captain *Wormly*'s guests in crossing the creek, and had a kind reception from them all, which answered (if not exceeded) my expectation.

Sir *Thomas Lundsford*, Sir *Henry Chickly*, Sir *Philip Honywood*, and colonel *Hamond* were the persons I met there, and enjoy'd that night with very good chear, but left them early the next morning, out of a passionate desire I had to see the governor, whose care for my preservation had been so full of kindness.

Captain *Wormly* mounted me for *James Town*, where the governor was pleased to receive and take me to his house at *Greenspring*, and there I pass'd my hours (as at mine own house) until *May* following; at which time he sent me for *Holland* to find out the king, and to sollicite his majesty for the treasurer's
place

place of *Virginia*, which the governor took to be void by the delinquency of *Claybourne*, who had long enjoy'd it. He furnish'd me with a sum of money to bear the charge of this sollicitation; which took effect, tho' the king was then in *Scotland*. He was not only thus kind to me (who had a more than ordinary pretence to his favour by our near affinity in blood) but, on many occasions, he shew'd great respect to all the royal party, who made that colony their refuge. His house and purse were open to all that were so qualify'd. To one of my comrades (major *Fox*) who had no friend at all to subsist on, he shew'd a generosity that was like himself; and to my other (major *Morrison*) he was more kind, for he did not only place him in the command of the fort, which was profitable to him whilst it held under the king, but did advance him after to the government of the country, wherein he got a competent estate.

And thus (by the good providence of a gracious God, who helpeth us in our low estate, and causeth his angels to pitch tents round about them that trust in him) have I given as faithful an account of this signal instance of his goodness to the miserable objects of his mercy in this voyage, as I have been able to call to a clear remembrance.

VIRGINIA:

More especially the South part thereof, Richly and truly valued : *viz.*

The fertile *Carolana,* and no lesse excellent Isle of *Roanoak*, of Latitude from 31. to 37. Degr. relating the meanes of raysing infinite profits to the Adventurers and Planters.

The second Edition, with Addition of

THE DISCOVERY OF SILKWORMS,

with their benefit.

And Implanting of Mulberry Trees.

ALSO

The Dressing of Vines, for the rich Trade of making Wines in VIRGINIA.

Together with

The making of the Saw-mill, very usefull in *Virginia*, for cutting of Timber and Clapbord to build withall, and its Conversion to many as profitable Uses.

By *E. W.* Gent.

LONDON,

Printed by *T. H.* for *John Stephenson*, at the Signe of the Sun below Ludgate. 1650.

Force's Collection of Historical Tracts.

Vol. III.—No. 11.

To the Supreme Authority of this Nation, The Parliament of ENGLAND.

Right Honorable :

His Dedication in it selfe unworthy the honour of an address to your Grandeurs, and of a foile too dead in shaddow to approach neer your most vigorous luster, reposes it selfe yet upon a confidence that in imitation of that God (of whom you are in power the proper Representatives) who vouchsafed graciously to accept a poore paire of Turtles from those whose abilities could not ascend to a more rich oblation, you will be pleased to cast a favourable aspect upon this humble offering, as proceeding from a grateful cleere and sincere intention whose desire being strongly passionate to present Your Honours with something more worthy the auspice of a beginning Yeare, is circumscribed by a narrownesse of abilities and fortunes.

And indeed my loweness had prompted me to have found out a more humble Patron for this Treatise; but since the Interest of that Nation you have so happily restored to its just and native liberty is the principall ayme intended in it, since the publick acknowledgement of the world unites in this common testimony, That God hath subscribed to all your Heroic and Christian undertakings with his own broad seal of Victory, with his owne field word, Go on and prosper : led you through the red sea of bloud into the Land of Canaan, into the Harvest and Vintage of Israel, since Pharoah and his mighty ones have been swallowed up in the rapid current in the hideous cataracts of their ambitious opposition, and have by loud and convincing testimonies (testimonies attracting the admiration of your friends, and confounding the malice of your enemies) made it a blessed object of your consideration that the preservation and fixure requires a blessing no lesse sublime, and a vertue no lesse exalted than the acquisition and tenure of conquests, made good in the eyes of Christendome by vindicating the English Honour upon the British Ocean with a Puissant Navy, a formidable subject of amazement to the Forraine Enemies of your Sion, by a strong winged prosecution of the Irish Assassinates, a spacious lettred example to teach English Mutineers what they may expect by the red sentence of justice upon Irish Rebells :

All

All indeavours holding forth the way to improve the interest of this Nation, are improperly addressed to any other then your selves, who as you have been the unexampled instruments of our unpiniond liberty, ought to be the sole Iudges of whatsoever may relate to our future felicity.

We should have suspected the sincerity of History in its delineation of the Majesty which sat upon that August, and venerable Roman Senats, after having made the Land tremble under the terrour of their Armies, the sea to labour under the burthen of their numerous Navies, after having delivered all power oppressing the universal liberty to the revenging beak of their victorious Eagles, and minted the Governments of the world by the Roman Standard; had not the Concentricity of your undertakings, had not the Homogeniousnesse of your actions and felicity, vindicated and asserted the honour of antiquity, and raysed your reputations upon so high a wing of glory, that Posterity will be lost in the same mist of jealousie and incredulity of your owne augustnesse, yet for ever want the revivall of such examples the restauration of such presidents to confirme them.

And to the end you may in all things either parallell or transcend that Romane greatnesse, of which you are the inimitable exemplary, who inriched the heart and strengthened the armes of their Dominions by dispersing Colonies in all Angles of their Empire, Your pious care hath already layed a most signall foundation by inviting incouragements to undertakers of that nature: In the pursuit whereof let me beg the liberty in this paper, under your Honours Patronage to publish the many pressing and convincing reasons which have and may induce you to prosecute a designe of such universall concernment.

1. It will disburthen this Nation of many indigent persons, who having formerly perhaps enjoyed a fulnesse of abused or forfeyted plenty, & at the present reduced to an inequality of such subsistence, are commonly prompted to their owne and other mens ruine by making the high wayes (which should be as public and inviolable a sanctuary as the most sacred places) an ambuscado to innocent Travellers, by which interruption of passages, there is commonly occasioned a decay and disincouragement of commerce, and dayly examples informs us, that Prisons at present are almost as full of criminall as indebted persons.

2. It will take off all Parish charges, in providing for destitute Minors and Orphans, whereof there at present a burthensome multitude, whereby the Parishes so freed, may with greater

greater alacrity and ability, part with contributory moneys to maintaine, recruite, and incourage your Armies and Navies.

3. Those Orphans so provided for may by Gods blessings upon their labours become happy and wealthy instruments, advantageous to the place of their nativity in particular, and their whole Nation in generall. Whereas the condition of their birth and the usual way of exposing them, makes them capable of no more gainfull calling then that of day-labourers, or which is more frequent hereditary beggers.

4. The republic in its present constitution abounding with so dangerous a number of male contents, who commonly like Shrubs under high and spreading Cedars, imagine the spacious height of others to be the cause of their owne lowness, may by this means be honourably secured, and such men removing their discontents with their persons, will have a brave and ample theater to make their merits and abilities emergent, and a large field to sow and reap the fruit of all their honest industrious and public intentions.

5. It will to admiration increase the number of Ships and Seamen, (the brazen wall of this Nation) all materialls to advance Navigation, being abundantly to be furnished out of those Countries and the more ingenious Passengers by conference and disputation with the knowing Mariner, will take great delight, satisfaction, and ambition, to attaine to the Theory of that knowledge, while the less capable being acccustomed and assigned to an usuall part in the toyle thereof, and instructed by the ordinary Seaman, will bee brought to a good readinesse therein and speedy perfection.

6. All Materialls for shipping, as Timber, Cordage, Sailes, Iron, Brasse, Ordnance of both mettals, and what ever else we are necessitated to supply our wants with out of the Easterne Countries, who make it not unusuall to take advantages of their neighbours necessity, and often times upon a pretence of difference or misintelligence betwixt us, embrace an occasion to over-rate or over-custome their commodities, or (a reall quarrell widening) sell it to other Nations from whence we are forced to supply our selves at a second or third market.

7. It will give us the liberty of storing a great part of Europe with a larger plenty of incomparable better fish, then the Holander hath found meanes to furnish it withall, and will make us in no long tract of time, if industriously prosecuted, equall, if not transcend him in that his most benificiall staple.

8. It will be to this Common wealth a standing and plentifull magazine of Wheat, Rice, Coleseed, Rapeseed, Flax,

Cotton,

Cotton, Salt, Pot-ashes, Sope-ashes, Sugars, Wines, Silke, Olives, and what ever single is the staple of other Nations, shall be found in this joyntly collected.

9. It will furnish us with rich Furrs, Buffs, Hides, Tallow, Biefe, Pork, &c. the growth and increase of Cattell in this Nation, receiving a grand interuption and stop, by killing commonly very hopefull yong breed to furnish our markets, or store our shipping, meerly occasioned by want of ground to feed them, whereas those Provinces afford such a large proportion of rich ground, that neither the increase of this or the succeeding age can in any reasonable probability overfeed the Moiety.

10. By it many of your Honours Reformadoes and disbanded souldiers being dismist with the payment of such part of their arrears as your owne judgement (guided by the rule of your immense disbursements) shall thinke a convenient recompence, by transporting themselves thither may change their desperate fortunes into a happy certainty of condition, and a contented livelyhood, which will be a meanes not only to disburden this Republick (as before) but to remove all those clamors usualy disturbing your public consultations, and to win upon them by your bounty to invert all those fearfull imprecations, with which they would (as much as in them lies) unblesse your proceedings, into a joyfull and fervent concurrence of prayers to the Almighty to shoure downe blessings upon your heads, who, next under him, are the glorious and visible instruments of their increasing happinesse.

11. It will be a generous and moving incouragement to all industrious and publick spirits, to imploy those parts with which God and nature hath blessed them in the discovery of such happy inventions as may drive on hopefull designs with a lesser number of hands then is usually assigned to them, which issues of the brain are legitimate and geniall to beginning Plantations, where the greatest want is that of people: but for our own or other popular Kingdoms where we are commonly overprest with a greater multitude of labourers then imployers, by much lesse acceptable, since our indigent people look upon such Engins meerly as Monoppolies to engrosse their livelihood.

12. It will adde a very considerable increase to the Revenue of your Honours own Customs, and I shal assume the liberty in all humility to offer up to your more advised deliberation by way of supplement to your incomes, whether such malefactors as the letter of the law dooms to death, yet leaves a latitude for extent of mercy in the bosome of the Judges, whose release oftentimes proves not only ruinous to them so discharged, since

not

not seldome they returne to their vomit, but pernicious to the Common-wealth reinvaded by their insolencies and disorders, might not be made instrumentally serviceable to the State, if (as it is frequent in other Countreys, where they are condemned to the Gallies) by way of reparation for their crime, they were sentenced to serve a quantity of years according to the nature of their offences, which expired, they should enjoy all immunities with others, and by this course be reduced and accustomed to a regular course of life. Of these a thousand transported and employed by an understanding improver, would by their labour advance an income of forty thousand pounds sterling *per annum*, at the least, and so proportionably according to their number.

That all these, and many inestimable benefits may have their rise, increase, and perfection from the South parts of Virginia, a country unquestionably our own, devolved to us by a just title, and discovered by John Cabot *at the English expences, who found out and tooke seisure, together with the voluntary submission of the Natives to the English obedience of all that Continent from* Cape Florida *Northward, the excellent temper of the air, the large proportion of ground, the incredible richnesse of soile, the admirable abundance of Minerals, vegetables, medicinall drugs, timber, scituation, no less proper for all European commodities, then all those Staples which entitle* China, Persia, *and other the more opulent Provinces of the East to their wealth, reputation, and greatnes (besides the most Christian of all improvements, the converting many thousands of the Natives) is agreed upon by all who have ever viewed the Country: To which the judgement of the most incomparable* Ralegh *may be a convincing assertion, whose preferring of that Country before either the North of* Virginia *or* New-England, *though it may sufficiently command my submission and acquiescence; yet for more particular satisfaction be pleased to accept these reasons for such prælation.*

1. The apparent danger all the Colonies may be in if this be not possessed by the English, to prevent the Spaniard, who already hath seated himself on the North of Florida, and on the back of Virginia in 34, where he is already possessed of rich silver Mines, and will no doubt vomit his fury and malice upon the neighbour Plantations, if a prehabitation anticipate not his intentions, which backt with your authority, he understands too much of your power, and is too sadly acquainted with your admirable successes and generous resolutions, not to sit downe by any affronts offered to those under the wings of your protection,

to

to attempt any thing against such who are immediately your owne Colony, lest thereby he administers matter of a fire, to which his owne fortunes in the Indies must be a fewel, and himselfe raked up in its ashes.

2. But the South of Virginia having a contiguous Ledge of at the least one hundred Ilands, and in the middest of those the incomparable Roanoak, the most of them at the same distance from the Continent that the Ile of Wight is from Hampshire, all of hazardous accesse to Forrainers, and affording a secure convenience from surprizall by the Natives, will if possessed and protected by your power, be as an inoffensive Nursery to receive an infant Colony, till by an occasion of strength and number, we may poure our selves from thence upon the Mayneland, as our Ancestors the Saxons from the Isle of Tanet into Brittaine.

3. It dispences a moderate equality of heat and cold between the two violent extreams thereof in *Barbadoes* and *New England*.

It will admit of all things producible in any other part of the World, lying in the same Parallel with China, Persia, Japan, Cochinchina, Candia, Cyprus, Sicily, *the Southern parts of* Greece, Spain, Italy, *and the opposite Regions of* Africa.

4. It hath besides all Timber for shipping, the best and reddest Cedars, and Cypresse trees that may be found in any Countrey.

5. And lastly, the planting of this Collony will open a most compendious passage to the discovery of those more opulent Kingdomes of China, Cochinchina, Cathaya, Japan, the Phillipines, Summatra, and all those beauteous and opulent Provinces of the East Indies, which beyond dispute lye open to those Seas which wash the South-West parts of Virginia, through whose bosome all those most precious commodities which enable the Chinesie, Cathayan, Persian, and Indostant Empires, may more conveniently, speedily, with more security and lesse expences be transported thence from Spawhawn or other remoter Provinces to Gombroon, by a long dangerous and expensive Caravane, and from thence to Surat, where when arrived the doubling of the Line, Calentures Scurvies, with a long train of diseases and Famine attend its transportation into our owne Countrey.

6. Whereas by expandeing our selves to both sides and Seas of Virginia, our commerce to those noble Nations lies open in short and pleasant voyages to the encouragement, enriching and delight of the Seamen, and personal adventurers, who will share in the delicacies and profits of those Kingdoms, without participating in the miseries attending our present voyages thither. The

Cargason

Cargason being easily conveyed, by much the greater part of the way, through Navigable Rivers, and from the Eastern shore of Virginia in a month, or at the largest six weekes time into England.

And by this meanes the Hollander, Spanyard, and Portugall, (who by the supine negligence of this Nation; and its Merchant Adventurers) do with insufferable insolence Lord over us in both the Indies, when they shall to the unknitting of their joints perceive by your nursing care over the Infancy of your Colonies, that they are arrived under your auspice, to cover both the Seas with numerous Navies, and your Honours eye of indulgence and providence waking to their security will be content laying aside all other passions to wave future affronts and injuries, or fall a deserved sacrifice to your offended justice.

And that this address may appear the more seasonable, I have (without any privity or relation to his person) taken leave to intimate to your Honours, that there is a Gentleman whom the publick reputation and testimony of those who have the happines to know him render of excellent abilities, integrity, and a never shaken affection to your cause, in all its crisis and dangers through which God with a clew of success hath been your conduct) who hath already undertaken for the transportation of some men thither; and only waits for your Honours approbation and authority, the world taking notice, hopes and encouragement from thence, that as this Colony is like to be the eldest of your legitimate daughters in that nature, so by your indulgence she shall have the happynesse not to be the youngest in your affection.

May that God who hath begirt your house with a Grove of Lawrell, continue the advance of those Victories till the whole Nation be crowned with Olives: May no sin, no ingratitude of ours divert his protecting hand from us, his assistant arme from you: May the generations to come in admiration of your virtue and gratitude for their by you derived happines, make every heart your monument, wherein to embalme your memory whilst the Histories of all Nations and times enrich their Annals with your names as the most serious and triumphant part of all examples and transactions. And lastly may your owne thankfulnes to him from whom these dispensations of mercy have distilled like the dew of Hermon upon your heads and borders so continue in your bosoms, that when you shal be ripe for translation, he whose instruments you are, may welcome you with the approbation of, Well done good and faithfull servant,

Which are the undisguised wishes of
Your Honours most humble, obedient,
and faithful Servant. *Ed. Williams.*

To the worthy Gentlemen, Adventurers and Planters in *VIRGINIA.*

My loving Friends:

I *Thought it convenient heere briefly to minde you of those Necessaries, that if wanted there, would greatly prove your prejudice, and render you obnoxious to many evils, which are these.*

Necessaries for Planters.

For Aparell: Provide each man 1. *Monmouth Cap,* 1. *Wastcoat,* 1. *Suit of Canvase, Bands, Shirts, Shooes, Stockings, Canvase to make sheets, with Bed and Bolster to till in Virginia,* 1. *Rugge, and Blankets.*

For Armes: Provide 1. *Suit of complete light Armour, and each man* 1. *Sword,* 1. *Musket or Fowling Peece, with Pouder and Shot convenient.*

For Houshold stuffe: Provide one great Iron Pot, large and small Kettles, Skellets, Frying pannes, Gridiron, Spit, Platters, Dishes, Spoons, Knives, Sugar, Spice, Fruit, and Strong water at Sea for sicke men.

For Tools: Provide Howes broad and narrow, Axes broad and narrow, Handsawes, two-band-sawes, Whipsaws, Hammers, Shovels, Spades, Augors, Piercers, Gimblets, Hatchets, Handbills, Frowes to cleave pale, Pickaxes, Nayls of all sorts, 1. *Grindstone, Nets, Hooks, Lines, Plowes: All which accomodation wherewith each to be well furnished, together with his Transportation, which is ordinarily* 6l. *a man, and* 3l. *a tun his goods, may amount unto* 20l. *a man, charges.*

Nor needs the carefull Adventurer much doubt what Wares may prove his profit there. For any Commodities of this Country are good Merchandize transported thither. viz. Strong waters, Haberdashers wares, Ironmongers wares, Drapers wares, Stationers wares, and many other wares which those sterill witted Americans doe easily admire. But your judgements are sufficient. And likewise I have further discovered them in the insuing Treatise of the Incomparable VIRGINIA. So wishing you all prosperous happinesse and happy prosperity heere, and in the world to come eternall blisse, I rest

Your faithfull

Servant,

E. W.

Virginia *in Generall, but particularly* CAROLANA, *which comprehends* Roanoak, *and the Southern parts of* Virginia *richly valued.*

THE scituation and Climate of *Virginia* is the Subject of every Map, to which I shall refer the curiosity of those who desire more particular information.

Yet to shew that Nature regards this Ornament of the new world with a more indulgent eye then she hath cast upon many other Countreys, whatever *China, Persia, Japan, Cyprus, Candy, Sicily, Greece,* the South of *Italy, Spaine,* and the opposite parts of *Africa,* to all which she is parallel, may boast of, will be produced in this happy Country. The same bounty of Summer, the same milde remission of Winter, with a more virgin and unexhausted soyle being materiall arguments to shew that modesty and truth receive no diminution by the comparison.

Nor is the present wildnesse of it without a particular beauty, being all over a naturall Grove of Oakes, Pines, Cedars, Cipresse, Mulberry, Chesnut, Laurell, Sassafras, Cherry, Plumtrees, and Vines, all of so delectable an aspect, that the melanchollyest eye in the World cannot look upon it without contentment, nor content himselfe without admiration. No shrubs or underwoods choake up your passage, and in its season your foot can hardly direct it selfe where it will not be died in the bloud of large and delicious Strawberries : The Rivers which every way glide in deepe and Navigable Channels, betwixt the brests of this uberous Countrey, and contribute to its conveniency beauty and fertility, labour with the multitude of their fishy inhabitants in greater variety of species, and of a more incomparable delicacy in tast and sweetnesse then whatever the European Sea can boast of : Sturgeon of ten feet, Drummes of six in length ; Conger, Eeles, Trout, Salmon, Bret, Mullet, Cod, Herings, Perch, Lampreyes, and what ever else can be desired to the satisfaction of the most voluptuous wishes.

Nor is the Land any lesse provided of native Flesh, Elkes bigger then Oxen, whose hide is admirable Buffe, flesh excellent

lent, and may be made, if kept domesticke, as usefull for draught and carriage, as Oxen. Deere in a numerous abundance, and delicate Venison, Racoones, Hares, Conyes, Bevers, Squirrell, Beares, all of a delightfull nourishment for food, and their Furres rich, warme, and convenient for clothing and Merchandise.

That no part of this happy Country may bee ungratefull to the Industrious, The ayre it selfe is often clouded with flights of Pigeons, Partriges, Blackbirds, Thrushes, Dottrels, Cranes, Hernes, Swans, Geese, Brants, Duckes, Widgeons, Oxeyes, infinites of wilde Turkeyes, which have been knowne to weigh fifty pound weight, ordinarily forty.

And the native Corne of the Country Maiz, is so gratefull to the Planter; that it returneth him his entrusted seed with the increase of 2 or 3 hundred interest, so facilely planted, that one man in 48 hours may prepare as much ground, and set such a quantity of Corne, that he may be secure from want of Bread all the yeere following, though he should have never so large an appetite to consume it, and have nothing else to live upon. Nor is it above three, or at the most foure months intervall betwixt the time of planting and gathering. Planted in March, April, or May, it is ready for the Barne in June, July, and August; and of this by a provident management, you may have yeerely three or foure Harvests. The stalk bruised yields a juice as big as Rice, pleasant as Sugar, and the green Ears boyled in such juice is comparable in agreeablenesse to the palats to what ever our Pease, Sparagus, or Hartichoke, hath eyther for satisfaction or delicacy. Nor is the Corne difficult in preservation, for in six or seven yeares there is scarce any sensibility of its corruption.

But lest our palats should have so much of curiosity as to dislike what ever is not native to our owne Country, and wheat is justly esteemed more proper this happy soyle, though at the first too rich to receive it, after it hath contributed to your wealth by diminution of its owne richnesse, in three or four crops of Rice, Flax, Indian Corne, Coleseed, or Rapeseed, will receive the English wheat with a gratefull retribution of thirty for one increase, every Acre sowed with wheat will produce six, seven, or eight Quarter of the graine intrusted. And though Mr. *Bullocke* be pleased to under-rate it at halfe the crowne the bushell, which in the Canaries will yeeld ten and twelve shillings, and in Spaine eight, yet even in that proportion you are recompenced with six, seven, or eight pound the Acre, of which two men by a discreet division of their time, will plow, reape, and in at the least 60 Acres.

Which though it may appeare a matter of admiration, yet I
shall

shall easily make it apparrant by the following Narration, in which such is the exactnesse of the Ayre in this Country, that you may have five sucessive Harvests of the same grain in different seasons. For though a man and a boy with much ease may plow an Acre every day, the ground being pliable of a rich blacke and tender mold, and no frosts or snowes, no usuall droughts or raines to hinder the going of the plow, yet I shall allow a month for the plowing of twelve Acres, and thus plowing in September, October, November, December, and January, you may have your severall Harvests in June, July, August, and September, which may easily bee inned by the same hands the labour not falling in a glut upon them, but the Corne ripening according to its severall seasons.

And thus by two mens labours onely you have a gratefull returne of at the least three hundred and sixty Quarters of Wheat, which will at that under rate formerly mentioned, *viz.* 2s. 6d. yeeld so many pounds sterling: Nor is there such difficulty in the threshing, as may be at first sight suspected, since it may easily be tread out with Oxen, as it is usuall in Italy and other Countries.

The first Wheat being reaped, if you desire a croppe of Barley, the same Land plowed in *July*, will returne its ripe increase in *September*, so that from one and the same piece of ground you may have the benefit of two different Harvests.

But the Rice (for production of which this Countrey is no lesse proper then those Lands which have the greatest reputation of fertility) sowed, yeelds a greater encrease with the same labour 40 Acres of this plowed if valued but at 7s. 6d. the Bushell, will yeeld 600l. all done by two men and a Teame of Oxen, who may by other labour in the intervall betwixt the committing the seed to ground, and its ripening, fall upon Coleseed or Rape-seed, infinitely rich Commodities with the same facility.

The objection, that the Countrey is overgrowne with Woods, and consequently not in many Yeares to bee penetrable for the Plough, carries a great feeblenesse with it. For there are an immense quantity of Indian fields cleared already to our hand by the Natives, which till wee grow over populous may every way be abundantly sufficient, but that the very clearing of ground carries an extraordinary benefit with it, I will make apparent by these following Reasons.

1. If wee consider the benefit of Pot-ashes growne from ten to fifty pound the Tunne, within these twenty yeares, and in all probability likely to encrease by reason of interdicting Trade
betwixt

betwixt us and the Muscovite, from whence we used to supply
our selves ; We shall finde the employment of that very Staple
will raise a considerable summe of Money, and no man so imployed can (if industrious) make his labour less than one hundred pound, *per annum* : For if wee consider that those who labour about this in England give twelve pence the bushell for
Ashes, if wee consider to how many severall parts of the Countrey they are compelled to send man and horse before they can
procure any quantity to fall to worke upon ; if wee consider
some of the thriftiest, and wise, and understanding men, fell
Wood on purpose for this Commodity, and yet not withstanding
this Brigade of difficulties finde their Adventures and Labours
answered with a large returne of profit, wee who have all these
things, already at our owne doore without cost, may with a confidence grounded upon reason expect an advantage much greater, and clearer profit.

Nor can wee admit in discretion, that a large quantity of those
should not finde a speedy Market, since the decay of Tymber
is a defect growne universall in Europe, and the Commodity such
a necessary Staple, that no civill Nation can be conveniently
without it.

Nor are Pipestaves and Clapboard a despicable commodity, of
which one man may with ease make fifteen thousand yearely,
which in the countrey it selfe are sold for 4l. in the *Canaries* for
twenty pound the thousand, and by this means the labour of one
man will yeeld him 60l. *per annum*, at the lowest Market. If
all this be not sufficient to remove the incumbrance of Woods,
the Saw mill may be taken into consideration, which is in every
respect highly beneficiall by this Timber for building houses,
and shipping may be more speedily prepared, and in greater
quantity by the labour of two or three men, then by a hundred
hands after the usuall manner of sawing.

The Plankes of Walnut-trees for Tables or Cubbords, Cedar
and Cypresse, for Chests, Cabinets, and the adorning magnifi-
cent buildings, thus prepared will be easily transported into
England, and sold at a very considerable value.

But that in which there will be an extraordinary use of our
woods is the Iron mills, which if once erected will be an unde-
caying Staple, and of this forty servants will by their labour
raise to the Adventurer foure thousand pound yearely : Which
may easily be apprehended if wee consider the deerenesse of
Wood in England, where notwithstanding this great clog of difficulty, the Master of the Mill gaines so much yearely, that he
cannot but reckon himselfe a provident Saver.

Neither

Neither does *Virginia* yeeld to any other Province whatsoever in excellency and plenty of this Oare : And I cannot promise to my selfe any other then extraordinary successe and gaine,
if this noble and usefull Staple be but vigourously followed.

And indeed it had long ere this growne to a full perfection, if
the treachery of the Indians had not crushed it in the beginning
and the backwardnesse of the *Virginia* Merchants to reerect it,
hindred that Countrey from the benefit arising from that universall Staple.

But to shew something further, what use may be made of
Woods besides the forementioned Wallnut Oyle, at the least a
fourth part of the Trees in *Virginia* being of that *species*, is an
excellent Staple, and very gainefull to the industrious Labourer.

Nor is it a contemptible profit that may be made of Woods, if
by boaring holes in divers trees, of whose vertues wee are yet
ignorant, and collecting the juce thereof, a scrutiny be made
which are fit for Medicinall Liquor and Balsomes; which for
Gummes, Perfumes, and Dyes, and heere I may justly take occasion to complain of our owne sloth and indulgence, if compared to the laborious Spanyard, who by this very practice have
found out many excellent Druggs, Paints, and Colours, meerely
by bruizing and grinding Woods, probably convenient for such
experiments : which if boyled, and a white peece of cloth steep-
ed in the boyling liquor, will by its tincture discover what colour
it is capable to give, and if many should faile in the tryall, yet
does it not fall under the probability, but that divers noble and
usefull mysteries of Nature may be discovered by some such
perforations and scrutinies. Nor are the many Berries commonly of an excellent collour and lustre unfit for such experiments; since the labour is little or nothing, and the issue if suc-
cesfull of remarkable advantage. And this the Spanyard hath
experimented to the encrease of gaine and reputation ; and
above this is so signally curious and industrious, that he hath
discovered many rare and delightfull colours, not onely by the
meanes before mentioned, but by bruizing and boyling divers
Fish-shells, the brightnesse and variety of colours giving him a
just reason to pursue such curious examens.

The French relations of their Voyages to *Canada*, tell us
that the Indians and themselves falling into a contagious disease,
of which Phisitians could give no Reason or Remedy, they
were all in a short space restored to their health meerely by
drinking water, in which Saxifrage was infused and boyled,
which was then discovered to them by the Natives, and wee justly entertaine beliefe that many excellent Medicines either for

conservation

conservation of Nature in her vigour or restauration in her decadence may be communicated unto us, if projection of this stampe be so much incouraged by hopes or reward of honour, as to be put in practice.

By this Improvement of Woods, the Ground comming to bee cleared, wee have a soile fit to produce what ever is excellent in Nature, the Vine and Olive which Naturally simpathize together, will thrive beyond belief, nor need it be any interruption to Tillage, since the Vintage and Harvest always fall out in different Seasons.

That wild Vines runne naturally over *Virginia*, ocular experience declares who delighting in the Neighbourhood of their beloved Mulberry-trees inseparable associates over all that Countrey, and of which in this their wildnesse Wines have beene made, of these Vines if transplanted and culitivated, there can be made no doubt but a Rich and Generous Wine would be produced: But if wee set the Greeke Cyprian Candian or Calabrian Grape, those Countries lying parallell with this, there neede not be made the smallest question but it would be a Staple which would enrich this Countrey to the envy of France and Spaine, and furnish the Northern parts of Europe, and China it selfe where they plant it not, (of which more hereafter) with the Noblest Wine in the World, and at no excessive prices.

And from this Staple 'tis not unworthy of our most serious consideration, what an occasion of wealth would flow upon this Nation : Virginia when well peopled being able to match Spaine in that his Soveraigne Revenue, and the State by addition to their Customes for exportation thereof according to the mode of France and Spaine, would in no short time be sensible of this most inestimable benefit : To which if wee joyne the Profits of our Olives, wee may (Gods favourable hand blessing our industry) be the happiest Nation in Europe.

Nor need wee be at that charge for Caske under which Spaine labours, where ever wee cast our eyes upon this Fortunate Countrey wee may finde Timber proper for it.

For the advance of which noble Staple, I should propose that the Greeke, and other Rich Vines, being procured from the Countries to which they are geniall, every Planter in that Countrey might be enjoyned to keep a constant Nursery, to the end when the ground is cleared, that they may be fit for removal, and the Vineyard speedily planted.

Further that some Greeke, and other Vignerons might be hired out of those Countries to instruct us in the labour, and lest their envy, pride, or jealousie of being layd aside when their

mysterie

mysterie is discovered, may make them too reserved in communicating their knowledge, they may be assured, besides the continuance of their Pension of a share in the profits of every mans Vintage, which will the more easily perswade them to be liberall and faithfull in their instructions, since the publick advance of this designe cannot miscarry without a sensible losse to their particular interest.

That before their going over a generall consultation may be had whith them what ground is proper, what season fit, what prevention of casualities by bleeding or splitting, what way to preserve or restore Wine when vesseld, which *species* of Wine is fittest for transportation over, or retention in the Countrey, which for duration, which for present spending : It being in experience manifest that some Wines refine themselves by purge upon the Sea, others by the same meanes suffer an evaporation of their spirits, joyne to this that some Wines collect strength and richnesse, others contract feeblenesse and sowernesse by seniority.

These consultations drawne to a head by some able person, and published to be sent over in severall Copies to Virginia, by the inspection of which people might arrive at such competent knowledge in the Mystery, that the reservation or jealousies of those Vignerons, could not but be presently perceived and prevented.

But from hence no occasion should bee derived to breake or fall short of any contract made with those Vignerons, who are to be exactly dealt with in performance of Articles, every way made good unto them, with all just respects to win upon them, and the non-performance of this hath beene the originall cause why Virginia at this day doeth not abound with that excellent commodity. Those contracted with as hired servants for that imployment, by what miscariage I know not, having promise broken with them, and compelled to labour in the quality of Slaves, could not but express their resentment of it, and had a good colour of justice to conceale their knowledge, in recompence of the hard measure offered them, which occasioned the laying aside of that noble Staple, the diligent prosecution whereof, had by this time brought Virginia to an absolute perfection in it, and to a great degree of happinesse and wealth which would attend it.

And had this beene as happily followed as it was prudently intended, that excellent Country had not hung downe its desolate head in so languishing a condition as the disrespect cast upon her, till of late yeares had reduced her to. Nor had the

poore

poore Planter (who usually spends all the profits of his labour in forraigne Wines) been impoverished by the want of it : but with delight might have shaded himselfe under his vine, reaped the benefit of it in Autumne, and buried all the memory and sense of his past labours in a cheerfull rejoycing by his owne harth with the issue of his owne vineyard.

And from hence might Barbadoes, St. Christophers, and all our Islands in the Indies, have richer, better, and by much cheaper, wines transported to them from a place much neerer in distance then Spain or the Canaries) and which doubles the benefit such intercourse together, would draw them to an association in power as well as communication of Staples.

Were this brought to a just perfection no other Nation could upon a quarrell betwixt Us, and Spaine, and France, reape a benefit by selling us their Wine at a third Market. And what wee vend now for it (that being made Native to us) might be returned in Bullion, to the apparent enriching of the Commonwealth, and the impoverishing of our Enemies, or at the least Friends deservedly suspected.

All Authors of Agriculture unanimously consent that neither Arable Pasture, Meadow, or any other Grounds are so benigne genuine, or proper for planting Vines in, as those cleared Lands are, wherein not Shrubs, but Tall Trees were standing. And wee must want a parrallell in any part of the World to compare with Virginia for tall and goodly Timber-trees cleared of all under Woods, to which when cleared your Vines may be removed (the very removeall of them, as indeed of all other, giving an addition to their perfection (the excellency of transplantation being more particularly insisted upon heereafter.) But in the clearing of these woods it will be a saving of labour, and a delight to the Vine, besides other profits following to leave the Mulberry trees standing there, being such a happy correspondence together such a mutuall love ingrafted in them by Nature, that wee well may conclude with this Axiome, that the same Nature joynes all her excellencies together by an association of simpathies.

Nor does she wave that her happy order in Incomparable *Virginia,* where the soile and climate that fits the one, is equally amiable to the other, their loves and hates happily according, what the one shunnes, the other flies from, what the one affects, challenges the others embraces, and were not this soile and climate most geniall and proper Nature her selfe (whose productions are never uselesse) would never have crowned the Virgin Brow of this unexampled Countrey, with such a universall

plenty

plenty of them, or with such a voluntary League have united them every where together.

VIRGINIA *compared to* PERSIA.

BUT to illustrate this with another argument : Let us compare this felicity-teeming *Virginia*, as it is scituated from 31 degrees of Latitude to 40. with other Countries, seated in the same degrees which opens us a method of observing what Commodities Nations so planted abound with, which found wee shall discover in this excellent Virgin a disposition ingrafted by Nature to be Mother of all those excellencies, and to be equall (if not superior) as well in all their noble Staples, as in nearenesse to their particular enricher the perpetually auspicious Sunne. And this to whome *Virginia* owes the publication and portract of her incomparable beauty ; Mr. *Harriot* the noble Mathematician delivers us by a happy instance in finding out for her a noble Sister of the same Latitude, the most glorious *Persia*, innobled as much by this comparison as in her Empire. And those who have travelled and viewed *Persia*, unanimously relate wonders of her admirable fertility in all sorts of Graine and Fruits, with an unexpressible abundance of Silke and Wines: In which this her rich-bosomed Sister claimes an equalty in her plenty of Mulberries, Silke, and Gums, Vines, Maiz, Rice, and all sorts of Graine: onely as a fuller-dowryed Sister she merits a priority in fertility, pleasure, health, and temperature, a Virgin Countrey, so preserved by Nature out of a desire to show mankinde fallen into the Old age of the Creation, what a brow of fertility and beauty she was adorned with when the World was vigorous and youthfull, and she her selfe was unwounded with the Plough-shares, and unweakened by her numerous future teemings.

Another eye-witnesse of this Victorious Empire, delivers to memory that *Covazan* in a Province of that Countrey, is so incomparably fruitfull, that Dearths are never knowne, nor Famine ever suspected in it, that in one onely City called Ery, there is such an inestimable store of Silke, that there might be bought in one day in that City as much Silke as will lode three thousand Camells. And he is little conversant with experience or History, who is ignorant that the abundance of Silke Native to that Countrey and Climate, is almost the sole Staple of that mighty Empire, by which never-to-be exhausted Treasure of Silkes the sinewes and vitalls of the Persian Empire, the Sophy to the generall good of Christendome, keepes both the hornes
of

of the Ottoman Moone from compleating their ambitious Circle. And if the English East-India Company of Merchants were not wrong-byassed by the factions and sinister ambition of some men in Authority amongst them, a great part of that wealthy Staple might be transported into England, and by that meanes dispersed over all parts of Europe to the enriching and honour of this Nation.

The digression upon this Parallell hath diverted me from ampliation upon the publick benefit, which may devolve into this republick by the Olive, which being genuine to the Vine, will by a happy consent of nature indisputably flourish in a vast abundance, and by a transportation into the warmer Regions, where the heate or scarcity of Cattle causeth a like indigence of Butter, will be a Staple of inestimable value, and of no smaller conducement to our owne shipping, into those provinces neere the Equinox, or in those voyages where the doubling of the Line either putrifies, or makes it of a taste little pleasing or agreeable to the palate.

VIRGINIA *compared to* CHINA.

BUt to leave Persia and descend to a more wealthy and powerful parallell, the richest and mightiest Empire in the World, lies in the same latitude and climate with our fortunate Virginia; namely China, divided from it only by the Southsea, and (which will bee a part of another discourse) not of any long distance from it, agreeing with it in multitude of Staples. China is stored with an infinite number of Mulberry trees to feede Silkewormes with, and vends silke in such a vast proportion, that in one onely City *Lempo*, which some call *Liempo*, the Portugeses, have with no small admiration, observed that one hundred and sixty thousand pound weight of silk hath beene caried out in one Shippe in the onely space of three Moneths.

Into *Cambula* the chiefe City of Tartary (as Authors of great repute and credit, and one who was personally there, reports) there comes every day from China, a thousand waggons laden with silke. Nor is China lesse happy in its multitude of navigable Rivers, in its wonderfull fertility of all sorts of graine, Maiz, Rice, &c. of which it receiveth every yeere three or foure most plentifull Harvests. Rivers stored with an incredible quantity of Fish and Fowle, enriched and ennobled with numerous Mines of Gold, Silver, Brasse, Iron, and other Mettalls, Quicksilver, Nitre, Allum, Pretious stones, Pearles, Muske,

Cotton,

Cotton, Sugars, Rubarb, China Root, vast proportions of Flax, Furres extraordinary rich. To this happinesse of soile and situation, they associate an equall felicity of parts and industry, by which they pretermit not one span of ground which they assign not to particular and profitable uses, and by an ingenious division of the ground according to the quality of the soyle, designe the drier part for wheat and barly, That* which is more visited with an improving moysture, to Rice and Sugar; Ascents and Mountaines to groves of Pines and Chestnuts, betweene·which are planted Maiz Panicle, and all kinde of Pulse. In other proper places are Mulberry Groves, Gardens, Orchards, Flax, and in a word no spot of ground misimployed from its proper advantage.

And that Virginia is parallell in neerenesse of Staples, as well as neighbourhood to the sunne, to that celebrated Empire, what multitudes of Fish to satisfie the most voluptuous of wishes, can China glory in which Virginia may not in justice boast of ? What Fowles can she make ostentation of, in which Virginia can be esteemed inferiour ? Can China, insolent with her prosperity, solely lay clayme to a more singular honour for her affluence in Maiz and other grain, for the maintenance and luxury of her plenty-wanton Inhabitants, without an open injury to her equall, to her Mayden sister, to our incomparable Virginia ? Are her Mulberries springing from a voluntary bounty of Nature lesse numerous or usefull then those to which China hath added all the assistance which could be expected from advantages of transplantation, or an industrious people ? If China will descend to particulars, to compare Quantity and Quality of Fish and Fowle, Let her shew us Turkies of 50 pound weight, Let her instance an example of one hundred and fifty Fowle, to reward the labour of three charges of shot and powder, Let her publish a president so worthy of admiration (and which will not admit beliefe in those bosomes where the eye cannot be witnesse of the action) of five thousand fish taken at one draught neere Cape *Charls*, at the entry into Chesapeak Bay, and which swells the wonder greater, not one fish under the measure of two feet in length. What Fleets come yeerely upon the coasts of New found Land, and New England for Fish, with an incredible returne ? Yet tis a most assured truth, that if they would make experiment upon the South of Cape Cod, and from thence to the coast of this happy Countrey, they would find Fish of a greater delicacy, and as full handed plenty, which though Foraigners know not, yet if our owne Planters would make use of it, would yield them a Revenue which cannot admit of any diminution,

whilest

whilest there are Ebbes and Flouds, Rivers feed and receive the Ocean, or Nature fayles in (the Elementall Originall of all things) Waters.

There wants nothing but industrious spirits and incouragement, to make a rich Staple of this commodity ; and would the Virginians but make Salt pits, in which they have a greater convenience of Tides (that part of the Universe by reason of a full influence of the Moone upon the almost limitlesse Atlantick causing the most spacious Fluxes and Refluxes, that any shore of the other divisions in the World is sensible of) to leave their pits full of Salt-water, and more friendly and warme Sunbeames to concoct it into Salt, then Rochel, or any parts of Europe. Yet notwithstanding these advantages which prefer Virginia before Rochel, the French King rayses a large proportion of his Revenues out of that Staple yearly, with which he supplyes a great part of Christendome.

And if from this Staple the miserable French can procure a subsistence, some of them a comfortable livelyhood, notwithstanding all the private oppressions of their grinding Landlords, the Publick Tallies, Subsidies, Aides, Imposts, and other hard Titles of authorized Rapine. What shall wee imagine the freeborne English in a Countrey where he owes no Rent to any but to God and Nature, where he has Land to satisfie his desires in its extent, his wishes in its fertility, where free-quarter is a word onely understood by Report, may expect of profit and content both in this Staple of Salt, in that of Wines made in those Countries, where either the Spanish insolence and exactions, the French extortions, or the Turkish Imperiall Robberies, though in the highest degrees of exorbitance, are not of force so to disincourage the Inhabitants from attendance upon the Vineyard, which notwithstanding all those Horse-leaches of Imposition, returnes them such a profit as make them keepe a middle path betweene the ascent of Riches, and precipice of Poverty.

Nor would it be such a long intervall (Salt being first made) betwixt the undertaking of this Fishing, and the bringing it to perfection ; for if every servant were enjoyned to practice Rowing, to be taught to handle Sailes, and trimme a Vessell, a worke easily practised, and suddainely learned, the pleasantnesse of Weather in fishing season, the delicacy of the Fish, of which they usually feede themselves with the best, the encouragement of some share in the profit, and their understanding what their owne benefit may bee when their freedome gives them an equallity, will make them willing and able Fisher-men and Seamen.

To

To adde further to this, if we consider the abundance, large-
nesse, and peculiar excellency of the Sturgeon in that Countrey,
it will not fall into the least of scruples, but that one *species* will
bee of an invaluable profit to the buyer, or if wee repeat to our
thoughts the singular plenty of Herrings and Mackarell, in
goodnesse and greatnesse much exceeding what ever of that
kinde these our Seas produce, a very ordinary understanding
may at the first inspection perceive that it will be no great difficulty to out-labour and out-vye the Hollander in that his almost
onely Staple : Which wee may also sell at a cheaper Market
then in common estimation ; if wee revolve the Salt to be our
owne, which they buy from France, or fetch from the Isle of
May, and that the very fraight of Passengers (of which allured
by this improvement, and the publick approbation, there will be
constant multitudes) in our owne Shippes will at the least defray 3 fourths of the charges.

I should not unwillingly heare (though I dispaire ever to
know it for a certainety) that *China* did exceede us in fishing ;
for were it granted, wee should not imagine those watry Inhabitants so circumscribed and limited to one part of the Ocean
especially the same Climate and Latitude, inviting them as not
to visit our opposite shore of Southwest *Virginia* in as great
variety and plenty.

And to the more curious and able Persons I shall offer what
singular object it were of variety and plenty, if they would take
the advantage of some tides and seasons, when the resort of fish
is greatest to stoppe the Returne of them out of some Creeke
perpetually flowing with Salt by Sluces, or such other invention :
Heere would those great ones generate and produce till even
they laboured with their owne Multitude, if permitted to increase two or three yeares, who might with very small charge
be maintained, and yearely render to the proprietar an Ocean
of Fish in a narrow confine of Water.

Nor were it unworthy the labour to make an experiment whether the Sturgion himselfe might not receive a kinde of Domes-
tication in that narrow circumscription, especially if wee let it
descend into our thoughts, that (by small perforations in the
sluces he perpetually admits a Renovation and change of salt
Water) he may receive the same benefit of Liberty, namely
variety of Water, which he delights in when unconfined, and
admitting the Originall Breeder not to thrive well by such im-
prisoning, yet customes ascending as high as Nature in the
Breed, would make that Familiar to them, which peradventure
might have been offensive to the first Spawner, and should they
delight

delight (as in some seasons of the yeare Fishes doe vary theit Resorts) at any time in fresh water; A large Pond digged neare having either Springs to feede it, or Raines to fill it, might by communication of a Sluce receive both them and Salmon, when they seeke after the Freshes.

And that Fishes may be unwilded, and become Domestick, History will sufficiently informe us, wherein are delivered Reports of some who growne more particularly intelligent, were distinguisht by names, and understood themselves so called: and *Martiall* in one of his Epigrams to *Cæsar*, (I meane *Domitian*) tells the Prince speaking of Fishes so instructed, *Quid quod nomen habent & ad Magistri Nomen quisq sui venit citatus?* And further, *Manumq lambit*, a thing, which though a Poet, and consequently bold, even to untruths, yet he durst never have obtruded upon *Cæsar*, whom himselfe makes a party in the experiment.

And to adde something to what hath formerly beene delivered of Balsomes and Colours, why from the Livers and most unctuous parts of those more delicate Fishes, may not curiosity finde a means to extract an Oyle, which (if it be not Medicinall, though I am enclined by severall Reasons to believe·the affirmative) may notwithstanding artificially distilled after its first extraction prove a delicacy for the Tables of Princes and Great Ones, especially for Sauces, and other Confections which Luxury hath found out for the irritation of dull and retreating appetites. But I cannot believe it to be deprived of its particular virtue in Physicall operations, and the industrious conclusions of our Ancestors have by such probations discovered many rich Mysteries of Nature; whilst wee either glutted with our owne pienty of Receipts, or out of a too fond a Reverence wee pay to antiquity acquiesce in their prescriptions, as in the *ne plus ultra*, the *Hercules* Pillars of Wisdome, beyond which there were no passage, or else feare every innovation brings inconveniences in his Traine, which opinion if it had possessed those our Ancestors, the World had continued in ignorance, and must for ever have layne sick of an incurable folly in the Fooles Hospitalls.

For what concernes the Flax of *China*, that wee may not lose the smallest circumstance of Parallell with *Virginia*, Nature her selfe hath enriched this her bosome Favourite with a voluntary plant which by art, industry, and transplantation may be multiplyed and improved to a degree of as plentifull, but more excellent Nature: Which because of its accession to the quallity of Silke, wee entitle Silke Grasse: Of this Queene
Elizabeth

Elizabeth had a substantiall and rich peece of Grograine made and presented to Her. Of this Mr. *Porey* in his discovery of the great River Chamonoak, to the South of *James* River, delivers a Relation of infinite Quantity, covering the Surface of a Vast Forest of Pine-trees, being 60. miles in length.

It had beene wished that the injunction given to every Planter to set so many thousand Plants of this kinde had been effectually prosecuted: The intermission whereof hath beene a prejudice not easily imaginable: Nor is it yet too late to effect it, and in all probability by transplantation it may thrive beyond comparison larger, and the skinne of it growne more tender and delicate, may arrive to some equality with the labour of the Silke-worme, if it be managed by such Rules of Nature best sute with its production.

For Hempe there is a naturall kinde of Hempe, a *species* of Flagg in that Countrey, from which being boyled you may strippe a long and fine skinne, not onely proper for Cordage, but the finer sort singularly usefull for Linnen ; of this two hundred weight hath been sent into England, of which hath beene made excellent Cordage, and very good Linnen. This, by observation of the soile it growes in, and transplanted into Grounds of like, but richer property, would together with the Silke-grasse make a Staple of admirable Returne and Profit ; Provided every Planter had an injunction for this, as well as the former to sow or set a convenient proportion, to which his owne profit (quickned with the imposition of a mulct in case of neglect) would easily invite him. And by this meanes would *Virginia* not onely furnish her owne people, but supply other Nations with Stuffes and Linnen.

To the Brasse of *China*, wee shall oppose the *Virginian* Copper (or Gold, for yet it is doubtfull) for by a concurrent Relation of all the Indians, justified to severall English of Quality, particularly to the Earle of *Southampton*, in Mr. *Poryes* Narrative, to Sir *William Berkely*, all seconding Mr. *Heriots* Report, that within ten dayes West toward the setting of the Sunne, the Natives of that Countrey gathered a kinde of a Red Sand falling with a streame issuing from a Mountaine, which being washed in a sive, and set upon the fire speedily, melts and becomes some Copper, which they shew us, but as they say much softer. We shall only suppose it to be Copper, contrary to the opinion of divers knowing men, who apprehend it for a Richer Metall ; but melting with such ease two parts in five turnings to a Solid Metall, the other three parts being peradventure not any thing of the Oare, but onely such Rubbidge, as

joyned

joyned to the Oare in rouling, and this falling meerely from the superficies of the Mountaine, yet a Rich Copper; what eye enlightned with the smallest beame of Reason, will not conclude it for an extraordinary accession of Wealth to this Countrey? and why may not the intralls of this Minerall be Gold, since the skinne and crust of it is Copper? Nature her selfe oftentimes dealing after the mode of divers great men, delighting to lay an unregarded outside over her Richest Linings.

To proceed in continuation of our comparison with China, if it abound more in visible Silver (of which with our abundance of Staples may quickly put us into a condition of entring into completion with) yet cannot *Virginia* in all probability be destitute of that Metall: For besides divers conjectures grounded upon naturall circumstances: Mr. *Gage* in his Relation of the Indies, assures us that the Spanyards have found out a rich Silver Mine on the back side of Florida Westward, in 34 degrees of Latitude, and the farther they extend their search Northward, the more Rich and Pure the Mines discovered improve themselves.

Nor shall wee plead inferiority in Pearles with China or Persia, since Mr. *Heriot* assures us of a large quantity of Pearles found amongst the Natives, spoyled by their ignorance in boring of them, and defacing their orientall lustre, by exposing them to the fire. These were found amongst the Indians at Roanoak, and the Relations of the Natives on all hands unanimously concur that the South and West of this opulent Contrey was stored with such abundance and variety, that the Indians used to make and adorne Babies with them: And one of the English had collected a Bracelet of very orientall Pearle, to the number of five thousand, which were all lost in the Returne to England.

If China suppose a merit of precedency in Muske, Virginia may justly oppose them with her Musk Rat, or Muscassus, which in all probability cannot but be the same; for it is a tradition received into the Number of truths, that the Confection of their Muske in that Countrey is bruizing and burying a certaine Creature to putrefaction of which this Odour is effected, and it is very open to conjecture that this Musk-Rat or Muscassus, whose flesh and skinne are extraordinary redolent and durant, and of which there is an infinite plenty, by such order may be brought to the same perfection. Neither is it so improbable that this Odour should proceed from putrefaction, which is naturally an abhorrence to the Nosthrill: for if you apply too neare to the substance of the Muske, there is an occult subolency of such a putrefactive originall. Neither are all excretions

of

of Nature in themselves offensive to the sense of smelling, for the Fluxe of the Civit-Cat is accounted amongst our most soveraigne Perfumes : And this experimented will be a Staple of noble use, and no lesse benefit.

Nor shall wee yeeld the Laurell of preeminence in Richnesse of Furres to China, if the Furres of Beavers, Otters, Martines, and above all Black Foxes (which are upon some part of this Continent) may pretend any title to Richnesse : And yet have wee beene hitherto so supinely negligent to permit the Dutch and the French to carry away most of this pretious Commodity, to trade in our Rivers, under-sell us, and which discovers either an implacable malice or insatiable avarice, trade with those Indians (of whom wee have no reason to nourish any great confidence) for Muskets and Powder.

To conclude, what ever else China may presume to boast of: Whether Nitre, Allum, Quicksilver, Rhubarb, and China Root, of which some wee have already discovered: If wee consider the parallell in Latitude, the equality of temperate Climate, the parity in soile, and its fertility, the similitude in brave Navigable Rivers, the unanimous congruity and consent in divers knowne Commodities, wee shall have an ample basis to ground conjectures upon, that what ever singularity of Nature that Nation may imagine her selfe Victorious over others, will be found equall in this Garden of the World, this æmulous Rivall of China, Virginia : And the Chineses may with as great justice deny the Europeans the benefit of both eyes, as boast that they precede in any thing except Antiquity of habitation, and a long experienced industry, this great Luminary of the new World Virginia.

What ever other commodities, the Novelty of inhabiting this amorous Virgin hath made it appeare defective in, as Sugar, Indigo, Cotton, Ginger, and other advantageous Staples, wee shall appeale to all who have seene this unexampled Countrey ; (we meane Roanoak, and the more Southerne parts, and those Countries towards the fertile Mangoack) whether it be guilty of any contrariety, distemper, or extremity, which might hinder their production. The Sunne, which in other Countreys makes his visit in Flames and Droughts, heere casts his auspicious Beames, and by an innocent and complimentall warmth, courts the bosome of this his particular favourite, hastening and disposing its wombe for ripe productions, which salute him in an absolute perfection. Winter Snowes, Frosts, and other excesses, are heere only remembred, never known. The purling Springs and wanton Rivers every where kissing the happy soyle into a

perpetuall

perpetuall verdure, into an unwearied fertility: no obstructions in your expectations, attempt and hope them, prosecute and enjoy them.

Nor have we in design to lay any imputation upon the Barbadoes, which already aboundeth to admiration, with the Staples last mentioned, yet it will become our charity to wish the Country as healthfull, as it is fruitfull; that it may answer the expectation and merit of its most industrious and publicke spirited Planters, who have given a brave example to all, by the effects of their industry and unwearied constancy. From a thing almost lost to memory, (at the least to reputation) they have raysed the honour of that Island, to be a subject of admiration for wealth and Staple, and that so little a circumference of Ground should be able to vent the value of two hundred and fifty thousand pound yeerely, as some Merchants have maintayned, not only addes to the weight and measure of their just estimation, but increases the favourable wishes of all lovers of industry, that they had a larger proportion of ground to improve upon.

And if an invincible sloth doth not possesse us in Virginia, (wee meane the South) why should not wee rayse an equall or greater profit upon as fertile and convenient a soile? especially if we consider the populousnesse of the place, has so raysed the price of Land there, which we have heere gratis, where number of inhabitants doe so little take from our abundance, that they adde to our wealth, security and plenty, and the sole meanes to increase and improve upon Staples.

We have made it apparant that what ever China hath of Staple or delicaoy, is produced or producible in this above-example Virgin. But to shew that even China her selfe must in some things give place to this more happy Mayden, *Terra sigillata*, or *Lemnia*, (as peculiar an income to the Grand Signiors Treasury, as that of Salt is to the French Kings) and of which China can no way boast, is native to this Countrey; Vines are eyther not naturall, neglected, or not understood by the Chineses, but in this incomparable soyle the Grape presents it selfe every where to your delighted prospect. And what shadow can there be of scruple that Wines well cultivated, and issuing from a rich Grape, will not be as commodious a Staple to that voluptuous and gluttonous Nation, who wanton away their wealth in banquets, as the Wines of France and Spaine are to the more Northerne and lesse abstenious Nations of Europe.

There needs no objection be made against this Staple; for the Southwest part of Virginia being once discovered, the Sea laid open and that passage compleat in all its numbers, the pleasure

of

of the commerce, the richnesse of returnes, and the extraordinary quicknes of the profit, will invite so many to come over and plant that commodious quarter of Virginia, that as we shall never labour with too numerous a multitude of inhabitants, so we shall not have any great occasion to complaine of the paucity of Planters.

Nor is Tobacco in those Indian seas (especially cured as in Virginia, and of that strength and excellency) a commodity of inconsiderable commerce, particularly if wee call to minde what gayne there is by the exchange for Indian commodities, so that any ordinary understanding may comprehend that although Tobacco should yeeld but three pence the pound in India, yet by way of barter with those Nations where the returne quadruples the value in England, the gaynes gotten by it might be very considerable.

But if we may beleeve Printed Relations (and the person delivering it so cleerely, is, in my opinion, worthy of all credit) Tobacco from Surat to Moco yeeld ten for one profit, returned in Eastridge feathers to England, you have six to one profit; but this is for those Planters who are so infected with that disease of the Countrey, that they cannot admit of any other Staple, though more gainefull and lesse laborious. Yet is not Tobacco without its virtues: for the Spaniard hath found out, besides the use of it in smoke, (or the smoky use) that the juice thereof (when greene) applyed to any wound cut, sore, and without any distinction, whether greene, festered, or cankered, will heale it speedily, and almost miraculously ; the leafe bruised or stamped, and applied to any bite or sting of a venemous quality, to any wound made by a poysoned arrow, the green leafe heated in hot ashes, and laed upon any part of the body afflicted with aches, will worke effects answerable to the most powerfull operations of Nature.

The Benefit and part of the Silke-worme mystery treated of.

BUT to show to the World that wee may equall the best of the Westerne Kingdomes in this noble mystery of Nature the Silke-worme: That France and Italy are much below this Mignon of Glory and Profit, the universally advantageous Virginia, wee shall upon those infallible demonstrations of Nature, make evident, having the clew of truth, reason, and modesty to direct us.

It

It will not be denied by any, whose forehead is not too brazen, that no Countrey is so proper for adventitions as its owne Native Commodities, the seeds of things suffer a deterioration by changing the propriety of that soile which was geniall to them, and the exact order of Nature suffers a diminution, if wee imagine any other Climate or Region more proper for the perfection of any thing, then where it is originally produced.

Tellier affirmes that this mystery of the Silke-worme hath not been experimented in Europe above a thousand yeares, being transmitted to our Climate out of the Asiatick World, in so much that Italy hath not beene above 200 yeares enriched with this industrious Creature, France received it from Italy, and it is observed, that the warmer the Region, by so much larger and stronger encrease and texture receive they from the labour of this admirable and naturall Weaver. France being of a colder temper then Italy, their Wormes are weaker, in the more Northerne part of that Kingdome from one ounce of seed they profit five or sixe pound of Silke increase, worth at the least 20s. *per* pound, in Languedock, and the warmer Provinces the same quantity is increased to 7, 8, or 9l. but in Brescia, of Calabria seede, they use usually to make eleaven or twelve pound of Silke from the same originall proportion.

The poore people in both those Kingdomes buy their Mulberry leaves to feede this profitable and industrious Spinner, and the very charge of those leaves amounts to a full halfe of all other their expences.

The nobility of Italy and France (the Grand Duke of Tuscany himselfe, descending into a part of this profit) make up a considerable part of their Revenue from their Trees, the Leaves of every one being valued according to their goodnesse and quality, from five shillings to twenty and upwards, so that divers make an income of three, four, five, sometimes a thousand pound, from the sole profit of their Mulberry trees.

The Grand Duke from the sale of his, rayses an income *communibus annis*, of sixty thousand Ducats.

Yet divers Gentlemen in Italy make a larger increase of profit, by setting out their Mulberry trees to necessitous people, for halfe the gaine arising from the worme so fed. Those poore contribute their seed, employ their labour, and are at all expences in bringing the silke to perfection ; yet notwithstanding when completed, the Gentleman who sets out his Trees, divides the moyety of the entire profit, for the hire of his Leaves only, yet are these people, maugre this difficulty, comfortable gayners.

And

And the same *Tellier* is bold to affirme, that *non obstante* the disagreeablenesse of the Country to that worme, in the Kingdome of France from the sole revenue now of Silke, arises a greater intrade then from their Corne, Oyle and Woad put together, which grow in that Kingdome in vast proportions. And another French Author affirmeth, that the benefit of the Silke-worme, (of which France hath had no triall till within these fifty yeeres) ariseth to four Millions *per annum*, sterling, and this he pretends to have all circumstances of truth and certainty, drawne from an exact computation to confirme it.

If France (an almost improper Countrey for this improvement) can rayse within the verge of fifty yeeres, so large and numerous a revenue, what shall we imagine Italy (a warmer Region, and by much more convenient, although not altogether Native for this inriching creature) may meerely upon this Staple returne in their Treasury, having besides the advantage of Climate, a hundred and fifty yeeres precedency in the mystery, and their seed more·strong, better fed, and less subject to diseases and casualties?

But Virginia a Countrey which Nature hath no lesse particularly assigned for the production, food, and perfection of this Creature then Persia or China, stored naturally with infinities of Mulberry-trees, some so large that the leaves thereof have by Frenchmen beene esteemed worth 5l. in which the indigenall and naturall Worme hath beene found as bigge as Wallnuts, and the using in the South thereof in admirable plenty and excellence; if this mystery were but duly followed, and industriously promoved, might be a Magazine for all the Westerne World, and singly in her selfe outvy France, Spaine, and Italy, in all their advantages collected.

Heere the Leaves are onely sold by nature, who requires no other satisfaction then industry to make use of her bounty. Timber to erect their Fabricks is provided, and costs no more then preparing a benevolent Sunne, and a Serene Sky, contributing their indulgence to its perfection. No narrow assignation of Ground (richer then the most fertile France or Italy can pretend to, or boast of) to plant those Trees on, if not neare enough to the setled Plantations; in briefe, all the conveniences imaginable to assist and advance this to the Noblest Commerce in the World, if neglect and sloth make us not ingratefull to our selves, and nature, by abusing our selves, by not using her bounty.

To further this happy designe, let us descend into an unequall comparison: Let us compare our most incomparable
Virginia,

Virginia, where the Mulberry and the Worme are aboriginall to Italy, where they are onely adventitious: Let us imagine our owne Worme of that strength and greatnesse onely equall to those of Brescia and Italy, where the usuall ofcome from sixe ounces of seede is 72. or at least 60 pound weight of Silke, and adhearing to this Parallell; let us see the apparency in the profit.

A man and a boy, if their hands be not sleeping in their pockets, will feede as many Wormes as come of sixe or eight ounces of seed till they be past their foure first sicknesses, and within some 14 dayes of spinning: Indeed the last 14 dayes require a more extraordinary diligence and attendance, a more frequent and carefull feeding, because in that time they conceive, gather, and store up the disposing matter from whence the Silke comes, which by an incomprehensible mystery of Nature, they after as it were vomit out of their mouthes, and spinne out of their bowells. At this more particular season, there is a necessity of adding the labour of three or foure helpes more (to which Women or Children are as proper as Men) which is an inconsiderable accession considering the gaine arising from it.

That you may know the reason why Women, Children, lame and impotent persons are as fitting to attend the last fourteene dayes, as Men, will appeare by their labour, which is nothing but to feede them within doores, cleanse, dry, and perfume their lodgings, with some strengthning, but not overstrong odour.

And as one skilfull in this noble mystery is sufficient for the employing, overseeing, and directing hundreds under him, so (the skill being rather experimentally to be taught, then built upon long and ambiguous precepts) he may bee able to perfect all those under him, within the five or six weekes time of their imployment in the full understanding the mystery. And the better to incourage both the teacher and learner of the mystery, the master should be invited by reward to be liberall in communicating his knowledge, and those under his instruction encouraged by arguments of honour and profit proposed to the best proficient, would disperse seeds of emulation and diligence, since every one would imploy himselfe seriously to engrosse and appropriate to himselfe the reputation and advantage in the victory.

And in boyes and children, disputations frequently set on foot, with some slight distinction of merit, would make all that are ingeniously disposed, quicken their observation and diligence, to gaine the credit of prelation. Though to take off all disincouragement

couragement or despayre, from those lesse apprehensive and docible, in this noble and gainefull Trade of Silke, there is no such absolute necessity layd upon them to be supersticiously and precisely curious in observing the Booke Rules, and written Precepts, that upon the omission or unpunctuall observation of any of those Precepts in hatching, lodging, feeding, and tending of the Silke-wormes, wee should imagine such minute deviations might occasion an improsperity or generall failing: for wee will admit something may be wanting either in materialls, accommodation, or precisenesse of knowledge; yet may the worke (a higher and irresistible cause not interrupting it) prosper and succeede, notwithstanding such defect, to the great contentment and gaine of them which keepe them.

Let us imagine it to be granted that the indigency of the person improving the incommodiousnesse of the place, or want of House-roome, which the Bookes exactly tye us to, be in many things preterregular (though such a supposition may fall upon any other part of the World more justly then Virginia, where all materialls and conveniency answer our exactest wishes) yet will dayly examples confirme us, that in Languedoc, Provence, and other parts of France, and as many in Spaine and Italy, amongst the common sort of that exaction tyred people, that one poore low-rooft Cottage, and one Roome in it is all the house extent they have to take their sleepe in, dresse their miserable dyet, and serve themselves of for use and retirement; yet does this industrious Creature (such are the blessings with which God rewards the sweat of Industry) thrive as happily (and sometimes answer labour with a greater felicity) as those which the curiosity of Richer persons fit with all commodiousnesse of Chamber feeding, and attending, which is a speaking encouragement that no man should despaire, but reposing a cheerefull confidence in the blessing of the Almighty, with this Resolution, that what ever meanes, what ever curiosity, art, or precept, may contribute towards the preparing and facilitation of a worke, yet the end, the event must depend on his eternall goodnesse to crowne it, and all our labours projected with never so great a Talent of humane wisdome and experience, must conclude with this never failing truth: That except the Lord build the house their labour is but lost that build it: Except the Lord keepe the City, the Watchman watches but in vaine. Wee must therefore lift up our hearts and eyes with thankefullnesse unto the Hills, unto the Monntaine of Israel, and Rock of *David*, from whence those streames of blessings must acknowledge their sole, their originall Fountaine,

which

which may serve as an admonition, that neither the whole, nor any part of the worke should be begunne without applying our devotions to him : Let it therefore be the Morning Omen to the worke, and the Evening auspice, Lord prosper the worke of our hands, prosper good Lord our handy workes. After the Reposall of this confidence in God; let him apply himselfe with his greatest industry and ability, with this comfort and assurance, that he cannot but make a considerable returne : Though wee should be much injurious to Art (the noble right hand and Midwife to Nature) if wee should deny a more promising probability of a riper and fuller gaine the more curious and observant he is in following all the approved experiments, Rules, directions, and precepts thereunto belonging.

But the chiefest aime and intention of those Rules are to illustrate the perfection of this Art, and to informe your knowledge, and better your future experience and preventionall care, if any misadventure arrive, or miscarriage in the Silke-wormes, or if they prosper not equally this yeare with the last ; for by inspection upon them you may understand the cause and reason of such misadventure, and with it the remedy ; and this also takes away all dispaire or disincouragement for men, commonly men till they are convinced in the naturall cause of a disaster or failing attribute, all such mischances to Nature, or else impute the non-thriving to their owne misfortune by a ridiculous opinion that they are not ordained to be fortunate in this or that Mystery, so freequently does Fortune incurre the blame of humane neglect or ignorance.

Besides wee are to imprint in our knowledge, that no Rules can have so much of generality and exactnesse, which will not admit of deviations arising from some particular and variable circumstances. Wee must not therefore conforme the nature of the Climate to our Rules, but our Rules to it, in which wee must resume to your deliberation how, and in what one Climate differs from another, how the constitution of this yeare varies from the next, or the precedent, the immediocrities of heate, cold, drought, and moisture, serenity, or mists, &c. The manner of their lodgings, the quality of the winde to be admitted or excluded : To temper a season inclining to a preternaturall coolenesse with an artificiall heate, to refresh and infrigidate the Aire in times of immoderate heate, by admitting the cooling Aire and Windes proceeding from a cooler Quarter, and this to be observed with a more particular care ; when they spinne their Silke, that Creature then being very obnoxious to be stifled with too much heate.

There

There must be likewise a providentiall regard in a moist sea-son, that the Mulberry leaves be carefully dryed after their gathering, before they be administred for food to the Silke-worme: But if the season pertake more of drought it will be wisedome to let the leaves lye and shade a little after their gathering, that they may have them coole and refreshing, and in seasons of temperature and continued droughts, it may be very requisite to water the Roots of the Mulberry-tree, which will be a refreshing to the leaves, and this is usually practised in Spaine; especially if the Mulberry-tree be seated in a hot or dry ground, which otherwise must not be so prescribed without particular caution.

Nor is it below our consideration to weigh the condition of the place in which the Mulberry is planted, if in a sower foule or wet soile to collect what inconvenience that food may bring unto your worme, and therefore if your necessity will admit it to avoyd such wholly, if not to use them with such qualifica-tions as may make them least offensive.

After having regard to the nature of the ground your Tree receives its juce from, the quality of the season, in which you gather them : it falls next to your consideration to compare the kinde and nature of the Tree, together with the kinde and na-tuae of their seed, worme, and silke, and directing your selfe by an exact observation of particular circumstances, so to make exceptions, and to order every thing with judgement and discre-tion thereafter, that your Bookes and experience may by that meanes walke hand in hand together.

But time and observations will affoord you many experiments, out of which perhaps some more rules of Art may be framed, in divers particulars, more consenting to the Country and Cli-mate of Virginia. Which finding, after good triall thereupon made, it will become the reputation of a good Patriot in gene-rall, and a good Master of a family in particular, to digest them into such a regular order and method, that the publication there-of may be a common benefit to all, and a private memoriall to particulars.

For since in Persia and China it does not fall under likeli-hood, that they can oblige themselves to observe all particulars in its strictest limitation, where such an infinite quantity of silke passeth through the hands of the people, it is very agreeable to reason that in a Climate of the same nature and parallell, name-ly Virginia, there may be rules found out of far lesse brevity, and more pertinency, then have yet been considered or published.

And yet where all these Rules are curiously observed, they
make

make not onely in Spaine and Italy, but in the colder parts of France a far greater gaine (the quantity of adventure and time considered) by this chargeably feeding of Silk-wormes, then by any other commodity whatsoever.

But to avoid that inconvenience of fetching leaves a far off, or attending the growth of your owne Mulberries, or that necessity which makes the poorer sort of our owne miserable people to lodge them in that Roome which is their Kitchin, their Chamber, their all. With what ease and conveniency may there be a house set up in the middle of a Grove of Mulberries, naturally growing, where the Silkewormes, in a dry Cabinet of Boords, after the maner of Sicily, may be kept (described more largely in the Bookes which treat of this Silkeworme, then can bee expected in this paper) set up with stones in it, in case the Countrey and season require it, eyther to correct the ill sents, or (if so be they are seated in cold, moyst, or shady places, of which your owne sense and experience will quickly acquaint you) to give the ayre a temper and qualification, which if not prevented, may destroy your worke by killing the Silkeworme.

And this Lodge built for them, the season of the yeere will invite your selfe and family (I mean such part of your family as you assigne to this worke) to lodge there also, the time being at the most but six weekes, and for the first moneth, one third of your family will be sufficient to feed them, but the last 14. dayes; the other 2. thirds will be requisit that the wormes may bee more often and plentifully fed the well feeding at that time contributing much to their strength and perfection, and consequently to the improving your expected silke, both in quantity and quality.

That all may be invited and courted to this undertaking, in this glorious Countrey, Nature hath left us destitute of no materialls. To erect these slight silken lodgings, will be no more expences, then your labour; nor is that any greater, then to cut out some posts and studdes, fit them, and set them up, then to cleave and saw out small quarters, rafters, plankes, pales, and boards, to make and set up the sides of the house, in stead of more substantiall walls, and to cover the roofe in stead of Tile. For the effecting of all which with the lesser trouble, that Countrey affords abundance of Woods, which will runne out, slit, and cleave into long lengths and breadths, which by the directnesse of the Ground will rive in a manner, as if they had beene sawne for the worke. All which must be so close layd, joyned, and nayled together, the one still lapt over the other, that no Winde or Raine may penetrate therein to offend that laborious Creature, and this may easily be prevented,

if

if such chinkes and open places as you shall discover bee stopped up with Lome, Clay, and Lime, of which materialls in those Countreyes you will finde no want. And to this purpose the Indian Mats, and the like things may be made good use of in this way, which will be sure to keepe out Winde and perhaps Raine : But to these things your owne inventions, *pro re nata*, will abundantly furnish you with matter of preventing casualties : Nor will it bee unseasonable to repeat the extraordinary convenience of Saw-mills, which in this case will be in a high degree serviceable to you, and of this the whole Colony will be beneficially sensible in boards, Plankes, housing, Silkworm-lodgings, Timber, shipping, and all particular kinde of uses.

And this once erected, with what speed may such a house be clapped up together, with a few nailes one lopping over another, either long like a Bowling-Alley, that the functions of the Family may be distinct, and no offensive heat or sent disturbe the Worme in his curious operations.

Or being in doubt of surprisall, some Families going into the Woods together may equally joyne together, and those woodden houses (still observing that the Roomes where the wormes are may be set end and end together, that so the Kitchins and their lodgings may be still the two extreames) may be cast into the forme of a Fort which pallisadoed, and your house sentinelled by halfe a dozen of good Dogges, wilbe a sufficient defence against all the Natives of the Countrey.

And this may be in case they worke not in common, which if by compact they agree upon, the Lodging for the wormes may be cast in the middle of such a circle, the Timber houses round about shading them from over much heat, wind or moisture, and the necessary fires there made, will throughly cleere the ayre of all vapours and mists which may disorder this innocent Spinner. The Silke Harvest ready, and the encrease brought to a just estimation : The Cohabitors may according to the agreement made betwixt them, returne with their Dividends, and this removall into the Woods will have the same nature of content which the Citizens take in a time of vacation and City wearinesse (Citizens being never so weary as when they have no worke) to visite the delights of the Countrey, though with different ends ; since these in their Voyages of pleasure expend, the other both save and encrease their stock and treasure. These Boards (the worke ended) being taken downe are serviceable for seaven yeares together, and easily erected or renewed.

I am not altogether of advice, that the Indians be hired to assist you in these Remoter Workes, as sensible how apt they and the Divell their Tutor may be to embrace an occasion of being treacherous; but if they could be brought to worke by Parties (well watched and Spyes amongst themselves set over them) in the middest of our most populous Plantations, with their Wives and Children, who will easily runne through this curious, but not heavy labour and may be sufficient pawnes for the Indian fidelity, if cunningly divided, they would be very serviceable in this kinde for a small Reward, and peradventure might be made great use of for this worke heereafter by undertaking it themselves, which may be manifested for these Reasons.

1. First, the Indian is naturally curious and very ingenious, which they shew in all their works and imitations: the only thing that frights them from bringing any work to perfection, is the labour attending it.

2. But to feed his curiosity, there is nothing in the world more proper then this curious atome of Nature the Silkeworme: to see this untaught Artist spin out his transparent bowels, labour such a monument out of his owne intralls, as may be the shame, the blush of Artists, such a Robe that Solomon in all his glory might confesse the meannesse of his apparell, in relation to the workemen, cannot but bring them to admiration ; and that those spirits whose thoughts are of a higher wing then ordinary, may bee convinced of a divine power óf the hand of God in the Creation: which gaynd upon him, it will not be impossible to drive him to an acknowledgement of Redemption, if private ends or any other respect then that to Gods glory, possesse not those who should cover a multitude of sinnes, by winning a soule to his Creator, and forcing him from the jawes of his Destroyer.

3. In this curiosity there is little or no labour (a thing which they abhorre) their women and children will bee sufficient to goe through with it: and if they could but be brought to it, our Trade with them for silke would be of greater consequence, then all their Furs or other commodities put together.

4. By this meanes it were possible to fasten Cloaths upon them, which if once it were effected, that which Mr. *Bullocke* excellent patly calls, The Universall not of Nature, Ambition would cement them to a more orderly course of life, and one still striving to outvie the other in bravery of habits: there would be no labour under Heaven like this, to reduce them to civility, the toyle thereof being inconsiderable, and the profit great to him in respect of his now trifling Merchandise : and

to

to us by trading with them, might bee returned for 5s. the pound at the most in commodities.

5. By this means would he be brought to plant great quantities of Mulberry trees round about his Plantation, which according to his constant inconstancy, evermore shifting, would necessarily, our owne numbers increasing, fall into our hands and possession, or if he should against the tide of his nature abide by them, yet a very inconsiderable trifle would buy the propriety from him.

6. The Silkeworme harvest lighting at such a season of the year, wherein he by improvidence hath wasted all his Breadcorne, at which time he usually retires into the Woods to seeke a thinne subsistence, by the allurement of this great profit he would undoubtedly stay at his Plantation, and allow us a share in his increase of Silke, for such provision of Maiz as would maintaine him, and this would be a large accession of profit to the English.

7. Admitting Virginia in its whole extent from *Cape Henry* Southward (as a worke so easily compassed, and such profit ensuing thereupon, especially to the Weroances or Reguli, who have many Wives, Slaves, and Children, would hardly faile from being a universall labour) to containe in all thirty thousand people, of which the fourth part or more men, if this Staple be followed by them, and our vigilance preventing any Traffick of other Nations with them, it will yeeld the Colony of course a trade with them worth cleare a hundred thousand pound *per annum.*

Neither doe I comprehend a sufficient Reason why in so happy a Climate as that of Virginia ; there may not be a double Silke Harvest : This I am sure of, that there are secrets in Nature of retardation as well as acceleration of Springs, and both being industriously brought to the experiment, the acceleration anteceeding the first Spring, and the retardation postvening the latter by three weekes, (which may easily be effected by election and distinction of ground to plant in) and at the latter end of the Harvest the seeds being disposed and ripened for production, will without doubt produce an effect answerable to the most inestimable profit intended by it.

That the election of Ground may doe this, wee may see by freequent examples betwixt things well cultivated, and that which is never transplanted from its first wildnesse, and there are many presidents round about us, where in one and the same Towne, one and the same fruit have oftentimes three Weekes distance of time betwixt their unequall maturity ; the naturall

warmenesse

warmenesse or coldnes of the Ground occasioning the advance
or procrastination of fruits according to its severall disposition.

Nor can such a course be any interruption to Harvest or Vintage, both comming much after the season of the Silke worme,
though I should (in submission to better judgement) conceive
that with transplantation of trees (such as they would have
come later then ordinary, for that purpose being loosed from the
Ground neare upon the ascent of their sap would spring for
that season according to their expectation later then is usuall,
and the next yeare its novelty of ground having made it wanton
will come much earlier, and more improved then those whose
fixure to the place of its first pullulation keepes its selfe to its
former constancy, and by this meanes the later Harvest would
not be at the most three Weekes time after the (usuall) income
of the first.

And without doubt the Chineses and Persian could not vend
such vast quantities of Silke, with which they farshion so huge
a part of the World with one single Harvest, which though wee
are at present ignorant of, yet what should discourage us from
delivering such conjectures to a tryall, since the examen of it is
not without probability, nor the discovery without an extraordinary certainety of profit?

Those who will object that notwithstanding 200 years practice Italy hath not discovered this mystery, or if discovered,
found it destitute of successe, may be pleased to receive this
Answer: That there is an immense disproportion betwixt the
happyest Region of Italy, and the South of the excellent Virginia. Italy (and that annually) is subject much to inclemency of
Winters, in respect of our more temperate Maiden, where
Snows and black Swans are alike Prodigies ; the cold there is
rather like a Phletomy to tame the Plethorick abundance of
Springs, then dead it : Nor are the Springs of Italy so early as
ours in that Climate, and the Mulberry shooting forth later then
all other Trees by much, may by this meanes of transplantation
and heat of soile, be equall with the first, and by that early
apparence give day-light to this and other more abstruse
Magnalia.

I have insisted so much the longer upon this Mystery of the
Silkworme, because (if it were handled by a better pen, judgement, and ability) it is every way noble and sublime, so much
worthy the knowledge, not onely for the benefit (which extraordinary rich how ever) but for the admiration of Nature, who
hath abreviated all the Volums of her other Miracles into this
her

her little, but exact Epitome, like that Artist who contracted the whole body of Iliads and Odysses into a Nutshell.

Besides what wee have sayd of Silke wee shall find the Indian profitable to himselfe, and as in the Staple of Wines, of which when he has received the whole knowledge, wee cannot make the least tittle of doubt, but he will with all eagernesse prosecute it : First, because it concernes his belly, to which no people under Heaven are more indulgent; and secondly, his Wife and Children who plant his Corne may take the charge of the Vineyard with not much more labour. But that which turnes to our advantage is, that the Indian communicating the knowledge of the Grape to his Neighbours, and they transmitting it all along as far as New Spain, will stir up the Spanish jealousie to interdict all Viti-culture amongst them, and as far as the extent of his power can fathome to prosecute severely all such Natives as shall make it a subject of their industry to the prejudice of Spaine. This must of necessity make strong combinations and leagues against the Spanish Tyranny, which though they are not of themselves able to shake off, yet will the Spanyard feare to extend himselfe further (except in such strength as at present his condition denies him) knowing the Indians unextinguishable thirst of Revenge, and his laying hold of all opportunities to put in execution, with all the powers of his understanding cruelty and malice.

And thus shall the Spanyard in case he attempts our supplantation be constantly discovered by the siding Indian, and if there be a necessity to prevent his malice, by turning his designe upon his owne head, infinite occasion of intelligence may wee have from the enraged Native, how to attaque him in his strongest security, where either the distance or impassability of the way will make him confident and carelesse.

Further use may be made of the Native in fishing after Pearle, to which if wee allure him by a constant Trade with him for them, his owne profit will quickly enlighten his desire of more, and that desire quicken his industry.

That Virginia affordes multitude of Pearles, Mr. *Lane* is sufficient to give publick information, where he tells us a Relation delivered to him of a Weroance, who had so great quantity of Pearle, and did so ordinarily take the same, as that not onely his owne skinnes that he weareth, and the better sort of his Gentlemen and Followers are set with the sayd Pearle ; but also his beds and houses are garnished with them, and that he hath such quantity of them that it is wonder to see : These are Mr. *Lanes* words exactly.

Nor is there any difficulty in the discovery of this, or ingross-

ing

ing the Trade; especially since wee are the Masters of the Countrey, and if any other Nation should attempt to partake in the benefit of our Trade, the strength of Virginia is at present such as may repell by violence, all Forraigne incroachments upon their trade and livelyhood.

The Indians unanimously consent that twenty two miles beyond the Falls, is a Rocke of Chrystall, and this they evidence by their arrowes very many whereof are headed with it. And that 3 dayes journey from thence, is a Rocke or Hill of Silver Oare. Beyond which, over a ledge of Hills, by a concurrent Relation of all the Indians, is the Sea, which can be no other but that Sea which washes the shore of China, &c.

That this report of a great Sea Southwest beyond the Mountains, cannot have the least of fiction or confederacy, since all the Indians from Canada to Florida, doe unjarringly agree in the Relation, is obvious to the meanest apprehension.

The discovery whereof, if we fall upon it by degrees, will bee a worke of no long time or difficulty, but the unexpressible profit and glory of the action, will rayse the noble head of this above example Countrey to such a high Zenith of wealth, power, and lustre, that it will be reputed a very remarkable degree of felicity to any Nation which shall reach to such a Verticall point of glory, as to bee reputed but our second in these most noble considerations.

By this meanes what wealth can there be in those richest provinces of the World, in those Countries which Nature created for her Cabinets of excellency, which we shall not discover? What discover without a power of Appropriation? What opulency does China teeme with which shall not be made our owne by the Midwifry, by the Juno Lucina of this virtuall passage? This by a happy transmigration, by an innocent Magick will convert that Countrey, (which by a swelling denomination, yet without not some pretence of Reason its Natives call by a Title signifying all under Heaven) into our Maid of admiration and envy Virginia. Her Silke-worm shall spinne for Carolana, her Cloth of Gold be weaved for Roanoak. The English name shall keepe company with the Sunne, and those Nations who owe him a particular adoration shall honour it as the next thing sacred. The Easterne Nations oppressed with the slavery of those illustrious horseleeches their princes, will come under our shadow, and by a thicke repayre to our most glorious and happy Mayden, live with us in that liberty, which Nature in their Creation intended to the noblest of his creatures Mankind. And by this recourse all those curiosities of Art, in which those Easterne Nations transcend Europe, will bee conveyed to us
with

with their persons. Cattell and Horse in which they abound, will be sold to us for nothing, for European trifles, whilest the more necessary Staples of this our Westerne World, will be sold at advantages not convenient to be mentioned. The voyage short, easie, rich, and pleasant. No doubling of the Line, no calentures, scurvies, or other longpassage diseases, to affright or distast the laborious Seaman : whereas now the enfeebling and destroying of Mariners is almost an unavoidable consequence of those long and dangerous, rather circumferences then voyages.

But lest we should sing a Pæan before a victory, it will not bee unworthy our labour to discourse what meanes may be used in this Discovery. Which it should misse in its prosecution, (for which fayling there is not the least shadow of probability) yet might carry a vast profit to recompence all your paynes and expences.

That it must not bee attempted at the first heat, but must have more recourses then one to the fire of a Triall, will bee made apparent by these reasons.

First, the inconveniency or non feysibility of carrying so much provison as will serve the Discoverers, whose number, in my opinion, cannot bee lower then two hundred, if wee let slide into our deliberation the many unknowne Nations, through whose territories we are to make our passage, and which by common estimation, are much more numerous in the Inland, then Marine Countreyes.

Next, admit wee undertake and compasse it with such a number, yet the discovery not being capable of secresie amongst such a multitude of undertakers, the publick resentment of such a felicity approaching, not suffering people to be silent; wee should have this arrive to the Spanyards knowledge, who will roule all stones under Heaven to dispossesse or prepossesse, and indeed the danger his Peru, Chili and Philippines, by such seating, may lie obnoxious to, will adde spurres to his inclination to prevent us, which till wee bee in a condition to resist, may be effected with our absolute ruine.

The safest way therefore is, by degrees to steal upon the design, and take our way thither, by ceasing of places of advantage, very frequently found in that Country, which wee may progressionaly fortifie at every twenty or five and twenty miles distance, and to these places we may constantly send supplies of victualls and ammunition, not only for the men there Garrisond, but for our owne reception and maintenance in the Discovery : and these men standing continually upon their guard, may (I meane those most remote) by conference with the Indians, dis-

cover

cover with much ease, of what distance, what accesse, what harbours, what frequentation, and by what people the neighbour Sea consists of ; to take with them exemplars of all Mineralls, Drugges, Dies, Colours, Birds and Beasts, drawne to the life in colours, which (by an invitation of reward) will be a surer meanes of discovery, (if any such be) then by multitudes of people, whose number commonly (as in the example of *Fernando Soto* in Florida) hastens no other discovery, but that of unavoydable famine, and being usually, either through necessity, or a disordred manner of living irregular and ungoverned, fright the inhabitants from all commerce and conference or else make them join in a confederacy to abuse and remove them by telling their unwelcome Company, golden lies, and miracles of Countreys farther distant, where they are likely to find small satisfaction for their covetousnes or hunger.

Reason and experience will condemne us of folly, if wee should refuse to profit by commendable examples, though proceeding from Enemies or Friends suspected : It will be therefore an incitement irreproveable to commend to our owne imitation the Custome which the industrious Spanyard practiseth in his designe of discoveries : Every one of the associates carry a little horne about their necks in such journeys, by which meanes if the errour of the night or thickenesse of the Woods occasion any separation betwixt them, or an Ambuscado of Enemies make the passage doubtfull, by winding of that Horne, presently notice is given to the rest, who upon receiving the sound give the first winder notice of their residence, to which they may repaire, or testifie their apprehension and readinesse to prevent all hostile stratagems.

The same indefatigable Nation in their passage over Rivers, presently make themselves light Canoas after the Indian mode, with which entring themselves and swimming their Horses (whose heads they keepe above water by a coller fastened to the Boat) they overcome difficulties of currents, which to any other but those seeme insuperable, and indeed their labour in this kinde show them of admirable Resolution and Constancy.

Though wee may entertaine grounds of hope and confidence, that this discovery of the South Sea may be made without any tedious Land-journey, since it is certain that from the great confluence of Waters in the Gulfe of St. Laurence, foure mighty Rivers receive their sourse, the first whereof pouring it selfe North into Canada, another running Eastward into the Sea called Hunsons River, the third running Westward into the Maine are already discovered, but the fourth upon which wee

have

have reason to fixe high expectation bending Southward to Florida, washes all the backside of Virginia, and may in all probability discharge it selfe into the South Ocean, which if it suit with our conjectures, Virginia will have by that meanes a double accession of security and convenience.

For our security it will be a naturall bar betwixt us and the jealous Spanyard, who if he should injustly continue the possession of our Florida, which is indisputably English; yet thus divided from us by a vast River full of Islands, and places convenient to command the Channell fortified and maintained by our Nation, he is too full of providence and caution to attaque us, if once in so good a posture.

For the conveniency which sufficiently speakes it selfe the ease of transportation by water, and all in our owne Chanell, the saving of Land charges, and probability of a more speedy passage, are prespicuous arguments to commend it.

And to confirme the probabilities of this passage by the Lake the more strongly, the Indians of Canada confessed to *James Cartier* that it is but a Moneths sayling, from thence to go to a Land where Cynamon and Cloves are gathered. Others told the same person, that from the place where they left their Pinnace, there is a River which goeth South-West, from whence there is a whole Moneths sayling to go to a certain Land, where there is neither Ice nor Snow seene, where the Inhabitants doe continually War one against the other, where there is great store of Orenges, Almonds, Nuts, and Apples, with many other sorts of Fruits. What ever beliefe other men bestow upon this Relation, I know not; but truely in such a generall concordance of Reports, where there can be no roome left for confederacy or designe, to be perswaded of the truth therein, cannot have any vitious tincture of facility or credulity.

But it is time to remit these high and noble atchievements to the prosecution of those who have more power and ability, who may give such a discovery the honour of their names, and transfer a perpetuall illustrious memory to posterity, we shall onely suppose it faisible and hope the effects will answer such supposition.

Which if it should faile, why may not Virginia in her future felicity of Silke be a new China and Persia to Europe? why may not all the spicery of the East flourish with an equall successe in this our most justly tempered Climate? already can Virginia boast of Cinamon, which if transplanted might not be inferiour unto any? why may not the Cloves perfume Virginia with as aromatick redolency as the Philipine Gardens.

Our

Our aire is more serene, better tempered then theirs, nor have we any more sense of Winter to hinder the ascent of sap then the Moluccians, if it be any thing more harsh in cold, yet is it but a check to a peradventure too forward Spring. What multitude of flowers have our late Gardens in England seen non native to this soyle or Climate? Fruits thought solely proper to Italy and Spaine flourish here to the envy of those Countries, who see often times the Colonies in a happier degree of prosperity then the Mother, for Fruit and Flowers.

But these designements must be the Daughters of time, curiosity and industry, to whom a way may be made passable, and easie, by that uncabinetting and deciphring of Nature, Garden Philosophy, what harsh disposition in the World will not be lenified and refined by these curious conclusions? *Dioclesian* could postpose the science of governing Mankinde to the knowlege of managing his Scions, to see those Plants grow up, which his own laureld hand had set, watred and attended, and accord·ingly flourish, was in a manner the production of so many Children, who in this have the advantage, that their florescence is not subject to selfe-deprivation, give them but an acceptable ground, a bounteous Aire, and an arriding Sunne and they answer the most exact desires of the Setter or Ingrafter; but Children, let them have all the Auxiliares of a full Fortune, warmth of education, and heat of encouragement, by some private disease of the genius, by some secret malignity in nature, or its right hand custome, seldome or neuer thrive according to the wishes of the Parent, they are either too ranke with insolence, too much parched with rashnesse, or withered with infamy and luxury, that those which planted them instead of delight in that which they esteemed their Masterpeece, have nothing but a Spring of indignation, or an Autumn of Melancholly to answer their expectation, and are so far from contentment at their groweth that they would have reckoned it amongst the Smiles of their fortunes, that no warmth of theirs had contributed to their production, no indulgence to their continuance and education.

These allurements are for those whose delights onely are interested and devoted to this retired activity; but those who looke further will finde (that which is rarely or never contingent to other contentments) this pleasure to be attended with an inestimable profit, and one of the most certaine returnes in nature: But this fertility-labouring Countrey, especially in its Southerne beauties, in its Roanoak excellencies, like to a Princesse, all compos'd of Bounty, suffers no addresse to be made unsatisfied.

Gentle

Gentle Winters to court your seed, warme Springs to marry them to perfect Masculine ripenesse, nothing but ingratitude and indiligence to delay or divert its liberality, hitherto (like those confined Virgins in a barbarous Seraglio) it hath suffered the imputation or injury of sterility by a non-complacency in its Savage Amourists, the abundance of perfection having put them into a satiety or incapacity of enjoyment.

The truth of this being abundantly manifest, an apparent profit and delight inviting the able and industrious ; necessity must be the next argument to those whose Poverty can pleade no excuse for their indiligence ; yet this laborious necessity is not so ingratefull as in England, and in other more thick-peopled Countries, what ever you sweat for in this bounteous Region, is crowned with a recompenee amazing your expectation ; such things as make poverty and life wearisome, contempt of, or impossibility of any melioration to their condition are things heere never charged upon honest indigence, or denyed to a commendable industry, nor can they palliate their sleepe and sloth with a pretence of wanting materialls to worke upon, or plead that such things as should employ them must be first had out of England, since there is enough abundantly and naturally in that unpresidented Countrey to employ their industry, to enrich their labour.

Though Silke-grasse is unquestionably a Staple which will bee Neighbour to the profit of the Silke-worme, though the naturall Hempe-flagge may be a Merchandize in time equal to English Flax, though the Sarsaparilla be an extraordinary vendible Commodity, though Pipestaves be so beneficiall, that with not many drops an extraordinary workeman may make his labour worth sixty pounds *per annum*.

Though he has fish there, and in such abundance that the attending diligently upon two seasons, onely returnes him a Reward of one hundred pound sterling in Sturgion, Salmon, Herings, Mackrell : Pot-ashes a rich and never decaying Staple, &c. Yet since against this an objection may be made what course they may take for their provisionall subsistence. Those who apprehend such doubts will be pleased to receive this answer, in which if they are sensible of Reason they cannot faile to receive satisfaction.

There is no man will ever be denyed the loane of Corne for his house-spending, and seed till the Harvest ; if he be a single man he may prepare as much ground if cleared, and set as large quantitie of Corne for his owne spending and repayment of what borrowed, in two dayes space as will abundantly suffice him twelve Moneths.

Admit

Admit there be no cleared Ground, yet if he but unbarke the Trees one foot round after the Indian mode to prevent the shade occasioned by the leaves, which such unbarking quite destroyes, the Corne (set betwixt those Trees) will thrive and prosper exceedingly, and their Ground thus prepared will last seaven or more yeares successively, and this worke cannot last him above five dayes at the longest.

If he have a Family, his Wife and Children will be able to beare part in that labour, and many others.

For Provision of flesh, if he can use his peece he may, even at his labour in the Woods, have opportunity of killing Venison, Hares, Wild-foule (in their season innumerable) and Fish, of which the Rivers are all times plentifully furnished, and of great delicacy ; if in all this abundance he is yet apprehensive of Famine, wee shall refer him to the number of those who are afraid to be starved for meat in a Cooks shop.

Besides what a small summe of money will buy your Cattell, and Swine in Virginia ? Whose feeding costs them nothing but thankes to God, who has spread that superficies of that noble Countrey with perpetuall fruit and verdure. Poultry in infinite variety and plenty, the forbearance of whose encrease for a small terme of years will make them so numerous, that they may alwayes have a full table.

The West-Indie Potatoe (by much more delicate and large then what wee have heere growing) besides that it is a food excellently delicious and strongly nourishing, fixes himselfe wherever planted, with such an irradicable fertility, that being set it eternally grows : of this an extraordinary pleasing and strong drinke may be composed.

Nor is the Maiz lesse commendable for bread then malting, of both which in its use it affordeth a peculiar goodnesse and convenience : And I am much to learne how a poore man can in justice complaine of want, when he is as it were besieged with such plenty : This for provision may abundantly satisfie, but if he can be content to forbeare debauches and profusenesse for the first three yeares he may by any of the meanes aforesaid arrive to such a condition of thriving, that he may allow himselfe a large latitude of expences (that first three yeares once expired) without much empairing his fortunes.

But since all men either by constitution of age, oppression of yeares, or different education, are unable or improper for the Fish-net or Hatchet, I shall offer them a way which may be lesse laborious and peradventure more gainefull ; yet before I descend to this, I must take leave by digression to enlarge something which I have already hinted on, namely the benefit of transplantation.

The

The removing and transposition of Wild Plants, doth with an experimented happinesse wonderfully mitigate and engentile their lesse noble nature ; whether (as an Author delivers it very elegantly) it be by reason that the nature of Plants, as of men, is desirous of Novelty and peregrination, or because that at their parting from their former grounds they leave their that ranke wildenesse virulency and ill quality from the Forest, where is first rooted the greatefull novelty and allurement of a well cultivated soyle makes it receive a new by exiling it from the old savagenesse and indomestication of its first seat and nature.

Since then the removing of Wild Plants addes so much to their improvement and melioration confirmed by naturall Reason and unerring experience : Why may not the diligent labour by removeall and transposing this excellent Staple of Silke grasse, make it thrive equally in greatnesse and goodnesse, there needs no more art to be used then that of comparing the soile (transplantations into worse grounds being naturally improsperous) and though there appeare now somewhat of trouble (though nothing of labour) in peeling the silky skinne of, yet that it may be broken as Flaxe or cleared by some Instrument (the Commodity richly rewarding the nobility of any invention) to this purpose ; time and further experience will no doubt to the publick enriching of the Colony and this Nation make apparent. In this any one which is not sworne a servant to ease and sloth, may with a small toile reape a considerable profit.

Next, what will not those Vines produce if well husbanded after their transplantation, and in this most delightfull labour the gain is so apparent that almost the blindest judgement may perceive it.

Orenges, Lemons, Pine-aples, Plantanes, Peaches, Apricocks, Peares, Aples, in a word all sort of excellent Fruits will grow there in full perfection : you may sleepe whilst they are growing, after their setting or engrafting, there needes no more labour but your prayers, that they may prosper, and now and then an eye to prevent their casualities, wounds or diseases.

Sugars, Indigos, Cotton, and Ginger, require a greater industry ; but if wee consider the difference betwixt the two Climates of Barbadoes and Virginia, the immoderate heat of the first and the exact temper of the other, the labour though it may require as frequent handling, yet is by much lesse toylesome.

In a word, if a man be yet timerous of a thriving condition in this Countrey ; I shall with his pardon believe him, distrustfull of Gods providence ; or if he be so vitiously disposed as to
hope

hope after a Land where he may enjoy an undisturbed plenty without the sweat of his browes, the Maps are so extreamely deficient in the description of such a Countrey, that I must desire him to looke for a new World and Kingdome, for such an easie accommodation.

If any make an Objection why this Countrey stored with all these Riches, furnished with all these Staples, hath so long held downe her head in the lownesse of a desperate condition? Why being capable to crowne her browes with Garlands of Roses and plenty, she sate desolate amongst the Willowes of neglect and poverty? Let them but recall their Memory, how by the prevailency of *Gondamore* the Corporation was dissolved, their patent cancelled, to which if wee adde the cooperation of the Indian treachery in their first massacre, they will cease their wonder at its languishing condition, and convert it to a full admiration, how that Colony could ever raise her endangered head out of those Gulfes of distraction, in which the Gold of Spaine, the disincouragement of the Court, the discontent of the better sort of Planters, and the desperate negligence of the more inconsiderable had in humane opinion irrecoverably involved her.

But the incomparable Virgin hath raised her dejected head, cleared her enclouded reputation, and now like the Eldest Daughter of Nature expresseth a priority in her Dowry; her browes encircled with opulency to be believed by no other triall, but that of experience, her unwounded wombe full of all those Treasuries which indeere Provinces to respect of glory, and may with as great justice as any countrey the Sunne honours with his eye-beames, entitle her self to an affinity with Eden, to an absolute perfection above all but Paradize.

And this those Gentlemen to whom she vouchsafes the honour of her Embraces, when by the blessings of God upon their labours sated with the beauty of their Cornefield, they shall retire into their Groves checkered with Vines, Olives, Mirtles, from thence dilate themselves into their Walkes covered in a manner, paved with Orenges and Lemmons, whence surfeited with variety, they incline to repose in their Gardens upon nothing lesse perfumed then Roses and Gilly-flowers. When they shall see their numerous Heards wanton with the luxury of their Pasture, confesse a narrownesse in their Barnes to receive their Corne, in bosomes to expresse fully their thankefulnesse to the Almighty Authour of these blessings, will chearefully confesse: Whilst the Incomparable Roanoak like a Queene of the Ocean, encircled with an hundred attendant Islands, and

the

the most Majestick Carolana shall in such an ample and noble gratitude by her improvement repay her Adventurers and Creditors with an Interest so far transcending the Principall.

※※※※※※※※※※※※※※※※※※※※※※※※※※※

A valuation of the Commodities growing
and to be had in *Virginia :* valued in the year, 1621.

And since those Times improved in all more or lesse, in some ⅓, in others ½, in many double, and in some treble.

IRon, ten pounds the Tun.
Silke Coddes, two shillings six pence the pound.
Raw silk, 13s. 4d. the pound, now at 25s. and 28. *per* pound.
Silke grasse to be used for Cordage, 6d. the pound : but we hope it will serve for many better uses, and so yeeld a far greater rate, whereof there can never be too much planted. Of this Q. *Elizabeth* had a silk Gowne made.
Hemp, from 10s. to 22s. the hundred.
Flax, from 22s. to 30s. the hundred.
Cordage, from 20s. to 24s. the hundred.
Cotton wooll, 8d. the pound.
Hard pitch, 5s. the hundred.
Tarre, 5s. the hundred.
Turpentine, 12s. the hundred.
Rozen, 5s. the hundred.
Madder crop, 40s. the hundred : course madder, 25s. the hundred.
Woad, from 12s. to 20. the hundred.
Annice seeds, 40s. the hundred.
Powder Sugar, Panels, Muscavadoes and whites, 25s. 40. and 3l. the hundred.
Sturgeon, and Caveare, as it is in goodnesse.
Salt, 30s. the weight.
Mastick, 3s. the pound.
Salsa Perilla wild, 5s. the hundred.
Salsa Perilla domestick, 10s. the hundred.
Red earth Allenagra, 3s. the hundred.
Red Allum, called Carthagena Allum, 10s. the hundred.
Roach Allum, called Romish Allum, 10s. the hundred.
Berry graine, 2s. 6d. the pound : the powder of graine, 9s. the pound : it groweth on trees like Holly berries.

Masts

Masts for shipping, from 10s. to 3l. a peece.

Pot-ashes, from 12s. the hundred, to 14. now 40. and 35s, the hundred.

Sope-ashes, from 6s. to 8s. the hundred.

Clapboard watered, 30s. the hundred.

Pipe staves, 4l. the thousand.

Rape-seed oyle, 10l. the tun, the cakes of it feed Kine fat in the Winter.

Oyle of Walnuts, 12l. the tun.

Linseed oyle, 10l. the tun.

Saffron, 20s. the pound.

Honey, 2s. the gallon.

Waxe, 4l. the hundred.

Shomacke, 7s. the hundred, whereof great plenty in Virginia, and good quantity will be vented in England.

Fustick yong, 8s. the hundred.

Fustick old, 6s. the hundred, according to the sample.

Sweet Gums, Roots, Woods, Berries for Dies and Drugs, send of all sorts as much as you can, every sort by it selfe, there being great quantities of those things in Virginia, which after proof made, may be heere valued to their worth. Aud particularly, we have great hope of the Pocoon root, that it will prove better then Madder.

Sables, from 8s. the payre, to 20s. a payre.

Otter skins, from 3s. to 5s. a piece.

Luzernes, from 2s. to 10. a piece.

Martins the best, 4s. a piece.

Wild Cats, 18d. a piece.

Fox skins, 6d. a piece.

Muske Rats skins, 2s. a dozen : the cods of them will serve for good perfumes.

Bever skins that are full growne, in season, are worth 7s. a piece.

Bever skins, not in season, to allow two skins for one, and of the lesser, three for one.

Old Bever skins in mantles, gloves or caps, the more worne, the better, so they be full of fur, the pound weight is 6s.

The new Bevers skins are not to bee bought by the pound, because they are thicke and heavy Leather, and not so good for use as the old.

Pearles of all sorts that ye can find : Ambergreece as much as you can get : Cristall Rocke : send as much as you can, and any sort of Minerall stones, or earth that weighs very heavy.

Preserve the Walnut trees to make oile of, & cut them not down : so also preserve your Mulberry and Chestnut trees very carefully.

In

In the month of June, bore holes in divers sorts of Trees, wherby you shall see what gums they yield, and let them bee well dried in the Sun every day, and send them home in very dry caske.

F I N I S.

THE TABLE.

That

*That the Silke-worme is as naturall to Virginia, as Persia, or
China.* p. 31.
*That Mulberry-trees proper for this Mystery grow there by
nature.* p. 19.
*That it may with much facility be set on foot, and with great
felicity brought to perfection.* p. 36.
*That in this the Indians may easily be brought to be coadju-
tors.* p. 38.
That Virginia may admit of a double Silk-harvest. p. 39.
*That the Silk-grasse of Virginia may prove a Staple of incom-
parable richnesse.* p. 24.
*That there is a naturall Hempe in Virginia excellent for Cor-
dage and Linnen.* p. 25.
*That there is a rich Copper (with great probability of a Gol-
den) Mine in Virginia.* ibid.
That there is great probability of rich Silver Mines. p. 26.
*That Sugar, Cotton, Ginger, Indigo, and Pepper will grow
in the South of Virginia with equall fertility, and much
more conveniency then in Barbadoes.* p. 27.
That Muske and Civet may both be made in Virginia. p. 26.
*That from the Terra Sigillata, equall in goodnesse to the best,
will be yeelded an incredible Revenue to the undertaker, and
that it is there in vast abundance.* p. 28.
*That there is no exact necessity to observe all the prescribed
rules written by Masters in the Silk-worme mystery; that
example and observation will diminish the number of these
rules, and the conveniency of Virginia for that Creature
may much abreviate them.* p. 33. 34. 35.
*That all the Spiceryes of the Philippines and other Countries
may grow in Virginia in equall felicity, the place affording
as happy, an aire, and a soile fitting in its variety for their
general production.* p. 45.
*That the excellencies of transplantation to meliorate what ever
transplanted may be with lesse charges and greater probability of thriving in Virginia, then elsewhere made experiment of.* p. 46.
*That ground may be prepared even in woody places for setting
Corne, Vines, and Potatoes, without any eradication, or fell-
ing of trees, with great speed and little labour.* p. 48.
*That there is a Rock of Chrystall in Virginia, already dis-
covered, and the place where.* p. 42.
*That if the English will but equall or imitate the industry of
the Spanyard, what ever has been discovered in New Spaine,
Peru, and Chili may be (by meanes there set down) laid
open to such their attempts.*

That

*That as the Indian may be invited to practise the Silk-worme
mystery, so with as probable hopes of successe he may be
gained upon to plant the Vine and Olive.* p. 41.

*That his planting the Vine will cement him to the English to
the disadvantage of the Spaniard.* ibid.

*That the South-west Passage may easily be found out by a
constant intelligence and information of the Natives: from
whence a trade and commerce may be driven with China and
Cathaya.* p. 44.

*That a fishing trade may be driven in Virginia, which for
excellency and plenty may be greater then that of Holland,
and in conclusion to make the Staple of fish a rich, delightfull, and unlaborious knowledge.* p. 21. 22. 23. 24.

*That Salt in Virginia may be made in greater abundance and
conveniency, then at Rochel.* p. 22.

*That some parts of Virginia abound with Pearle, and that
the Indian may be serviceable in fishing for them, himselfe
allowed a small share in the profit arising from so rich a
Merchandise.*

*That who ever can but satisfie for his owne transportation,
neede not trouble himselfe for any stock to set up with, since
so many severall wayes are proposed for his enriching and
maintenance.*

*Lastly, it may evidently appeare through all the passages of the
whole booke, that Virginia duly considered for exactnesse of
temperature, goodnesse of soyle, variety of Staples, and ca-
pability of receiving what ever is produced in any other part
of the World, gives the right hand of preheminence to no
Province under Heaven.*

AS a Supplement to all which, since so many objections have
beene, and are dayly made, lest a wilfull silence might
believe their scruples as authentick as reason it selfe ; such as
have beene made to me have had this answer returned them,
with which I desire to satisfie and communicate to all others
who may have the same doubts.

Why rather doe wee apply our selves to the South of Virginia, then the North? Why to a new where in probability all
things may be wanting, rather then an old Colony where already
there is great abundance?

To this may be returned, that the South of Virginia is more
proper then the North, by reason of its fertility and aptnesse
to produce all those Staples of Sugar, Cotton, Ginger, which
the colder aire in the North will not permit to flourish : That
the

the South is more proper, may appeare by the large quantity of
Palmetoes which have been found there, who cannot flourish
in any Countrey in which there may be so much as an appearance of Winter.

Neither need wee so much feare a want or non-abundance in
this new Colony, our nearenesse to Virginia and New England
being able plentifully to furnish us with all sort of Cattle at a
cheaper rate then in England, and the very reputation of this
place once planted will quickly invite so many men as know by
experience or information the excellence of the place, to remove
what ever is theirs out of those more cold Countries to joyne
issue with us in the better Sunbeam'd Carolana.

Another objection is, what security wee may expect from the
Natives, who looke upon us as Intruders upon the Land of their
Nativity, and seeing the South of Virginia in like manner to be
possessed as the North, whether they will not in all probability
attempt what ever rage, malice, and treachery can dictate to
them to oppose the beginnings of such possession to our extirpa-
tion, to which they will be more enabled (say they) since wee
are at the first seating not likely to be so numerous, or so well
fortified to resist them, as in the North of Virginia, where already
they have committed two massacres notwithstanding the length
of yeares to secure the implanters, and their large numbers.

Wee should attribute too much of the Bug-beare to the Indian
armes, to believe that 10 of our men well appointed are not
able to give law to their 100 aided with all the advantages of
animosity and revenge, to which by nature I must confesse them
prone, but their cowardise is so great, that they never act any
thing but upon the score of anticipation or security; a nights
march and the dawne of the day are the onely opportunities
which they take to revenge former hostilities upon their sleeping enemies: he which considers the desperate security the
English then lived in, the fatall entercourse to the admission of
them into their houses, into the heart of all their plantations
without any jealousie (I had almost said discretion) will rather
admire they were not totally massacred, then but in part attempted ; and yet to shew the invincible basenesse and Cowardise of those Savages, then when in the heat of their revenge
and hight of bloud, fury, and successe (when all Cowards but
themselves are irrisistably desperate and pushing on their fortune) one man that was master but of a heart and pitch-forke,
hath been known stave off and affright ten of those assassinates ; nor were any that had the generosity to oppose, or the
discretion to keepe good their houses massacred by them.

The

The basenesse of these incomparable Poltrons considered, what cause should there be to feare them? yet to show how those which through ignorance or doubt of their attempts may be sufficiently secured, these remedies have been proposed and are resolved upon to remove all future attempts of that nature.

Our first seating will be upon as pleasant Islands as eye may delight, into which all accesse must be by water. The Indian (first bought out of those Seas, which a most inconsiderable trifle will purchase and prohibited fishing there, with a severe punishment to all those who shall against such prohibition appeare with their Canoas upon the waters) cannot assemble upon the main to our prejudice, or gather together their Canoas without our notice; besides a small thing will buy spyes amongst themselves to discover all such practises; a knife or a hatchet will make them betray their neighbours, or which is more, their kindred.

When our numbers (by the blessing of God) shall enable us to grow upon the maine, the same price which bought them out of Islands will purchase them out of the continent (I meane such a part of it as will sufficiently serve 100000. Inhabitants) in the bounds whereof no Indian shall appeare without an uncountrefaitable mark of permission, and spies used as before; we may make use of their intelligence concealing the Authors, which will make those so discovered attribute to miracle what we receive by information, and peradventure enter into a superstitious beliefe of our præscience of their machinations, which will deter their attempting the like for the future.

Another objection which is usually made, whether this part of Virginia may not be too hot as the North of that Continent is too cold, considering the constitution of the English not proper to endure it, the extreams of either being alike distastfull.

Though it be certaine that all over those Countries drawing near the Center of the Sun a constant Brise arises and continues from 9. to 3. with a great mitigation during the violence and height of the Sun, and that during those intervalls, servants are so indulged as not to labour without doors, yet it is certain that the violentest of heats in that Southern is not hotter then some dayes which we feele in England.

And though ancient Philosophy may stumble at the doctrine (able to make reason herselfe almost blear-eyed) yet those no lesse signall experiencers of the modern will tell us, that the causes of moderation and habitability of those regions proceed from that which imposed upon our Patriarchs of learning, who

upon

upon favourable conjecture that the (supposed dangerous) neighborhood of the Sun, and the rapid transit of the celestiall bodies, with the perpendicularnesse of direct rayes could not but perpetually exile all cold and moisture as non-naturall and forreine to their immediat residence. Neither had reason any allegations to the contrary, till experience opened its eye-lights by this demonstration, for moisture is never more violent in those (which we call torrid) regions then when the Sun is in his nearest visits; from hence arise winds and impetuous showers dayly, from hence the Sun having (in a degree of debauch) caroused too much in his spacious and sweaty journey, over the Ocean does there discharge it; whereas in his abscence he receives no more of those moist vapours then he can temperately and healthfully concoct.

Besides, these frequent showers do not only coole and refresh the otherwise parching earth, but adde as much to its fatnesse and improvement, as the innundations of Nilus, Niger, and Zaire in Africa, and makes the earth invulnerable against the Sun's hostility & arrowy beams: and as in an Alembick a fire of heat and violence enlargeth the quantity of vapours, which stifled as it were and issulesse are converted into waters, but the fire being but meanly eager, drinks up those vapours in their exhaustion; so the Sun in the greatnesse in the Giantism of his strength, onely exhales (not digests) that quantity of vapours which he is inforced to disgorge in showers, which draughts of his are in his lesser heat in a more temperate quantity imbibed and concocted.

Nor deserves it a lesse part of consideration, that in that part of the world in which there are so many unbounded Gulphs, such immense Rivers and inlets, the vapours and exhalations cannot but adde coolnesse and moisture to the neighbouring Elements of earth and aire: and which is an indisputable reason the almost equall length of days and nights dividing perpetually the time into equall portions causeth a lesse heat then presented it selfe to the consideration-slumber of the ancients, which is confirmed by the Philosophick Poet in these Verses.

Quodq^e die solis violento in canduit astu,
Humida nox reficit paribusq^e refrigerat horis.

Nights what e're dayes burn with o're heated powers,
Coole and refresh by their length-equal'd houres.

Joyne to this the plentifull discent of Dewes greater then unexperienced imagination can comprehend them, and in dispensation of the moisture equall to petty showers behealth the dayes with coolenesse and freshnesse, which added to the

neighbourhood

neighbourhood of such an unfathomed depth, such an unem-
braceable greatnesse with their spacious fluxes resolve the
heated aire into a healthfull moisture : But nearer the Poles
the continuance of the Sunne, the almost no nights and long
lived dayes make of those parts more insufferably hot, then
nearer an equall division of night and light, and this cause
makes the Summer hotter in Russia then in England.

I had not dwelt so long upon this discourse, but onely to
show that if the Centre and head-quarters of the Sunne perpetually assigned betwixt the Tropiques be capable of coolenesse and habitability : What shall Virginia a Region as fortunately and temperately seated as the noblest Countries under
Heaven expect of moderate heates, and a by-these-infertiled
surface ?

To those other Questions how people shall trnsport themselves if of fortunes ? how the lesse able be transported ? what
conditions they are to expect ? I shall not doubt but publick
bils will make manifest to them, and that speedily. For the
other what meanes to live there ? what way of improvement
upon meanes ? the book is referred unto for directions : But if
that appeare unsatisfactory (that and all things humane being
subject to failings) I owe too much to my owne and that Countrey, not to give them further satisfaction to the best of my
knowledge ; And if they please to collect the Stationers name
and residence from the Frontispiece of the Booke, I am confident he out of his humanity and good affection, will either signi-
fie to them where I may prefer my addresses to their information,
or where I shall be to attend them, and withall contribute my
best knowledge in what may be usefull to them, or bring them
to such of higher quality as may give them plenary satisfaction.

It is my opinion (but the more ripe judgement of others)
that this Countrey well husbanded, and peopled, will in regard
of its variety of Staples, be such a constant entercourse of
Traffick to our Merchant Adventurers, as to free them totally
from all those dangers which they now groane under, either by
open hostility of knowne, or under hand dealing of private
Enemies Trade will be so secured among our selves of all those
Staples which France and Spaine sell us with a hand full of
exaction and causelesse expostulations, that nothing but the
casualties of the Sea will contribute to cast down countenances
upon the Exchange or making our Merchants Bankrupt.

And that this may want no poore contribution of mine : The
Reader will be pleased to take notice that a booke fully discovering the whole mystery of the Silke-worme, the whole art
of

of the Vine, and the conversion of the Sawmill to infinite other
as profitable uses, will shortly be published, in which the
Authour as in this will reckon it amongst his happinesses, if he
can at all be availeable to private instruction, or the publick
benefit

F I N I S

A LETTER

FROM

Mr. JOHN CLAYTON

Rector of Crofton *at* Wakefield *in* Yorkshire,

TO THE

ROYAL SOCIETY,

May 12. 1688.

Giving an Account of several Observables in Virginia, and in his Voyage thither, more particularly concerning the Air.

Force's Collection of Historical Tracts.

Vol. III.—No. 12.

A Letter from Mr. John Clayton *Rector of* Crofton *at* Wakefield *in* Yorkshire, *to the Royal Society,* May 12. 1688. *giving an Account of several Observables in* Virginia, *and in his Voyage thither, more particularly concerning the Air.*

Aving oftentimes been urged to give an Account of *Virginia*, by several of the Worthy Members of the Royal Society, I cannot but, as far forth as I am able, obey Commands whereby I'm so much honour'd, and shew my Respect by my ready Compliance; tho' I am so sensible of my own Weakness and Incapacity to answer your Expectations, that before-hand I must Apologize for my self. And indeed by Sea I lost all my Books, Chymical Instruments, Glasses and Microscopes, which rendred me uncapable of making those Remarks and Observations I had designed, they were all cast away in Captain *Win*'s Ship, as they were to follow me; and *Virginia* being a Country where one cannot furnish ones self again with such things, I was discourag'd from making so diligent a Scrutiny as otherwise I might have done, so that I took very few Minutes down in Writing; and therefore, since I have only my Memory to rely on, which too has the Disadvantage of it's own Weakness, and of the Distance of two Years since now I left the Country, if future Relations shall in some small Points, make out my Mistake, I thought this requisite to justify my Candor; for I ever judg'd it villanous to impose in matters of Fact; but Descriptions of things that depend on Memory may be liable to Mistakes; and yet the Sincerity of the Person that delivers them intire. But hereof I shall be as cautious as possible, and shall rather wave some things whereof I have some Doubts, and am uncapable now of satisfying my self, than in any sort presume too far. The Method I design is, first, to give an Account of the Air, and all such Observations as refer thereto ; then of the Water, the Earth and Soil ; the Birds, the Beasts, the Fishes, the Plants, the Insects ; and lastly, the present State of the Inhabitants : But at present I shall neither trouble you nor my self with any more than an Account of what refers to the Air alone, being conscious the honourable Society may receive such a Glut with the Imperfection of this, as to excuse me from a farther Relation.

But

But before I begin, perhaps it may not be impertinent to acquaint you with some things that happen'd in our Voyage. We sail'd in the Ship *Judith*, Captain *Trim* Commander, 'twas Flyboat built, about 200 or 250 Tuns; she sprung a considerable Leak. When the Captain had made long and diligent Search, had tried all Methods that Sea-men use upon such Occasions, or he could think of, all in vain, and that the Leak encreased, he came pensively to consult me. Discoursing with him about it, and understanding that the Ship was cieled within; so that though the Leak might possibly be in the Fore-part, it would fill the whole Cavity betwixt the Cieling and the Planks, and so run into the Hold at all the Crevices of the Cieling up and down: I thereupon conceived, that where it burst in betwixt the Cieling and the Planks, it must needs make some Noise. He told me, they had endeavoured to find it out that Way, and according to custom had clapt Cans to their Ears to hear with; but the working of the Ship, the Tackle and the Sea made such a Noise, that they could discover nothing thereby. I happily bethought my self of the Speaking Trumpet; and having one which I had contrived for some other Conveniences, of a differing Shape from the common Sorts, I bid him take it and apply the broad End to the Side of the Ship, the narrow End to his Ear, and it would encrease his Hearing as much as it augmented the Voice the other Way, and would ward the Ear the too from the Confusion of foreign Noise. Upon the first Application, accordingly they heard it, tho' it happened to be at a considerable Distance; and when they removed the Trumpet nigher, they heard it as if it had been the Current of a mighty River, even so distinctly, as to have Apprehensions of the bigness and figure of the Hole that the Water came in at; so that cutting there the Cieling of the Ship, they immediately stopt the Leak.

In the Sea I saw many little things which the Seamen call Carvels; they are like a Jelly, or Starch that is made with a cast of Blue in it; they Swim like a small Sheeps Bladder above the Water, downwards there are long fibrous Strings, some whereof I have found near half a Yard long. This I take to be a Sort of Sea-Plant, and the Strings its Roots growing in the Sea, as Duck-weed does in Ponds. It may be reckon'd among the Potential Cauteries; for when we were one Day becalm'd, getting some to make Observations thereof, the sportful People rub'd it on one anothers Hands and Faces, and where it touch'd it would make it look very Red, and make it smart worse than a Nettle. In my Return for *England* we struck a Hauks-bill Turtle, in whose Guts I found many of these Carvels; so that it's manifest

fest they feed thereon. 'Tis commonly asserted by the Seamen, that they can smell the Pines at *Virginia* several Leagues at Sea before they see Land, but I could receive no Satisfaction as to this Point; I could not discern any such thing when at a moderate Distance, I fear much of this may be attributed to Fancy; for one Day there came three or four full Scent to tell me they were certain they smelt the Pines; but it afterwards prov'd that we were at that Time two hundred Leagues from the Shoar, so that I was satisfied that was therefore meer Fancy. Indeed we thought, by the general Accounts of the Ship, that we had been just on the Coast, but all were deceived by a Current we met with, that at that Time set about South-East, or East South-East, which when once becalmed we tried thus: We hoised out a Boat, and took one of the Scuttles that covered one of the Hatches of the Ship, tying thereto a great Weight, and a strong long Rope, we let it sink a considerable Depth, and then fastning it to the Boat, it serv'd as an Anchor, that the Boat could not drive; then with the Glass and log Line we found the Current set, as I say, Eastward, at the rate of a Mile and a half an Hour. This Current is of mischievous Consequence, it does not always run one way, but as it sets sometimes as we proved Easterly, so does it as they say, set at other Times Westerly, whereby many Ships have been lost; for then the Ships being before their Accounts, they fall in with the Land before they are aware. Thus one Year many Ships were lost on Cape *Hattarasse*, and thereabouts.

Of the AIR.

THE Cape called *Cape Henry*, lies in 36½ of the Northern Latitude. The Air and Temperature of the Seasons is much govern'd by Winds in *Virginia*, both as to heat and cold, driness and moisture, whose Variations being very notable, I the more lamented the Loss of my Barometers and Thermometers, for considerable Observations might be made thereby, there being often great and suddain Changes. The Nore and Nore-West are very nitrous and piercing, cold and clear, or else stormy. The South-East and South hazy and sultry hot: Their Winter is a fine clear Air, and dry, which renders it very pleasant: Their Frosts are short, but sometimes very sharp, that it will freeze the Rivers over three Miles broad; nay, the Secretary of State assured me, it had frozen clever over *Potomack* River, over against his House, where it is near nine Miles over:

I

I have observed it freezes there the hardest, when from a moist South East, on a sudden the Wind passing by the Nore, a nitrous sharp Nore-West blows; not with high Gusts, but with a cutting brisk Air; and those Vales then that seem to be shelter'd from the Wind, and lie warm, where the Air is most stagnant and moist, are frozen the hardest, and seized the soonest; and there the Fruits are more subject to blast than where the Air has a free Motion. Snow falls sometimes in pretty Quantity, but rarely continues there above a Day or two: Their Spring is about a Month earlier than in *England*; in *April* they have frequent Rain, sometimes several short and suddain Gusts. *May* and *June* the Heat encreases, and it is much like our Summer, being mitigated with gentle Breezes that rise about nine of the Clock, and decrease and incline as the Sun rises and falls. *July* and *August* those Breezes cease, and the Air becomes stagnant that the Heat is violent and troublesome. In *September* the Weather usually breaks suddenly, and there falls generally very considerable Rains. When the Weather breaks many fall Sick, this being the Time of an endemical Sickness, for Seasonings, Cachexes, Fluxes, Scorbutical Dropsies, Gripes, or the like which I have attributed to this Reason. That by the extraordinary Heat, the Ferment of the Blood being raised too high, and the Tone of the Stomach relaxed, when the Weather breaks the Blood palls, and like over-fermented Liquors is depauperated, or turns eager and sharp, and there's a crude Digestion, whence the named Distempers may be supposed to ensue. And for Confirmation, I have observed the carminative Seeds, such as warm, and whose Oil sheaths the acid Humors that ever result from crude Digestions. But Decoctions that retain the Tone of the Stomach, as I suppose, by making the little Glands in the Tunicles of Stomach, squeeze out their Juice, (for what is bitter may be as well offensive to the Stomach, as to the Palate) and then Chalibiates that raise the decayed Ferment, are no bad Practice; after which, I conceive, Armoniack Spirits might be very beneficial. But their Doctors are so learned, that I never met with any of them that understood what Armoniack Spirits were: Two or three of them one Time ran me clear down by Consent, that they were Vomitive, and that they never used any thing for that Purpose but Crocus Metallorum, which indeed every House keeps; and if their Finger, as the Saying is, ake but, they immediately give three or four Spoonfuls thereof; if this fail, they give him a second Dose, then perhaps Purge them with fifteen or twenty Grains of the Rosin of Jalap, afterwards Sweat them with *Venice* Treacle, Powder of Snake-root, or *Gascoin's*
Powder;

Powder; and when these fail *conclamatum est.* But to return. 'Tis wonderful what influence the Air has over Men's Bodies, whereof I had my self sad Assurances; for tho' I was in a very close warm Room, where was a Fire constantly kept, yet there was not the least Alteration or Change, whereof I was not sensible when I was sick of the Gripes, of which Distemper I may give a farther Account in it's proper Place. When a very ingenious Gentlewoman was visited with the same Distemper, I had the Opportunity of making very considerable Observations. I stood at the Window, and could view the Clouds arise: for there small black fleeting Clouds will arise, and be swiftly carry'd cross the whole Element; and as these Clouds arose, and came nigher, her Torments were encreased, which were grievous as a labouring Womans; there was not the least Cloud but lamentably affected her, and that at a considerable Distance; but by her Shrieks it seemed more or less, according to the Bigness and nearness of the Clouds. The Thunder there is attended often with fatal Circumstances: I was with my Lord *Howard* of *Effingham* the Governor, when they brought Word that one Dr. *A.* was killed therewith after this Manner. He was Smoaking a Pipe of Tobacco, and looking out at his Window when he was struck dead, and immediately became so stiff, that he did not fall, but stood leaning in the Window, with the Pipe in his Mouth, in the same Posture he was in when struck: But this I only deliver as Report, tho' I heard the same Account from several, without any contradicting it. These things are remarkable, that it generally breaks in at the Gavel End of the Houses, and often kills Persons in, or near the Chimney's Range, darting most fiercely down the Funnel of the Chimney; more especially if there be a Fire, (I speak here confusedly of Thunder and Lightning) for when they do any Mischief, the Crash and Lightning are at the same Instant, which must be from the nearness of the Cloud. One Time when the Thunder split the Mast of a Boat at *James* Town, I saw it break from the Cloud, which it divided in two, and seemed as if it had shot them immediately a Mile asunder, to the Eye: It is dangerous when it thunders standing in a narrow Passage, where there's a thorough Passage, or in a Room betwixt two Windows; tho' several have been kill'd in the open Fields. 'Tis incredible to tell how it will strike large Oaks, shatter and shiver them, sometimes twisting round a Tree, sometimes as if it struck the Tree backwards and forwards. I had noted a fine spreading Oak in *James Town* Island, in the Morning I saw it fair and flourishing, in the Evening I observed all the Bark of the Body of the Tree, as if it had

been

been artificially peeled off, was orderly spread round the Tree, in a Ring, whose Semidiameter was four Yards, the Tree in the Center; all the Body of the Tree was shaken and split, but its Boughs had all their Bark on; few Leaves were fallen, and those on the Boughs as fresh as in the Morning, but gradually afterwards withered, as on a Tree that is fallen. I have seen several vast Oaks and other Timber Trees twisted, as if it had been a small Willow that a Man had twisted with his Hand, which I could suppose had been done by nothing but the Thunder. I have been told by very serious Planters, that thirty or forty Years since, when the Country was not so open, the Thunder was more fierce, and that sometimes after violent Thunder and Rain, the Roads would seem to have perfect casts of Brimstone; and 'tis frequent after much Thunder and Lightning for the Air to have a perfect sulphureous Smell. Durst I offer my weak Reasons when I write to so great Masters thereof, I should here consider the Nature of Thunder, and compare it with some sulphureous Spirits which I have drawn from Coals, that I could no way condense, yet were inflamable; nay, would burn after they pass'd through Water, and that seemingly fiercer, if they were not over-power'd therewith. I have kept of this Spirit a considerable time in Bladders; and though it appeared as if they were only blown with Air, yet if I let it forth, and fired it with a Match or Candle, it would continue burning till all were spent. It might be worthy Consideration likewise, whether those frequent Thunders proceeded from the Air's being more stagnant, the Motion of the Winds being impeded by the Trees, or whether the Motion of the Winds being obstructed by them below, the Motion might not be more violent aloft; and how far that may promote Inflammability; for Stacks of Hay or Corn that ferment with Moisture, never burn, unless when brisk Winds blow, that agitate and fan the little fermenting Sparks, and often kindle them into an actual Fire. And Observance of the Meteors there might perhaps not be impertinent, as both what are more rare, and what are more frequent, as of *Gosimore* in great Abundance, and of those small Cobwebs in a Morning, which some have supposed to be Meteors: *Ignes fatui*, though there be many boggy Swamps and Marshes, are seldom, if any are seen there. There be frequent little sorts of Whirl-winds, whose Diameter may be sometimes not past two or three Yards, sometimes forty, which whisking round in a Circle, pass along the Earth, according to the Motion of the Cloud, from whence they issue; and as they pass along with their gyrous or circular Motion, they carry aloft the dry Leaves into the Air, which fall again often in places far remote. I have seen them

descend

descend in a calm Sun-shine Day, as if they had come from the Heavens in great Showers thereof, so that all the Elements seemed filled therewith. And I could perceive them to descend from on high as far as I could possibly discern a Leaf. I remember a roguish Expression of a Seaman, otherwise silly enough, who wondering thereat, cry'd out, *Sure now 'tis manifest there is a World above! And now with them 'tis the Fall of the Leaf.* But to proceed, I thought this made it manifest, whence many preternatural Showers have happen'd. I remember at Sir *Richard Atherton's* in *Lancashire*, some few Years ago, there fell a great Number of the Seeds of Ivy-berries; at first we admir'd what they were, for they were cover'd with a thin Skin that was red, and resembled the Figure of a small Wheat Corn; but afterwards they fully manifested what they were; for many sprouted and took Root. I suppose they were carry'd aloft by some such Whirl-wind, and let fall there. I have purposely gone into the Place where I perceived this Gust, which is notorious enough by the Noise it makes, with ratling the Leaves as it carries them aloft, and have found a fine sharp Breeze of Wind.

Yours, &c.

Mr.

Mr. Clayton's *second Letter, containing his farther Observations in* Virginia.

BEing honour'd with the Thanks of the Society for my last, and receiving by my worthy Friend Dr. *Moulin* their Commands to proceed, I have added here my Observations of the Waters, and part of the Earth and Soil. I shall wave both Complements and Apologies, since I have greater Respect and Honour for the Society than I can possibly express, and have no reason to suspect their Favour, whose Candidness I so signally proved in my last.

Of the WATER.

'TWixt the two Capes, the Southern, called *Cape Henry*, the more Northerly, called *Cape Charles*, there runs up a great Bay, called the Bay of *Cheesepeak*; nine Leagues over in some places; in most seven, which lying West, Nore and South, divides *Virginia* into two unequal Parts. On the East Side of this Bay there lies a narrow Neck of Land, which makes the Counties of *Northampton* and *Accomack*. On the West Side of the Bay there branch forth four great Rivers, *James River, York River, Rapahanack* and *Potomack*, that rise from a Ridge of Mountains, whereof more in the Sequel. These Rivers plentifully water all the other Parts of *Virginia*, emptying themselves into the great Bay. The Mouth of *James River*, which is the most Southerly of them, and the Mouth of *Potomack*, which is the most Northerly, may be a hundred Miles Distance: But as I have been credibly inform'd that the Falls of *James River* are not past thirty Miles from *Potomack*, which is a vast large River nine Miles over in many Places. I have been told it was navigable nigh two hundred Miles, much higher than any of the other Rivers: Whence I conclude, in future Times, it will be the most considerable for Trade when the Country comes to be inhabited further up into the main Land. The other Rivers are much about three Miles over a-piece. And *James River* is navigable at least eighty Miles. Within four or five Miles of *James Town, James River* and *York River* are not past four or five Miles asunder. Yea, Sloops of considerable Carriage may sail up the Branches of the two Rivers, till they come within a Mile the one of the other; for I take it to be no more from Collonel *Bollard's* to Major *Troop's* Landing, and

and I believe they may come much about as near again as Collonel *Cole's*, and several other Places. *York River* is distant from
Rapahanack in some places not past ten or twelve Miles, *Rapahanack* from *Potomack* not past seven Miles in one Place, tho'
it may be sixty in others. The Heads of the Branches of the
Rivers interfere and lock one within another, which I think is
best expressed after the Manner that an *Indian* explained himself once to me, when I enquired how nigh the Rivers of *Carolina*, *Virginia* and *Maryland* arose out of the Mountains, from
those that ran Westerly on the other Side of the Mountains, he
clapt the Fingers of one Hand 'twixt those of the other, crying,
they meet thus; the Branches of different Rivers rising not past
a hundred Paces distant one from another: So that no Country
in the World can be more curiously watered. But this Conveniency, that in future Times may make her like the *Netherlands*, the richest Place in all *America*, at the present I look on
the greatest Impediment to the Advance of the Country, as it is
the greatest Obstacle to Trade and Commerce. For the great
Number of Rivers, and the Thinness of the Inhabitants, distract
and disperse a Trade. So that all Ships in general gather each
their Loading up and down an hundred Miles distant; and the
best of Trade that can be driven is only a Sort of *Scotch* Ped-
ling; for they must carry all Sorts of Truck that trade thither,
having one Commodity to pass off another. This (*i. e.*) the
Number of Rivers, is one of the chief Reasons why they have
no Towns: for every one being more sollicitous for a private
Interest and Conveniency, than for a publick, they will either
be for making forty Towns at once, that is, two in every Country, or none at all, which is the Country's Ruin. But to return,
the Tides in these Rivers regularly ebb and flow about two Foot
perpendicular at *James Town;* there is there, as they call it, a
Tide and half Tide; that is, it flows near two Hours along by
the Shore, after that it is ebb in the Channel; and again, it ebbs
near two Hours by the Shore, after that it is Flood in the Channel. This is great Advantage to the Boats passing up and down
the River, I suppose this is caused by many Creeks and Branches
of the Rivers, which being considerable many, tho' only three
or four Miles long, yet as broad as the *Thames* at *London*,
others ten Miles long, some above twenty, that have little fresh
Water which they carry of their own, but their Current primarily depending upon the Flux and Re-flux of the Sea. So
that after the Tide is made in the Channel, it flows by the Shore
a considerable Time afterwards, being that those Creeks are still
to fill, and therefore as it were draws up a Source upwards by
the

the Shore; and likewise when the Tide returns in the Channel, the Creeks that could not so readily disburse their Water, being still to empty themselves, they make an Ebbing by the Shore a considerable Time after that it is Flood, as I say, in the Channel. So far as the salt Waters reach the Country is deemed less healthy. In the Freshes they more rarely are troubled with the Seasonings, and those endemical Distempers about *September* and *October*. This being very remarkable, I refer the Reason to the more piercing Genius of those most judicious Members of the Society : And it might perhaps be worthy the Disquisition of the most Learned to give an Account of the various Alterations and fatal Effects that the Air has on humane Bodies, especially when impregnated with a marine Salt; more peculiarly when such an Air becomes stagnant : This might perhaps make several beneficial Discoveries, not only in Relation to those Distempers in *America*, but perhaps take in your *Kentish* Agues, and many others remarkable enough in our own Nation. I lately was making some Observations of this Nature, on a Lady of a delicate Constitution, who living in a clear Air, and removing towards the Sea-Coast, was lamentably afflicted therewith, which both my self and others attributed to this Cause, she having formerly upon her going to the same, been seized in the same Manner. But to return : There is one thing more in reference to this very thing very remarkable in *Virginia* : generally twice in the Year, Spring and Fall, at certain Spring-Tides, the most of the Cattle will set on gadding, and run, tho' it be twenty or thirty Miles, to the River to drink the salt Water, at which Time there's scarce any stopping of them, which the People know so well, that if about those Times their Herds are strayed from their Plantations, without more Sollicitation they go directly to the Rivers to fetch them home again. As for the Waters in the Springs in general, they are, I think, somewhat more eager than those in *England*. In that I have observed, they require some Quantity more of Malt to make strong Beer than our *English* Waters, and will not bear Soap. I have try'd several by infusing of Galls, and found little difference in the Colours, turning much what the Colour of common Sack in Taverns. I tried two Wells at Collonel *Bird's* by the Falls of *James River*, several Wells near *James Town*, some Springs in the *Isle of Wight County* : There's a Spring in the *Isle of Wight*, or *Nanzamond County*, vents the greatest Source of Water I ever saw, excepting *Holy-Well* in *Wales*, but I had not Opportunity to make Experiments thereof. I tried likewise some Springs on the Banks of *York River*, in *New Kent* and *Glocester*

ter

ter County, but found them vary very little as to Colour. I could not try any thing as to their specifick Gravity, having neither Aquapoise, nor those other Glasses I had contrived peculiary for making such Experiments, they being all lost with my other things. I had Glasses blown would hold about five Ounces, others abont ten Ounces, with Necks so small, that a Drop would make a considerable Variation; with these I could make much more critical and satisfactory Observations as to the specifical Gravity of Liquors, having critical Scales, than by any other Way yet by me tried. I used this Method to weigh Urines, which Practice I would recommend to the inquisitive and critical Physicians. I had made many Observations hereof, but all Notes were likewise lost with my other things. Yet I have begun afresh; for there are more signal Variations in the Weights of Urines than one would at first imagine; and when the Eye can discover little, but judge two Urines to be alike, they may be found to differ very much as to Weight. By Weight I find Observations may be made of Affections in the Head, which rarely make any visible Alterations in the Urine. I have found two Urines not much unlike differ two and twenty Grains in the Quantity of about four or five Ounces: But let them that make these Essays weigh all their Urines when cold, lest they be thereby deceiv'd. But to return to the Spring Waters in *Virginia*. There's a Spring at my Lady *Berkley*'s, called *Green-Spring*, whereof I have been often told, so very cold, that 'tis dangerous drinking thereof in Summer-time, it having proved of fatal Consequence to several. I never tried any thing of what Nature it is of.

There be many petrifying Waters; and indeed I believe few of the Waters but participate of a petrifying Quality, tho' there be few Pebbles or paving Stones to be found in all the Country. But I have found many Sticks with crusty Congelations round them in the Ruins of Springs, and Stones figured like Honey-Combs, with many little Stars as it were shot in the Holes. And nothing is more common than petrify'd Shells, unless you would determine that they are Parts of natural Rock shot in those Figures, which indeed I rather think; but thereof hereafter. Mr. Secretary *Spencer* has told me of some Waters participating much of *Alome* or *Vitriol* towards *Potomack*. Up beyond the Falls of *Rapahanack* I have heard of poisonous Waters. But these I only mention as a Hint to further Enquiry of some others, for I can say nothing of them my self.

A

A Continuation of Mr. John Clayton's Account of Virginia.

Of the Earth and Soil.

WHEN you make the Capes of *Virginia*, you may observe it low Land, so that at some Distance the Trees appear as if they grew in the Water; and as you approach nigher to emerge thence. For a hundred Miles up into the Country, there are few Stones to be found, only in some Places, Rocks of Iron Oar appear, which made me expect to have found many Waters turn Purple with Galls, but never met with any. Providence has supplied the common Use of Stones, by making the Roads very good : So that they ride their Horses without shoeing them ; which yet are more rarely beaten on their Feet, than ours are in *England*, the Country and Clime being dry, their Hoofs are much harder; for I observed, that take a Horse out of the wet Marshes, and Swamps, as they there call them, and ride him immediately, and he'll quickly be tender-footed. In some Places, for several Miles together, the Earth is so intermix'd with Oyster-shells, that there may seem as many Shells as Earth; and how deep they lie thus intermingled, I think, is not yet known : For at broken Banks they discover themselves to be continued many Yards perpendicular. In several Places these Shells are much closer, and being petrified, seem to make a Vein of a Rock. I have seen in several Places, Veins of these rocky Shells, three or four Yards thick, at the Foot of a Hill, whose Precipice might be twenty Yards perpendiular, whose Delf, I suppose, shot under the Hill; pieces of these Rocks broken off, lie there, which, I suppose, may weigh twenty or thirty Tuns a-piece, and are as difficult to be broken as our Free-stone. Of these Rocks of Oyster-shells that are not so much petrified, they burn and make all their Lime; whereof they have that store, that no Generation will consume. Whether these were formerly Oysters, which left by the subsiding Seas, (as some suppose, that all that Tract of Land, now high Ground, was once overflowed by the Sea) were since petrified, or truly Stones, *sui Generis*, I leave to the honourable Society to determin. But when I consider the constant and distinct Shooting of several Salts, Nature's Curiosity, in every thing, so far exceeding that of Art, that the most ingenious, when referr'd thereto, seem only endued with an apish Fondness, I cannot think any thing too difficult or wonderful for

Nature ;

Nature; and indeed I do not apprehend, why it may not be as feasible to suppose them to have been Rocks, at first shot into those Figures, as to conceive the Sea to have amass'd such a vast Number of Oyster-shells one upon another, and afterwards subsiding, should leave them cover'd with such Mountains of Earth, under which they should petrify: But not to launch forth too far into those Disputes, since I must modestly remember to whom I write. Often, in the looser Banks of Shells and Earth, are found perfect Teeth petrified, some whereof I have seen, could not be less than two or three Inches long, and above an Inch broad: Tho' they were not maxillary Teeth, the Part that one might suppose grew out of the Jaw, was polished, and black, almost as Jett; the Part which had been fasten'd in the Jaw and Gums, was brown, and not so shiningly polished, or smooth; if they were, as they seemed to be, really Teeth, I suppose, they must have been of Fishes. The Back-bone of a Whale, and as I remember, they told me of some of the Ribs, were digg'd out of the Side of a. Hill, several Yards deep in the Ground, about four Miles distant from *James Town*, and the River. Mr. *Banister*, a Gentleman pretty curious in those things, shew'd me likewise the Joynt of a Whale's Back-bone, and several Teeth, some whereof, he said, were found in Hills beyond the Falls of *James River*, at least, a hundred and fifty Miles up into the the Country. The Soil in general is sandy: I had designed, and I think it might be worth a critical Remark, to observe, the difference of Soils seem appropriated to the several Sorts of Tobacco: For there is not only the two distinct Sorts of sweet-scented, and Aranoko Tobacco, but of each of these be several Sorts much different, the Seeds whereof are known by distinct Names, they having given them the Names of those Gentlemen most famed for such Sort of Tobacco, as of *Prior* Seed, &c. Nay, the same Sort of Seed in different Earths, will produce Tobacco much different, as to Goodness. The richer the Ground, the better it is for Aranoko Tobacco, whose Scent is not much minded, their only Aim being to have it specious, large, and to procure it a bright Kite's Foot Colour. Had not my Microscopes, &c. Tools to grind Glasses, been cast away, with my other things, I had made some critical Enquiries into their several Natures, I would have examined what Proportions of Salts, all the Sorts of Earths had afforded, and how Water impregnated with their Salts, would have changed with infusing Galls, how with the Syrup of Violets, and how they would have precipitated Mercury, or the like, and so far forth as I had been able, examined them by the several Tryals of Fire. I conceive Tobacco

bacco to be a Plant abounding with nitro-sulphureous Particles ;
for the Planters try the Goodness of their Seed, by casting a
little thereof into the Fire; if it be good, it will sparkle after the
Manner of Gun-powder: So will the Stalks of Tobacco-leaves,
and perhaps has something analagous to the narcotick Sulphur
of *Venus*, which the Chymists so industriously labour after. The
World knows little of the Efficacy of its Oil, which has wonderful Effects in the curing of old inveterate Sores, and scrophulous
Swellings, and some, otherwise applied and qualified. The
Goodness of Tobacco I look on primarily consists in the Volatili-
ty of its Nitre: And hence the sandy Grounds that are most impregnated therewith, and whose nitrous Salt is most volatile, for
such Grounds are quickliest spent, yield Tobacco's that have
the richest Scent and that shortly become a pleasant Smoak ;
whereas, in Tobacco that grows on stiff Ground, the Salts seem
more fix'd, and locked up in the Oyl, so that whilst new, 'tis
very heady and strong, and requires some time for its Salts to
free themselves, and become volatile ; which it manifests, by its
having an urinous Smell. The same Reason satisfies, why Tobacco that grows on low Lands as far as the Salts, tho' the Plant
be never overflowed with salt Water, yet the Ground that feeds
the Plant being impregnated with salt Water, that Tobacco
smoaks not pleasantly, and will scarcely keep Fire ; but do all
that a Man can, will oft go out, and gives much trouble in frequent lighting the Pipe, 'till after it has been kept some considerable Time: Which may be assign'd to the more fixt saline
Particles of the marine Salt in these Plants ; which require more
time ere they be rendered volatile. Here it might be worthy of
an Enquiry into the nature of Filtration of Plants, since we may
hence gather, Particles of the marine Salt are carried along with
the *Succus Nutritius* of the Plant ; concerning which, if it were
not too much to deviate from the Matter in hand, I should offer
some Reflections of my own, which the learned Society might
perhaps improve: For I think thence might be made many
happy Conjectures as to the Virtues of Plants. So where we
see Plants, or Trees of an open Pore growing low, we shall find
their Juice has subtile Parts ; So have all Vines, whether the
grape Vine, or briony, or a smilax, or the like. If a gummous
Plant or Tree, that grows low, and close pored, it abounds with
acid Spirits, as *Lignum Vitæ*, &c. if it grow tall, and be open
pored, it abounds with a subtile volatile Spirit, as your Firs, and
the Turpentine Tree. But to insist no further herein, than as
this may be applicable to the present Discourse: For I have
observed, that that which is called Pine-wood Land, tho' it be a
sandy

sandy Soil, even the sweet-scented Tobacco that grows thereon, is large and porous, agreeable to Aranoko Tobacco, and smokes as coarsely as Aranoko: Wherefore 'tis, that I believe the Microscope might make notable Discoveries towards the Knowledge of good Tobacco: For the closer the Composition of the Leaf, the better the Tobacco; and therefore the Planters and Merchants brag of the Substance of their Tobacco; which Word, did they always take it in a true Sense, for the Solidness, and not mistake it for the Thickness, it would be more consonant to a true Observation: For as I said of the Pine-wood Tobacco, some of it is thick and not solid, and differs from the best Tobacco, as Buff does from tanned Leather; so that if the Tobacco be sound and not rotten, you may give a great guess at the Goodness of Tobacco, when you weigh the Hogsheads, before you see them: For if an equal Care be taken in the packing of them, the best Tobacco will weigh the heaviest, and pack the closest. Now I said, that the sweet-scented Tobacco most in vogue, which was most famed for its Scent, was that which grew on sandy Land; which is true, if you would smoak it whilst new, or whilst only two or three Years old; but if you keep the stiff Land Tobacco, which is generally a Tobacco of great Substance five or six Years, it will much excel: for tho' the sandy Land Tobacco abound with a volatile Nitre at first, yet the stiff Land Tobacco abounds with a greater Quantity of Nitre, only that it is locked up in its Oyl at first, and requires more time to extricate it self, and become volatile; but the Pine-wood Land having little of the Nitro-sulphureous Particles, neither is, nor ever will make any thing of a rich Smoak. Discoursing hereof some Days since, to a Gentleman of good Observation, that has been versed with maulting, he assured me, to back this my Supposition, or Hypothesis, he had observed, that Barley that grew on stiff Ground, required more time considerably to mellow, and come to Perfection, than that which grew on light Land. Having proceeded thus far to speak of Tobacco, I shall add one or two things more. The Planters differ in their Judgments about the time of planting, or pitching their Crops: Some are for pitching their Crops very early, others late, without any Distinction of the nature of the Soils; and 'tis from the different Effects that they find, in that, sometimes early, sometimes the late planting succeeds: But they have not the reason to judge of the Cause, to consider the Accidents of the Year, and the difference of the Soils. In sandy Grounds they need not strive so much for early Planting, the Looseness of the Earth, and the kind natur'd Soil, yielding all that it can, easily and speedily,

and

and Sand retaining the Heat, makes the Plants grow faster. But in stiff Soils, if the Crops be not early pitched so that during the Season of Rains it have got considerable Roots, and shot them some depth, if early Droughts come, it so binds the Land, that the Roots never spread or shoot deeper, or further than the Hill that they are planted in: For they plant them as we do Cabbages, raising Hills to set every Plant in, about the bigness of a common Mole - hill : observing this on the Plantation where I lived, that it was stiff Ground, I advised them to plant their Crops as early as possible ; and in order thereunto, I tried several ways to further the Plants ; but not to trouble you with the several Experiments that I made, in reference thereto : What I found most advantageous was, by taking an Infusion of Horsedung, and putting thereon Soot, and then my Seeds ; this I kept forty eight Hours in an ordinary digestive Heat, I had two Beds left me to sow, in the midst of those the People sowed, and the quantity of Seed that they generally allotted to the same Quantity of Ground ; when I sowed, I mix'd Ashes with the Seed, having decanted the Liquor, that the Seed might sow the evener : The effect was, that my Plants came up much sooner, grew swifter, and I had five Plants for one more than any of the other Beds bore ; I left the Country shortly after, and so no certainty of the final Result. There are various Accidents and Distempers, whereunto Tobacco is liable, as the Worm, the Fly, firing to turn, as they call them, Frenchmen, and the like. I proposed several ways to kill the Worm and Fly, as by Sulphur and the like ; but had no Opportunity to experiment it : I shall set down that I had most hopes of, which perhaps may give a Hint to others to try or improve. Tobacco-seed is very small, and by consequence so is the young Plant at first, that if gloomy Weather happen at that time, it breeds a small Fly, which consumes the Plume of the Plant ; now it being early in the Year when they sow the Seed, *viz.* about the fourteenth of *January,* they cover the Ground, to secure, as well as they can, their tender Plants, from the niping Frosts, that may happen in the Nights ; they cover them only with a few Oak-leaves, or the like ; for Straw they find apt to harbour and breed this Fly : I therefore would advise them to smoak Straw with Brimstone, once in two or three Nights, and so they might cover them securely, with that which would preserve them infinitely beyond the Covering with Oak-boughs ; indeed, I would advise them to keep peculiarly so much of their *Indian* Corn-blades, which they gather for their Fodder, for this very purpose, being, as I conceive, much the best, there being no Chaff to foul their Beds,
and

and prejudice them when they should weed them.   What they
call firing is this: When Plants are of small Substance, as when
there has been a very wet and cold Season, and very hot Weather suddenly ensues, the Leaves turn brown, and dry to Dust:
The Cause I conceive to be hence: The Plant being feeble,
and having a small quantity of Oyl, which makes the more solid
part of the Plant, the Earth being suddainly heated by the Sun's
fiercer Beams, the Roots are rather scorched and dried up in
the Earth, than nourished; so that the Plant consisting only
of watry parts, is consumed, as it were by Fire: sometimes
hopeful Plants, when by a sudden Gust some Master Veins are
broken; if suddain Heat ensues, they likewise fire: For being
not come to Maturity, and being deprived of the Supports of
Life and Vegetation they likewise perish, are dried up, and fall
to Dust.   *French-men* they call those Plants, whose Leaves do
not spread and grow large, but rather spire upwards, and grow
tall; these Plants they don't tend, being not worthy their Labour.   Were they so critical, I believe, they might have great
guess what Plants were most likely to turn *French-men*, by observing whether the Roots of the Plants run downwards, as those
whose Branches are aptest to spire upwards: For tho' I have
not made positive Proof thereof, I have something more than
bare Fancy for my Conjecture; I have pulled up some of these
French-men, and compared them with the Roots of some other
Plants, and found them much longer than others; and 'tis ob-
servable, loose Soils, and sandy Ground are more subject thereto
than the stiff Land. The Country of it self is one entire Wood,
consisting of large Timber Trees of several sorts, free from
Thickets or Under-Wood, the small Shrubs growing only on
Lands that have been clear'd, or in Swamps; and thus it is for
several hundreds of Miles, even as far as has yet been discovered.   But that shall be reserved 'till another Opportunity.

I am, &c.

Mr.

Mr. John Clayton, *Rector of* Crofton *at* Wakefield, *his Letter to the* Royal Society, *giving a farther Account of the Soil, and other Observables of* Virginia.

I Shall here present you with a continuation of my Remarks on the River, Soil, and Plants of *Virginia*. And first, as to the River on the other side the Mountains, said to ebb and flow. I have been assured by Col. *Bird*, who is one of the most intelligent Gentlemen in all *Virginia*, and knows more of *Indian* Affairs than any Man in the Country, that it was a Mistake; for that it must run into a Lake, now called *Lake Petite*, which is fresh Water; for since that time a Colony of the *French* are come down from *Canada*, and have seated themselves on the back of *Virginia*, where *Fallam* and the rest supposed there might be a Bay, but is a Lake, to which they have given the Name of *Lake Petite*, there being several larger Lakes 'twixt that and *Canada*. The *French* possessing themselves of these Lakes, no doubt will in short time be absolute Masters of the beaver Trade, the greatest number of Beavers being catch'd there. The Colonel told me likewise, that the common Notion of the Lake of *Canada*, he was assured was a Mistake, for the River supposed to come out of it, had no Communication with any of the Lakes, nor the Lakes one with another, but were distinct. But not to ramble after here-say, and other Matters; but to return to the parts of *Virginia* inhabited by the *English*, which in general is a very fertile Soil, far surpassing *England*, for there *English* Wheat (as they call it, to distinguish it from *Maze*, commonly called *Virginia* Wheat) yields generally 'twixt Fifteen and Thirty fold, the Ground only once plow'd; whereas 'tis a good Crop in *England* that yields above eight Fold, after all their Toil and Labour. And yet in truth 'tis only the barrennest Parts that they have cultivated, by tilling and planting only the High-Lands, leaving the richer Vales unstirr'd, because they understand not any thing of Draining. So that the richest Meadow-Lands, which is one third of the Country, is Boggy, Marsh, and Swamp, whereof they make little Advantage, but lose in them abundance of their Cattle, especially at the first of the Spring, when the Cattle are weak, and venture too far after young Grass. Whereas vast Improvements might be made thereof; for the generality of *Virginia* is a sandy Land with a shallow Soil: so that after they have clear'd a fresh piece of Ground

Ground out of the Woods, it will not bear Tobacco past two or three Years, unless Cow-pened; for they manure their Ground by keeping their Cattle, as in the South you do your Sheep, every Night confining them within Hurdles, which they remove when they have sufficiently dung'd one spot of Ground; but alas! they cannot improve much thus, besides it produces a strong sort of Tobacco, in which the Smoakers say they can plainly taste the fulsomness of the Dung. Therefore every three or four Years they must be for clearing a new piece of Ground out of Woods, which requires much Labour and Toil, it being so thick grown all over with massy Timber. Thus their Plantations run over vast Tracts of Ground, each ambitious of engrossing as much as they can, that they may be sure to have enough to plant, and for their Stocks and Herds of Cattle to range and to feed in; that Plantations of 1000, 2000, or 3000 Acres are common, whereby the Country is thinly inhabited; the Living solitary and unsociable; Trading confused and dispersed; besides other Inconveniences: Whereas they might improve 200 or 300 Acres to more Advantage, and would make the Country much more healthy; for those that have 3000 Acres, have scarce cleared 600 Acres thereof, which is peculiarly term'd the Plantation, being surrounded with the 2400 Acres of Wood: So that there can be no free or even Motion of the Air, but the Air is kept either stagnant, or the lofty sulphureous Particles of the Air, that are higher than the tops of the Trees, which are above as high again as the generality of the Woods in *England*, descending when they pass over the cleared Spots of Ground, must needs in the violent Heat of Summer, raise a preternatural Ferment, and produce bad Effects. Nor is it any Advantage to their Stocks, or Crops; for did they but drain their Swamps, and Low-lands, they have a very deep Soil, that would endure planting twenty or thirty Years, and some would scarce ever be worn out, but the longer the better, for they might lay them all Winter, or when they pleased in Water, and the Product of their Labour would be double or treble, whether Corn or Tobacco; and that this is no fond Projection, (though when I have discoursed the same to several, and in part shewn them how their particular Grounds might be drained at a very easie rate) they have either been so conceited of their old way, so sottish as not to apprehend, or so negligent as not to apply themselves thereto. But on the Plantation where I lived, I drain'd a good large Swamp, which fully answered Expectation. The Gentlewoman where I lived, was a very acute ingenious Lady, who one Day discoursing the Overseer of her Servants, about pitching

ing

ing the ensuing year's Crop; the Overseer was naming one place
where he designed to plant 30000 Plants, another place for
15000, another for 10000, and so forth, the whole Crop designed to be about 100000 Plants: Having observed the Year before he had done the like, and scattered his Crop up and down
the Plantation, at Places a Mile, or a Mile and a half asunder,
which was very inconvenient, and whereby they lost much time.
I interposed, and asked, why they did not plant all their Crop
together? The Fellow smiled as it were at my Ignorance, and
said, there was very good Reason for it. I replied, that was it
I enquired after. He returned, the Plantation had been an old
planted Plantation, and being but a small Plot of Ground, was
almost worn out, so that they had not Ground all together that
would bring forth Tobacco. I told him then they had better
Ground than ever yet they had planted, and more than their
hands cound manage. He smil'd again, and asked me, where?
I then named such a Swamp. He then said scornfully, he
thought what a Planter I was; that I understood better how to
make a Sermon, than managing Tobacco. I replied with some
warmness, tho' I hoped so, that was Impertinence, and no Answer. He then said, that the Tobacco there would drown, and
the Roots rot. I replied, that the whole Country would drown
if the Rivers were stopt, but it might be laid as dry as any Land
on the Plantation. In short, we discoursed it very warmly, till
he told me, he understood his own Business well enough, and
did not desire to learn of me. But the Gentlewoman attended
somewhat better to my reasoning, and got me one Day to go
and shew her how I projected the draining of the Swamp, and
thought it so feasible, that she was resolved to have it done; and
therefore desired me I would again discourse her Overseer, which
I did several times, but he would by no means hearken thereto,
and was so positive, that she was forced to turn him away, to
have her Servants set about the Work; and with three Men in
thirteen Days I drained the whole Swamp, it being sandy Land,
soaks and drains admirably well, and what I little expected, laid
a Well dry at a considerable distance. The Gentlewoman was
in *England* last Year, and I think Dr. *Moulin* was by when she
asked me, to teach her how she might make her Tobacco that
grew in the Swamp less, for it produced so very large, that it
was suspected to be of the *Aranoko* kind: I told her, though the
Complaint was rare, yet there was an excellent Remedy for
that, in letting every Plant bear eight or nine Leaves instead of
four or five, and she would have more Tobacco, and less Leaves.
Now you must know they top their Tobacco, that is, take away
the

the little top-bud, when the Plant has put forth as many Leaves
as they think the richness of the Ground will bring to a Substance ; but generally when it has shot forth four or six Leaves.
And when the top-bud is gone, it puts forth no more Leaves,
but Side-branches, which they call Suckers, which they are
careful ever to take away, that they may not impoverish the
Leaves. I have been more tedious in the Particulars, the fuller
to evince how resolute they are and conceitedly bent to follow
their old Practice and Custom, rather than to receive Directions
from others, tho' plain, easie and advantageous. There are
many other Places as easie to drain as this, tho' of larger Extent, and richer Soil, for some of which I have given Directions,
and have only had the return perhaps of a flout afterwards:
Even in *James Town Island*, which is much-what of an oval
Figure, there's a Swamp runs diagonal-wise over the Island,
whereby is lost at least 150 Acres of Land, which would be
Meadow, and would turn to as good Account as if it were in
England: Besides it is the great Annoyance of the Town, and
no doubt but makes it much more unhealthy. If therefore they
but scoured the Channel, and made a pretty ordinary Trench
all along the middle of the Swamp, placed a Sluce at the Mouth,
where it opens into the back Creek ; for the Mouth of the Channel there is narrow, has a good hard Bottom, and is not past
two Yards deep when the Flood is out ; as if Nature had designed it beforehand: They might thus drain all the Swamp absolutely dry, or lay it under Water at their pleasure. I have
talked several times hereof to Mr. *Sherwood*, the Owner of the
Swamp, yet nothing is essayed in order thereto. And now since
we are speaking of *James Town*, give me leave to adjoyn some
Reflections as to the Situation and Fortifications of the Place.
The natural Situation of the Place is such, as perhaps the World
has not a more commodious Place for a Town where all things
conspire for Advantage thereof.

    James Town Island is rather a *Peninsula*, being joyned to the
Continent by a small Neck of Land, not past twenty or thirty
Yards over, and which at Spring-tides is overflowed and is then
an absolute Island. Now they have built a silly sort of a Fort,
that is, a brick Wall in the shape of a Half-Moon, at the beginn-
nig of the Swamp, because the Channel of the River lies very
nigh the Shoar ; but it is the same as if a Fort were built at *Chel-
sea* to secure *London* from being taken by Shipping. Besides
Ships passing up the River are secured from the Guns of the
Fort, till they come directly over-against the Fort, by reason the
Fort stands in a Vale, and all the Guns directed down the River,

that

that should play on the Ships, as they are coming up the River, will lodge their Shot within ten, twenty, or forty Yards in the rising Bank, which is much above the Level of the Fort; so that if a Ship gave but a good Broad-side, just when she comes to bear upon the Fort, she might put the Fort into that Confusion, as to have free Passage enough. There was indeed an old Fort of Earth in the Town, being a sort of *Tetragone*, with something like Bastions at the four Corners, as I remember; but the Channel lying further off to the middle of the River there, they let it be demolished, and built that new one spoke of, of Brick, which seems little better than a blind Wall, to shoot wild Ducks or Geese.

If they would build a Fort for the Security of the Town and Country, I conceive it should be on *Archer's Hope Point*, for that would stop the Ships from passing up the River, before they come to the Town, and would secure the Town from being blocked up by Sea. The Channel at *Archer's Hope Point* lies close by the Shoar, and makes such an Angle there by reason of *Hog Island*, that going up or down the River, let the Wind be where it will, they must there bring the contrary Tack on Board, and generally when they about the Ship as they call it, they are so near the Shoar, that a Man may almost fling a Finger-stone on Board. How much this hinders the Motion of a Ship, and what Confusion it must be to them to bring a contrary Tack on Board, whilst they have all the Guns of a Fort playing so nigh upon them, may readily be conceived. *Archer's Hope* is a neck of Land, that runs down three Miles long, not much past half a Mile broad betwixt the main River and *Archer's Hope Creek*, which has large Marshes and Swamps; so that a Citadel built upon the Point, would almost be impregnable, being it could be attack'd no way but one, which is so narrow a slender Neck of Land, that it would be difficult to take it that way: And it would secure *James Town* from being blocked, being it would not be past a Mile by Water, to the Point of *James Town Island*. The Island is so surrounded with Water and marshy Land, that the Town could never be bomb'd by Land. But now to return to the Reflections of improving, and manuring of Land in *Virginia*; hitherto, as I have said, they have used none but that of Cow-penning; yet I suppose they might find very good Marl in many Places, I have seen both the red and blew Marl at some Breaks of Hills: This would be the properest Manure for their sandy Land, if they spread it not too thick, theirs being, as I have said, a shallow, sandy Soil, which was the Reason I never advised any to use

Lime,

Lime, tho' they have very good Lime of Oyster-shells; but that's the properest Manure for cold Clay Land, and not for a sandy Soil. But as most Lands have one Swamp or another bordering on them, they may certainly get admirable Slitch, wherewith to manure all their Uplands. But this, say they, will not improve Ground, but clods and grows hard; 'tis true, it will do so for some time, a Year or two at the first; but did they cast it in heaps, and let it lie for two or three Years after a Frost or two had seized it, and it had been well peirced therewith, I doubt not it would turn to good Account: And for this too I have something more than bare Conjecture; for discoursing it once with a good notable Planter, we went to view a Heap thereof, that casually he had cast up 'twixt three and four Years before, and we found it not very binding, but rather a fine natural Mould, whereupon he did confess, he then remembred that out of a Ridge of the like Mould he had very large Plants, which must have been of the like Slime or Slitch cast up before: But said, that himself and others despaired of this Manure, because they had taken of this Slitch fresh and moist out of the Swamp, and fill'd Tobacco Hills with it, and in the midst of it planted their Plants, which so bound the Roots of their Plants, that they never came to any thing. But he said, he then saw his Error, yet I have not heard he has remembred to correct it. But 'tis strange in how many things besides they are remiss, which one would think *English* Men should not be guilty of. They neither House nor Milk any of their Cows in Winter, having a Notion that it would kill them; yet I persuaded the afore-mentioned Lady where I lived, to milk four Cows the last Winter that I staid in the Country, whereof she found so good effect, that she assured me she would keep to my Advice for the future; and also as I had further urged, house them too, for which they have mighty Conveniences, their Tobacco Houses being empty ever at that time of the Year, and may easily be fitted in two or three Days time without any Prejudice; whereby their Cattle would be much sheltered from those pinching sharp Frosts that some Nights on a sudden become very severe. I had another Project for the Preservation of their Cattle proved very successful; I urged the Lady to sow her Wheat as early as possible she could, so that before Winter it might be well rooted, to be early and flourishing at the first of the Spring: So that she might turn thereon her weak Cattle, and such as should at any time be swamp'd, whereby they might be recruited and saved, and it would do the Wheat good also. I advised her likewise to save and carefully gather her *Indian* Corn-tops, and Blades, and all

her

her Straw, whatever could be made Fodder, for her Cattle; for they get no Hay, tho' I was urging her to that too, and to sow *Saintfoin;* for being a sandy Soil, I am confident it would turn to very good Account. They have little or no Grass in Winter, so that their Cattle are pined and starved, and many that are pined and starved, and many that are brought low and weak, when the Spring begins, venture too far into the Swamps after the fresh Grass, where they perish; so that several Persons lose ten, twenty or thirty Head of Cattle in a Year: I observed this was much owing to their Inadvertency and Error in their way of managing and feeding them; for they get little Fodder, but as they think Corn being more nourishing, feed them with their *Indian* Corn, which they give them Morning and Evening; they spend thus a great Quantity of Corn, and when all's done, what signifies two or three Heads of Corn to a Beast in a Morning? it makes them only linger about the Houses for more; and after that sweet Food they are not so prompt to brouze on the Trees, and the coarse Grass which the Country affords; so that thus their Guts shrink up, and they become Belly-shot as they call it. I advised therefore never to give them any thing in a Morning, whereby as soon as they were set forth of the Cow-pens, they would fall a feeding, and tho' they filled their Bellies only with such coarse Stuff as had little Nourishment in it, yet it would keep out their Bellies, and they would have a better Digestion; and then when they were come home at Nights, to fodder them, beginning with Straw and their coarsest Fodder, which they would learn to eat by degrees, before they tasted that which was more delicate, and whilst their Digestion was strong, would yield them Nourishment to keep them still so; afterwards when the Winter pinched, their fine Fodder then would stand them in stead; and hereby they might preserve their weakest Cattle. By these Methods, and the Help of the Wheat-patch, she, the Gentlewoman where I lived, saved all her Cattle, and lost not one in two Winters after, that I staid there; besides she saved above Twenty Barrels of Corn, as I remember that she told me she used to spend upon her Stock; and a Barrel of Corn is commonly worth Ten Shillings. Nay further, the last Spring she fed two Beasts a Bullock and a Cow, fat, upon her Wheat, with the Addition only of a little boiled Corn, and yet the Wheat was scarce eat down enough. But to return again to the Nature of the Earth, which may be pretty well gathered from what I have already said; I have observed, that at five or six Yards deep, at the Breaks of some Banks, I have found Veins of Clay, admirable good to make Pots, Pipes or the like of, and whereof I

suppose

suppose the *Indians* make their Pipes, and Pots, to boil their Meat in, which they make very handsomely, and will endure the Fire better than most Crucibles : I took of this Clay, dryed, powdered, and sifted it ; powdered and sifted Potsherds, and Glass ; three parts, two parts and one part as I remember, and therewith made a large Crucible, which was the best I yet ever tried in my Life ; I took it once red hot out of the Fire, and clapt it immediately into Water, and it started not at all. The Country abounds mightily with iron Oar, that as I have been assured by some upon Tryal, has been found very good. There are Rocks thereof appear at the precipice of Hills, at the foot whereof there runs a River fit for a Forge, and there's Wood enough to supply it with Charcoal ; as I have heard there was formerly some Persons undertook the Work, and when they had made but a small Quantity of Iron, which proved very good, the *Indian* Massacre happened, and they being higher seated than the then inhabited Part of the Country, were all cut off, and the Works demolished ; so that it has frighted others I think from the like attempt ; besides, such a Work requires a greater Fund, and Bank of Money to carry it on, than any there are able to lay out ; and for Persons in *England* to meddle therewith, is certainly to be cheated at such a Distance ; some *Indians* brought Col. *Bird* some black Lead, whereof he told me there was great Store. There's very curious Chalk towards the Falls of *Rapahanock* River, which they burn, and make a delicate White-wash of it. The Secretary of State Col. *Spencer*, has assured me, there were vitriolick or alluminous Earth on the Banks of *Potomack*. And thus far of what my Memory supplies me, referring to the Earth ; in the next place I shall give a short Account of the Birds.

Of the B I R D S.

I Had indeed begun once whilst I was in that Country to have made a Collection of the Birds, but falling sick of the Griping of the Guts, some of them for want of care corrupted, which made them fling others away that I had thoroughly cured ; for I was past taking care of them my self, there remaining but small hopes of my Life.

There are three sorts of Eagles, the largest I take to be that they call the grey Eagle, being much of the Colour of our Kite or Glead.

The second is the bald Eagle, for the Body and part of the Neck being of a dark brown, the upper part of the Neck and
Head

Head is covered with a white sort of Down, whereby it looks very bald, whence it is so named.

The third is the black Eagle, resembling most the *English* Eagle, they build their Nests much after the manner of that Dr. *Willoughby* describes, and generally at the top of some tall old Tree, naked of Boughs and nigh the River-side, and the People fell the Tree generally when they take the young; they are most frequently sitting on some tall Tree by the River-side, whence they may have a Prospect up and down the River, as I suppose to observe the fishing-Hawks; for when they see the fishing-Hawk has struck a Fish, immediately they take Wing, and 'tis sometimes very pleasant to behold the Flight; for when the fishing-Hawk perceives her self pursued, she will scream and make a terrible noise, till at length she lets fall the Fish to make her own Escape, which the Eagle frequently catches before it reach the Earth or Water. These Eagles kill young Lambs, Pigs, &c.

This fishing-Hawk is an absolute Species of a Kings-fisher, but full as large or larger than our Jay, much of the Colour and Shape of a Kings-fisher, tho' not altogether so curiously feather'd; it has a large Crop as I remember; there is a little Kings-fisher much the same in every respect with ours.

If I much mistake not, I have seen both Goss-Hawk, and Falcon; besides there are several sorts of the lesser Kind of Stannels.

There is likewise the Kite and the Ringtail.

I never heard the Cuckow there to my remembrance.

There's both a brown Owl and white Owl, much what as large as a Goose, which often kills their Hens and Poultry in the Night; the white Owl is a very delicate feathered Bird, all the Feathers upon her Breast and Back being Snow-white and tipp'd with a punctal of Jet-black: besides there is a Barn Owl much like ours; and a little sort of Scritch-Owl.

There's both the Raven and the Carrion-Crow; I do not remember I ever saw any Rooks there. Dr. *Moulin* and my self, when we made our Anatomies together, when I was at *London*, we shewed to the *Royal Society*, that all flat-billed Birds that groped for their Meat, had three pair of Nerves, that came down into their Bills; whereby as we conceived they had that Accuracy to distinguish what was proper for Food, and what to be rejected by their Taste when they did not see it; and as this was most evident in a Duck's Bill and Head, I draw'd a Cut thereof, and left it in your Custody: A Duck has larger Nerves that come into their Bills than Geese or any other Bird that

that I have seen and therefore quaver and grope out their Meat the most: But I had then discover'd none of these Nerves in Round-bill'd Birds: But since in my Anatomies in the Country, in a Rook I first observed two Nerves came down betwixt the Eyes into the upper Bill, but considerably smaller than any of the three pair of Nerves in the Bills of Ducks, but larger than the Nerves in any other round-bill'd Birds; and 'tis remarkable these Birds more than any other round-bill'd Birds seem to grope for their Meat in Cow-dung and the like: Since I have found in several round-bill'd Birds the like Nerves coming down betwixt the Eyes, but so very small that had I not seen them first in a Rook I should scarce have made the Discovery; in the lower Bill there are Nerves have much the same Situation with the flat-bill'd Birds, but very small, and scarce discernable, unless to the Cautious and Curious.

The night Raven, which some call the *Virginia* Bat, is about the Bigness of a Cuckow, feathered like them but very short, and short Leg'd, not discernable when it flies, which is only in the Evening scudding like our Night Raven.

There's a great sort of ravenous Bird that feeds upon Carrion, as big very nigh as an Eagle, which they call a Turky Bustard, its Feathers are of a duskish black, it has red Gills, resembling those of a Turky, whence it has its Name; it is nothing of the same sort of Bird with our *English* Turky Bustard, but is rather a Species of the Kites, for it will hover on the Wing something like them, and is carnivorous; the Fat thereof dissolved into an Oil, is recommended mightily against old Aches and Sciatica Pains.

I think there are no Jackdaws, nor any Magpys; they there prize a Magpye as much as we do their red Bird.

The *Pica Glandaria*, or Jay, is much less than our *English* Jay, and of another Colour, for it's all blue where ours is brown, the Wings marbled as curiously as ours are, it has both the same Cry, and sudden jetting Motion.

There are great Variety and Curiosity in the Wood-peckers, there's one as big as our Magpye, with blackish brown Feathers, and a large scarlet Tuft on the top of the Head: There are four or five sorts of Wood-peckers more, variegated with green, yellow and red Heads, others spotted black and white, most lovely to behold. There's a Tradition amongst them, that the Tongue of one of these Wood-peckers dryed will make the Teeth drop out if pick'd therewith, and cure the Tooth-ach (tho' I believe little of it, but look on it ridiculous) yet I thought fit to hint as much that others may try; for sometimes such old

Stories

Stories refer to some peculiar Virtues, tho' not to all that is said of them.

There be wild Turkies extream large; they talk of Turkies that have been kill'd, that have weigh'd betwixt 50 and 60 Pound weight; the largest that ever I saw, weigh'd something better than 38 Pound; they have very long Legs, and will run prodigiously fast. I remember not that ever I saw any of them on the Wing, except it were once: Their Feathers are of a blackish shining Colour, that in the Sun shine like a Dove's Neck, very specious.

Hens and Cocks are for the most part without Tails and Rumps; and as some have assured me our *English* Hens after some time being kept there have their Rumps rot off; which I'm the apter to believe, being all their Hens are certainly of *English* breed. I'm sorry I made no anatomical Observations thereof; and Remarks about the Use of the Rumps in Birds, which at present I take to be a couple of Glands, containing a sort of Juice for the varnishing of the Feathers; having observed all Birds have much recourse with their Bills to the Rumps when they dress their Plumes, whereby they scud thro' the Air more nimbly in their Flight.

Partridges there are much smaller than ours, and resort in Covies as ours do; their Flesh is very white, and much excels ours in my mind, *Sed de gustibus non est disputandum.*

Their Turtle-Doves are of a duskish blue Colour, much less than our common Pigeon; the whole Train is longer much than the Tails of our Pigeons, the middle Feather being the longest. There is the strangest Story of a vast Number of these Pigeons that came in a Flock a few Years before I came thither; They say they came thro' *New England, New York* and *Virginia,* and were so prodigious in Number as to darken the Sky for several Hours in the place over which they flew, and brake massie Boughs where they light; and many like things which I have had asserted to me by many Eye-witness of Credit, that to me it was without doubt, the Relators being very sober Per-sons, and all agreeing in a Story: Nothing of the like ever happen'd since, nor did I ever see past ten in a Flock together that I remember. I am not fond of such Stories, and had suppressed the relating of it, but that I have heard the same from very many.

The Thrush and Feldfare are much like ours, and are only seen in Winter there, accordingly as they are here.

Their mocking Birds may be compared to our singing Thrush-es, being much of the same Bigness; there are two sorts, the grey and the red, the gray has Feathers much of the Colour of

our

our grey Plovers with white in the Wings like a Magpye; this has the much softer Note, and will imitate, in its singing, the Notes of all Birds that it hears, and is accounted much the finest singing Bird in the World. Dr. *Moulin* and I made in our Anatomy many Observations of Singing-Birds to this effect : The Ears of Birds differ much from those of Men and Beasts, there's almost a direct Passage from one Ear to the other of Birds, so that prick but the small Membrane call'd the Drum on either Ear, and Water poured in at one Ear will run out at the other : But this is not all, but what is much more remarkable, they have no Coclea, but instead thereof there's a small Cocleous or twisting Passage that opens into a large Cavity that runs betwixt two Sculls, and passes all round the Head ; the upper Scull is supported by many hundreds of small Thread-like Pillars or Fibres, which as we supposed had another use also, to break the Sound from making any confused Eccho, and to make it one and distinct ; this Passage we observed betwixt the two Skulls was much larger in singing Birds than in others that do not sing, so very remarkable that any Person that has been but shew'd this may easily judge by the Head what Bird is a singing-Bird, or has Aptitude thereto, tho' he never saw the Bird before, nor knew what Bird it were : This has often made me reflect how much the Modification of Voices depends upon the Accuracy of the Ear, and how deaf Persons become dumb : and since I have observed that many Children, that have an acute Wit enough, that are slow of Speech, that is, long before they speak, are much longer before they can pronounce those Letters that are Sharps, as *g. h. r.* and never have an Aptitude to learn to sing. Hence I judge that Songs that have many Sharps in them are the difficultest to sing well, and discover any Persons Skill upon the trial of Musick most. This I suppose only, having no Skill in Musick my self, nor having ever discoursed any Person about it. As I remember we shewed some of these things to the *Royal Society*, and I drew some Cuts thereof, and gave the Doctor, upon Promise that he would put these and many other our joint Observations in Print, but I hear he is since dead. I have anatomized most sorts of Creatures, and never found any four-footed Creature with an Ear like a Bird, unless a Mole ; and a Mole has an Ear much like them, with a very thin double Scull, and a great Cavity like a Bird, and is very acute of hearing ; the Scull by reason of the large Cavity is very slender and easily crush'd, so that a Mole is quickly kill'd with a Bruise on the Scull like a Lark, and upon the Bruise the Membranes of the Scull turn black ; whence *Segerus*'s Mistake,

Membranæ

Membranæ Cerebri in superficie exteriori omnino nigræ visæ.
But when I have taken care not to bruise the Scull the Membranes were not black at all, both *Segerus* and *Severinus* I think had some perceptions of the different Structure of a Mole's Ear, but not any thing of its Analogy to a Bird's Ear; they speak of a Bone *Egregie pumicosum:* And *Segerus* says there's a *Ductus ad ossis usque petrosi cavitatem protensus, plurimis fibrillis Membraneis annectabatur.* But to return, this mocking Bird having its Name from *Mimicking* all other Birds in singing, is a wonderful mettled Bird, bold and brisk, and yet seems to be of a very tender Constitution, neither singing in Winter, nor in the midst of Summer, and with much Difficulty are any of them brought to live in *England*.

The red Mocking is of a duskish red, or rather brown; it sings very well, but has not so soft a Note as the gray mocking Bird.

Of *Virginia* Nightingale, or red Bird, there are two sorts, the Cocks of both sorts are of a pure Scarlet, the Hens of a duskish Red; I distinguish them into two sorts, for the one has a tufted Cops on the Head, the other is smooth-feather'd. I never saw a tufted Cock with a smooth-headed Hen, or on the contrary; they generally resorting a Cock and Hen together, and play in a Thicket of Thorns or Bryars in the Winter, nigh to which the Boys set their Traps, and so catch them and sell them to the Merchants for about six Pence apiece; by whom they are brought for *England;* they are something less than a Thrush.

There's a Bird very injurious to Corn, they call a Blackbird; I look on it a sort of Starling, for they cry something like them but do not sing, are much what of the same bigness, have Flesh blackish like theirs; they resort in great Flocks together, they are as black as a Crow all over, their Bills and all, only some of them have scarlet Feathers in the Pinions of their Wings. *Quære,* whether a distinct Species?

They have a Lark nothing differing from our common Lark; they have another Bird which they call a Lark that is much larger, as big as a Starling; it has a soft Note, feeds on the Ground, and, as I remember, has the specifical Character of a long Heel; it is more inclined to yellow, and has a large half Moon on its Breast of yellow; if it have not a long Heel, *Quære,* whether a Species of the Yellow-hammer?

They have a Martin very like, only larger than ours, that builds after the same manner. The honourable Col. *Bacon* has remarked for several Years, that they constantly come thither on the tenth of *March*, one or two of them appearing before, being seen hovering in the Air for a Day or two, then go away,

and

and as he supposed, returned, with the great Flock. The Colonel delighted much in this Bird, and made like Pigeon-holes at the end of his House with Boards purposely for them.

Their Swallow differs but little from ours.

They have a Bird they call a Blue-bird, of a curious azure Colour about the bigness of a Chafinch.

There be other sorts of Goldfinches variegated with orange and yellow Feathers, very specious and beautiful.

Sparrows not much different from the *English*, but build not in the Eaves of Houses that ever I saw.

The Snow-bird, which I take to be much the same with our Hedge-sparrow; this is so called because it seldom appears about Houses but against Snow or very cold Weather.

The humming Bird that feeds upon the Honey of Flowers: I have been told by some Persons, that they have kept of these humming Birds alive, and fed them with Water and Sugar: they are much the smallest of all Birds, have long Bills and curious coloured Feathers, but differ much in Colour.

Herons three or four several sorts, one larger than the *English*, feathered much like a *Spanish* Goose.

Another sort that only comes in Summer Milk white, with red Legs very lovely to behold.

The Bittern is there less than in *England*, and does not make that sounding Noise that ever I heard.

Curlews something less than our *English*, tho' bigger than a Wimbrel.

The Sandpiper much resembling the *English*.

The Snipe, two sorts, one resembling ours, the other much less.

The Tewits are smaller than the *English*, and have no long Toppins, but just like a young one that begins to fly.

There are a great number of wild Swans.

Wild-geese and Brent-geese all winter in mighty Flocks, Wild-ducks innumerable, Teal, Wigeon, Sheldrakes, Virginia-didapers, the Black-diver, &c.

In my return home for *England May* 1686. off the Banks of *Newfound-land*, when we were, according to Account, a Hundred Leagues from the Shoar, we saw several prodigious floating Islands of the Ice, no less to our Wonder than Terror, for they were very dangerous: I got the Master to sail one Day as nigh one of them as we securely durst, which we judged to be full a League in length, and was higher above Water than the top of our Main-mast; the Snow drove to and fro upon it as upon a large Plane. There was a great Flock of small Black-divers,

that

that were not much bigger than a Feldfare, came to us a little before, but all of them then left and betook themselves to this Island of Ice. They dived the constantliest, and the longest at a time of any Bird that ever I saw. We saw, as I remember, nigh thirty of these Islands of Ice. Captain *Rider* being some few Days later in his Passage, and bearing more to the *Nore,* told me, he saw many more of these Islands of Ice, and some much larger.

There are in *Virginia* a great many Cormorants; several sorts of Gulls, and in about the Bay many Bannets. Thus much for the Birds,

Yours, &c.

A Con-

A Continuation of Mr. Clayton's *Account of* Virginia.

Of the Beasts of Virginia.

THERE were neither Horses, Bulls, Cows, Sheep, or Swine, in all the Country, before the coming of the *English*, as I have heard, and have much reason to believe. But now among the *English* Inhabitants there are good Store of Horses, though they are very negligent and careless about the Breed: It is true there is a Law, that no Horse shall be kept stoned under a certain size, but it is not put in Execution. Such as they are, there are good Store, and as cheap or cheaper than in *England*, worth about five Pounds apiece. They never shoe them, nor stable them in general; some few Gentlemen may be something more curious, but it is very rare; yet they ride pretty sharply, a Planter's Pace is a Proverb, which is a good sharp hand-Gallop. The *Indians* have not yet learnt to ride, only the King of *Pomonkie* had got three or four Horses for his own Saddle and an Attendant, which I think should in no wise be indulged, for I look on the allowing them Horses much more dangerous than even Guns and Powder.

Wild Bulls and *Cows* there are now in the uninhabited Parts, but such only as have been bred from some that have strayed, and become wild, and have propagated their kind, and are difficult to be shot, having a great Acuteness of Smelling. The common rate of a Cow and Calf is 50*s.* sight unseen; be she big or little, they are never very Curious to examine that Point.

Their *Sheep* are a midling Size, pretty fine fleeced in general, and most Persons of Estate begin to keep Flocks, which hitherto has not been much regarded, because of the Wolves that destroy them; so that a piece of Mutton is a finer Treat than either Venison, Wild-goose, Duck, Widgeon, or Teal.

Elke, I have heard of them beyond the Inhabitants, and that there was one presented to Sir *William Berkly*, which he some time kept.

Deer, there are abundance of brave red Deer, so that a good Woodsman, as they call them, will keep a House with Venison; the *Indians*, they say, make artificial sorts of Heads of Boughs of Trees, which they consecrate to their Gods, and these they put on to deceive the Deer when they go a Shooting, or Hunting, as they call it, and by mimicking the Feeding of the Deer, they by degrees get within Shot.

Swine,

Swine, they have now in great abundance, Shoats or Pork-rels are their general Food ; and I believe as good as any *West-phalia*, certainly far exceeding our *English*.

Rackoone, I take it to be a Species of a Monky, something less than a Fox, gray-hair'd, its Feet formed like a Hand, and the Face too has likewise the resemblance of a Monky's, besides being kept tame they are very Apish : They are very prejudicial to their Poultrey, as I remember.

An *Opossum*, as big and something shaped like our Badgers, but of a lighter dun Colour, with a long Tail something like a Rat, but as thick as a Man's Thumb ; the Skin of its Belly is very large, and folded so as to meet like a Purse, wherein they secure their Young whilst little and tender, which will as naturally run thither, as Chicken to a Hen ; in these false Bellies they will carry their Young, they also feed on and devour Corn.

Hares, many will have them to be a Hedge-Rabbet, but I know not what they mean thereby. I take them to be a perfect Species of Hares, because I have seen Leverets there with the white Spot in the Head which the old ones have not, so it is in *England ;* and the Down is perfectly of the Colour of our Hares, they sit as our Hares do, and make no Holes and Burrows in the Earth ; true they are but about the bigness of an *English* Rabbet, and run no faster ; they generally take into some hollow Tree within a little space, which then the People catch by gathering the withered Leaves, and setting them on fire within the hollow of the Tree, and smoaking of them so till they fall down, sometimes they take long Bryars, and twist them in the Down and Skin, and so pull them forth.

Squirrels, there are three sorts. The first is the great Fox Squirrel, much larger than the *English*, and gray, almost as a common Rabbet. These are very common, I have eaten of them at the best Gentlemen's Tables, and they are as good as a Rabbet. The second is the flying Squirrel, of a lighter dun Colour, and much less than the *English* Squirrel ; the Skin on either side the Belly extended is very large betwixt the Fore-Leg and Hind Leg, which helps them much in their skipping from one Bough to another, that they will leap farther than the Fox-Squirrel, though much less, yet this is still rather skipping than flying, though the Distinction be well enough. The third is the Ground-Squirrel, I never saw any of this sort, only I have been told of them, and have had them thus described to me, to be little bigger than a Mouse finely spotted like a young Fawn ; by what I further apprehended, they are an absolute sort of Dor-Mouse, only different in Colour.

Musk-Rats,

Musk-Rats, in all things shaped like our Water-Rats, only something larger, and is an absolute Species of Water-Rats, only having a curious musky Scent : I kept one for a certain time in a wooden Chest ; two Days before it died it was extraordinary odoriferous, and scented the Room very much ; but the Day that it died, and a Day after the Scent was very small, yet afterwards the Skin was very fragrant ; the Stones also smelt very well. They build Houses as Beavers do, in the Marshes and Swamps (as they there call them) by the Water-sides, with two or three ways into them, and they are finely daubed within. I pulled one in pieces purposely to see the Contrivance : There were three different Lodging-Rooms, very neat, one higher than another, as I conceive purposely made for Retirement when the Water rises higher than ordinary ; they are considerably large, having much Trash and Lumber to make their Houses withal ; I suppose they live mostly on Fish.

Batts, as I remember at least two sorts ; one a large sort with long Ears, and particularly long stragling Hairs. The other much like the *English*, something larger I think, very common.

I never heard of any *Lions*; they told me of a Creature killed whilst I was there, in *Glocester* County, which I conceived to be a sort of Pard or Tyger.

Bears there are, and yet but few in the inhabited part of *Virginia;* towards *Carolina* there are many more. There was a small Bear killed within three Miles of *James City* the Year that I left the Country, but it was supposed to have strayed, and swam over *James River*. They are not very fierce, their Flesh is commended for a very rich sort of Pork ; but the lying Side of the Bear, as I remember, is but half the Value of the other, Weight for Weight.

There are several sorts of *Wild-Cats* and *Poll-Cats*.

Beavers build their Houses in like manner as the Musk-Rats do, only much larger, and with pieces of Timber make Dams over Rivers ; as I suppose either to preserve their Furs dry in their Passage over the Rivers, otherwise to catch Fish by standing to watch them thereon, and jumping upon them on a sudden ; they are very subtil Creatures, and if half the Stories be true that I have been told, they have a very orderly Government among them ; in their Works each knows his proper Work and Station, and the Overseers beat those young Ones that loiter in their Business, and will make them cry, and work stoutly.

Wolves there are great store; you may hear a Company Hunting in an Evening, and yelping like a pack of Beagles ; but they are very cowardly, and dare scarce venture on any thing
that

that faces them ; yet if hungry, will pull down a good large Sheep that flies from them. I never heard that any of them adventured to set on Man or Child.

Foxes, they are very much like ours, only their Fur is much more grisled, or gray ; neither do I remember ever to have seen any Fox-holes but of this I am not positive.

Every House keeps three or four mungrel *Dogs* to destroy Vermin, such as *Wolves, Foxes, Rackoons, Opossums*, &c. But they never Hunt with Hounds, I suppose, because there are so many Branches of Rivers, that they cannot follow them. Neither do they keep Grey-hounds, because they say, that they are subject to break their Necks by running against Trees, and any Cur will serve to run their Hares into a hollow Tree, where after the aforesaid manner they catch them.

They have great store both of Land and Water *Tortoises*, but they are very small, I think I never saw any in that Country to exceed a Foot in length ; there is also another sort of Land-Tortoise, different from the common sort, with a higher ridged Back, and speckled with a red sort of Spots.

Frogs they have of several sorts, one of a prodigious largeness, eight or ten times as big as any in *England*, and it makes a strange Noise, something like the bellowing of a Bull, or betwixt that and the hollow sounding Noise that the English Bittern makes.

Another very common sort, which they call *Toads*, because black, but I think differs nothing from our black Frog. They have Toads also like ours in *England ;* and another small sort of Frog, which makes a Noise like Pack-horse Bells all the Spring long. Another little green Frog, that will leap prodigiously, which they therefore call the flying Frog. There is frequently heard in the Woods a shrill sort of Noise, much like that which our shrew-Mouse makes, but much sharper ; I could never learn the certainty what it was that made this Noise, it is generally in a Tree, and some have asserted to me, that it was made by the green Frog, yet I scarcely believe it. Mr. *Banister* assured me it was made by a sort of *Scarabæus* Beetle, that is I think full as big as the humming-Bird ; but neither do I believe that, and for this Reason, for I never saw that Beetle so low as the Salts, but always as high up in the Country as the Freshes, and that Noise is frequent all over the Country.

Lizards, that are gray and very common, the Snakes feed much on them, for I have taken several of them out of the Bellies of Snakes.

Snakes, about seven several sorts. The rattle-Snake, so called

ed from certain Rattles at the end of the Tail : These Rattles seem like so many perished Joints, being a dry Husk over certain Joints, and the common Opinion is, that there are as many Rattles or Joints, as the Snake is Years old. I kill'd four or five, and they had each eleven, twelve, or thirteen Joints; but the young Ones have no Rattles of a Year or two, but they may be known notwithstanding, being very regular diced or checker'd, black and grey on the Backs. The Old shake and shiver these Rattles with wonderfull Nimbleness when they are any ways disturbed; their Bite is very deadly, yet not always of the same Force, but more or less mortal, accordingly as the Snake is in Force or Vigour, and therefore in *June* or *July* much worse, and more mortal, than in *March* and *April*. This Snake is a very majestick sort of Creature, and will scarce meddle with any thing unless provok'd ; but if any thing offend it, it makes directly at them. I was told a pleasant Story of an old Gentleman, Col. *Cleyborn* as I remember was his Name, the same that sent the Rattle-Snakes to the *Royal Society* some Years since. He had an odd Fancy of keeping some of these Snakes always in Barrels in the House, and one time an *Indian* pretending to charm them so as to take them by the Neck in his Hand without biting of him; the old Gentleman caused a rattle-Snake to be brought forth; the *Indian* began his Charm with a little Wand, whisking it round and round the rattle-Snake's Head, bringing it by degrees nigher and nigher, and at length flung the Switch away, and whisked his Hand about in like manner, bringing his Hand nigher still and nigher, by taking less Circles, when the old Gentleman immediately hit the Snake with his Crutch, and the Snake snap'd the *Indian* by the Hand, and bit him very sharply betwixt the Fingers, which put his Charm to an end, and he roared out; but stretch'd his Arm out as high as he could, calling for a String, wherewith he bound his Arm as hard as possibly he could, and clapped a hot burning Coal thereon, and singed it stoutly, whereby he was cured, but looked pale a long while after. And I believe this truly one of the best ways in the World of curing the Bite either of Viper or mad Dog. I was with the honourable Esquire *Boyle*, when he made certain Experiments of curing the Bite of Vipers with certain *East-India* Snake-stones, that were sent him by King *James* the Second, the Queen, and some of the Nobility, purposely to have him try their Virtue and Efficacy : For that end he got some brisk Vipers, and made them bite the Thighs of certain Pullets, and the Breasts of others : He applied nothing to one of the Pullets, and it died within three Minutes and a half, as I remember; but I

think

think they all recover'd to which he applied the Snake-stones, tho' they turned wonderful pale, their Combs, &c. immediately, and they became extream sick, and purged within half an Hour, and the next Morning all their Flesh was turned green to a wonder, nevertheless they recovered by degrees. The manner of the Application was only by laying on the Stone, and by two cross-Bits of a very sticking *Diaculum* Plaister binding it on, which he let not lie on past an Hour or two, but I think not so long, took the Stone off, and put it into Milk for some time ; some Stones were of much stronger Virtue than others. I proposed a piece of unquench'd Lime-stone to be apply'd to see whether it might not prove as powerful, but know not whether ever it was tried. But here one telling Mr. *Boyle* the Story of this *Indian*, he approved the method of Cure, and said, an actual Cautery was the most certain Cure. The Poison, both of Viper and mad-Dog (as I conceive) kill by thickning of the Blood, after the manner that Runnet congeals Milk when they make Cheese. Vipers, and all the viperous Brood, as rattle-Snakes, &c. that are deadly, have I believe their poisonous Teeth fistulous, for so I have observed that Vipers Teeth are, and the rattle-Snakes very remarkable, and therefore they kill so very speedily by injecting the Poison through those fistulous Teeth into the very Mass of Blood ; but the bite of mad-Dogs is oft of long Continuance before it get into and corrupt the Mass of Blood, being it sticks only to the outsides of the Teeth, and therefore when they bite thro' any thickness of Cloaths, it rarely proves mortal, the Cloaths wiping the Poison off before it come to the Flesh. A Girl that was bit about *New-Years Day*, continued well till *Whitsuntide*, when coming to see certain Friends in our parts, she fell very ill, and being a poor Girl, they came to me ; it pleased God I recovered her. Sometime after she returned to give me thanks for saving her Life, being two Persons that were bit with the same Dog, were dead, whilst she remained under Cure, and therefore she was the fuller convinc'd she owed her Life to me ; but of this I shall give a more particular Instance by and by. But the Poisons of Vipers seem to be like the injecting of Liquors into the Veins of Creatures ; Dr. *Moulin* and I made many Experiments of this Nature together, and I have made many more by my self. We once, I remember, injected half a Dram of Allom into the jugular-Vein of a Dog before the *Royal Society*, (the Allom being only dissolved in a little Water) which within something less than one Minute's time was so absolutely dead, as not to have the least convulsive Motion ; and I have done the like with many other things besides Allom, but

with

with some things it is more curdled and broken, than with others; and will differ much both as to colour and consistence. Salt-Petre kills much as quickly as Allom, but then the Blood in the Heart looks very florid, smooth, and even. I wish some Person of Observation and Leisure would prosecute these sorts of Experiments, and make Injections of the several things most used in Physick into the Veins of Creatures, both in Quantities, and into different Veins, as into the thigh-Veins of some Dogs, and Jugulars of some others, and in much lesser Quantities of such things as kill suddenly; for in the little time I have spent in these sort of Experiments, I easily perceive notable Discoveries might be made thereby: One Dog that lived became lame and gouty; another with Quick-Silver died in about sixteen Weeks time, consumptive, and I discovered Quick-Silver in the impostumated parts of his Lungs. *Query,* Whether some Persons that have been flux'd, or used Quick-Silver Ointments, and the like, and afterwards become consumptive, owe not their Distemper to the abusive use of a most excellent Remedy? Much after the same manner, the subtile Quick-Silver getting into the Mass of Blood by degrees, through its Ponderosity settles in the Lobes of the Lungs, and causes Ulcers there. But to return: The Poison of Vipers and mad-Dogs I suppose kill by thickning of the Blood, as many malignant Fevers also do; in all which Cases, I look on volatile Salts to be the properest Physick, as keeping the Blood from congealing. I had a singular Instance hereof in a Gentleman of *Yorkshire,* bit with a Grey-hound on the *Thursday,* not three Minutes before the Dog died mad; he bit him in several places of the Hands, as he was giving him a Remedy: The *Monday* following the Gentleman was very ill, and came to our Town to an Apothecary his Acquaintance, who knowing not what to do, desired my Assistance. When I came, the Gentleman could talk, but every two or three Minutes he had violent Fits, and would tell us when they were over, that his Brains worked like Birm in an Ale-Fat, and seemed to froth up at every Fit. The Apothecary had no volatile Salt of Vipers; so I took the volatile Salt of Amber, and ordered him ten Grains in Treacle-Water every half Hour: He told me every Dose seem to clear his Brain, and cool it as perfectly as if a Bason of cold Water were poured on his Head, but it returned by degrees again: Having then a volatile Salt by me that vomits very well, I gave him a Dose thereof; it worked very well, and he was much better after it: I then ordered him to continue the volatile Salt of Amber once every four Hours, and at each two Hours end, that is betwixt, *Spec. Pleres Archonticon* and
Rue

Rue powder'd ana gr. 15. whereby he was so well recovered, that within two Days he would needs go home, to look after some urgent Affairs, and afterwards found himself so well, that he forgot to return, and perfect the Course ; and I heard no more of him for half a Year, when I was fetched one Morning to him in great haste.   He had been abroad, play'd the good-Fellow, and in his return home having rode a great Day's Journey, being weary, and I suppose finding himself indisposed, he staid all Night in our Town, it being fortunately in his way.   In the Morning when he should have got up, he could not stand, whereupon the Apothecary was sent for, and a Surgeon to bleed him, which was accordingly done, but he grew worse ; for in this Case I look upon bleeding to be very prejudicial, as well as in most malignant Fevers, for thereby the Spirits are diminished, and the Blood congealed the sooner.   When they had done all they could, and the Symptoms still increased, they at length sent for me.   I never saw Man or Creature in that Agony in all my Life, that I found him in, senseless, and mad, when at best, but every Minute the fiercest shiverings ran through him, his Eyes would first roll and then set, as if ready to start out of his Head, but above all, the Swelling and Luctation at his Breast, was as if he would burst, which went off with a prodigious sigh :   All this I judge the effects of the heart labouring to discharge it self of the stagnating Blood, and the Nervous Convulsions as Consequences thereof.   And I am the more confirm'd in this, from what I saw in a Woman that was bit also with a mad-Dog in the Leg, and fell ill the very day that she had paid the Chirurgeon for her Cure ; and notwithstanding all that could be done, growing worse, they sent for me ; I went, and found her with what is called a *Hydrophobia :* She would look earnestly after Drink or Water, and seem to desire it, but as soon as she began to drink, away it went, be it what it would, with the greatest Violence she could possibly fling it.   I gave her the Vomit hereafter and also before mentioned, but she got but little of it down, and I had no more with me ; nevertheless it so brought her to her self, that she could answer Questions, and I asked her, whether she was afraid of the Drink and Water, when she flung the Cups in that violent manner from her? She said no ; but when she offered to drink, her Breast and Heart would not let her.   I asked whether through any Aversion or Fear ? She said no, she was very thirsty ; but when she offered to drink, it struck to her Heart, and stopped her Breath.   That is, as I apprehend, the cold Drink passing down the Throat struck a Chilness in the Blood, and made it readier to stagnate: Besides the very Act

of

of Drinking, hindring the free Breathing, conduced also much thereto: and therefore the Heart was so suddenly oppress'd, that she could not forbear flinging away whatever she had in her hand. She complained also of a great Rigor and Stiffness or Straitness of the Muscles of her Breast; so that possibly the spirituous Liquor that flows in the *Genus Nervosum* may be congeal'd as well as the Blood; or the same effects may be supposed notwithstanding to be the result of the condensed Blood clogging both the Heart and Lungs, so that the Breast may seem to be straitned therewith. The same I judge to be the cause of all the violent Luxations in this Gentleman, whose Fingers I looked on, and found the Places where he had formerly been bit turned blackish, and much inflamed about them, which confirmed me in my Sentiment, that it was a Relapse of its former Distemper, that is, of the Bite of the mad-Dog. I told them, if any thing in the World would save his Life, I judged it might be the former Vomit of volatile Salts; they could not tell what to do, nevertheless such is the Malignancy of the World, that as soon as it was given, they ran away and left me, saying, he was now certainly a dead Man, to have a Vomit given in that Condition. Nevertheless it pleased God that he shortly after cried, *this Fellow in the Black has done me good*, and after the first Vomit, came so to himself, as to know us all. I vomited him every other day with this Vomit for three times, and made him in the interim to take volatile Salt of Amber, and the aforesaid Powders, and to wash his Hands, and Sores in a strong salt Brine: to drink Posset-Drink with Sage and Rue, and by this Course, and the Blessing of God, his Life was saved, and he perfectly cured, for it was now four Years since, and he had had no Relapse. I have cured several others by the same Method. Coll. *Spencer*, the Secretary of State in *Virginia*, a very serious and ingenious Gentleman, told me that his Servant brought him word once that a Sow having farrow'd, a rattle-Snake was got into the Den, and had killed the Piggs. The Colonel went to see the Snake, which they said was still coyl'd in the Den; there followed them two or three mungrel Curs, and they sat one of the Dogs at the Snake, which was too quick for the Dog, and snapt him by the Nose, whereupon he set a howling, and run immediately into the adjacent River, and died very shortly after. Another of the Dogs upon the like attempt was bit by the Snake also, and fell a howling, and frothing, and tumbling; but being he dyed not so soon as the other Dog did, they fetched some of the Herb which they call Dittany, as having a great traditionary Virtue for the Cure of Poisons; they pounded it,

and

and adding a little Water, express'd the Juice, and gave the Dog frequently thereof, nevertheless he dyed within a Day or two. The howling of the Dogs he supposed gave notice to the Sow, and made her come furiously brisling, and run immediately into her Den; but being likewise bit by the Snake, she set up a terrible Squeak, and ran also into the River, and there died.

A Gentlewoman, that was a notable female Doctress, told me, that a Neighbour being bit by a Rattle-Snake, swelled excessively; some Days afterwards she was sent for, who found him swelled beyond what she thought it had been possible for the Skin to contain, and very thirsty. She gave him *oriental Bezoar* shaved, with a strong Decoction of the aforesaid Dittany, whereby she recovered the Person: To the best of my Remembrance, it was he that told me, asking him afterwards, what he felt when the Snake first bit him? He said, it seemed as if a flash of Fire had ran through his Veins.

Besides the Rattle-Snake there is the Blowing-Snake, an absolute Species of a Viper, but larger than any that I have seen in *Europe;* it is so called, because it seems to blow, and spread its Head, and swell very much before it bite which is very deadly. It is remarkable that there is none of their Snakes there, make any of that hissing Noise that ours in *England* make, but only shoot out their Tongues, shaking them as ours do, without any Noise at all; this is a short thick sort of Snake, there is another sort of Deadly Snake, called the *Red-Snake;* I once narrowly escaped treading on the Back of one of them: They are of an ugly dark brown Colour, inclining to red; their Bellies are of a more dusky White, with a large streak of vermilion Red on either Side; this too is of the Viper kind, but is not so short, but its Tail is more taper and small. The *Horn-Snake* is, as they say, another sort of deadly Snake; I never saw any of them, unless once, shortly after my Arrival in that Country, which I cannot attest to be the Horn-Snake, for I could not distinctly view it, being in a Thicket of *Sumach;* it was perch'd up about two Foot high in a *Sumach* Branch, its Tail twisted about the Shrub, and about a quarter of a Yard stood bolt forward, leaning over the forked Branch thereof: I could not see the Horne, which they say it has in its Front, wherewith it strikes, and if it wounds, is as deadly as the Rattle-Snake's Bite. The Gentleman that was with me, told me it was the Horn-Snake; but being in hast, and on Horseback, and the Snake in a Thicket, I could not see the Horn; but had I thought I should never have seen more of them, I should have took a little Pains to have been better satisfied. This I think may not improperly be referred to the *Dart-Snake.*   The

The *Black-Snake*, is the largest I think of all others, but I am sure the most common; I have kill'd several of them full six Foot long, their Bite is not deem'd mortal, but it swells, and turns to a running Sore; they feed upon Lizards, Mice, Rats, Frogs, and Toads, which I have taken out of their Bellies. I was once a Simpling in the Woods, on a fair Sun-shine Day, when I saw a Snake crawling on a Tree that was fallen, and licking with its forked Tongue as it moved; I stood still to observe it, I saw it lick up small Insects and Flies with wonderful Nimbleness, catching them betwixt the Forks of its Tongue.

The *Corn-Snake*, most like the Rattle-Snake of all others in Colour, but the Checker are not so regular, neither has it any Rattles: They are most frequent in the Corn-Fields, and thence I suppose so called; the Bite is not so venomous as the Black-Snakes.

The *Water-Snake*, a small Snake, I never saw any of them above a Yard long, though I have sometimes seen Forty or Fifty at once; they are of an ugly dark blackish Colour: They say, they are the least venomous of any.

THE REFORMED

VIRGINIAN

SILK–WORM,

Or, a Rare and New

DISCOVERY

OF

A speedy way, and easie means, found out
by a young Lady in *England*, she having made
full proof thereof in *May*,
Anno 1 6 5 2.

For the feeding of Silk-worms in the Woods, on
the Mulberry-Tree-leaves in *Virginia*: Who after fourty
dayes time, present their most rich golden-coloured
silken Fleece, to the instant wonderful enriching
of all the Planters there, requiring from
them neither cost, labour, or hind-
rance in any of their other employments whatsoever.

And also to the good hopes, that the *Indians*, seeing and finding that there is neither Art, Skill, or Pains in
the thing: they will readily set upon it, being by the
benefit thereof inabled to buy of the *English* (in
way of Truck for their Silk-bottoms) all
those things that they most desire.

LONDON,
Printed by *John Streater*, for *Giles Calvert* at
the *Black-Spread-Eagle* at the West end
of *Pauls*, 1 6 5 5.

Force's Collection of Historical Tracts.

VOL. III.—No. 13.

TO THE Reader.

Ingenious Reader,

I Have in my *Legacy of Husbandry* bequeathed something unto thee concerning *Silk-worms,* which hath wakened many to search after the means to advance that part of *Husbandry.* But because the *Letter* of King *Iames* to the *Lords Lievtenants* of the severall *Shires* of England, *for the increasing of Mulberry Trees, and the breeding of Silk-worms, for the making of Silk in this Nation,* had not annexed unto them in that *Treatise* the *Instructions* tending to that purpose, and being but few, wholly out of print, and very much desired: I thought good upon the occasion of the printing of this *Letter* to those of Virginia, to publish it also for the benefit of those who shall be willing to employ themselves in this way of industry, which seemeth to be brought unto a more perfect and speedy accomplishment than heretofore hath been known either here or in France, as by the contentes of this adjoyned *Letter* (wherein the *Experiment* of a vertuous *Lady* of this *Nation* for the breeding of *Silk-worms,* is addressed unto the *Planters* of Virginia) is set forth to encourage both them and others to set upon this work, to benefit themselves and the *Nation* thereby. And truly the *Gentleman* who doth address this *Letter* to the *Planters* of the *Virginian Colonie* is much to be commended for his affection to the publick, because he doth not conceal (as some *Muck-worms* do for private ends) the *Advantages* which may be reaped by singular industrious *Attempts* or experiments of profit; but desires the benefit of others, even of all, to be encreased. And it were to be wished, that every one to whom *God* (from whom comes every good & perfect gift) doth impart any rare and profitable *Secret of Industry,* would open himselfe towards his *Brethren,* as this publick-hearted *Gentleman* doth; then would all hands be set a work, and every one would become instrumentall to serve himselfe and his *Neighbours* in Love, and overcome the burthen of povertie, which for want of employment and decay of *Trade,* doth lie so heavie upon very many, whose burthens might be either born, or made easie, if all the gifts of *God* were made use of, for the end for which he doth bestow them, namely, to profit withall towards others, as it becommeth the *Members of*
the

To the Reader.

the same Christian, and Human, and Nationall Society; for the same rule holds in all these respects among such as understand what it is to be a good Commonwealths-man in the State, as well as in the Communion of Saints: And to this good and generous inclination, which I wish may more and more abound in them with the grace of God, I shall leave thee and rest,

Thy most assured and faithfull servant,

SAMUEL HARTLIB.

Instructions

Instructions *for the increase and Planting of* Mulberry-trees.

What ground is fit for the Mulberry-seeds, *how the same is to be ordered, and in what sort the seeds are to be sowed therein.*

He ground which ought to be apointed for this purpose, besides the natural goodness of it, must be reasonably well dunged, and withall so situated, as that the heat of the Sun may cherish it, and the nipping blasts of either the North wind or the East, may not annoy it : The choice thereof thus made ; that the seeds may the better prosper, and come up after they be sown, you shall dig it two foot deep, breaking the clods as small as may be, and afterwards you shall divide the same into severall Beds of not above five foot in breadth, so that you shall not need to indanger the Plants by treading upon them, when either you water or weed them.

The Mulberry seeds you shall lay in water for the space of 22 hours, and after that you shall dry them again half dry, or some what more, that when you sow them they may not cleave together : Thus done, you must cast them upon the foresaid Beds, not altogether so thick as you use to do other garden Seed, and then cover them with some fine earth (past through a Sive) about half an inch thick. In dry weather you shall water them every two days at the farthest, as likewise the plants that shall come of them ; and keep them as clean from weeds as possibly you can.

The time in which you ought to sow them for your best advantage, is either in *March, April,* or *May,* when frosts are either altogether past, or at the least not so sharp, or of so long continuance, as to indanger their upspring.

There is yet another way to sow them, and that is as followeth : you shall (being directed by a strait line) make certain furrows in the Beds above mentioned, of some four fingers deep, & about a foot in distance the one from the other : After this, you shall open the earth with your hands, on either side of the aforesaid furrows, some two fingers from the bottom, and where you

have

have so opened it, shall you sow your seeds ; and then cover them half a finger thick with the earth which before you opened.

When the Plants that are sprung up of the Seeds, are to be removed, and how they are to be planted the first time.

IN the moneths of *September, October, November, December, March,* or *April,* the next yeer after the Seeds are sown, you may remove their plants, (or in the moneth of *January,* if it be not in frosty weather) and set them in the like Beds as before, and about one foot the one from the other, but first you must cut off their roots about eight inches in length, and their tops about half a foot above their roots, more or lesse, according to the strength of the said plaints, for the weaker they be the lesse tops you shall leave them. In this sort you may suffer them to remain weeding and watering them (as need shall require) till they be grown six foot in length above their roots, whereunto when once they have attained, you may cut their tops, and suffer them to spread, alwayes having a care to take away the many branches or succours, that may any way hinder their growth untill they be come to their full length of six foot, as aforesaid.

When, and how the Plants are to be removed the second time, and in what manner they are to be planted where they shall remain.

IN the moneths aforesaid, (according as your plants are waxen strong) you may remove them either into the hedges of your fields, or into any other grounds. If in hedges, you must set them 16 foot the one from the other : if in other ground, intending to make a Wood of them 18 foot at the least. But a moneth before you do remove them, you must make the holes (wherein you purpose to set them) about four foot in breadth, and so deep as that their roots may be well covered, and some half a foot of loose earth left under them, having alwayes a special care so to place them, that they may receive the benefit of the Sun, and not to be shadowed or over-spread by any neighbouring trees.

When, and how the Eggs of the Silk-wormes are to be hatched, and how to order the Wormes that shall come of them.

VVHen the leavs of Mulberry-trees begin a little to bud forth, take the eggs of your Silk-worms, and lay them in a piece of Say, or such like stuff, and in the day time carry them in some warm place about you, in a little safe box, but in the night either lay them in your bed or between two warm pillows, untill such time as the Wormes begin to come forth : then take a piece of paper of the wideness of the said box, and having cut it full of small holes, lay it within the same upon the eggs, and

upon

upon that again some few Mulbery-leaves, to which the Wormes as they are hatched, will continually come. These leaves with the Wormes upon them, you must still remove into other boxes, laying fresh leaves as well on those that are removed as on the paper where the eggs are; and this is the course which must be duly kept and observed, untill such times as all the Wormes be come forth of their shels, still keeping their boxes warm, as aforesaid; but no longer about you, but untill the Wormes begin to come forth, out of which boxes you may safely take them, when once they have past their second sicknesse, and feed them upon shelves of two foot in breadth, and 18 inches one above the other.

The said shelves are not to be placed in any ground-room, nor yet next unto the tiles, but in some middle room of your house which openeth upon the North and South, that you may the more conveniently give them either heat or aire, according as the time and season shall require. Besides you must not make them close unto the Wals, but so as you may passe about them the better to look unto the Wormes, and keep them from Rats and Mice, which otherwise might devoure them. You must observe the times of their comming forth, and keep every one, one or two dayes hatching by themselves, that you may the better understand their severall sicknesses or sleepings, which are foure in the time of their feeding. The first commonly some twelve dayes after they are hatched, and from that time at the end of every eight dayes, according to the weather, and their good or ill usage, during which time of every sicknesse, which lasteth two or three dayes, you must feed them but very little, as onely to relieve such of them, as shall have past their sicknesse before the rest, and those that shall not fall into their sicknesse so soon.

The whole time that the Worms do feed, is about nine Weeks, whereof untill they come unto their first sicknesse, give them young Mulbery-leaves twice every day, but few at a time; from thence untill their second sickness, twice every day in greater quantity; and so from their second to their third sicknesse, increasing the quantity of the leaves, according as you perceive the Wormes to grow in strength, and clear of sicknesse: from the third untill their fourth sickpesse, you may give them leaves thrice every day, and the fourth being past, you may let them have so many as they will eat, always having a care that you give them none, but such as are dry, and well aired upon a Table or cloth, before they be laid upon them, and withall gathered so neer as may be; at such times as either the Sun or Winde hath cleared them of the dew that falleth upon them.

For the feeding of Worms you need observe no other order then this, lay the Mulberry-leaves upon them, and every two or
three

three dayes remove them, and make clean their boxes, or shelves, unlesse in times of their sicknesse, for then they are not to be touched ; the leaves which you take from them when you give them fresh to feed upon, you must lay in some convenient place, and upon them a few new leaves, to which the Worms that lay hidden in the old, will come, and then you may passe them with the said new leaves to the rest of the worms : And now lest any thing should be omitted, which serves to perfect the discovery of so excellent a benefit, I will advise you to be very diligent in keeping clean their Boxes, or shelves, as being a speciall means whereby to preserve them ; wherefore when you intend to do it, you shall remove them together with the uppermost leaves whereon they lie, unto other boxes or shelves, for with your hands you may not touch them, till they have throughly undergone their third sicknesse, and then may you passe them gently with clean hands, without doing them any harm : provided that the party that commeth neer them smell not of Garlick, Onions, or the like. The first five weeks of their age you must be very carefull to keep them warm, and in time of rain or cold weather, to set in the room where they remain, a pan with coals, burning in it now and then some Juniper, Benjamin, and such like, that yieldeth sweet smels.   But afterwards unlesse in time of extraordinary cold, give them aire, and take heed of keeping them too hot, being alwayes mindfull to store the room with herbs and flowers which are delightfull and pleasing to the smell.   As the wormes increase in bigness, you shall disperse them abroad upon more boards, or shelvs, and not suffer them to lie too thick together : and if you finde any of them broken, or of a yellow glistering colour inclining to sickness, cast them away, lest they infect the rest, and sort such as are not sick, the greatest and strongest by themselves, for so the lesser will prosper the better.

When and how to make fit rooms for the worms to work their bottoms of silk in, and in what sort the said bottoms are to be used.

AS soon as by the clear amber-coloured bodies of your worms, you shall perceive them ready to give their silk, you must (with heath made very clean, or with the branches of Rosmary, the stalkes of Lavender, or such lik) make Arches between the foresaid shelves.

Vpon the branches and sprigs whereof, the wormes will fasten themselves, and make their bottoms, which in fourteen days after the worm beginneth to work them, you may take away ; and those which you are minded to use, for the best silk, you must either presently winde, or kill the worms which are within them,

by

by laying the said bottoms two or three dayes in the Sun, or in some Oven after the bread baked therein is taken out, and the fierceness of the heat is alaid. The other bottomes which you intend to keep for seed, you must lay in some convenient warme place, untill the worms come forth, which is commonly some six-teene or twenty days from the beginning of their work: and as they do come forth you must put them together upon some piece of old Say, Grogeran, the backside of old Velvet, or the like, made fast against some Wall, or Hangings in your house.

There they will ingender, and the Male having spent himselfe, falleth down, and in short time after dieth, as also doth the Fe-male when she hath laid her egges, which egges, when you per-ceive them upon the Say or Grogran, &c. to be of a grayish co-lour, you may take them off gently with a knife, and having put them into a piece of Say or such like, keep them in a covered box amongst your woollen cloaths, or the like till the year following: But not in any moist room, for it is hurtfull for them, neither where there is too much heat, least the wormes should be hatch-ed before you can have any food for them.

The making of a Wheel, as likewise the way to winde the said silk from the bottoms, can hardly be set down so plainly as to be rightly understood: Wherefore when time shall serve, there shall be sent into every County of this Kingdom, a Wheel ready made, and a man that shall instruct all such as are desirous to learn the use thereof: Till when, I will commend these brief instructions to be carefully considered of all such as are willing to benefit either themselvs or their Country, that being skilfull in the Contemplation, they may the readier, and with less errour apply themselves to Action, which painfull industry, with Gods assistance, will quickly perfect.

An Extract of a Letter from Germany, *concerning Silk-worms, written to S. H, Esquire.*

AS for keeping of Silk-worms I must confess I have spent likewise some time in the ordering and observing of them inasmuch as this very yeare (1653) I have had from them so much good Silk (and equal to that which is brought either out of *Persia* or *Italy*) as have made mee two paire of Stockings. And I have found by experience that they may be kept as well in *Germany* as in other Countries, and that Mulberry-trees will grow in abundance upon our Lands; wherefore I have often wished that the Emperour (of *Germany*) would follow the most laudable example of the K. of *France*, who having forbidden the importation of foraigne Silk into his Kingdom hath thereby so much obliged the industry of the People of *France*, that they are
come

come to a great perfection in this Silken Manufacture. But concerning the Experiments of making Silk out of Nettles or out of Flax, I never have tried either of them.   Only I remember that I have seene once a very fine and delicate yarne or thred, which was made purely out of Nettels.   I do not believe, that those Artist of *Hamburg* and *Wolfenbuttel* which you have named unto mee in your Letter, will communicat their Skil for a publique good, as long as they can get their own comfortable subsistance by it.

A Letter written by Mr. Ra. Austen, *from* Oxford, *Febr.* 18. 1654. *Imparting his Experiments about Silk-worms and how to wind off the Silk from the Bottoms, when the Worms have done spinning?*

COncerning my experiences about Silk-worms, I only say thus much. That I am fully satisfied upon good and sure grounds that the keeping of them (store of them) in these parts would be of very great profit, could we but get Mulbery leaves sufficient to feed them.   For upon my own knowledge and experience (last yeare) upon some thousands of them, I see what might be by more.   For my great doubt and question was satisfied about the winding of the Silke from the Bottoms, when the Worms have done spinning.   I plainly see it is very easy, Children of 6. or 7. yeares old can apprehend it, and do it.   For the Worms having done spinning, which is within 4. or 5. dayes of their beginning, through out-most silke is ravelled off, and the end is found immediately, which runnes on (5. or 10. or 16. or more bottoms together) in a bason of water, a little gum drag mixed. Some Bottoms (if the Worms were strong and well fed) run without breaking scarce once or twice till all be off, and such as break, are quickly found again.   The truth is, if the Worms are scanted of leaves, their silk is so small, that it holds not so well as that of lusty Worms. I saw many brave Skains of Silk wound off the last yeare, and help't to do part of it myself.   Now the great matter is, How to propagate Mulberry-trees enough.   As for the ordinary way, by boughes, we can have but few that way. I am from time to time experimenting other wayes by Seed, Inoculating, Grafting, &c : what will be the result, as yet I know not : I doubt not, but God will in his good time bring to light and set on foot many good and worthy designes, more then are in these Nations.   We had need to labour to be of the like Principles of that worthy person, whose Paper you enclosed, patiently and humbly to waite the Lords season, and to designe for God in all we go about, which will crowne our endeavours with comfort and success.   *A*

A Rare and new discovered speedy way, and easie meanes of keeping of Silk-worms, being thus made knowne to the Colony in V I R G I N I A.

HEarken wel you beloved Planters, to what in these few lines I shall declare unto you ; and is thus sent you in Print, that all of you may communicate the great and superlative good and benefit will be unto every one of you : *who so is wise, will ponder these things*, and give the praise and glory to God, the Author of all good Inventions, how Providence having brought this to pass for all your exceeding great happiness and increase of store of wealth, with so much ease, so little labour, no cost unto you ; and in so short a time as fourty daies, this wealth flowes in upon you.

You now I conceive desire to know it, and I am as willing to impart it unto you : thus then in brief, in a plain manner, that all may understand it,

The same Lady, who last year sent you her Books of *Health and Wealth*, (who hath the happiness to beare the honourable name of your incomparable Countrey) continuing her sincere affections to the advancing of your welfares in all kindes ; and amongst the rest in this rich work of Silk, knowing *Virginia* to be in all respects most proper for it, (as by a late Book sent you published by Mr. *Williams,*) not onely in regard of the Climate being the same with *China*, from whence the infinite quantity of silk comes, but abounding (as it doth) with Mulberry-trees naturally growing there, and exceeding it by the Silkworm-bottoms found in her Woods. She hath I say this Spring found out (by the speciall blessing of God upon her intentions) so rare, so speedy, and so costless a way and means for the feeding of Silkwormes ; by the triall and experiment she so luckily made, to the admiration of all that have seen or heard of it, as a thing scarce credible ; because not heretofore thought of, nay, as it were, held impossible by such Authours as have written of the ordering and feeding of Silkworms : that this her invention being thus made known unto you, her beloved friends in *Virginia*, she is most confident, and assures herself you will all there instantly without further delay (which will be the joy of her heart) become great and rich Masters of this noble Silk-work to all your unspeakable wealth.

The way to speedy wealth was by some hundreds of you to remove some 60 miles, miles South by land, and to attempt the discovery of the Westerly Sea, ont he border of Virginia, and both two very easily atchieved, &c.

The lady hath of these Silk bottoms in her Cabinet as Jewels to convince the incredulous, as they are ten times bigger then any in Europe to admiration, and of infinite incouragement to the work.

Do

Do but as she hath done; follow but with good courage your cheerfull leader, and doubtless you shall finde (what she desires you may,) namely, *Great profit and pleasure* in an honest imployment. This Silken-Mine will be to you of more benefit then a Mine of silver.

In the beginning of *May* last 1652, when her young Mulberry-tree in her Garden began to put out its buds, then her Silkworm-eggs began to hatch, as the nature of this wise creature is, when her food begins once to appear, she comes forth of her shell: she presently laying a Mulberry-leafe upon these little crawling creatures, they came all upon it instantly; then she carried the leafe and them upon it to the tree, upon whose leaves they made hast to be; and there they day and night fed themselves, creeping from leafe to leafe, and branch to branch at their own liberties most pleasing to themselves; they grew and thrived wonderfully, and surpassed in largness of body those other wormes she kept in her chamber (she having been many a year a Mistris of Silkworms, and kept them by the Book-rules) this good and prosperous beginning heightened her hopes.   The wormes, as their nature is, cast off or slipped out of their skins four severall times, still growing greater and greater to the singular delight and content of their Mistris. About 45 dayes thus feeding upon the leaves, they began that rare and glorious work of spinning their Silk-bottomes upon the leaves and branches of the tree; such a gallant sight to behold, it ravished the Spectators, and their Mistris joy was crowned with excess of happiness herein and hereby, apparently finding the incomparable felicity this would prove to her dearly beloved *Virginia*, (for so you must give her leave to call it,) for she concluded, and so must all you, that this being thus effected in *England*, how much more with assured confidence will the wormes live, feed, and spin in *Virginia*? she upon serious and due consideration of this thing, gave God hearty and humble thanks.

And what can any of you now wish, for more incouragement? the full proof is made, the work (or rather let me call it) the pleasure is effected with so much ease, so little cost, hazard or pains, as all may admire it.

'Tis not the hundreth part of your care, labour,
or

Marginal notes:

Contrary to Book Rule, these eggs were purposely exposed to aire, cold, winds, and frost, being laid & spawned on a wall in a chamber, and there remained all winter long to try the vertue of the Eggs, &c. And twice before they come out of their bottoms, six times in all.

The seventh, they appear, then come out, a gallant silken white-winged Fly,

No weather it seems hurts them there; from heat and rains they shelter themselves under the great leaves as with a shield, but neither do harm them, how easie is a canvasse covering reared over the trees to save them from either.

or toyl you take about your Tobacco, and an hundred times (as I may say) all things put together more gain and profit to you then you make by Tobacco, which in truth is but smoak and vapour, but this a reall-royall-solid-rich-staple Commodity.

And yet if you will have still smoak, so this neither will nor can hinder your labour in that, or take from you any other employment you have a minde unto.

Consider, consider I pray you (beloved friends) your incomparable happiness in this thing, and bless God for it. Surely I should much wrong your judgements and patience if I should spend any more arguments to perswade you to this so great benefit to you, and should be like to him that to manifest the clear Sun-shine at noon-day, brought in a candle.

In a word, there's nothing is or can be wanting but your true thankfulness to God for compleating this happy invention, and your present speedy putting it in practice.

Yet give me leave, before I bid you adieu, to add the incomparable joy this Lady hath, who is confidently perswaded (her daily prayers are to God for it) that this new invented way of thus keeping Silkworms on the Trees; it requiring neither skill nor pains, (this last being the only *Remora*, in the Savages nature, which witholds them from attempting any thing of labour) that when the Indians shall behold and see you begin the business, they will with all alacrity set upon it likewise, and imitate you. And that you to incourage them (as well you may) do agree with them, that for every pound-weight of Silk-bottoms they bring unto you, you give them (as well it deserves) 5 *shil.* worth in any Commodities they desire.

And thus by the blessing of Almighty God, there may be good hope of their civilizing and conversion; so that they may be likewise great gainers both in body and soul by this thing. And if this prove so, (Gods mercies and workes being far beyond our capacities) how much then indeed will *Virginia's* happiness be every way raised to the height of Blisse. The promise being made, *That they that be wise shall shine as the brightness of the Firmament, and they that turn many to righteousnesse, as the stars for ever and ever;* which the God of wisdome and power grant to you all in *Virginia*, and so, Lord, prosper this work in their hands, Lord, prosper their handy-work; good luck I wish you all in the name of the Lord, *Amen, Amen, Amen.*

Memorandum, that you take notice, that the Birds will eat up the Silkworms on the trees, so that care must be had (and it's easily prevented by severall wayes and means, as you will devise) to scare away the birds; if all fail, a boy may be set that may affright them all away with some noise, or by nets encompassing

passing the trees, and the birds will also carry the Silk-bottoms off the trees, if they be let there remain; but thats soon prevented, by taking them speedily away.   And this of the birds is the chief reason, that *Virginia* abounds not with plenty of the naturall wilde Silkworms, they devouring most of them: and it's a wonder how any at all escape them, but that God preserves some few of the race, that his power and wisdome may be seen, and the aptnesse of the Countrey to invite you to the work.

For their Bottom being ten times bigger then ours, what mighty great Worms must they be, and what incouragement is this to the businesse, and how much more silk they make then ours, &c. Till you can try and gain the Egg and seed of your naturall gallant large Silk worm: which is chiefly that we must endeavour to store ourselves with, no Eggs comparable to hers, &c.

It will be good for you to incourage the Savages, when they finde any bottoms in the woods, to bring them to you, that you may get of the race, and seed to increase it.   Some say, the originall Silkworm is produced by the corruption of the old Mulberry-tree and leaves, by the Sunne and moisture.   But that none of you may want a stock to begin your Silk-work, the Lady aforesaid hath sent you store of Silkworm-eggs to be distributed amongst you: and if you begin but with an 100 eggs this year, they will next year be above 1000; for one female Silk-fly will lay 3, 4, 500 at a time, all things more and more concurring to your incouragement.

Now the two Propositions that tend to infinite welfare, benefit, and wonderfull advantage both to *England* and the Colony joyntly, are those that follow, they which upon no terms are to be omitted to be published and effected.

First, that with all speed some kinde of Coyne be sent to *Virginia,* that may be authorized to passe there for their Commerce and better trading.   But whether all silver somewhat valued above its worth, or part silver and part copper, is left to the wise judgments in that case.   But of this confidently be assured, that without some kinde of coyn or other, that Colony can no way prosper or thrive, nor any staple-commodities be set up, or Artificers in any kinde follow their professions: for Tobacco being now their money, and that with which all Commerce is driven, and paiments made in, and passeth from man to man: all men are set upon that thing with the neglect of all other rich and solid innumerable Commodities that are in that land to be had: and till this remedy of Coyne be applied, there can be no prosperity in that Colony. Were not the thing as apparent to all mens understandings as light is from darknesse; I should alledge many reasons for it, but it's so needlesse to spend time about it, as it might well be thought a great absurdity.   What then remains? but that some publique spirited Patriot that would immortalize

his

his name and honour in the procuring of this so necessary a thing to be speedily effected, wherein also as the generall good he shall do, so the benefit will be ever great to those that shall undertake the carrying over this Coyne; be it what it will be, all men know it so well what the gain will be, as there's no need to name it in particular manner, they cannot wish for more profit then that will be to the undertakers, and the Colony will with all their hearts be content with it, and esteeme them happy and thrice happy Benefactours.

The second thing is, that a Publication be procured and sent to the Colony in *Virginia*, declaring unto them, that there shall be liberty for all men to bring from thence for the space of ten years to come, any commodity that they shall there raise, into *England*, Custome and Excize free, (Tobacco onely excepted, which may pay double Custome, if so thought fit:) and further that to what value of money such commodities shall be sold for here in *England*, (being rated at the Custome-house at their entry;) it shall be lawfull to carry out to *Virginia* any Commodities again to the same proportion & worth, Custome and Excize free.

These two reasonable things granted; as they shall infinitily with all speed advance the Plantation, so shall they (all things duly weighed in the scale of prudence) be no lesse beneficiall to *England*, as all men that have their eyes in their heads, and English hearts in their bodies, see and apparantly know, nothing more sure and certain; and all stable and needfull Commodities brought out of all-liberall-*Virginia* into *England* at a very reasonable rate and price, much cheaper then now we have them, and are fain to fetch them with great hazard from doubtfull friends, or Heathen Nations, to their great enriching and our own impoverishing, as to all knowing men is most apparent; we shall be free from the usurpation of forreign Princes and States in our Estates, Lives, Liberties and shipping: and we may conclude boldly and rejoycingly, that Providence hath provided this all-sufficient Countrey of *Virginia* against these times, and to these intents, that hence we may have all we want from our own brethren, our Navy there increased to what number we please, for this incomparable land affords naturally all whate're belongs to the building and rigging of a Navy in all compleat manner from top to toe, as may be said; and by a safe, a sure, certain, easie, near at hand westerly discovery, (part by land, and part by Rivers and Seas) contract all the riches of the South-sea, the *Molocos, Philipines,*

Sir Francis Drake was An. 1577 in a Westerly Sea one the back of Virginia, in 37 degrees in opposite to the head of James Town in Virginia and he sailed from that Countrey which he called Nova Albion, in an

China,

open Sea to the
Molocos and
China, and so
that also this
way a trade may
be made to those
places to the
back of Virginia,
&c.

China, &c. by **3000** leagues neerer to us, without molestation by any Prince or Pirat, and shall
not need at all to be troubled, if *Rushia, Poland,*
Denmark, Sweden, Norway, Germany, yea
France, Spain, Italy, Constantinople, were removed 5000 times more distant from us: for in
one word, what ever these Countreys afford, either
necessary or superfluous, all-sufficient *Virginia* within its limits
will produce unto us.   And shall there not I say then now be
found a zealous Patriot, that will stand up for his Countrey, and
procure these things to be done out of hand? Now God forbid;
I commit the businesse to God, having done what I conceive my
part is, who onely have good wishes, and daily prayers to attend
this enterprize, which God prosper, *Amen.*

POSTSCRIPT.

At a friends importunity, (the former part sent to the Presse)
I am thus enforced to make this Addition, and upon the great
hopes that upon triall it will be found, that you may have two
Silk-harvests in one six moneths time; of the eggs a second
brood may be hatched in *June,* and so fed by Mulberry-leaves,
though then it may be it must be in an house, that then for the
promoting of such a good designe nothing of incouragement may
be wanting, nor any obstructions in the businesse, under pretence
of wanting needfull housing for to feed the wormes in.   Thus
much I will assure you,

That the slightest and simplest kinde of housing or coverture
(though the books are too superstitious and ceremonious in the
rules which are many that they give concerning the ordering of
the worm, which are not so necessary as they pretend;) I assure
you, you will abundantly content and satisfie this, though noble,
yet most humble creature, even with any habitation to do her
work in.   And to this intent I now declare unto you, (that all excuse may be taken from you) that the poor simple people in *Italy,*
Spain, Languedock, Provence, &c. do keep and feed their Silk-
worms in the same low earthen-floored Rooms, wherein themselves lodge and do all their houshould-affairs, feeding them on
shelves and on tables, giving them leaves without any more curiosity, and they thrive and prosper with them as well as in the
greatest Cities and stately chambers of the greatest rich mens
Palaces.

Sicily.   And that in *Sicilie* and *Calabria,* the common
Silk-Masters there do at time of year in the Spring,
set up only slight boarded houses in the fields round about the
Mulberry

Mulberry groves, and placing shelves in the inside of them, two foot one above the other to the roof, and a table all a long the midst of the room, they strowing their leaves on these shelves and table, there feed their wormes, and there they spin in the room their Master lies for the space of five or six weeks time, and they have abundance of silk without more ado, and a man and a boy will tend all the worms that come of six ounces of eggs, and those wormes will spin 60 pound-weight of silk, and that but at 20 *shil.* the pound, is worth 60 *ls.* in ready money, a sufficient gain to allure a man to the work I tro; but the gain by the naturall worme multiplying will farre exceed it. And I may not forget yet more that the Persian manner is to pitch up onely tents of *Canvas,* and Booths round their Mulberry-woods, and there-under they strow the Mulberry-tree-leaves on the ground : there

The great gain of the Silk-works in a house, how much more in the trees, will it be to you. The simplest and slightest houses or coor-tures will be sufficient for the Worm to feed in, and live and spin ; let no man doubt it, &c.

their wormes feed and live and spin, and do well in all kindes, the *Persians* living also the time of five weeks in the tents. Thus all these examples do manifestly prove unto you, that very simple and slight housing and a little coverture will content the Silk-worms, and they will thrive well in them. And thus you see that very poor and slight houses in *Virginia* will do the deed. Nay rest assured that the very Savages houses built but with Poles Arbor-wise, and covered top and sides with mats, will be abundantly satisfactory to the wormes, and they will thrive in them as you shall finde upon triall. And let me tell you, being desirous that you may do all things with the least cost and labour to you, and to invite also the Savages to the work for their own gain ; do but take your Reeds and small Canes in *Virginia,* and run but a strong needle and threed thorow the Reeds which will hold them together, and so you may presently make shelves and tables with them as narrow and as broad as you please ; and in truth you shall finde this kinde of shelf and tabling to feed your worms on much better in many respects then boards : but you may make triall of the Persian way also by strowing your leaves on the ground in these houses, and so feed them, and so your second brood of Silk-worms may also be thus kept and nourished in this kinde of housing and coverture ; Experience is the Mistris of fools, faith the Proverb : and it is not an unwise mans part often to make trials, though to some men they may seem impossibilities, yet rare and strange

Concerning the winding off your Silk, this Lady hath sent you one of the wheels, so that by it all of you may make the like to do that work, so you shall want nothing to speed the work.

things have upon triall often been found out ; and if you would
but

but shew the Savages samples of all kinde of things, you should soon by them know more in a moneth what is in that Countrey to be had then you have done these 40 years; and for reward they would bring in of all kindes unto you, what they have and you desire to know, so a sudden discovery may be made of all things in that land to your infinite gain.

To conclude with this *Memento,* that there are nine things that appear, are of no or small difficulty to you and the Savages to enterprize, and get gain and wealth to be produced from these Commodities; I will but name them and leave them to your better judgements and thoughts.

1 This Silke, so easie, speedy, and profitable a thing.

2 The Silk-grasse naturally there growing, which to the *Indians* the onely labour is of putting it up, and bringing it to you at such a price; a rich Commodity if known.

3 The planting Vines, small labour, little cost, long enduring.

4 The multiplying of Cunny-warrens, so easie a thing, the wool of a skin now worth 8 pence, which is more then the body, yet the flesh is considerable meat; the wooll is and will be very vendible for this new Invention, not onely of these fine light hats now sold at 15 and 20 *shil.* but the spining of the wool, and making stockings of it as fine as those of silke.

5 The increasing of abundance of Bees for wax and honey, their food so plentifull in *Virginia,* as in no Land more, and if with an hatchet you do but slash your Pine-trees, Firre-trees, Locus, and other trees, there will store of liquor come out of them, on which the Bee will gather infinite store of honey and wax, as in *Russia* and other Countreys they do.

6 The planting of Sugar-canes, that being no more laborious then the Indian wheat, setting it, and once set in good Land they grow eight or ten years, and the Indians pains will onely be to cut them yearly down, and sell them to you.

7 That of the Cotton-tree is the like for many years, gathering of the cods of woll from them, as we do Roses from the Rosebushes.

8 That of Ginger soon done, the planting and the gathering of it.

9 That of grafting your Crab-trees with Apples and Pears for Sider and Perry, you knowing that a man in one day will graft an 100 stocks, and they will grow night and day, while you eat, sleep, and play, and last 100 years to your great gain and profit.

I may not further inlarge my self for the present, these are but tastes and hints for your better wits to worke on: so with a thousand good wishes, I bid you adiew.

Floreat ***VIRGINIA.***

The

The fashion of the Botome.

The Silk Bottome of the
naturall Worm in *Virginia*, found
there in the Woods, is ten Inches about,
and six Inches in length to admiration : & whereas ours in *Europe* have their Sleave and loose Silke on
the outside ; and then in a more closer covering they in-
tombe themselves. These rare Worms, before they
inclose themselves up, fill with Silke the great
emptinesse, and afterwards inclose themselves in the middle of it, so they
have a double Bottom.

The loose Sleave Silk is all on the outside of this compass,
for if that were reckoned in, the compasse of the Bottom would
far exceed this proportion : But this is sufficient to be the Wonder of the whole World : to the Glory of the Creatour, and Exaltation of *VIRGINIA*.

A Loving Advertisement to all the Ingenious Gentlemen-Plan-
ters in Virginia *now upon the Designe of* Silk.   By V. F.
Gentlemen,

SVch hath bin the singular favour of Providence to you and the
Lady, that since the publishing of this Book ; it hath so happily lighted into the hands of divers worthy persons, being not
only Gentlemen-Travellers of credit, & Merchants of reputation ;
but likewise wonderfully taken with the lóve of *Virginia*, and no
less zealously affected to the advancement of the Silk-trade in that
Land, which they judge (not of their experience and knowledge of
what they have and observed in the Easterly parts of the World,
where abundance of Silk is made) that no part of the World is
more proper for Silk then Al-suffieient-*Virginia :* In regard of
the excellency of the temper of the Climate, which naturally
produceth not onely Mulberries for food, but the Silk-worme itselfe, in that wonderful greatness of the wilde Silk-bottom : which
as they say, The whole Vniverse affords not, nor brings forth
the like to their own small admiration. And that there is no greater quantities of them found or seen they conclude, it is in regard
of the birds who are their natural enemies, & devoure most of
them.   And these Gentlemen are confident, that you did not
know & practise those ways and meanes, for the feeding and preservation of them, as in some far remote Regions is practised by
those Nations, that are expert Masters of Silk-wormes, *Virginia*
would instantly abound with great store of Silk, and surpass all
those Countreyes in that rich commodity, and you all become
with great speed and small cost, or litle labour one of the happiest, wealthiest people that the World affords. And to the intent
that such a blessing may not be longer wanting to you, they have
out of their superlative benigne affections, and publike spirit, imparted to the Lady these ensuing Relations, with their earnest
desires and advises, that you all in *Virginia* may out of hand be
made partakers of them.   And then knowing them, you may no
longer live in gross darknes and ignorance of so great a treasure
that you are possessors of, and may now have and enjoy the full
use and benefit of, which hitherunto hath most straingely been
hidden from the eyes of body and mind ; They conceiving that
the chief cause thereof hath been the pernicious blinding smoak
of Tobacco, that thus hath dimmed and obscured your better intellectuals; but when you begin to put these wayes & means in
practice, they say you will blesse your selves (as they do) that
you have not in this long time discovered the infinite wealth and
happiness that will arise unto you out of Silk. But not longer to
detain from you this most precious eye-salve, for the speedy curing of your infirmity, and making you all rich (which is your
main aime in that new world).   *Hearken*

Hearken well so these Informations, which the Lady earnestly desires may thus be with all speed made known to you all.

THe one Traveller declared, That he passed a Countrey where he saw those people had their Silk-worms feeding on their Mulberry-trees in the fields & there they live & spun their Bottoms on the trees, And to protect this noble profitable creature & to defend it from the birds, they used a most slight, simple, plain invention speedily effected & of no cost or labour to them, which was certain great sheets of Reeds or Canes, that they hung over and about their trees, tied to certain poles that incompassed them. And in this easie manner they obtained great abundant quantities of silk, to their wonderful inriching. The sheets of Reeds were joyned together by a needle and thred, running through each Reed at several equal distances, and so drew them close and firm together. This for you to imitate, is in every respect to your wonderfull happiness.

Another of these Travellers saith, That he passed a Countrey where the inhabitants did make large Tents or Boothes all of Reeds and Canes, and in them placed shelves and tables made likewise of Reeds, on which they fed their Worms, strewing leaves on them. These tents they set up round about their Mulberry-Groves, and with much celerity, and no cost.

A third Gentleman and Merchant, that lived long in the farthest parts of *Turkey*, affirmeth, That there the inhabitants begin every Spring, *March*, to feed their Worms, and continue it till *October*, six moneths time : their Worms hatching & rehatching, one generation or brood succeeding the other : so that they have three harvests of silk-bottoms, in that space of time, every five or six weeks one : they feed their Worms in great long Barns made of Reeds or Canes, the walls and roofs of them, and shelves as aforesaid, and the Wormes when they have done feeding, spin their bottoms upon the reedy walls and roofs ; and that they have two crops of leaves from their trees : for those trees that have their leaves pull'd off in *March*, *April*, and *May*, do re-leave again, and have new and fresh leaves in *June*, *July* and *August*, wherewith they feed their latter generation or brood of Wormes very profitably.

And in confirmation of this, you shall know, the same hath been found true in *England*, that the Mulberry-tree will leave twice in a Summer, the Lady had the experience of it, and therefore much more will it do with you, which will be a most singular advantage to you.

I must not omit to add what these Gentlemen farther advise, that you can never sufficiently augment the store of food for this Noble Creature : for store of food is the main foundation, upon whose

whose speeding the Silk-trade is to be erected : for if that be not wanting, no obstruction can be in it.   For the glorious Worm is so infinite in multiplication, with that celerity as is incredible, so that she will never be defective unto you : they therefore counsell, that you graft your Mulberries with all care and speed upon these severall trees, upon which they will exceedingly thrive, *viz.* the *Popler*, the *Elme*, the *Chesnut, Beech, Quince, Medler, Fig, Peare, Apple*, and *Cornell*-trees.   And also upon any other trees, of which upon a trial you find the Worm will taste or eat their leaves. Likewise that you set of your Mulberry-slips as big as your thumb, about two foot long : and put them into good wel-digg'd ground in *September*, setting them a foot in the ground, bruising the ends of them, and watering them the next Summer well, if need be : in the same manner as in *Kent*, they set the Codling-slips.   That you also cause the *Indians* to bring unto your habitations all the young Mulberry-trees that are within an hundred miles of your Colony.   But let me acquaint you that they admire what some Gentlemen Planters of credit tell them ; that your brave Wormes do not onely live, feed, and spin upon the Mulberry-trees in the Woods, but do the same upon the *Poplar*-trees, *Plum*-trees, and *Apple*-trees :: such an incouragement to the *Silk-trade*, the World (say they) never yet heard of before, which must needs lift you up to a most speedy and incomparable height of wealth and riches, in a moment of time.

And by your gentle patience and generosity, give me leave to propound unto you, the earnest request the Lady hath to all of you ; that you please to inform her (being also the desire of many others) how it comes to pass that your Wormes get to your severall trees, not only to the *Mulberry*, but to others : For in no other Countreys the *Silk-worme*-flie doth use her wings to flie with : so that yours must either do it (and so at time of yeer couple and flie to sundry trees ; and there lay their eggs which remain till Spring again) or that your trees do naturally ingender and produce the Wormes (as it is conceived, the original of them so hapned at first) but which way soever it be, it's rare and remarkable ; and proves *Virginia* to be one of the most superlative Countreys in all the Vniverse for the *Silk-trade;* and none comparable unto the excellency of its naturall temper for *Silk.*

Then that you also inform her all you can of the nature, actions, qualities and dispositions in all kindes of this most wonderfull Creature, every way so admirable, what by any *English* or *Savage* hath bin any way observed in her : when her eggs first hatch, then how long time she is feeding before she spins, upon what part of the trees she fastens her Bottom ; How long she continues in her Bottom before she comes out a Fly, then when they couple, where they lay their eggs, upon what part of
the

the trees ? How long they live after that time ? For these in the old World never eat after they once begin to spin : how large in bigness and compass are commonly their bottoms ? if all of one colour, or divers ? In what part of the Countrey are most of them seen and found ? what do the *Savages* call them, or know any use of them ; what birds are they that most devoure them ? (for did they not, they would swarm all the Land over in a very few yeers) ; if any thing besides birds be hurtfull to them ? Their greatness and doubleness of their Bottoms are wonderful, none ever known to be so, which argues the strength and richness of this noble Worm, her vigour and hardnes exceeds, that can endure all wethers and seasons both alive and in her eggs. A great incouragement to you all that she is not a nice curious kinde of *Silkworme;* but stout and robustous, that will require little care or attendance, of small cost unto you. But her food and protection is all she requires, and pays you ten thousand-fold for what you bestow on her. That you please to send of her Bottoms to satisfie all men, who are like the Queen of *Sheba*, much better trust their eyes than eares ; some of their eggs likewise upon that which they lay them, and the *Fly* (though dead) which will many a yeer retain her perfect form in a box : do not the wormes hatch and spin twice or thrice in a Summer ?

Let me add one Petition more, and I have done. *viz.* That some of your precious Silk-grass may be sent the Lady, who is confident upon the triall she will make of it, she will give you so pleasing an account and so profitable unto you, in making known unto you what an unknown wealth you have : she prays you (and all is for your own gain) to bore and cut all your trees (a most easie thing) and thereby you shall discover presently, what rich Gums, what Balsoms, what Oils, and precious healthful Liquours they will yield you for profit & necessity : For all men know that many kindes of trees do yield most pleasant and healthsome Wines (as I may call them) for man to drink ; so also you will finde out all sorts of Dies and Colours (instantly done) : cut and bruise all kindes of your Woods, Barks, and Leaves of Trees, Roots, Berries, Nuts, Fruits, Plants, Weeds ; and but boil them in a Skillet, and then put in a little piece of white Woollen or Linnen cloth with some Allom, and you shall instantly finde and see what rich Colours they will make. What is *Indico* but a Weed, so *Woad* and *Madder?* What is *Brasil, Fustick, Logwood*, and many more kinde of Dies, but Woods ? what Coucheneal the rich Scarlet die, but a Fly, or the excrements of the *Indian* Fig-tree ? what is the new found rich dying stuff of 25. *l.* a Tun, but of a tree that is brought from the Island of *Liberty*, neer Cape *Florida* where Captain *Sailes* plants ? And shall *Virginia*

ginia not yield a drop of good Liquour or Colour? It cannot be; if but a triall thus easie were made.

By burning of all kinde of Woods and Gums, you'le soon finde by your nose what sweet Perfumes they yield. And by the ponderousness or weight of earths, you may know if Minerals or not? Let it be known also, if you have not Waters of more than ordinary qualities; for taste, colours, smell, weight, hotness, or coldness? there is much depends upon them. And you shall know if they proceed out of any Minerals, by taking a glass full, and putting into it a Gall beaten to powder, which will turn the water into a reddish colour: and send samples of all kinde of strange earths, and of all other kinde of things without fail. And lastly, (if it be not too much presumption to beg the favour to receive that honour from you) which she no wayes deserves nor can hope to requite: To inform her what be the things, the wayes, the means to advance *Virginia's Prosperity,* if they may be procured and effected. If any errour be committed in telling you all this: there is hope your pardon may be obtained, seeing your onely good and benefit hath caused all this that hath been said: and the zeal of your wealth and happiness hath drawn all to this length:

Sirs, you have the faithful testimonies of those aforesaid worthy Gentlemen, and nothing can be now wanting unto you but putting all in practice, what they have declared; and for your good are such invitations and incouragements unto you, that more cannot be wished for. There remains nothing but humble thanks to God, and to these Gentlemen your due respects, whom God hath made such Instruments for your happiness, hoping their noble courteous examples will allure all other Gentlemen Travellers to cast into this good work some mites of their further knowledges, and every man to contribute his prayers and help to to this or any other hopefull designe: seeing the consequence of them may be so good and great, not only to the *English* Nation at home and abroad; but to the poor *Savages* their welfare of souls and bodies, which God grant.

An Other Advertisement.

THe Silk-Trade, (unlesse we will be deaf to Reason and Experience) cannot be denyed the precedency of all Trades that are at this day a foot, in either World: And that in regard of its great and certain gain in so small a time; A man and a Boy being able to tend as many Silk-worms in two Moneths space, as will yeeld you sixty pounds: *which *According to that is made in Sicille by a Man and Boy.* done, they leave you ten Moneths free for any other imployment. In regard of its small skill, lesse pains, care and labour, no hazard, no cost or charge;

charge, (more then a twelve-penny Reel) no troublesome tools
or Implements : in regard of its incredible ease and pleasure, as
not requiring strength of Body, of Wit, of Purse, any stock to begin with, only hands and eyes to gather leaves and feed the
Worms with, or protect them from the Birds : if kept on the
Trees (their natural Mansion :) Admitting of all Ages, (for a
Child can do all that belongs to it) all Sexes, all Qualities, (a
most fit recreation for Ladies, especially being begun and ended
in the two pleasantest Moneths of the year, *March* and *April*.)
And all Callings too ; for if Saint *Paul* made Tents, who can
plead exemption from tending Silk-worms ?

*Again, Silk is lesse chargeable in Ware-House, *A most proper*
Fraight, &c. then any other Commodity, and yet *implyment for*
none more durable, lasting, neat, vendible, nor *the lasie* Indi-
more easily transportable : for Five hundred *ans.*
pounds worth of Silk, fraights lesse, and takes up lesse room then
ten pounds worth of Tobacco.

Now where Worms and Food abound naturally, and the Inhabitants are born with Brains, the advancement of the Silk Trade
must needs be proportionable : upon which double score *Virginia* hath the advantage of any place in the yet discovered
World ; I mean for Worms and Food, which may be thus several-
ly demonstrated. Their Worms (partly annually produced by
heat and moysture as our Caterpillars and other Insects each
Spring, partly by Eggs which have escaped the Birds who are
the greatest cause of their scarsity (which otherwise would swarm
over all the Land) devouring them when they are Worms, Eggs
and Bottoms) exceed ours not only in strength, hardinesse and
greatnesse, (being when Flyes as big as mens Thumbs) but also
in the largeness of their Bottoms, which are as big as Limons ;
(for Mr. *William Wright* of *Nansamond* found of them above
seven inches round) and one of them weighs more then a score
of ours ; insomuch that whereas a Thousand of our Worms made
but one pound of Silk, worth at most here 30s. a pound, a thousand of their natural Worms will make ten pounds of Silk, worth
here twenty shillings the pound. And certainly they need not
object or be troubled at the somewhat more coursnesse of their
Silk, since they from the same number of Worms receive ten
pounds in mony for our thirty shillings.

As for their Food, the *Virginia* Worms feed not only on the
Mulberry (their sole food in all other parts of the World) but
also on the Crab, Plum, Poplar ; Oake, Apple, Cherry and Po-
hickerry-tree leaves, with sundry other shrubs and bushes. For
proof whereof, Mistresse *Mary Ward* sent over to her Couzen
ten bottoms taken from Apple trees. Esquire *Ferrar* her Kinsman likewise sent her ten more, pulled off from Oaks and divers
shrubs

shrubs. Mr. *Laurence Ward* some taken from the Pohickerry tree, Mr. *Wright* from the Cherry tree. So Dr. *Russel* and others.

The Objection, or rather groundlesse surmise of the Worms being hurt by Thunder in *Virginia*, is sufficiently cleared, not only by the Natural Worms living so well, and thriving there so admirably on the trees ; but also by trial made there this Spring of our Worms. That ever to be honoured Noble Squire *Diggs* having (at his very great charge) sent for two *Armenians* out of *Turky* skilful men, and made ten pound of Silk, which had not want of Eggs hindred him, would have been so many Thousand pounds.

Nothing then wants to make *Virginia* rival *Peru* for wealth, more then to perswade the Planters to provide themselves this Winter (to lose no more time) of as many of the Natural Worms bottoms as possibly they can. They will now be found in the Woods on the dis-leaved trees, though most of them are spun by the Worms on the tree leaves, which falling to the ground, they perish with them ; and this is another great cause that so few bottoms are to be found. The Bottoms thus gotten must be carefully kept in some long boxes till the Flyes come forth, happily in February or March. For they remain in their bottoms 300. dayes, ours but 20. so that their Eggs (whereof one female will lay a spoonfull, suppose 500.) lye unhatched but about nine dayes, ours nine moneths.

When your Worms are hatched, you may keep them either on the trees (being assured that they will live on that kind of Tree whatsoever it be from whence you took your Bottoms) and then you shall need onely to protect them from the Birds ; or else in some slight kind of housing, Reedy arbors, Indian mansions, or what else you can devise there cheapest and speediest, and then your onely labour and care is to give them leaves, which you may either strip off, or clip from off your Trees, or if you will, lop off little branches (which may perhaps prove a good way for you: for thereby the leaves will remain the longer fresh) and give them to your Worms, who for the labour of every Man and Boy thus imployed only in two moneths time, will repay you with threescore pounds worth of Silk.

> Your own Experience (Gentlemen) will I hope ere this time twelv-moneth certifie you of the truth that is here set down, unless you shall rather chuse to hugg your own poverty, and make much of that slavery and drudgery you wear out your selves with, in toyling about that contemptible, beggarly *Indian* Weed,

T O B A C C O

The Copy of Esquire *Diggs* his Letter, to his much honoured freind, *John Ferrar*, Esquire at his house at little Gidding, in Huntingtonshire. From *Virginia*, June 21. 1654.

Sir,

I *Have received your many and severall Letters, printed papers, and Quæries; and, would my occasions have permitted, I should ere this, have given you that due thanks you deserve, and punctually have answered all your judicious and pleasing Quæries: But I was so taken up in sending dayly for Mulberry-leaves, as they are now so far scattered from my present Plantation, that I could not possibly answer your expectations; That onely difficulty made me to make but 400. pound weight of Silk-bottomes, which I caused to be wound of 7. or 8. l. of Silke in a day: Sir, I doe very well approve of your last well printed Paper, sent the Colony for making triall of the Naturall Silk-worme, but such was my ill happe, that I could not this spring meet with any of those Bottoms, but shall this next Winter procure of them, all I can; Sir, I am now confident I have conquered all the great feared difficulty of this rich commodity, and made its sweet easy and speedy Profitt so evident to all the Virginians (and that it doth not at all hinder their too much beloved* Tobacco, *but that they may proceed with both together) that now I doubt not (nor they) but that in a short time here will be great quantities made of Silke; you in* England *will reape much advantage, and gaine many waies by it, (more then most men can yet see) and I by Gods blessing the comfort and joy, in setting up so noble, so beneficiall, a staple vendible commodity. My people differ very little from the rules set down in your, Mr.* Williams *his Booke, and as Esquire* Samuell Hartlib *hath also directed in his advertizement of Silk-worms unto us; only in the hatching of the Worms-Eggs, they are more curious, of which I shall, when I have more time, give you a more particular accompt: I made 10. l. of seed or Eggs this spring to give away to diverse Planters, that are very earnest (seeing so great a benefit before their eyes) to become also Silk-masters, you need not feare it but that this next spring there will be divers tryalls made of the hopefull Naturall Worms, that you so highly prize (and not without good cause) and which is more, perhaps they may fall one after another and be re-hatched that we may have a double Silk harvest in one summer (as you have formerly hinted to us). Pray Sir will you be pleased at this time to excuse my too much brevity in this great business of so much concernment, of so much happiness to this Country, and attribute it to my great hast, and much business upon the ships sudden departure, having many*

more

more dispatches to make to Freinds; But in my next, I shall make you double amends; I pray present my service to the vertuous Lady Virginia: Sir I daily pray for your long life, and well-fare, and now rest.

Sir your most humble Servant,
Edward Diggs.

A Way Experimented by Mr. Farrar, *to make the Gummy-hard Naturall* Virginia *Bottoms (which hetherto by no art could be prepared to unwind by reason of the Gummy hardness) to unwinde with ease, to the great advantage of the Planters of the Silk-trade in* Virginia.

YOu must take Sope-boylers lye or liquor, which is very sharp and strong, and set that in a vessel over the fire till it be warme, then put in as many of your hard gummy Bottoms as you please, and let them rest in that liquor, till it be scalding-hot, and so remain half a quarter of an houre more or less, till they be so dissolved, that you may take out one and find it fit to unwind; which you must thus doe.

First put the Bottoms into scalding clean water, and having layen a while therein, then take them out and proceed to unwind them as the custome is.

In case Sope-boylers lye or liquor be not to be had, you may make a strong liquor of the Ashes of any Wood, with boyling water, the stronger the better, and this may and will also perform the work. And this is just as you make a lye to buck clothes withal. Only note it must be very strong made.

An Extract out of a very Ingenious Gentlemans Letter from Dublin, *Concerning the Reformed* Virginian *Silk-worm.*

I Thank you for your *Virginian* Paper. Me thinkes the Experiment is most Natural to my apprehensions, that the Worms should feed and thrive best upon the leaves growing on the Trees, rather then in the Houses, and that they, like other Caterpillers (of whom these are a sort) did at first breed so, and that Houses were rather an Invention for expediency,

But their Proposition about Money to be carried to *Virginia*, I utterly dislike; even somuch as if it were possible, I would banish Money from *Ireland.*

An Animadversion upon the Letter from Dublin.

I like not the Gentlemans Reason why he likes the Proposition concerning feeding of Silk-worms upon the Trees.

For

For almost all Plants, even the most rare now in use were Originally (namely since the deluge) wild and past muster amongst Weeds, & are improved to such a degree of excellency to the eye, nose or palat, by industry and home-helps and contrivances : So *Iohn Tradeskin* by *Lambeth*, by the advantage of putting his Trees, and other Plants into a warm house in winter or a stow, nurses up those things faire and fragrant, which would without that help either dye or be dwarft. This is the reason why tame Pigeons or Conies are larger, and breed better, and oftner then wild. Yet I conclude not against the thing it self ; for questionles, that the leaves have more heart, fresh and greene, then halfe withered, if the cause of their withering were known or considered, But I can say little to this, as having no experience,

A new observation, concerning the feeding of Silk-worms with Lettice, imparted from Dublin.

I Have only to present you with some observations I made concerning the feeding of Silk-worms (meeting here accidentally with a kinswoman of mine that keepes great store of them) which generally is beleeved only to be don, with *Mulberry* leaves : the contrary of which is here by some practised, *viz.* to feede them with Lettice ; which the worms eat very readily, grow as big as those that are fed with Mulberry leaves & spin as much Silk : They will also eate the hearb called *Dantedelyon*, but whether that will so well agree with them as *Lettice*, *I* have not tried, but with *Lettice* they will thrive very well, eating nothing else all the yeare.

More Observations concerning the feeding of Silk-worms with Lettice,

SIR,

MY good Cosen Mr. *W.* sent me the letter, you wrote to him ; and the note sent you out of *Ireland*, that intimated the happy success the Gentlewoman had then in keeping Silk-worms, not only on the Mulberry-tree-leaves, but with Lettice leaves, the thing you much desired that my Daughter should have made known unto her. Truly Sir your singular humanity and goodness in all things more and more extends it selfe for the publique benefit of all, and I see to the particular satisfaction of your Freinds, though Strangers to you yet those that have daily cause more and more to honour you, as we justly do. Sir, this your favour is both by my-self and Daughter so much resented as it requires from us, very hearty and particular thanks to be tendered to
your

your worth. She is a lover of Rarities in these kinds, and to try
conclusions upon her Silk-worms, and no way envious, but much
rejoyces to hear that any have had that good success with Lettice as you write of, and shall her-self againe make a third triall
in that kind, for she hath 2. yeares last past tryed her-self to have
kept some with Lettice leavs & so did & they thrivd as well as
those kept with Mulberrys, but stil when the time of spinning
came they would not spin, but then dyed and this put her out of
heart to try further, yet I may tell you, she perswaded a Gentleman near her to keep some with Lettice 25. daies and then fed
them with Mulberrys at last, and these did very well and spun
as good Bottoms as those wholly kept with Mulberry leaves.
But now she resolves upon your intimation of the experiment
made in *Ireland* to try a third time, and to give you an accompt
of her success in *June* next, if God permit.

And now Sir she presents this printed inclosed paper to your
worthy judgment, if you find not it matter of consideration and
reason for her to send it as a second new yeares gift to *Virginia*,
hoping that it may do good there to the Planters and informe
them of much truth, and invite them to the business of Silk, which
God grant, *Amen.*

This other paper of Ryming lines (for Verses they deserve
not the name) yet being that what her Brother a young Scholar
hath collected out of Letters, that were sent her from *Virginia*
and given her, she also sends you to further informe you of things
done, last spring.

Thus worthy, Sir, with the due respects of both our kindest
salutes, wishing you all happiness in this and the better world,
I rest ever.

Yours in all love and service

Littell *Gidding Huntingshire*   *JOHN FERRAR.*
this 28. *Novemb.* 1653.

SIR,
She makes bold to present you with a sample of *Virginia*
Silk-grass sent her by a freind. It's a rarity, and she hopes will
delight you who have such a publique Spirit to rejoyce, and further a Common good; as she hath great hopes this will prove a
commodity next to the Silk there, as skilfull men and Artists do
assure her of it, and thousands of poor people will be set a work
with it, if it prove there to be in quantity.

Upon

Upon the most Noble, Virginian natural Silk-Worm
her wonderful, various, plentiful food; The infinite, speedy, great wealth she will produce to her
protector; (in 45. days the time of her feeding)
with small labour, cost, or skill, (learnt in an houres
space by any child.) The singular aptness of that
rare Superlative Climate, in Breeding them on so
many several kinds of Trees in her Woods where
they live, Feed and Spin, their mighty large,
strange, double-bottoms of Silk : To the admiration of this our Old World; but to the exaltation
and glory of incomparable *Virginia,* in the New.

*W*Here *Wormes and Food doe naturally abound,*
   A Gallant Silken Trade must there be found :
Virginia *excells the World in both,*
Envie nor Malice can gaine say this troth.
Many a man the causes faine would heare,
How these rare Worms came first or still come there.
Insects produced are by heat and moisture
Who in strange shapes and formes do oft appeare.
In Spring our trees the Caterpillers reare ;
Their trees likewise these noble creatures beare.
And some proceed from eggs that scaped are
From their enemies sight, which thing is rare.
They feed not only on the Mulberry
Which in our World sole food is held to be
For all such precious Worms of that degree :
But Popler, Plum, Crab, Oake, and Apple tree,
Yea Cherry, and tree called Pohickery :
So on the Shrubs and Bushes feed full many
Her Worms are huge whose bottoms dare
With Lemmons of the largest size compare.
And twenty one of ours will sure poize less
Then one of theirs for weight and ponderousness.
Master William Wright *of* Nansamound
Found Bottoms above seven Inches round.

                                        And

And though the Silk prove not all out so fine
As Persian, *that's no let to the designe.*
For since a thousand of our Bottoms make
But one pound of fine Silk, you'l ten pounds take
From theirs.   If we at Thirty shillings sell
Our pound, for twenty they'l afford theirs well.
The paines that's taken is alike in either
But the gaines by theirs eight times greater:
Then, we confined are to the Mulberry
For food, their Worms have great Variety.
Her dainty coloured flies and large Worms
In length and bigness do surpass mens Thumbs.
Whereas ours short of little fingers come.
Our flies come out in twenty days and lay
Eggs, theirs not still three hundred as they say
O wondrous thing! a Worm to fast so long
And then come out a painted Fly so strong.
Nine months full out our eggs unhatch't remaine
Nine daies in Spring makes theirs revive againe
A Planter (I *wish they had him named*)
A spoonfull eggs from one fly he gained
Which to five hundred at least amounted
Loe shortly endless they must be counted.
In March *they first begin to live and feed*
In Aprill *they have done the Silken deed*
The sweetest, pleasantst time in all the yeare.
You to this Wealth the chanting Birds will cheare
And ten moneths time they leave you with great ease
To spend it in what profit you shall please.
Rare Worms who feeding five and forty daies
On leaves of sundry Plants and shrubs repaies
Their keepers with fine Silke which wants no strength
And yet extends itselfe some miles in lenght
And for the labour of a Man and Boy
They gaine you Sixty pounds which is no toy.
If you from Birds protect them on the trees
(*Their naturall mansions*) *t'will them best please*
Your paines is spar'd in giving them the leaves
By which alone you gaine their Silken sleaves
For non-parrel Virginia *in her Woods,*
Brings forth as all men know these precious goods:
Where thousand fleeces fit for Princes *Robes*
On Virgin-trees shall hang in Silken Globes.
The noble Worm so hardy, stong and stout
No weather ill is able them to rout.

The

The reasons why the numbers are so small
Less Cruell Birds devoure most of them all
When they are Worms yea Eggs or Silken ball.
Most bottoms likewise on the leaves are spun
Both falling to the ground do perish soon
Those only found that spun are on the branch
Not by their care but providentiall chance
Which only show themselves when all is bare
To Find in Summer any'tis most rare.
If to prevent both dangers you intend
A Reedy-Arbourwell will doe't, you'l find
Or slightest coverture in any kind
The skill and paines to all each Child can do :
As you shall find on triall tis most true.
And may in Wealth compare with rich Peru.
And for all Tooles that appertaine thereto
A Twelve-peny Reele is all it will cost you,
No wit, no strength, no purse, no stock will need
But Eies and hands, the Worms to guard and feed.
And thus you see done is the Silken deed :
Which brings you so great wealth with so much speed.
Five hundred pounds worth of rich Silk, all know
Fraights less then ten pounds in poore Tobacco
Silkes are no trash, no toy, nor Pedlars ware ;
Staple, good, and ready chinke every where.
Twenty shillings a pound t'will yield you cleare
And Ships to fetch it will come flying there.
Queenes of the best edition need not scorne
In her owne Livery to serve this Worm :
Only to give her leaves is all she craves
And in reward with Silk shee'l make you brave.
Out of her rich belly by her mouth spun
Weaves it into a most curious bottom
Which by a Reele turning with hand of man
Is wholly wound off most neatly againe.
To feed Silk-Worms no Caling can disdaine
Seeing they yeild you so much honest gaine
No imployment in the World so likely
To make so soone your lasie Savage Wealthy.
For his Silk bottoms in exchange shall have
From English, *what he so needs, begs, and craves*
Red coats, hose, shooes, knives, they highly deeme
Jewes-Trumps, Bells, Beads, all toys, no less esteeme.
If all be thus the cause you now demand
Why hath this knowledg been thus long detain'd

And

And but now by the Ladies Books inflam'd
Ignorance of Planters so strange hath been
Till now ne're knew nor dreamt of this rich thing.
Confest it is, that of't some they have seene
Regardlesly, but ne're did them esteeme.
Which loss of Wealth and Honour they'l regaine
And Virgins *Counsell follow will amaine.*
The happy onset they this Spring have made
Assures them all a stately pretious trade.
Sir Henry Chichly *that Heroick Knight*
Affirmes ther's not an ingenuous Wight
In Virginia *but makes all speed he can*
To be e're long a Silken noble man.
And say, Colonel Ludlow *certifies*
That thence from Silk great profit will arise ;
Yea worthy Bernard *that stout Colonel*
Informes the Lady the work most facile
And of rich Silken stuffs, made shortly there
He hopes that he and others shall soone weare.
So major John Westrope *saith, Silk will be*
A gallant designe for their brave Country.
Thunder was that, that some men onely doubt
But triall made this Spring puts that feare out.
In all Lands where Worms are kept tis wonder
To heare that any were harm'd by thunder.
Their naturall Worm proves this more truer.
Mr. Gorge Lobs *that prudent old Planter*
Tells her that Worms ne're spun Silk daintier.
Lets give those Gentlewomen their full dues
Mistress Garret *and* Burbage *for Silk clues*
That Colonells Wife needs not farr to rove
Her Court affords a pleasant Mulberry Grove :
But noble Diggs *carries the Bell away*
(Lass ! want of eggs made so small the essay)
His two Armenians *from Turky sent*
Are now most busy on his brave attempt
And had he stock sufficient for next yeare
Ten thousand pound of Silk would then appeare
And to the skies his worthy deeds upreare.
Loe here what mistress Mary Ward *hath sent*
And to her Lady Cosin she presents
Ten rare Bottoms took from her Apple tree
That all England may it beleeve and see.
Her honour'd Kins-man Esquire Ferrar,
To confirme and make the wonder greater

The

Ten more likewise hath sent her, which he found
On stately Oakes and Shrubs that kiss the ground
And Doctour Russell *that learn'd Phisitian*
Hath with his, made a full addition.
For things more slowly do affect the minde
Which eares do heare then those that eies do find.
Now from smoke Virginia *shall be raised*
And throughout the World be duly praised.
Ah Blest be God that now in his due time
This Silken light apparently doth shine
 Then come, O come with sacred Lays
 Let us sound the Almightys praise

I. F.

To the most Noble deserving Esquire *Diggs:* upon the Arrivall
of his two Armenians out of *Turky* into *Virginia*.

Courage, brave Sir: sith Ayde from God is sent
Proceed, go on, drive forth thy great intent.

A

A Comparison between the gain and labour of
TOBACCO *and* **SILK.**

TObacco requires 9 moneths time, much care and labour, both without and within dores, and a mans Crop is commonly 15 hundred weight of Tobacco, and this at two pence a pound is 14 pound gain.

Silk requires six weeks time, if done in a house, and by the labour of a man and boy, in gathering leaves, and tending the worms that come of six ounces seed, there is by so many worms spun as much Silk as will weigh sixty pound weight, and this but at 20 *shil.* a pound, yeelds 60 *l.* in ready money.

Tobacco, leaves a man but 3 moneths in the year for other business.

Silk, leaves a man ten moneths time in the year, for any other imployments.

14 pounds a man gaines by his Crop of Tobacco.

60 pounds a man and boy gains by his Crop of Silk.

Then let all men judge which is the more gainfull.

But what will be the gain and profit, by the worms feeding and spinning on the Trees is more considerable, and also the naturall *Virginia*-worms bottome exceeding ours in *Europe* 20 times in bigness, and in weight: what a Treasure then will this be, and no labour, cost, hazard, expence of time at all, a Boy onely to keep away the Birds from eating the Silk-worms on the Trees, &c.

Thus

Thus learned Bartas *upon this noble `&` admirable Creature.*

YEt may I not this *Wonderous Worm* pass by,
  Of fly turn'd Worm, and of a *Worm a Fly.*
Two Births, two Deaths, here Nature hath assign'd
  her,
Leaving a *Posthume,* dead-live Seed behind her;
Which soon transforms the fresh and tender leaves
Of *Thisbes* pale tree, to those tender sleaves
(On Ovall Clues) of soft smooth silken **Flax,**
Which more for us then for her self she makes.
O precious fleece ! which only did adorne
The sacred loins of Princes heretofore :
But our proud age, with prodigall abuse
Hath so profan'd the old honorable use :
That Shifters now, that scarce have bread to eat
Disdain plain Silk, unless it be beset
With one of those brave Metals, whose desire
Burns greedy soules with an impartiall fire.

Had Du Bartas *fully known all the vertues and rarities in this incomparable Creature, even a miracle in Nature, he would have inlarged his Poems in a more ample manner in the praise of it, to the great honour of the Creatour.* Cui Gloria, *Amen.*

Homo Vermis.

Wee all are creeping Worms of th' earth,
Some are Silk-Worms great by birth,
Glow-Worms some that shine by night,
Slow-Worms others, apt to bite,
Some are muck-Worms slaves to wealth,
Maw-Worms some that wrong the health,
Some to the publique no good willers,
Cancker-Worms and Cater-pillers ;
Found about the earth wee'r crawling,
For a sorry life wee'r sprawling,
Putrid stuff we suck, it fills us,
Death then sets his foot and kills us.

FINIS.

LEAH and *RACHEL,*

OR,

the Two Fruitfull Sisters

VIRGINIA,

AND

MARY-LAND:

Their Present Condition, Im-

partially stated and related.

VVITH

A Removall of such Imputations as are scandalously cast on those Countries, whereby many deceived Souls, chose rather to Beg, Steal, rot in Prison, and come to shamefull deaths, then to better their being by going thither, wherein is plenty of all things necessary for Humane subsistance.

By *John Hammond.*

Eccles. 22. v. 8.
If children live honestly and have wherewith, they shall put away the shame of their Parents.

LONDON,
Printed By *T. Mabb,* and are
to be sold by *Nich. Bourn,* neer the Royall
Exchange, 1 6 5 6.

Force's Collection of Historical Tracts.

VOL. III.—No. 14.

TO

His Honoured and Worthy Friends
the Worshipfull William Stone *Esquire, Governour ;*
and Leivt. General of the Province of Mary-land.

A N D

Mr. James Williamson *of* Rapahanock *in*
Virginia *Gentleman.*

Gentlemen,

AS yee both are Eminent in your Places, and are as well beloved where ye live; and that your loves to each other are such, as I wish the Vnion between *Virginia* and *Mary-land* to be, my Subject being concerning both places: I know none more fit then your selves to Dedicate it to, (not so much for your kindnesses, which I have often tasted of) as that the truth hereof under your Patronage may obtain belief and credit: I crave your Pardons, for intruding this unknown to you, and using your names to so mean a piece; I have certified you wherefore I did it; to which I add, that

(4)

I am desirous the whole country may note your affections to each other; And that I dare in *England* own and Entitle him my Governour; that in *Mary-land* I fled for submitting to. I shall no further enlarge here more, then to let you know, that I am to those Countries and Your selves, an

Humble Servant, and Well-wisher

whilest I am

Jo. Hammond.

To

TO

Those two worthy Commanders

and Marriners, Capt. *Iohn Whittie*, Commander
of the good Ship, the *Freeman*, now bound for
Virginia; And Capt. *Sam. Tilghman*, Commander
of the *Golden Fortune*, now bound for the
Province of *MARY-LAND*.

SIRS,

AS I have made choice of two *Honourable Gentlemen, the
one belonging to* Virginia, *the other to* Mary-land; *So I
thought it not impertinent equally with them to Dedicate
this to you two living in* England, *and Vsing the Trade of*
Virginia *and* Mary-land, *that your selves may judge and testifie,
who well know the Country, that I have not added to their
worths, but rather been sparing of what is justly their dues:
For it is a received errour amongst the many slanders cast on
these places, that we are sworn neither to Speak nor Write but
glossingly of them; If we are so sworn, they cannot believe
yee are; and therefore will credite your Affirmations, both
places speak worthily of you, both for affable usage of your
Passengers, and noble deportments towards the inhabitants in
those Countries; and so are yee both noted, that I wish yee
were as well known to all strangers desirous to ship themselves
thither, as to us that have lived there: They then would as
much covet to be your Passengers, as we that by experience
have felt and known your goodnesse; many other Gentlemen
of good repute uses the Trade: but this I dare affirm, that
though they may be had in equall esteem, yet men more generally beloved and applauded I have not known, using that
Course than your selves: You know I flatter not; therefore I crave no excuse, unlesse for my presumption in this attempt; but seeing unknown to your selves, I have published
your names here in Print, pray call me not to account for it:
This Book I confess is not worthy of it, nor I of your angers;
but how ever ye see it is past, &* litera scripta manet, *yee must
either buy up and burn all, or ye will be found here, and I
hope not blemisht in it, nor in owning the truth of,*

Your reall Servant,

JOHN HAMMOND.

Leah

Leah *and* Rachell, *or the two fruit-*
full Sisters of Virginia *and* Mary-land ; *their pre-sent condition impartially stated and related.*

IT is the glory of every Nation to enlarge themselves, to encourage their own forraign attempts, and to be able to have of their own, within their own territories, as many several commodities as they can attain to, that so others may rather be beholding to them, then they to others ; and to this purpose have Encouragements, Priviledges and Emunities been given to any Discoveries or Adventurers into remote Colonies, by all politique Common Wealths in the world.

But alas, we Englishmen (in all things else famous, and to other Countries terrible) do not onely faile in this, but vilifie, scandalize and cry down such parts of the unknown world, as have been found out, setled and made flourishing, by the charge, hazzard and diligence of their own brethren, as if because removed from us, we either account them people of another world or enemies.

This is too truly made good in the odiums and cruell slanders cast on those two famous Countries of *Virginia* and *Mary-land*, whereby those Countries, not onely are many times at a stand, but are in danger to moulder away, and come in time to nothing ; nor is there any thing but the fertility and natural gratefulnesse of them, left a remedy to prevent it.

To let our own Nation (whose common good I covet, and whose Common-wealths servant I am, as born to no other use) be made sensible of these injuries: I have undertaken in this Book to give the true state of those places, according to the condition they are now in ; and to declare either to distressed or discontented, that they need not doubt because of any rumour detracting from their goodnesses, to remove and cast them-

selves

selves and Fortunes upon those Countries, in which if I should
deviate from the truth ; I have at this present carping enemies
in *London* enough, to contradict and cry down me and this, for
Impostours. It is not long since I came from thence (God
knows sore against my will) having lived there upward of one
and twenty years ; nor do I intend (by Gods assistance) to be
long out of it again : and therefore can by experience, not hear-
say (as *Bullock* and other lying Writters have done, who at
randome or for their own private lucre have rendred their
Books rediculous and themselves infamous lyars, nor will I like
them, over extoll the places, as if they were rather Paradices
than earthly habitations; but truly let ye know, what they are,
and how the people there live.) Which when impartially viewed, will undoubtedly clear up those Foggy Mists, that hath to
their own ruine blinded and kept off many from going thither,
whose miseries and misfortunes by staying in *England* are much
to be lamented, and much to be pittied.

In respect these two Sister Countries (though distinct Governments) are much of one nature, both for produce and manner of living ; I shall only at present, Treat of the elder Sister
Virginia, and in speaking of that include both : And ere I
leave off, shall in particular rehearse the unnaturall usage *Mary-
land* the younger Sister, hath had, not by *Virginia*; but by
those Vipers she hath received and harboured with much kind-
nesse and hospitalitie.

The Country is reported to be an unhealthy place, a nest of
Rogues, whores, desolute and rooking persons ; a place of intolerable labour, bad usage and hard Diet, &c.

To Answer these several calumnies, I shall first shew what it
was ? next, what it is ?

At the first settling and many years after, it deserved most of
those aspersions (nor were they then aspersions but truths) it
was not settled at the publique charge ; but when found out,
challenged, and maintained by Adventurers, whose avarice and
inhumanity, brought in these inconveniences, which to this day
brands *Virginia*.

Then were Jayls emptied, youth seduced, infamous women
drilled in, the provisions all brought out of *England*, and that
embezzelled by the Trustees (for they durst neither hunt fowl,
nor Fish, for fear of the *Indian*, which they stood in aw of,
their labour was almost perpetuall, their allowance of victual
small, few or no cattle, no use of horses nor oxen to draw or
carry, (which labours men supplyed themselves) all which caused a mortality ; no civil courts of justice but under a Marshall
law,

law, ho redresse of grievances, complaints were repaied with stripes, moneys with scoffes, tortures made delights, and in a word all and the worst that tyrany could inflict or act, which when complained of in *England*: (but so were they kept under that it was long ere they would suffer complaints to come home) the bondage was taken of, the people set free, and had lands a signed to each of them to live of themselves, and enjoy the benefit of their own industry; men then began to call what they laboured for their own, they fell to making themselves convenient housing to dwell in, to plant corne for their food, to range the wood for flesh, the rivers for fowle and fish, to finde out somwhat staple for supplie of cloathing, to continue a commerce, to purchase and breed cattle, &c. but the bud of this growing happinesse was again nipt by a cruell Massacre committed by the Natives, which again pull'd them back and kept them under, enforcing them to get into Forts (such as the infancy of those times afforded: they were taken off from planting; their provisions destroyed, their Cattle, Hogs, Horses, &c. kill'd up, and brought to such want and penury, that diseases grew rife, mortality exceeded; but receiving a supply of men, amunition and victuals out of *England*, they again gathered heart, pursued their enemies, and so often worsted them, that the *Indians* were glad to sue for peace, and they desirous of a cessation) consented to it.

They again began to bud forth, to spread further, to gather wealth, which they rather profusely spent (as gotten with ease then providently husbanded, or aimed at any publique good; or to make a Country for posterity; but from hand to mouth, and for a present being; neglecting discoveries, planting of Orchards, providing for the Winter preservation of their stocks, or thinking of any thing staple or firm; and whilest Tobacco, the onely Commodity they had to subsist on bore a price, they wholy and eagerly followed that, neglecting their very planting of Corn, and much relyed on *England* for the chiefest part of their provisions; so that being not alwayes amply supplied, they were often in such want, that their case and condition being related in *England*, it hindred and kept off many from going thither, who rather cast their eyes on the Barren and freezing soyle of *New-England*, than to joyn with such an indigent and sottish people, as were reported to be in *Virginia*.

Yet was not *Virginia* all this while without divers honest and vertuous inhabitants, who observing the general neglect and licensiousnesses there, caused Assemblies to be call'd and Laws to be made tending to the glory of God, the severe suppression

of

of vices, and the compelling them not to neglect (upon strickt punishments) planting and tending such quantities of Corn, as would not onely serve themselves, their Cattle and Hogs plentifully, but to be enabled to supply *New-England* (then in want) with such proportions, as were extream reliefs, to them in their necessities

From this industry of theirs and great plenty of Corn, (the main staffe of life) proceeded that great plenty of Cattel and Hogs, (now innumerable) and out of which not only *New-England* hath been stocked and relieved, but all other parts of the *Indies* inhabited by Englishmen.

The inhabitants now finding the benefit of their industries, began to look with delight on their increasing stocks: (as nothing more pleasurable then profit) to take pride in their plentifully furnished Tables, to grow not onely civil, but great observers of the Sabbath, to stand upon their reputations, and to be ashamed of that notorious manner of life they had formerly lived and wallowed in.

They then began to provide and send home for Gospel Ministers, and largely contributed for their maintenance ; But *Virginia* savouring not handsomely in *England*, very few of good conversation would adventure thither, (as thinking it a place wherein surely the fear of God was not) yet many came, such as wore Black Coats, and could babble in a Pulpet, roare in a Tavern, exact from their Parishoners, and rather by their dissolutenesse destroy than feed their Flocks.

Loath was the Country to be wholy without Teachers, and therefore rather retain these then to be destitute ; yet still endeavours for better in their places, which were obtained, and these Wolves in sheeps cloathing, by their Assemblies questioned, silenced, and some forced to depart the Country.

Then began the Gospel to flourish, civil, honourable, and men of great estates flocked in: famous buildings went forward, Orchards innumerable were planted and preserved ; Tradesmen set on work and encouraged, staple Commodities, as Silk, Flax, Pot-ashes, &c. of which I shall speak further hereafter, attempted on, and with good successe brought to perfection ; so that this Country which had a mean beginning, many back friends, two ruinous and bloody Massacres, hath by Gods grace out-grown all, and is become a place of pleasure and plenty.

And having briefly laid down the former state of *Virginia*, in its Infancy, and filth, and the occasion of its scandalous aspersions : I come to my main subject, its present Condition and Hapinesse (if any thing can be justly called happy in this

transatory

transatory life (otherwise then as blessings which in the well using whereof, a future happinesse may be expected.)

I affirme the Country to be wholesome, healthy and fruitfull; and a modell on which industry may as much improve it self in, as in any habitable part of the World; yet not such a Lubberland as the Fiction of the land of Ease, is reported to be, nor such a *Vtopian* as Sr. *Thomas Moore* hath related to be found out.

In the Countries minority, and before they had well cleared the ground to let in ayre (which now is otherwise) many imputed the stifling of the wood to be the cause of such sicknesse; but I rather think the contrary; for divers new Rivers lately settled, where at their first comming upon them as woody as *James* Rivers, the first place they setled in, and yet those Rivers are as healthy as any former setled place in *Virginia* or *England* it self: I believe (and that not without reason) it was only want of such diet as best agreed with our English natures, good drinks and wholesome lodgings were the cause of so much sicknesses, as were formerly frequent, which we have now amended; and therefore enjoy better healths;' to which I add, and that by experience since my comming into *England*, and many (if not all *Virginians* can do the like,) that change of ayre does much alter the state of our bodies: by which many travellers thither may expect some sickness, yet little danger of mortality.

A Geographicall description of the Country I shall not attempt (as having little skill in the Mathematicks) enough of that hath been formerly Written; nor is it a place now to learn to discover. I shall abhor to spirit over any; but go along with such as are voluntarily desirous to go thither, and lead them with my blunt relation (for truth knows little of eloquence) aboard the Ships thither bound, and carrying you into the Country, shew you the courtesie of the place, the disposition of the Inhabitants, the commodities, and give all sorts of people advice how and where to set down for their present benefit and future accommodation.

If any are minded to repair thither, if they are not in a capacity to defray their own charges (if they are I wish they might and so be at their own disposing) let them not be seduced by those mercinary spirits that know little of the place, nor aime at any good of theirs, but onely by foysting and flattering them to gain a reward of those they procure them for; beware them, for it is not only hab nab whether ye go to a good service or a bad, but scandalous to your selves to be so seduced, and it
were

were good and very just that such vagabond people were severely punished, as great betrayers of their own Nation, for ye cannot imagine but their are as well bad services as good; but I shall shew ye if any happen into the hands of such crooked dispositions, how to order them and ease your selves, when I come to treat of the justice of the Country, which many being ignorant of suffer inconveniences, which by this they may prevent.

Let such as are so minded not rashly throw themselves upon the voyage, but observe the nature, and enquire the qualities of the persons with whom they ingage to transport themselves, or if (as not acquainted with such as inhabit there, but go with Merchants and Mariners, who transport them to others,) let their covenant be such, that after their arrival they have a fortnights time assigned them to enquire of their Master, and make choyce of such as they intend to expire their time with, nor let that brand of selling of servants, be any discouragement to deter any from going, for if a time must be served, it is all one with whom it be served, provided they be people of honest repute, with which the Country is well replenished.

And be sure to have your contract in writing and under hand and seal, for if ye go over upon promise made to do this or that, or to be free or your own men, it signifies nothing, for by a law of the Country (waving all promises) any one coming in, and not paying their own passages, must serve if men or women four years, if younger according to their years, but where an Indenture is, that is binding and observing.

The usual allowance for servants is (besides their charge of passage defrayed) at their expiration, a years provision of corne, dubble apparrell, tooles necessary, and land according to the custome of the Country, which is an old delusion, for there is no land accustomary due to the servant, but to the Master, and therefore that servant is unwise that will not dash out that custom in his covenant, and make that due of land absolutely his own, which although at the present, not of so great consequence; yet in few years will be of much worth, as I shall hereafter make manifest.

When ye go aboard, expect the Ship somewhat troubled and in a hurliburly, untill ye cleer the lands end; and that the Ship is rummaged, and things put to rights, which many times discourages the Passengers, and makes them wish the Voyage unattempted: but this is but for a short season, and washes off when at Sea, where the time is pleasantly passed away, though not with such choise plenty as the shore affords.

But when ye arrive and are settled, ye will find a strange alteration,

ration, an abused Country giving the lye in your own approbations to those that have calumniated it, and these infalable arguments may convince all incredible and obstinate opinions, concerning the goodnesse and delightfulnesse of the Country, that never any servants of late times have gone thither; but in their Letters to their Friends commend and approve of the place, and rather invite than disswade their acquaintance from comming thither. An other is this, that seldom (if ever) any that hath continued in *Virginia* any time, will or do desire to live in *England*, but post back with what expedition they can; although many are landed men in *England*, and have good Estates here, and divers wayes of preferments propounded to them, to entice and perswade their continuance.

The Country is as I said of a temperate nature, the dayes, in summer not so long as in *England*, in winter longer; it is somewhat hotter in *June, July* and *August* then here, but that heat sweetly allayed by a continual breaze of winde, which never failes to cool and refresh the labourer and traveller; the cold seldom approaches sencibly untill about *Christmas*, (although the last winter was hard and the worst I or any living there knew) and when winter comes, (which is such and no worse then is in *England*,) it continues two monthes seldom longer, often not so long and in that time although here seldom hard-weather keep men from labour, yet there no work is done all winter except dressing their own victuals and making of fires.

The labour servants are put to, is not so hard nor of such continuance as Husbandmen, nor Handecraftmen are kept at in *England*, I said little or nothing is done in winter time, none ever work before sun rising nor after sun set, in the summer they rest, sleep or exercise themselves five houres in the heat of the day, Saturdayes afternoon is alwayes their own, the old Holidayes are observed and the Sabboath spent in good exercises.

The Women are not (as is reported) put into the ground to worke, but occupie such domestique imployments and houswifery as in *England*, that is dressing victuals, righting up the house, milking, imployed about dayries, washing, sowing, &c. and both men and women have times of recreations, as much or more than in any part of the world besides, yet som wenches that are nasty, beastly and not fit to be so imployed are put into the ground, for reason tells us, they must not at charge be transported and then mantained for nothing, but those that prove so aukward are rather burthensome then servants desirable or usefull.

The Country is fruitfull, apt for all and more then *England* can or does produce, the usuall diet is such as in *England*, for the

the rivers afford innumerable sortes of choyce fish, (if they will take the paines to make wyers or hier the Natives, who for a small matter will undertake it,) winter and summer, and that in many places sufficient to serve the use of man, and to fatten hoggs, water-fowle of all sortes are (with admiration to be spoken of) plentifull and easie to be killed, yet by many degrees more plentifull in some places then in othersome, Deare all over the Country, and in many places so many, that venison is accounted a tiresom meat, wilde Turkeys are frequent, and so large that I have seen some weigh neer threescore pounds; other beasts there are whose flesh is wholsom and savourie, such are unknowne to us; and therefore I will not stuffe my book with superfluous relation of their names; huge Oysters and store in all parts where the salt-water comes.

The Country is exceedingly replenished with Neat cattle, Hoggs, Goats and Tame-fowle, but not many sheep; so that mutton is somwhat scarce, but that defect is supplied with store of Venison, other flesh and fowle; The Country is full of gallant Orchards, and the fruit generally more luscious and delightfull then here, witnesse the Peach and Quince, the latter may be eaten raw savourily, the former differs and as much exceeds ours as the best relished apple we have doth the crabb, and of both most excellent and comfortable drinks are made, Grapes in infinite manners grow wilde, so do Walnuts, Smalnuts, Chesnuts and abundance of excellent fruits, Plums and Berries, not growing or known in *England*; graine we have, both *English* and *Indian* for bread and Bear, and Pease besides *English* of ten several sorts, all exceeding ours in *England*, the gallant root of Potatoes are common, and so are all sorts of rootes, herbes and Garden stuffe.

It must needs follow then that diet cannot be scarce, since both rivers and woods affords it, and that such plenty of Cattle and Hogs are every where, which yeeld beef, veal, milk, butter, cheese and other made dishes, porke, bacon, and pigs, and that as sweet and savoury meat as the world affords, these with the help of Orchards and Gardens, Oysters, Fish, Fowle and Venison, certainly cannot but be sufficient for a good diet and wholsom accommodation, considering how plentifully they are, and how easie with industry to be had.

Beare is indeed in some place constantly drunken, in other some, nothing but Water or Milk, and Water or Beverige; & that is where the goodwives, (if I may so call them) are negligent and idle; for it is not for want of Corn to make Malt with (for the Country affords enough) but because they are sloath-

full

full and carelesse: but I hope this Item will shame them out of those humours, that they will be adjudged by their drink, what kinde of Housewives they are.

Those Servants that will be industrious may in their time of service gain a competent estate before their Freedomes, which is usually done by many, and they gaine esteeme and assistance that appear so industrious: There is no Master almost but will allow his Servant a parcell of clear ground to plant some Tobacco in for himself, which he may husband at those many idle times he hath allowed him and not prejudice, but rejoyce his Master to see it, which in time of Shipping he may lay out for commodities, and in Summer sell them again with advantage, and get a Sow-Pig or two, which any body almost will give him, and his Master suffer him to keep them with his own, which will be no charge to his Master, and with one years increase of them may purchase a Cow Calf or two, and by that time he is for himself; he may have Cattle, Hogs and Tobacco of his own, and come to live gallantly; but this must be gained (as I said) by Industry and affability, not by sloth nor churlish behaviour.

And whereas it is rumoured that Servants have no lodging other then on boards, or by the Fire side, it is contrary to reason to believe it: First, as we are Christians; next as people living under a law, which compels as well the Master as the Servant to perform his duty; nor can true labour be either expected or exacted without sufficient cloathing, diet, and lodging; all which both their Indentures (which must inviolably be observed) and the Justice of the Country requires.

But if any go thither, not in a condition of a Servant, but pay his or her passage, which is some six pounds: Let them not doubt but it is money well layd out (yet however let them not fail) although they carry little else to take a Bed along with them, and then few Houses but will give them entertainment, either out of curtesie, or on reasonable tearms; and I think it better for any that goes over free, and but in a mean condition, to hire himself for reasonable wages of Tobacco and Provision, the first year, provided he happen in an honest house, and where the Mistresse is noted for a good Housewife, of which there are very many (notwithstanding the cry to the contrary) for by that means he will live free of disbursment, have something to help him the next year, and be carefully looked to in his sicknesse (if he chance to fall sick) and let him so covenant that exceptions may be made, that he work not much in the hot weather, a course we alwayes take with our new hands (as they call them) the first year they come in.

If

If they are women that go after this manner, that is paying their own passages; I advise them to sojourn in a house of honest repute, for by their good carriage, they may advance themselves in marriage, by their ill, overthow their fortunes; and although loose persons seldome live long unmarried if free ; yet they match with as desolute as themselves, and never live handsomly or are ever respected.

For any that come over free, and are minded to dyet and quarter in another mans house, it matters not whether they know on what term or conditions they are there; for by an excellent Decree, made by Sir *William Berkly* , when Governour ; (as indeed he was the Author of many good Laws :) It was ordered, that if any inhabitant received any stranger Merchant, or border into their houses, and did not condition in Writing with him or them so entertained on what tearms he received them, it should be supposed an invitation, an no satisfaction should be allowed or recovered in any Court of Justice ; thereby giving notice that no stranger coming into the Country should be drilled in, or made a purchase of under colour of friendship : but that the Inhabitants at first coming shall let them know how they mean to deal with them, that if they like not the terms they may remove themselves at pleasure ; a Law so good and commendable, that it is never like to be revoked or altered.

Now for those that carry over Families and estates with a determination to inhabit, my advice is that they neither sojourn for that will be chargeable ; nor on the sudden purchase, for that may prove unfortunate ; but that they for the first year hire a house (for seats are always to be hired) and by that means, they will not onely finde content and live at a cheap rate, but be acquainted in the Country and learn the worth and goodnesse of the Plantation they mean to purchase ; and so not rashly intangle themselves in an ill bargain, or finde where a convenient parcell of Land is for their turns to be taken up.

Yet are the Inhabitants generally affable, courteous and very assistant to strangers (for what but plenty makes hospitality and good neighbourhood) and no sooner are they settled, but they will be visiting, presenting and advicing the stranger how to improve what they have, how to better their way of livelihood.

Justice is there duly and daily administred ; hardly can any travaile two miles together, but they will finde a Justice, which hath power of himself to hear and determine mean differences, to secure and bind over notorious offenders, of which very few are in the Country.

In every County are Courts kept, every two moneths, and
oftener

oftener if occasion require, in which Courts all things are determined without exceptions ; and if any dislike the proceedings of those Courts, they have liberty to appeal to the Quarter Court, which is four times a year ; and from thence to the Assembly, which is once or oftner every year : So that I am confident, more speedy Justice and with smaller charge is not in any place to be found.

Theft is seldome punished (as being seldome or never committed ; for as the Proverb is, where there are no receivers, there are no thieves ; and although Doores are nightly left open (especially in the Summer time) Hedges hanging full of Cloathes ; Plate frequently used amongst all comers and goers (and there is good store of Plate in many houses) yet I never heard of any losse ever received either in Plate, Linnen, or any thing else out of their Houses all the time I inhabited there.

Indeed I have known some suffer for stealing of Hogs, (but not since they have been plentifull) and whereas Hogstealing was once punished with death, it is now made penal, and restitution given very amply to the owner thereof.

Cases of Murther are punished as in *England*, and Juries allowed, as well in Criminal causes, as in all other differences between party and party, if they desire it.

Servants complaints are freely harkened to, and (if not causlesly made) there Masters are compelled either speedily to amend, or they are removed upon second complaint to another service ; and often times not onely set free, (if the abuse merit it) but ordered to give reparation and damage to their servant.

The Country is very full of sober, modest persons, both men and women, and many that truly fear God and follow that perfect rule of our blessed Saviour, to do as they would be done by ; and of such a happy inclination is the Country, that many who in *England* have been lewd and idle, there in emulation or imitation (for example moves more then precept) of the industry of those they finde there, not onely grow ashamed of their former courses, but abhor to hear of them, and in small time wipe off those stains they have formerly been tainted with ; yet I cannot but confesse, there are people wicked enough (as what Country is free) for we know some natures will never be reformed, but these must follow the Fryers rule, *Si non caste, tamen cante ;* for if any be known, either to prophane the Lords day or his Name, be found drunk, commit whoredome, scandalize or disturb his neighbour, or give offence to the world by living suspiciously in any bad courses ; there are for each of these, severe and wholsome laws and remedies made, provided

and

and duly put in execution : I can confidently affirm, that since my being in *England*, which is not yet four moneths, I have been an eye and ear witnesse of more deceits and villanies (and such as modesty forbids me to utter) then I either ever saw or heard mention made of in *Virginia*, in my one and twenty years aboad in those parts.

And therefore those that shall blemish *Virginia* any more, do but like the Dog bark against the Moon, untill they be blind and weary; and *Virginia* is now in that secure growing condition, that like the Moon so barked at, she will passe on her course, maugre all detractors, and a few years will bring it to that glorious happinesse, that many of her calumniators, will intercede to procure admittance thither, when it will be hard to be attained to; for in smal time, little land will be to be taken up ; and after a while none at all ; and as the Mulberry Trees grows up, which are by every one planted, Tobacco will be laid by, and we shall wholy fall to making of Silk (a Sample of 400l. hath already been sent for *England*, and approved of) which will require little labour ; and therefore shall have little use of Servants ; besides, Children increase and thrive so well there, that they themselves will sufficiently supply the defect of Servants: And in small time become a Nation of themselves sufficient to people the Country : And this good policy is there used ; As the Children there born grow to maturity, and capable (as they are generally very capable and apt) they are still preferred and put into authority, and carry themselves therein civilly and discretly ; and few there are but are able to give some Portions with their daughters, more or lesse, according to their abilities ; so that many comming out of *England* have raised themselves good fortunes there meerly by matching with Maidens born in the Country.

And therefore I cannot but admire, and indeed much pitty the dull stupidity of people necessitated in *England*, who rather then they will remove themselves, live here a base, slavish, penurious life ; as if there were a necessity to live and to live so, choosing rather then they will forsake *England* to stuff *New-Gate, Bridewell*, and other Jayles with their carkessies, nay cleave to tyburne it selfe ; and so bring confusion to their souls horror and infamine to their kindred or posteritie, others itch out their wearisom lives in reliance of other mens charities, an uncertaine and unmanly expectation ; some more abhorring such courses betake themselve to almost perpetuall and restlesse toyle and druggeries out of which (whilst their strength lasteth) they (observing hard diets, earlie and late houres) make

hard

hard shift to subsist from hand to mouth, untill age or sicknesse takes them off from labour and directs them the way to beggerie, and such indeed are to be pittied, relieved and provided for.

I have 'seriously considered when I have (passing the streets) heard the several Cryes, and noting the commodities, and the worth of them they have carried and cryed up and down; how possibly a livelihood could be exacted out of them, as to cry Matches, Smal-coal, Blacking, Pen and Ink, Thred-laces, and a hundred more such kinde of trifling merchandizes; then looking on the nastinesse of their linnen habits and bodies: I conclude if gain sufficient could be raised out of them for subsistance; yet their manner of living was degenerate and base; and their condition to be far below the meanest servant in *Virginia*.

The other day, I saw a man heavily loaden with a burden of Faggots on his back, crying, Dry Faggots, Dry Faggots; he travailed much ground, bawled frequently, and sweat with his burthen: but I saw none buy any, neer three houres I followed him, in which time he rested, I entered into discourse with him, offered him drink, which he thankfully accepted of (as desirous to learn the mistery of his trade) I enquired what he got by each burden when sold? he answered me three pence: I further asked him what he usually got a day? he replyed, some dayes nothing some dayes six pence; some time more, but seldome; me thought it was a pittifull life, and I admired how he could live on it; And yet it were dangerous to advise these wretches to better their conditions by travaile, for fear of the cry of, a spirit, a spirit.

The Country is not only plentifull but pleasant and profitable, pleasant in regard of the brightnesse of the weather, the many delightfull rivers, on which the inhabitants are settled (every man almost living in sight of a lovely river) the abundance of game, the extraordinary good neighbour-hood and loving conversation they have one with the other.

Pleasant in their building, which although for most part they are but one story besides the loft, and built of wood, yet contrived so delightfull, that your ordinary houses in England are not so handsome, for usually the rooms are large, daubed and whitelimed, glazed and flowered, and if not glazed windows, shutters which are made very pritty and convenient.

Pleasant in observing their stocks and flockes of Cattle, Hoggs, and Poultry, grazing, whisking and skipping in their sights, pleasant in having all things of their own, growing or breeding without drawing the peny to send for this and that, without which, in England they cannot be supplyed.

The

The manner of living and trading there is thus, each man almost lives a free-holder, nothing but the value of 12. d. a year to be paid as rent, for every 50. Acrees of land ; firing cost nothing every man plants his own corne and neede take no care for bread : if any thing be bought, it is for cõmodity, exchanged presently, or for a day, payment is usuall made but once a year, and for that Bill taken (for accounts are not pleadable.)

In summer when fresh meat will not keep (seeing every man kils of his own, and quantities are inconvenient, they lend from one to another, such portions of flesh as they can spare, which is repaied again when the borrowers kils his.

If any fall sick, and cannot compasse to follow his crope which if not followed, will soon be lost, the adjoyning neighbour, will either voluntarily or upon a request joyn together, and work in it by spels, untill the honour recovers, and that gratis, so that no man by sicknesse loose any part of his years worke.

Let any travell, it is without charge, and at every house is entertainment as in a hostery, and with it hearty welcome are stranger entertained.

In a word, *Virginia* wants not good victual, wants not good dispositions, and as God hath freely bestowed it, they as freely impart with it, yet are there aswel bad natures as good.

The profit of the country is either by their labour, their stockes, or their trades.

By their labours is produced corne and Tobacco, and all other growing provisions, and this Tobacco however now lowrated, yet a good maintenance may be had out of it, (for they have nothing of necessity but cloathing to purchasse) or can this mean price of Tobacco long hold, for these reasons, First that in England it is prohibited, next that they have attained of late those sorts equall with the best Spanish, Thirdly that the sicknesse in Holland is decreasing, which hath been a great obstruction to the sail of Tobacco.

And lastly, that as the mulbery tree grows up, tobacco will be neglected and silke, flax, two staple commodities generally fallen upon.

Of the increase of cattle and hoggs, much advantage is made, by selling biefe, porke, and bacon, and butter &c. either to shipping, or to send to the Barbadoes, and other Islands, and he is a very poor man that hath not sometimes provision to put off.

By trading with Indians for Skine, Beaver, Furres and other
commodities

commodities oftentimes good profits are raised ; The Indians are in absolute subjection to the English, so that they both pay tribute to them and receive all their severall king from them, and as one dies they repaire to the English for a successor, so that none neede doubt it a place of securitie.

Several ways of advancement there are and imployments both for the learned and laborer, recreation for the gentry, traffique for the adventurer, congregations for the ministrie (and oh that God would stir, up the hearts of more to go over, such as would teach good doctrine, and not paddle in faction, or state matters ; they could not want maintenance, they would find an assisting, an imbracing, a conforming people.)

It is knowne (such preferment hath this Country rewarded the industrious with) that some from being wool-hoppers and of as mean and meaner imployment in England have there grown great merchants, and attained to the most eminent advancements the Country afforded. If men cannot gaine (by diligence) states in those parts.) I speake not only mine owne opinion, but divers others, and something by experience) it will hardly be done (unlesse by meere lucke as gamsters thrive, and other accidentals in any other part whatsoever.

Now having briefly set down the present state of *Virginia* not in fiction, but in realitie, I wish the juditious reader to consider what dislike can be had of the Country, or upon what grounds it is so infamously injured, I only therein covet to stop those blackmouthed babblers, that not only have and do abuse so noble a plantation, but abuse Gods great blessing in adding to England so flourishing a branch, in perswading many souls, rather to follow desparate and miserable courses in England, then to ingage in so honourable an undertaking as to travile and inhabite there ; but to those I shall (if admonition will not worke on their recreant spirits) only say. Let him that *is filthie be filthie still.*

Mary-

Mary-lands Additions.

HAving for 19. yeare served *Virginia* the elder sister, I casting my eye on Mary-land the younger, grew in amoured on her beauty, resolving like Jacob when he had first served for Leah, to begin a fresh service for Rachell.

Two year and upward have I enjoyed her company with delight and profit, but was enforced by reason of her unnatural disturbances to leave her weeping for her children & would not be comforted, because they were not; yet will I never totally forsake or be beaten off from her.

Twice hath she been deflowred by her own Inhabitants, stript, shorne and made deformed ; yet such a naturall fertility and comelinesse doth she retain that she cannot but be loved, but be pittied; and although she would ever have vailed to *Virginia* as her elder, yet had not these two fatall mischiefs hapened, she would ere long have spread her self as largly, and produced as much in every respect as *Virginia* does or could doe.

Mary-land is a province not commonly knowne in England, because the name of *Virginia* includes or clouds it, it is a Country wholy belonging to that honorable Gentleman the Lord of *Baltamore*, granted him by Pattent under the broad Seal of England long since, and at his charge settled, granted for many reasons, and this for one; that *Virginia* having more land then they could manure or look after in convenient time, first the Duch came and tooke from the English much land which they still hold, next the Swead, who intrenched neerer and had not this Pattent came and prevented it, Dutch, Swead, French & other strangers had pend up our Nation with in the bounds of *Virginia*, whereas now they have now all *Mary-land*, as it were their own, it being only granted for the use of Brittaines and Irish.

It

It is (not an Island as is reported, but) part of that maine adjoyning to *Virginia*, only separated or parted from *Virginia*, by a river of ten miles broad, called *Patomack* river, the commodities and manner of living as in *Virginia*, the soyle somewhat more temporate (as being more Northerly) many stately and navigable rivers are contained in it, plentifully stored with wholsome springs, a rich and pleasant soile, and so that its extraordinary goodnes hath made it rather desired then envied, which hath been fatall to her (as beauty is often times to those that are endued with it) and that the reader may thoroughly be informed how she hath suffered. I shall in brief relate, and conclude.

It is to be understood that in the time of the late King; *Virginia* being whol for monarchy, and the last Country belonging to England that submitted to obedience of the Common-wealth of England. And there was in *Virginia* a certaine people congregated into a Church, calling themselves Independents, which daily encreasing, severall consultations were had by the state of that Coloney, how to suppresse and extinguish them, which was daily put in execution, as first their Pastor was banished, next their other Teachers, then many by informatiõs clapt up in prison, then generally disarmed) wᶜʰ was very harsh in such a country where the heathen live round about them) by one Colonel *Samuel Mathews* then a Counsellor in *Virginia* and since Agent for *Virginia* to the then parliament, and lastly in a condition of banishment, so that they knew not in those streights how to dispose of themselves.

Mary-land (my present subject) was courted by them as a refuge, the Lord Proprietor and his Governor solicited to, and severall addresses and treaties made for their admittance & entertainment into that province, their conditions were pittied, their propositions were harkened to and agree on, which was that they should have convenient portions of land assigned them, libertie of conscience and priviledge to choose their owne officers, and hold courts within themselves, all was granted them, they had a whole County of the richest land in the province asigned them, & such as themselves made choyce of, the conditions of plantations (such as were common to all adventurers) were shewed and propounded to them, which they extreamly approved of, and nothing was in those conditions exacted from them, but appeales to the Provincial court, quit-rents, and an oath of fidelitie to the Proprietor: An assembly was called thoroughout the whole Country after their comming over (consisting aswell of themselves as the rest) and because there

were

were some few papists that first inhabited these themselves, and others of being different judgments, an act passed that all professing in Jesus Christ should have equall justice, priviledges and benefits in that province, and that none on penaltie (mentioned) should disturb each other in their several professions, nor give the urging termes, either of Roundheads, sectarie, Independent, Jesuit, Papist, &c. Intending an absolute peace and union; the Oath of Fidelitie (although none other then such as every Lord of a manner requires from his tenant) was over hauled, and this clause added to it (provided it infring not the libertie of the conscience.)

They sat downe joyfully, followed their vocations chearfully, trad increased in their province, and divers others were by this incouraged and invited over from *Virginia.*

But these people finding themselves in a capacitie not only to capitulate, but to oversway, those that had so received and relieved them.

Began to pick quarrells, first with the Papists, next with the oath, and lastly declared their aversness to all conformalitie, wholy ayming (as themselves since confessed) to deprive the Lord proprietor of all his interest in that country, and make it their own: with unworthiness? What ingratitude? with unparalled inhumanitie was in these practices made obvious.

Amongst others that became tenants in this aforesaid distress was one *Richard Bennett* Merchant, who seated and settled amongst them, and so (not only owed obedience to that government, but) was obliged as a man received in his pretended distresse, to be a gratfull benefactor upon the setting forth of a fleet intended for the reducement of *Virginia,* the said **Bennet** and one *Claiborne* (a pestilent enemie to the wel-faire of that province and the Lord Proprietor, although he had formerly submissively acknowledged he owed his forfeited life to the said proprietor, for dealing so favorably with him for his misdemeanors, as by his treacherous letters under his hand (now in print) is manifest, and many other acts of grace conferred on him, having a commission directed to them and others (who miscarried by sea) to reduce *Virginia* (not Mary-land, for they were in obedience to the Common-wealth of England, and great assistance to the said fleet) although they knew Mary-land to be excluded and dasht out of their Commission, yet because the commission mentioned the Bay of Chesapeack) in which Mary-land was (as well as *Virginia*) yet they were resolved to wreth and stretch their commission to the prejudice of Mary-land and becomming abbetters and confederats with those serpents

pents that have been so taken in, presumed to alter the government and take away the governours Commission, putting in others in their place, *viz.* a Papist in cheife, and one more, who misgoverning the Country, they were excluded, and the former governor restored with an addition of Commissioners of their owne creatures, and as taking power from them, untill further knowledge from England, driving herein at their own interest.

The governour (so restored) being truly informed that their proceedings were illegal; held Courts and proceeds as if no such alteration had been made, issues out Writs (according to order) In the name of the Lord proprietor, but they require and command them to do it in the name of the Keepers of the Liberties of England, according to act of Parliament, to which answer sufficient was given, that they never were in opposition to the present power, they had taken the Engagement, & for the tenure or form of writs, they were not compelled by vertue of that act to make them other wise then they always had done, for by Patent from the late K. they had power to issue out in the Proprietors name, and never had used the Kings name at all, therefore that act requiring all Writs formerly issuing out in the late Kings name, now to revolve to the Keepers of the Liberties of England, was no way binding to them, who had never used the kings name at all.

But it was not religion, it was not punctilios they stood upon, it was that sweete, that rich, that large Country they aimed at; and therefore agrees amongst themselves to frame petitions, complaints, and subscriptions from those bandetoes to themselves (the said *Bennet* and *Claiborne*) to ease them of their pretended sufferings, and then come with arms, and againe make the Province their own, exalting themselves in all places of trust and command, totally expulsing the Governer, and all the hospitable Proprietors, Officers out of their places.

But when his Highnesse (not acquainted with these matchinations) had owned and under his hand and signet acknowledged Cap. *Will. Stone* (the former governor) Governor for the Lord *Baltamore* of his Province of *Mary-land*, he again endeavored to reasume the government, and fetched away the records from those usurpers, proclaimed peace to all not obstinate, and favorably received many submissives, who with seeming joy returned, bewailing their unworthy ingratitude & inhumanitie, blaming the unbridled ambition and base averice of those that had misled them.

The Province consists of foure Counties already inhabited, viz. St. *Maries*, *Calverton*, *An Arundal* and *Kent*. St. *Maries* and

and *Calverton* submitted, *An Arundall* and part of *Kent* opposed.

The Governor desirous to reclaim those opposing, takes a partie about 130. persons with him, and sailes into those parts, one *Roger Heamans* who had a great ship under him, and who had promised to be instrumentall to the governor, to wind up those differences (being *Judas*-like, hired to joyn with those opposing Countries) and having the Governour and his vessells within reach of his Ordnance, perfidiously & contrary to his undertaking and ingagments, fires at them and enforces them to the first shore to prevent that mischief.

The next morning he sends messengers to those of *An Arundall* to treat, and messengers aboard that *Shittlecock Heamans*, but all were detained ; and on the 25. of *March* last (being the next day and the Lords day) about 170. and odd of *Kent* and *Anne Arundall* came marching against them, *Heaman* fires a pace at them, and a small vessel of *New-England* under the command of one *John Cutts* comes neere the shore and seazes the boats. provision and amunition belonging to the Governour and his partie, and so in a nick, in a streight were they fallen upon.

The Governour being shot in many places yeilds on quarter, which was granted ; but being in hold, was threatned (notwithstanding that quarter given) to be imediatly executed, unlesse he would writ to the rest to take quarter, which upon his request they did, twentie odd were killed in this skirmish, and all the rest prisoners on quarter, who were disarmed & taken into custodie.

But these formerly distressed supplicants for admittance, being now become High and Mighty States, and supposing their Conquest unquestionable, consult with themselves (notwithstanding their quarter given) to make their Conquest more absolute, by cutting off the heads of the Province, *viz*. the Governor, the Counsel and Commanders thereof : And so make themselves a Counsel of War, and condemn them to death : Foure were presently executed, scilicet, Mr. *William Eltonhead*, one of the Councel ; Capt. *William Lewis*, Mr. *John Legate* Gentleman, and *John Pedro ;* the rest at the importunity of some women, and resolution of some of their souldiers (who would not suffer their designe to take thorough effect, as being pricked in Conscience for their ingratitudes) were saved, but were Amerced, Fined and Plundred at their pleasures : And although this was prophetiquely foreseen by diverse eminent Merchants of *London*, who Petitioned his Highnesse for

prevention,

prevention, and that his Highnesse sent a gracious command to
Bennet, and all others, not to disturb the Lord *Baltamores* Officers, nor People in *Mary-land*, but recalled all Power or pretence of Power from them; yet they still hold, and possesse (in
defiance of so sacred a mandate) the said Province of *Mary-*
land, and sent an impious Agent home to Parlie whilest they
plundred; but he hath long since given up his account to the
great avenger of all injuries: Although sticklers (somewhat
more powerfull, but by many degrees more brazen fac't then
his spirit could bare him forth to appear) now labour to justifie
these inhumanities, disorders, contempts, and rebellions; so
that I may say with the Prophet *Jeremiah*; How doth the Citty
sit solitary that was full of people? How is she become as a wid-
dow? She that was great amongst the Nations, and Princesse
amongst the Provinces? How is she become tributary. Thus
have they brought to desolation, one of the happiest Plantations that ever *Englishmen* set foot in, and such a Country (that
if it were again made formall) might harbor in peace and plenty
all such as *England* shall have occasion to disburthen, or desire
to forsake *England*.

A pious consideration of these distractions is by his Highnesse taking notice of, and these controversies are by him referred to the Hearing, and Report of those two Honourable and
judicious Gentlemen the Lords *Whitlock* and *Widdrington*,
whose Pains and Moderation in Hearing, and mildly disputing
indifferently the condition of these uproars, gives not onely
hopes of relief, but have added to their renowns, by all those
that (as observed) have been present at the severall Hearings,
an account whereof will ere long be published in print.

Upon determination whereof, it must be concluded that a
settlement will follow, and then many families will flock over to
inhabit these ruines, the fertility of the Province will (in short
time) make good (excepting the blood spilt which can never be
recalled nor satisfied for.)

Let this be no discouragement to any to goe over, for it will
now be more firmly settled then ever, and so throughly, setled
that neither envy nor deceipt can again ever shake it.

And being so setled, I know no country (although I have
have travelled many) that I more affect, more esteem, that
which profits delights, and here is both absolute profit, reall delight; I shall forget my undertaking in the beginning of my
booke, which was not to over extall the Country: for should I
indeed give it its due commendations, I should seem to be
suborn'd; but in few words, it is that Country in which I desire

to

to spend the remnant of my dayes, in which I covet to make my grave.

This I have not written for profit, for it is known I have given away the copy, and therefore am the less to be mistrusted for a deluder, for popular applause I did it not, for in this pregnant age, my lines appear so harsh and disordered, that I would not have affixed my name to it, but in obedience to those commands that so require it, and to prevent the imputation of a libeller, the maine drift and scope I have herein aimed at, is to discover *Virginia* and *Mary-land*, and stand up in their just defences when caluminated, to let many that pine in *England* know, they are to their ruines deluded, that are frighted from going thither, if their wayes of livelihood be not certaine in *England*.

Post

Post-script.

A Word to the Governour and Counsell in Virginia.

Gentlemen,

AS I have done your Country of *Virginia* justice in standing up in its defence, so I expect and entreat the like from you; I know ye are honest and understand your selves; I cannot except nor speake against any of ye, but *Will. Claiborne,* whom ye all know to be a Villaine, but it is no more blemish to your degree, to have him of your societie, then it was to the Apostles to have Iudas of theirs, I have had injury by him by palpable cousinages done me, as I shal one day demonstrate. But for the decree of your court against one Captaine *Thomas Thoroughgood,* late Commander of the Shipp *Cressent.* I desire you to consider of it again and reverse it for these reasons following.

I was an inhabitant of *Mary-land* of two years standing, proscribe to die by the rebells of the Bay. I fled disguised to *Virginia,* came a bord his Ship by an unknowne name, made my condition, not my person known to him, and he charitably brought me for *England,* otherewise I had causelesly been put to death. For which letters certifies us in *England,* that ye have amersed him in deep penalties, by an acted of Assembly made against masters or Commanders of ships that shall carrie away

any

any of the inhabitants of your colonie without a pass.

First, know I was no inhabitant of *Virginia*, but *Mary-land*, a government ye have nothing to doe with.

Next I came with my Governours consent, Captaine *William Stone* who in *England* justifies Captaine *Thoroughgoods* bringing me home: and here I must and will abide such censure or vindication as the supreame power of *England* shall find me to have merited; and therfore I humbly request ye to peruse and reverse that order against him for bringing me for *England*.

I shall hereafter give such an account to *Virginia* of my actions from time to time, that they shall be fully satisfied; I never deserved the least injurie either from any Government, nor any private person, since I first inhabited there. But that shall be a subject particular: and a peece not usefull in *England*, but only to scatter in *Virginia* amongst my friends, whos good opinion I covet, and that they may know in many odiums I have been wronged, and that I am the man that have seene affliction.

FINIS.

Virginia's Cure:

OR

An ADVISIVE NARRATIVE

CONCERNING

VIRGINIA.

DISCOVERING

The true Ground of that CHURCHES
Unhappiness, and the only true Remedy.

As it was presented to the Right Reverend Father in
God *GVILBERT* Lord Bishop of LONDON,
September 2. 1661.

Now publish'd to further the Welfare of that
and the like PLANTATIONS:
By *R. G.*

And this Gospel of the Kingdome shall be preach'd in all the world,
for a witness unto all Nations, and then shall the End come,
Mat. 24. 14.
Is it time for you O ye to dwell in your ceiled houses, and this House
lie waste? Now therefore thus saith the Lord of Hosts, Consider
your wayes, Hag. 1. 4, 5.

London, Printed by *W. Godbid* for *Henry Brome* at the Signe of
the *Gun* in *Ivy-lane*, 1 6 6 2.

Force's Collection of Historical Tracts.

Vol. III.—No. 15.

Virginia's Cure:

OR,

An Advisive NARRATIVE

CONCERNING

VIRGINIA.

TO shew the unhappy State of the Church in *Virginia,* and the true Remedy of it, I shall first give a brief Description of the Manner of our Peoples scatter'd Habitations there; next shew the sad unhappy consequents of such their scatter'd Living both in reference to themselves and the poor Heathen that are about them, and by the way briefly set down the cause of scattering their Habitations, then proceed to propound the Remedy, and means of procuring it; next assert the Benefits of it in reference both to themselves, and the Heathen; set down the cause why this Remedy hath not been hitherto compass'd: and lastly, till it can be procured, give directions for the present supply of their Churches.

That part of *Virginia* which hath at present craved your Lordships Assistance to preserve the Christian Religion, and to promote the Building Gods Church among them, by supplying them with sufficient Ministers of the Gospel, is bounded on the North by the great River *Patomek,* on the South by the River *Chawan,* including also the Land inhabited on the East side of *Chesipiack Bay,* called *Accomack,* and contains above half as much
Land

Land as *England;* it is divided into several Counties, and those
Counties contain in all about Fifty Parishes, the Families whereof
are dispersedly and scatteringly seated upon the sides of Rivers ;
some of which running very far into the Country, bear the *English* Plantations above a hundred Miles, and being very broad,
cause the Inhabitants of either side to be listed in several Parishes.
Every such Parish is extended many Miles in length upon the
Rivers side, and usually not above a mile in Breadth backward
from the River, which is the common stated breadth of every
Plantation belonging to each particular Proprietor, of which
Plantations, some extend themselves half a mile, some a mile,
some two miles, some three miles, and upward upon the sides of
those Rivers, many of them are parted from each other by small
Rivers and Creeks, which small Rivers and Creeks are seated
after the manner of the great Rivers.   The Families of such
Parishes being seated after this manner, at such distances from
each other, many of them are very remote from the House of
God, though placed in the middest of them.   Many Parishes as
yet want both Churches and Gleabes, and I think not above a
fifth part of them are supplyed with Ministers, where there are
Ministers the People meet together Weekly, but once upon the
Lords day, and sometimes not at all, being hindred by Extremities of Wind and Weather : and divers of the more remote Families being discouraged, by the length or tediousnesse of the way,
through extremities of heat in Summer, frost and Snow in Winter, and tempestuous weather in both, do very seldome repair
thither.

By which brief Description of their manner of seating themselves in that Wildernesse, Your Lordship may easily apprehend
that their very manner of Planting themselves, hath caused them
hitherto to rob God in a great measure of that publick Worship
and Service, which as a Homage due to his great name, he requires to be constantly paid to him, at the times appointed for it,
in the publick Congregations of his people in his House of Prayer.

— Hinc illæ Lachrymæ.

This Sacriledge I judge to be the prime Cause of their long
languishing improsperous condition, for it puts them under the
Curse of God, according to that of *Malachy* 3. 9. *Ye are cursed with a Curse, because ye have robbed me.*   Which Curse we
find executed upon the Jews, after such a manner, as any observing Person that knows *Virginia,* need not doubt to conclude,
that it hath been long executed upon her Planters in the same
kind and manner, as it is express'd to have been upon the Jews,

in

in *Hag.* 1. 9. *Ye looked for much, and loe, it came to little : and when ye brought it home, I did blow upon it : Why, saith the Lord of Hosts? because of mine House that is wast, and ye run every man to his own house.* By which Scriptures (comparing their Sins of Sacriledge together) it appears, that the Curse of God was executed upon the Jews, for the same Sacriledge *Virginia's* Planters are guilty of, the same Sin of robbing God of his publick Worship and Service in his House of Prayer. For, was the Curse of God upon the Jews for not building his House according to the Prophet *Haggai's* Sentence? But why did God regard his House, but for the recieving the due tribute of his publick Honour, Worship, and Service in it? Or was his Curse upon them for detaining his Tythes and Offerings? But why did God regard these, but for the maintenance and continuance of his publick Worship, and Service in his House? The Conclusion therefore is, that their great Sin of Sacriledge, for which the Curse of God was denounced and executed vpon them, was, that they robbed God of his publick Worship and Service in his House at the times appointed by God for it.

Which if *Virginia's* Planters do, it matters not whether they do it, by neglecting to build Churches, Houses of God amongst them, (which in great part they are guilty of;) or by with holding, or not assuring the maintenance of the Ministery of Gods publick Worship, Word, and Sacraments (which I cannot wholly excuse them of) or by planting themselves after such a manner, as may disable them to attend as constantly upon such Sacred publick Ministrations in the House of God, as the Equity of the Fourth Commandement, the positive Evangelical Duties, to be performed in publick Congregations, and the Law of the Church doth require (of which they are generally guilty) whether they rob God any of these wayes, the Sin hath the same stamp of Sacriledge, and therefore the same Curse attending it. But long experience hath ascertained, and the before described manner of their Planting makes it evident, that whilest our Planters in *Virginia* continue as at this day, dispersedly and remotely planted from the House of God, they will continue to rob God in a very great measure of his publick Worship and Service in his House of Prayer. Which is the same Sin the Jews were Cursed for, and must needs put them under the same Curse of God.

But though this be the saddest Consequent of their dispersed manner of Planting themselves (for what Misery can be greater than to live under the Curse of God?) yet this hath a very sad Train of Attendants which are likewise consequents of their scatter'd Planting. For, hence is the great want of Christian Neighbourhood, or brotherly admonition, of holy Examples of religious

gious Persons, of the Comfort of theirs, and their Ministers Administrations in Sicknesse, and Distresses, of the Benefit of Christian and Civil Conference and Commerce.

And hence it is, that the most faithfull and vigilant Pastors, assisted by the most carefull Church-wardens, cannot possibly take notice of the Vices that reign in their Families, of the spiritual defects in their Conversations, or if they have notice of them, and provide Spiritual Remedies in their publick Ministery, it is a hazard if they that are most concerned in them be present at the application of them : and if they should spend time in visiting their remote and far distant habitations, they would have little or none left for their necessary Studies, and to provide necessary spiritual food for the rest of their Flocks. And hence it is that through the licentious lives of many of them, the Christian Religion is like still to be dishonoured, and the Name of God to be blasphemed among the Heathen, who are near them, and oft among them, and consequently their Conversion hindred.

Lastly, their almost general want of Schooles, for the education of their Children, is another consequent of their scattered planting, of most sad consideration, most of all bewailed of Parents there, and therefore the arguments drawn from thence, most likely to prevail with them chearfully to embrace the Remedy. This want of Schooles, as it renders a very numerous generation of Christians Children born in *Virginia* (who naturally are of beautifull and comely Persons, and generally of more ingenious Spirits then these in *England*) unserviceable for any great Employments either in Church or State, so likewise it obstructs the hopefullest way they have, for the Conversion of the Heathen, which is, by winning the Heathen to bring in their Children to be taught and instructed in our Schooles, together with the Children of the Christians. For as it is the Beauty and Glory of Christian Graces, shining in the lives of Christians, which must make the Heathen that are men, in love with the Christian Religion ; so it is that love, which can only perswade them to bring in their Children to be taught and instructed in it : But as it is unlikely that such love should be wrought in them by the Glory of Christian Graces, appearing in the Christians lives ; who (as now planted) are for the most part destitute of the ordinary means of Grace : so granting that this might be, yet it is very unlikely that any raticall Heathen should be perswaded to commit their Children to the teaching and education of such Christians, whom they shall perceive to want Schooles of learning (the means of both) for their own.

It were easie to adde to these a heap of evill consequents of their scattered Planting, which hinder their Temporal, as well

as

as Spirituall happinesse. But I forbear, it being a task unsuit-
able for my Profession, and for that I know the Remedy to be
the same for both, and the removing the one will be the removing
of the other.

Onely for conclusion of this part, discovering *Virginia's* Disease and Misery, Your Lordship may be pleased to represent to
your thoughts the Evills of the fore-mentioned consequents of
their scattered Planting in reference to the poor Heathen; The
effecting whose conversion, should be the great end designed by
all, who would be subservient to the Providence of God, in
Transporting our Colonies thither.

The Heathen enter frequently into some of the remote dispers'd habitations of the Christians, the premises considered,
what can they see which should make them in love with their
Religion? They see their Families disordered, their Children
untaught, the publick Worship and Service of the great God they
own, neglected; neglected upon that very day, which they heare
call'd the Lords Day, and to be by the Christians peculiarly set
a part for it; yea so farre neglected, that some of the Heathen
have complained it was the worst of the seven to them, because
the servants of the Christians Plantations nearest to them, being
then left at liberty, oft spend that day in visiting their *Indian*
Towns, to the disquiet of the Heathen, but certainly to the great
Scandall of the Christian Religion, and little hopes have the
poor Heathen of redresse, whilst they see that Day so far neglected by the Christians, that in many Parishes they see no publick
holy Assemblies of our people, no Ministers provided for the
holy Ministrations of such Assemblies, no Churches erected and
consecrated for such publique Sacred Ministrations; or such in
such desolate Places, and so remote from many of their habitations that an ingenuous Christian would blush to tell a Heathen,
that They are the houses of the Christians great God, that made
the Heaven and the Earth of nothing, in which he is honoured,
worshipp'd, prayed unto, and his heavenly will taught from his
holy Word: for if a sober discreet Heathen (and there are many
such) should reply, Why hath not every Parish one of them, and
Ministers belonging to them? why do not the Christians build
their houses nearer them, that they may come oftner to them?
why are they not better built? why will not all the Christians of
a Parish bestow as much cost in building the house of their great
God, as one particular Christian among them bestows upon his
own house? what defence could an ingenuous Christian make,
which should not at once both shame himself and the Christians
he would defend?

If then Sacriledge were so goodly a thing in the Heathens
account,

account, as to make them in love with the Christians and their Religion for it, they see the Christians robbing God in all the fore-mentioned particulars, robbing him of his Days, Churches, Ministers, publick Worship and Service. But I can truly affirm (by what I have learn'd among divers Nations of those Heathen) that it is a Sin, which those Heathen by the Light of Nature do most detest and abhorre, and the holy Scripture gives Testimony to it: *Mal. 3. 8. Will a man rob his God? will a Heathen do it?* Can they then observe it in the Christians, and not abhorre and detest both them and their Religion for it? and in stead of acknowledging them a seed which the Lord hath blessed, think on the contrary that both they and their offspring are a Generation whom the Lord hath cursed.

No hopes therefore of bringing the Heathen in love with the Christian Religion; whil'st so many evill and scandalous consequents attend the Christians scatter'd manner of planting in that wildernesse. And their scatter'd Planting being the cause of such consequents, the consequents will remain, so long as that continues, as at this day it doth. I have hitherto forborn to mention the great danger that many of the Christians are in, of being destroyed by the Heathen, as formerly hundreds of them have been, because this consideration doth so easily offer it self upon the fore-mention'd description of their scattered Seating: By which and the sad consequents of it, if your Lordship shall please to contemplate the deplorable Estate and condition of the poor Church in *Virginia* (which implores your aid) it will present to your charitable heart such a moving object of your fatherly Care, Pitty, and Compassion, as will employ all your Interest in the Kings Grace and Favor, and your utmost power and endeavours to procure the Remedy.

The cause of their dispers'd Seating was at first a priviledge indulged by the royall Grant of having a right to 50 Acres of Land, for every person they should transport at their own charges: by which means some men transporting many Servants thither, and others purchasing the Rights of those that did, took possession of great tracts of Land at their pleasure, and by Degrees scattered their Plantations through the Country after the manner before described, although therefore from the premisses, it is easie to conclude, that the onely way of remedy for *Virginia's* disease (without which all other help will only palliate not cure) must be by procuring Towns to be built, and inhabited in their several Counties. Yet lest any man be hereby injured in his just Right, even this Remedy ought to be procured after such a manner, as the present manner of planting themselves, their poverty and mean condition will permit. According to which,

which, whether the building Towns in each County of *Virginia*, will be best promoted by reviving a former Act of that Country for Markets in Stated places of each County, where whatsoever should be transported into that Colony was onely to be sold (which Act was perhaps over-hastily repealed the next ensuing Assembly held *March* 27. 1656. for in my hearing, they who were the chief Agents in repealing it, have more then once repented it) or whether they may best be promoted by some other way (it being out of my Sphere) I dare not presume to determine, Your Lordship will best inform your self in this by consulting with *Virginia's* present Honourable Governour Sir *William Berkly*, or their late *Edward Diggs* Esq;

What way soever they determine to be best, I shall humbly in obedience to your Lordships command endevour to contribute towards the compassing this Remedy by propounding,

1. That your Lordship would be pleased to acquaint the King with the necessity of promoting the building Towns in each County of *Virginia*, upon the consideration of the fore-mentioned sad Consequents of their present manner of living there.

2. That Your Lordship upon the fore-going consideration, be pleased to move the pitiful, and charitable heart of His gracious Majesty (considering the Poverty and needs of *Virginia*) for a Collection to be made in all the Churches of his three Kingdomes (there being considerable numbers of each Kingdome) for the promoting a work of so great Charity to the Souls of many thousands of his Loyal Subjects, their Children, and the Generations after them, and of numberlesse poor Heathen; and that the Ministers of each Congregation be enjoyned with more then ordinary care, and pains to stirre up the people to a free and liberal Contribution towards it; or if this way be not thought sufficient, that some other way be taken to do it.

3. That the way of dispencing such collections for sending Work-men over for the building Towns and Schooles, and the assistance the persons that shall inhabit them shall contribute towards them may be determin'd here, by the advice of *Virginia's* present or late Honourable Governours if in *London*; and whom they shall make choice of for their assistants (who have formerly lived in *Virginia*;) and that the King (if he shall approve what is so determined) may be humbly Petitioned to authorize it by his special command, lest what is duely ordered here, be perverted there.

Fourthly, That those Planters who have such a considerable number of Servants, as may be judged may enable them for it, if they be not willing (for I have heard some expresse their willingnesse, and some their aversnesse) may by His Majesties Authority

Authority be enjoyned, to contribute the Assistance that shall be thought meet for them, to build themselves houses in the Towns nearest to them, and to inhabit them, for they having horses enough in that Country, may be convenienc'd, as their occasions require, to visit their Plantations.   And the Masters who shall inhabit the Towns, having Families of Servants upon remote Plantations, may be ordered to take care, that upon Saturdays Afternoon (when by the Custome of *Virginia*, Servants are freed from their ordinary labour) their Servants (except one or two, left by turns to secure their Plantations) may repair to their Houses in the Towns, and there remain with their Masters, until the publick Worship and Service of the Lords Day be ended.

Fifthly, That for a continual supply of able Ministers for their Churches, after a set term of years. Your Lordship would please to endevour the procuring an Act of Parliament, whereby a certain number of Fellowships, as they happen to be next proportionably vacant in both the Universities, may bear the name of *Virginia* Fellowships, so long as the Needs of that Church shall require it; and none be admitted to them, but such as shall engage by promise to hold them seven years and no longer; and at the expiration of those seven years, transport themselves to *Virginia*, and serve that Church in the Office of the Ministery seven years more, (the Church there providing for them) which being expired, they shall be left to their own Liberty to return or not: and if they perform not the Conditions of their Admittance, then to be uncapable of any Preferment.

These things being procured, I think *Virginia* will be in the most probable way (that her present condition can admit) of being cured of the forementioned evils of her scatter'd Planting.

For hereby her Planters will be convenienced to give God the honour due unto his Name, by attending constantly in full Congregations upon his publick Worship and Service, they will enjoy the benefits of Christian Offices, of frequent civil commerce and Society, which begets mutual confidence, trust, and friendship, the best groundwork for raising Companies of the best qualified, and most able persons to combine in Designs, most advantagious to their own and the publick Weal; they will enjoy the benefits of vertuous Examples, of publick Catechizing and Instructing their Children and Servants in the Principles and Duties of the Christian Religion, according to the Constitutions of the Church of *England;* whereby not only Children and Servants, but Parents and Masters who are ignorant, may (without being ashamed) be enlightned with true saving knowledge, and their Children in Schools of Learning, may grow up to be serviceable both in Church and State. And by good Discipline and

careful

careful tending, in well order'd Societies, under faithful Teachers and Magistrates, both Parents and Children would by the grace of God grow into habits of Christian Living, and the light of their Graces and good works shining before the Heathen, would above all other Oratory prevail with them, both to be desirous to learn themselves, and to bring their Children to be taught in the Christians Schools, how to glorifie the same God with them.

That the former benefits will accrue to themselves, needs no Proof; the experience of all united well order'd Christian Societies, sufficiently confirms it.

That the latter (*viz.* the gaining the Heathen to the Christian Faith) will be the hopeful Consequent of their habitual Christian living, of the united light of their graces and good works shining before the Heathen; I shall (not presuming to inform Your Lordship, but not knowing to whom this Paper may be communicated) make bold to add a brief Confirmation of it. First, by the testimony of that vertuous Heathen Emperour *Alexander Severus*, who when he perceived two of his Servants to be perswaded to receive the Christian Faith, by the Eloquent Orations *Origen* had made before him to prove the Truth of it. *I perceive* (saith he) *Ye do wonder at the Learning of* Origen, *whereby ye are induced to embrace the Christian Profession : But truly, the Humility and Charity of the Christian People, which I do hear of, and daily behold with my Eyes; do much more move me to believe that their Christ is God, then all his Eloquent Perswasions.*

This Heathen Emperour understood the Language of *Origen*; and (as the History relates) was much moved with the convincing perswasive Arguments *Origen* used, to prove the Truth of the Christian Faith : yet he professeth he was much more perswaded to believe it, by the Humility and Charity, the graces and vertues, which appeared in the Christians lives, which he heard of, and daily beheld. But the Heathen in *Virginia* neither understand the Christians language, nor the Christians theirs; and although they did understand it, I think it too barren to express the Christian Religion by, and therefore they have no other arguments left to convince them of the Truth of the Christian Faith, and to perswade them to embrace it. But only (which that Emperor acknowledged most perswasive) the amiablenesse of Christian Graces and Vertues shining in their lives, whose excelling beauty and benefit, when they appear in united Societies of Christians, they may well perswade any rational Heathen, that they are most conducing to procure the true happinesse of all united Societies and Communities of Men, and therefore the Religion, that teacheth them, above all other to be embraced.

This

This Consideration enforced the accute *Acosta*, after he had spent 17 years in conversing with the Heathen in that new world (though he was of a Church that pleads much for Miracles) ingenuously to confesse, that the greatest, and even the only Miracle necessary to the Conversion of those Heathen, is the gracious lives of Christians, agreeable to that Christian Faith they professe, and in this he subscribes but to St. *Chrysostome* affirming the same concerning the conversion of the Heathen in his dayes. But long before *Chrysostome*, the Prophet *Isaiah* foretold the power of this Miracle, how powerful the glory of the Lord shining in the gracious lives of Christians should be, to further the conversion of the Gentiles. *Isa.* 60. 2, 3. Where speaking of the Church under the Gospel, *The Lord* (faith he) *shall arise upon thee, and his glory shall be seen upon thee,* and what followes? *the Gentiles shall come to thy Light, and Kings to the brightnesse of thy rising.* What is this Light, and Brightnesse, and Glory, which should be seen upon the Church under the Gospel, which should invite the Gentiles to come into it? The same Prophet tells us *Isa.* 62. 2. *The Gentiles shall see thy Righteousness, and all Kings thy Glory.* 'Tis the Righteousnesse, the Holynesse, the graces shining in the lives of Christians; 'tis this should make their *Seed known among the Gentiles, and their off-spring among the People:* So that *all that see them should acknowledge them that they are the Seed which the Lord hath blessed. Isa.* 61. 9. And this should make them bring their Sons and Daughters to be nurst up at the Churches breasts. *Isa.* 49. 22, 23. *Isa.* 6. 4.

But when were these Prophecies fulfilled?

Two times are only remarkable for fulfilling them by Gods ordinary way of Converting Heathen (except the way of Converting them by Miracles) and those were,

First, The Times of Persecution, when the Faith, Constancy, Meeknesse, Patience, and Charity of the Christian Martyrs shined so bright in the Heathens eyes, through the Flames, Wounds, and Tortures they endured, that it made them wonder at the glory of the Lord, which was seen upon them, and fall in love with the Christian Religion, which brought forth such glorious Fruits in them: But neither doth this reach all States of the Church, not particularly *Virginia's,* so long as the Christians have the upper hand of the Heathen, which God grant may continue till the End of Times.

2. The times of the Churches peace, when the Christians in their united Societies, having the Liberty of their publick holy Assemblies in the House of God, did constantly attend upon the Service of God in them, and the Heathen comming in among
them,

them, and beholding the comely order and beauty of their holy worship, perceiving their Unanimity and Uniformity in the same faith and worship of the same God, were so convinced of all and judged of all, that the secrets of their hearts were made manifest, and they fell down upon their faces and worship'd God, and confessed that God was in them of a Truth, as the Apostle saith Infidels would do such a Case. 1 *Cor.* 14. 24, 25. And therefore no doubt but many of them did.

And as for those of the Heathen who lived in the Cities and Towns with the Christians, or near unto them, and yet frequented not the Christians Churches (which I suppose few of them would wholly omit, men being generally of the *Athenians* temper, inquisitive after what seems new to them) but if there were (as 'tis possible) any considerable numbers of such rigid Heathen; yet even these beholding the comely order of the Christians Government, the amiablenesse of their Conversations, their Meeknesse, Humility, Charity, their Righteousnesse shining as the Light, and their just dealing as the Noon-day : In sum, seeing the light of their good works, they were allured, and won by degrees to glorifie the same God with them : and these latter I take to be chiefly meant by the visible righteousnesse and glory of the Church, under the Gospel, which the Prophet *Isaiah* foretold (for he saith it should be seen) which should be so prevailing with the Heathen; these the most ordinary wayes (though there were other) of Converting them to Christianity; which Interpretation, besides that it is cleared by the words of the Text cited, and the evidence of the matter, it exactly agrees with the judgement of the Learned *Acosta* and St. *Chrysostome* before mentioned.

Object. But it may be objected, that *neither of these, nor perhaps any other Ecclesiatick Writers, have told us, that Christians for this end ought to be united in Societies in Towns, that it is the glory of the graces and virtues of many Christians shining, not in scatter'd Corners, but in visible united Societies, which is so perswasive and powerfully prevailing with the Heathen to embrace the Christian faith; nor do they use any arguments to perswade Christians to live together in Towns and to incorporate into Societies for this end.*

Answer. And no marvel; how could we reasonably expect it from them? The Christians whom they knew dispers'd through the then inhabited parts of the World (except *Hermites* whose condition of life is not here spoken of) were united in such Societies; planted together in the House of God, so as they might
constantly

constantly attend upon the publique sacred Ministrations of his
Word and Worship ; and their light best shine before men to the
glory of God. Therefore for this manner of Christians living together, as there was no need to argue ; so they might charitably
hope, there never would be, Christians being bound to it by vertue of Christs command. To seek first the Kingdome of God
and the Righteousnesse thereof, and to depend upon his promise,
for adding all other things to them ; of which Duty, that they
might be daily minded, Christ hath taught them by the method
of that daily Prayer, which he hath set them, as to beg of God,
so to seek the Hallowing of his Name, the advancement of his
Kingdome, and the doing of his will before their daily Bread ;
from whence it follows, that it is the Duty of all Christians to
take care in the first place, so to unite their habitations in Societies, after such a manner, as they may be best convenienc'd constantly to attend upon the publick Ministery of Gods holy Word,
Sacraments, and Worship (which conveniency only Towns and
Villages afford ;) because God hath ordained the publick Ministery of these to be the means by which (through his blessing
upon the due using them) his Name should be glorified, his Kingdome advanc'd, and his will perform'd, and hath exprest it to be
his will, that he will be glorified before all the People ; honoured
and praised in the great Congregations, and therefore calls for it
by his Word, *Psal.* 100. *O go your way into his Gates with
thanksgiving, and into his Courts with praise; be thankfull
unto him and blesse his name.*

And perhaps it may be truly affirmed, that *Virginia's* Planters were the first considerable numbers of Christians in the
whole world, which first violated this stated Order of Christ, (I
say not in a remote desert, and in the sight of the Heathen,
which hugely aggravates their fault) but the first that ever planted themselves after such a manner *(Hermites* as before excepted, whose manner of Life *Virginians* profess not) as might
make their due and constant attendance upon the publick worship and Service of God impossible to them, and consequently
disable them to glorifie the Name, and advance the Kingdome of
God, in the way God hath ordained and commanded.

It may suffice therefore for answer to the Object, to say, that
if neither ancient, nor modern Writers have told us, that Christians (if they have Liberty) ought to live together in visible united Societies, in Cities, Towns or Villages, for the fore-mentioned ends ; it was, because they knew no present need of writing
any thing of it, nor could charitably conjecture there would be
any for the Future.

But deer bought experience hath taught, that it is now necessary,

cessary, which hath made me thus far presume upon Your Lordships Candor and Patience for this brief asserting it; There being no other Remedy for *Virginia's* Malady, but by reducing her Planters into Towns.

Object. The common Objection against this way of being reduced into Towns, which I have often heard among them, is, *that they shall be undone by it in their Estates.*

Answer. For Answer to which it may suffice to say,

1. The most knowing and prudent among them, have judg'd the contrary, and that it would be the only way to enrich them, and therefore have both wish'd and endeavour'd it though in vain, witnesse the above-mention'd Act for Markets, contrived by the prudent *Edward Diggs* Esq; their sometime Governour, and the very many attempts and contrivances to compasse it, made and devised by the most Noble lover of *Virginia* Sir *William Berkely* their present Governour.

2. It will be the most probable way of securing both their Persons and Estates against all attempts of the Heathen, the Rumours whereof (frequently spread through that Countrey) do oft affright them, for hereby, either the Heathen will be gained, after the manner before specified, or their power not fear'd.

3. Only Persons that are able will be enjoyned it, according to the Tenour of the fourth Proposition, and perhaps Collections being made, and dispers'd according to the 2, and 3. Propositions, or agreeable Sums of money raised by a Rate set upon every Hogshead of *Tobacco* imported into *England*, according to the Honourable Sir *William Berkleys* Proposition in his view of *Virginia*, Workmen may be provided for them and the Planters be at little Charge, besides affording them Assistance and Dyet, which they have in so great Plenty in that Countrey, that Countrey, that very few or none will account the affording that, any impairing to their Estates. If none of these answers will satisfie such Objectors.

4. Yet let them consider seriously what hath been before asserted; That while they continue their present manner of scattered living (whereby they necessitate themselves to rob God of his due publique Worship and Service) they will continue under the Curse of God, but by uniting their habitations in Towns, they will make themselves capable of giving God his due honour in his house of Prayer in the great Congregations of his People, and consequently of procuring his blessing; for them that honour God, God will honour, *and they that are planted in the house of the Lord, shall flourish in the Courts of the house of*
our

our God. Psal. 92. 13. Now whether their living under the Curse, or under the Blessing of the Almighty will best improve their Estates, let themselves judge.

These things considered, men may wonder why the attempts made by the fore-mentioned Honourable Governours to reduce *Virginia's*-Planters into Towns did never succeed, and perhaps it may be hard for any that never lived among them rightly to conjecture. But the truth in plain *English* is this,

Whatsoever is of publick concernment in *Virginia*, is determined by their Grand Assemblies, which are usually held once a year, and consist of Governour and Councell, which make the upper house, and the Burgesses which represent the People, and make the lower house, and are chosen out of every County by the People, after the manner that Burgesses are chosen for Parliaments in *England*, and are more or fewer according as the People agree, who are to defray their charges. Whatsoever passes into an Act of Assembly, must be agree'd upon by the Major part of Burgesses, and these are usually such as went over Servants thither, and though by time and industry, they may have attained competent Estates; yet by reason of their poor and mean education they are unskilful in judging of a good Estate either of Church or Common-wealth, or of the means of procuring it. No marvell therefore, if the best proposals, which have been made to such persons, for reducing them into Towns, offending in the least against their present private worldly interest (though never so promising for the future) have been from time to time bandied against by such Major parts of their Burgesses, and the fewer wise heads over-voted by them.

And if at any time it hath so happened, that the Major part of the Burgesses have been so meetly qualified and tempered, as to enact any thing tending to such a publique good; The following Assemblies have usually repealed it. The consideration of which, is the true ground of the whole third Proposition: of the Contents of which and the rest, if Your Lordship shall become the blessed procurer. The forlorne Church which is now scattered in desolate Places of that wildernesse, without any comlinesse, which should make her desired, and sought after, may (though Gods blessing) in a few years, gain such beauty, wealth, and ornament, as may either enable her to nurse up Children of her own, to become her servants in the Gospel, or allure Strangers to court her for the Favour, and if it shall please God to prolong your Honourable dayes, till you shall hear of the promised blessed fruits of your labour of love and charity for that poor Church, (which God grant in mercy for his name and Churches sake) what ravishing joy and contentment will affect
your

your pious and charitable heart, to contemplate at this distance, the Glory of the Communion of Saints, in their united holy Societies and Assemblies; the constant beauty of their publique Worship; of their holy Sacrifices of prayers and praises offered in a comely order in their publique congregations.

To contemplate the poor Church (whose plants now grow wilde in that Wildernesse) become like a garden enclosed, like a Vineyard fenced, and watch'd like a flock of Sheep with their Lambes safely folded by night, and fed by day; all which are the promised fruits of well ordered Towns, under Religious Pastours and Magistrates, with what joy, and delight may you likewise think upon their comely and most ingenious Children, like hopefull plants growing up in Nurseries of learning and piety, and when their time of fruit is come, Transplanted into the enclosed gardens of God, and becoming fruitfull and usefull trees of righteousnesse; which is the promised happinesse and benefit of well ordered Schooles, in well governed Towns.

And lastly, what rejoycing will it be to your most Christian heart, to behold the glorious issue of that Prophecy, concerning the calling the Gentiles fulfilled in those numerous herds of Heathen in *Virginia.* Isa. 11. 6. &c. *The Wolfe shall dwell with the Lambe, the Leopard shall lye down with the Kid, &c.* To contemplate the Heathen, who in that Prophesie are likened to Wolves, Leopards, Lyons, Bears, Aspes, and Cockatrices; couching quietly & harmlesly in the same fold of Christs Church with the Sheep and Lambes of Christ, which will be the hopeful Consequent of well ordered Towns and Schooles. And the procuring these, the only true effectual Remedy for *Virginia's* Disease, as hath been shewed.

But this is a Work of time to compasse; and we have an *English* Proverb, *Whilst the grasse growes, the Steed Starves,* before this can be compassed, many poor Christians there, may perish for want of their souls food, where there is no vision the people perish, and that is the case of the far greater part of that Colony.

For encouragement therefore of Ministers to adventure thither to help them, I humbly propound,

First, That your Lordship be pleased to procure, that the next grand Assembly in *Virginia* may enact. That what *Tobacco* any Parish agrees to pay their Minister, shall be payed of the best *Tobacco* of every Mans own Crop, and with Cask, otherwise experience hath shewed, that a Ministers livelyhood there will be very uncertain.

Secondly, That at the same Assembly it be Enacted, that every Parish chuse a Vestry (in case they have not one already chosen)

chosen) and the Vestry of each Parish be enjoyned to subscribe what quantity of Corn and Tobacco of the best of their own Crops, with Cask, they will allow a sufficient Minister yearly.

Thirdly, That in the next and every Assembly, the Act for paying 15 *l.* of Tobacco *per annum,* for every Tythable person, in every Parish destitute of a Minister (which Act was made at an Assembly *March* 27. 1 6 5 6.) be carefully executed, and strict Enquiry made, whether the Tobacco due by that Act, be duely collected, and employed to the ends express'd in that Act, *viz.* Building Churches, purchasing Gleabes, and stocks of Cattel to belong to them. And if any Parish hath imployed any part of such Arrears to any other use, that they be enjoyned to make them good again.

Fourthly, That the Act made in the same Assembly concerning disposing intestate estates to publick uses, in case no Administratour of Kin to the diseased Proprietour appears) may serve in the first place the needs of the Church, for furnishing each Parish with Gleabes, and the Gleabes with Stocks of Cattel, before any part of such estates be employed to any other use.

Fifthly, that there being divers persons already in the Colony fit to serve the Church in the office of Deacon, a Bishop be sent over, so soon as there shall be a City for his See, as for other Needs of that Church, so also, that after due Probation and Examination, such persons may be ordained Deacons, and their Duty and Service be appointed by the Bishop.

Sixthly, That the Ministers that go thither, be not hired by the year, as is now usual, but firmly instituted and inducted into Livings of stated value by the Subscriptions of their Vestries, according to the second Proposition.

Seventhly, That all Ministers desirous to go to *Virginia,* and not able to transport themselves, be acquainted with an Act of Assembly of that Country, whereby it is provided, that whatsoever sufficient Minister, shall not be able to pay for his transportation, any Merchant that shall defray the charge of it (if such Minister agree not with him upon other conditions) shall receive 20 *l. Sterling* for his passage, from the Parish that entertains him, or two Thousand pound of Tobacco, who shall also repay any Sums of money disburs'd for his accommodation, and the Minister to be free to choose his Parish, which shall make such disbursements for him.

This is all I can think meet to propound at present, only for a Conclusion I shall add for the Encouragement both of Bishop and Ministers, that shall adventure thither out of pity and compassion to the souls of so many of their poor Brethren, that as their reward will be great in Heaven, so also, they shall (in a

very

very pleasant and fruitful Land) meet with a People, which generally bear a great love and respect to their Ministers; And (if they behave themselves as becommeth their high calling) they shall find their ready help, and assistance in their Needs; and (which should be much more encouraging) they will find a People, which generally bear a great love to the stated Constitutions of the Church of *England,* in her Government and publick Worship; which gave us (who went thither under the late Persecutions of it) the advantage of Liberty to use it constantly among them, after the Naval force had reduced that Colony under the power (but never to the obedience) of the Usurpers.

Which Liberty we could not have enjoyed, had not the People generally express'd a great Love to it. And I hope even this will be a consideration (not of least regard) to move Your Lordship to use all possible care and endevour to supply *Virginia's* Needs with sufficient Orthodoxe Ministers, in the first place, and before any other of our forraign Plantations which crave your help, because in the late times of our Churches Persecution, her people alone, cheerfully and joyfully embraced, encouraged, and maintained the Orthodoxe Ministers that went over to them, in their publick Conformity to the Church of *E N G-L A N D,* in her Doctrine and stated manner of Public Worship.

F I N I S.

DATE D

DEC 3 '76		
MAY 25 '78		
AUG 16 1979		
APR 27 1981		
JUL 1 1981		
SE 12 '83		
OC 3 '89		
24 '89		
GAYLORD		